TOMORROW'S ORGANIZATIONS

The Scott, Foresman Series in Management and Organizations

Charles E. Summer, Advisory Editor
University of Washington

Boddewyn, COMPARATIVE MANAGEMENT AND MARKETING

Elbing, BEHAVIORAL DECISIONS IN ORGANIZATIONS

Filley and House, MANAGERIAL PROCESS AND ORGANIZATIONAL BEHAVIOR

Hampton, Summer, and Webber, ORGANIZATIONAL BEHAVIOR AND THE PRACTICE
   OF MANAGEMENT, Revised

Jun and Storm, TOMORROW'S ORGANIZATIONS: CHALLENGES AND STRATEGIES

Perrow, COMPLEX ORGANIZATIONS

Reeser, MANAGEMENT: FUNCTIONS AND MODERN CONCEPTS

Turner, Filley, and House, STUDIES IN MANAGERIAL PROCESS AND ORGANIZATIONAL
   BEHAVIOR

Wadia, THE NATURE AND SCOPE OF MANAGEMENT

Young, MANAGEMENT: A SYSTEMS ANALYSIS

TOMORROW'S ORGANIZATIONS:

CHALLENGES AND STRATEGIES

Jong S. Jun
Department of Public Administration
California State University, Hayward

William B. Storm
School of Public Administration
University of Southern California

Scott, Foresman and Company
GLENVIEW, ILLINOIS   BRIGHTON, ENGLAND

Acknowledgments

PART ONE

"On Attending to the Future" by Bertrand de Jouvenel
from *Environment and Change: The Next Fifty Years,*
edited by William R. Ewald, Jr. Copyright © 1968 by
Indiana University Press. Reprinted by permission of
the publisher.

"Why Speculate Far Ahead?" by Herman Kahn and
Anthony J. Wiener. Reprinted with permission of The
Macmillan Company from *The Year 2000: A Frame-
work for Speculation on the Next Thirty-Years* by
Herman Kahn and Anthony J. Wiener. Copyright ©
1967 by The Hudson Institute, Inc.

"Beyond Theory Y" by John J. Morse and Jay W.
Lorsch from *Harvard Business Review* 48 (May-June
1970), © 1970 by the President and Fellows of
Harvard College. All Rights Reserved. Reprinted by
permission.

"Organization Government: The Prospects for a Truly
Participative System" by William G. Scott from *Public
Administration Review* 29, no. 1 (January-February
1969). Reprinted by permission.

From "Today's Problems with Tomorrow's Organiza-
tions" by Chris Argyris from *Journal of Management
Studies* (February 1967). Reprinted by permission of
Basil Blackwell, Publisher.

"Beyond Bureaucracy" by Warren Bennis. Copyright ©
July-August, 1965 by *TRANS-action,* Inc., New Brunswick, New Jersey. Used by permission.

From "A New Corporate Design" by Jay W. Forrester
from *Industrial Management Review* 7, no. 1 (Fall
1965): 5–18. © Industrial Management Review Association, reprinted by permission.

PART TWO

"Changes in Inner Human Experience and the Future"
by James F. T. Bugental. Chapter 22 of *Toward Century 21,* edited by C. S. Wallia, © 1970 by Basic Books,
Inc., Publishers, New York.

"New Light on the Human Potential" by Herbert A.
Otto from *Saturday Review* (December 2, 1969):
14–17. Copyright 1969 Saturday Review, Inc.

"Complex Man in the Complex Organization," a re-
titled excerpt by Edgar H. Schein from Edgar H.
Schein, *Organizational Psychology,* © 1965, pp. 60–
63. Reprinted by permission of Prentice-Hall, Inc.,
Englewood Cliffs, New Jersey.

"Interpersonal Relationships: U.S.A. 2000" by Carl R.
Rogers. Reproduced by special permission from *The
Journal of Applied Behavioral Science* 4:3 (July-
August-September 1968): 265–80. © 1968 by *The
Journal of Applied Behavioral Science* and Carl R.
Rogers. Reprinted by permission of the author and
the publisher.

"Humanistic Elements in Group Growth" by Jack R.
and Lorraine M. Gibb from *Challenges of Humanistic
Psychology,* ed. by J. F. T. Bugental. Copyright ©
1967 by McGraw-Hill, Inc. Used by permission of
McGraw-Hill Book Company.

"The Causal Texture of Organizational Environments"
by F. E. Emery and E. L. Trist from *Human Relations*
18, no. 1 (1965): 21–32. Reprinted by permission of
Plenum Publishing Corporation.

From "Organization-Environment Interface" by
Paul R. Lawrence and Jay W. Lorsch from *Developing
Organizations: Diagnosis and Action.* Copyright ©
1969 by Addison-Wesley Publishing Company, Inc.,
Reading, Mass. Reprinted by permission.

"Change by Design, Not by Default" by Robert R.
Blake and Jane Srygley Mouton. Reprinted from
S.A.M. Advanced Management Journal of the Society
for Advancement of Management 35, no. 2 (April
1970): 29–34.

"Bureaucracy and Innovation" by Victor A. Thompson
from *Administrative Science Quarterly* (June 1965).
Reprinted by permission of *Administrative Science
Quarterly* and the author.

"Innovation-Resisting and Innovation-Producing Organizations" by Herbert A. Shepard from *Journal of
Business* 40, no. 4 (October 1967): 470–77. Copyright
1967 by the University of Chicago.

PART THREE

From "Society As a Complex Adaptive System" by
Walter Buckley. Reprinted from Walter Buckley, ed.,
Modern Systems Research for the Behavioral Scientist
(Chicago: Aldine Publishing Company, 1968). Copy-
right © 1968 by Walter Buckley. Reprinted by permis-
sion.

"Organizational Cybernetics and Human Values" by
Richard F. Ericson from *Academy of Management
Journal* (March 1970). Reprinted by permission of
Academy of Management Journal and the author.

"Mixed Scanning: A 'Third' Approach to Decision
Making" by Amitai Etzioni from *Public Administra-*

A. CHAPTERS OF THIS TEXT CORRELATED WITH CONTEMPORARY

Contemporary Textbooks in Organization Theory and Behavior	Scott and Mitchell, *Organization Theory* (Irwin, 1972)	Argyris, *Integrating the Individual and Organization* (Wiley, 1966)	Kelly, *Organizational Behavior* (Irwin, 1969)	
Table of Contents				
Part One				
1. Challenges of the Future	20		14	
2. Tomorrow's Organizations	20	13	14	
Part Two				
3. Understanding Tomorrow's Man	5	2	4,14	
4. Interpersonal Competence and Group Growth	7	2,5	5,11,12	
5. Organizational Environments and Adaptation	7	1,4	6	
6. Breakthroughs in Change and Innovation	15,16	6,8	10	
Part Three				
7. Open Systems, Cybernetics, and Decisions	4,9	1-5	11	
8. Exchange, Motivation, and Role Theory	5,10,11	2,11	6	
9. Phenomenology: The Search for New Perspectives		2	14	
Part Four				
10. General Strategies for a Changing Organization		8		
11. Structural Change, Technology, and Self-Management	3,14	9,10	5,6	
12. Behavioral Change and Organization Development	15,16	6,8	10	
13. New Roles for Proactive Administrators	13	9	3	
14. Organization Research and Policy Development	18,19		1	

TEXTBOOKS IN ORGANIZATION THEORY AND BEHAVIOR

Silverman, *The Theory of Organizations* (Basic Books, 1971)	Davis, *Human Relations at Work* (McGraw-Hill, 1972)	Likert, *Human Organization* (McGraw-Hill, 1967)	Katz and Kahn, *The Social Psychology of Organizations* (Wiley, 1966)	Filley and House, *Managerial Process and Organizational Behavior* (Scott, Foresman, 1969)
Chapter Numbers				
7,10	26	1,2	1,14	19
4	3,5,26	9	12	
9	23	4	12	12,14
1,2,5	11–14	10	2,3,6	4,6
7	9	2	10,12	18
2,3	2,20,21	7	2,3,10,14	5,6,7
7	2,3	9	7,12	1,13,14
6,7,10				
		10	13	17
5	17,18	2	4,13	4
	10	7	13	
8	6,7,8	4	11	16
		8	9	2

B. CROSS-REFERENCE OF THIS TEXT WITH OTHER MAJOR TEXTBOOKS IN ORGANIZATION THEORY AND BEHAVIOR

Contents	Author	Book Title and Publishers	Chapter numbers
Part One			
1. Challenges of the Future	Bennis	Changing Organizations (McGraw-Hill, 1966)	1,2
	Schmidt	Organizational Frontiers (Wadsworth, 1970)	1,2,3
	Bennis and Slater	The Temporary Society (Harper and Row, 1969)	1,2
	Drucker	The Age of Discontinuity (Harper and Row, 1969)	1–8
	Lippitt	Organizational Renewal (Appleton-Century, 1969)	16
	Gross	Organizations and Their Managing (Free Press, 1968)	Part IV
2. Tomorrow's Organizations	Bennis and Slater	The Temporary Society	3,4
	Maslow	Eupsychian Management (Irwin, 1965)	entire book
	Hicks	The Management of Organizations (McGraw-Hill, 1972)	32
Part Two			
3. Understanding Tomorrow's Man	Schein	Organizational Psychology (Prentice-Hall, 1970)	4
	Lippitt	Organizational Renewal	4
	Gardner	Self-Renewal (Harper and Row, 1963)	entire book
	Jourard	The Transparent Self (D. Van Nostrand Co., 1970)	entire book
4. Interpersonal Competence and Group Growth	Argyris	Interpersonal Competence and Organizational Effectiveness (Irwin, 1962)	1,2
	Zaleznik and Moment	The Dynamics of Interpersonal Behavior (Wiley, 1964)	entire book
	Hicks	The Management of Organizations	8–11
	Athos and Coffey	Behavior in Organizations (Prentice-Hall, 1968)	3,6,7
5. Organizational Environments and Adaptation	Gross	Organizations and Their Managing	6,7
	Vickers	Towards a Sociology of Management (Basic Books, 1967)	4
	Hicks	The Management of Organizations	5
6. Breakthroughs in Change and Innovation	Thompson	Bureaucracy and Innovation (Univ. of Alabama, 1969)	entire book
	Argyris	Organization and Innovation (Irwin, 1965)	1,7
	O'Connell	Managing Organizational Innovation (Irwin, 1968)	1,9
	March and Simon	Organizations (Wiley, 1958)	7
	Press and Arian	Empathy and Ideology (Rand McNally, 1966)	1,2
Part Three			
7. Open Systems, Cybernetics, and Decisions	Buckley	Sociology and Modern Systems Theory (Prentice-Hall, 1967)	3,6
	Buckley	Modern Systems Research for Behavioral Scientists (Aldine, 1969)	entire book
	Seiler	Systems Analysis in Organization Behavior (Irwin, 1967)	1,8
	Schein	Organizational Psychology	2,6

Contents

Preface

In *Tomorrow's Organizations,* the orientation is toward meeting organizational needs implied by the changing conditions of our era. Today's organizations, with their inheritance of rationalism and technocracy, are locked into a set of values, procedures, and techniques that renders them almost incapable of proactive change. Many organization managers appear unaware of the social, political, economic, and cultural changes rapidly taking place. We believe there is a need for a new type of organization—and new values and processes to go with it.

To this end, we review a variety of contemporary organization theories and attempt to develop an integrated theory that pulls together the most useful possibilities. We hope that you will find, in these pages, new ways of thinking about complex organizational problems, current *and* future, internal *and* external, that will serve your needs in more than immediate operational terms. The fate of tomorrow's organizations depends upon today's strategies. The year 2000 is already with us: Its top managers and professors are in our offices and classrooms today.

Tomorrow's Organizations has five essential parts, including the General Introduction. Our introductory essay reviews the current organizational dilemma and suggests the need for a new theory. We also set the stage for the four major parts that follow. We introduce each part, in turn, with an integrative essay.

Part One offers two chapters dealing with future challenges and the design of future organizations. In Part One we make a normative statement that the process of organization is a viable means for problem solving, but only where the organization is fashioned in terms of the times.

Part Two brings together new human values, the development of interpersonal competence and group growth, and adaptation to changing environments. Part Two also emphasizes the need for adaptability to continuous change and innovation.

Part Three re-emphasizes the integrated perspective mentioned in the General Introduction. New and integrated theories are necessary to understand and develop the dimensions of tomorrow's organizations. Thus, Part Three directs attention to open systems theory, cybernetics, decisionmaking, exchange theory, motivation, and role theory, among others. In addition, Part Three introduces the phenomenological approach as a useful perspective.

In Part Four we endeavor to systematize approaches to integrated organizational change.

Preceding this preface are two charts: Chart A correlates the chapters of *Tomorrow's Organizations* with the chapters of contemporary textbooks; Chart B cross-references specific textbooks that may be of supplementary value to each chapter of *Tomorrow's Organizations.*

We wish to thank all contributors to this volume for the perspectives they offer. We have benefited greatly from the ideas and criticism of our students and colleagues in the California State University at Hayward and the University of Southern California. We are also indebted to Professor Charles E. Summer, whose suggestions on the organization of the book have been of great value; to Professor Charles Perrow, who gave a most helpful critical review of our introductions and our selection of the readings; and to the editors at Scott, Foresman and Company, for their invaluable assistance in preparing this book for publication.

Finally, we express our appreciation for the patience and understanding of our wives, Soon Ye and Harriet.

J. S. J.
W. B. S.

General
Introduction

During the initial seven decades of the twentieth century, theories about how man may best use organizations to help achieve his goals have passed through a metamorphosis ranging from extremely simple forms to varieties of great complexity and sophistication. The end of that development is by no means in sight; indeed, a whole new era in the study of organizations appears to be opening.

Most of the elements of contemporary organization theory were born in this century; in large part, they were developed to meet the needs of the burgeoning industrial revolution. Early theory was simple and practical, falling generally within the rubric of "scientific management" as defined by Frederick W. Taylor sixty years ago. The term initially referred more to the study of work, especially work measurement, than to the many processes which have subsequently been covered by this designation; yet, such study rapidly gave way to the broad range of activities known as industrial engineering. Such engineers were concerned with system refinement to achieve maximum "efficiency" and production within each organizational unit.

Before long, technological developments brought the more advanced nations into a second industrial revolution, one based upon information processing rather than upon the simple mechanical activities characteristic of the first period. Two developments have been central to this breakthrough: the invention of machines that could convert observations into symbols and that could feed those symbols back into the machines in such a way as to regulate their behavior in terms of "real time" and, secondly, the invention of the electronic digital computer. In combination, such devices, with their decisionmaking capability, created the basis for automation. They also offered management various opportunities to experiment with the social system of organizations in ways which had not been readily available within the framework of scientific management. In response to that opportunity, modern management generally has chosen to use these newfound skills simply to impose, in a more sophisticated way, the efficiency criteria of Taylor's period. The organization-as-machine thus ran more smoothly insofar as its *systems* were concerned, but the negative imposition on its *members* was much the same as ever.

The reason for such a choice by management appears to have been that, through most of the period of organizational change and development, people assumed the technology associated with the work itself—the job—could not be altered except to increase the efficiency with which it was performed. Thus, the nega-

1

tive effects experienced by people as a result of scientific management were largely reinforced by management science. While students of organization were often preoccupied by social and psychological aspects of work situations, their research and experimentation was normally restricted to nontechnological domains that were less directly related to production; they did not undertake to modify technical arrangements if such manipulation threatened the overt indicators of efficiency. Instead, they accepted the technological system as a given element and attempted to create a positive human environment around it. The result was that the sociopsychological environment became almost wholly a factor of the technology involved, and, as such, was grossly conditioned by the latter needs rather than those of the human beings doing the work.

This emphasis has always created problems, and the problems have become more acute as changes have occurred both in the nature of the work being done and among the workers doing it. While millions of additional workers are now employed in activities such as public health, recreation, education, and similar occupations in the United States, the number of workers employed in such areas as agriculture, mining, and manufacture, for example, has literally decreased by millions during the past few decades. Furthermore, the immigrants who fleshed out the employment needs of farm, mine, and industry—many all too often illiterate, ignorant of English, and devoid of training or skill—have given way to a new generation of workers with technical or professional qualifications. In place of the dependent, near-slave status of the immigrants, we now have a rapidly growing force of mobile, independent, well-educated employees. These new workers have long since met the basic requirements of survival and shelter and have reached a level higher up on Maslow's hierarchy of needs. They seek belonging and esteem. Some have progressed to the desire for self-actualization—and it is becoming clear that, in the foreseeable future, millions more will seek that level of achievement. Such developments supply the ingredients for major changes in the manner whereby we organize and manage our public and private enterprises. The use of management science simply to refine the technical system is no longer enough. Both the new workers and their new roles imply the need for a theory that will make maximum use of both technical and behavioral knowledge. The problems that organizations are having to confront suggest the need for a theory which will create a flexible and adaptive organization that can learn to adapt its responses to changes in the environment. The purpose of this volume is the explication of means for achieving such an organization.

That purpose is significant for a number of reasons. There are the obvious values of making maximum use of technical capabilities generated by what has been called the second industrial revolution and of matching organizational processes to the characteristics implicit in contemporary man. Further, and of central importance, is the need to muster resources to the fullest extent in order to confront problems which must be solved as we move into the next century. We are presently aware that tomorrow's world will include acute problems of overpopulation, shortages of food, resource exhaustion, ecological deterioration, and other matters which, in combination, raise the specter of nonsurvival or, at best, sharp reduction in the quality of life as we know it. Coming to grips with those threats implies two particular courses of action: building new organizations to attack specific problems and, secondly, effecting changes in established organizations—a process which may help society achieve control over unfavorable intervening variables.

For a Better Future

This age of rapid social and technological development and impending emergency impels us to learn how new concepts in organization theory may be utilized more rapidly in order to initiate changes in organization behavior. A salient feature of public and private organizations, both past and present, has been the relative inability of administrators to use properly the existing body of knowledge both for improving the effectiveness of their organizations and for facilitating their adaptation to changing environments. Most administrators inherit a legacy of ignorance and habit which requires them to operate their organizations with traditional and inappropriate concepts of organization theory which offer little relevance to contemporary situations and future responsibilities. There seems always to be a severe lag in the application of what is known about organizations and about human behavior in actual management situations. The lag becomes more acute—and less acceptable—as the rate of change increases. The lag implies that we are overly committed to theories and techniques we have employed in the past and which we still retain in order to achieve a modicum of success with our organizations. Appropriate solutions for today's problems within organizations and the quality of our plans for a better future depend upon our capacity to change the perceptions held by administrators. Those perceptions include views about man and his environment, about the capability of organizational change, and about the limitations of the cultural commitment we have inherited—a commitment which favors rational-scientific solutions to all problems. We must break away from habits which favor traditional organizational systems, structures, techniques, and hierarchies—habits which, ironically, cause us to organize automatically in terms of stylized routines.

We take the position that circumstances will make it literally inevitable that tomorrow's organizations will display more consciousness of new ideas that have been developed by behavioral scientists to deal with special demands of a turbulent environment and that those ideas will be utilized. With the ever-increasing knowledge we now have, the problem-solving method used by our predecessors is no longer applicable; contemporary problems and future problems will not be solved in traditional ways. Part of the agony of this era is generated by our clumsy efforts to do tomorrow's job with yesterday's tools.

Our purpose in this book is not to describe or advocate any one theory; instead, the purpose is to stress that an integration of many theories provides an alternative view for studying organizational phenomena and adapting our organizations for their future environment. The effort to integrate knowledge is too often neglected, with the result that we frequently are forced into an acceptance of positions which are too *purely theoretical* to accommodate the realities of the operational world. In the next section, we shall take a look at some of these theories and introduce an integrating approach.

Perspectives in Organization Theory

Arnold Rose described two kinds of sociological imagination in social research—the macro and micro.[1] He pointed out that sociologists may have a superb capacity for one kind of sociological imagination but that they may be almost blind with respect to the other. The same effect appears to occur in organizational research and theory-building because a similar characterization may be made between macro-level and micro-level approaches. We believe literature now justifies adding a third perspective—the phenomenological—and from these three we suggest that a fourth perspective can be extracted: an integrated approach which contains the main properties of the initial three.

The macro perspective in organization theory manifests a holistic orientation, placing its emphasis on the total system and its major subsystems. Macro theory assumes the gestalt property of the organization process, where the product is more than the sum of its parts. The theory of bureaucracy, modern systems theory, and rational decisionmaking theory incorporate that approach. Macro-oriented research moves from a general theory to measurement of the impact resulting from the application of that theory. The impact is defined in terms of the effects upon people working in the system. Theory revision then stems from hypotheses drawn from such measurement.

Micro theory, as its name implies, is concerned with what has been considered the smallest element of the organizational equation—human capabilities and behavior. In micro-level research, organizational phenomena are keyed and explained in terms of psychological variables. Role theory, the theory of motivation, and exchange theory are typical examples of the micro perspective. They have in common a strong emphasis on empirical investigation of human problems in complex organizations. Here, research goes from hypotheses developed from research on individual and group behavior to the development of a general theory which accommodates behavioral data. The research is geared toward the effectiveness of the larger construct—the organization—rather than the individual as he functions in the system.

Though micro and macro approaches tend to flow into each other and to lack clear distinction, theory at each of these levels does offer a somewhat different frame of reference. Moreover, the study of organizational theories drawn from both perspectives reveals that they are indeed sufficiently distinct that neither of them explains the sum of internal and external problems characteristic of complex organizations today. No single theory explains precisely the pluralistic realities of both human and organizational values. The extent to which these realities can be subjected to analysis and comprehension may depend on introducing a new frame of reference which accommodates the diversity of both knowledge and human consciousness. In this regard, the phenomenological perspective provides another useful approach to the study of human organizations. The phenomenologi-

cal orientation to organization theory is either implicit or explicit in the work of many behavioral scientists, including the writings of March and Simon, Cantril, Giorgi, Snygg and Combs, C. Wright Mills, and many others. Generally speaking, phenomenology is a point of view rather than a theory. A point of view implies simply a perspective, whereas theory attempts to make concrete predictions and explanations on the basis of interrelated assumptions.

Certain concepts in phenomenology provide significant dimensions for understanding human organizations. Since Chapter 9 in this book addresses phenomenology as it relates to the study of organizations, only major properties of the view are listed:

1) The view provides a frame of reference for studying authentic behavior of the individual as related to the phenomenal self and, to an extent, to the phenomenal world.
2) It considers the possibilities and potentialities of the human being.
3) Phenomenology takes into account the meaning of time, consciousness, and action.
4) It accounts the temporal nature of human learning and human knowledge.
5) It considers the multiple realities between individual, group, organization, community, and society.
6) It assumes the complementary nature of theories.
7) Phenomenology emphasizes the meaning of reality and the objective definition of the situation.

Previously it was noted that phenomenology offers a perspective rather than a theory. Certainly its very nature suggests that it includes the integration of the micro and macro theories, but the essence of phenomenology is such that explanation, evaluation, and interpretation are not its product. Rather, it offers a position from which to view phenomena in an unbiased way, thereby suggesting new possibilities. It does not, then, offer a framework for integrating existing theories into a new formulation. For this purpose, we need a fourth perspective.

What we have said of these three approaches clearly implies the need for an integrative framework which continually and openly draws upon their different perspectives and knowledge to help resolve the complex problems which complex organizations normally encounter. Each approach offers very significant values which must be drawn together into an integrative theory. The integrative process is the central objective of this book. In the following paragraphs are set forth reasons for integrating currently available knowledge for the study and operation of modern organizations.

A Normative Assumption

It is becoming increasingly necessary to integrate the knowledge, theory, and methodology being developed by organizational theorists and behavioral scientists in order to comprehend possibilities and strategies. Through such means, we may learn to determine relevant goals. The knowledge which has been gathered by micro theorists provides many possibilities for organizational innovation and creativity, while the macro level of knowledge offers invaluable explanations of organizational control and organizational processes. Both categories will be of significant use in organizational policymaking. Adopting one particular theory for policymaking cannot develop a fully meaningful policy.

Continuous Search for New Knowledge

Obviously, man has only a limited capability in searching for knowledge; yet, the possibility of developing new knowledge is always present. The continuous learning process which underlies the accumulation of human knowledge should be accompanied by continual organizational change.

The integration of our knowledge of organizational theory is incomplete; a further integration of old and new knowledge may uncover many new ideas which will facilitate organizational accommodation to reality in a proactive rather than a reactive manner. To achieve such an accommodation in a very complex and turbulent world will draw heavily upon every resource we can muster.

Construction of a New Reality

Knowledge about the history, culture, and processes of organization is, of course, an essential part of explaining the totality of organizations, but such macro-level knowledge suffers in that it is hard to relate to those aspects of human behavior which directly affect organizational goals. This suggests that, in the typical human organization, we should construct a new and integrated reality which combines the individual and the organization. In developing Karl Mannheim's idea of "functional and substantial rationalities," for example, C. Wright Mills pointed out that rationality without reason in an organization is not commensurate with freedom. "Freedom," says Mills, "is not merely the chance to do as one pleases; neither is it merely the opportunity to choose between set alternatives. Freedom is, first of all, the chance to formulate the available choices, to argue over them—and then, the opportunity to choose. That is why freedom cannot exist without an enlarged role of human reason in human affairs."[2] Here Mills has suggested one form of an "integrated reality" wherein the individual's relation to the organization is more directly based on the *real* nature of the individual as opposed to the individual viewed strictly as a worker.

Projection of the Future

The imaginative use of organizational knowledge can provide both the endogenous and exogenous forces which appear

relevant to a prediction of the future. A
more imaginative analysis of existing
knowledge frequently leads to new knowledge with which to confront future challenges. As man develops more knowledge
and learns from new experience, he acquires increasing capability to create his
future. In this respect, the phenomenological perspective offers conceptual
thoughtways whereby man may perceive
many new possibilities for change and development. Through those thoughtways,
man may at least partially free himself
from the encapsulation of his language,
perception, and experience to formulate
an unlimited number of insights into the
phenomenal world around him, thereby
greatly enlarging his ability to grope with
paradoxes and ambiguities, to see order in
them, and to project more freely and
imaginatively into the future. Thus the
phenomenological perspective directly and
immediately enlarges the possibilities inherent in micro and macro theories. The
enlarged, value-free perspective gives
them new dimensions and offers them
new possible meanings and uses.

Imperatives for
Tomorrow's Organizations

The extraordinary complexity of both the
environments and the organizations of
today and tomorrow implies need for new
ways to understand and respond to organizational problems. To comprehend
contemporary organizational reality and to
bring continuous adaptative capability to
the system, the integrated approach considers three important elements: man, environment, and change. The liberation of
contemporary and future organizations
from continued envelopment by traditional, essentially bureaucratic theory depends upon both understanding and the
effective use of new ideas and findings
about those three elements.

A Fresh Look at the Concept of Man

We believe that exploring new ideas about
the nature of man, his relationships with

other individuals, his place in various organizations, and what tomorrow's organizations have to offer him are important both in understanding contemporary organizational problems and in planning for the future. We need to know
more about human behavior in order to
develop better and more realistic organizational goals. Organizations must
learn to accommodate in better fashion
the two contradictory elements in the
construction of their goals and behaviors
—organizational rationality and the existence of human nonrationality. The
former assumes the possibility of *control*
of organizational functions, while the latter recognizes the limitations imposed by
divergent human behavior. Probably "human reality" should be accepted as the
most important variable in explaining the
totality of organizational phenomena; the
human reality offers the diversity of ideas,
knowledge, and experience which will increasingly be the lifeblood of effective organizations. The recognition and acceptance of this diversity introduces
boundless possibilities and alternative
meanings to organization. If one rejects
this view and elects instead to emphasize
control of organizational activities, he is
choosing to reduce the individual to the
mechanical roles of bureaucratic theory,
to deny his fellowman the expansion toward self-actualization, and he is choosing
to set the state for continual contest between the system and its members.

The insidious processes of bureaucratization in complex organizations have
brought about not only the impersonalization and alienation of individuals but also
an inevitable tendency for the structure to
become abstract; in turn, that pattern has
produced and emphasized "rationalization" and "efficiency" as organizational
values. The development of science and
technology, and, particularly, development during the past century, has resulted
in the increased emphasis on rational
approaches to our problems, with less
concern for possible humanistic considerations. In some ways the highly rationalized complex organizations which have

evolved at this time seem like "sand cas-
tles," built of innumerable particles held
together by ephemeral and abstract
means. As in the case of the castle builder
who attempts in vain to retain the integrity of his sandy construct against the
forces of wind, tide, and passing people,
the builders of organizations appear to be
trying to retain their artificial systems and
relationships in the face of more natural
internal and external forces which seem
likely to be the final victors. The survival
of complex human organizations is likely
to be jeopardized in the future if administrators continue to view the processes of
organizational structure and control.

The human being is a complex organism
which has a variety of needs and values
to fulfill. The organization-as-process view
must eventually recognize and take into
account the numerous and varied aspects
of human nature. We must learn to build
organizations that are held together not by
rules and standard procedures but by the
forces of individual and group identification—identification with organizational
goals and systems—and organizational
awareness of the psychobiological realities of the human being. We include here
a summary of characteristics attributable
to man—characteristics which offer implicit stipulations for the instrumental use
of human beings in an organization.[3]

A) Human Needs and Values
   Man requires the satisfaction of his
   survival needs.
   Man strives for social satisfaction.
   Human beings have a need for self-
   esteem.
   Human beings insist that society
   should offer hope that their aspirations and potentials will be fulfilled.
   Human beings require freedom to
   exercise choices.
   Human beings seek a value system
   or system of beliefs to which they
   can commit themselves.
B) Possibility of Man's Development
   Human beings continuously seek to
   enlarge and enrich the quality of
   their satisfactions.

Human beings are creatures of hope.
Humans have the capacity to make
changes and the desire to use this capacity.
C) Authentic Being
   People want to experience a sense of
   their own worthwhileness.
   The average human learns, under
   proper conditions, not only to accept
   responsibility but also to seek responsibility.
D) Change
   Man continuously tends to change
   his role relationships.
   Man is not static, but continues to
   develop as he encounters new experiences.
   Man is shaping the man of the future—consciously or not.
   Man has a useful image of space and
   time.
E) Adaptation
   Man is adaptable to change.
   Under the proper climate, man is
   willing to adopt more innovative and
   risk-taking behavior.

Proponents of the scientific management and human-relations schools of organizational thought have viewed man in
his "natural state," seeing him as a creature that would do only what was required to fulfill its economic and social
needs. The early theories were essentially
mechanistic in that they neither recognized the potential of man nor a hope in
people. Similarly, they did not posit the
ways in which this relatively untapped
"human resource" could be developed to
benefit both the individual and the organization. The above list on the "nature
of complex man" reveals a far different
set of assumptions about man and his role
in modern organizations. New concepts of
man view him as a separate entity capable
of fluidity, growth, and tremendous constructive and innovative change.

No individual is likely to achieve fully
the properties suggested in the above list.
It is doubtless part of man's nature that
he may forever fall short of achieving his
needs and values in a complete sense. But

our new assumptions about man imply that a proper contemporary organization must adopt a far different managerial strategy to deal with the complexities of human nature that can now be characterized by implicit differences in capabilities, needs, values, motivations, and perceptions. The task for tomorrow's organizations includes not only shaping an "adaptable man" rather than a "static" or "finished" man but also teaching an open and receptive attitude toward change and a desire to learn.

Environment

Complex organizations in a state of change must properly be viewed in relation to their complex environments. In an organization, man interacts and transacts with his environment, as does the organization with its environment. Each gives to the environment, takes from it, and, in a dynamic exchange with it, in turn becomes changed. Interactive processes of adaptation and growth involve numerous variables, not all of which bear the same significance nor have the same interactive value. However, the central problem of environmental transactions is that an organization interacts with multiple environments rather than a few stipulated and controlled ones. That is, there are transactions with the total environment and many subenvironments. In addition, the multiple goals of organizations involve interdependent activities with different environmental and clientele-oriented relationships. Thus, an effective, changing organization requires continuous research upon—and feedback from—its changing environments. Human organizations, unlike mechanical and organic systems, have the ability continually to modify their basic goals, structures, and procedures. Walter Buckley describes this as the "morphogenic process" in modern sociocultural systems. Whereas traditional organizational theory tended to overlook or to oversimplify that capability, modern theory is increasingly aware of the value of the "morphogenic process" and is at-

tempting to maximize it. Such maximization also requires the integration of both macro and micro theories and the overlay of a phenomenological perspective.

Relating the organization to various environments provides three essential opportunities: the chance to optimize for the survival of the organization; the chance to reduce the risk and uncertainty involved in organizational goals; and the opportunity to discover the possibility for new alternatives. These characteristics are depicted in Figure 1 (see p. 9).[4]

Figure 1 introduces a desirable iterative process: present organization—present environment—future environment—future organization—and so on. Through this process, the organization may continuously learn about its present environment and may project the future environment with appropriate consideration of new organizational forms to meet various challenges. Perhaps the most important implication of this process is that the organization is able to develop new goals or to revise established goals in order to achieve its organizational objectives. Organizational processes should always open up broad alternatives and improve the possibility of discovering new objectives and goals when the organization has predicted the future environment. Adequate knowledge about our environment increases the probabilities for organizational survival and reduces the risks involved in policymaking.

Change

The concept of the "temporary society" offers what may be the best descriptive term for modern organizations. Nothing ever remains the same as it was at the moment it is observed. Findings in organizational research indicate the predominance of change; the process of change is inevitable and constant. The organization is in a constant state of change not only because it consists of individuals who are in a constant state of change but also because it functions in a continually changing environment. It is the individual

Figure 1   Organization and Its Environment

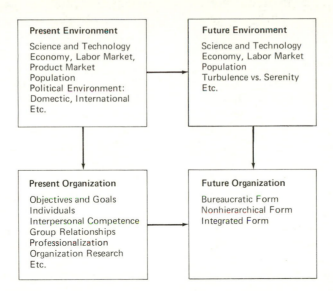

who breaths life into the organization, and it is the collective behavior, modified by internal and external forces, which defines the nature of organizational goals.

The integrated approach stresses the need for continual organizational change to shape and accommodate the future. This implies the need for a conceptual framework for change. Figure 2 offers such a schema.

The integrated approach to change suggests a frame of reference which administrators and change agents can consider a

conceptual tool for developing the capability for alterations in the structures and processes of existing organizations. The integrated use of knowledge developed from different perspectives or theories should increase organizational capacity both to adapt and to change in the present environment and to project and to shape the future environment. Increasing the change capability of the organization implies a sharp increase in its innovativeness, which, in turn, offers such rewards as improved consistency between short-

Figure 2   Conceptual Framework for Integrated Organizational Change

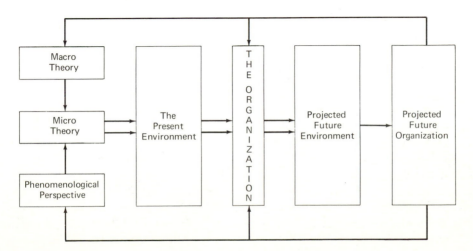

term and long-term goals, encouragement of individual development, greater emphasis on interpersonal competence and trust among members, and increased reliance on professionalization. Implied, too, are reduced emphases on formalization, control, authority and power, and the abstract and regulated life of the bureaucracy.

A useful distinction has been drawn between organizational change and the "changing organization." Both are extremely dynamic processes, but they are different. Organizational *change* involves identifying and programming needed changes, accommodating resistance to change, and dealing with the ambiguity which attends change. The concept of *changing* implies processes of continual feedback, evaluation, and adaptation. Problems of direction, resistance, and ambiguity are handled through socialization and training processes, the cybernetic support system, and the open nature of relevant systems. To achieve the condition of *changing* implies a whole new set of perspectives related to dealing with people and systems in organizational settings; instead of controlling the organizational variables, the administrator would set variables to function in terms of human capabilities, system flexibility, and overall identification with goals and objectives. We suggest that tomorrow's world will need increasing emphasis on change capability and that the changing organization—Buckley's morphogenic model—may well be the model for the future.

This implies that new knowledge is needed both about man and about systems. We need to improve our skills for projecting the future environment and the organizational forms and processes that will become necessary. We must learn to consider man and the future environment in as many different dimensions as possible rather than seeing them in the terms we find relevant to our needs today. This reinforces the value of the phenomenological perspective, while at the same time, it illustrates the need for further refinement of knowledge available through

macro and micro theory-building and research. Our product should be organizations which properly employ the qualities of the view of man, while at the same time, they should contribute to his development. Such organizations must have the capacity to monitor the environment, to make reasonable estimates of the implications of what they find and to adapt automatically to new conditions and potentials. The new condition would reflect the creative, growing, and adaptive quality of the mature person, while at the same time, it would make appropriate use of the superb support systems currently being developed.

Strategies for Integrated Change

The integration of new ideas, processes, and hardware to achieve organizational change and changing cannot be accomplished unless there is a high level of organizational capacity for adaptation. Such integration requires new strategies for organizational change. First, structural flexibility is needed to relate the organization to its environment with more fidelity. Recently, many top administrators in bureaucratic structures (in other words, complex organizations) have begun to recognize that the rigidity of bureaucracy makes its adaptation to the changing environment almost impossible. Managers from private organizations may be more aware of that fact than those in government organizations. The rigid bureaucratic structure may continue to be at least partially applicable in those organizations which strive for a high degree of predictability in short-term output and which demand that their members precisely conform to institutional goals. Certainly such rigidity is not encouraged for most research and development organizations. In those organizations, creativity and initiative is valued, and considerable uncertainty attends schedules and eventual products.

A further reason for structural flexibility is that modern organizations tend to have multiple conflicts and multiple sources of power; they reflect the pluralistic policy process and are a component of that process. By definition, pluralistic policy determination accommodates a broad diversity of interests. While the pluralistic system has many limitations such as frequent overaccommodation to external rather than internal pressures, it is and will be a continuing feature of organizational life. For the organization to function within such a force field the internal structure must be much more amenable to adaptive change than is typical of the present situation.

A second strategy, perhaps the most important one, is the administrator's use of knowledge. The administrator's willingness to search for new ideas, to experiment with them, and to adopt those which are promising proves to be a useful and accurate measure of the speed of organizational change and adaptation. How may we begin to develop new thinking and to design the new organizations we must have to accommodate the increasingly turbulent environment? There are many ambiguities in managing complex organizations, but we believe the following considerations will prove to be significant. In general, the enlightened administrator will:

1) show willingness to provide the incentives and opportunities for development of the individual's potential abilities.
2) provide the climate for creativity and innovation, for risk-taking, and for ensuring organizational support for such activities.
3) identify environmental forces relevant to the organization and establish workable relationships with those forces.
4) constrain administrative discretion to fit the bonds imposed by internal and external human restraints and system restraints.
5) proactive rather than reactive organizational policies and management.

6) show awareness of the significance of time dimensions.
7) display consciousness of both short-term and long-term goals and possibilities.
8) employ skillful awareness and accommodation of behavioral dimensions in formulating and implementing means toward goals.
9) make the organization reflect, in its behavior, acceptance of responsibility for the pursuit of social goals in its own social grouping and in the larger society.
10) assure that the organization offers the "slack" necessary for the psychological security of members and that it supplies the resources necessary for organizational research, for risk-taking, for personal development, and so forth.

Organizational research represents a third important strategy. Involved is both the effective use of existing knowledge and participation in the search for new knowledge. Organizational research aims at the integration of the knowledge and methods developed by behavioral scientists into the ongoing processes of the organization. This implies openness, trial and error, experimentation, measurement of results, and so forth. To survive and grow, organizations must engage in continuing research on the relevance of knowledge to their present and future condition. The activities associated with organizational research must be oriented toward the future. Such an orientation necessitates new research methods, new thinking toward people, new relationships with clients, new involvements of professionals in the organization, new information, new technology, and possibly even new ways of making policy.

Organization research may offer the means to measure the adequacy of existing policies. Organizational development through time implies a thorough investigation of existing policies, a determination of the successes and failures of those policies, and the identification of alternative possibilities. The sum of those activities is of potential value not only to private organizations that are fighting for survival and growth in a changing market system but also to public organizations which have a responsibility to the public for viable policies which directly deal with societal issues, change, and development.

Summary

Today's organizations, with their inheritance of rationalism and technocracy, are locked into a set of values, procedures, and techniques which render them so reactively oriented that they are almost incapable of proactive change. Their administrators appear to be unaware of the challenges that are rapidly mounting around them—challenges to both the organization and the general society. Thus, our concern in this book is with the problems of organizational adaptation to a changing environment and with the development of tomorrow's organizations. Both of these purposes depend upon new uses of new knowledge. Through such uses we may achieve a better understanding of complex human behavior, grasp the implications of organizations conceived as open systems, and begin to comprehend the totality of the organizational phenomenon. The development of such new uses calls for a new theoretical perspective which integrates a variety of theories and knowledge by pulling together the broad range of possibilities.

An integrated perspective in organization theory necessarily implies the use and understanding of various theories in formulating meaningful organizational goals and generating responsible policy choices. An integrated overview for the changing organization is significant for the development of the modern organization as a whole, both in relation to its present and its future environments. As modern organizations become more and more complex and increasingly interact with the powerful forces of human behavior and an expanding environment, changing organizations will require new roles for administrators. Updated management roles are needed in order to facilitate the adaptation of new knowledge and to initiate various change processes. Needless to say, only through the accumulation of new knowledge can administrators ever hope to be able to design and redesign organizations that effectively confront both contemporary difficulties and foreseeable future problems and contingencies. In order to expect continuous organizational development, tomorrow's organizations must carry on vastly different research activities. Such research activities are necessary to avoid unintended consequences, to correct internal mistakes, and to develop plans for action. All these strategies for tomorrow's organizations depend upon a capacity for adaptation and a new-style management that will cope with the changing needs of both tomorrow's man and his organizations.

References and Notes

1. Arnold M. Rose, "Variations of Sociological Imagination," *American Sociological Review* 34, no. 5 (October 1969): 623–30.
2. C. Wright Mills, *The Sociological Imagination* (New York: Grove Press, Inc., 1959), p. 174. Berger and Luckman, who introduced a dialectical perspective upon the theoretical orientation of the social sciences, suggest the construction of a new reality between social phenomena and individual existence. See Peter L. Berger and Thomas Luckman, *The Social Construction of Reality* (Garden City, N.Y.: Doubleday and Company, Inc., 1966).
3. These indicators are based upon studies by such scholars as Abraham Maslow, Hadley Cantril, and Douglas McGregor.
4. Figure 1 is a modified version of one which was developed by a member of a Manchester Business School Graduate Seminar, "Integrated Organizational Strategy," *The Journal of Management Studies* 6, no. 1 (February 1969): 106.

Part One *The Different Future*

INTRODUCTION TO PART ONE

The initial two chapters of this book include a discussion of the environment of the future and the kinds of organizations which appear likely to fit the new conditions. We shall proceed from the conviction that the future—including, of course, the next few decades—will be different in many dramatic and significant ways from what we now know or have known in the past.

The challenges of the future have attracted many writers from virtually every substantive viewpoint. Works focusing on this subject have ranged from science fiction and cartoons to scholarly endeavors such as *Toward the Year 2000, Mankind Two Thousand, The Year 2000, Toward the Year Two Thousand Eighteen, The Next Ninety Years,* and *Twenty-First Century: The Control of Life.* Most of these works are products of future-oriented research and of academic meetings carried out by such organizations as the Hudson Institute, the Commission on the Year 2000 of the American Academy of Arts and Sciences, the American Institute of Planners, the World Future Society, and Les Futuribles in Paris. Current on the list is *The Limits of Growth,* produced under the prestigious auspices of The Club of Rome and scholars at M.I.T.

Without exception, the writings and seminars of the futurists express the concept that a "different future" is rap-idly taking form and that, as such, it offers many promising and exciting possibilities as well as some awesome threats. The efforts of these organizations and writers are geared to projecting possible futures and using such predictions to draw inferences about important elements of societies that are to come. The future clearly presents many serious challenges in such areas as space science, technology, industry, thermonuclear power, urbanization, transportation, biomedical engineering, ecology, consumption of energy, educational systems, and so forth. We may reasonably assume that all of these will have a great effect upon the quality of future human life.

A phenomenon which will relate to future conditions—and will considerably affect them—will be the organizational form and style which evolves from our current models and potential strategies. We may not be able to predict the exact conditions the future environment may hold for tomorrow's organizations, but we do know that future societies will be at least as dependent on organizations as they are today and that the alternatives in the form and operation of organizations will have much to do with the nature of the future and the level of its creativity and achievement. We have become increasingly aware of the fact that what happens in the operation of our organizations has much to do with the achievement of our societal goals and the solution of our problems. We know, too, that the way organizations are established and managed relates intimately to the growth and development of individuals in the society.

Tomorrow's Environment

Among the more obvious features of the environment of most countries in the year 2000 will be the increase in population and the highly urbanized character of many societies. Population estimates range from 300 to 330 million people in the United States, while the trend toward urbanization in the U.S. appears likely to continue at such a rate that, by the year 2000, between 80 and 90 percent of the population will be urban. Obviously, population growth and rapid urbanization will create and reveal many complex problems which will affect every aspect of life as the millenium ends.

Another major effect on many future societies will be caused by economic growth. Kahn and Wiener estimate that if current trends in U.S. industrialization continue, the Gross National Product, currently just over one trillion dollars, will be more than three trillion dollars by the year 2000.[1] The United States already has more than half its labor force employed in service-oriented rather than production-oriented jobs. Many writers predict that the ratio of highly trained professional workers to production workers will continue to increase rapidly.

This trend toward a more service-oriented, affluent, learned, "knowledgeable" society appears likely to continue at an accelerating rate. Futurists argue that the combined effects of industrialization, scientific knowledge, and technological change may produce a completely new industrial society in the U.S. by the year 2000; indeed, America already is experiencing a new industrial revolution. The industrial period has been described by various writers as the postindustrial society, the postmodern society, the supraindustrial society, and the knowledge society. Daniel Bell[2] describes five dimensions of the postindustrial society: (1) the creation of a service economy; (2) the preeminence of the professional and technical class; (3) the centrality of theoretical knowledge as the source of innovation and policy formulation in the society; (4) the possibility of self-sustaining technological growth; and (5) the creation of a new "intellectual technology."

The new postindustrial society will probably mean a much greater development of human resources and professionalization in the future; one can hardly visualize any other way that it could function. The needs of a complex, dynamic economy will demand more knowledge and higher job mobility. After all, scientific and technological developments affect the level of education required of the labor force. Since science and technology, as well as other areas of knowledge, are changing at an increasingly rapid rate, we may assume that education and training will necessarily become a continuous element in almost everyone's life. Additional training, even formal education, is already needed by most administrators, physicians, engineers, and many other professionals for "retooling" and "self-renewing." Warren Bennis and Philip Slater point out that we are already beginning an era when a man's knowledge and intellectual approach may be obsolete before he has even begun his chosen career.[3]

The Futuristic Orientation: Its Relevance for Tomorrow's Organizations

Changing environments have always stimulated change in both private and public organizations, but the policy-shaping responses of many such organizations have too often been reactive and piecemeal. More and more, it appears clear that the process of transition from the industrial to the post-industrial era is engendering organizational dysfunction, societal unrest, personal alienation, discontent with bureaucracy, and many additional organizational and personal reactions. Many of those ills appear to be the outcome of the incremental method of achieving change—a method exercised by most of our organizations as well as our political system. In view of our unfortunate experiences in this regard, we may well find it advantageous, in our large organizations, to develop more of a "forwardist" or future-oriented administrator as compared to the traditional, conservative administrator characteristic of past organizations. In de Jouvenel's terms, policymakers or administrators must anticipate changing conditions in the future and introduce changes in organization to avoid unexpected problems. Other authors argue for the development of *proactive* capability to the extent that the organization more directly and vigorously creates its own future.

The essays in Chapter 1 stress the proactive orientation. A selection especially pertinent to organization theory and management is that of Bertrand de Jouvenel, a leading futurist, who argues that the "forwardist" manifests and values "a care for improvement which in itself comprises not only the term of 'more' but the term of 'better.' " Improvement in the quality of human life, in turn, necessitates a better understanding of human resources—and such understanding should be reflected in development of more appropriate goals for new organizations.

The second paper, by Kahn and Wiener, points out that "the different future" depends on today's policy choices. More precisely, the speculating about future events implies the anticipation of future problems and the initiation of effective long-range plans and programs. In contrast to these initial articles, Robert Biller indicates that we may anticipate possible procedural differences between an industrial society and a postindustrial society. He maintains that changes in a post-industrial era should be expected to effect a proactive orientation rather than a reactive, reformist character and that such changes should bring about not only a fusion of knowledge and action in policy formulation but also an effective dialectical analysis of past and present experiences with change directly related to future planning.

One common emphasis among these three viewpoints is the importance of policy research within a context of social phenomena, social action, and social change. Organizations must anticipate problems at an early stage by conducting policy research. Effective policymaking requires projections based on reliable information. How to develop human beings for innovation and change, how to encourage the use of new knowledge, how to be aware of technological forces and their impact on change, and how to relate current goals to future goals—these are distinct challenges for today's organizations. Clearly, a futuristic, "forwardist" orientation in the administration of today's organizations has direct relevance to a different and better future.

Shaping Tomorrow's Organizations Today

Chapter 1 addresses a number of possibilities for designing organizations to meet the challenges of tomorrow. In a way, of course, the year 2000 is already with us. Peter Drucker has expressed this very well.

What we do now and in the next few years, in our business as well as in our classrooms, will very largely determine the one crucial quality of 'the year

2000': the vision, self-respect, and performance capacities of leaders of tomorrow's America. . . . Tomorrow's vision is today's work assignment.[4]

The clear implication is that today's organizations should begin to shape and design new organizations for the new man who will be employed in tomorrow's organizations and who will be the human part of the environment of the future. There are several purposes implicit in changing and reshaping today's organizations. Three essential purposes are: to minimize risk in decision outputs, to forecast future problems as early as possible, and to cope with unexpected challenges. After all, increased knowledge and rapid technological change have brought many unprecedented problems to business and public organizations—how to find new ways for using and managing professionals, how to devise structural changes for handling organizational innovation and change, how to employ new techniques for managing information (particularly computer systems), and how to bring about the appropriate amount of system decentralization are but a few of those problems. Significantly, those issues circumscribe many of the major changes that have occurred in management in the past fifty years. Despite their importance, however, the solution of those problems represents hardly more than a start toward meeting the needs of today's and tomorrow's organizations.

The one thing that can be said about the future with any degree of certainty is that contemporary societal complexity will become more apparent, more pressing, and, doubtless, more dysfunctional. There are many "straws in the wind" today which suggest that society faces vastly different, possibly far more intense problems in the future than have been encountered thus far; the result is expected to be increasing turbulence, paradox, and ambiguity. Once again, the basic reason for those developments may well be the explosion of knowledge and technology. In the past, the knowledge explosion has given rise to large organizations—a development which is likely to continue. Short of devastation by an ecological or nuclear disaster, nothing we are now measuring suggests anything other than the likelihood that organizations, in whatever new form they take, will be even more complex in the more complex environments of the future.

Another certain trend is that many more socially significant functions will be performed by large organizations, both private and public, in the future. It is already happening; despite many handicaps, large organizations are presently becoming increasingly involved with many socially significant activities. This book is premised, in part, on the conviction that much more needs to be done in this regard. Some organizations are now beginning to function in a more socially conscious manner. Indeed, organizations have too often been destructive of such entities as individuality, a sense of community, the public interest, growth, develoment, change, and so forth. They have produced much of the impersonalization, alienation, dehumanization, normlessness, and powerlessness which characterize our times. The rejection of responsibility for social costs, particularly by many of the hugest industrial corporations, has contributed immensely to the destruction of our environment as well as some of the physical and human resources of those organizations. These are matter of vital, central significance to society; no society can achieve true greatness while strong destructive qualities are maintained within the social system. That modern organizations are becoming aware of the serious nature of these matters, are finding ways of combatting self-defeating policies that downgrade human dignity, and are creating people-building management techniques which are functional to organizational needs and goals is a development of historic significance. We may assume that such techniques, as will be described in this volume, will be refined and expanded in the future.

Other features of today's organizations which appear especially promising are the growing interdependence among many of them, the subtle blending of the lines between public and private, and increasing diversity in each of the two sectors. This is most noticeable in the granting of contracts by the federal government for private research. It is also apparent in business organizations to the extent that owners and managers are becoming more concerned with education and training for employees. Another characteristic of the interdependence of organizations is the increased exchange of professionals. In the field of public administration, for instance, there has been more reliance on private enterprise in introducing new ideas for change. The survival problems of business organizations, with their motivations for profit and productivity, altogether have accelerated more change, innovation, and risk taking than have public organizations. However, Kahn and Wiener predict that in the postindustrial society, business organizations will no longer be the major source of such innovation and change. Public organizations will have to play a more dynamic role in societal development; they will have to become accountable for social involvement and for developing internal management procedures that will combat some of the human problems of our time. For many organizations, public as well as private, such internal procedures may prove to be more important to society than the substantive program for which the organization was established.

If public administration has made any major innovative contributions to management, these could be systems analysis and PPBS (Programming-Planning-Budgeting Systems). Both of these tools suffer from a lack of proper accounting for political and human dimensions in their analytical methods; however, the fact that such management techniques are far from perfected should not discourage their application in appropriate circumstances. With careful consideration and refinement, they may serve as useful means for rational planning and policy development. Admittedly, determining what the right strategies are for societal change is no easy task, but it is fairly evident that the methods and structures which government has used in the past are not appropriate for solving today's problems or the problems of tomorrow.

The discussion above, while far from being comprehensive about the future responsibility of large organizations, does suggest many of the reasons why today's organizations must respond to increasing knowledge and complexity. The responses have been minimal thus far; they do not get to the center of the problems. Unless organizations face up to the task of redesigning their systems to be flexible in using people more creatively and more constructively and to adapting to the turbulent environment, the future may be far less satisfactory than the present.

New Organizations in Perspective

Organizations in the future will be composed of people with different needs and values. They will be effectively coordinating their efforts for the accomplishment of multiple goals. The goals of the organization will be more widely shared among people in the organization than is the case today. We believe we can assume a sort of "authentic organization" which characterizes the responsibility for its own existence in relation to human existence, a dialectical consideration of man-and-organization. An authentic organization encourages the individual's full realization of his potential and his realistic life goals. In relating to administrative dogma and to society, such an organization represents a revolt against certain tendencies inherent in modern technology and superrationalism. Thus, the authentic organization emphasizes the restoration of corresponding authentic human values within the confinement of organizational procedures. On the other hand, the term *inauthentic organization* implies an organization which not only fails to provide adequate service for its members and clients but also fails to assume any responsibility for society. It only promotes rational-organizational goals; it is the kind of organization which reflects Douglas McGregor's "Theory X."

Thus tomorrow's organization (presumably "authentic" in our terms) is essentially a "human organization," but it retains, at the same time, a rational mode of existence. On the one hand, such an organization assumes the necessity of being humanistic; on the other hand, it must consider and account the rationality of organizational goals. The goals and policies of new organizations will be related to the consciousness of policymakers and organizational members and will gain their interpretation of reality from empirical organizational and social phenomena. Goal seeking and goal-oriented behavior in general are characteristic of modern organizations; furthermore, most individuals tend to behave purposively, their behavior being regulated by conscious goals and intentions. If all the goals and policies are prescribed in the rules of management, they may not lead to effective action because they conflict with the goals and needs of both the individual and the group. When individuals commit themselves to organizational objectives, they expect to exert influence in the achievement of those objectives. Thus the more "meaningful" an organization's goals are, the more likely they are to motivate and guide people's actions and to generate commitment to organizational activities. This concept suggests many ways wherein typical public and private organizations might broaden their goals, making them more socially relevant.

Approaches to Tomorrow's Organizations

We note that the study of the future must remain highly probabilistic, since future events obviously involve a thousand "ifs" and "maybes." Future events will be affected by the availability of imaginative hypotheses for guiding thought and development, by limitations on the amount of knowledge brought to bear on policy issues, by unexpected human intervention, and by particular challenges which cannot be foreseen. In other words, no one condition or guideline is adequate to the task of forecasting because of the inevitable uncertainty about the course of events as well as a relative degree of uncertainty in the decisionmaking processes. Since it is hazardous to predict single events or historical turning points, we will sketch some broad possibilities likely to be found in tomorrow's world. Such a course is preferable because what is desired is not a decision guide for particular situations but a broad apparatus to aid in delineating how the future may be approached. There is no clairvoyance involved; future problems may be considered from many perspectives.

In this vein, we will describe possible means for inquiry into tomorrow's organizations and search for answers to questions concerning organizational phenomena which appear likely to be critical. Although speculation about tomorrow's organizations is exciting and challenging, as this orientation considers the possibility of improving human life through new organizational modes, no fully systematic approaches to the subject have yet been made. The purposes of an organization have been variously defined throughout the history of organization theory. Weber, Taylor, Fayol, and other classic writers theorized about organizations in terms of the essentially mechanical criteria of rationality and efficiency as their frame of reference, whereas today's behavioral scientists emphasize the analysis of human organizations through behavioral, psychological, and structural inquiry. For the purposes of this volume, we suggest three means for studying tomorrow's organizations. None is as systematic as we might wish, but the three offer a useful range of perspectives.

Historical-Descriptive

This approach analyzes organization in historical perspective. A basic assumption in this context is that the more complex are the social and organizational problems which need to be solved, the more management requires a system of coordination and control to ensure productivity and the accomplishment of goals. The historical approach associates virtue with the progress of an industrial society based upon powerful bureaucratic structures and processes. Thus, organization research generally aims at the identification of major structural and procedural variables which make for organization success. Normally, these include such matters as hierarchy, division of labor, centralization of authority, specification of rules, elaboration of measurements, specialization, and so forth. Theorists using this approach attempt to coordinate human actions through controlled structural elements. Briefly, then, this approach predicts tomorrow's organization from the knowledge of the past.

Utopian

Under this term we introduce two perspectives which, though normally in opposition with each other, may, under the utopian approach, be joined. These are a strong normative stance combined with a technological perspective. Students who evaluate human organizations through the behavioral frame of reference often identify themselves with a normative bias favoring deep concern for the latent human values in organization. This has led to development of a variety of scenarios based on behavioral and psychological dimensions to describe (and prescribe) tomorrow's organizations. In this context, organization is defined as a system of human values; organizations must justify their existence in terms of these values. Within the utopian paradigm exists the possibility of creating a new organization through technology and of taking full account of human values as well as structural needs. A computer system could supply an information-handling center which would coordinate human activities in human growth terms, the management of policy information, and normal organizational procedures. The increasing application of such technological possibilities to organizational processes can be expected to foster more interest in the changing of human behavior as well as changing organizational structures and processes. In brief, this approach would create tomorrow's "perfect" organizations by putting together a normative humanistic position—the complex motivational and behavioral variables in modern organizations and the various dimensions of organizational subsystems—though the extraordinary capability of our evolving technology.

Multidimensional

The multidimensional approach builds upon the historical evolution of organizations, but it also assumes the possibility, even the likelihood, that many contemporary structural variables will be discontinued at a future time. This approach assumes multiple contingencies among structural and behavioral variables. Social and organizational phenomena are viewed as a complex interrelated web of multiple realities unavailable to easy stereotyping, control, or long-term projection. This frame of reference represents organizational development and problem solving through the integration of organizational and individual needs in a "sociotechnical system." It takes advantage of environmental forces to achieve organizational change. In this context, tomorrow's organizations evolve partly as logical projections of historical characteristics, partly as reflections of normative possibility, and partly as proactive manifestations of the accommodation of environmental realities, the organizational system, and the needs of members in the organization.

Organizational Forms for Tomorrow

In Chapter 2 are included a number of papers which deal more generally with what is implied by "tomorrow's organizations." The essays provide many insights into the process of constructing a new organizational and social reality for future organizations. For the most part, they not only argue that organizations should democratize various processes so that more members "get into the decisionmaking act" but also that organizations must become increasingly aware of their responsibilities toward individuals and toward the environment.

We turn now to the design of new organizational forms. In most respects, recent developments relating to future organizational forms or the design of new organizations have been divergent and difficult to integrate into a meaningful conceptual framework. With some simplification and projection, however, we can discern three main forms of "future organizations." These three models are natural projections

from the three approaches presented in the previous section: [See below].

Historical approach ⟶ Bureaucratic model

Utopian approach ⟶ Nonhierarchial model

Multidimensional approach ⟶ Integrated model

Many scholars have emphasized the continuous existence through human history of the *bureaucratic* or hierarchical model of organization. Others argue that the bureaucratic form will characterize the future just as it has characterized the past by dint of its persistent and often irrefutable logic. The organizational form of large contemporary administrative organizations, public and private, tends to reflect this complex pyramidal type of structure, with its emphasis on formal authority and procedure, work measurement, files, and so forth. The bureaucratic form appears likely to be continued unless top executives adopt some radical changes that are presently seen in only a few places. Indeed, organizations of the near future will probably continue to manifest bureaucratic characteristics to some degree, even though their forms and processes are substantially modified by accommodation to new theory. The model appears likely to persist for the next few decades even though it has been subjected to many strains and adjustments. The bureaucratic model features:

1) A pyramidal arrangement of its hierarchy
2) Formal division of work, based on task specialization
3) Clearly defined authority, chain of command, and communication
4) A merit system based on technical competence
5) Prescribed rules and regulations
6) Accountability
7) Decisionmaking power centered at the top

A fundamental assumption underlying this "mechanical model" is that bureaucracy will achieve a higher degree of efficiency and greater productivity as long as the pyramidal hierarchy and its associated values exist and are permitted to control the system. McGregor's Theory X, reviewed in the article by Morse and Lorsch, describes assumptions about human nature and human behavior which attend the traditional bureaucratic model.[5] The evolution of bureaucracy has paralleled the industrial revolution and has contributed to its success. Because of its past successes and its rational qualities, bureaucracy, as an organizational model, continues to attract most management people in government and industry; it continues to be used extensively with few changes in its various fundamental forms. Morse and Lorsch argue that the hierarchical model still serves with usefulness and effectiveness those organizations with high-level task performance and precise productivity needs.

In recent years the bureaucratic model has been criticized by more humanistically oriented scholars, many of whom sponsor an alternative, herewith termed the *nonhierarchical model* (or "beyond bureaucracy" model). Some of the basic features of the nonhierarchical model are:

1) A new concept of man based on behavioral science research findings
2) A new concept of shared power based on freedom and reason
3) Elimination of hierarchy
4) Favorable organizational policies toward individual effectiveness
5) Information system widely shared among members

These factors are elaborated in the essays of Bennis and Forrester. While Forrester suggests elimination of the superior-subordinate relationship that tends to be based on the use of technological systems, Bennis posits the end of bureaucracy in order to serve changing human needs in the organization. He argues that the social structure of tomorrow's organizations will be adaptive and rapidly changing "temporary systems." Maslow's eupsychian management is another example of a nonhierarchical model which assumes a flexible utopian system which will develop the intrinsic needs of individuals—particularly the need for self-actualization.[6] Stressing a strong value orientation, this theory argues that tomorrow's organizations must be designed to fit people rather than to fit job tasks. Forrester says that the development of science and technology provides a new opportunity for designing a nonhierarchical organization which will increase structural flexibility, innovation, and individual freedom of action. Most existing organizations are built upon a rigid hierarchical structure, and they incorporate information monopolies so characteristic of bureaucracy. In the new organization, individuals will have much greater internal mobility, more access to information, and an increased feeling of shared power.

Most bureaucratically-oriented managers have trouble with nonhierarchical theory and remain unconvinced despite increasing evidence in support of such organizational patterns. Public administrators, especially, tend to take a dim view of this approach. They are familiar with traditional concepts of management, and they are (perhaps overly) aware of the need for stabilization of their systems; instability and flexibility are perceived as threats to their power and control and as catalysts for political risks that they prefer to avoid. Bureaucratic administrative theory offers them a convenient hideout wherein they may pursue their goals with little visibility (or vulnerability) to either their clientele or their legislative overviewers.

The third form can be entitled the *integrated model* (also called the mixed model); it fits very well the premise of this book—that, for most areas of organization and management, the most appropriate model is one which draws on major features of other, often more extensive models. The integrated approach includes well defined opposition to the classic bureaucratic model, but it is not as extreme in its critique as is the second model. Rather, it represents a selective amalgam of hierarchical necessities with a strong dash of humanism. As the selections by both Argyris and Morse & Lorsch point out, the traditional organizational form tends to be effective for routine decisionmaking and noninnovative activity. But organizations such as those in research and development appear to gain in effectiveness through the triadic qualities of less formalized decisionmaking processes, more value placed on innovation and creativity, and vastly increased personal autonomy for members. The integrated model attempts to meet both kinds of need. The following significant features are encouraged under the integrated model:

1) Participative management
2) New, nonauthoritarian leadership styles
3) Risk taking and mutual trust
4) The accounting of both technical skill and interpersonal competence
5) More power and control to lower levels of the hierarchy
6) Adaptive change capability in relation to the turbulent environment

Chris Argyris' matrix organization accentuates the above elements. By maximizing these elements, tomorrow's organizations will become more effective problem-solving systems and will be more competent in rewarding experimentation and in learning from new experiences. Scott emphasizes the role of the institution and its social responsibility for promoting humanism and pluralism. His ideas about organizational government offer an organizational guarantee of due process in handling individual grievances and conflicts, and they embody the concept that leaders should encourage member participation in making organizational policies and decisions. The encouragement of participation should make it easier for people to represent their own interests and their unit interests in the process of goal setting in future organizations. As reviewed by Morse and Lorsch, McGregor's Theory Y is another effort to integrate individual and organizational goals.[7]

Rensis Likert, in *The Human Organization,* also adopts an integrated view, stressing shared power in the relationship between management and employees, multiple coordination among groups in the problem-solving process, and more reflection of human values in achievement of organizational goals.[8] In view of these various considerations, we propose that the integrated model is the most likely to be successful in accommodating today's organizations to tomorrow's needs. The model encourages not only the search for possibilities in integrating individuals and organizations but also a continuous integration of sociopsychological characteristics of members into the more "rational" elements of the system—and the selection of the latter by imaginative appraisal of need rather than by rote and by rule. This form appears especially useful for launching the transition from a more traditional model, since it does not imply the complete rejection of established forms and practices; yet, it may also be most representative of "tomorrow's organizations."

Impact of Organization Forms

With three general models briefly described, a further consideration of the consequences of each of the three forms is in order. The different models produce different organizational outcomes. Since there are a variety of out-

Table 1   Organizational Forms and Their Possible Outcomes

Forms	Produc- tivity	Conflict	Satisfac- tion	Change	Innova- tion	Aliena- tion
Bureaucratic						
Nonhierarchical						
Integrated						

comes and since the outcomes depend upon which model is selected, there must be careful consideration to needed or anticipated values. Table 1 offers a frame of reference for considering alternatives.

In this introduction we will not address the measurement of productivity, conflict, satisfaction, change innovation, and alienation, although these are important organizational qualities about which there are many research findings. Our interest here is simply to discuss the relationships between organization form and the consequent outcomes as revealed in contemporary literature.

Since the bureaucratic model assumes high behavioral conformity of individuals into various organizational roles, objectives, and goals, this form of organization generates high predictability and system stability; in turn, there is greater productivity in short-run terms. The bureaucratic organization may survive for a short period of time in a turbulent environment, but the organization has made important trade-offs to achieve its extra efficiency and productivity. Among these are survival capability, innovativeness, the ability to change and adapt, and others. During the existence of the bureaucracy, members tend to be alienated, hostile, and less participative in organizational activity. The model is likely to include among members a low satisfaction in terms of personal development, low self-esteem, and very little self-actualization even at the upper levels. On the other hand, it may offer high satisfaction with economic rewards. In the bureaucratic organization, conflict is considered detri-

mental to organizational performance; it is not considered a desirable basis for organizational change, as is the case with both alternative models. Top administrators are considered responsible for introducing and establishing change; any change-oriented plan or idea must be approved by them. There is little room for either innovation or creativity.

The nonhierarchical model, on the other hand, assumes the unpredictable quality of human nature. Accordingly, different organizational situations require an analysis of complex human behaviors. Productivity cannot be guaranteed unless the human factor is considered in the process of goal formulation: Various human processes are stressed rather than productivity and the accomplishment of intended goals. Both conflict and deviant behavior are major sources of innovation and change. Conflict is indeed functional; under stable conditions, the generation of conflict may be necessary to bring new types of change into the organization.[9] Increased satisfaction of a variety of human needs and values will eventually develop high productivity in human organizations. There is little problem with alienation when such needs are satisfied.

The integrated model suggests that productivity and satisfaction are outputs of an effective collaboration among members—both employees and management. In the process of integration, the organization must offer attractive goals to its members. In the terms of this model, conflict and deviant behavior may be either functional or dysfunctional processes; rather than eliminating conflict, this model would regulate the source of conflict.[10] Presumably, one could structure an organization which was capable of admitting no conflict—either all conflicts would be resolved by the system or the organization would screen them all out. Many would argue that this extreme state of "no conflict" would represent a condition of no change. Fortunately, organizations are made of people, who, being human, can be expected to interact, aspire, have ideas and needs, compete, and, in additional ways, generate conflict. Growth and change, in turn, are the end products of conflict.

Today's public organizations and large private organizations are generally structured in such a manner as to screen out the very change mechanisms scholars are so fond of extolling. Pondy argues that we have "spent much more time avoiding conflict than resolving it."[11] Pondy's point is well taken. After all, public organizations, in particular, are structured in such a way that they are not comfortable in conflict situations. While the environment is characterized by turbulence and conflict, the structure used to deal with open, unstructured, and unstable reality is itself extremely orderly, hierarchical, and based on premises which are unreal. The bureaucratic model used by public agencies cannot cope with various contemporary environmental forces; such a model is out of alignment with the environment in which the organization must exist and change. Innovation and creativity in the integrated model depend, among other things, upon risk-taking ability among policymakers and members of the organization, high interpersonal competence among executives and members, structural flexibility, autonomy.[12]

Organizations are responsible for reducing individual alienation and developing an authentic relationship with members. The integrated model appears to be the only one that offers those qualities in a form in which they may be realized and put to use.

Summary

In order to meet the challenges of tomorrow and to bring the changes needed in modern organizations, three organizational forms were presented in this introduction. Each of the organizational models will elicit different consequences in the organizational process. Although the bureaucratic model will exist in "the different future," it appears to offer many negative consequences, and long-term survival appears unlikely for that model. Many scholars in the field of public administration argue that public policymakers are now actively pursuing societal goals that are inconsistent with what may very likely be the basic trends of culture ten to thirty years into the future; the reason is that there is an inconsistency between short-term and long-term goals due to the incremental nature of public policymaking. Yet bureaucratic organizations tend both to extend and to accentuate such disparity!

Given the problems associated with the bureaucratic model in comparison with the possibilities offered by the nonhierarchical and integrated models, we believe it likely that the latter will slowly but surely replace the former. The "authentic organization" of tomorrow's world will be more closely related to either the nonhierarchical or the integrated models. We believe that organizational goals are likely to be accomplished best when individual members feel their personal goals and needs are reflected in both their organizational role and the management process. We see the general trend in organizational theory to be oriented toward these two models with their more humanistic and more futuristic focus.

A task for today's organizations is to restructure the system to accommodate a broader variety of conflicts and deviant behaviors, using them as triggers for problem solving and change. Such activity represents appropriate risk taking and experimentation today as a preface for the increased change capability needed tomorrow.

References and Notes

1. Herman Kahn and Anthony J. Wiener, *The Year 2000: A Framework for Speculation on the Next Thirty-Three Years* (London: The Macmillan Company, 1969).

2. Daniel Bell, "The Measurement of Knowledge and Technology," in *Indicators for Social Change,* Eleanor B. Sheldon and Wilbert E. Moore, eds. (New York: Russell Sage Foundation, 1968), pp. 152–61.

3. Warren G. Bennis and Philip E. Slater, *The Temporary Society* (New York: Harper and Row, Publishers, 1968).

4. Peter F. Drucker, ed., *Preparing Tomorrow's Business Leaders Today* (Englewood Cliffs, N.J.: Prentice-Hall, Inc., 1969), p. 290.

5. Douglas McGregor, *The Human Side of Enterprise* (New York: McGraw-Hill Book Company, 1960), pp. 33–34.

6. Abraham Maslow, *The Eupsychian Management* (Homewood, Illinois: Richard D. Irwin, Inc., 1965).

7. See also Douglas McGregor, *Human Side,* pp. 59–243.

8. Rensis Likert, *The Human Organization* (New York: McGraw-Hill Book Company, 1967).

9. See Magoroh Maruyama, "The Second Cybernetics: Deviation-Amplifying Mutual Causal Processes," *American Scientist* 51 (1963): 164–79.

10. Walter Buckley, *Sociology and Modern Systems Theory* (Englewood Cliffs, N.J.: Prentice-Hall, Inc., 1967).

11. Louis R. Pondy, "Organizational Conflict: Concepts and Models," *Administrative Science Quarterly* 12, no. 2 (September 1967): 297–319.

12. Chris Argyris, *Organization and Innovation* (Homewood, Ill.: Dorsey Press, 1965).

Chapter 1 Challenges of the Future

ON ATTENDING TO THE FUTURE

Bertrand de Jouvenel

Technology

Modern civilization as we know it today, owes its inception and development to a change, slowly started and progressively accelerated, in the esteem granted to the mechanical arts. The term *mechanical arts* was used to designate both the activities serving material needs and the skills and knowledge required for such performance—what is now called technology. As late as the latter part of the seventeenth century, the great jurist Domat noticed as a fact that such arts brought no consideration. (It may be of interest to stress that architecture was not counted among them, but among the liberal arts.)

Progress in the mechanical arts was long hampered by such lack of consideration, by lack of means, and by legal restraints upon changes in practices. Lack of consideration further caused dynamic personalities to escape upward into spheres where they had to be careful to dissociate themselves from their previous activities or those of their fathers. Recounting how all this changed would imply sketching the rise of present civilization.

It is enough to point to the growing recognition and power of the entrepreneur which marked the first half of the nineteenth century, and to that second great step, characteristic of our day, the huge moral and material credit granted to research and development.

Our indebtedness to progress in the mechanical arts can be apprehended immediately by looking to the condition of the common man in countries where such arts have remained underdeveloped: How very much better it is in countries where these arts are advanced! But is it good enough? And if not, should we expect its improvement in the mood of passive excitement of children awaiting the toys which technology shall hang on Christmas trees to come?

Have we no dream of the good life? No picture of the social scene as inviting each human plant to fully flourish in its unique manner? Of course we have, and for this reason we are assembled.

Whatever degree of implementation of such a dream we may hope for, technology plays therein a permissive role. It allows us to move in that direction, it does not lead us there of itself.

Indeed there is some reason to worry about *whither* technological progress would lead us, if we left it to lead, as it presently does. Who would deny that it exerts a shaping influence upon Society? It is therefore to be regretted that its main orientations are imparted by concerns quite alien to the improvement of daily life.

However important and beneficial their role had been before that, the great social promotion of technologists came only through World War II. [T]he now current expression of research and development was coined to describe the process of organized downflow from high science to weaponry, and the first city of science and technology was that where the atom bomb was prepared.

Since then, resources devoted to research and development have so far increased as to nearly equal two-thirds of those addressed by the nation to its housing. The main motors of this huge advance were public agencies with missions of power or prestige. It is striking that in the two industries which alone use a good half of industrial research and development, no less than 72 percent of the scientists and engineers so employed are working for the aforesaid agencies.

It may well be presumed also that these agencies' programs attract the best technological talent: For the problems to be dealt with are here most intricate, therefore most exciting to the mind, and the public agency favors pushing ever further, while the progress is naturally more bounded if one works for an employer looking to consumer sales.

It is of no mean social consequence that such ambitious and richly endowed programs have gathered in their service a new intellectual elite, numerous, highly concentrated, youthful and dynamic. This elite cannot fail to exert an influence within the nation for again bolder programs, and also an influence abroad, on their fellow professionals who admire and wish to emulate their exploits.

Therefrom issues a strong propensity for technologists to "take off" from the more pedestrian and humdrum tasks, which may be more serviceable to everyday life. Perhaps unconsciously, this makes up a powerful intellectual lobby, demanding tasks suiting its high talents.

The pressure of high talents for great tasks is the only explanation I can find for our building on both sides of the Atlantic supersonic transport planes. They are certainly not meant for the improvement of daily life: They will bring a minor economy of time to a small minority of the population at the financial cost of the great majority and to the considerable inconvenience of all. This was noted in the most recent conference of the American Economic Association.

There is indeed very little content of service to the greater number in publicly financed research and development; notable, in view of our declared aims of technical assistance to the under-developed countries, is an almost total absence of research for techniques suited to conditions very different from ours in climate, customs, and man-to-resources ratios.

It is the more regrettable that publicly financed technology should turn its back upon the cares of ordinary men, in that consumer-serving technology requires correctives. From the operations of a firm proceed two material outflows, an outflow of goods to be sold, and an outflow of nuisances inflicted. It is the logic of enterprise that what matters is the ration of goods outflow to factor inputs, while the outflow of nuisances is "not its business." Therefrom we have such practices as strip-mining in Kentucky, which is the best method if you consider only the coal you are getting, and not the volume of soil you are munching and tossing away.

Discards do not enter the economic picture of the firm; even worse, they do not enter the economic picture of the nation. National accounts are indeed nothing other than an aggregation of the accounts of firms, so that the flows of nuisances, as they have no place in business accounting therefrom, have no place in national accounting. But, if nuisances have no place in the economic picture, they do have their place in the actual life of people. Their presence is occasionally stressed by some ominous incident: Thus hundreds of thousands of Englishmen and Frenchmen, last spring, saw their prospects of vacation darkened by the black muck flowing out of the wrecked *Torrey Canyon,* a suddenly apparent manifestation of the generally invisible creeping process which poisons our environment. This event found the best scientists ignorant of remedies. Wardley Smith, chief scientific officer at the Ministry of Technology's Warren Spring Laboratories, has just reviewed the occurrence. He said that while the method used had been to spray with detergents, in retrospect it might have been better to attempt collection of the oil reaching the beaches by mechanical means or even by hand. About three hundred suggestions, he said, had been received from scientists all over the world. Some were impractical, others were rejected after trial. "We had no suggestions," he reflected, "where we could really say 'this is the answer' and none which embarked us on new lines of research." The situation, he concluded, would be no better in the event of a second such accident. This admirably honest statement makes it clear that, endowed as we are in technologies of Doing, we are miserably poor in techniques of Undoing, which the progress of Doing shall make ever more necessary.

Far more tragic is the history of the Aberfan disaster. The tribunal of inquiry quotes the dramatic testimony of that one child who survived, his description of that huge wave of earth and boulders he saw rushing at them, rearing over the schools and which came down upon them crushing at one blow that community's whole generation of children. Whence this murderous wave? From the slipping of a coal tip, that is, of a pile of discards from the mine. As the report makes clear, while great care was taken as to the mining operations proper, none was shown in the disposal of the refuse, which was, so to speak, discarded from attention. May this awful event warn us that the menace of our discards is hanging over us!

We must mend our ways. Our economic operations will have to be conducted in the future, not only with an eye to the successive lessening of labor inputs relative to output, but also and increasingly with an eye to the lessening of noxious discards.

Indeed, if we take a long view as we are here invited to do, then, according to Nieburger of UCLA, it is the very problem of continued human existence upon Earth which is raised by our waste products. The economy of our advanced countries is based upon a gigantic consumption of energy. If, as one hopes, the remainder of Mankind gradually tends toward our standards of such consumption, then the human species must gradually poison itself out of existence, unless we change the form of such consumption so

as to minimize the noxious wastes therefrom.

It is worth stressing the reversal which has occurred in the kind of worry to which energy consumption gives rise. In my youth there was some worry about the exhaustion of energy stores. This ghost has been laid low but not without research, in the form of exploring for oil, and in the form of working out the use of nuclear energy. Similarly, the ghost of atmosphere poisoning can be laid low, but not without adequate research and implementation of its findings. The reversal of preoccupation is from worry about lack of means to worry about the consequences of bad ways.

I have used here the expression of "bad ways": The ways alluded to are indeed "good" in the sense of short-term efficiency; they can be recognized as "bad" only by reference to their long-term consequences.

The Forwardist

This "goodness-badness" quality makes up the essence of the operational problems encountered by the future-oriented mind. As I shall now have to speak a good deal about the man so engaged, let me for short give him a name: the Forwardist. Purposely the term is noncommittal, as I know from my own lengthy experience that a man of this disposition may be engaged in a variety of specific roles to which more definite denominations, such as forecaster or planner, properly apply.

Taken in general, the social function of the Forwardist can be loosely described as that of calling attention to more or less remote consequences, thus giving these weight in the minds of some actors or decisionmakers. This function required hard (and risky) intellectual labor, tending to the perception of consequences: It is socially operational insofar as it does actually affect conducts and decisions.

It is most apt to affect decisions when it is meant to do so by decisionmakers themselves, who call upon forwardists. Such is eminently the case of the in-house services set up by governments since World War II, whose mission it is to supply the authorities with frequently revised previews of the impending course of the economy during the 18 months immediately ahead (such is the span of economic forecasting properly so called). Forwardists cast in this role are expressly required to warn of the troubles present courses are leading to, troubles the simplest forms of which are recessive tendencies and unemployment increases, or on the other side balance of payments troubles or price rises, whether associated or not. It is the intent of the authorities to act upon such predictions so as to falsify some of their unpleasant aspects. The prediction which is actually given out to the public is a second version (usually with a 12-month span only), which takes into account the improvements expected from the corrective measures taken or proposed by the Executive.[1]

The operational effectiveness here stems from the demand of the decisionmakers for the forecast, which they obtain from experts of their own choice, deemed trustworthy for this subjective reason, and for an objective reason: It is pretty clear how things will go for as short a time as 18 months, in the absence of intervention, because the present momentum does determine the near future in the economic realm.

Again in the economic realm, Forwardists are called by the authorities to a second function, planning (which covers a four- or five-year period envisaged three years ahead from its inception). There is no question here of predicting how things will have turned out eight years hence: The intention is to map out a design for the fastest feasible overall economic growth during the plan period, a design which, after two years of extensive discussion (involving a variety of public agencies, business executives, union leaders, and economists) shall have acquired (through testing and amendments) sufficient credibility to bring about from a variety of agents voluntary behaviors apt to implement the design. It would be quite out of order to go into the intricacies of the mental exercise; but I do want to stress that it is very closely behavior bound. Let me clarify. The planner must respect what is known of government propensities; he has to write into his sketch such government demands upon resources, in volume and in kind, which are the most likely, regardless of the unfavorable judgment he may pass upon some of them. He must respect what is known of consumer preferences: He has to write in that pattern of consumer spending which the known linkage of shifts in kind, with increases in per capita volume, leads him to expect even though some slightly different pattern, lessening pressure on the least elastic supply sectors, would permit the accommodation of a somewhat higher rate of growth. He must respect what is known of firms' investment determinants, of the role played in such determination by cash flow, prospects, and incentives. In short, his plan must embody no behaviors which are in the least unlikely, however desirable they may seem to him. Finally, whatever government measures may be proposed to further the implementation of the plan, their acceptance, or that of near equivalents, must be highly plausible.

From what has been said, it should be clear that the planner makes no choices for society: I can find for his activity no better analogy than the designing of a delivery system; the goods (and services) to be delivered are those wanted by the government, by the consumers, and by producers for the servicing of the two aforesaid (in good logic, as Kuznets pointed out long ago, investments, or at least so-called productive investments, should be adjuged intermediary, not final, products).

Contrary to legend, the planner, at least in France, not only makes no decision—having no powers—but makes no proposition as to *what* shall be obtained by society; his design bears solely upon the *how,* the expediting of deliveries—filling a maximum of orders within a given period. And it is because his function is purely instrumental that he is trusted.

Orientation

But, of course, the very urge which carries a man to planning activities is a care for improvement which, in itself, comprises not only the term of "more" but the term of "better." Planning for more is, by itself, psychologically rewarding in that the faster the pace of the social caravan (thought of as ranked by income), the faster the emergence of its tail from the deserts of sheer want. But, to pursue the metaphor, as to the vanguard and body of the caravan, one does care about the kind and quality of the land one is moving into. In short, the Forwardist wants to raise questions of *orientation.*

Such questions can be raised in many ways, which, to my mind, can be divided into two great categories: questions which arise from the consideration of active causes, and questions which arise from the consideration of goals.

In the first category, I place all the forward speculations aroused by some obviously increasing cause, whose various impacts upon society one imagines and assesses, some good and some bad. Many minds, especially in the U.S., start out from some important technological change. Most favored presently is the computer theme. This gives rise: (a) to thoughtful and valuable estimates of the changes which the progress of computers is apt to bring into organization and labor deployment; (b) to promises, which seem to me wild, about a consequent mutation in productivity increases, leading shortly

into a world without work; (c) to fears, not unfounded but possibly excessive, about the consequent change in the status of the individual: To a central computer a person becomes a collection of registered attributes.

In Europe we are more apt to start from a waxing social phenomenon; Michael Young has written a fascinating book, *The Rise of the Meritocracy,* upon the kinds of social problem [*sic*] raised by meritocracy, a society where positions are granted according to diplomas, with a rapid obsolescence of dated diplomas.

One of my own favorite starting points for this kind of speculation is the impact upon social relations of the increasing place taken in society by the very large and many-tiered organization (business or administrative). It seems to me difficult to consider such hierarchies without regarding them as apt to produce a classified society: Relations naturally tend to establish themselves laterally between people lodged within the same stratum. Another consequence of such integration into large organizations is that decisionmaking and responsibility tend to be increasingly concentrated. These two developments seem to work the first against social democracy, the second against political democracy.

Another increasing trait which attracts my attention is the continual lengthening of the period of education. I wonder whether maintaining young people upon school benches well beyond their majority is not in flagrant contradiction with the spirit of youth which wants to be up and doing, and whether this contradiction is not apt to produce restlessness in students, and a decline of forcefulness in adults.

I have given instances of speculations based upon consideration of a single cause. Such speculations naturally bring in their train speculations about remedies, and the likelihood of their adoption.

Here a trivial illustration must suffice. The public is well aware of the problem arising from the motor car, in terms of traffic congestion, noise, and air pollution.

Speculation bears, therefore, not upon the unquestioned progress of the evils, but upon the *validity* of the remedies applied and upon the *acceptability* of those which come to mind. In the case of the historic towns of Europe, the enlargement of streets is an immensely costly and quantitatively futile remedy; on the other hand, the exclusion from these towns of any but minicars electric powered is not presently acceptable to the public. Beyond this and regarding the long term, the question can be raised whether the continuing process of human agglutination, fostered by the age of railways, does not represent a lag of social practices, relative to the facilities given by the wonderful change in communications and flexible means of transport. Were I president of a motor company, I would commission research on a nonagglutinated pattern of life and work.

I turn now to my second category of long-term speculations, those which are not based upon the progress of a single definite cause, but those which are aimed at progress toward a certain goal. When speculating from causes, there are many plausible starting points, but, when speculating toward a goal, there seems but one, and that is the quality of ordinary daily life.

Take the time-budget of a whole family for a whole year. You will find that very much the greatest part thereof is spent in the home. Other places, work places, schools, playgrounds (here a blanket term including libraries and meeting places, and even street corners), and transport also take a substantial slice. This immediately shows that our attention should be addressed to the qualitative improvement of homes, work places, schools (this is surely the most satisfactory chapter in the U.S.), and playgrounds and to the quantitative lessening of mandatory transport. Qualitative improvement means not only gains in convenience but gains in charm. A lovely setting is a permanent influence upon our disposition: So Jefferson thought when he planned the Univerity of Virginia.

So thought Ledoux when he devised the charming milltown of Chaux. It has been the folly and crime of industrial civilization utterly to forget that "hands," as they were so tellingly called, have eyes and ears that are sensitive to sights and noises.

This forgetfulness must now be repaired, and let me, with all due respect, say to architects that it is not repaired when they build what is immediately striking rather than what is continuously pleasing, when they give proof of their engineering skill rather than of their understanding of human beings.

A better understanding of human beings—this seems the essential condition for a better future. We need such understanding in order to move intellectually from goals stated in broad terms toward better specifications; we need such understanding also in order to move in fact, since such moving depends upon human conducts; and for that we must be able to make estimates of how people shall react to this or that warning, vision, facility, or incentive.

It is clear enough from the allocation of research funds that the understanding of human beings is not presently regarded as a main subject of interest. It is even clearer from public discourse and, indeed, from public decisions, that, whatever progress may have been achieved in such understanding in scientific circles, no trace thereof has come through upon the public scene. Any schoolboy has a more complex image of the atom than the highest scientists of the nineteenth century, but hardly any public statement reveals any but the most naive standard image of man. This may indeed be due to the heavy sententiousness which is a professional obligation of politicians.

Progress in our mastery of nature has come from a progress in understanding it; similarly, our progress in the service of men requires a progress in our understanding of them. It is sure to come; let us, however, beware of its coming from the carrying over of the technologies applied in the material realm, which would lead us straight into an Orwellian world. It must be remembered that here our purpose is to serve and not to utilize, to favor the diverse blooming of human plants, not to raise men as wheatears in Iowa. Let us therefore draw our inspiration from the gentle art of gardening.

Note

1. The services referred to are, in the U.S., the Council of Economic Advisers, in France, the Direction de la Prévision. In France there are two yearly sessions of in-camera criticism of such forecasts by a body including out-of-house experts, which is known as the Commission des Comptes de la Nation.

WHY SPECULATE FAR AHEAD?

Herman Kahn and Anthony J. Wiener

There are many good reasons for trying to imagine what the world may be like over the next thirty-three years. The most important, of course, is to try to predict conditions in reasonable detail and to evaluate how outcomes depend on current policy choices. If only this were feasible, we could expect with reasonable reliability to change the future through appropriate policy changes today.[1] Unfortunately, the uncertainties in any study looking more than five or ten years ahead are usually so great that the simple chain of prediction, policy change, and new prediction is very tenuous indeed.

It is not that the period beyond the next decade (the approximate limit of usefulness of most policy research studies) is too far away to be of interest. It is short in terms of many human concerns: A child born this year [1967] will be only thirty-two years old on January 1, 2000, and many of today's adults will probably still be taking active roles in the first third of the twenty-first century. Useful or interesting as such long-range predictions would be, it is simply too difficult to make them well, and even more difficult to estimate how this relatively distant future depends on current policies.

Nevertheless, at the minimum, such studies, even if only partially successful, contribute to interesting lectures, provo-

cative teaching, and stimulating conversation, all of which can broaden horizons and increase creativity—by no means negligible benefits. More important, these studies can affect basic beliefs, assumptions, and emphases. Probably most important, at least for us at Hudson Institute, is that long-range studies provide a context in which to do five- to ten-year studies that can and do influence policy choices. Thus a long-range perspective is useful to policy planners and policy research analysts generally. Line decisionmakers, in government and industry, in contrast to staff analysts, will ordinarily find extremely long-range studies less useful; they may be still less useful, in a narrow professional sense, for various specialists, though even here they can still be of some heuristic value.

Another important, but unfortunately often unattainable, objective for a long-range study is to anticipate some problem early enough for effective planning. Whether this can be accomplished more or less directly (as opposed to stimulating or providing a perspective for a later study or plan) depends, of course, on the issue and the question: Some variables change much more slowly and reliably than others, and some questions need much better answers than others. Trends or events that depend on large, aggregative phenomena are often more amenable to long-range planning than those that depend on unique circumstances or special sequences of events. Projects, such as educating an individual, carrying out city planning, projecting recreational demands, formulating antipollution, or perhaps population control policies, can normally be usefully considered much further in advance than problems of international relations or subtle and complex national security issues. This is true because gross, long-term trends are far more recognizable and projectable than complex sequences of unique events, such as those that will determine tomorrow morning's headlines.

There are also problems of timing. Programs, policies, and doctrines, as well as governmental and military systems, usually change relatively slowly in response to current decisions, yet at the same time are changing rapidly as a result of decisions made in the past. In the late 1950s and early 1960s decisions were made on political and strategic programs (and military procurement) that [in 1967] will play a large part in determining the foreign alliances, political commitments, and military capabilities of the United States in the late 1960s and early 1970s. Today [1967] decisions are being made that will heavily influence our situation and commitments in the early and mid 1970s. Thus between now [1967] and about 1970 we are working in a changing context, and with changing instrumentalities, which were largely decided upon in the quite different conditions of at least five years ago. At the same time, our current needs and decisions find relatively little immediate response. In short, we can often do least to change sociopolitical situations that are closest to us and about which we know the most, while we may have the greatest influence over those future situations of which we know relatively little, even about our preferences. Thus to paraphrase the old French adage *"si la vieillesse pouvait; si la jeunesse savait"*—if the past only could; if the present only knew.

One answer, a partial one, to these

problems at the national policy level is deliberately to build greater flexibility into both systems and programs. To the extent that we succeed in this, policymakers and decisionmakers of the future will be freed from some of the material, technological, and political constraints which otherwise could prevent them from responding appropriately to the circumstances in which they find themselves. Although this kind of flexibility is extremely valuable, it is difficult to achieve and may be expensive in both resources and, in some cases, the sacrifice of advantages associated with commitment strategies or the need for continuity. It is certainly expensive in thought. If it is desirable for a decisionmaker to be able to "muddle through," how—in this world of accelerating changes and global political involvements—does he acquire the capability for muddling through? What are the parameters of that flexibility which all concede the policymaker of the future is likely to need? One answer . . . is to plan in a way that accommodates a large range of events. Options should be provided not only for the important long-run choices which are most likely to occur, but also for less likely choices insofar as they would present significant dangers or opportunities, and if preserving the options would not require giving up too much in current terms.

Thus, in policy research we are not only concerned with anticipating future events and attempting to make the desirable more likely and the undesirable less likely. We are also trying to put policymakers in a position to deal with whatever future actually arises, to be able to alleviate the bad and exploit the good. In doing this, one clearly cannot be satisfied with linear or simple projections: A range of futures must be considered. One may try to affect the likelihood of various futures by decisions made today, but in addition one attempts to design programs able to cope more or less well with possibilities that are less likely but that would present important problems, dangers, or opportunities if they materialized.

New and rapidly innovating technologies; vast political, social, and economic upheavals accompanying the worldwide mushrooming of population; the continued development of mass communication; and the less spectacular but equally consequential processes of urbanization, industrialization, and modernization are obvious facets of the second half of this century. It is a truism that the pace with which such changes are taking place has reduced the reliability of practical experience as a guide to public policy and has diminished the usefulness of conventional judgment in dealing with social problems. On the other hand, traditional or unalterable factors in man, societies, and culture continue to play important, even decisive, roles.

Policymakers in many fields, given so much new information to assimilate, so many new variables to assess, and so little experience directly relevant to the new problems, can no longer be as confident of the applicability of traditional wisdom and can no longer rely as much on the intuitively derived judgments that once seemed adequate to resolve issues and to achieve fairly well-understood social goals. It is very difficult not to underestimate or overestimate the overall significance of new developments and tendencies: scientists, engineers, and managers who deal directly with modern technology and who are also interested in broad policy issues often seem to overestimate its likely social consequences, and go to extremes of optimism or pessimism, while those more oriented to the cultural heritage—whether they are unschooled conservatives or liberal, literary intellectuals —equally often seem to bank too heavily on historical continuity and social inertia. The problem, of course, is to sort out what changes from what continues, and to discern what is continuous in the changes themselves.

This kind of study of the long-range future has, after some decades of disrepute, become once again a matter of scholarly interest. Indeed, it has become fashionable if not faddist. More or less systematic and serious efforts to explore the shape and possibilities of the future are under way in several places in the United States, Europe, and Japan. One thing which distinguishes some of these new efforts from the earlier work, or speculation, of individual writers and thinkers is their emphasis on sustained, cooperative, and relatively systematic effort. Several disciplines are enlisted in a common effort of analysis and interactive speculation. These efforts are hardly likely to replace individual visions of the future of the kind we already know, such as those of H. G. Wells, Aldous Huxley, and George Orwell, to take only the best-known recent examples in English. Such personal works of imagination—nearly all of them in fact passionately aimed at changing the future—are likely to prove more influential than more systematic and "reasonable," but correspondingly more prosaic, efforts. On the other hand, a properly led and integrated interdisciplinary project is more likely to incorporate the relevant insights, if any, from a range of academic and technical disciplines. It is also more likely, if this is an objective of the study, to address realistic policy issues in the form in which they are likely to arise. Sometimes, of course, such projects are trying to study important issues whether or not they have yet been perceived or felt to be important. In this case, while a competent interdisciplinary study is not necessarily more likely than a political fantasy to arouse the interest and concern of decisionmakers, the former should, at least, contain recommendations in a form decisionmakers can eventually use.

Of course, such interdisciplinary research may fail to achieve its objectives. For example, much interdisciplinary research results in congeries of reports rather than in integrated and unified discussions. Interdisciplinary projects that are organized as committees of equals are most likely to have this difficulty.

There is also a risk of falling between the stools of rigor and relevance: One may relax the requirement of being academically "sound" and "well grounded" so far (perhaps in order to be able to address interesting and important issues) that the work is of low quality; on the other hand, one may try so hard to be explicit and "objective" (perhaps so that there will be tangible empirical and analytical issues about which to argue) that the project is ultimately diverted from the more interesting and important issues—those that are hard to formulate and perhaps even partially "unresearchable." Despite these difficulties, good policy research projects are indeed more likely to produce hard documentation, explicit issues, or relatively objective speculation. The argument will then be carefully formulated and more productive than a discussion concerning intuitive assumptions, tastes, or values. (Such discussions are not necessarily futile, but it is difficult to avoid conducting them so abstractly, ir-

relevantly, or otherwise out of context that issues are not joined. It is rare for any cumulative growth in understanding to result from a series of such discussions.) And while only the great novelists and prophets can impart an intense sense of drama and excitement, even quite minor poets, seers, and publicists may achieve some of this quality. We hope that in this venture into speculation we have not been so austere as to exclude this flavor entirely, or so interested in the important, or sensational, as to be irresponsible.

Note

1. Of course, there is no doubt that actions taken today can change the future. The problem, to which we return in our concluding chapter, is that the changes may be unintended, undesirable, and unpredictable.

CONVERTING KNOWLEDGE INTO ACTION: TOWARD A POSTINDUSTRIAL SOCIETY[1]

Robert P. Biller

The efficacy of what we as a society can do is related to the quality of the procedures we use to identify policy alternatives and translate them into action. The procedures we now employ are the products of particular historical circumstances. In general, they are based upon assumptions evolved from the industrialization of this society. These procedures not only may now cost more to employ than they are worth; they may not result either in the construction of desirable policy alternatives or the organizational forms necessary to their implementation. This note suggests some of the dimensions of an alternative set of procedures.

The United States has developed and employed a reformist model of politics

and organizational change. As a society, we have learned to respond to the emergence of new policy issues and/or the deterioration of past resolutions of policy issues. As a new policy issue becomes recognized, or as an old one deteriorates sufficiently, we have learned how to activate political processes in order to accomplish a particular change. We have learned how to build organizations, again counting on a reformist change model either to create new ones or deal with old ones requiring change. We have depended on "new brooms" (elections, appointments), "independent analysis" (audits, consultants, clientele interest groups), faith (in new people, or people with different backgrounds), and/or various control procedures (budgetary reviews, planning cycles, managers' decisions)—whose implementation appeared assured by virtue of their authority positions—to initiate and effect necessary changes. We found this reformist model of change, expressed in both politics and organizations, to be generally satisfactory. Catastrophe seemed to be avoided. [N]o other procedure seemed feasible, and we appeared, in general, to have the time and other resources necessary to make it work.

The consequences of increasing complexity and rapid change are now amplified through a society characterized by increasing interdependency. It is difficult to understand, much less control, the consequences of particular problems or policy "solution." The number of problems requiring attention appear to increase simultaneously with the decrease of interval between problem emergence and its potential criticality. It becomes more difficult to know what information you need, and more difficult to gather and test its accuracy, in proportion to the extent the

time allowable for these operations decreases. It becomes harder to assess with confidence the consequences of alternatives or the degree of risk which they represent.

It is not simply that the procedures designed for other conditions no longer work well. It is rather that to employ them may be counterproductive as well as ineffectual. That is, to pour gasoline on a fire in order to extinguish it, is not only unlikely to work well, it is likely to create a more serious dilemma than the one with which you began. It is probably at the level of premises, assumptions, and implicit decision rules that the differences between reformist change procedures and the possibility of an alternative are most clearly revealed. The following items [in Table 1] suggest some examples of these differences.

The argument is not that a reformist set of change procedures is wrong. It is that such procedures are insufficient when confronting conditions of complexity, change, and uncertainty.

Table 1   Examples of Premises, Assumptions, and Decision Rules Characteristic of Where We Have Been Versus Where We Might Be Going

Premises, Assumptions, and Decision Rules	Where We Have Been (Reform Strategy of an Industrial Society)	Where We Might Be Going (An Alternative of a Postindustrial Society)
(1) Locus of Meaning	Man is a creature who, though inherently social, acquires *meaning* (both to himself and others) in terms of his *skin-bounded self.*	Man is a creature who, though inherently a discrete entity, acquires *meaning* (both to himself and others) in terms of those relationships which he establishes with his *extended self* (i.e., others).
(2) Nature of Reality	*Social reality* exists independent of particular men. They are, as individuals, likely to be as effective as they are able to *learn it* well. The trouble is that they are limited creatures who learn it imperfectly. They get into trouble by violating those laws which they have imperfectly apprehended. *They do not learn well enough* and do not recognize the limitations implied by their "uninformed" state.	*Social reality* is an artifact of particular men which they are continuously *constructing.* They are, as individuals, likely to be as effective as they are able to construct it in efficacious ways. The trouble is that they are godlike creatures who tend to comprehend perfectly what they have constructed. They get into *trouble* by so consistently following those laws (routines) which they have constructed. *They learn too well,* and do not recognize the tentativeness with which they ought to regard the "truth" they have discovered.

(3) Man and Culture	Men are products of their experience. They are affected and molded by the experience they have. They are products of their culture. They are embedded in it (i.e., reactive).	Men's experiences are their products. They come to know themselves and each other by virtue of the experiences they have. Their culture is their product. It is the home they construct for themselves (i.e., proactive).
(4) Response to change	Rapid social change is a transient phenomenon—needing to be weathered and . . . accommodated.	Rapid social change is a permanent phenomenon—needing to be facilitated and capitalized upon.
(5) Politics and Governance	Politics is primarily positive—thrashing out what people can agree ought to be done and implementing the program implied by these agreements (setting targets and meeting them). A governed society unavoidable.	Politics is primarily negative—thrashing out what people can agree ought not to be done and implementing the programmatic changes implied by these agreements (setting limits and avoiding them). A self-governing society unavoidable.
(6) Knowledge Adequacy	Our knowledge is adequate (truth content high and generalizable) for prescription ("We ought to do. . . .").	Our knowledge is inadequate enough (truth content unknown and generalizable only with the acceptance of risk) to support prevention ("We oughtn't to do. . . .").
(7) Constitutions	Making a constitution work is harder than writing one.	Continuously discovering what sort of constitution it might be worthwhile to have is harder than making a written one work.
(8) Efficacy Criterion	The problem is basically one of reform (how to put right what is wrong).	The problem is basically one of institutionalizing change procedures (recognizing that things put right are unlikely to stay right, and making correctability criteria as important as correctness ones).
(9) Personal Clocks	Secure in our mortality (ultimately we do not have to bear the full consequences of our actions—"others" in space and time will bear some of them) we act as if we were eternal (trying to put things "right"—and attempting to institutionalize these fixes).	Secure in our immortality (ultimately our extended "selves" must bear the full consequences of our actions) we act as if we were transient (trying to discover ways by which those things we discover to be "wrong" can be corrected—and attempting to institutionalize those processes of change which may increase subsequent error-correction capacity).
(10) Knowledge Risks	We know more than we apply, and the problem is one of transmitting and using this knowledge.	We know less than we apply, and the problem is one of trying to prevent the transmitting and use of nonsense.
(11) Knowledge Dilemmas	We know what ought to be done and the crucial problem is discovering how to do it well.	We know how to do things and the crucial problem is discovering what ought to be done.
(12) Organizational Focus	Manage the "inside" of an organization well, and it will be possible to have effective external relations. (Emphasize the internal.)	Manage the boundary transactions of an organization well, and it will be possible to have effective internal arrangements. (Emphasize the environmental.)

(13) Members and Clients	*Few* people are *"in"* public organizations or engaged in making public policy, while *many* are independently served by such organizations and policies.	*Most* people are *"in"* public organizations and/or engaged in making public policy, while *few* are independently served by such organizations and policies.
(14) Planning Strategy	Walk softly but carry a big stick. *Plan before you act.* Develop the basis for as much commitment as possible before initiating a proposal or program.	Walk loudly but carry a small stick. *Act as a way of planning.* Develop no more commitment on your own or others' part than you develop information on the probable consequences of your action.
(15) Technology and Politics	*Technology* may provide the *solutions* to politically "caused" problems (urban development, NASA spillovers, etc.).	*Politics* may provide the *solutions* to technologically "caused" problems (sonic boom, ecology, genetics, etc.).
(16) Ephemeral Man or Organization?	Men come and go, but *organizations persist.* Organizations take on an independent character which affects those who participate within them.	Organizations come and go, but *men persist.* Men take on an independent character which affects those interdependency networks called organizations.
(17) Duration and Permanence	The expected *half-life* of organizations, purposes, roles, statuses, tasks, technologies, etc., is *long.*	The expected *half-life* of organizations, purposes, roles, statuses, tasks, technologies, etc., is *short.*
(18) Organizational Dilemmas	Making stable programs, organizations, and policies flexible and *adaptive* is the critical issue. Assuring *responsive* performances for the unique is the problem.	Making the flux represented by programs, organizations and policies *stable* is the critical issue. Assuring *responsive* performances for the average is the problem.
(19) Natural State	Organizations are inherently *stable* and change only as the consequence of particular events. If it is to occur, change must *be "caused"* planned change usually means *do something.*	Organizations are inherently *changeful* and stabilize only as the consequence of particular events. If it is to occur, *change must not be prevented;* planned change usually means *stopping something* you are doing.
(20) Change Strategy	It is easiest to produce *change* by focusing on the *parts* or components; they are more discrete, controllable, and mutable.	It is easiest to produce *change* by focusing on the *interdependencies* between parts or components; they are more critical to sustained change.
(21) Change Leverage	The critical problem in ensuring the "responsiveness" of public organizations is to develop more effective scanning and open-information processing *within* those organizations so that they can sense when adaptation is required.	The critical problem in ensuring the "responsiveness" of public organizations is to develop more effective scanning and open-information processing among the *environmental constituents* of these organizations so that they can elicit adaptation when it is required.
(22) Sequence of Institutionalization	You *decide* what you want to do and *build* an increasingly *institutionalized* organization to do it.	You *start doing something* and *codify* an organization's way of doing it and the value members attach to it only *to the extent warranted by the stability of the problem faced.*

(23) Ends and Means	Rationalize action in terms of the *efficacy of goals.* Acceptance of goals implies means. ("If something is worth doing, it's worth doing well.")	Rationalize goals in terms of the *efficacy of action.* Acceptance of means serves as a basis upon which goals may be inferred. ("If something isn't worth doing well, it certainly isn't worth doing.")
(24) Bases of Commitment	Seek to develop commitment to sensible *goals* in order to make possible the emergence of consistent action.	Seek to develop commitment to sensible *action* in order to make possible the emergence of overall objectives.
(25) Problems and Organization	Allow the availability of solutions to determine the ways in which problems are recognized, defined, and dealt with. *Assign problems* to organizations.	Allow the configuration of problems to determine the way in which solutions are recognized, defined, and dealt with. *Construct organizations* if problems are worth solving.
(26) Specialists and Generalists	"We are becoming *too specialized.*" We are increasingly bound by the codified precedents of certified society—which require the investments of more resources. Try to create generalists or interstitial role specialists.	"We are *not specialized enough.*" We are increasingly free from those codified investments seen now to be avoidable—and can use these resources to pay for more differentiation. Try to create the conditions under which specialists find themselves rewarded for coordinating themselves.
(27) Complexity and Simplicity	The problems occasioned by uncertainty, complexity, and rapidity of change require larger investments in *organizational* machinery. (Build better.)	The problems occasioned by uncertainty, complexity, and rapidity of change require larger investments in *disorganizational* machinery. (Discount faster.)
(28) Centralization and Decentralization	Centralize *or* decentralize large organizations on the basis of which form of symptomology is least costly. (unresponsiveness—irresponsibility) (*Balance-off* the tension.)	Centralize *and* decentralize large organizations simultaneously on the basis of double-constraint systems which feed on the inherent differences of advocacy. (*Design and use* the tension.)
(29) Risk and Rationality	Rationality results from minimizing the *costs* of information.	Rationality results from minimizing the *risks* of information unavailability.
(30) Managerial Roles	The task of the manager is to *make good decisions* and to be sure that these decisions are *amplified* through the organization.	The task of the manager is to make sure that *good decisions get made* and to be sure that *blockages* preventing their amplification *are removed.*
(31) Conflict Expression	*Avoid and suppress* the expression of conflict. It is evidence that someone does not understand what needs to be done, is inadequate, etc. (Maintenance oriented)	*Cultivate and facilitate* the expression of conflict. It is evidence that alternatives that might become necessary are being tested and explored. (Adaption oriented)
(32) Consensus and Confrontation	*Consensus is necessary,* and confrontation may be *tolerable* (as long as it is transient). Confrontation may be productive of catastrophe if allowed to extend beyond marginal questions.	*Confrontation is necessary,* and consensus is *tolerable* (as long as great premium is not placed upon it). Consensus may be productive of error if allowed to extend beyond the original conditions which produced it.

An alternative to the reformist model of organizational and political change would be based upon and deal with the contingencies reflected above in the right-hand column. It would be directed not toward the spasmodic formulation and reformulation of policies and organizations, but, rather, to the creation of policies and organizations supportive of sustained change over time. Such an alternative would take as the central task the attempt to institutionalize a process of change, rather than process the change of institutions. It would need to comprehend rather than deny those conditions of complexity, change, interdependency, and uncertainty which acted to confound the reformist model. It would address itself to those conditions likely to be encountered in the transition to a postindustrial society. Some of the major attributes of such an alternative would include the following:

1) It would be action based. The need for high quality information is imperative and the time and resources required to assure such information in isolation is prohibitive. It would respond by attempting continuous and self-conscious action to elicit information for the continuous evolution of more preferred outcomes and strategies.

2) It would fuse knowledge and action. To have different people thinking and acting, or the same people thinking and acting at different points in time, is likely simply to make thought impractical and action uninformed.

3) It would be informed by a continuous cycle of feedback and evolution, and the change processes involved would be sustained rather than episodic. To hope for quick studies and recommendations that are "right" and that will be implemented is to ask otherwise human and responsible people to act in a superhuman and irrational fashion.

4) It would lock together those people who are most likely to be the beneficiaries of risks, benefits, and other consequences—in organizational relationships that roughly correspond to the proportional risk undertaken —rather than attempting to maintain our present member-client distinctions.

5) It would attempt to learn from experience, but not be bound by it. Those people involved in this alternative (i.e., affected by it) must find themselves rewarded for digesting the past but discounting that part of it which is not useful. It would assume that futures are to be actively created, not simply inherited, and that the efficacy of using the past to predict the future must be explicitly tested rather than implicitly assumed.

6) It would encourage actors to determine the degree of risk it is reasonable for them to undertake, and to be self-conscious rather than implicit about the constraints they face. A climate of trust should facilitate this.

Note

1. I appreciate the support provided by NASA that made possible the contribution of these thoughts to the December 1969 Project Blueprint meeting at the University of Southern California School of Public Administration.

Chapter 2 Tomorrow's Organizations

BEYOND THEORY Y

John J. Morse and Jay W. Lorsch

During the past 30 years, managers have been bombarded with two competing approaches to the problems of human administration and organization. The first, usually called the classical school of organization, emphasizes the need for well-established lines of authority, clearly defined jobs, and authority equal to responsibility. The second, often called the participative approach, focuses on the desirability of involving organization members in decisionmaking so that they will be more highly motivated.

Douglas McGregor, through his well-known "Theory X and Theory Y," drew a distinction between the assumptions about human motivation which underlie these two approaches, to this effect:

Theory X assumes that people dislike work and must be coerced, controlled, and directed toward organizational goals. Furthermore, most people prefer to be treated this way so they can avoid responsibility.

Theory Y—the integration of goals—emphasizes the average person's intrinsic interest in his work, his desire to be self-directing and to seek responsibility, and his capacity to be creative in solving business problems.

It is McGregor's conclusion, of course, that the latter approach to organization is the more desirable one for managers to follow.[1]

McGregor's position causes confusion for the managers who try to choose between these two conflicting approaches. The classical organizational approach that McGregor associated with Theory X does work well in some situations, although, as McGregor himself pointed out, there are also some situations where it does not work effectively. At the same time, the approach based on Theory Y, while it has produced good results in some situations, does not always do so. That is, each approach is effective in some cases but not in others. Why is this? How can managers resolve the confusion?

A New Approach

Recent work by a number of students of management and organization may help to answer such questions.[2] These studies indicate that there is not one best organizational approach; rather, the best approach depends on the nature of the work to be done. Enterprises with highly predictable tasks perform better with organizations characterized by the highly formalized procedures and management hierarchies of the classical approach. With highly uncertain tasks that require more extensive problem solving, on the other, organizations that are less formalized and emphasize self-control and member participation in decisionmaking are more effective. In essence, according to these newer studies, managers must design and develop organizations so that the organizational characteristics *fit* the nature of the task to be done.

While the conclusions of this newer approach will make sense to most experienced managers and can alleviate much of the confusion about which approach to choose, there are still two important questions unanswered:

1) How does the more formalized and controlling organization affect the motivation of organizational members? (McGregor's most telling criticism of the classical approach was that it did not unleash the potential in an enterprise's human resources.)
2) Equally important, does a less-formalized organization always provide a high level of motivation for its members? (This is the implication many managers have drawn from McGregor's work.)

We have recently been involved in a study that provides surprising answers to these questions and, when taken together with other recent work, suggests a new set of basic assumptions which move beyond Theory Y into what we call "Contingency Theory: the fit between task, organization, and people." These theoretical assumptions emphasize that the appropriate pattern of organization is *contingent* on the nature of the work to be done and on the particular needs of the people involved. We should emphasize that we have labeled these assumptions as a step beyond Theory Y because of McGregor's own recognition that the Theory Y assumptions would probably be supplanted by new knowledge within a short time.[3]

The Study Design

Our study was conducted in four organizational units. Two of these performed the relatively certain task of manufacturing standardized containers on the high-speed, automated production lines. The other two performed the relatively uncertain work of research and development in communications technology. Each pair of units performing the same kind of task were in the same large company, and each pair had previously been evaluated by that company's management as containing one highly effective unit and a less effective one. The study design is summarized in Table 1.

The objective was to explore more fully how the fit between organization and task was related to successful performance. That is, does a good fit between organizational characteristics and task requirements increase the motivation of individuals and hence produce more effective individual and organizational performance?

An especially useful approach to answering this question is to recognize that an individual has a strong need to master the world around him, including the task that he faces as a member of a work organization.[4] The accumulated feelings of satisfaction that come from successfully mastering one's environment can be called a "sense of competence." We saw this sense of competence in performing a particular task as helpful in understanding how a fit between task and organizational characteristics could motivate people toward successful performance.

Organizational Dimensions

Because the four study sites had already been evaluated by the respective corporate managers as high and low performers of tasks, we expected that such differences in performance would be a preliminary clue to differences in the "fit" of the organizational characteristics to the job to

Table 1 Study design in "fit" of organizational characteristics

Characteristics	Company 1 (predictable manufacturing task)	Company 2 (unpredictable R&D task)
Effective performer	Akron containers plant	Stockton research lab
Less effective performer	Hartford containers plant	Carmel research lab

be done. But, first, we had to define what kinds of organizational characteristics would determine how appropriate the organization was to the particular task.

We grouped these organizational characteristics into two sets of factors:

1) Formal characteristics, which could be used to judge the fit between the kind of task being worked on and the formal practices of the organization.
2) Climate characteristics, or the subjective perceptions and orientations that had developed among the individuals about their organizational setting. (These too must fit the task to be performed if the organization is to be effective.)

We measured these attributes through questionnaires and interviews with about 40 managers in each unit to determine the appropriateness of the organization to the kind of task being performed. We also measured the feelings of competence of the people in the organizations so that we could link the appropriateness of the organizational attributes with a sense of competence.

Major Findings

The principal findings of the survey are best highlighted by contrasting the highly successful Akron plant and the high-performing Stockton laboratory. Because each performed very different tasks (the former a relatively certain manufacturing task and the latter a relatively uncertain research task), we expected, as brought out earlier, that there would have to be major differences between them in organizational characteristics if they were to perform effectively. And this is what we did find. But we also found that each of these effective units had a better fit with its particular task than did its less effective counterpart.

While our major purpose in this article is to explore how the fit between task and organizational characteristics is related to motivation, we first want to explore more fully the organizational characteristics of these units, so the reader will better understand what we mean by a fit between task and organization and how it can lead to more effective behavior. To do this, we shall place the major emphasis on the contrast between the high-performing units (the Akron plant and Stockton laboratory), but we shall also compare each of these with its less effective mate (the Hartford plant and Carmel laboratory respectively).

Formal Characteristics

Beginning with differences in formal characteristics, we found that both the Akron and Stockton organizations fit their respective tasks much better than did their less successful counterparts. In the predictable manufacturing task environment, Akron had a pattern of formal relationships and duties that was highly structured and precisely defined. Stockton, with its unpredictable research task, had a low degree of structure and much less precision of definition (see Table 2, p. 44).

Akron's pattern of formal rules, procedures, and control systems was so specific and comprehensive that it prompted one manager to remark: "We've got rules here for everything from how much powder to use in cleaning the toilet bowls to how to cart a dead body out of the plant."

In contrast, Stockton's formal rules were so minimal, loose, and flexible that one scientist, when asked whether he felt the rules ought to be tightened, said: "If a man puts a nut on a screw all day long, you may need more rules and a job definition for him. But we're not novices here. We're professionals and not the kind who need close supervision. People around here *do* produce, and produce under relaxed conditions. Why tamper with success?"

Table 2 Differences in formal characteristics in high-performing organizations

Characteristics	Akron	Stockton
(1) Pattern of formal relationships and duties as signified by organization charts and job manuals	Highly structured, precisely defined	Low degree of structure, less well defined
(2) Pattern of formal rules, procedures, control, and measurements systems	Pervasive, specific, uniform, comprehensive	Minimal, loose, flexible
(3) Time dimensions incorporated in formal practices	Short-term	Long-term
(4) Goal dimensions incorporated in formal practices	Manufacturing	Scientific

These differences in formal organizational characteristics were well suited to the differences in tasks of the two organizations. Thus:

Akron's highly structured formal practices fit its predictable task because behavior had to be rigidly defined and controlled around the automated, high-speed production line. There was really only one way to accomplish the plant's very routine and programmable job; managers defined it precisely and insisted (through the plant's formal practices) that each man do what was expected of him.

On the other hand, Stockton's highly unstructured formal practices made just as much sense because the required activities in the laboratory simply could not be rigidly defined in advance. With such an unpredictable, fast-changing task as communications technology research, there were numerous approaches to getting the job done well. As a consequence, Stockton managers used a less structured pattern of formal practices that left the scientists in the lab free to respond to the changing task situation.

Akron's formal practices were very much geared to *short-term* and *manufacturing* concerns as its task demanded. For example, formal production reports and operating review sessions were daily occurrences, consistent with the fact that the through-put time for their products was typically only a few hours.

By contrast, Stockton's formal practices were geared to *long-term* and *scientific* concerns, as its task demanded. Formal reports and reviews were made only quarterly, reflecting the fact that research often does not come to fruition for three to five years.

At the two less effective sites (in other words, the Hartford plant and the Carmel laboratory), the formal organizational characteristics did not fit their respective tasks nearly as well. For example, Hartford's formal practices were much less structured and controlling than were Akron's, while Carmel's were more restraining and restricting than were Stockton's. A scientist in Carmel commented: "There's something here that keeps you from being scientific. It's hard to put your finger on, but I guess I'd call it 'Mickey Mouse.' There are rules and things here that get in your way regarding doing your job as a researcher."

Climate Characteristics

As with formal practices, the climate in both high-performing Akron and Stockton suited the respective tasks much better than did the climates at the less successful Hartford and Carmel sites.

Perception of structure
The people in the Akron plant perceived a great deal of structure, with their behavior tightly controlled and defined. One manager in the plant said:

"We can't let the lines run unattended. We lose money whenever they do. So we make sure each man knows his job, knows when he can take a break, knows how to handle a change in shifts, etc. It's all spelled out clearly for him the day he comes to work here."

In contrast, the scientists in the Stockton laboratory perceived very little structure, with their behavior only minimally controlled. Such perceptions encouraged the individualistic and creative behavior that the uncertain, rapidly changing research task needed. Scientists in the less successful Carmel laboratory perceived much more structure in their organization and voiced the feeling that this was "getting in their way" and making it difficult to do effective research.

Distribution of influence

The Akron plant and the Stockton laboratory also differed substantially in how influence was distributed and on the character of superior-subordinate and colleague relations. Akron personnel felt that they had much less influence over decisions in their plant than Stockton's scientists did in their laboratory. The task at Akron had already been clearly defined and that definition had, in a sense, been incorporated into the automated production flow itself. Therefore, there was less need for individuals to have a say in decisions concerning the work process.

Moreover, in Akron, influence was perceived to be concentrated in the upper levels of the formal structure (a hierarchical or "top-heavy" distribution), while in Stockton influence was perceived to be more evenly spread out among more levels of the formal structure (an egalitarian distribution).

Akron's members perceived themselves to have a low degree of freedom vis-à-vis superiors both in choosing the jobs they work on and in handling these jobs on their own. They also described the type of supervision in the plant as being relatively directive. Stockton's scientists, on the other hand, felt that they had a great deal of freedom vis-à-vis their superiors both

in choosing the tasks and projects, and in handling them in the way that they wanted to. They described supervision in the laboratory as being very participatory.

It is interesting to note that the less successful Carmel laboratory had more of its decisions made at the top. Because of this, there was a definite feeling by the scientists that their particular expertise was not being effectively used in choosing projects.

Relations with others

The people at Akron perceived a great deal of similarity among themselves in background, prior work experiences, and approaches for tackling job-related problems. They also perceived the degree of coordination of effort among colleagues to be very high. Because Akron's task was so precisely defined and the behavior of its members so rigidly controlled around the automated lines, it is easy to see that this pattern also made sense.

By contrast, Stockton's scientists perceived not only a great many differences among themselves, especially in education and background, but also that the coordination of effort among colleagues was relatively low. This was appropriate for a laboratory in which a great variety of disciplines and skills were present and individual projects were important to solve technological problems.

Time orientation

As we would expect, Akron's individuals were highly oriented toward a relatively short time span and manufacturing goals. They responded to quick feedback concerning the quality and service that the plant was providing. This was essential, given the nature of their task.

Stockton's researchers were highly oriented toward a longer time span and scientific goals. These orientations meant that they were willing to wait for long-term feedback from a research project that might take years to complete. A scientist in Stockton said:

"We're not the kind of people here who need a pat on the back every day. We can wait for months if necessary before we get feedback from colleagues and the profession. I've been working on one project now for three months and I'm still not sure where it's going to take me. I can live with that, though."

This is precisely the kind of behavior and attitude that spells success on this kind of task.

Managerial style

Finally, the individuals in both Akron and Stockton perceived their chief executive to have a "managerial style" that expressed more of a concern for the task than for people or relationships, but this seemed to fit both tasks.

In Akron, the technology of the task was so dominant that top managerial behavior which was not focused primarily on the task might have reduced the effectiveness of performance. On the other hand, although Stockton's research task called for more individualistic problem-solving behavior, that sort of behavior could have become segmented and uncoordinated, unless the top executive in the lab focused the group's attention on the overall research task. Given the individualistic bent of the scientists, this was an important force in achieving unity of effort.

All these differences in climate characteristics in the two high performers are summarized in Table 3.

As with formal attributes, the less effective Hartford and Carmel sites had organization climates that showed a perceptibly lower degree of fit with their respective tasks. For example, the Hartford plant had an egalitarian distribution of influence, perceptions of a low degree of structure, and a more participatory type of supervision. The Carmel laboratory had a somewhat top-heavy distribution of influence, perceptions of high structure, and a more directive type of supervision.

Competence Motivation

Because of the difference in organizational characteristics at Akron and Stockton, the two sites were strikingly different

Table 3   Differences in "climate" characteristics in high-performing organizations

Characteristics	Akron	Stockton
(1) Structural orientation	Perceptions of tightly controlled behavior and a high degree of structure	Perceptions of a low degree of structure
(2) Distribution of influence	Perceptions of low total influence, concentrated at upper levels in the organization	Perceptions of high total influence, more evenly spread out among all levels
(3) Character of superior-subordinate relations	Low freedom vis-à-vis superiors to choose and handle jobs, directive type of supervision	High freedom vis-à-vis superiors to choose and handle projects, participatory type of supervision
(4) Character of colleague relations	Perceptions of many similarities among colleagues, high degree of coordination of colleague effort	Perceptions of many differences among colleagues, relatively low degree of coordination of colleague effort
(5) Time orientation	Short-term	Long-term
(6) Goal orientation	Manufacturing	Scientific
(7) Top executive's "managerial style"	More concerned with task than people	More concerned with task than people

places in which to work. But these organizations had two very important things in common. First, each organization fit very well the requirements of its task. Second, although the behavior in the two organizations was different, the result in both cases was effective task performance.

Since, as we indicated earlier, our primary concern in this study was to link the fit between organization and task with individual motivation to perform effectively, we devised a two-part test to measure the sense of competence motivation of the individuals at both sites. Thus:

The *first* part asked a participant to write creative and imaginative stories in response to six ambiguous pictures.

The *second* asked him to write a creative and imaginative story about what he would be doing, thinking, and feeling "tomorrow" on his job. This is called a "projective" test because it is assumed that the respondent projects into his stories his own attitudes, thoughts, feelings, needs, and wants all of which can be measured from the stories.[5]

The results indicated that the individuals in Akron and Stockton showed significantly more feelings of competence than did their counterparts in the lower-fit Hartford and Carmel organizations.[6] We found that the organization-task fit is simultaneously linked to and interdependent with both individual motivation and effective unit performance. (This interdependency is illustrated in Figure 1.)

Putting the conclusions in this form raises the question of cause and effect. Does effective unit performance result from the task-organization fit or from higher motivation, or perhaps from both? Does higher sense of competence motivation result from effective unit performance or from fit?

Our answer to these questions is that we do not think there are any single cause-and-effect relationships, but that these factors are mutually interrelated. This has important implications for management theory and practice.

Contingency Theory

Returning to McGregor's Theory X and Theory Y assumptions, we can now question the validity of some of his conclusions. While Theory Y might help to explain the findings in the two laboratories, we clearly need something other than Theory X or Y assumptions to explain the findings in the plants.

For example, the managers at Akron worked in a formalized organization setting with relatively little participation in decisionmaking, and yet they were highly motivated. According to Theory X, people would work hard in such a setting only because they were coerced to do so. According to Theory Y, they should have been involved in decisionmaking and been self-directed to feel so motivated. Nothing in our data indicates that either set of assumptions was valid at Akron.

Conversely, the managers at Hartford,

Figure 1 Basic Contingent Relationships

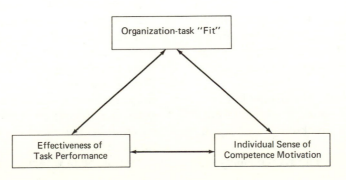

the low-performing plant, were in a less formalized organization with more participation in decisionmaking, and yet they were not as highly motivated like the Akron managers. The Theory Y assumptions would suggest that they should have been more motivated.

A way out of such paradoxes is to state a new set of assumptions, the Contingency Theory, that seems to explain the findings at all four sites:

1) Human beings bring varying patterns of needs and motives into the work organization, but one central need is to achieve a sense of competence.
2) The sense of competence motive, while it exists in all human beings, may be fulfilled in different ways by different people depending on how this need interacts with the strengths of the individuals' other needs—such as those for power, independence, structure, achievement, and affiliation.
3) Competence motivation is most likely to be fulfilled when there is a fit between task and organization.
4) Sense of competence continues to motivate even when a competence goal is achieved, once one goal is reached, a new, higher one is set.

While the central thrust of these points is clear from the preceding discussion of the study, some elaboration can be made. First, the idea that different people have different needs is well understood by psychologists. However, all too often, managers assume that all people have similar needs. Lest we be accused of the same error, we are saying only that all people have a need to feel competent; in this *one* way they are similar. But in many other dimensions of personality, individuals differ, and these differences will determine how a particular person achieves a sense of competence.

Thus, for example, the people in the Akron plant seemed to be very different from those in the Stockton laboratory in their underlying attitudes toward uncertainty, authority, and relationships with their peers. And because they had different need patterns along these dimensions, both groups were highly motivated by achieving competence from quite different activities and settings.

While there is a need to further investigate how people who work in different settings differ in their psychological makeup, one important implication of the Contingency Theory is that we must not only seek a fit between organization and task, but also between task and people and between people and organization.

A further point which requires elaboration is that one's sense of competence never really comes to rest. Rather, the real satisfaction of this need is in the successful performance itself, with no diminishing of the motivation as one goal is reached. Since feelings of competence are thus reinforced by successful performance, they can be a more consistent and reliable motivator than salary and benefits.

Implications for Managers

The major managerial implication of the Contingency Theory seems to rest in the task-organization-people fit. Although this interrelationship is complex, the best possibility for managerial action probably is in tailoring the organization to fit the task and the people. If such a fit is achieved, both effective unit performance and a higher sense of competence motivation seem to result.

Managers can start this process by considering how certain the task is, how frequently feedback about task performance is available, and what goals are implicit in the task. The answers to these questions will guide their decisions about the design of the management hierarchy, the specificity of job assignments, and the utilization of rewards and control procedure. Selective use of training programs and a general emphasis on appropriate management styles will move them toward a task-organization fit.

The problem of achieving a fit among

task, organization, and people is something we know less about. As we have already suggested, we need further investigation of what personality characteristics fit various tasks and organizations. Even with our limited knowledge, however, there are indications that people will gradually gravitate into organizations that fit their particular personalities. Managers can help this process by becoming more aware of what psychological needs seem to best fit the tasks available and the organizational setting, and by trying to shape personnel selection criteria to take account of these needs.

In arguing for an approach which emphasizes the fit among task, organization, and people, we are putting to rest the question of which organizational approach—the classical or the participative—is best. In its place we are raising a new question: What organizational approach is most appropriate given the task and the people involved?

For many enterprises, given the new needs of younger employees for more autonomy, and the rapid rates of social and technological change, it may well be that the more participative approach is the most appropriate. But there will still be many situations in which the more controlled and formalized organization is desirable. Such an organization need not be coercive or punitive. If it makes sense to the individuals involved, given their needs and their jobs, they will find it rewarding and motivating.

Concluding Note

The reader will recognize that the com-plexity we have described is not of our own making. The basic deficiency with earlier approaches is that they did not recognize the variability in tasks and people which produces this complexity. The strength of the contingency approach we have outlined is that it begins to provide a way of thinking about this complexity, rather than ignoring it. While our knowledge in this area is still growing, we are certain that any adequate theory of motivation and organization will have to take account of the contingent relationship between task, organization, and people.

References and Notes

1. Douglas McGregor, *The Human Side of Enterprise* (New York, McGraw-Hill Book Company, 1960), pp. 34–35 and pp. 47–48.
2. See, for example, Paul R. Lawrence and Jay W. Lorsch, *Organization and Environment* (Boston, Harvard Business School, Division of Research, 1967); Joan Woodward, *Industrial Organization: Theory and Practice* (New York, Oxford University Press, Inc., 1965); Tom Burns and G. M. Stalker, *The Management of Innovation* (London, Tavistock Publications, 1961); Harold J. Leavitt, "Unhuman Organizations," *HBR* (July-August 1962), p. 90.
3. McGregor, *Human Side*, p. 245.
4. See Robert W. White, "Ego and Reality in Psychoanalytic Theory," *Psychological Issues,* 3, no. 3 (New York, International Universities Press, 1963).
5. For a more detailed description of this survey, see John J. Morse, *Internal Organizational Patterning and Sense of Competence Motivation* (Boston, Harvard Business School, unpublished doctoral dissertation, 1969).
6. Differences between the two container plants are significant at .001 and between the research laboratories at .01 (one-tailed probability).

ORGANIZATION GOVERNMENT: THE PROSPECTS FOR A TRULY PARTICIPATIVE SYSTEM[1]

William G. Scott

The fact that administrative organizations are political systems has not been ignored by theorists.[2] But this commonplace insight is not exploited. Administration deals with governmental issues. It is praised or condemned for how well it handles the allocation question of *who gets what, how, why, when, and where* in the organizations it governs. This question has economic, sociological, and psychological dimensions. But power is also part of its content, and power must be treated in the political and governmental order, as well as in the other behavioral disciplines.

As management thought is surveyed over time, we discover that the major ideologies of administration have reflected obliquely the governmental character of organizational relationships. I say *obliquely* [Emphasis added.] because the creeds of management have roots elsewhere than in political science. This creates inconsistencies both in theory and application. Administrators are told for example to expect satisfactory outcomes from democratic (participative) management. However, democratic management is currently treated as a psychotherapeutic technique. But if democratic management is anything, it is first a governmental phenomenon. Yet, this obvious notion receives little systematic attention in the literature.

I say something about the pitfalls of managerial ideologies in this paper, in keeping, I hope, with the theme of alienation, decentralization, and participation. . . . My main objective, however, is to estimate the probability for a system of government in formal organizations which is consistent with democratic values and which also accords with the aims of two leading managerial creeds.

Before making a proposal for representative government in organizations, I shall discuss the evolution of managerial ideologies, and give an interpretation of the present state of management ideology that exposes some of my prejudices. I conclude with the proposal for representative government and a dismal forecast of the chance it has.

The Evolution of Managerial Creeds

Scientific management was administration's first creed. It was the first to embody utopian idealism and practical programs of implementation. From it grew human relations and industrial humanism on one evolutionary branch and management science on another. It seems strange to call these four belief systems creeds of organization government. Nevertheless, this is what they are for two reasons. First, they describe and, in a sense, prescribe certain quasi-political processes in organizations. Second, they have a utopian vision of "good" organization government.

The creeds are primarily concerned with:

1) A description of internal relationships between two organizational sovereignties—the management elite on the one hand and the popular domain (everybody else) on the other.
2) A prescription of the rights and limits of these two sovereignties.
3) A conceptualization of power as a means to resolve conflict between the sovereignties.

Secondarily, the creeds' utopian aims hope to achieve:

1) Mutual satisfaction of organizational goals and the needs of individuals in the organization.
2) Integration of the individual into the

organizational system for his own and the corporate good.

3) Maximization of the organization's potential to adapt to change.

Scientific management was born to resolve conflict between the two great sovereignties in organizations. It planned to do so within the economic framework. Mutuality of interests in constantly expanding productivity is the key to this creed. The scientific management pioneers felt that conflict between the management and the people could be settled if an organization's government achieved distributive justice in the allocation of economic resources.

Human relations came later, but it is philosophically a close cousin to scientific management. Both human relations and scientific management held that power should vest in management governing in the interests of ownership. But they also believed that the preeminence of managerial sovereignty is sustained by eliminating the causes of discontent among the governed.

Though there are no principal differences in the goals of scientific management and human relations, their means are not the same. Human relations extended the motivational horizons of management beyond the economic to the social and the psychological. It also introduced the small group (the informal organization) to management thinking. Such motivational factors as participation and democratic leadership were recommended as major techniques for accomplishing higher productivity and greater individual satisfaction in organizations. This led the human relationists to speak of the "integration of interests" between individuals and organizations. Integration of interests is a shorthand notation for the bundle of human relations techniques which are useful to management for resolving conflict between the sovereignties across a wider spectrum of human needs than those accounted for by scientific management.

In the evolutionary scheme of things, scientific management and human relations dominated a period in management thought roughly from 1900 to 1960. Their orientation in the ideological order was toward the relationships *between* the two sovereignties with the objective of resolving conflicts seeming to arise inevitably from the midst of their confrontations.

But these early creeds did something else. They introduced administrators to the idea that science has many helpful things to say about running organizations. The modern creed of management science traces its quantitative point of view to scientific management. Human relations brought the first systematic application of the behavioral sciences to management and organizations. Industrial humanism draws heavily upon behavioral science research to give it the stamp of empirical legitimacy.

Thus, scientific management and human relations left administration with the science-based legacies of management science and industrial humanism. However, we must quickly add that change occurred in the ideological order as well as in the scientific order. For ideological reasons, industrial humanists seem unwilling to rest with the continued dominance of the management hierarchy over the popular domain, and management scientists are not content to languish in the role of technical specialists or staff advisors. Science came to the service of ideology, or maybe it was the other way around. But this is of no consequence because science and ideology are hopelessly entangled in contemporary management creed.

Contemporary Management Creeds

Three creeds have made the modern management scene. We have mentioned two of them: management science and industrial humanism. The third, pluralism, does not seem to have roots in any earlier management creed. It apparently has grown from the so-called social responsibility of business arena. In this section, descriptions are given of the values I believe these creeds endorse.

Industrial Humanism

Industrial humanism emerged as a branch in the evolutionary tree of management thought when it occurred to the shamans of this movement that democratic leadership and participation are *more* than motivational devices to be used by managers to get action out of subordinates. They began to see in them and in advanced techniques like sensitivity training the way to achieve major redistribution of organizational power to suit the ideals of democratic liberalism. This shift in attitude by the spiritual leaders of the movement created a distinctly different texture to the meaning of democracy in industrial humanism as contrasted with human relations.

Industrial humanism is composed of a series of assumptions about the nature of man and the outlook for the "human condition." The industrial humanists:

1) Assume the dignity of man plus the need of protecting and cultivating personality on an equal rather than hierarchical basis.
2) Assume there is a steady trend in the "human condition" toward the perfectibility of man.
3) Assume that organizational gains are basically the gains of people in them and that the benefits (or satisfactions) flowing from these gains should be distributed as rapidly as possible to those responsible for them.
4) Assume that those who are in organizations should be, in the last analysis, the source of consent for those who make policy and establish controls.
5) Assume that change in organizations should be the result of full awareness of alternatives and consensus by participants.[3]

From the standpoint of the administrative posture toward organizations, this means that autocracy must be replaced by democracy, flexibility must be built into the organization, power equalization between the sovereignties must be sought, and the climate of the organization must be designed to satisfy a wide range of human needs.

These are the humanist imperatives. They are consistent with the humanist view that man is by nature antiautocratic, antihierarchical, and antitotalitarian. That man is "ungood" is because he has been corrupted by evil institutions, repressed by power, and generally kept in an unfulfilled state.

To be compatible with twentieth-century forces of change and reform,[4] as the industrial humanists see them, organizations have to be designed to help everyone in them realize their desires for self-determination and self-realization. The recipients of this help are supposed to be those in the popular sovereignty as well as those in the administrative core. (But as things have developed, management is the main beneficiary of industrial humanism's payoff.) In any event, freedom and self-realization, the main reasons for organizational modification, are themselves consequences of other dynamics like education, advancing technology, and rapid social change.

Industrial humanism's plans for organizational change rest upon assumptions about the nature of man, the direction of movement of social forces, and the ideals of liberalism. Both men and organizations need to be remade to correspond with these assumptions. The underlying imperative from the standpoint of organizations is that bureaucracy must give way to democracy as the prevailing mode of government. This is the point where the operational models of industrial humanism appear.

These models carry labels like Theory X–Theory Y, Systems 1,2,3,4, organizational development, the managerial grid, and planned change.[5] By the time this is published, there may be more. But regardless, these models are components of the industrial humanist syndrome. They support a cluster of values similar to those described previously as peculiar to industrial humanism. However, the models use different techniques.

The models are made operational through programs. For example, the organizational development model creates program mixtures of various interventions including research and diagnosis, counseling, and a dose of sensitivity training. Each OD potion is brewed especially for the ailments of each client. Therefore, the kind and amount of the interventions will differ in programs. But all programs have in common the application of behavioral sciences to reconstitute man and organization in the image of industrial humanism's values.

Management Science

Commenting on classical management theory, of which scientific management is a part, Joan Woodward says, " . . . [scientific management] was developed in a technical setting but independently of technology."[6] Scientific management was not tuned into the times in the ideological sense. However, management science, sired by technology and mothered by the quantitative tradition of scientific management, is a well-adjusted offspring.

Technology, or as Ellul calls it, *La Technique,* is a recent event.[7] It cannot predate the turn of the century by much. This is because *La Technique* is more than mechanization, automation, computerization, or applied science. It is a sociotechnical paradigm which is solely dedicated to the rational *quest* for the one best way of innovating, producing, and distributing material goods and service. This quest and its outcomes are not merely the means for the betterment of humanity. Maybe this was the way *La Technique* started, but it has been mutated into an end quite apart from human values and goals.

Technological determinism, which this description suggests, is the bogey of the modern philosophers of humanistic enlightenment. Because as they correctly perceive, *La Technique* does its own thing, and those individuals, organizations, cultures, and nations which want to participate in its material affluence must knuckle under to its rational, nonhuman imperative.

Management science is part of this imperative. As an ideology, it is beyond computer fiddling or linear programming. Rather, it is a massive application of rational values to all planes of organizational life and government. It is the final extension of scientific management (hinted at by the inversion of the words) made possible by progress in the natural and behavioral sciences.

The proximate organizational consequence of management science is the rise of the technical elite. Management science is not a force for democratic government of organizations, even though some humanists feel it is. Instead, it creates technical aristocracy. This follows from the assumptions it makes about man and the direction of humanity.

Management science assumes that man is pleasure seeking and comfort loving. He is both the creator and consumer of affluence. Man is a producer and avid consumer of material well-being. From these motivations arise the morality of production and consumption.[8] They are probably the only moral foundations of the technological society since they are essential to the dynamics of *La Technique.*

The technical elite emerges as the power in the technical society.[9] They alone are prepared to run organizations rationally in the interest of all. Rationality is the key input of the technical elite. Education, information, and skill are the sources of their power. Ultimately they are responsible for the things hedonistic producers consume. How can a creed fail, even though it is aristocratic and totalitarian, when it combines functional expertise and rationality of an elite with a materialistic, achievement-motivated rank and file?

Management science has in its grasp the opportunity to achieve an integration of interests between the sovereignties of management and the people which eluded scientific management and human relations. From *La Technique,* through management science, emerges a new order of harmony in organization government based upon rationality and material well-being.

Pluralism

Pluralism, as I said before, is not a creed indigenous to management thought. It is related to that incorporeal area known as the social responsibility of business. The social responsibility theorists deal with many things, including the social, economic, and political mechanisms in society which impose constraints on the behavior of businessmen: for example, impersonal regulatory forces which cause management to act responsibly whether it wants to or not. Traditionally, such constraints are treated as property (the interest of ownership), the consumer (sovereignty of the purchaser to buy or not), the public (generally expressing its sentiments through government regulation), and, finally, the economic system (the constraints imposed by competition).

For reasons which we cannot examine here, these traditional constraints fall short of regulating in ways consistent with the social good: that is, according to criteria of distributive and corrective justice. They have too many loopholes through which unscrupulous power seekers and greedy money grubbers can manipulate unfair advantage. So many loopholes exist that no less an observer than Adolf Berle makes his final appeal for responsibility to the individual "corporate consciousness."[10]

The pluralists, not forsaking either the traditional constraints or corporate consciousness, add to the list of controls the counterbalance of interest among institutions. The varying interests of business, labor, government, and the military, and to a lesser degree consumer groups, or-

ganized religion, education, and a huge number of voluntary associations counterbalance one another like a multipoled seesaw. This balancing off among competing claimants to power and resources is thought by the pluralists to be beneficial to the general health of society and individual freedom.[11]

Constitutionalization is allied to the notion of counterbalances in the pluralistic framework. Constitutionalization is a process of negotiation in the system by which exchanges are bargained between interest groups, and a sort of law governing their relationships evolves. The collective bargaining agreement between labor and management has frequently been referred to as the "constitution of industrial government." Similarly, negotiations between automobile manufacturers and their franchised agencies take on the character of law governing their mutual interests.[12]

The point of this overlong excursion into the area of social responsibility is to emphasize that, by and large, the pluralists deal with macro phenomena of *inter*-institutional and *inter*organizational arrangements. Their bag has been to view the world as islands of despotism in a sea of constitutional pluralism accompanied by the hope that equity, justice, and social good comes out of it all.

Of late, pluralism has shifted its perspective. Some writers are now saying that pluralistic principles apply to *intra*-organizational government.[13] They find numerous interest groups around the "pluralistic bargaining table" determining the destiny of their organization. The "dynamic interaction" of such groups, representing specialties like personnel, engineering, marketing, finance, production, and research and development, negotiating within the framework of the constitutional process, is believed to produce the same salutary results as those worked by pluralism on the macro level of society. Professional managers preside over this pluralistic exercise in their organizations facilitating the transactional process among groups. All of this creates much good, for as in Davis' words, "among pluralists the utopian vision of the good organization is that *truth* arises from looking at an issue from many points of view and then delicately balancing those points of view."[14]

Obviously the usefulness of pluralism on either the macro or micro levels of society is to protect against the tyranny of an elite. Such is the destiny of pluralism. As this review of contemporary management creeds ends, one is struck by the supreme optimism of each creed. Its zealots perceive their values, goals, and programs of government providing man and organizations with a kind of worldly salvation. It is a world of freedom from domination and repression as in the case of industrial humanism and pluralism, while in the case of management science, it is a world of comfort and rationality.

An Appraisal of Contemporary Management Creeds

All the management creeds make bright promises. However, I will not equivocate about my attitude toward them. With the exception of management science, I am unconvinced by their arguments. I summarize my appraisal of these ideologies in four propositions, which I expand in this section.

1) Management science will dominate the ideology of organization government.
2) Industrial humanism is not an alternative to management science, or a softener of its impact. Rather, industrial humanism is the behavioral science adjunct of management science.
3) Pluralism is not a viable alternative ideology of organization government.
4) The form of organization government which we may expect is an elite aristocracy with power vesting in the technicians.

These propositions predict a bleak future for democracy. However, far from being extreme, the forecast is tenable, and

not too distant from the central concerns of many well-known contemporary social critics. Problems do not appear in the descriptive topologies of the creeds which were discussed in the last section. Rather, they grow from the ways in which the creeds interact. Thus, an elaboration on the propositions entails a discussion of the relationships among the creeds.

Management Science and Industrial Humanism

Of all the linkups among the creeds, the least apparent but the most important is the one between management science and industrial humanism. Superficially, these creeds seem to polarize in their positions on organizational government. Industrial humanism offers man freedom and self-determination. Management science offers man comfort and organizations rationality. These creeds appear to create totally different kinds of organizational governments. Industrial humanism rests with power-equalization and democracy. Management science stands with an autocracy of the technical elite.

The unreflective see *La Technique* as a blessing without mitigation. They insist that technology will post impressive victories over the Four Horsemen of the Apocalypse. No doubt technology and management science will work wonderments in this respect. But there is more to the quality of life than freedom from pestilence, famine, war, and death. There are values like grace, dignity, human difference, cultural diversity, and spiritual transcendence which observers from Max Weber to Ellul, Marcuse, von Bertalanffy, and Galbraith fear will be blotted out by the rational imperative of *La Technique*.[15] Humanism ought to stand as a bulwark between ourselves and technology.

Without question this is the ideological posture of the leading figures in the industrial humanism movement. The difficulty is the credibility gulf between the words of their ideology and the actions of their programs. It seems unlikely, if we believe

Ellul, that organizations will implement programs which run counter to the technical imperative. Thus, are we to accept as evidence that, since industrial humanist programs are installed by management, they are consistent with technical values rather than human values? Strong reasons exist for believing that a convergence has occurred between industrial humanism and management science at the level of program implementation.

We must examine at least one of these reasons in depth. Industrial humanism re-enforces the technical imperative in the behavioral sphere. While industrial humanism is a checkered picture, it is fair to say that much of the humanists' efforts has been aimed at the creation of effective managerial teams, stressing such qualities of behavior as "openness, confrontation, and authenticity" in interpersonal relations. The chief means for accomplishing this is through sensitivity training. But now the emphasis is shifting toward organizational development. Its goal is to change organizations to be supportive of the values of reconstituted individual managers.

For the management of many organizations, industrial humanist techniques are highly functional, if we accept as evidence the growing popularity of its programs. (They have made *Look* and *Life*.) Naturally the question is, functional for what? Obviously these programs are functional because they supply management with a human technology entirely consistent with the values of *La Technique.* They represent a quest based in behavioral science for better interpersonal relationships among the technicians who compose the governing elite of organizations.

The quest for improved relationships among this elite is supremely important. The logic of technique cannot tolerate behavior which gets in the way of an elite's rational performance of organizational processes. Industrial humanism supplies mechanisms to "deal" with nonrational behavior so that effective managerial teams are formed and maintained. This is not to say that humanist techniques eliminate nonrational behavior and conflict. Far from it. Rather, human feelings, attitudes, and interpersonal and intergroup conflict are anticipated, "accounted for," and directed into channels which are organizationally beneficial. Humanist techniques are, therefore, rational, technical methods for the management of conflict within the elite.

For the elite itself, these techniques provide ways of looking inward, into the heart of the relationships among those in governing power. The elitist is self-oriented, group-oriented, and task-oriented. Humanist methods are perceived as devices to realize the goals and satisfactions growing out of these orientations. Industrial humanist programs secure the pathways of understanding and communication necessary for running organizations according to the larger designs of *La Technique.*

Thus, industrial humanism's focal point is the resolution of conflict *within* the sovereignty of the managerial elite. Neither scientific management nor human relations dealt with conflict among the members of the elite. As we said, these creeds were oriented toward intersovereignty conflict. The confluence of management science and industrial humanism provides the technical elite with programs for *intra*sovereignty conflict resolution.

This merger is essential and inevitable. The power of the technical elite rests upon functional expertise, which is the source of their legitimacy as the leaders of organizational government. Their main obligation is to fulfill the minimum expectation of the participants and clients of the modern organization. It is *unimpeded rationality.* The programs of industrial humanism make this possible.

Management Science and Pluralism

The argument that pluralism is an alternative to management science is even less compelling than the case for industrial humanism as an alternative. But as we said before, some pluralists see the destiny of their ideology as an offset to the autocracy of the technical elite. However, this is far from a universally held opinion. For example, Kariel[16] points out that technology is a force for concentration of power in society rather than fragmentation. He shows that on the national political scene, technology has resulted in the consolidation of power confounding the original intention of the constitution to sustain local autonomy and individual freedom against a central government.

Others as well, like C. Wright Mills,[17] have observed a decline of pluralism and the rise of the power elite. More recently Galbraith[18] writes of the emerging technostructure. These commentaries suggest things are run from the rarified atmosphere of high positions in society crosscutting government, labor, and business. In the light of these observations, the major institutions in our society, which should offset each other, unite, in Marcuse's words, in a "higher unification," which has little to do with democracy, justice, or social good.[19] Rather, the aim which is actually served is the rational quest for the one best way. This is the goal that animates the technological society. The quest is facilitated in the consolidation of power, not in its diffusion.

We cannot pursue this line of analysis. However, we must ask that since society in the macro order cannot resist the advent of consolidation, how can the management of individual organizations expect to promote pluralism?

Our society has a pluralistic tradition. This tradition is reflected in our Constitution and in our culture. The innumerable associations in our society attest to our commitment to diversity. As a people, we have been suspicious of power without regulation. Pluralism for us is a cultural mode that currently is threatened by technology.

If we move from the level of society to the level of localized despotism, like the corporation or government agency, no such tradition is found. Why should modern administrators steeped in the traditions of centralized command suddenly cultivate pluralism when it is clearly against the tide of technologically based concentration to do so? Little in the literature of pluralism suggests an answer beyond appealing to the constitutional process.

Hopefully, through the negotiations entailed in this process, each interest group will find its concerns represented in the "law" of the organization. This is a vague kind of yearning because it assumes an equivalence of power among interest groups. Such parity is *not* one of the facts of organizational life. Those with power impress their will on others. They have a disproportionate voice in the legislation of policy and distribution of resources. Since an elite controls the system of sanctions they can limit choice and thereby regulate the behavior of others in the organization. Those who are not in the elite are vulnerable to tyranny because they are without "equal protection" and access to an "impartial judicial system."

Constitutionalization is no more or less than an amoral process by which power is allocated to those who have the most persuasive claim to legitimacy. As we said before, the technical elite bases its legitimacy to govern organizations on functional expertise. Therefore, constitutionalization is not a servant of either democratic or totalitarian ideology. Rather, it is a servant of both. Which ideology prevails depends on determinates outside of any particular organization. Technological determinism is the categorical imperative of modern organizations. If pluralism arrives in organizations at all, it will arrive stillborn.

A Proposal For Organization Government

Daniel Defoe was put in the pillory for making his proposal to eliminate religious dissent in England. I expect nothing so dramatic from mine. It will probably be ignored. In any event, time is running out for the humanists and the pluralists. Neither seems to be able to offset the dehumanization and consolidation of organizations resulting from technological determinism. The industrial humanists are in management science's camp already. However, some restructuring is possible at the organizational level which would resist domination by the technical elite and delay technological determinism. I have in mind structural changes and innovations in organization government which are consistent with the values of democracy, participation, and power fragmentation.

The changes I propose in the mechanisms of organizational government are the *structural minimums* necessary to achieve the goals of humanism and pluralism. But I hasten to add, organizational leaders must be dedicated to the belief that the spirit and style of democratic government is a good to be fostered by these mechanisms. This belief has to be shared by those led. Changes in structure without devotion to the ideals of justice and democracy is just as futile as such devotion without support of implementing institutions and mechanisms of government.

My proposal, while structural, is congruent with the ideology of industrial humanism and pluralism. It has two imperatives:

1) The structured separation of governmental power in organizations.
2) The structural guarantee of due process in organizations.

In short, I am proposing as an ideal-type model that the principles of representative government contained in the Constitution of the United States, and certain of its amendments, in other words, the 14th, become incorporated as values and program focal points in the creeds of industrial humanism and pluralism.

With all the prattle about democracy in the management literature, I have not seen, especially among the humanists, a serious treatment of representative government in administrative organizations. It is felt that somehow, as we have said, pluralism and democracy are achieved by countervailing institutions and psycho-therapy. However, if we assume that each organization is a governmental system, then we could also assume that principles of representation might apply. One such principle is the separation of governmental power held by management. The cause of democracy is not advanced if organizations are politically structured like Persian satrapies.

In the interest of democracy and pluralism, management ought not to monopolize the power to legislate, execute, and adjudicate. Two of these powers (the legislative and the judicial) should be differentiated into subgovernmental systems, separated from each and from the executive function which management retains.

Beyond this is the need for guarantees of due process. Such guarantees are in two categories.

1) There must be a guarantee that all members of an organization have access to a fair and impartial judicial system which assures that corrective justice is implemented without prejudicing the future of the individual appellant in the organization. This can happen only when the judicial system in the organization is outside management control. The grievance system negotiated between unions and management works along this line. But the protected organizational participants are restricted to union members and the scope of legitimate grievances is limited to violations of the terms of the collective bargaining agreement.

    I propose a sweeping "appeal system" which gives all members of an organization an avenue for redress if they feel their rights have been abrogated. At the *minimum,* the last step in such a system should be to an independent judge, in no way connected with the management hierarchy.[20] The structure of corrective justice requires the judicial function be separated from the other functions of government which management performs, an orderly, accessible procedure for settling disputes, and a guarantee to the individual that no reprisals will result from using the procedure.

Procedural due process is relatively uncomplicated conceptually, and programs for implementing appeal systems in organizations are fairly simple. However, this cannot be said for the other dimension of due process.

2) There must be a guarantee that the citizens of organizations participate in legislative affairs where rights are formulated. The question is, who are the citizens of organizations? For a beginning I suggest the ownership and the employees. Employees may be subdivided into management, technical support personnel, and rank and file.

It seems to me that each of these groups have direct and roughly differentiated interests in the legislative aspects of organizations. For the sake of pluralism and democracy these interests should be represented in policymaking activities. Representation of these interests must be guaranteed so that all, even dissenting minorities, are not excluded from the legislative process. Such a guarantee can exist only when there are mechanisms of government which allow expression of diverse interest. Such guarantees assure that all interests are heard even in the face of overwhelming power of the executive elite. This power, based upon technical knowledge and control of economic resources, ought to be reduced to par with the voting power of the organizational citizenship. It is a matter of detail whether representation of the citizenship is direct or through a constituency system. Large organizations tend toward the latter approach. For example, the Priest Senate in the Catholic Church is composed of elected delegates, who are responsible to their constituency in the dioceses.

What is more important is a commitment to democratic procedures which permit expression of a diversity of interests. It means a commitment to a system of government which probably would be less efficient than a technical autocracy. This commitment has to be made by all members of the political community of the organization, not just management. Owners, staff, and rank and file as well would have to say, "There are values of government, beyond the autocracy required by the rational quest for the one best way, which we wish to see manifested in our organization. We intend to insure that these values materialize in policy through structural guarantees of representation. This is the one way we can be sure our interests are served today and will be served in the future."

The Case for a Truly Participative System of Organizational Government

Whether or not one feels a case can be made depends on the optimistic or pessimistic state of one's psyche. I am pessimistic for two reasons.

First, I do not believe the organizational citizenship has the will to sacrifice a single quanta [*sic*] of rationality for those values of a truly participative government which conflict with the quest for the one best way. I am not imputing to this citizenship a lack of moral conviction necessarily. The web of technological determinism has too completely enfolded its beneficiaries. The expectations of organizational citizens are nearly entirely in the technical and material orders. Each element of the citizenship anticipates rational behavior from the other. Taken together they expect efficient organizational performance. The technical elite are supposed to accomplish this. For their part, the elite, at once a segment of the citizenship but preeminent among citizens, perceive rationality as their unique role. Where can this chain be broken?

Second, there might be some hope for breaking it if the managerial elite and the industrial humanists endorse the cause of representative government in organizations. But I do not see this leadership coming from the practice or from the intellectuals.

Management supports democracy as long as it remains in the never-never land of "authentic confrontations, meaningful dialogue, interpersonal competence, and loving-kindness." But management is less supportive of organizational forms which enfranchise employees and reenfranchise ownership in the legislative process. In a grudging way management may institute judicial procedures as long as they are controlled by the managerial hierarchy using incumbent executives as the judges. However, something as "radical" as my modest proposal is likely to give the most liberal administrator a serious trauma.

Managers are blessed at least with a refreshingly pragmatic attitude toward organizational reform. "If it works in the interest of rationality, we'll use it." Such cannot be said for the curiously schizophrenic position of the industrial humanists. The humanists *qua* ideologists should embrace a plan of governmental reform by structural change to foster representation of interests and to assure corrective justice. But the humanists are so opposed to one kind of structure, bureaucracy, that they are blind to other kinds of structures which are supportive of their values.

This mild myopia could be fixed if it were not for the program side of industrial humanism. The humanists cannot recommend programs to their clients which fail to correspond with the rational interests of the organization. A system of organization which has both the form and spirit of representative government could not conform to the rational imperative. Therefore, in programs, and by default in ideology, separation of power and due process are disregarded. Instead, there is brave talk about individual self-realization, team effectiveness, and supportive organizational climates.

So here in truncated fashion are the reasons for my pessimism. I imagine the main question now is what individual strategies should a person adopt given little hope for self-determination or assurance

of justice in organizational life? He could, as a physicist friend of mine suggests, "lie back and enjoy the material affluence." Or he could assume the guise of the simple-minded boy on the cover of *Mad* magazine and say "who's worried, not me." Or he could become a true creature of his environment.

This strategy was stated by one of my students in a *very* early morning business school course in organization theory. We were discussing the kinds of utility created by organizations with different objectives. The question always arises during these discussions of the utility created by universities. This student said that the university creates educated people. I asked if he considered himself a product of the university or a participant in the more lofty enterprise of learning which includes himself, his fellow students, and the professor. I hoped he would agree to the latter. But instead he replied, "that's right prof. I'm a product and I'm going to be consumed by a big company."

References and Notes

1. The first three parts of this paper are based upon two previous articles, "Technology and Organization Government . . . ", *Academy of Management Journal* (September 1968), pp. 301–13, and "A Fragment on Government," *The Personnel Administrator* (September-October 1968), pp. 22–23.
2. A recent anthology has a number of the basic articles dealing with this subject. See D. Hampton, C. Summer, and R. Webber, *Organizational Behavior and the Practice of Management* (Glenview, Ill.: Scott, Foresman and Co., 1968), chapters seven and nine. See also William M. Evan, "Public and Private Legal Systems," in William M. Evan, ed., *Law and Sociology* (New York: The Free Press of Glencoe, 1962), pp. 165–84; James L. Price, *Organizational Effectiveness* (Homewood, Ill.: Irwin-Dorsey, 1968), chapters three and four; and William G. Scott, *The Management of Conflict* (Homewood, Ill.: Irwin-Dorsey, 1965).
3. These tenets of democratic liberalism were paraphrased from the views of a well-known political scientist of the 1930's. See Charles E. Merriam, *The New Democracy and the New Despotism* (New York: McGraw-Hill Book Company, 1938), pp. 12–38.

4. Consult Warren G. Bennis, *Changing Organizations* (New York: McGraw-Hill Book Company, 1966).
5. The names often associated with these models are: Douglas McGregor, Rensis Likert, Richard Beckhard, Robert Blake, and Warren Bennis.
6. Joan Woodward, *Industrial Organization: Theory and Practice* (London: Oxford University Press, 1965), p. 35.
7. Jaques Ellul, *The Technological Society* (New York: Alfred A. Knopf, Inc., 1965).
8. Ibid., pp. 301–02.
9. See "The Big Business Executive, 1964," *Scientific American*, 1965, Special Report, pp. 1 and 9. This report says that in 500 of the largest American manufacturing firms, 74 percent of the top executives have college degrees. Of these, 33 percent have their degrees in some branch of science or engineering.
10. A. A. Berle, Jr., *The 20th Century Capitalist Revolution* (New York: Harcourt Brace Jovanovich, Inc., 1965), chapters three and five.
11. For example, Richard Eells and Clarence C. Walton, *Conceptual Foundations of Business* (Homewood, Ill.: Richard D. Irwin, 1961), pp. 360, 363; and Keith Davis and Robert L. Blomstrom, *Business and its Environment* (New York: McGraw-Hill Book Company, 1966), pp. 9, 326–27.
12. Evan, *Law and Sociology*, p. 179, although as Evan points out, it took some "persuasion" from the public sector to curb manufacturers in forcing terms on their agencies.
13. See "comments" by Keith Davis and Sherwood Gordon in the communication section of the *Academy of Management Journal* (December 1968).
14. Ibid.
15. See Nisbet's interpretation of Weber in Richard A. Nisbet, *The Sociological Tradition* (New York: Basic Books, Inc., Publishers, 1966), especially pp. 292–300 and Julian Freund, *The Sociology of Max Weber* (New York: Pantheon Books, Inc., 1968), pp. 17–24. The standard references to the other social critics cited are Ellul, *Technological Society*, Herbert Marcuse, *One Dimensional Man* (Boston: Beacon Press, 1964), Ludwig von Bertalanffy, *Robots, Men, and Minds* (New York: George Braziller, 1967), and John Kenneth Galbraith, *The New Industrial State* (Boston: Houghton Mifflin Company, 1967).
16. Henry S. Kariel, *The Decline of American Pluralism* (Stanford, Calif.: Stanford University Press, 1961).
17. C. Wright Mills, *The Power Elite* (New York: Oxford University Press, 1957).
18. Galbraith, *Industrial State*.
19. Marcuse, *Dimensional Man*, p. 51.
20. See Scott, *Management of Conflict.* In my research on organizational appeal systems, I found the U.A.W. with a structure like this. Of the business firms surveyed (there are 800 respondents), I discovered just two which referred the final settlement of appeals in unilaterally-granted systems to an outside arbitrator. In all the other firms with such systems, incumbent managers adjudicated disputes.

TODAY'S PROBLEMS WITH TOMORROW'S ORGANIZATIONS

Chris Argyris

There is a revolution brewing in the introduction of new organizational forms to complement or to replace the more traditional pyramidal form. I believe, on the basis of some recent research, that the new forms are basically sound. However, because of the methods used to introduce them and because of those used to maintain them, many of the unintended self-defeating consequences of the older structures are reappearing.

Two major causes for this revolution are the new requirements for organizational survival in an increasingly competitive environment and the new administrative and information technology available to deal with complexity. W. L. Wallace summarizes these requirements as: (1) the technological revolution (complexity and variety of products, new materials and processes, and the effects of massive research); (2) competition and the profit squeeze (saturated markets, inflation of wage and material costs, production efficiency); (3) the high cost of marketing; and (4) the unpredictability of consumer demands (due to high discretionary income, wide range of choices available, and shifting tastes).[1] To make matters more difficult, the costs of new products are increasing while their life expectancy is decreasing.

Requirements of Tomorrow's Organizations

In order to meet these challenges, modern organizations need: (1) much more creative planning; (2) the development of valid and useful knowledge about new products and new processes; (3) increased concerted and cooperative action with internalized long-range commitment by all involved; and (4) increased understanding of criteria for effectiveness that meet the challenges of complexity.

These requirements, in turn, depend upon: (1) continuous and open access between individuals and groups; (2) free, reliable communication, where (3) interdependence is the foundation for individual and departmental cohesiveness and (4) trust, risk taking, and helping each other is prevalent, so that (5) conflict is identified and managed in such a way that the destructive win-lose stances with their accompanying polarization of views are minimized and effective problem solving is maximized. These conditions, in turn, require individuals who: (1) do not fear stating their complete views; (2) are capable of creating groups that maximize the unique contributions of each individual; (3) value and seek to integrate their contributions into a creative total, final contribution; (4) rather than needing to be individually rewarded for their contributions, thus (5) finding the search for valid knowledge and the development of the best possible solution intrinsically satisfying.

Unfortunately, these conditions are difficult to create. Elsewhere[2] I have tried to show that the traditional pyramidal structure and managerial controls tend to place individuals and departments in constant interdepartmental warfare, where win-lose competition creates polarized stances, that tend to get resolved by the superior making the decisions, thereby creating a dependence upon him. Also. there is a tendency toward conformity, mistrust, and lack of risk taking among the peers that results in focusing upon individual survival, requiring the seeking out of the scarce rewards, identifying one's self with successful venture (be a hero), and being careful to avoid being blamed for or identified with a failure, thereby becoming a 'bum.' All these adaptive behaviors tend to induce low interpersonal competence and can lead the organization, over the long run, to become rigid, sticky, less innovative, resulting in less than effective decisions with even less internal commitment to the decisions on the part of those involved.

Some people have experimented by structuring the organization in such a way that people representing the major functions (marketing, engineering, manufacturing, and finance) are coerced to work together. Unfortunately, the pyramidal structure does not lend itself to such a strategy. As Wallace points out, the difficulty is that typically each function approaches the business problems inherent in the product from a somewhat different point of view: Marketing wants a good product at a low price; production, a product that is easily produced; engineering, a product that outclasses—engineering wise—all other products, etc.[3] None of these stances tends to lead to the resolution of conflicting ideas into a decision that tends to integrate the best of each view.

The Matrix Organization

One of the most promising strategies to induce cooperation and integration of effort on crucial business problems is the development of project teams and the matrix organization. These administrative innovations were created initially to solve the complex problems of coordination and scheduling of large defense projects. They have been adapted and used by many other organizations because of their potential promise. The future role of the team approach and matrix organization is, in my opinion, an important one for administration.

A project team is created to solve a particular problem. It is composed of people representing all the relevant managerial functions (for example, marketing, manufacturing, engineering, and finance). Each member is given equal responsibility and power to solve the problem. The members are expected to work as a cohesive unit. Once the problem is solved, the team is given a new assignment or disbanded. If the problem is a recurring one, the team remains active. In many cases, especially in the defense programs, the project manager is given full authority and responsibility for the completion of the project including rewarding and penalizing the members of the team. An organization may have many teams. This results in an organization that looks like a matrix; hence the title of matrix organization. (See figure on p. 64.)

Problems with the Matrix Organization

How effective are the project teams and the matrix organizations? In order to begin to answer that question, I have been conducting some research in nine large organizations utilizing a matrix organization structure. In preliminary interviews the executives reported that the matrix organization and team approach made sense, but that they found them very difficult to put into actual practice. People still seemed to polarize issues, resisted exploring ideas thoroughly, mistrusted each other's behavior, focused on trying to protect one's own function, over-emphasized simplified criteria of success (for example, figures on sales), worked too much on day-to-day operations and short-term planning, engaged in the routine decisions rather than focus more on the long-range risky decisions, and emphasized survival more than the integra-

tion of effort into a truly accepted decision.

Others found fault with the team approach for not providing individuals enough opportunity to get recognition in their own functional departments for their performance on the team. Still others insisted that individuals sought to be personally identified with a particular accomplishment; that it wasn't satisfying for them to know that their group (and not they) obtained the reward. Finally, some said that during their meetings the teams got bogged down in focusing on the negative—in other words, what had not been accomplished.

Why are these new administrative structures and strategies having this trouble? I do *not* believe the concept of the matrix organization is inherently invalid. I believe the answer lies in the everyday *behavior styles that the managers have developed, in the past, to survive and to succeed within the traditional pyramidal organization.* The behavior styles needed for the effective use of the matrix organization are, I believe, very different. Also, the group dynamics that are effective in the pyramidal structure are different from those that will be effective in the matrix organization. Thus I do not agree that the comments above are "natural" for all people. They are "natural" for people living under the pyramidal concept. For example, groups *can* be created where individuals gain success from seeing integrated decisions; where recognition *does* come more from success and less from compliments from others, where overcoming barriers and correcting faults and failures are not perceived as negative.[4]

A second important cause for the ineffectiveness of the matrix type organization lies in the very processes that have given it birth. Again, the difficulty has been that the birth processes used were more applicable to the pyramidal than to the matrix organization. In short, I am suggesting that a basic problem has been that a new form of organization has been introduced in such a way as to make difficulties inevitable and that the leadership

Representatives of	Project 1	Project 2	Project 3
Manufacturing			
Engineering			
Marketing			
Finance			
	Team 1	Team 2	Team 3

styles that the executives use to administer the matrix organization, on the whole, compound the felony. In order to illustrate my point I should like to take one of these nine studies and discuss it in some detail. The case that I have selected to discuss approximates the other eight. The variance among the cases was not high. More importantly, the establishment of a project and program approach had the most careful thought and analytical competence brought to bear on it by the top management. It is a study of a multi-million-dollar organization that decided to reorganize its *product planning* and *program review* activities into a team approach which resulted in a matrix organization. These two activities have been the ones most frequently organized into a matrix organization. The study lasted about one year. I interviewed all the top executives involved (25), asked them to complete questionnaires, and observed, taped, and analyzed nearly 35 meetings of the teams, ranging from 45 minutes to two and one-half hours in length.

.   .   .

A New Philosophy of Organizing and Managing People

One of the most important first steps is to communicate to the people that the matrix organization is not a simple extension of the traditional pyramidal structure. The pyramidal structure acquires its form from the fact that as one goes up the administrative ladder (1) power and control increase; (2) the availability of information increases; (3) the degree of flexibility to act increases; (4) the scope of the decisions made and the responsibilities involved increase. Implicit in the matrix organization are almost opposite tendencies. For example, power and control are given to the individual and/or to the groups who have the technical skill to accomplish the task, no matter what their organizational level. Thus a team could be composed of five people representing all different levels of authority (on the traditional chart), who are equal. The group could be chaired by the individual with the least organizational authority. The individual or groups are given responsibility and authority to make decisions of the widest necessary scope.

If we may extrapolate to the probable matrix organization of the future, Forrester suggests that the organization will eventually eliminate the superior-subordinate relationship and substitute for it the individual self-discipline arising from self-interest created by a competitive market mechanism within the system. The individual would negotiate continuously changing relationships. Each individual would be a profit center whose objective would be to produce the most value for the least activity; who would have the freedom to terminate as well as to create new activity, who would have access to all the necessary information. The organization of the future would be rid of internal monopolies which is the usual status of most traditional departments.[5]

Although I would agree with Forrester, I believe that the organizations of the future will be a combination of the old and the new forms of organization. I believe that the old forms are going to be more effective for the routine, noninnovative activity that requires little, if any, internal commitment by the participants. However, as the decisions become less routine, more innovative and require more commitment, the newer forms such as the matrix organizations will be more effective.

In addition to being able to differentiate clearly between the old and the new forms, the future executive must also be able to know the conditions under which he will use the different organizational forms.[6] Moreover, he will need to become skillful in several different kinds of leadership styles, each of which is consistent with a particular form. For example, an authoritarian leadership style is more consistent with the traditional structure; a participative style with the link pin organization defined by Likert and a style that develops risk taking and trust for the matrix organization.

Leadership Style and Matrix Organizations

If recent research is valid, then the majority of executive leadership styles conform to the traditional pyramidal style. This is not surprising since leadership styles and organizational design would naturally go together. The findings that did surprise us were (1) the degree to which the executives believed in leadership styles that were consonant with the matrix organization, and (2) the degree to which they were *unaware* that they were *not* behaving according to their ideals.[7]

Another important first step therefore is to help executives become more aware of their actual leadership style. Unless they develop such awareness, they are not going to be able to unfreeze their old styles, develop new ones, and, most importantly, switch from one style to another as the administrative situations and the organization structure used is changed. Unless the switching from one style to another can be clearly identified by the person and the receivers, confusion will result.[8]

Another finding that surprised us about executive decisionmaking was how many executives focused on keeping people "happy." Indeed, the most frequently cited reason for not being open with another was the fear that it might upset the receiver (and thus upset the sender). The most frequently cited reason for not bringing two groups together who are locked in interdepartmental warfare was that it would simply "involve personalities and nothing but harm could come of it." Although the executives that we studied were happiness-oriented in their behavior, they were not in their attitudes. They believed in strong leadership that could call a spade a spade and let the chips fall where they may. Again according to the observations, the spades were called spades and the chips placed on the line, but in private settings where few could be witnesses, or by such deft and diplomatic processes that few people, including the targets, were aware of what was happening. I cannot refrain from adding that there seemed to be a strong correlation between those executives who were critical of the field of "human relations" as one whose objective was to make people happy and the degree of their blindness to the fact that they tended to do the very same thing when they were actually leading.

The Management of Tension

Executives in the matrix organization will also need to learn, if I may be permitted to oversimplify, that there is productive and unproductive or crippling tension. The unproductive or crippling tension is tension that a person experiences but which he cannot control. The reason he cannot control the tension may be external (pressure from his superior) or internal (inability to control his own demands on himself, plus the accompanying feelings of impatience and guilt aimed at himself).

Productive tension is that tension that the individual can control and which comes from accepting new challenges, taking risks, expanding one's competencies, etc. These are the very qualities that are central to the matrix organization. Thus the executive of the future will have to learn how to define internal environments that challenge people, stretch their aspirations realistically, and help them face interpersonal reality. Some examples are financial controls that reward people for risk taking; organizational situations that are optimally undermanned; incentive systems that reward excellence (not average performance), work that is designed to use people's complex abilities. To put this another way, we need to develop competence in manipulating the environment but not the people. (They should have the freedom and responsibility to choose if they will enter the new environment).

The Management of Intergroup Conflict

The matrix organization is composed of teams which in turn are populated by representatives of the traditional line functions. As we have seen, this leads to much intergroup conflict within the team as well as between teams.

Instead of trying to stamp out intergroup conflict as bad and disloyal, the executives need to learn how to manage it so that the constructive aspects are emphasized and the destructive aspects are de-emphasized. This means that the organization needs to put on the table for diagnosis the interdepartmental fires, the incidents of throwing the dead cat over into the other department's yard, the polarized competitive warfare where success is defined by the participants in terms of which side won rather than the contribution to the whole. The executives will have to learn how (1) to bring the groups together; (2) where each discusses and seeks, in private, to agree on its views and attitudes toward the other and toward self; (3) then the representatives of both groups talk together in the presence of the other group members, followed by (4) private discussion to establish the way they are perceived by others in order (5) to

develop (through representatives) an understanding of the discrepancy between their and other's views.[9]

The Executive Educational Activities

Most organizations send their executives to university executive programs or to internal executive programs usually designed following the concept of the university. I do not want to get into philosophical discussions about the nature of university education at this point. I would like to point out, however, that *there may be a discrepancy between the characteristics of university education and the needs of the matrix organization.*

The university has typically assumed that learning (1) is for the individual; (2) occurs when it is given; (3) is tested by contrived examinations of the knowledge acquired; (4) need not be relevant to any immediate problem; (5) should be designed and controlled by the educator; it is the task of the educator to define the problems, develop ways to solve them, and define the criteria for evaluation who passes and who does not. The matrix organizations require education that (1) focuses on individuals in team systems and (2) it occurs where the problem is located; (3) is learned by the use of actual problems, and (4) is tested by the effectiveness of the actual results, and (5) is controlled by those participating in the problem (aided by the educator as a consultant).

Executive education in the matrix organization will focus on system effectiveness. This means that the central educational department will now become an organizational development activity. It will have systems as its clients. A small team of consultants will enter the system and develop a diagnosis of its human and technical effectiveness. These data will then be fed back to representatives at all levels of the system to generate, at the grass-roots level, action recommendations. A steering committee composed of representatives of the client system and the organizational development will then prepare a long-range educational program designed to increase the immediate as well as the long-range effectiveness of the system.

Classes may then be held at the plant location or at a central facility, depending upon the resources needed, the time available, the availability of the "students," as well as the faculty. Teams, and not disconnected individuals, will study together for the majority of technical and management subjects. These teams will be actual working teams. This will place pressure on the faculty to develop learning that is valid for the real problems of the team and motivate the students to learn, since it is their problems upon which the education is focusing.

To put this another way, education will be for organizational and system diagnosis, renewal, and effectiveness. It will be held with groups, subject material, and faculty that are organic to the organization's problem. One of the dangers of this education is the possibility that it will focus on the trivial, short-range problems. The quality control in this area will depend partially on the diagnostic competence of the faculty. In defining the problem, they can help the organization to get to the underlying and basic causes. The students can also help by being alert to the validity of the education that is being offered to them.

Some critics wonder if teams of people working together can be pulled away from work. The answer, in my experience, is affirmative. The fear, for example, that the company will be in trouble if the top team leaves for a week, has been quietly exploded in several cases. The explosions have been quiet lest, as one president put it, "it was learned how well things ran while the top management was away."

More importantly, this new type of education is central to the work of the system. Thus, the team is not being pulled away from work. Indeed, in many cases, it is pulled away *in order to work.* Systems, like cars, need to have their organizational hoods opened and the motor checked and tuned. Unless this mainte-

nance work is done, the system will deteriorate as certainly as does an automobile.

Finally, the concern of being away physically from the location should be matched with the concern about the number of hours being consumed needlessly while at work. In the studies listed previously, I have found that as many as half the meetings and as much as three quarters of the time spent at meetings are not productive and worse than unnecessary.

Organizational Change

Anyone who has planned major organizational change knows (1) how difficult it is to foresee accurately all the major problems involved; (2) the enormous amount of time needed to iron out the kinks and get people to accept the change; (3) the apparent lack of internal commitment on the part of many to help make the plan work, manifested partly (5) by people at all levels resisting taking the initiative to make modifications that they see are necessary so that the new plan can work. In preparing this article, I reviewed my notes from thirty-two major reorganizations in large organizations in which I played some consulting and research role. I did not find one that could be labeled as fully completed and integrated three years after the change had been announced (and in many cases had gone through several revisions). That is, after three years there were still many people fighting, ignoring, questioning, resisting, blaming, the reorganization without feeling a strong obligation personally to correct the situation.

As I mentioned above, I believe the reasons for this long delay are embedded in the change strategy typically used by management. To refer to the diagram, the basic strategy has been for the top management to take the responsibility to overcome and outguess the resistance to change. This strategy does tend to succeed because management works very hard, applies pressure, and, if necessary, knocks a few heads together (or eliminates some). However, as we have seen, the strategy creates resisting forces that are costly to the organization's effectiveness, to its long run viability and flexibility, as well as to the people at all levels.

Reducing the Resisting Forces

What would happen if management experiments with the strategy of reducing the restraining forces by involving, at least, the management employees at all levels in the diagnosis, design, and executive of the change program? For example, in one organization a plan of reorganization was begun by getting all levels involved in diagnosing the present problems of the organizations. Groups were formed (which met only twice for several hours each time) to diagnose the effectiveness of the present organization. These groups were initially composed of people from various functions but holding positions of about equal level. Each group brainstormed as much as it desired to get out of the problem. They were not asked to suggest solutions at this time because (1) no one group would have a total picture of the organization, and therefore (2) its recommendations could be incomplete and misleading, with the added danger of (3) each group becoming attached to their suggestions, and finally (4) people tend to be hesitant about enumerating a problem if they are asked for solutions and do not have any.

The results of these diagnostic sessions were fed to a top-level steering committee which contained representatives of all the major managerial levels. This committee had the diagnoses collated, analyzed, and developed into an integrated picture. Wherever they found holes and inconsistencies in the diagnoses they made a note of them. Eventually they had compiled a lengthy list of major questions to be answered before the overall diagnosis could be accepted as valid. These questions were fed to small task forces whose composition was specifically designed to be able to answer the questions. Thus, in this phase, the groups were composed of managerial personnel from many functions and levels who were relevant to the question being asked. These task forces were disbanded as soon as they provided the answers to the questions.

The third phase was one where the steering committee tried to develop a new organizational structure. In achieving this objective the steering committee began, for the first time, to suggest arrangements of individuals and groups tasks that could be threatening to various interests. This led to the members becoming more involved, cautious, and at times, defensive. Members who, up to this point, had felt free to be objective were beginning to feel themselves slipping into the role of protecting the groups toward which they had the closest attachment.

At this point, the task force went to the education group and asked for a course in such subjects as how to deal with intergroup rivalries and issues, with emotionality in groups, and with hidden agendas. This course was quickly but carefully planned. The steering committee members reported that it was a great help to them. It was especially helpful in welding them into a more fully functioning open, confronting of issues, and risk-taking group. They also reported that as the members' confidence and trust in their group increased, the more willing they were to invite, at the appropriate time, members of departments whose future roles were being discussed so that the problems could be discussed and solved jointly.

The fourth phase was the preparation of a final but still tentative plan. It was fully discussed with the top executives until it represented a plan that they liked. This plan was then discussed systematically with key representatives of all the departments. Alterations were invited and carefully considered. Two members of the steering committee were members of top management who had authority to represent the top in approving most changes.

During the fifth phase, two kinds of data were collected. First a questionnaire was sent to all who had participated asking them for any individual comments about the plan as well as any comments about the effectiveness of the process of change to date. This diagnosis uncovered, in several cases, new ideas to be considered as well as several suggestions to be reexamined because they were developed in groups where individuals felt that they had been pushed through by a small but powerful clique.

The final plan was then drawn up with a specific timetable (which had been discussed and accepted by the people below). The top management, with the help of the steering committee, then put the new organizational plan into action. These phases took nearly seventeen months. However, once the plan became policy (1) the resisting forces and the tensions were much lower than expected on the basis of previous experience; (2) wherever they existed there were organizational mechanisms already established and working to resolve them; (3) the internal commitment to the new policy was high (it is ours not theirs), and thus (4) changes were made as they became necessary without much fanfare or difficulty.

One of the most important outcomes of this type of change strategy was that it provided a living educational experience for individuals and groups on how to work together; on how to develop internal commitment among the members of the organization; and how to reduce the unnecessary and destructive win-lose rivalries. Thus the change program became an opportunity for education at all levels. The result was that a new system had been created which could be used for future changes and to increase the capacity of the organization to learn.

Even with these results, I have encountered some managers who wonder if an organization can take this much time

for changing organizational structure. In my experience, although time is a critical factor, it is a false issue. Time will be taken, whether management is aware of it or not, by people to ask all the questions, make all the politically necessary moves, develop all the protective devices, and create all the organizational escape hatches that they feel are necessary. The real issue is whether the time will be used constructively and effectively so that the organization can learn from its experiences thereby increasing its competence in becoming a problem-solving system.

References and Notes

1. W. L. Wallace, "The Winchester-Western Division Concept of Product Planning" (New Haven: Olin Mathieson Chemical Corporation, January 1963), pp. 2–3.
2. Chris Argyris, *Interpersonal Competence and Organizational Effectiveness* (Homewood, Ill.: Richard D. Irwin, Inc., 1962) and "Interpersonal Barriers to Decision Making," *Harvard Business Review* (March 1966).
3. W. L. Wallace, "Product Planning."
4. Chris Argyris, *Organization and Innovation* (Homewood, Ill.: Richard D. Irwin, Inc., 1965); Edgar Schein and Warren Bennis, *Personal Growth and Organizational Change Through Group Methods* (New York: John Wiley & Sons, Inc., 1965).
5. Jay W. Forrester, "A New Corporate Design," *Industrial Management Review* 7, no. 1 (Fall 1965): 5–18.
6. Elsewhere I have suggested some examples of the decision rules that could be developed within the organization so that all concerned coud be clear when to use the different structures. Chris Argyris, *Integrating the Individual and the Organization* (New York: John Wiley & Sons, Inc., 1964).
7. Chris Argyris, "Interpersonal Barriers."
8. For some concrete examples of how this may be achieved, see my article quoted above in the *Harvard Business Review*, in March 1966.
9. Robert R. Blake, Herbert A. Shepard, and Jane S. Mouton, *Managing Intergroup Conflict in Industry* (Houston: Gulf Publishing Co., 1965).

BEYOND BUREAUCRACY: WILL ORGANIZATION MEN FIT THE NEW ORGANIZATIONS?

Warren Bennis

Most of us spend all of our working day and a great deal of our nonworking day in a unique and extremely durable social arrangement called "bureaucracy." I use the term "bureaucracy" descriptively, not as an epithet about those "guys in Washington" or as a metaphor a la Kafka's *Castle* which conjures up an image of red tape, or faceless and despairing masses standing in endless lines. Bureaucracy, as I shall use the term here, is a social invention, perfected during the industrial revolution to organize and direct the activities of the business firm.

It is my premise that the bureaucratic form of organization is becoming less and less effective; that it is hopelessly out of joint with contemporary realities; the new shapes, patterns, and models are emerging which promise drastic changes in the conduct of the corporation and of managerial practices in general. In the next 25 to 50 years we should witness, and participate in, the end of bureaucracy and the rise of new social systems better suited to twentieth-century demands of industrialization. (Sociological evolutionists substantially agree that 25 to 50 years from now most people in the world will live in industrialized societies.)

Corsica, according to Gibbon, is much easier to deplore than to describe. The same holds true for bureaucracy. Basically, bureaucracy is a social invention which relies exclusively on the power to influence through rules, reason, and law. Max Weber, the German sociologist who developed the theory of bureaucracy around the turn of the century, once described bureaucracy as a social machine:

Bureaucracy is like a modern judge who is a vending machine into which the pleadings are inserted together with the fee and which then disgorges the judgment together with its reasons mechanically derived from the code.

The bureaucratic "machine model" Weber outlined was developed as a reaction against the personal subjugation, nepotism, cruelty, emotional vicissitudes, and capricious judgment which passed for managerial practices in the early days of the industrial revolution. The true hope for man, it was thought, lay in his ability to rationalize, calculate, to use his head as well as his hands and heart. Thus, in the bureaucratic system social roles were institutionalized and reinforced by legal tradition rather than by the "cult of personality"; rationality and predictability were sought for in order to eliminate chaos and unanticipated consequences; emphasis was placed on technical competence rather than arbitrary or "iron whims." These are oversimplifications, to be sure, but contemporary analysts of organizations would tend to agree with them. In fact, there is a general consensus that the anatomy of bureaucracy consists of the following "organs":

1) a division of labor based on functional specialization.
2) a well-defined hierarchy of authority.
3) a system of rules covering the rights and duties of employees.
4) impersonality of interpersonal relations.
5) promotion and selection based on technical competence.

It does not take great critical imagination to detect the flaws and problems in the bureaucratic model. We have all *experienced* them:

1) bosses without (and underlings with) technical competence.
2) arbitrary and zany rules.
3) an underworld (or informal) organization which subverts or even replaces the formal apparatus.
4) confusion and conflict among roles.
5) cruel treatment of subordinates based not on rational or legal grounds but upon inhumanity.

The tremendous range of unanticipated consequences provides a gold mine of material for comics like Charlie Chaplin and Jacques Tati who capture with a smile or a shrug the absurdity of authority systems based on pseudologic and inappropriate rules.

Almost everybody, including many observers of organizational behavior, approaches bureaucracy with a chip on his shoulder. It has been attacked for many reasons: for theoretical confusion and contradictions; for moral and ethical reasons; on practical grounds such as its inefficiency; for methodological weaknesses; for containing too many implicit values and for containing too few. I have recently catalogued the criticisms of bureaucracy, and they outnumber and outdo the ninety-five theses tacked on the church door at Wittenberg in attacking another bureaucracy. A small sample of these:

1) Bureaucracy does not adequately allow for personal growth and the development of mature personalities.
2) It develops conformity and "groupthink."
3) It does not take into account the "informal organization" and the emergent and unanticipated problems.
4) Its systems of control and authority are hopelessly outdated.
5) It has no adequate juridical process.
6) It does not possess adequate means for resolving differences and conflicts between ranks, and most particularly, between functional groups.
7) Communication (and innovative

ideas) are thwarted or distorted due to hierarchical divisions.
8) The full human resources of bureaucracy are not being utilized due to mistrust, fear of reprisals, etc.
9) It cannot assimilate the influx of new technology or scientists entering the organization.
10) It modifies personality structure so that people become and reflect the dull, gray, conditioned "organization man."

Max Weber, the developer of the theory of bureaucracy, came around to condemn the apparatus he helped immortalize. While he felt that bureaucracy was inescapable, he also thought it might strangle the spirit of capitalism or the entrepreneurial attitude, a theme which Schumpeter later developed. And in a debate on bureaucracy Weber once said, more in sorrow than in anger:

It is horrible to think that the world could one day be filled with nothing but those little cogs, little men clinging to little jobs and striving towards bigger ones—a state of affairs which is to be seen once more, as in the Egyptian records, playing an ever-increasing part in the spirit of our present administrative system, and especially of its offspring, the students. This passion for bureaucracy . . . is enough to drive one to despair. It is as if in politics . . . we were deliberately to become men who need 'order' and nothing but order, who become nervous and cowardly if for one moment this order wavers, and helpless if they are torn away from their total incorporation in it. That the world should know no men but these: It is such an evolution that we are already caught up in, and the great question is therefore not how we can promote and hasten it, but what can we oppose to this machinery in order to keep a portion of mankind free from this parcelling-out of the soul, from this supreme mastery of the bureaucratic way of life.

In what ways has bureaucracy been modified over the years in order to cope more successfully with the problems that beset it? Before answering that, we have to say something about the nature of organizations, *all* organizations, from mass production leviathans all the way to service industries such as the university or hospital. Organizations are primarily complex, goal-seeking units. In order to survive they must also accomplish the secondary tasks of (1) maintaining their internal system and coordinating the "human side of enterprise"—a process of mutual compliance here called *reciprocity*—and (2) adapting to and shaping the external environment—here called *adaptability*. These two organizational dilemmas can help us to organize the pivotal ways in which the bureaucratic mechanism has been altered—and found wanting.

Reciprocity primarily covers the processes which can mediate conflict between the goals of management and the individual goals of the workers. Over the past several decades a number of interesting theoretical and practical resolutions have been made which truly allow for conflict and mediation of interest. They revise, if not transform, the very nature of the bureaucratic mechanism by explicit recognition of the inescapable tension between individual and organizational goals. These theories can be called, variously, *exchange, group, value, structural, situational*—depending on what variable of the situation one wishes to modify.

The *exchange* theories postulate that wages, incomes, and services are given to the individual for an equal contribution to the organization in work. If the inducements are not adequate, men may withdraw and work elsewhere. This may be elaborated upon by regarding "payments" to individuals as including motivational units. That is to say, the organization provides a psychological anchor in times of rapid social change and a hedge against personal loss, as well as position, growth and mastery, success experience, and so forth—in exchange for energy, work, commitment.

Management tends to interpret motivation in economic terms. Man is logical; man acts in the manner which serves his self-interest; man is competitive. Elton Mayo and his associates were among the first to see human *affiliation* as a motivating force, to view industrial organization as a *social* system as well as an economic-technical system. A manager, they stated, should be judged in terms of his ability to sustain cooperation. In fact, once a cohesive, primary work group is seen as a motivating force, a managerial elite may become obsolete, and the work group itself becomes the decisionmaker. This allows decisions to be made at the most relevant point of the organization, where the data are most available.

Before this becomes possible, however, some theorists believe that the impersonal *value* system of bureaucracy must be modified. In this case the manager plays an important role as the instrument of change in interpersonal relations. He must instill values which permit and reinforce the expression of feeling, experimentalism, and norms of individuality, trust, and concern. Management, according to R. R. Blake, is successful insofar as it maximizes a "concern for people"—with "concern for production."

Others believe that a new conception of the *structure* of bureaucracy will create more relevant attitudes towards the function of management than formal role specifications now do. If the organization is seen as organic rather than mechanistic, as adapting spontaneously to its needs, then decisions will be made at the critical point and roles and jobs will devolve on the "natural" organizational incumbent. The shift would probably be from the individual level to cooperative group effort, from delegated to shared responsibility, from centralized to decentralized authority from obedience to confidence, from antagonistic arbitration to problem solving. Management centered upon problem solving, that assumes or relaxes authority according to task demands, has most concerned some theorists who are as much interested in an organization's success and productivity as in its social system.

However, on all sides we find a growing

belief that the effectiveness of bureaucracy should be evaluated by human *situation* as well as economic criteria. Social satisfaction and personal growth of employees must be considered as well as the productivity and profit of the organization. The criticism and revisions of the bureaucratic organization tend to concentrate on the internal system and its human components. But although it appears on the surface that the case against bureaucracy has to do with its ethical-moral posture and the social fabric, the real coup de grace has come from the environment.

Bureaucracy thrives in a highly competitive, undifferentiated and stable environment, such as the climate of its youth, the Industrial Revolution. A pyramidal structure of authority, with power concentrated in the hands of a few with the knowledge and resources to control an entire enterprise was, and is, an eminently suitable social arrangement for routinized tasks.

However, the environment has changed in just those ways which make the mechanism most problematic. Stability has vanished. As Ellis Johnson said, " . . . the once-reliable constants have now become galloping variables."

The factors accelerating change include:

1) the growth of science, research and development activities, and intellectual technology.
2) the increase of transactions with social institutions (and their importance in conducting the enterprise)—including government, distributors and consumers, shareholders, competitors, raw material and power suppliers, sources of employees (particularly managers), trade unions, and groups within the firms. There is also more interdependence between the economic and other facets of society, leading to greater complications of legislation and public regulation.
3) competition between firms diminishing as their fates intertwine and become positively correlated.

My argument so far, to summarize quickly, is that the first assault on bureaucracy arose from its incapacity to manage the tension between individual and management goals. However, this conflict is somewhat mediated by the growth of a new ethic of productivity which includes personal growth and/or satisfaction. The second and more major shock to bureaucracy is caused by the scientific and technological revolution. It is the requirement of *adaptability* to the environment which leads to the predicted demise of bureaucracy and to the collapse of management as we know it now.

A forecast falls somewhere between a prediction and a prophecy. It lacks the divine guidance of the latter and the empirical foundation of the former. On thin empirical ice, I want to set forth some of the conditions that will dictate organizational life in the next 25 to 50 years.

The Environment

Those factors already mentioned will continue in force and increase. Rapid technological change and diversification will lead to interpretation of the government—its legal and economic policies—with business. Partnerships between industry and government (like Telstar) will be typical. And because of the immensity and expense of the projects, there will be fewer identical units competing for the same buyers and sellers. Or, in reverse, imperfect competition leads to an oligopolistic and government-business controlled economy. The three main features of the environment will be (1) interdependence rather than competition; (2) turbulence rather than steadiness, and (3) large-scale rather than small enterprises.

Population Characteristics

We are living in what Peter Drucker calls the "educated society," and I think this is the most distinctive characteristic of our times. Within fifteen years, two-thirds of our population living in metropolitan areas will have attended college. Adult education programs, especially the management development courses of such universities as M.I.T., Harvard, and Stanford, are expanding and adding intellectual breadth. All this, of course, is not just "nice," but necessary. For as Secretary of Labor Wirtz has pointed out, computers can do the work of most high school graduates—cheaper and more effectively. Fifty years ago education used to be regarded as "nonwork" and intellectuals on the payroll (and many of the staff) were considered "overhead." Today, the survival of the firm depends, more than ever before, on the proper exploitation of brain power.

One other characteristic of the population which will aid our understanding of organizations of the future is increasing job mobility. The lowered expense and ease of transportation, coupled with the real needs of a dynamic environment, will change drastically the idea of "owning" a job—or "having roots," for that matter. Participants will be shifted from job to job and even employer to employer with much less fuss than we are accustomed to.

Work Values

The increased level of education and mobility will change the values we hold about work. People will be more intellectually committed to their jobs and will probably require more involvement, participation, and autonomy in their work. (This turn of events is due to a composite of the following factors: (1) positive correlation between a person's education and his need for autonomy; (2) job mobility places the educated in a position of greater influence in the system; (3) job requirements call for more responsibility and discretion.)

Also, people will tend to be more "other-directed" in their dealings with others.

David McClelland's studies suggest that as industrialization increases, "other-directedness" increases; so we will tend to rely more heavily on temporary social arrangements, on our immediate and constantly-changing colleagues.

Tasks and Goals

The tasks of the firm will be more technical, complicated, and unprogrammed. They will rely more on the intellect than muscle. And they will be too complicated for one person to handle or for individual supervision. Essentially, they will call for the collaboration of specialists in a project or team form of organization.

Similarly there will be a complication of goals. "Increased profits" and "raised productivity" will sound like oversimplifications and cliches. Business will concern itself increasingly with its adaptive or innovative-creative capacity. In addition, *meta*-goals will have to be articulated and developed; that is, supragoals which shape and provide the foundation for the goal structure. For example, one meta-goal might be a system for detecting new and changing goals; another could be a system for deciding priorities among goals.

Finally, there will be more conflict and contradiction among diverse standards of organizational effectiveness, just as in hospitals and universities today there is conflict between teaching and research. The reason for this is the increased number of professionals involved, who tend to identify as much with the supragoals of their profession as with those of their immediate employer. University professors can be used as a case in point. More and more of their income comes from outside sources, such as private or public foundations and consultant work. They tend not to make good "company men" because they are divided in their loyalty to professional values and organizational demands.

Organization

The social structure of organizations of the future will have some unique characteristics. The key word will be "temporary"; there will be adaptive, rapidly changing *temporary systems.* These will be "task forces" organized around problems to be solved. The problems will be solved by groups of relative strangers who represent a set of diverse professional skills. The groups will be arranged on organic rather than mechanical models; they will evolve in response to a problem rather than to programmed role expectations. The "executive" thus becomes a coordinator or "linking pin" between various task forces. He must be a man who can speak the diverse languages of research, with skills to relay information and to mediate between groups. *People will be differentiated not vertically, according to rank and role, but flexibly and functionally according to skill and professional training.*

Adaptive, problem-solving, temporary systems of diverse specialists, linked together by coordinating and task evaluating specialists in an organic flux—this is the organizational form that will gradually replace bureaucracy as we know it. As no catchy phrase comes to mind, let us call this an *organic-adaptive* structure.

As an aside—what will happen to the rest of society, to the manual laborers, to the less educated, to those who desire to work under conditions of high authority, and so forth? Many such jobs will disappear; other jobs will be automated. However, there will be a corresponding growth in the service-type occupations, such as those in the "war on poverty" and the Peace Corps programs. In times of change, where there is a discrepancy between cultures, when industrialization and, especially, urbanization proceeds rapidly, the market for men with training and skill in human interaction increases. We might guess that approximately 40 percent of the population would be involved in jobs of this nature, 40 percent in technological jobs, with a 20 percent bureaucratic minority.

Motivation

Our above discussion of "reciprocity" indicated the shortcomings of bureaucracy in maximizing employee effectiveness. The "organic-adaptive" structure should increase motivation, and thereby effectiveness, because it enhances satisfactions intrinsic to the task. There is a harmony between the educated individual's need for meaningful, satisfactory, and creative tasks and a flexible organizational structure.

Of course, where the reciprocity problem is ameliorated, there are corresponding tensions between the individual's involvement in his professional community and his involvement in his employing organization. Professionals are notoriously "disloyal" to organizational demands.

There will, however, also be reduced commitment to work groups, for these groups, as I have already mentioned, will be transient and changing. While skills in human interaction will become more important, due to the growing needs for collaboration in complex tasks, there will be a concomitant reduction in group cohesiveness. I would predict that in the organic-adaptive system people will have to learn to develop quick and intense relationships on the job, and learn to bear the loss of more enduring work relationships.

In general I do not agree with Clark Kerr, Harold Leavitt, and others in their emphasis on a "New Bohemianism" in which leisure—not work—becomes the emotional-creative sphere of life. They assume a technological slowdown and leveling off, and a stabilizing of social mobility. This may happen in a society of the distant future. But long before then we will face the challenge of creating the new service-type organizations with an organic-adaptive structure.

Jobs in the next century should become more rather than less involving; man is a problem-solving animal and the tasks of the future guarantee a full agenda of problems. In addition, the adaptive process itself may become captivating to many. At the same time, I think that the future I described is not necessarily a "happy" one. Coping with rapid change, living in the temporary work systems, setting up (in quick-step time) meaningful relations—and then breaking them—all augur social strains and psychological tensions. Learning how to live with ambiguity and to be self-directing will be the task of education and the goal of maturity.

In these new organizations, participants will be called on to use their minds more than at any other time in history. Fantasy, imagination, and creativity will be legitimate in ways that today seem strange. Social structures will no longer be instruments of psychic repression but will in-creasingly promote play and freedom on behalf of curiosity and thought. I agree with Herbert Marcuse's thesis in *Eros and Civilization* that the necessity of repression and the suffering derived from it, decreases with the maturity of the civilization.

Not only will the problem of adaptability be overcome through the organic-adaptive structure, but the problem we started with, reciprocity, will be resolved. Bureaucracy, with its "surplus repression," was a monumental discovery for harnessing muscle power *via* guilt and instinctual renunciation. In today's world, it is a lifeless crutch that is no longer useful. For we now require structures of freedom to permit the expression of play and imagination and to exploit the new pleasure of work.

A NEW CORPORATE DESIGN

Jay W. Forrester

During the last fifteen years there have emerged several important new areas of thinking about the corporation, its purpose, and its management. When brought together, these ideas suggest a new kind of organization that promises major improvements in the way the corporation can serve the needs of man. As yet, no such synthesis has been implemented.

In technology we expect bold experiments that test ideas, obtain new knowledge, and lead to major advances. But in matters of social organization we usually propose only timid modifications of conventional practice and balk at daring experiment and innovation. Why? Surely it is not that present organizations have proven so faultless. Nor can it be a matter of risk, for we spend far more and drastically affect the lives of more people with scientific and product experiments, many of which fail, than would be necessary in experiments with new concepts of corporate design. Perhaps we are victims of a preoccupation with scientific experiment. Perhaps knowledge is so compartmentalized that no one person sees at the same time the evidence of need, the possibility of improvement, and the route of advance. Perhaps we are reluctant to permit changes in the framework of our own existence. But it is time to apply to business organizations the same willingness to innovate that has set the pace of scientific advance.

Basis for a New Organization

Innovation can only be based on new ideas. These are now available. Four areas of thought, developed in the last two decades, form the foundations for the new type of organization that is here proposed. These four areas cover quite different aspects of the corporation, but together they offer a mutually enhancing basis for a new type of enterprise:

1) New thinking in the social sciences indicates that moving away from authoritarian control in an organization can greatly increase motivation, innovation, and individual human growth and satisfaction.[1]

2) Critical examination of trends in the structure and government of corporations suggests that the present superior-subordinate basis of control in the corporation should give way to a more constitutional and democratic form.[2]

3) Recent research into the nature of social systems has led to the methods of "industrial dynamics" as a way to design the broad policy structure of an organization to enhance growth and stability.[3]

4) Modern electronic communication and computers make possible new concepts in corporate organization to increase flexibility, efficiency, and individual freedom of action.[4]

When these four lines of thinking are synthesized into a new, internally consistent structure, we find that they point to a very different kind of organization from that common in business today.

Characteristics of the New Organization

The proposed organization can perhaps best be conveyed by discussing eleven of its most conspicuous characteristics.

Elimination of the Superior-Subordinate Relationship

The influence of organizational form on individual behavior is central to the proposed corporate structure. A substantial body of thought, derived from several centuries of politics, national government, economics, and psychology, exposes the stultifying effect of the authoritarian organization on initiative and innovation and suggests that, whatever the merits of authoritarian control in an earlier day, such control is becoming less and less appropriate as our industrial society evolves.

From industrial history, the social sciences, and the observation of contemporary organizations, there emerges a relationship between the methods used for organizational control and the effectiveness and growth of individuals within the organization. The authoritarian and bureaucratic control structure molds individual personality so that the environment is seen as capricious, and lacking in orderly structure and in cause-and-effect relationships. Consequently the individual feels little hope of changing that environment and is not open to information and observations that would lead to improvement. (See the reference by Hagen.)

If the authoritarian hierarchy with its superior-subordinate pairing is to be removed, it must be replaced by another form of discipline and control. This substitute can be individual self-discipline arising from the self-interest created by a competitive market mechanism.

To depart from the authoritarian hierarchy as the central organizational structure, one must replace the superior-subordinate pair as the fundamental building block of the organization. In the new organization, an individual would not be assigned to a superior. Instead, he would negotiate, as a free individual, a continually changing structure of relationships with those with whom he exchanges goods and services. He would accept specific obligations as agreements of limited duration. As these are discharged, he would establish a new pattern of relationships as he finds more satisfying and rewarding situations.

The guiding policy structure and accounting procedures of the system must be so adjusted that the self-interest of the individual and the objectives of the total organization can be made to coincide.

Education within the organization must then prepare each individual to use his opportunities in that self-interest.

The nonauthoritarian structure implies internal competition for resource allocation. Prices of individual skills, capital, and facilities would rise to the highest level that could be profitably recovered by the various managers who sell to the outside economy. An internal price that is higher than an external price for the same resource would reflect a more efficient and effective internal use of that resource than is possible in the external economy. Such internal competitive allocation of resources would contrast to allocation by central authority as is now practiced by industrial corporations.

Individual Profit Centers

If resources are allocated not by the edict of higher authority but according to the value of the resource to the individual members of the organization, there must be a basis on which each member can estimate that value. In our economy outside the corporation, price is established in the long run by competitive conditions at a level that allows a profit to both buyer and seller. To achieve a counterpart within the new organization, each man or small team (partnership) should be a profit center and a decision point responsible for the success of those activities in which the center chooses to engage.

Much has been written about profit centers in the corporation. In the larger corporations, profit responsibility is often decentralized to divisional profit centers. Yet, even in the most extensive present use of the profit center concept, only a tiny percentage of the individuals in the organization are personally involved in a profit center frame of reference to guide their own decisions and actions.

The profit center concept is very different from the budget center concept which is so common in financial planning and control. In a budget center the individual governs himself relative to a negotiated expenditure rate. The objective within the budget center is often to negotiate the highest expenditure rate possible (because salary and status are associated with number of employees and size of budget) and then to spend the full budget. Indeed, there are often pressures to overspend because next year's budget is related to this year's expenditures. The budget measures performance in terms of cost compared to promised cost and not in terms of cost compared to accomplishment.

The budget system of control sets up two conflicting chains. On one side are the functional activities responsible for accomplishing the work of the corporation—research, engineering, production, and sales. In each of these functional areas are pressures to accomplish as much as possible, to hire as many people as possible, and to spend as much money as possible. Since these tendencies toward excess can not go unchecked, there must be an opposing group, such as the controller's office, to impress financial restraint on the first group. The resulting conflict between pressures toward excesses and restraint of those pressures can only be resolved at higher authoritarian levels in the corporation. Once a control system is established that is not based on self-restraint, the authoritarian structure becomes necessary to resolve conflict. Efficiency, motivation, and morale decline rapidly as the command channels become choked, and as the decision-making point becomes so remote from operations that first-hand knowledge is inadequate for sound decisions.

In contrast to a budget center, a profit center values activity and resources in terms of the difference (profit) between input costs and a sale price that is acceptable to others in a competitive market. The incentive is to maximize the difference between cost and value, to produce the most value for the least cost, and to reduce expenditure of time and resources where this can be done without a more than corresponding reduction in the value of the product. To be effective, rewards at the profit center, both financial and psychological rewards, must depend on profit and not on expenditure rate.

The way in which the profit accounting is done and the manner in which rewards depend on profit become of the utmost importance when these are the measures of success. The possible rules for this accounting cover a broad range. It is here that the self-interest of the individual is determined. It is in the profit center accounting rules that the individual meets the policy structure of the organization. It is here that individual self-interest and the objectives of the organization must coincide if a unity of purpose is to be sustained. It is here that the proper balance must be struck between long and short term objectives. It is here that the intended pressures must be created for adequate planning, for quality, for integrity, and for stability and growth of the organization as a whole.

The profit center provides the incentive to start new activity but, perhaps even more important, it must create pressures to discontinue old activities. Stopping an activity at the right time is one of the most important management functions. Too often, termination is delayed because it must be forced on an operational group having personal incentives to continue. In this conflict, termination can be imposed only when the external evidence for stopping the activity becomes overwhelming. Since emphasis should focus on the total life cycle of an undertaking—successful beginning, successful mid-life management, and successful termination or transfer—profit center accounting for determining personal compensation should usually occur at the closing of an account and be measured against a compounded return-on-investment basis that extends over the total life of the activity.

The detailed accounting procedures are beyond the scope of this paper. Initially the accounting rules can only be tentative because they will almost certainly need to be changed after observation of the pressures they create in the organization. Unintended pressures or inadequacy of

unintended pressures must be corrected at their source by changing the accounting methods, not by building a body of compensating rules that would have to be implemented by a superimposed authoritarian control structure.

In the profit center structure there will be similarities to the various legal entities in the outside economy. Some persons will offer personal services as advisors and consultants, others as contractors taking engineering and manufacturing commitments at a bid price, some as promoters and entrepreneurs to coordinate internal resources to meet the needs of the market, and still others in the role of informed investors to allocate the financial resources of the organization where the promise is greatest. Several procedures of the outside economy, such as the cost-reimbursement contract, which reduce the incentive for efficiency and tend to reimpose the budget method of control, would be prohibited.

Objective Determination of Compensation

If each profit center is designed to provide a sufficient measure of performance and if the centers correspond to individual people or small groups of people, then salary and bonus compensation can be determined automatically from the accounts of the center. Each man identified with the center would have a status similar to that of an owner-manager.

Above-average performance, as shown in the profit center accounts, would lead to bonus payments, perhaps distributed into the future to give greater personal income continuity. If high performance persists, repetitive bonus payments would be the signal, according to a formula, for base salary increases to transfer more of the man's compensation to a stable income basis.

An "objective" determination of salary here means one that is not the subjective setting of one man's income by the judgment (often interpreted as whim or caprice) of a superior. Instead, income results from the value set on the man's contribution by peers who negotiate for his service. For this peer evaluation to produce more effective internal alignments, there must be enough internal mobility so that the man can find the more satisfying situations. He must have unhampered freedom to test the value of his contribution in a variety of competing outlets. The objective measure of value rests on the freedom to move away from any situation which he believes to result in an unfair evaluation of his worth.

Policymaking Separated from Decisionmaking

Policies and decisions are conceptually very distinct from one another although they are intermingled and confused in much of the management literature.

Policies are those rules that guide decisions. The policy treats the general case and at least partially defines how specific decisions under that policy are to be made. Conversely, a decision takes the status and information of the system and processes it in accordance with the guiding policy to determine current action.

In their effect on human initiative and innovation, four measures of policy are important—freedom, accessibility, source, and consistency:

By the first measure, policies can differ in freedom, that is, the extent to which they determine the encompassed decisions. A fully defining policy completely determines the decision as soon as the values of the input variables are available; that is, when the existing conditions that are recognized by the policy have been measured, the rules of the policy are explicit and complete and the decision can be routinely computed. Such a policy leaves no freedom of action and can be automatized in a computer as are the policies for ordinary accounting procedures. On the other hand, a policy can establish a boundary within which the decisions must be made but with freedom remaining to adjust the decisions to personal preference or to information that was not foreseen by the policy.

By the second measure, policies can differ in accessibility, that is, the extent to which they are known to the decisionmaker. That decisionmaker is in a difficult and frustrating position who must act without being able to discover the policies which are to govern his actions. This inaccessibility of the guiding policies may arise for any number of reasons—the policies may exist but be undetectable, they may exist and be known but be subject to capricious change; or they may be nonexistent until a decision has been made which then may precipitate a contrary and retroactive policy.

By the third measure, policies can differ in source. Personal satisfaction with policies probably varies along the axis marked at one end by self-determined policies that govern one's own and others' decisions to, at the opposite extreme, policies imposed by another who establishes those policies unilaterally for his own benefit. In a democracy, the source of policy is intermediate between these extremes, being established by compromise between the citizens in a search for the greatest average satisfaction.

By the fourth measure, policies can differ in consistency, that is, freedom from internal contradiction. Often one finds policy structures in which the parts are so fragmented and unrelated that the separate policies operate at cross purposes. Examples are seen in emphasis on evergreater sales even with hesitance and conservatism in expanding productive capacity, in stress on quality and customer satisfaction even while overloading the organization till it can perform only poorly, and in the unresolved conflict between pressures for short-term success and long-term strength. Contradictory policy is apt to arise where policy is an interpretation of decisions rather than vice versa. When decisions are made on the basis of local expediencies and policy is formulated to fit, the policy structure becomes an assembly of unrelated pieces. If policy is to be internally self-supporting and consistent, it must reflect a systems awareness. Each part of the policy structure must be appropriate not only to its local objective but must interact with other policies in a manner consistent with the overall objectives of the total system. In the complex feedback system structure of an economic enterprise, consistent policy can hardly be created in bits and by happenstance.

As measured along these four dimensions—freedom, accessibility, source, and consistency—policy often operates in a manner that is unfavorable to individual effectiveness. Policy is most suppressive of innovation when it completely defines action and states exactly what is to be done. Policy is most frustrating to initiative when it is undeterminable and subject to future definition and retroactive application. Policy is most antagonizing when it is imposed on a subordinate for the benefit of the superior. Policy is most confusing when it is internally inconsistent and provides no guide for resolving conflicting pressure. These undesirable extremes are closely approached in some corporations.

By contrast, the more successful corporations are characterized by policies that give coordination without confinement, clarity of forbidden action, objectives that balance the interests of all, and consistency that reduces unresolved conflict. Yet it would appear that only the rare corporation goes far enough in even one of these four measures of desirable policy, and none go far enough in all.

Policy should allow freedom to innovate and should have the fewest restrictions compatible with the coordination needed to insure overall system strength, stability, and growth. Policy should be accessible, clear, and not retroactive. The source of policy should be a process that ensures some consensus by those affected that it is a just compromise for the common good. Policies should be consistent by being designed as parts of a total policy structure that creates the desired dynamic behavior in the resulting system. Recent advances in the theory of dynamic systems and in system simulation using digital computers demonstrate that it will

be possible to design internally consistent policy structures directly, rather than inferring corporate policy from the implications of past decisions.

Creating such a policy structure, and maintaining it as conditions change and new insights are acquired, would be a full-time task for a small number of the most capable men in a corporation. The past and present of the corporate system must be studied as a background for designing policy changes which will create pressures and incentives toward an improving future.

Policymaking ought to be separated from the distractions of operational decisionmaking; otherwise, short-term pressures will usurp time from policy creation, which can always be postponed to the future. Policymaking ought to be separated from decisionmaking to give a more objective and impartial outlook to policy design. Policymaking ought to be separated from decisionmaking so that the source of the policy is specific and responsibility for policy is clear.

Restructuring Through Electronic Data Processing

Vast amounts of electronic communication and computing equipment have already been installed for business data processing. Yet, the equipment is used almost entirely for tasks of the type that were previously done manually. Emphasis has been on doing more data processing within the earlier patterns, or on reducing the cost of work already being done.

The inadequacy of today's data processing objectives is exposed by industrial dynamics studies of corporate systems that show how behavior depends heavily on classes of information channels and decisions that are not today being supported by the electronic equipment. In these more important channels, information flow is haphazard, information is late, information is biased by human filtering, and error is frequent. Computers provide the incentive to explore the fundamental relationship between information and corporate success.

Part of the policy design task is to identify the relative importance of the various decision points and to determine the quality and fidelity needed in each information input. When this is done, information channels will be emphasized which are very different from those presently receiving attention.

Information networks can take several forms. The networks of most organizations are in the form of a complex mesh with many information repositories and large numbers of interconnecting channels. Another kind of network, made possible by the digital computer, takes the form of an information storage and computing hub with radiating spokes to each source or destination.

In the mesh network type of information system that is now common, the task of information storage and processing is subdivided to many small centers. Information is handled in batches, and files lag behind the status of the real-life system that they represent. Also, much of the information must be processed in series through several centers, and there are large "inventories" of in-process information scattered throughout the system. Information retrieved from the system to guide decisions does not reflect past actions that are still being recorded and processed. This is often true even in the simple accounting and sales information that is now being handled by electronic computers. It is universally true and seriously detrimental in those informal information channels and decisions at the higher management levels. The mesh network becomes impossibly complex as the number of centers increases, particularly if each center is allowed to interact with every other center. A partial simplification has been achieved in practice by restricting communication channels to the inverted tree pattern of the formal organization chart. When this is done, lateral communication becomes slow and circuitous.

In the mesh network, substantial time and energy are consumed by internal communication that is made necessary by the dispersed storage of information. As a result, the organization becomes preoccupied with itself. It becomes inward looking with vast numbers of internal channels, the maintenance of which draws attention away from the contacts between the organization and the outside world. The organization consequently makes too little use of new technical knowledge; it loses contact with new market trends; and it is insufficiently aware of customer attitudes. These communication difficulties can be alleviated through a complete restructuring of the information system.

Modern electronic equipment permits a rearrangement of the information system into a radial or star shape with all files at the center. "On line" use of computers for both data processing and internal communication can provide an information picture that is up to date and fully processed at all times. Partially processed inventories of information can be substantially reduced, along with a reduction of the internal communication needed to estimate conditions that are not yet reflected in the formal data.

With such a restructured system, information will be directly accessible to persons that now must operate with too little information either to permit good management or to establish a feeling of security and confidence. If the internal information can be reduced, energy can be turned to the even more challenging quest for external information—information about new technical developments, new management methods, new employees, customer satisfaction, product performance in the field, and changing markets.

Freedom of Access to Information

Much of the character and atmosphere of an organization can be deduced from the way it internally extends and withholds information. Corporations are almost all built on the authoritarian hierarchy structure but corporations differ greatly as to the basis on which authority and status are maintained within the hierarchy. In healthy organizations, authority tends to rest on generally recognized ability, ability which is great enough that it need not be excessively bolstered by information monopolies. In an authoritarian position that is not based on recognized ability, security may simply derive from the structure of the bureaucracy and the prerogatives of the office, or position may be maintained by withholding information from both superiors and subordinates.

To possess information is to possess power. A monopoly of information can give a form of security. There are [sic], in all organizations at all levels, a selective withholding and extending of information. Sole possession of information can make others dependent on oneself. Withholding of information can limit the scope and power of others' actions and reduce the threat to oneself. Control of information channels can isolate certain persons from the remainder of the organization and keep them within one's own sphere of influence.

Most persons in most organizations feel that they do not have access to all the information they need. Sometimes they lack the information specifically needed to accomplish their duties. Very often they lack the information needed to create a sense of security and a belief in the fairness and rationality of the system of which they are a part.

Information is often withheld to forestall questions about an authoritarian decision that has no rational defense. The availability of salary information illustrates the point. Wages of workers in a union situation may be generally known because the contract rules have been made explicit; information about individual compensation is made available to show that the rules are being followed. Conversely, there are rules to justify the wage so that a subjective decision need not be defended. At the top of the hierarchy, executive salaries are published to stockholders along with information to implicitly or explicitly justify those salaries. In public service, salaries are set by law and are public knowledge. It is in the middle level of the corporation that one finds the greatest secrecy in salary details; this middle level is where salary determination is most subjective and where a guiding policy is least available. One can generalize to the observation that the more obscure the reasons for a decision, the greater are the inclinations to hide both the decision and the information on which it was based.

An organization can be seriously handicapped by the loss of energy consumed in the struggle for information. Time is occupied by attempts to obtain and to hide information. Psychological energy is drained by the nagging belief that others are withholding information that one needs, and by concern lest others learn information that one hopes to withhold.

Just as the individual hoards information, so does the organization as a whole. Competitive position is often believed to rest on secrecy to a far greater extent than is the fact. Information is withheld from individuals inside the organization on the excuse that this keeps information from outsiders. Secrecy is a poor foundation for success compared with competence, and to maintain secrecy reduces competence.

Although one will never succeed in making all information fully available, the goal can be pursued. Access can be given to the information that is recorded in the formal data system of the corporation. Incentives, both the incentive of convenience and the incentives designed into the accounting system, can encourage the entry of information into the central data files, from which it can be electronically retrieved. Design studies of the corporate data system will show the importance of converting many of today's informal information channels to ones in which regular observations are measured and recorded.

A general principle of the new organization should be to give much wider and more ready access to information than is now the usual practice. This can be accomplished by reducing restrictions in information availability, by designing the social and incentive structure to favor the release of information, and to gather and record information in important channels that often remain on an informal basis.

Elimination of Internal Monopolies

On the national level, monopolies are forbidden because of their stultifying influence on economic efficiency. Yet within corporations monopolies are often created in the name of presumed efficiency and are defended as avoiding duplication of effort.

For most activities the economies of scale are not as great as commonly supposed. In many situations where economy is expected from a larger activity it is easy to see that lower efficiency is, in fact, resulting. Very often the problems of planning and coordination rise so rapidly that they defeat the economies from larger size. This is particularly true of many of the service activities such as shops, drafting rooms, and purchasing offices.

Even where the activity itself may become more efficient in terms of local measures, the efficiency of the total organization may suffer. For example, in the consolidation of model shops, higher shop efficiency may result from a greater load factor on machines and machinists. However, the consolidated shop, now administratively separated from the technical activities, is less responsive to need, required negotiation of user priorities, and may well cost substantially in the valuable technical and management time of senior people on whom the success of the organization depends.

It should be a principle of the proposed organization that every type of activity and service must exist in multiple. No person is limited to a single source for his needs. No person is dependent on a single user of his output.

Only by eliminating the monopolies of the normal corporate structure can one have the efficiencies and incentives of a competitive system and provide objective and comparative measures of performance.

Balancing Reward and Risk

The new organization should retain and combine the advantages of earlier organizational forms while minimizing their disadvantages. One wishes to combine the stability and strength of the large, diversified business organization with the challenge and opportunity that the small company offers to its founder-managers. At the same time one must avoid the stifling bureaucracy and compartmentalization that is frequent in large organizations wherein the central power holds the right to allocate resources and make decisions. For the larger companies, competition exists on the outside but has no direct and often little indirect personal influence on those inside, except at the top levels of management. Conversely, the extreme risk and threat of failure in the small organization must be minimized since this repels many who might become effective independent managers.

In today's "small-business" world, the risk to the budding entrepreneur is greater than it need be. In general he gets but one chance. There is no opportunity to practice and to improve ability if the first undertaking is not a success. Penalty for failure should be reduced to a tolerable level but not eliminated. This can be done by risk sharing, not unlike the concept of insurance against catastrophe. The penalties should be just high enough to identify and dissuade the manager who repeatedly fails. Rewards should attract and encourage the competent and be high enough so that a normal quota of success will more than carry the burden of occasional failures.

Offsetting part of the successes to cover the cost of the failures is now done by risk investors in the financial community but under circumstances unfavorable to the individual who seeks financial help. The investor is interested in a quick return on his investment. He has neither the skill nor the opportunity to substantially increase the ability of the new manager, or even to judge that ability in advance. The investor in new ventures is forced into a sorting process of trying prospective managers, staying with the successes, and dropping the failures as soon as they are so identified. Such a process must be contrasted with a more ideal one in which the individual grows from initially managing his own time, to managing small projects, to becoming an entrepreneur who matches customer needs to the abilities of the organization. This evolution without discontinuity from individual worker to entrepreneur can stop or be redirected at any point. At each stage a history of performance is available to the man and to his potential supporters as a basis for deciding the next stage of his growth.

It follows that specific undertakings must be small enough so that the total organization can survive any individual failure. A favorable overall ratio of success to failure must rest on the greater efficiency instilled in the organization, the greater competence created by the internal educational system, and the personal growth induced by the freedom, competitive challenge, and greater opportunities for the individual.

Mobility of the Individual

In the new organization, in contrast to the conventional corporation, the individual should have much greater freedom of internal movement and greater ease of voluntary exit, but more restraint on entry.

The nonauthoritarian structure with its internal competitive characteristics lays the basis for internal mobility so that work relationships can continually change toward those that are more satisfying. This potential mobility must be made real by an educational system that prepares the man for new opportunities and by an accounting system that creates pressures to prevent reversion to the superior-subordinate relationship. The latter is one of the many pressures that must be created by the design of the data-processing system. For example, mobility should be enhanced by limiting, in the profit-center accounting, the credit allowed for income from any one source that exceeds a specified fraction of the year's activity. This would create pressures on each individual to maintain several activity contacts, making it easier for him to gradually shift toward the ones that are more desirable.

Most corporations have reward structures designed to discourage men from leaving. Pension funds and stock options have rules that penalize the manager who leaves before retirement age. The worker is under similar pressures generated by pension rights and union seniority.

The negative consequences of this immobility are serious to the health of the organization just as immobility can retard a country's economic growth. Dissatisfied persons, who therefore lack dedication to their work, stay in the organization rather than finding a position elsewhere to which they are better suited. The suppressed turnover rate in personnel makes it easy for management to ignore undesirable internal conditions which might be quickly corrected if they were emphasized by a higher personnel departure rate. Furthermore, we can assume that people who are unwillingly present are less likely to grow to greater competence and responsibility. Finally, the restrictions on leaving fail in their primary purpose by having little effect on the most competent men whose self-confidence and security lie in outstanding ability.

The new organization should hold people because they want to be a part of its kind of society. Any rights or deferred compensation that have been earned by past performance should be readily transportable if the man decides to leave. In fact, one might go further and visualize a placement office to assist any member of the organization in looking for a more attractive outside opportunity. If he finds one, the organization should reexamine itself to see if it is failing to offer the superior environment that is one of its principal objectives. If the man does not find the outside more attractive, he may become even more dedicated to the organization of which he is a part.

Mobility from the outside into the new organization is a different matter. Life in the organization would be very unlike most people's prior experience. The organization would be suitable for only a small fraction of them. It may well be that, if he has adequate information on which to base his decision, a man can judge his own compatibility with the organization more accurately than those within can judge for him. The mutual decision by the applicant and the organization should be based on a deeper acquaintanceship than precedes employment in most companies. This might be achieved through a series of study and discussion seminars that would expose the applicant, and perhaps his wife also, to the philosophy, history, psychological basis, objectives, and people of the organization.

The growth and stability of the total organization would depend on the mix of human resources and their rate of entry. The overall policies must provide guidance and incentives for bringing in the proper skills. For this reason also, the inward mobility cannot be as free as interior or outward mobility.

Enhanced Rights of the Individual

Thoughtful writers on the evolution of the corporation have raised challenging questions about the sources and legitimacy of corporate power and its effect on those involved. By law, power rests with the stockholders; but in practice, stockholders have little control over either the acts or the selection of management. Considering the emerging concepts of social justice, there is serious doubt about the moral right of stockholders, acting through management, to the arbitrary power which can now be exercised over individual employees, particularly those in the middle-management and technical groups. The precedents set in the last several hundred years by changes in the form of national government suggest that corporate power will also evolve from the authoritarian toward the constitutional. With this evolution, the primary objectives of the corporation would change from the already diluted idea of existence primarily for profit to the stockholders and toward the concept of a society primarily devoted to the interests of its participants.

The present-day protection of the employee against the exercise of arbitrary power by the corporation is weak and unevenly distributed. Production workers, by joining together in unions, have won a few fundamental individual rights regarding seniority, grievance procedures, and rights of arbitration. But, as one moves up the corporate hierarchy, the subordinate has progressively less security against arbitrary decisions by the superior. It is in the technical and management levels, where initiative and innovation are so important, that we find most unrestrained that suppressor of initiative and innovation—capricious, arbitrary authority.

The new organization should develop around a "constitution" that establishes the rights of the individual and the limitation of the power of the organization over him. Corporate policy would be subject to corporate constitutional provisions just as the national constitution has supremacy over laws made by national legislative bodies. To complete the system, there must be means for "judicial review" by impartial tribunals to arbitrate disagreements and to interpret into illustrative precedent the operational meaning of the constitution and policies of the organization.

Education Within the Corporation

A modern national democracy rests on an extensive body of tradition and a high level of public education without which the democratic processes fail. This failure has been manifest in the turmoil during the formation of new nations. Without a foundation of education and tradition, premature democratic governments quickly revert to authoritarian regimes. By contrast, democracy in Western Europe and the United States now rests on a massive base of education and on deep traditions regarding the rights and responsibilities of the individual.

A corresponding foundation must support the new type of "industrial democracy" that is here being proposed. Such a base of education and tradition lies as far beyond the background possessed by today's average manager and engineer as the United States public background of democracy lies beyond that in the underdeveloped nations. The cycle of change can begin with education that guides practice which matures into different organizational traditions.

The more effective education of the future must permit man's transition to a new, higher level of abstraction in the economic process. The last such change in level of abstraction was man's entry during the last two centuries into our present industrial society. In the days of the craftsman, the most skilled in the population made the consumer products; but, in the more abstract atmosphere of industrialization, the most skilled have become the inventors and designers who create machines that, in turn, make the consumer products. The skilled designers now operate once removed from direct production.

At the same time, the structure for decision making changed radically to one in which the decisions are now more abstract because they are removed from the point of actual production. The need for coordinating many efforts caused a subdivision and specialization of decisionmaking, similar to the specialization that is so evident in actual manufacturing steps. Where the craftsman had hardly been aware of the distinction between deciding and doing, the industrial society separates the decision from the action. Decisionmaking is separated from the worker because the governing policy is implicit and subjective. It has not yet been clearly stated. Coordination has been possible only by centralizing decisionmaking in one individual so that consistency

might then come from all decisions being tempered by the same subjective policies. But for this coordination we pay a high price in personal values and in flexibility to innovate and to respond to changing circumstances. The separation of work from decisionmaking, with the authoritarian system that it implies, has been at the root of the growing dissatisfaction with the present trend in corporate government.

In leaving our present stage of economic evolution and moving to a future "automation society," we must pass through another transition in man's relationship to production. In this still more abstract society, we must pass through another transition in man's relationship to production. In this still more abstract society, the most skilled, on whom the production processes depend, will be those who create the machines which in turn make production machines which, again in turn, produce goods. The most skilled will then be twice removed from actual production. This new complexity of industrialization has already begun.

The conceptual changes in management which must accompany our progress into the automation society are as sweeping as the change to centralized decisionmaking that came with industrialization. In the new phase there must be another restructuring of the decisionmaking process.

Our understanding of the industrial system is now reaching a point where the policy necessary to guide coordinated decisions can be made explicit and the policy structure itself can be objectively studied and designed. As this explicit treatment of policy is achieved, policymaking and decisionmaking can be completely separated. Policymaking can then be executed by a central group; and decisionmaking, within the framework of the common policy, can be returned to the individual person.

In such a new industrial organization, education must serve two purposes that are not essential in an authoritarian corporate government. First, understanding of the growth and stability dynamics that interrelate psychology, economic activity, and markets must be adequate to permit design of a governing policy structure. Second, the citizens of the new corporate society must understand the origin, meaning, and purposes of the policy structure well enough to successfully conduct their affairs in a manner that combines individual freedom with group coordination.

In preparing men for our present industrialized society, we already devote a third of each lifetime to education. One might ask how a still higher level of education is to be achieved. There are several answers.

First, as we climb to the next level of conceptual abstraction, much of the earlier educational process condenses into a new, rational framework. Specifically, as we come to understand the fundamental structure and dynamics of social systems, we can learn explicitly and directly the general concepts which earlier had to be taught indirectly by historical incident or learned slowly from personal experience. Most present-day teaching in the humanities and in management is by the "case method" of retracing specific situations, leaving to the student the task of extracting some general principles from the apparently conflicting descriptions. Now, as it becomes possible to work directly with the pertinent system structures in the context of system theory and laboratory simulation, it becomes clearer how certain fundamental characteristics of social systems can produce the divese modes of behavior that are observed. An understanding of social systems can be acquired much more rapidly if learning can be based on an explicit system rationale than if this rationale is only dimly and intuitively perceived.

Second, time for education can be obtained in the work environment if the confusions and distractions in present practice can be reduced by a clearer structure and a more efficient coordinating process. Estimates indicate that many of today's organizations consume 25 percent or more of their potential effectiveness

trying to coordinate internal activity. Much of this coordination is necessary simply because the organization is overloaded and trying to produce beyond its true capability. As the organization tries to do more in the short run, the costs rise rapidly in terms of confusion, coordinating and planning personnel, resolving priorities, and pacifying dissatisfied customers. The toll is especially high at the creative levels of management and engineering. Policies that ensure slight underloading could leave the same actual productive output and make the time now lost through attempted overloading available for a continuing educational program.

Third, time for education will be economically feasible if it results in greater long-term effectiveness. Greater revenue resulting from a higher degree of initiative and innovation can be allocated partly to the educational program. If the organization maintains its vitality and continues to change in keeping with the times, it should sustain a high enough level of contribution to society to justify a perpetual rebuilding of the educational base.

Fourth, education might be more effective if it could be properly coordinated with a man's development. This would require a true educational opportunity as a continuing part of the work environment. Then it would be possible to shorten a man's formal education at the college level and defer the study of many areas until work experience has indicated their importance and until learning motivation is higher. For example, engineers early see the importance of science but they may be well launched on their professional careers before they see reason to understand psychology, the dynamics of industrial systems, law, or even effective writing.

What, then, should be the place of education in the corporate strategy? The arguments are persuasive that some 25 percent of the total working time of all persons in the corporation should be devoted to preparation for their future roles. This means time devoted to competence some five years in the future and does not include the learning that may be a necessary part of the immediate task. Over a period of years this study would cover a wide range—individual and group psychology, writing, speaking, law, dynamics of industrial behavior, corporate policy design, advances in science and engineering, and historical development of political and corporate organizations—the extent and sequence being tailored to the individual person.

Such an educational program would differ substantially from any now offered. It must be derived from the same foundations and social trends as the new corporation itself. It must be at the same time more practical, but also more fundamental and enduring, than existing advanced training programs in either technology or management.

The educational program must become an integral part of corporate life, not a few weeks or months once in a lifetime at another institution. The overall policies of the organization must create incentives that protect the time for education from encroachment by short-term pressures. Because self-development is so easy to defer, the responsibility for personal growth should probably be shared by the individual and a "career advisor" whose own compensation depends on the growth and success of his protégés.

Analogy to National Economic Structure

The central feature of today's corporation is its authoritarian power structure, with the superior-subordinate pair relationship as the fundamental building block. Ultimate authority for all decisions lies at the top, and this authority is delegated or withheld by the superior at each level. So entrenched in our thinking is this authoritarian structure that few people can visualize an alternative, yet our largest economic unit stands as a striking and successful contradiction.

The growth and strength of the United States as a whole rests on an economic structure in which the superior-subordinate relationship is absent. Legal entities, be they corporations or individuals, are related to each other as equals. Corporations, doctors, lawyers, shop owners, independent contractors, and private businessmen interact with one another in a structure based on self-interest, not on the right of one to dictate to another. The United States' economic structure is not an exact pattern for the new organization. Yet the constitution and legal structure of the country offer many clues to answering the more difficult questions about the proposed organization.

The profit center concept of the proposed organization brings into the corporation the same free-enterprise profit motive that we believe is essential to the capitalist economy. The objective determination of compensation is the same process that determines the profitability of legal entities in the outside economy.

The stress on separation between policy-making and decisionmaking has its counterpart in the separation, on the one hand, between congressional and executive branches of the government and, on the other hand, between the policies set by law and the decisionmaking freedom left to the independent economic units. Laws, viewed as policy to govern economic activity, tend to be boundary policy stating what cannot be done and leaving all else to the discretion of business decisionmakers. The counterpart of laws would be corporate policy designed to achieve adequate coordination while permitting individual freedom.

Freedom of access to information within the corporation has its equivalent in the freedom of the press.

Antimonopoly legislation rests on reasons that should prevail far oftener when corporations decide whether or not to combine similar functions.

Education as a major function of government has an equivalent in the emphasis that the corporation should place on preparing its people for the future.

Implementation of These Proposals

It is not implied that these ideas for a new corporate design are yet developed to a point where they would fit all types of businesses. But they do seem particularly suited to those industries which feel the impact of rapid change in science and technology and in which conventional management approaches have often been found wanting.

An experiment in organization should presume slow growth at first under conditions permitting revision because it must be realized that an enterprise as different as the one here proposed must test and evolve its most fundamental concepts as well as their implementation.

It does not seem likely that such sweeping changes could be implemented by gradual change within an existing organization. The new proposals represent a consistent structure; but they contain many reversals of existing practice. Introducing the changes piecemeal would place them in conflicting and incompatible environments; the changes would be contrary to existing traditions and would give rise to counterpressures high enough to defeat them.

The only promising approach seems to be to build a new organization from the ground up in the new pattern. It might be either a truly new and independent organization or a detached and isolated subsidiary of an existing corporation. It must

feel its way, modify ideas where necessary, and create success at each stage as a foundation for further growth.

References and Notes

1. Everett E. Hagen, *On the Theory of Social Change* (Homewood, Ill.: Dorsey Press, Inc., Div. of Richard D. Irwin, Inc., 1962). David D. McClelland, *The Achieving Society* (New York: Van Nostrand Reinhold Company, Div. of Litton Educational Publishing, Inc., 1961). Douglas McGregor, *The Human Side of Enterprise* (New York: McGraw-Hill Book Company, 1960). Rensis Likert, *New Patterns of Management* (New York: McGraw-Hill Book Company, 1961). Mason Haire, *Psychology in Management* (New York: McGraw-Hill Book Company, 1964).
2. Richard Eells, *The Government of Corporations* (New York: Free Press, Div. of The Macmillan Company, 1962). Richard Eells and Clarence Walton, *Conceptual Foundations of Business* (Homewood, Ill.: Richard D. Irwin, Inc., 1961). Adolf A. Berle, Jr., *The Twentieth-Century Capitalist Revolution* (New York: Harcourt Brace Jovanovich, Inc., 1954).
3. Jay W. Forrester, *Industrial Dynamics* (Cambridge, Mass.: M.I.T. Press, 1961). Edward B. Roberts, *The Dynamics of Research and Development* (New York: Harper & Row, Publishers, 1964). David Packer, *Resource Acquisition in Corporate Growth* (Cambridge, Mass. M.I.T. Press, 1964). Ole C. Nord, *Growth of a New Product* (Cambridge, Mass.: M.I.T. Press, 1963).
4. The literature is notably weak in treating the philosophy of how electronic data processing can, in the long run, lead to restructured organizations and to environments more attractive to the individual. There has been a tendency to stress the negative short-run trends rather than to develop the positive aspects.

Part Two   New Dimensions for Tomorrow's Organizations

INTRODUCTION TO PART TWO

Our concern in Part Two is with certain developments and possibilities which we believe will prove especially significant to the "next generation" of organizations. At the present time, criteria which have traditionally been employed to evaluate organizational effectiveness are becoming less and less appropriate. To achieve organizations characterized by humanistic and adaptive systems, traditional criteria of effectiveness must be reevaluated and updated.

Traditional theory has been concerned with such concepts as task specialization, hierarchical authority and responsibility, individual task performance, coordination and control, system refinement, and matters of this nature. As was emphasized in Chapter 2, these considerations do serve significant purposes in production-oriented organizations; in some form and degree, they will continue to be pertinent to most large organizations. They are, however, of secondary importance—and are even a threat—to adaptive, changing organizations and to organizations concerned with nonproduction-oriented, nonroutine activities. In the postindustrial world, far more organizations will have to deal with ambiguity rather than certainty, unscheduled rather than scheduled events, problem solving rather than "solutions," and additional tests of their internal systems. Criteria designed to achieve rationality and predictability will establish techniques and objectives diametrically opposite to the organizational needs of tomorrow.

Increasingly, the next generation of organizations will achieve effectiveness through different means. These will include: a higher level of applied knowledge about human beings, including their ability to interact with others; skillful, flexible adaptation to the organizational environment; acquisition of change capability to meet demands imposed by an unstable and unpredictable environment; and achievement of skills necessary for the continual use of innovation and creativity in the functioning organization.

Many of the knowledges and skills implied by these criteria are new. They have not been digested, integrated, and made operational as significant elements of modern organization theory or practice. To prepare for the refinement of these new criteria in functioning organizations, we must pay more attention to the following questions. What operational knowledge do we have about the nature of man? How may the interpersonal capability of individuals be developed so they can interact with organizational members and management more effectively? Typically, how free is man to communicate with others, to be open with them, and to experiment with new ideas? How may an organization properly relate to its environment and adapt to it? Is it really necessary for modern organizations to change and to innovate? In Part Two we offer some possible answers to these questions.

Tomorrow's Man and Complex Human Values

The essays included in Chapter 3 imply that a study of emerging human values can help today's management develop a new organization which will accommodate "the human variety." Bugental and Otto argue the possibility of developing a new kind of man for tomorrow's society, while Schein looks at both the old values and the new in complex, modern organizations. The Scientific Management and Human Relations Schools of organization and management theory had a great influence on modern thought, especially in the professionalization of management. However, many probing questions have been raised. Those questions have been addressed to assumptions underlying those schools of thought—assumptions about the nature of man and the proper way to use man in organizations. The complexity of large organizations inevitably presents a dilemma, with control of functions on the one hand and management's acknowledgement of human aspirations on the other. This is true no matter how well-intentioned management may be. Katz and Kahn express this very well:

The characteristic properties of bureaucratic structures . . . are responsible for some of the major dilemmas of our society. In the first place, the maximization dynamic with its push toward organizational growth . . . made possible a richer material life and . . . created corporate bigness and the nightmare of totality. In the second place, the use of role systems as a rational device for handling all problems has given us certain efficiencies but at the expense of some impoverishment of personal relations and loss of self-identity.[1]

Previous management schools of thought had assumed that individuals are motivated by extrinsic rewards of an economic or social nature. Underlying these assumptions is the conviction that man adapts himself to his environment; little consideration is given to the existential, humanistic nature of man or to man's adaptation of reality to his own situation and self-concept. In mentioning the existential and humanistic nature of man, we are not very much concerned with the existential thought typified by Kierkegaard, Jaspers, Heidegger, Camus, and Sartre. Their total viewpoint is, at best, only marginally optimistic and, at worst, is nihilistic. Camus is obsessed with death, while Sartre gives no credence to the possibilities suggested by human peak experiences.[2]

New views of man introduced by contemporary humanistic and existential psychologists consider human nature as it *can be* rather than expressing the negative view of man that has been so widespread in the past. Maslow, Bugental, Jourard, Rogers, Frankl, Cantril, Otto, and many others have recognized the need for understanding healthy, achieving, self-fulfilling individuals. They emphasize the optimistic view of man as potentially creative and innovative. For example, Maslow's "self-actualizing man" is characterized as a person with a high level of acceptance of himself and others, a "superior perception of reality," openness, capacity to appreciate, and an ability to take a statesman's view of the world, to feel that he is a part of the human race, and to manifest independence. Were we to add another dimension of self-actualizing man, it would be creativeness, which is different from Maslow's concept of spontaneity. Not every individual possesses true creativity, but self-actualizing will release the individual's talents and uncover unsuspected abilities. We know many of our social and cultural institutions stifle creativity and innovation, but most organizations are not aware of what can be done to foster these qualities. Otto sees that man's creative capacities may well be infinite. He asks how we can learn to develop and utilize those capacities when "negative conditioning" limits our confidence and our approach to life.

Describing "future man" is a difficult task which many scholars refuse to attempt, partly because they are more interested in the historical experiences of human beings and partly because they believe that the future of man is solely a factor of the past. On the other hand, a few humanistic psychologists have begun to analyze future man, to *perceive* him, to *comprehend* his implications, and to *form* him through adjustments in current practices and assumptions. Both Bugental and Otto argue that we can, in fact, shape tomorrow's man—that the human being is changeable. Bugental maintains that man constantly has new experiences and that he regularly learns and changes. Man has inner experiences and is aware of them. Man also expands his goals and values. Otto provides great insight into the possibility for continuous development of human potentialities. He suggests that today's man is utilizing less than 5 percent of his capability!

The positive image of humanistic future enhances the possibility of man creating new environments for himself. When an individual can come to grips with his needs by changing his circum-

stances, he does so. When an individual in an organization cannot achieve such need satisfaction, he is inclined to search for alternatives to accomplish what he perceives to be "realistic" for himself and what he thinks others want. Man tends to discover the possibilities for meeting his goals within the limits of available freedom and choice.

The complexity of human motivations and values is considered by Schein, who sees man as a complex creature having many motives for economic, social, and self-actualizing experiences. In complex organizations, man seeks both extrinsic and intrinsic incentives. Economic-rational reward still has its appeal to many employees. On the other hand, new values such as self-actualization are also emerging. These changing elements of human need and value suggest that effective organizational development must include a set of values related to the complex nature of man. If organizations can be established so as to nurture the creative, self-actualizing, responsible individual, whose worth is easily seen in relation to our suggested criteria for organizational effectiveness, then there is hope that "tomorrow's man" can be accommodated. Shaping such a man in today's organization presents challenges to both the individual and to management. Contemporary organization includes the whole spectrum of complex and rich human experiences to which these new humanistic and existential thoughts may be applied in the managerial process. We must not only find ways to accommodate the individual who is different; we must encourage each individual to *be* different by being his own "epic self," in Bertolt Brecht's sense. For Brecht, *epic man* constantly extends his horizons, changes his way of life, and moves in innovative, self-renewing directions.[3] We must cherish this man and accept this diversity as necessary to meet the accelerating rate of change that tomorrow's organizations and society must face.

Interpersonal Competence and Changingness

Achievement of an integrated meaning for organizational and social reality implies development of a better understanding of the relationship among members of groups as well as openness between individuals and management. Many writers today are beginning to emphasize interpersonal competence in their works.

Among these, the work of Chris Argyris is especially significant, partly because of its quality and partly because of the long involvement Professor Argyris has had with interpersonal competence. According to Argyris, interpersonal competence is the ability to cope effectively with interpersonal relationships. He lists three criteria for such effective interpersonal coping:

1) The individual perceives the interpersonal situation accurately. He is able to identify the relevant variables plus their interrelationships.
2) The individual is able to solve problems in such a way that they remain solved. If, for example, interpersonal trust is low between A and B, they have not solved the problem competently unless and until it no longer recurs (assuming the problem is under control).
3) The solution is achieved in such a way that A and B are still able to work with each other at least as effectively as when they began to solve their problems.[4]

An important aspect of interpersonal competence is *changingness* of the person—the individual's capacity for change. It is a latent *capacity* in the individual and a latent *function* in organizations. Carl Rogers suggests that change capability is inhibited in many organizations by pessimistic attitudes among administrators toward many long-range policies. He illustrates this with administrative refusal to face up to the problems of urban ghettos, the reality of air and water pollution, transportation problems, and many additional matters in the social arena. Rogers offers two bases of hope for survival. First is the ability of Western democratic structures to respond appropriately—at the very last "cliff-hanging" moment—to those trends which actually challenge their survival. Second is the magnetic attraction of the *experience* of change, growth, and fulfillment. Even though growth may involve intense pain and suffering, once the individual or group has tasted this changingness, persons are drawn to it as to a magnet. Thus, Rogers argues that, in the future, high interpersonal competence will be the natural built-in motivation for organizational growth and change rather than dependence upon (and submissive acceptance of) change introduced by top management. Interpersonal competence appears to be a vital ingredient of human ability in the achievement of the "changing organization" (see Bennis in Chapter 2) or the "morphogenic model" of Walter Buckley (in Chapter 7).

The importance of interpersonal competence is also related to group development. The Gibb article presents the constructive use of sensitivity training that will develop personal and group growth. Through the improvement of trust among members, the group can develop integration of goals and consensual decisionmaking. Gibb and Gibb claim that individual members can have an authentic feeling of collaboration and interdependence through effective feedback.

In sum, interpersonal competence must be fostered in tomorrow's organizations in order to yield a better relationship among organizational members and between workers and management and in order to produce a relationship that develops trust, openness and authenticity, integration of goals, and in turn, self-control and collaboration. A new form of organization is necessary, of course, to nurture interpersonal competence and to encourage management to take on the responsibility of being sensitive and behaviorally flexible.

The Turbulent Environment and Organizational Adaptation

A profound change in the way organizations interact with their environments and adapt to their demands will become evident in the coming decades. The essays in Chapter 5 emphasize that coping with turbulent, often paradoxical environmental demands will increasingly be the secret of the survival and growth of the organization.

Emery and Trist classify four "ideal types" of environment according to the degree of "system connectedness" that exists among components of the environment. Components are incorporated in relation to the system's actual and potential transactional interdependencies (both input and output). The four ideal types are: (1) the placid, randomized environment; (2) the placid, clustered environment; (3) a disturbed-reactive environment, and (4) a turbulent field (turbulent environment). The fourth type, the turbulent environment, is new to us and very important in understanding the setting of modern (and future) organizations. The turbulent environment consists of "dynamic properties arising not simply from the interaction of identifiable component systems, but from the field itself (the ground). The turbulence results from the complexity and multiple character of the causal interconnections. Individual organizations, however large, cannot adapt successfully simply through their interactions." Emery and Trist point out that the changed texture of the environment was not recognized by traditional management theory. Organization adaptation to the turbulent environment appears likely to be the most significant factor in the effective-

ness of tomorrow's organizations. In simple environments, predetermined solutions and strategies guide human actions and involve little risk, but in the complex, turbulent environment the adoption of a determined action includes a high degree of risk because future events always present new, often unforeseen possibilities for solving problems. Thus, continuous monitoring of the turbulent environment will normally have the effect of continually modifying organizational goals and policies by implying the need for new methods or by requiring new ways of doing things to meet various challenges. This reveals both the promise and risk of the adaptive organization; but, in survival terms, the promise far outweighs the risk. In these terms, the promise *is* survival while the risk is simply disturbance.

Organizational transactions with their environments typically may encounter any of three fundamental problems: (1) the environmental transactions cannot be explained by economic-rational criteria; (2) transactions involve whole-system adaptation; and (3) transactions assume that a social responsibility exists. Any of these is sufficiently threatening to place the entire concept of adaptive environmental transactions in jeopardy in the minds of many managers. Yet, such interaction is increasingly important for the organization's survival.

The article by Lawrence and Lorsch illustrates how human elements affect the quality of an organization's transactions with its environment. Improving the internal processes involving individuals and groups can improve the effectiveness of transactions. Sir Geoffrey Vickers notes that organizational adaptation is a response of the system as a whole, a continuous process of transaction and adaptation which accompanies economic, social, and political relationships.[5] Involved are both the adjustments of organizational members to the need for change and management accommodation to the implications of change. In this vein, West Churchman says that the possibility of improving systems depends upon understanding the properties of the whole system; the problem of system improvement is a problem of the "ethics of the whole system."[6]

Acceptance of social responsibility by an organization is not simple; the maximization of profit or productivity as a major goal does not describe the actual, complex boundaries of organizational transactions. Modern, large organizations tend to be increasingly aware of their responsibility for the social–economic-political impact of their functions. In recent years, large private organizations in the United States have allocated substantial financial resources and manpower to meet their social responsibilities. Their activities include manpower training programs, free management services for urban ghetto industries, the solving of pollution problems, increased aid to education, and other similar efforts. These represent a significant beginning, of course; but, thus far, there has been too little awareness of the *social values* inherent in the kinds of internal organizational processes which are the subject of this book. When organizational leadership recognizes the social relevancy of those processes, a long step will have been taken toward a more humanistic society. The recent research report made by the Committee for Economic Development succinctly states that:

Today it is clear that the terms of the contract between society and business are, in fact, changing in substantial and important ways. Business is being asked to assume broader responsibilities to society than ever before and to serve a wider range of human values. Business enterprises, in effect, are being asked to contribute more to the quality of American life than just supplying quantities of goods and services.

Inasmuch as business exists to serve society, its future will depend on the quality of management's response to the changing expectations of the public.[7]

New responses to changing environments have always posed a problem for public organizations. Their reaction to the turbulent social environment around them has normally been *against* change or adaptation and *for* maintenance of the *status quo.* Promotion of the "public interest," a concern of typical public organizations, may often represent a reactionary measure as against pursuing proactive behavior in favor of social change. This point suggests that a more socially relevant concept of the public interest may be needed throughout the whole system of public organizations. This new concept would emphasize humanistic values inside the organization as well as among both the clientele and the larger society. Developing organizational policies with a public-interest focus would, in these terms, have to take structural, procedural and managerial matters into consideration along with overt program goals. The process of developing human potential would replace bureaucratic management systems; clientele would participate in program development and execution; persons who will be related to programs (regardless of whether those persons are inside or outside the system) would participate, as they chose, in personal development seminars, etc. Such a model of public interest offered by public organizations would have a profound effect on practices employed in all other organizations.

Lawrence and Lorsch write that with regard to a rapidly changing environment, "the organization must be capable of creative and flexible problem solving to discover potential opportunities for conducting more favorable transactions." We would like to interpret that statement as an implication of the necessity for transactions that are more socially relevant and more valuable. In time, our organizations will have the capability to monitor and react to their environments in such a fashion that, in a flexible and creative way, they will be discovering ways to transact which are more socially pertinent and valuable. We believe that we should be ready for whatever mysteries the different future holds! Obviously, such a new organizational style implies the reduction of structural and procedural obsolescence, the development modes for flexibility and adaptation, and the increased research and implementation of human capability. At the present time, these possibilities are more than dreams, but to achieve them will require the development of skills, commitments, and values different from those which characterize the organizational world at the present time.

Proactive Change Versus Reactive

The inevitability of change is something we are learning to accept—even to anticipate—in organizations. Yet, there is much to be done in most organizations to achieve a condition of continuous change, in other words, change of a *proactive* rather than *reactive* nature. The complex, tumultuous environments of modern organizations supply an unavoidable impetus for development of at least some degree of change capability, as does the diversity and pluralism of the democratic political system. Further, modern organizations, often characterized as "open systems," learn to accommodate more direct relationships with clients and a more diverse range of member interests. These add further pressure for flexibility and change. The more different the relevant points of view and the more groups with conflict of interest, the more change is necessary; the principle applies to both public and private organizations.

In addition to all of the qualities which would appear to make modern organizations ongoing "systems of change," there is a strong tendency in our organizations to establish and maintain systems and techniques for getting things done. These, in turn, reduce change capability. Any change may be seen as a threat to administrators who have learned to consider organizational procedures as fixed and predictable. Administrators in established organizations generally want the structure and procedures to remain as they are; they know how to "do their thing" in the system, how to manipulate the power structure, and how to assure that their own needs and the needs of their unit are being met. It is only natural that they would be oriented toward the status quo. What we need today, however, is more proactive change to adapt social values and to shape our environment for a better society.

Regardless of the need or desire for change, we must consider yet another question of possible significance in the future: How much change can the human being assimilate; and at what rate of change may acceptance be achieved? Are we actually prepared physically and emotionally for Bennis and Slater's "temporary society?" Can we stand continual ambiguity, paradox, and uncertainty? Can people and organizations legitimately be expected to keep up with the ever-increasing rate of technological and societal change? Certainly it is reasonable to wonder whether man has a limited capacity for absorbing change. We can only speculate at this time, since more evidence is needed, and we are only now beginning to enter this new "changing" era. An interesting possibility is suggested by some writers who claim that, at the present time, we are socialized to seek stability and are upset by instability and change; they argue that we might just as readily socialize people to *instability* so that they would be upset by matters which were too structured and unchanging. Obviously, we need more knowledge, but certainly this latter notion should be born in mind. The notion implies that the issue may be no more than a matter of perspective, which could support the concept that man can accommodate to a far higher level of instability and ambiguity than he has regularly known in the past.

The short essay by Blake and Mouton indicates that managing change requires the systematic design of change as well as careful selection of appropriate change models—models suitable for the needs of the client system. They imply that, when change is not systematically introduced, it may be detrimental—even catastrophic—to organizational effectiveness. In discussing several basic elements for developing the ideal change model, they remind us again that organizational change must take into consideration the forces of internal organization as well as the outside environment.

Developing Innovative Capacity

Modern, complex organizations in the United States have always been dependent upon new ideas for survival and growth and on breakthroughs in innovation, but never have they been more determined in their search for new ways of doing things than they are today. Both Thompson and Shepard in Chapter 6 argue that, in the future, organizational survival will depend almost totally on achieving an innovative capability.

What is innovation? What type of individuals and organizations display innovativeness? Are there structural and/or managerial differences between innovative and noninnovative organizations? What type of organizational climate is necessary for innovation to occur? Answers to these questions are crucial for tomorrow's organizations.

The distinction between innovation and creativity is confused by many stu-

dents and is, admittedly, elusive. For our purposes, creativity implies *bringing something new into being,* whereas innovation suggests *bringing something new into use.*[8] Innovation occurs when an organization adopts something new for the first time, though it may have been done elsewhere for years. Creativity has occurred when the organization develops a completely new idea, product, or way of doing things not necessarily related to what has gone before. Pressure for adaptation may develop innovation and/or creativity. For example, Japanese business and industry went through a period of adaptation by imitation of foreign models. Subsequently, the country focused more on innovation (adaptive change) than on imitation in new product development. At the present time, Japanese industry is revealing a high level of true creativity in many areas.

As previously noted, organizational change, innovation, and creativity must depend to a great extent upon individuals in the organization. Large private organizations increasingly realize that the era addressed solely to productivity and efficiency has passed. What we now face is an exciting new era emphasizing humanization and democratization, sponsorship of innovation and creativity, and more services for members and clients. This development is a clearly discernable trend at the present—a trend which evidence suggests will become far more general in the future. It is a development with great social significance since it is humanist. Yet, it promises an organizational model which will achieve continuing high levels of adaptation, innovation, creativity, and problem solving.

Innovation as well as creativity is unable to flourish in an unfavorable environment. After all, no man can conceive of innovative work in an environment which affords him no motivation, no incentives, and no freedom. Psychologists have pointed out that most novelists and poets in nineteenth-century France were either born in Paris or found the opportunity in Paris for creative expression. The favorable environment was necessary to stimulate and to bring to fruition their native powers. Another example can be made of a government employee who was working at $32,000 per year (1970) for an important agency in the federal government. He was described as an honest, sincere but naive man who was critical of the waste and cost overruns in government programs in his field. He suggested some innovative ideas to top policymakers and had some direct interactions with them. At the end, he lost his job. The *Los Angeles Times* stated the case in an editorial: "Tell the truth and lose your job. . . ." This example suggests that one man alone cannot expect to be innovative or otherwise buck the rigid government system.

The conclusion to be drawn from this discussion is that if society wants to harvest innovativeness and creativeness, it must prepare the fields and offer receptive and appreciative climates for the growth of the unique forms of talent and ability associated with these qualities. Unfortunately, not many organizations are prepared to do this as yet. While it is obvious that tomorrow's organizations will be the product of choices we are making today, few managers foresee "the different future" sufficiently well to take advantage of the opportunity offered by our increased understanding of innovation and creativity. Minority groups in this country, aided by increasing freedom, education, and opportunity, produced many excellent writers, musicians, educators, and scientists. The accomplishments of minority groups serve to illustrate the effect of increasing the receptivity of the environment on creativity and growth. As they have experienced a more open environment, new stimuli, and new opportunities, they have responded with an exciting contribution to the American culture. We are aware that this society has not

yet provided enough opportunity for all people, but we find this a gratifying illustration of the possibilities for large-scale increase in innovative and creative capability. We anticipate that the models for tomorrow's organizations which we consider in this book may represent another means for society-wide increases in innovativeness and creativity.

Thompson and Shepard argue that typical conditions within bureaucracy are determined by a drive for productivity and greater organizational control, the result of which is an unfavorable climate for creativity and innovation. The needs of traditional, industrial-era organizations created the bureaucratic organizational model, which is designed to minimize interpersonal relations, stifle innovation, and function on essentially mechanical principles. Suggestions made by Thompson for alterations in the bureaucratic model in order to increase innovativeness include: increased professionalization, formation of a looser structure, decentralization of authority, creation of freer communications, developing project organization, rotation of assignments, the use of group processes, continual restructuring, implementing a different incentive system, and a variety of changes in management practices.

The organizational context needs to have more "slack" introduced to facilitate development of innovative activities and to absorb the costs resulting from errors ascribed to innovation. The organizational climate is unfavorable for both innovation and creativity when an organization has little slack. This is perhaps as useful a concept as any to describe the limitations of traditional organization behavior. The history of organizational development is, in some ways, little more than a continuing "scientific" effort to get *all* the slack out of structures, procedures, and behaviors. Now that we know how to "run the system," we must selectively reintroduce a form of *lifespace* into our organizations or they will strangle on the tautness of the costs associated with highly structured conditions. When organizations depend upon changingness for survival, innovation and creativity become critical and central variables. These, in turn, are dependent upon organizational slack or looseness to create the climate for their growth and opportunities. As Shepard notes in his article, "Innovation-Resisting and Innovation-Producing Organizations," innovation-producing organizations must continuously learn, develop new ideas, and adapt to both internal and external changes.

Summary

We introduced Part Two with some questions. Our intervening discussion implies that the readings in the four chapters which follow offer many possible answers to those questions. The chapters suggest that tomorrow's organizations will indeed feature "new dimensions," including capability to formulate broader organizational goals and to cope with the various social problems which attend organizational phenomena at present.

We see in the writings of Part Two that we know a great deal about the nature of man which, as we make it operational, should render man-in-organization a more self-actualizing, whole person. This offers the release of more creative energy into group, organizational, and societal activities—a condition which promises realization of many possibilities now only in prospect.

One dimension of this increased human capability is in interaction and communication with others. Many possibilities have been developed and refined for improving man's abilities to relate to his fellow beings. In the new organizations, with their reduced em-

phasis on formalism, this quality will prove of increasing importance and value.

Finally, a major dimension in future organizations will be a realization of the need to relate intimately to the environment, to sense its needs and changes, and to have, within the organization, a highly developed capability for both change and innovation in order for the organization and the environment to exist in harmony. The survival of organizations in the future will be tied directly to this adaptive capability.

Clearly, many present ways of doing things are inappropriate and inadequate to meet future challenges. Today's organizations will require drastic change and revision if complex problems are to be satisfactorily solved. We have learned that no person can develop his potentialities or be truly innovative and creative if the organizational environments in which he participates do not provide favorable climates. When one attempts to design a new organization which will cope with changing environments, one must consider the new dimensions we have introduced in this section. Part Three will address the matter of how several theories can be applied toward the explication of a variety of organizational dimensions and how those dimensions are relevant to the process of changing.

References and Notes

1. Daniel Katz and Robert L. Kahn, *The Social Psychology of Organizations* (New York: John Wiley & Sons, Inc., 1966), p. 459.
2. Colin Wilson, *Introduction to the New Existentialism* (Boston: Houghton-Mifflin Company, 1967), pp. 14–18.
3. One can sense Brecht's epic man best in his play, *Galileo*.
4. Chris Argyris, "Conditions for Competence Acquisition and Therapy," *The Journal of Applied Behavioral Science* 4, no. 2 (1968): 147.
5. Sir Geoffrey Vickers, *Towards a Sociology of*

Management (New York: Basic Books, Inc., Publishers, 1967). pp. 167–84.

6. West Churchman, *Challenge to Reason (New York: McGraw-Hill Book Company, 1968), p. 4.*

7. *Committee for Economic Development, Social Responsibilities of Business Corporations* (New York: Committee for Economic Development, June 1971), p. 16.

8. Everett M. Rogers, *Diffusion of Innovation* (New York: Free Press, Div. of Macmillan Company, 1962). Cited in Lawrence B. Mohr, "Determinants of Innovation in Organizations," *American Political Science Review* 63 (1968): 112.

Chapter 3   Understanding Tomorrow's Man

CHANGES IN INNER HUMAN EXPERIENCE AND THE FUTURE

James F. T. Bugental

Commercial passenger rockets will be in service by 1980. The first manned space-craft will land on Venus in 1990. A major program will be initiated on the development and utilization of nonlethal weapons by 1972. Directed energy beams, both lethal and incapacitating types, will be in use by 1989. By 1979 cross-country super-highways will provide limited automatic control with the emphasis on vehicle separation. By 1973 mass-produced large injection-molded, fully functional modules will be introduced for low-cost home construction. Home facsimile systems of a newspaper type will be available by 1978, and low-cost three-dimension television communication service will be available to reduce the need for business travel by 1977. The first controlled thermonuclear fusion power plant will be demonstrated in 1984, while by 1980 the synthesis of life matter will signal the opening of an enormous new era in biology. Commercial undersea units such as factories and motels will be in operation by 1995.

These are some of the predictions that the scientists and technologists of TRW have recently made to the public at large. They give a fascinating glimpse of what may be in the offing, and what many of us may live to see and experience. They picture a world changed in physical, technological, and social ways.

But they don't tell us what the inner experience of man is going to be like. Taking a weekend trip to an undersea motel, riding in a passenger rocket—what is it going to be like? Is it going to be the same old thing inside, or is there going to

be a difference? As a humanistic and existential psychologist, I am asked to say, "Where is man going? And what is man going to be in the midst of this rapidly changing world?" But it's quite another matter, as you will see, when one comes to make prognostic statements about human experience than when one tries to say what the future will be like in terms of hardware and the *things* with which humans deal.

An important reason for this difference is that what we can think of as "the state of the art," is easily manifest in the realm of hardware. Here is what I mean: We can look at the present methods of building houses, stores, garages, factories, schools, and so forth and clearly see before us how far we have progressed in our technology. Moreover, we can look to other fields, such as the design or building of special structures—say, for undersea life—and we can borrow from them. We select procedures, devices, and other parts of their technology and apply them as we choose to building a home or an office building. The state of the art is in many ways objective and identifiable when we're talking about physical and technological matters. But what is the state of the art, what is the stage of progress regarding man's inner experience?

Here we have a very different kind of problem to deal with. It's not as readily manifest; indeed, by and large, most of us in our culture have been trained to keep our inner experiencing concealed, so that any general conception of what most people experience must always be subject to question. I don't think that a public opinion survey or a laboratory procedure in a psychology department really tells us in any depth what it feels like to . . . [have been] a human being in 1969. We can look to religion and philosophy and try to get their answers, but I suspect that most of us would be dubious about accepting those as definitive of the human experience in 1969. And thus when we come to try to predict the inner experiencing of a person in 1988 or 2000, we lack the most important basis of prediction: a clear picture of where we are today.

Now there is a second important basis often used for prediction: extrapolation of a trend line. We go back to the past and find out what happened, and then follow the trend from the past through the present toward the future, extrapolating in that fashion. If we study the history of air travel for instance, it is possible to make reasonable prognostications on the basis of what has happened in the past 50 years, joined to what we know of our present situation, and thus to make informed guesses about the future. But here again when we turn to man's inner experiences, we lack adequate sources of information: What is it that men have generally experienced over the past years? To be sure, biographies, novels, and fiction of various kinds have frequently given us some piercing insights, but these have been chiefly into the experience of individuals and often unusual individuals. While we can generalize from these with some hope of having general validity, it is still fairly tenuous for most of us, taken as a whole.

Let us begin by making a quick estimate of what at least one aspect of our inner experience is like today. Generally, I think, we have expected of ourselves that we should have clear intentions and purposes; that we will have arrived at these by logical, defensible reasoning; that we will have worked out plans for arriving at their realization; and that all we feel and do will be consistent with these intentions and purposes. In this same fashion we have imagined that our minds

are like computers that could be fed vast amounts of relatively abstract information throughout our childhood and youth (a period society regards as wasted anyway; we can't do any useful work during that time, so we might as well be accumulating facts). Then we have expected that later all of this information will be well arranged on file, so that we could pull it out when we have worked out our intents and purposes. Thus, when the time came to live our lives—probably a few years after completing our educations, choosing our lifework, selecting a spouse—in other words, after making the key decisions of life—we would have everything properly organized to live out the program that we and society have so carefully prepared. Now I am being sarcastic, but I believe that this model is one that still is implicit in much of our thinking. To the extent that we have found our own experience not fitting into this neat and orderly state of affairs, we have tended to feel deficient in some manner and often have attributed this deficiency to laziness, guilt, mental inadequacy, or the pressure of outside demands. Clearly within this kind of model or perspective, there is no place for conflicting feelings, misgivings about choices, or unhappiness with outcomes. You are supposed to do it right the first time.

This summary fairly well fits the underlying implicit unformulated expectation of many of the people that I see as a psychotherapist. And these are people, by and large, from the upper socioeconomic, educational levels. They are well educated; often they are very successful in their vocations, but they are people who feel something is missing or something is not working out right in their lives, that they are not really experiencing being fully alive. So they come for help, because this unexpressed model that I have caricatured is operating.

Now what I want to do next is to offer some speculations, some hunches about what is happening to that inner model, to our inner experiences, and how that picture I presented may be changing. I think that changes are occurring in a number of areas, and I am going to pick out four of them to "freewheel about a little bit."

These areas are, first, expectations regarding the inner life, the subjective life—simply what it means to be me, how I feel in experiencing me inside. Second, the values by which I try to guide my life: What is it I am trying to do? How is it I am trying to be? Third, the kind of expectations we have regarding relationships with other people—what it means to be in a relationship with other people. And finally, the kinds of things or goals I'm working toward. I put all this in the first person, because what I am trying to convey is the feeling of subjective experience—not "him," "it," "her," but one's own subjective experiences.

The Meaning of Inner Experience

I think we are increasingly recognizing that there is competition among goals and values inside of us and that this is the normal state of affairs. It's not something gone wrong; it's the way it is. So that we expect a measure of conflict, rather than that clear single-mindedness that I was describing earlier. We expect conflict between things we want within ourselves and conflict between ourselves and others. We're beginning to recognize that most of the really important issues of life are ambiguous, rather than clear-cut. They're not either-or, not just black or white; there are many shades and many hues. Thus choice is an ever-present part of being human. Choice is not something we do once and then it's taken care of, but choice is a continuous process that goes on at each moment of experience.

One important implication of this continuing nature of inner alternatives with their resulting competition and conflict is that choice becomes more available. A professor of mine (the late George A. Kelly) once enunciated what I think is kind of a jewellike summary of this: He said, "The key to man's destiny is his ability to reconstrue what he cannot deny." I think that this is a very pregnant

statement. It uses the fact of interpretation of experience as a tool to free things. Someone else once observed, "My greatest opportunities all came to me cleverly disguised as insoluble problems." This is the same message—The univocality, the singleness with which we have seen many of life's issues in the past is beginning to be revealed as not really so. There is a great deal of ambiguity if we really perceive what we are up against. The possibility of reconstruing or reinterpreting is ever-present.

Perhaps part of the same observation is the recognition that every time we make a choice for something, we are letting go of or relinquishing other things. It has been said that every choice is a relinquishment. There are more things we consign to oblivion than we positively select at any given point. All of it together spells out a kind of end to the getting-set-to-live model of life that I was describing earlier—that model that said we line things up and then we live out our plan. Rather, it says that living is a continual process.

This then leads to a second part of this inner expectation that I think is important: first, that there is competition and conflict among the things we want, and second, there is a continually evolving character to being a human being. Being a person is not something that we get set or that we construct, once and for all. Typical of the neurotic, for example, is his feeling that whatever he is experiencing at the moment is the way it is going to be from here on. If he's depressed, then he sees the world as irredeemably bleak from now on. If he's angry, he feels that hostility will govern things henceforth. Typical of the healthy person is the recognition that there is a constant changing, flowing quality to experience. To try to convey the flavor of this, suppose we wanted to take a picture of a tree, and we want to get *the* right picture of it. Now just when shall we take it? What season of the year, or what time of day? When would we get *the* right picture of the tree? Recognizing that there's some problem, we might set up a movie camera and floodlights and photograph it 24 hours a day and 365 days a year. And then we will have many thousands and millions of frames, each one with a picture of a tree. Which one is the right picture of the tree? Well, I think we can recognize that there is no *right* picture of the tree, because there is no tree out there. We might better say that there is a "treeing" going on out there. There is a process going on, and the process is the constant evolution and change.

And so, there is a "being" going on in each person; there is not something static and fixed that is one way. It is a constant, evolving, changing thing. This focus on process, on the evolution of experience is something that changes our expectancies for ourselves. Perhaps you have experienced, as have I, the recognition that in some ways I always felt that one of these days I ought to get matters all worked out—to know what I was going to do, to get enough information, then to get organized with things worked out. Then gradually the recognition dawns that that day is never going to come—that there is always a new upset to the beautiful plan, a new challenge, a new opportunity, a new setback, so that it is a constantly evolving, changing experience. This means that the high value, which, in our culture, we place on consistency probably is in for change. Yet we still place a great deal of importance on it. We say, "John is always so optimistic," so when John is kind of pessimistic, everybody protests, "But John, you're always looking on the good sides of things." We try to keep each other consistent. It makes life simpler, I guess. But recognizing that consistency is really kind of antilife, the ability to change, to be inconsistent, to be fluctuating, is a part of genuine growth and evolution.

And then a third part of the change in inner experience, I think, is a recognition of the primacy of our feelings, of our emotions. We have had such an overemphasis on the explicit, on the verbal, on the objective, on the cognitive—and such an underemphasis on feeling, on body ex-perience, on the more inner living. One reason for this probably is that one part of the whole range of human experience, the so-called nonhedonic emotions such as anger, pain, fear, grief, and disappointment, have all been taken as signals of something wrong, and often as shameful. Thus in many ways we have tended to suppress these emotions. All of these feelings—are actually very important parts of human experience and are terribly important as signals to tell us what is going on in the organism and what needs attention. And yet we so often tend to cover those signals; we try to get people to stop feeling badly [*sic*] by suppression, by shutting off the awareness. However, I think this is changing, too.

Changing Human Values

Second, I wanted to describe changes in the values by which we guide life. I have already indicated one: the greater primacy that I think is beginning to be given to subjective experiencing. This is sometimes called the "psychedelic ethic," but by so terming it, I am by no means limiting it to the use of consciousness-expanding substances. The "psychedelic ethic" is the one that points to the primacy of the internal experiencing—to fantasy, to emotion, to body experience—as a primary value in itself, not just as means to some other end. This isn't a "kicks" philosophy as I am talking about it, but it is a recognition that the inner world is ultimately where each person lives—in his subjective experiencing.

Perhaps another part of this change in values would be a distinction between "shoulds" and "oughts." So much of our experience is hemmed in by the "shoulds." "You should do this, you should feel that, you shouldn't do the other thing," and so on. And most of these "shoulds," at least as I'm using the term now, are imposed from the outside. While the "oughts," as I'm using the word here, are those things that are intrinsic: If you want to keep alive, you'd better eat;

you ought to eat. "Oughts" are inherent or intrinsic to what it is one wants or what one is experiencing or doing, as opposed to the "shoulds," which are imposed and may not be essential at all to what it is being experienced.

This is related to the concept of situational ethics, which a number of people are describing now, and offering as a moral code based on the recognition of response to situations rather than obedience to abstract rules or principles.

Probably a third part of the change in values is the recognition of the finitude or limitedness of such values as perfection. So much of our culture has been founded on an idea that we have to perfect ourselves, to make our lives without defect. I think we are beginning to see that perfection as a value is actually often destructive, that it leads to a loss of humanness in experience. It may lead to discouragement or resentment as one fails again and again to achieve the demanded perfection. So it is not a counsel of futility to say that we ought to relinquish the value of perfection, but it is a counsel of realism, which makes greater effort and follow-through possible.

Perhaps we ought to include here, too, the increased recognition of the importance of mystery, of recognizing how much lies beyond our ken, how much more is potential than we ever know or ever realize.

And finally, among the changes in values, I would point to a change regarding sensuality and sexuality. Eroticism has long been seen as a negative value, a punished aspect of our experience. Now it is, I think, beginning to be seen as a positive value. The taboo on the erotogenic, that which arouses sexual feeling, is at such contrast with the rewards that we give artists, writers, actors, and others who can arouse other feelings—for instance, fear, horror, and violence. There was a comic strip recently that showed some kids being sent out to go to the movies. When they arrived at the movies, there were two billboards—one showing a children's matinee, a violent film, "The Kill," or

something like that. For the evening performance was "The Kiss," but that was labelled "For Adults Only." Obviously children should be protected from that.

I think the Danish experience with pornography is highly instructive in this regard. Recently Denmark dropped all legal restrictions against pornography, and the booksellers prepared for the rush by stacking their shelves with great quantities of pornographic material. However, now they are remaindering those items; no one wants pornography since it has become perfectly legal. It is only interesting when it is forbidden. It becomes relatively dull or only mildly interesting when it is no longer on the forbidden list. Indeed, one could argue that pornography probably has a real social value and protects us from acts of sexual violence; that it is clinically quite defensible.

Related here to the change in values about sensuality and sexuality are the facts that bodies and nudity may be seen as positive goods, rather than the traditional concepts of them as being dirty. For instance, I have a conviction that a usual Doris Day–Rock Hudson movie is much more obscene than something like "A Man and a Woman" or many more of these much more explicitly sexual, but to my mind, moral films. In the average Doris Day–Rock Hudson film, all values are made subservient to the technical virginity of the heroine, with a complete callousness toward the values of relationships, compassion, and friendship.

Responsibility in Human Relationships

Third, I wanted to describe changes in relationship. I think one of the things that is beginning to emerge is a recognition that 200 percent responsibility exists in every relationship. That is, each partner to a relationship, a friendship, a love affair, a marriage, or whatever, is totally responsible for what happens in the relationship. Now this seems to defy mathematics, but let me show you what I mean. There are always two partners to a relationship, and both partners to the relationship contribute to what happens. One doesn't "do it" to the other one; the "done to" one is in some way always cooperating, consciously or unconsciously. This recognition really changes the way you approach a relationship. It can transform it from kind of a bargaining, blaming, and accusation and defense kind of situation to one of genuine mutuality, because then there is the possibility of genuine meeting between people. One doesn't get "up" on the other by scoring points of blame, but there is a mutual working to see how the relationship may be made more fruitful. This is part of the point I made earlier—the fact that conflict can be expected in a relationship; any healthy relationship will have conflict in it. The poet says, "The only thing I have to give to you, my beloved, is my difference from you." In a way this is deeply true. The combination of difference with agreement is what makes a viable relationship. Only as that difference is made a positive source of nourishment for the relationship, can it grow and evolve. This leads, I think, toward a greater potential for genuine caring in the relationship. Caring is not the same as "taking care of," which is a kind of infantalizing, trying to control the other person's feelings, by what is said or done, rather than being genuine. In this regard, I think we are beginning to see that human pain is not something sacred, something terrible, but may be a very important part of life. People are not as fragile as we think they are. In encounter groups, encounter often exposes people to pain, but this can be a constructive and growth-evoking experience. The pain of relinquishing false images of oneself, of confronting and dealing with false bases of relationship can actually be purging and freeing. Someone has said, "Care for man may be the ultimate form of the worship of God."

Goals and Human Values

It seems to me that in the past we have all assumed that we knew what reality was. It is only in more recent days that we can let ourselves see that our grasp on reality is a very tenuous one. We do not know what is real in a relationship or in our own experience or in what we are doing in the world. There are many ways in which we practice deceptions. Expediency may often be seen as life-destroying, so that I see a freshened value to that which is genuine, which sheds pretension and seeks the authentic. This may come about through much more attention to here-and-now living rather than to deferred living, much more attention to immediacy of experience—not without regard for the future or respect for the past—but with more concern for the immediacy of experience as the point where things happen and where differences can occur. Perhaps a way of illustrating this is to notice how we value "play," seen as experience that is valued for itself, more than "work," which is seen as experience having value only for some other end, the payoff of which must follow after the work. Now, in this fashion, of course, the meaning of play is intrinsic, in the same fashion as a dedicated scientist plays in his laboratory or a novelist plays in his writing, if he is genuinely involved in it. The immediate experiencing is the thing, not the image that he builds, not the end-product in terms of some extrinsic performance. In the same way, we are beginning to see more of the importance of relationship as one of the goods, as one of the deeper values of being alive. Genuinely "knowing" another person, as opposed to "knowing about" another person, is a constructive, life-evoking experience.

Finally, we can say that all of this boils down to a kind of decline in what one can only think of as sort of a sacrilege—our attempts to constantly redesign human beings, to make them other than they really are. If we in the Christian tradition really believe we are made in the image and likeness of God, then when we keep trying to redesign people and say, "You shouldn't feel this, and you shouldn't have that impulse," we are really committing a great sacrilege: We are trying to redesign man and God too, and saying we can do a better job. Certainly we have committed this sacrilege, if such it be, in regard to sensuality and sexuality, anger and conflict.

My account so far is that of an objective observer of the human scene, but I suspect you will have also observed that my objectivity is tissue paper thin. I am really quite a biased pleader for change in the human experience. I would not pretend otherwise. I am deeply invested in this matter of being human, trying to experience my own life fully, and I work with people who are genuinely concerned about theirs, who spend hundreds of hours and thousands of dollars in the effort to become more human and to experience their own lives more deeply. For the most part my concern is expressed in trying to find my own way toward greater authenticity and in trying to help them to do so. However, I am also finding an increasing feeling of wanting to go further than just the work of the individual consultation hour.

In the physical sciences the great leaps forward have been made as new energy sources have been tapped. When we changed from muscle power to steam power, the entire scientific-technological enterprise took a great leap forward; then when we changed from steam to electric, another one; and from electric to atomic power, yet another. But we have not had anything similar to this progress in the human sciences. I think there is a tremendous power source in human concern and relationship, but that we are primitives, savages in the jungle when it comes to knowing how to handle that power source. Just as primitives of another day handled lightning or water power by inventing superstitions and rituals to try to deal with them, I think we have done the same thing with the power of human concern and relationship. We have primitive superstitions for most of what we do with this power. Maybe a new Einstein will come along who can really crack through the facade of superstition and teach us how to turn to account that great potential power of concern and relationship. In other words, what I want to do now is to call your attention to this source of human power, which I think is terribly impaired at the present time, but which may be crucially important when we find ways of releasing and channeling it. This we must do if we are ever going to close the gap between the physical sciences and the human sciences in time to save the human race.

Let me first give you a bit of background so you will understand what it is I am going to relate. Several years ago I was asked by the University of Alberta in Canada to conduct a 10-day human relations workshop. It was the kind of project called an "encounter group" or "sensitivity training," which seeks to help individuals explore their inner experiencing and their experiencing of each other, so as to make available to them a greater sense of awareness and greater degree of choice in how they experience their lives. During one evening meeting of that workshop, I had an experience that moved me very deeply. And afterward in my room I began writing in an effort to capture what that experience meant to me. I wrote:

I bought a new sweater yesterday afternoon. It was a nice sweater, and I paid more for it than I've ever paid for a sweater before. It will be a nice souvenir of a pleasant experience in Canada one May. I can afford to spend more for a sweater nowadays and to take time for pleasant visits to places as interesting as this. The practice of my profession goes well; my reputation is growing. I published a book earlier this year, and as the result of the attention to it, I now have a wider range of clientele from which to choose those I'll see. In short, after many years of struggle, the rewards of a kind of ruthlessness within myself and with my family are coming more abundantly. Now life is very good, and I am so very fortunate. Yet tonight it was all threatened to its very foundation, and I am really frightened.

My life was threatened tonight, and I mean no melodrama by phrasing it that way. I was threatened by two things that happened in our group meeting. The first thing that happened was that Lois (disguised name) discovered a fuller range of her own being. Let me tell you about that. Lois is a social worker for a large metropolitan social agency. Day after day she sees people who are in need of various kinds. She is efficient and has progressed well in her three years with the agency. Last night in our group we engaged in an exercise which consisted of shutting our eyes and extending our hands and moving about the room until we came in contact with people who were similarly groping about. And then, still without words or sounds, we would touch each other and try to make contact and communicate in some fashion. When the experience was over and we sat down to talk about it, Lois burst into tears. She said that she had suddenly realized that it didn't matter with whom she came into contact—that all the people were people, that these people were like people she saw in her work, and that they were people, too. Each person was a person in his own right. She sobbed as she told us, "I didn't know. I didn't know. The clients are people, too—each one of them."

Now at first reading this account may sound like an almost ridiculous or meaningless discovery. But see if you can let yourself think more deeply about it, then perhaps you can realize the profundity of Lois' awakening. She had discovered that within each person was a life, was an awareness going on.

Within each person was a seeking very like the seeking in the procedure I've just described—blindly groping to try to make contact, to try to be with someone, to try to find one's way. Like a person who's been blind since childhood suddenly gaining sight and seeing the world revealed in all its dimensions and color and movement, so Lois had discovered the humanity of each person whom she touched, each person who came to her in her professional work. The meaning of this became clearer as she talked on. "There's so much I could do," she said, "so much

that I could do, and so little that I do. If I could only really make a commitment to it, if I could only be there with those people."

The group was silent after Lois sobbed out her discovery, and we all watched her, each making his own inner interpretations. Then gradually some of the group began to talk. An older man said that he admired what Lois was saying and that he remembered himself having had such a feeling. A middle-aged woman said that Lois must not feel so badly, that there were so many people that needed help, and one could only do so much. A third argued that we all had to face this gap between what we saw could be done and what we were able to do. Still others spoke, and generally the tone of the comments was that this was a fine and wonderful discovery that Lois had made, one that most of us had already confronted, and that she would feel better after awhile. A number of people were particularly concerned to soothe her and to help her stop crying.

And that was the second thing that threatened my life tonight, for I became furious with the group. They insisted on reassuring Lois and soothing her, told her she'd soon forget the pain of her discovery, and I was angry at the group for trying to rob Lois of her grief and her guilt, of her struggle, of her newfound dignity as a person. For in discovering that other people were each human, each a person, Lois was discovering her own humanity, her own deeper roots. And I knew that I was angry with the group because they said to Lois the things that I've said to myself so often when I've opened my eyes, when I've really looked, when I've really touched. Lois spoke for one part of my awareness and the group for another part. And I feared Lois, and I was angry at the group. And I felt terribly alone.

Now let me be clear about what I am saying. First, I am saying that I am aware of so much more that could be done to make all of our lives more real, more humane. Second, I recognize that I do some things—even many things—about this recognition. Third, I know that I do but a small portion of what I might really do if I dared fully to commit myself. Fourth, I have many ways of hiding from my limited commitment, of reassuring myself that I am really doing all that needs to be expected. And fifth, I am guilty for compromising with my own potential and am less fully alive because of that self-deception. Now let me write about these in more detail:

First, I am aware of so much that I could be doing. I think of Granada, Mississippi, or Selma, Alabama, or we could add now the Arkansas State Prison. I think of the public institutions in any community, the jails, the hospitals, the orphanages, the crying need for committed, dedicated service. I think of children needing a home, children who could grow, given a chance in their lives, but children who will literally never have that chance. I think of people in genuine need of money, a friend, or devoted attention. I think about the hitchhiker. I think about being in a bus station about 2 o'clock one morning. There was a sick or drunk sailor whom everybody was sort of shunning, and I shunned him, too. I think about the whole obscene business of war in any form. I think about bad government or police brutality or the police falsely accused of brutality and trying to do a difficult job.

Of course, I do some things. I contribute to ACLU and NAACP and to all the right, proper causes. I debate with myself over which ones and how much. I try to take some comfort from the total of the money contributions, knowing all the time that it is a way of trying to buy off the guilt. I try to vote regularly and to inform myself about the issues and candidates, and I know how little I really know. In my practice I have a sliding scale for my fees, so that some people who might not otherwise be able to afford help can receive it, and I try to extend this to the so-called gatekeepers—you know, the teachers, ministers, and social workers who can importantly affect what's happening in the community. I work in programs as a consultant for social or community agencies that pay much less than if I used the same time for some of the industrial clients who could pay much more. I do all these things, but they are so very little, so comfortable, so convenient; and they do not really intrude on my life. And then I remind myself again of some of the needs of the jails, of the orphanages, of the loneliness. There are so many ways of soothing, of quieting and tranquilizing these feelings. Our culture is full of them. I tell myself I am doing all that could be reasonably expected; I tell myself that if I spread myself too thin, it wouldn't do anybody any good. I tell myself that others are certainly doing less, but that that's just the way the world is. Nobody can change it all overnight. Or, there are people who really do not want to be helped. Or I accuse myself of feeling I'm messianically able to change the world. And all the time I know I'm trying to quiet the voice of that guilt.

So what is it—what is it that full responsible awareness asks of me? Nothing less than to give up what I've spent 50 years building. Jesus said you must lose your life in order to gain it; I have always admitted that and admired that sentiment and kept it safely 2,000 years away. Now I'm not coming down with the religious shakes, so you can't dismiss me that way. I am just rediscovering that that man knew what he was talking about. The Buddha said the same thing, and many other great teachers as well. And Jesus said it is easier for a rich man to pass through the eye of a needle than to enter the kingdom of heaven. And I'm too rich, and we're all too rich—not rich in Rockefeller terms, but rich in a new sweater, a pleasant way of life, a stable world, at least for awhile. And so we look out of our window as a young woman is attacked and killed, and we don't want to get involved. And so we let our government buy guns and flamethrowers, and we do not want to get involved. It's warm and safe in our apartments, and it's cold and dangerous out there. And if we go out we may never, really never, find our way back. That's no metaphor, for if we do get *involved, really involved, we may sell our homes for the money we need for something more important. We may lose our community's respect; we may be attacked, denounced, hurt, or even killed. We may indeed be literally killed. The Reverend Mr. Reeb was; Mrs. Liuzzo was.*

So why should I or anybody else who's in his right mind even think about going out into the streets where the killers lurk? Why should I even consider the idea of jeopardizing, let alone giving up, what I've worked for through the prime years of my life? And the answer is so simple and so awful. I cannot be aware and not be concerned. I cannot be concerned and not take action. If I am to be fully alive, I must accept my awareness fully, my concern fully. From time to time I see this with awful clarity. And it's a searing vision.

So where does it all lead? Well, I will gradually lull myself into less intense confrontation of being aware and being concerned and being responsible. I will accept the reassurances that I give myself or that others so readily provide me, and I will enjoy my new sweater. But I find the time between these recognitions grows shorter, and the clarity increases. Once I kept them to myself, and then I began to hint about them to a few who were close to me. That was a big step, because it made the awareness more real, more immediate. Today I am telling you, and I am frightened of what lies ahead, and I am excited by what lies ahead.

This is what I wrote on that summer night and the next morning 2 years ago. I added another page later that morning.

Today I can see how my guilt and my not doing more of what I can do led me to split away from myself and from the group. Yet I can see too that the anger I felt was a purgative to free myself and my system of the accumulated self-deceptions. For there is much to be angry about in the world, and we are too seldom angry about the right things. We waste our anger on picayune trifles, while great injustice sweeps by unchallenged. We are guilty, and we need our guilt. We are angry, and we need our anger. For me the task is to wait for the maturing of that anger and guilt; only then can I express it as a whole person, to keep awareness open and avoid the easy self-deceptions that lull us so readily to sleep. With truly open awareness I can grow in my readiness to live out the responsibility. I have heard it said that the control of our emotions is what distinguishes man from the lesser animals. I do not think this is so. Rather it is how we accept and turn our emotions to account, that distinguishes us. When we do this with real concern, real love, then we are more ourselves, more true humans.

For some of us there comes a time of awakening to what it means to be alive and to be in the world. When this happens, the sense of potential, the sense of possibility, the sense of what we might do, is overwhelming—and very often quite frightening. If we've shared this experience with others, we often find that they try to reassure us, try to get us to see things less starkly, less demandingly. During a marathon group I conducted, one of the men in the group came to this kind of awful clarity of recognition. Once again the group moved in to reassure him, to quiet him. Probably the most telling blow that is struck in such times is the confrontation when someone says, "Who do you think you are, Jesus Christ?" The implication is that one must have delusions of grandeur to have such thoughts. But these aren't grand perceptions, when one really experiences them; they're awful, and maybe I need to use that word two ways—"awful" and "awe-filled."

I think my main concern would be to say, "Maybe you'd better think you're Jesus Christ." Maybe somebody had better quit dismissing the sense of urgency, the sense of demand about being human. I am calling, it seems to me, on myself and others to recognize that the most fateful challenges are not always the most self-conscious initially and certainly not the most gratifying or promising. If each of us says, "I am no Messiah; I cannot do very much; the problem is too big for one man," if all of us keep saying that, then there may not be a year 2000. Then the hardware merchants may win out. We need more people willing to stand up and shout,"No!"

NEW LIGHT ON THE HUMAN POTENTIAL

Herbert A. Otto

William James once estimated that the healthy human being is functioning at less than 10 percent of his capacity. It took more than half a century before this idea found acceptance among a small proportion of behavioral scientists. In 1954, the highly respected and widely known psychologist Gardner Murphy published his pioneering volume *Human Potentialities.* The early sixties saw the beginnings of the human potentialities research project at the University of Utah and the organization of Esalen Institute in California, the first of a series of "growth centers" that were later to be referred to as the Human Potentialities Movement.

Today, many well-known scientists such as Abraham Maslow, Margaret Mead, Gardner Murphy, O. Spurgeon English, and Carl Rogers subscribe to the hypothesis that man is using a very small fraction of his capacities. Margaret Mead quotes a 6 percent figure, and my own estimate is 5 percent or less. Commitment to the hypothesis is not restricted to the United States. Scientists in the U.S.S.R. and other countries are also at work. Surprisingly, the so-called human potentialities hypothesis is still largely unknown.

What are the dimensions of the human potential? The knowledge we do have about man is minimal and has not as yet been brought together with the human potentialities hypothesis as an organizing force and synthesizing element. Of course, we know more about man today than we did fifty years ago, but this is like the very small part of the iceberg we see above the water. Man essentially remains a mystery. From the depths of this mystery there are numerous indicators of the human potential.

Certain indicators of man's potential are revealed to us in childhood. They become "lost" or submerged as we succumb to the imprinting of the cultural mold in the "growing up" process. Do you remember when you were a child and it rained after a dry spell and there was a very particular, intensive earthy smell in the air? Do you remember how people smelled when they hugged you? Do you recall the brilliant colors of leaves, flowers, grass, and even brick surfaces and lighted signs that you experienced as a child? Furthermore, do you recall that when father and mother stepped into the room you *knew* how they felt about themselves, about life, and about you—at that moment.

Today we know that man's sense of smell, one of the most powerful and primitive senses, is highly developed. In the average man this capacity has been suppressed except for very occasional use. Some scientists claim that man's sense of smell is almost as keen as a hunting dog's. Some connoisseurs of wines, for example, can tell by the bouquet not only the type of grape and locality where they were grown but even the vintage year and vineyard. Perfume mixers can often detect fantastically minute amounts in mixed essences; finally there are considerable data on odor discrimination from the laboratory. It is also clear that, since the air has become an overcrowded garbage dump for industrial wastes and the internal combustion engine, it is easier to turn off our sense of smell than to keep it functioning. The capacity to experience the environment more fully through our olfactory organs remains a potential.

It is possible to regain these capacities through training. In a similar manner, sensory and other capacities, including visual, kinesthetic, and tactile abilities, have become stunted and dulled. We perceive less clearly, and as a result we feel less— we use our dulled senses to close ourselves off from both our physical and interpersonal environments. Today we also dull our perceptions of how other people feel and we consistently shut off awareness of our own feelings. For many who put their senses to sleep it is a sleep that lasts unto death. Again, through sensory and other training, the doors of perception can be cleansed (to use Blake's words) and our capacities reawakened. Anthropological research abounds with reports of primitive tribes that have developed exceptional sensory and perceptive abilities as a result of training. Utilization of these capacities by modern man for life-enrichment purposes awaits the future.

Neurological research has shed new light on man's potential. Work at the UCLA Brain Research Institute points to enormous abilities latent in everyone by suggesting an incredible hypothesis: The ultimate creative capacity of the human brain may be, for all practical purposes, infinite. To use the computer analogy, man is a vast storehouse of data, but we have not learned how to program ourselves to utilize these data for problem-solving purposes. Recall of experiential data is extremely spotty and selective for most adults. My own research has convinced me that the recall of experiences can be vastly improved by use of certain simple training techniques, provided sufficient motivation is present.

Under emergency conditions, man is capable of prodigious feats of physical strength. For example, a middle-aged California woman with various ailments lifted a car just enough to let her son roll out from under it after it had collapsed on him. According to newspaper reports the car weighed in excess of 2,000 pounds. There are numerous similar accounts indicating that every person has vast physical reserve capacities that can be tapped. Similarly, the extraordinary feats of athletes and acrobats—involving the conscious and specialized development of certain parts of the human organism as a result of consistent application and a high degree of motivation—point to the fantastic plasticity and capabilities of the human being.

Until World War II, the field of hypnosis was not regarded as respectable by many scientists and was associated with stage performances and charlatanism. Since that time, hypnosis has attained a measure of scientific respectability. Medical and therapeutic applications of hypnosis include the use of this technique in surgery and anesthesiology (hypnoanesthesia for major and minor surgery), gynecology (infertility, frigidity, menopausal conditions), pediatrics (enuresis, tics, asthma in children, etc.), and in dentistry. Scores of texts on medical and dental hypnosis are available. Dr. William S. Kroger, one of the specialists in the field and author of the well-known text *Clinical and Experimental Hypnosis,* writes that hypnotherapy is "directed to the patient's needs and is a methodology to tap the 'forgotten assets' of the *hidden potentials* of behavior and response that so often lead to new learnings and understanding." [My italics.] As far as we know now, the possibilities opened by hypnosis for the potential functioning of the human organism are not brought about by the hypnotist. Changes are induced by the subject, utilizing his belief structure, with the hypnotist operating as an "enabler," making it possible for the subject to tap some of his unrealized potential.

The whole area of parapsychology that deals with extrasensory perception (ESP), "mental telepathy," and other paranormal phenomena, and that owes much of its development to the work of Dr. J. B. Rhine and others is still regarded by much of the scientific establishment with the same measure of suspicion accorded hypnosis in the pre-World War II days. It is of interest that a number of laboratories in the U.S.S.R. are devoted to the study of telepathy as a physical phenomenon, with research conducted under the heading "cerebral radiocommunication" and "bioelectronics." The work is supported by the Soviet government. The reluctance to accept findings from this field of research is perhaps best summarized by an observation of Carl C. Jung's in 1958: "[Some] people deny the findings of parapsychology outright, either for philosophical reasons or from intellectual laziness. This can hardly be considered a scientifically responsible attitude, even though it is a popular way out of quite extraordinary intellectual difficulty."

Although the intensive study of creativity had its beginnings in fairly recent times, much of value has been discovered about man's creative potential. There is evidence that every person has creative abilities that can be developed. A considerable number of studies indicate that much in our educational system— including conformity pressures exerted by teachers, emphasis on memory development, and rote learning, plus the overcrowding of classrooms—militates against the development of creative capacities. Research has established that children between the ages of two and three can learn to read, tape record a story, and type it as it is played back. Hundreds of children between the ages of four and six have been taught by the Japanese pedagogue Suzuki to play violin concertos. Japanese research with infants and small children also suggests the value of early "maximum input" (music, color, verbal, tactile stimuli) in the personality development of infants. My own observations tend to confirm this. We have consistently underestimated the child's capacity to learn and his ability to realize his potential while *enjoying* both the play elements and the discipline involved in this process.

In contrast to the Japanese work, much recent Russian research appears to be concentrated in the area of mentation, with special emphasis on extending and enlarging man's mental processes and his capacity for learning. As early as 1964 the following appeared in *Soviet Life Today,* a U.S.S.R. English language magazine:

The latest findings in anthropology, psychology, logic, and physiology show that the potential of the human mind is very great indeed. "As soon as modern science gave us some understanding of the structure and work of the human brain, we were struck with its enormous reserve capacity," writes Yefremov (Ivan Yefremov, eminent Soviet scholar and writer). "Man, under average conditions of work and life, uses only a small part of his thinking equipment. . . . If we were able to force our brain to work at only half its capacity, we could, without any difficulty whatever, learn forty languages, memorize the large Soviet Encyclopedia from cover to cover, and complete the required courses of dozens of colleges."

The statement is hardly an exaggeration. It is the generally accepted theoretical view of man's mental potentialities.

How can we tap this gigantic potential? It is a big and very complex problem with many ramifications.

Another signpost of man's potential is what I have come to call the "Grandma Moses effect." This artist's experience indicates that artistic talents can be discovered and brought to full flowering in the latter part of the life cycle. In every retirement community there can be found similar examples of residents who did not use latent artistic abilities or other talents until after retirement. In many instances the presence of a talent is suspected or known but allowed to remain fallow for the best part of a lifetime.

Reasons why well-functioning mature adults do not use specific abilities are complex. Studies conducted at the University of Utah as part of the Human Potentialities Research Project revealed that unconscious blocks are often present. In a number of instances a person with definite evidence that he has a specific talent (let's say he won a state-wide contest in sculpture while in high school) may not wish to realize this talent at a later time because he fears this would introduce a change in life-style. Sometimes fear of the passion of creation is another roadblock in self-actualization. On the basis of work at Utah it became clear that persons who live close to their capacity, who continue to activate their potential, have a pronounced sense of well-being and considerable energy and see themselves as leading purposeful and creative lives.

Most people are unaware of their strengths and potentialities. If a person with some college background is handed a form and asked to write out his personality strengths, he will list, on an average, five or six strengths. Asked to do the same thing for his weaknesses, the list will be two to three times as long. There are a number of reasons for this low self-assessment. Many participants in my classes and marathon group weekends have pointed out that "listing your strengths feels like bragging about yourself. It's something that just isn't done." Paradoxically, in a group people feel more comfortable about sharing problem areas and hang-ups than they do about personality resources and latent abilities. This is traceable to the fact that we are members of a pathology-oriented culture. Psychological and psychiatric jargon dealing with emotional dysfunction and mental illness has become the parlance of the man in the street. In addition, from early childhood in our educational system we learn largely by our mistakes—by having them pointed out to us repeatedly. All this results in early "negative conditioning" and influences our attitude and perception of ourselves and other people. An attitudinal climate has become established which is continually fed and reinforced.

As a part of this negative conditioning there is the heavy emphasis by communications media on violence in television programs and motion pictures. The current American news format of radio, television, and newspapers—the widely prevalent idea of what constitutes news—results from a narrow, brutalizing concept thirty or forty years behind the times and is inimical to the development of human potential.

The news media give much time and prominent space to violence and consistently underplay "good" news. This gives the consumer the impression that important things that happen are various types of destructive activities. Consistent and repeated emphasis on bad news not only creates anxiety and tension but instills the belief that there is little except violence, disasters, accidents, and mayhem abroad in the world. As a consequence, the consumer of such news gradually experiences a shift in his outlook about the world leading to the formation of feelings of alienation and separation. The world is increasingly perceived as a threat, as the viewer becomes anxious that violence and mayhem may be perpetrated on him from somewhere out of the strange and unpredictable environment in which he lives. There slowly grows a conviction that it is safer to withdraw from such a world, to isolate himself from its struggles, and to let others makes the decisions and become involved.

As a result of the steady diet of violence in the media, an even more fundamental and insidious erosion in man's self-system takes place. The erosion affects what I call the "trust factor." If we have been given a certain amount of affection, love, and understanding in our formative years, we are able to place a certain amount of trust in our fellow man. Trust is one of the most important elements in today's society although we tend to minimize its importance. *We basically trust people.* For example, we place an enormous amount of trust in our fellow man when driving on a freeway or in an express lane. We trust those with whom we are associated to fulfill their obligations and responsibilities. The element of trust is the basic rule in human relations. When we distrust people, they usually sense our attitude and reciprocate in kind.

The consistent emphasis in the news on criminal violence, burglarizing, and assault makes slow but pervasive inroads into our reservoir of trust. As we hear and read much about the acts of violence and injury men perpetrate upon one another, year after year, with so little emphasis placed on the loving, caring, and humanitarian acts of man, we begin to trust our fellow man less, and we thereby diminish ourselves. It is my conclusion the media's excessive emphasis on violence, like the drop of water on the stone, erodes and wears away the trust factor in man. By undermining the trust factor in man, media contribute to man's estrangement from man and prevent the full flourishing and deeper development of a sense of community and communion with all men.

Our self-concept, how we feel about ourselves and our fellow man and the world, is determined to a considerable extent by the inputs from the physical and interpersonal environment to which we are exposed. In the physical environment, there are the irritants in the air, i.e., air pollution plus the ugliness and noise of megapolis. Our interpersonal environment is characterized by estrangement and distance from others (and self), and by the artificiality and superficiality of our social encounters and the resultant violation of authenticity. Existing in a setting that provides as consistent inputs multiple irritants, ugliness and violence, and lack of close and meaningful relationships, man is in danger of becoming increasingly irritated, ugly, and violent.

As work in the area of human potentialities progressed, it has become ever clearer that personality, to a much greater degree than previously suspected, functions in response to the environment. This is additional confirmation of what field theorists and proponents of the holistic approach to the study of man have long suspected.

Perhaps the most important task facing us today is the regeneration of our environment and institutional structures such as school, government, church, etc. With increasing sophistication has come the recognition that institutions are not sacrosanct and that they have but one purpose and function—to serve as a framework for the actualization of human potential. It is possible to evaluate both the institution and the contribution of the institution by asking this question: "To what extent does the function of the institution foster the realization of human potential?"

Experimental groups consistently have found that the more a person's environment can be involved in the process of realizing potential, the greater the gains. It is understandable why scientists concerned with the study of personality have been reluctant to consider the importance of here-and-now inputs in relation to personality functioning. To do so would open a Pandora's box of possibilities and complex forces that until fairly recently were considered to be the exclusive domain of the social scientist. Many scientists and professionals, particularly psychotherapists, feel they have acquired a certain familiarity with the topography of "intrapsychic forces" and are reluctant to admit the reality of additional complex factors in the functioning of the personality.

It is significant that an increasing number of psychologists, psychiatrists, and social workers now realize that over and beyond keeping up with developments in their respective fields, the best way to acquire additional professional competence is through group experiences designed for personal growth and that focus on the unfolding of individual possibilities. From this group of aware professionals and others came much of the initial support and interest in Esalen Institute and similar "growth centers" later referred to as the Human Potentialities Movement.

Esalen Institute in Big Sur, California, was organized in 1962 by Michael Murphy and his partner, Dick Price. Under their imaginative management the institute experienced a phenomenal growth, established a branch in San Francisco, and is now famous for its seminars and weekend experiences offered by pioneering professionals. Since 1962 more than 100,000 persons have enrolled for one of these activities.

The past three years have seen a rapid mushrooming of growth centers. There are more than fifty such organizations ranging from Esalen and Kairos Institutes in California to Oasis in Chicago and Aureon Institute in New York. The experiences offered at these growth centers are based on several hypotheses: (1) that the average healthy person functions at a fraction of his capacity; (2) that man's most exciting life-long adventure is actualizing his potential; (3) that the group environment is one of the best settings in which to achieve growth; and (4) that personality growth can be achieved by anyone willing to invest himself in this process.

Human potentialities is rapidly emerging as a discrete field of scientific inquiry. Exploring the human potential can become the meeting ground for a wide range of disciplines, offering a dynamic synthesis for seemingly divergent areas of research. It is possible that the field of human potentialities offers an answer to the long search for a synthesizing and organizing principle which will unify the sciences. The explosive growth of the Human Potentialities Movement is indicative of a growing public interest. Although there exist a considerable number of methods —all designed to tap human potential— work on assessment or evaluation of these methods has in most instances not progressed beyond field testing and informal feedback of results. The need for research in the area of human potentialities has never been more pressing. The National Center for the Exploration of Human Potential in La Jolla, California, has recently been organized for this purpose. A nonprofit organization, the center will act as a clearinghouse of information for current and past approaches that have been successful in fostering personal growth. One of the main purposes of the center will be to conduct and coordinate basic and applied research concerning the expansion of human potential.

Among the many fascinating questions posed by researchers are some of the following: What is the relationship of body rhythms, biorhythms, and the expansion of sensory awareness to the uncovering of human potential? What are the applications of methods and approaches from other cultures such as yoga techniques, Sufi methods, types of meditation, etc.? What is the role of ecstasy and play vis-à-vis the realizing of human possibilities? The exploration of these and similar questions can help us create a society truly devoted to the full development of human capacities—particularly the capacities for love, joy, creativity, spiritual experiencing. This is the challenge and promise of our lifetime.

COMPLEX MAN IN THE COMPLEX ORGANIZATION

Edgar H. Schein

Organization and management theory has tended toward simplified and generalized conceptions of man. Empirical research has consistently found some support for the simple generalized conception, but only some. Consequently, the major impact of many decades of research has been to vastly complicate our models of man, of organizations, and of management strategies. Man is a more complex individual than rational-economic, social, or self-actualizing man. Not only is he more complex within himself, being possessed of many needs and potentials, but he is also likely to differ from his neighbor in the patterns of his own complexity. It has always been difficult to generalize about man, and it is becoming more difficult as society and organizations within society are themselves becoming more complex and differentiated.

What assumptions can be stated which do justice to this complexity?

a. Man is not only complex, but also highly variable; he has many motives which are arranged in some sort of hierarchy of importance to him, but this hierarchy is subject to change from time to time and situation to situation; furthermore, motives interact and combine into complex motive patterns (for example, since money can facilitate self-actualization, for some people economic strivings are equivalent to self-actualization).

b. Man is capable of learning new motives through his organizational experiences, hence ultimately his pattern of motivation and the psychological contract which he establishes with the organization is the result of a complex interaction between initial needs and organizational experiences.

c. Man's motives in different organizations or different subparts of the same organization may be different; the person who is alienated in the formal organization may find fulfillment of his social and self-actualization needs in the union or in the informal organization; if the job itself is complex, such as that of a manager, some parts of the job may engage some motives while other parts engage other motives.

d. Man can become productively involved with organizations on the basis of many different kinds of motives; his ultimate satisfaction and the ultimate effectiveness of the organization depends only in part on the nature of his motivation. The nature of the task to be performed, the abilities and experience of the person on the job, and the nature of the other people in the organization all interact to produce a certain pattern of work and

feelings. For example, a highly skilled but poorly motivated worker may be as effective *and satisfied* as a very unskilled but highly motivated worker.

e. Man can respond to many different kinds of managerial strategies, depending on his own motives and abilities and the nature of the task; in other words, there is no one correct managerial strategy that will work for all men at all times.

Implied Managerial Strategy

If assumptions such as the above come closer to the empirical reality, what implications do these have for managerial strategy? Perhaps the most important implication is that *the successful manager must be a good diagnostician and must value a spirit of inquiry.* If the abilities and motives of the people under him are so variable, he must have the sensitivity and diagnostic ability to be able to sense and appreciate the differences. Second, rather than regard the existence of differences as a painful truth to be wished away, he must also learn to value difference and to value the diagnostic process which reveals differences. Finally, he must have the personal flexibility and the range of skills necessary to vary his own behavior. If the needs and motives of his subordinates are different, they must be treated differently.[1]

It is important to recognize that these points do not contradict any of the strategies previously cited. I am not saying that adhering to traditional principles of organization, or being employee-centered, or facilitating the work of subordinates is wrong. What I am saying is that any of these approaches may be wrong in some situations and with some people. Where we have erred is in oversimplifying and overgeneralizing. As empirical evidence mounts, it is becoming apparent that the frame of reference and value system which will help the manager most in utilizing people effectively is that of science and of systems theory. If the manager adopts these values toward man, he will test his assumptions and seek a better diagnosis, and if he does that he will act more appropriately to whatever the demands of the situation are. He may be highly directive at one time and with one employee but very nondirective at another time and another employee. He may use pure engineering criteria in the design of some jobs, but let a worker group completely design another set of jobs. In other words, he will be flexible, and will be prepared to accept a variety of interpersonal relationships, patterns of authority, and psychological contracts.

Evidence for Complex Man

In a sense, all of the researches previously cited support the assumptions stated in this section, but it will be helpful to review and to cite some additional studies which highlight human complexity and human differences. For example, both Whyte and Zaleznik in the studies previously cited showed that the background and pattern of motivation of rate-busters differed from that of underproducers. Both types were group deviants, but the reasons why one group was indifferent to group sanctions while the other group aspired to membership and was rejected were found in their different personal and social backgrounds.

The study of Vroom and Mann . . . showed that workers with different personalities preferred different leadership styles in their bosses. A similar example drawn from another type of organization, namely the prison, comes from Grusky's study.[2] Because the prison is a coercive organization which forces its inmates to be totally dependent and submissive, it should create primarily alienative involvement. Grusky hypothesized and confirmed that those prisoners who had submissive and dependent kinds of personalities would be relatively less alienated, more cooperative, and more positive about prison life. Both Pearlin[3] and Argyris[4] in studying the alienation of workers in typical industrial organizations found cases of workers who were not alienated because their personal needs and predispositions made them comfortable in a highly authoritarian situation which demanded little of them, either because they did not seek challenge and autonomy or because they genuinely respected authority and status.

In a recent study of four types of industrial workers, Robert Blauner[5] found evidence for very different patterns of alienation depending on the nature of the technology which was involved in the work. He defined alienation as being the resultant of four different psychological states which are in principle independent of each other: (1) sense of powerlessness or inability to influence the work situation; (2) loss of meaning in the work; (3) sense of social isolation, lack of feeling of belonging to an organization, work group, or occupational group; and (4) self-estrangement or sense that work is merely a means to an end, lack of any self-involvement with work.

Automobile workers on assembly lines were found to be alienated by all four criteria mentioned. At the other extreme, members of the printing trades felt a sense of influence, meaning, integration into the occupational group, and deep involvement in their work. Textile workers resembled automobile workers but were highly integrated into communities in which the traditional values taught them not to expect a sense of influence or meaning. These values in combination with paternalistic management practices made them feel reasonably content with their lot in spite of strong forces toward alienation. The fourth group, chemical workers, represented still another pattern. Because the continuous processes in chemical plants tend to be highly automated, the chemical worker has a great deal of responsibility for controlling the process, considerable autonomy and freedom, a close sense of integration with others on his shift and in the plant, and high involvement in the work because of the high responsibility. The variation in these four types of workers illustrates the danger of generalizing about alienation among factory workers, and the utility of more refined concepts of alienation and technology such as Blauner has developed.

Studies of the dominant motivational patterns which led men into management positions show similar variations. Although there is some agreement that managers, in comparison to other groups of similar socioeconomic status or to other occupations, are more concerned with power, achievement, income, and advancement, the variability within each occupational group is more striking than the difference between occupational groups. For example, in reviewing the literature Vroom finds that sales and personnel managers are more likely to have strong social or affiliative needs, while production managers tend to have strong needs to work with mechanical things. Higher levels of management are more likely to be concerned with desires for personal growth and needs for self-actualization and autonomy than lower levels of management.[6]

Gellerman, in discussing varieties of motives such as the ones mentioned, has pointed out that even economic rewards can and do have vastly different meanings to different people.[7] For some people, money represents basic security and love; for others, it represents power; for still others, it is a measure of their achievement in society; and for still others, it represents merely the means to the end of comfortable and sumptuous living. Thus it is difficult to judge even in the case of a given motive, what all of its symbolic meanings are to the person and how it is connected to other motives.

Another line of evidence comes from studies of *changes* in motivation as a result of organizational experience. It has been difficult to determine, for example, whether an alienated worker was a person without achievement and self-actualization needs when he first joined an organization, or whether he became that way as a result of chronically frustrating work experiences. The point is critical, because if motives are not capable of being elicited or stimulated, more emphasis should be placed on *selecting* those workers who initially display the patterns of motivation required by the organization; if, on the other hand, by changing organizational arrangements and managerial strategies, it is possible to arouse the kinds of motives desired, more emphasis should be given to helping *organizations change.*

I have already mentioned the evidence of case studies such as those done in companies which have adopted the Scanlon Plan. Workers who for years took an apathetic attitude toward organizational goals were able, with an organizational change, to become highly motivated and committed to such goals.

In one of the few field studies concerned with changes, Lieberman attempted to determine what *attitude* changes would occur as a result of shifting a man's role from union steward to foreman.[8] Those stewards who were promoted to foremen showed consistent attitude changes—from pro-union to pro-management—within a few months of the promotion. Because of economic reverses, the company had to demote some of these foremen. When their attitudes were studied again, it turned out that they had again adopted the attitudes of the worker group and abandoned their pro-management attitudes.

References and Notes

1. Theorists like Argyris, Likert, and McGregor have argued for more diagnostic ability and skill-flexibility in managers. My argument here summarizes theirs and attempts to make it more explicit and general. A similar analysis and generalization has also been made by W. G. Bennis in

"Revisionist Theory of Leadership, *Harvard Business Review* 39 (1961): 26 ff.

2. O. Grusky, "Authoritarianism and Effective Indoctrination: A Case Study," *Administrative Science Quarterly* 7 (1962): 79–95.

3. L. I. Pearlin, "Alienation from Work," *American Sociological Review* 27 (1962): 314–26.

4. C. Argyris, op. cit.

5. R. Blauner, *Alienation and Freedom* (Chicago: Univ. of Chicago Press, 1964).

6. V. H. Vroom, *Motivation in Management* (New York: American Foundation for Management Research, 1964).

7. S. W. Gellerman, *Motivation and Productivity* (New York: American Management Association, 1963).

8. S. Lieberman, "The Effects of Changes in Roles on the Attitudes of Role Occupants," *Human Relations* 9 (1956): 385–402.

Chapter 4 Interpersonal Competence and Group Growth

INTERPERSONAL RELATIONSHIPS: U.S.A. 2000[1]

Carl R. Rogers

I want to make it very clear at the outset that I am not making predictions about the year 2000. I am going to sketch possibilities, alternative routes which we may travel.

One important reason for refusing to make predictions is that for the first time in history man is not only taking his future seriously, but he also has adequate technology and power to shape and form that future. He is endeavoring to *choose* his future rather than simply living out some inevitable trend. And we do not know what he will choose. So we do not know what man's relation to man will be in this country 32 years from now. But we can see certain possibilities.

Man's Greatest Problem

Before I try to sketch some of those possibilities I should like to point to the greatest problem which man faces in the years to come. It is not the hydrogen bomb, fearful as that may be. It is not the population explosion, though the consequences of that are awful to contemplate. It is instead a problem which is rarely mentioned or discussed. It is the question of how much change the human being can accept, absorb, and assimilate, and the rate at which he can take it. Can he keep up with the ever-increasing rate of technological change, or is there some point at which the human organism goes to pieces? Can he leave the static ways and static guidelines which have dominated all of his history and adopt the process ways, the continual changingness which must be his if he is to survive?

There is much to make us pessimistic about this. If we consider the incredible difficulties in bringing about change in our great bureaucracies of government, education, and religion, we become hopeless. When we see how frequently the people take action which is clearly against their long-range welfare—such as the resolute refusal to face up to the problem of the urban ghettos—we become discouraged.

But I see two elements on the other side of the balance. The first is the ability of the Western democratic cultures to respond appropriately—at the very last cliff-hanging moment—to those trends which challenge their survival.

The second element I have observed in individuals in therapy, in intensive encounter groups, and in organizations. It is the magnetic attraction of the experience of change, growth, fulfillment. Even though growth may involve intense pain and suffering, once the individual or group has tasted the excitement of this changingness, persons are drawn to it as to a magnet. Once a degree of actualization has been savored, the individual or the group is willing to take the frightening risk of launching out into a world of process, with few fixed landmarks, where the direction is guided from within. So, in this field of interpersonal relations, though there is much reason for despair, I believe that, if our citizens experience something of the pain and risk of a growth toward personal enrichment, they will grasp for more.

With this context of uncertainty about our ability or willingness to assimilate change, let us look at some specific areas of interpersonal relationships as they may be.

Urban Crowding and Its Possible Effects

The world population will more than double in the next 32 years, a ghastly trend which will affect us in unknown ways. The population of the United States, which was comfortably remembered in my grammar school days in 1915 as 100 million, 52 years later reached 200 million, 22 years from now is predicted to reach 300 million, and in the year 2000 will be between 320 and 340 million, though hopefully it will be starting to stabilize itself at about that time. The great bulk of these millions will reside in a great megalopolis, of which there will probably be three. One trend which we may follow is to crowd more and more closely together, as we are now crowded in our ghettos. I understand that Philip Hauser, the noted demographer, has stated that, if all of us were crowded together as closely as the residents of Harlem, all of the people in the entire United States could be contained in the five boroughs of New York City. The future may resemble this, if we choose to push in more and more closely together.

Such crowding has consequences. Even in rats, as Calhoun[2] has so vividly shown, overcrowding results in poor mothering, poor nest building, bizarre sexual behavior, cannibalism, and complete alienation, with some rats behaving like zombies, paying no attention to others, coming out of their solitary burrows only for food. The resemblance to human behavior in crowded rooming house areas, the complete lack of involvement which permits people to watch a long-drawn-out murder without so much as calling the police, the poor family relationships—this could be a trend which will be carried even further by the year 2000.

On the other hand, we could learn to decentralize our great urban areas, to make them manageable, to provide not only for more efficiency but for warmer and more human interpersonal relationships. We could use more space, build smaller cities with great park and garden areas, devise plans for neighborhood building which would promote *humanization,* not dehumanization. What will the choice be?

Closeness and Intimacy in the Year 2000

In my estimation, one of the most rapidly growing social phenomena in the United States is the spread of the intensive group experience—sensitivity training, basic encounter groups, T-groups (the labels are unimportant). The growth of this phenomenon is rendered more striking when one realizes that it is a "grass roots" movement. There is not a university nor a foundation nor a government agency which has given it any significant approval or support until the last five or six years. Yet it has permeated industry, is coming into education, is reaching families, professionals in the helping fields, and many other individuals. Why? I believe it is because people—ordinary people—have discovered that it alleviates their loneliness and permits them to grow, to risk, to change. It brings persons into real relationships with persons.

In our affluent society the individual's survival needs are satisfied. For the first time, he is freed to become aware of his isolation, aware of his alienation, aware of the fact that he is, during most of his life, a role interacting with other roles, a mask meeting other masks. And for the first time he is aware that this is not a *necessary* tragedy of life, that he does not have to live out his days in this fashion. So he is seeking, with great determination and inventiveness, ways of modifying this existential loneliness. The intensive group experience, perhaps the most significant social invention of this century, is an important one of these ways.

What will grow out of the current use of basic encounter groups, marathons, "labs," and the like? I have no idea what *forms* will proliferate out of these roots during the coming decades, but I believe men will discover new bases of intimacy which will be highly fulfilling. I believe there will be possibilities for the *rapid* development of closeness between and among persons, a closeness which is not artificial, but is real and deep, and which will be well suited to our increasing mobility of living. Temporary relationships will be able to achieve the richness and meaning which heretofore have been associated only with lifelong attachments.

There will be more awareness of what is going on within the person, an openness to all of one's experience—the sensory input of sound and taste and hearing and sight and smell, the richness of kaleidoscopically changing ideas and concepts, the wealth of feelings—positive, negative, and ambivalent, intense and moderate—toward oneself and toward others.

There will be the development of a whole new style of communication in which the person can, in effect, say, "I'm telling you the way it *is,* in me—my ideas, my desires, my feelings, my hopes, my angers, my fears, my despairs," and where the response will be equally open. We shall be experimenting with ways in which a whole person can communicate himself to another whole person. We shall discover that security resides not in hiding oneself but in being more fully known, and consequently in coming to know the other more fully. Aloneness will be something one chooses out of a desire for privacy, not an isolation into which one is forced.

In all of this I believe we shall be experimenting with a new ideal of what man may become, a model very *sharply* different from the historical view of man as a creature playing various appropriate roles. We seem to be aiming for a new *reality* in relationships, a new openness in communication, a love for one another which grows not out of a romantic blindness but out of the profound respect which is nearly always engendered by reality in relationships.

I recognize that many individuals in our culture are frightened in the depths of their being by this new picture of man—this flowing, changing, open, expressive, creative person. They may be able to stop the trend or even to reverse it. It is conceivable that we shall go in for the manufactured "image," as on TV, or may insist more strongly than ever that teachers are *teachers,* parents are *parents,* bosses are *manipulators*—that we may rigidify every role and stereotype in new and more armor-plated ways. We may insist with new force that the only significant aspect of man is his rational and intellectual being and that nothing else matters. We may assert that he is a machine and no more. Yet I do not believe this will happen. The magnetism of the new man, toward which we are groping, is too great. Much of what I say in the remainder of this paper is based on the conviction that we are, for better or for worse, in labor pains and growth pains—turning toward this new view of man as becoming and being—a continuing, growing *process.*

Man-Woman Relationships

What do the coming decades hold for us in the realm of intimacy between boy and girl, man and woman? Here too enormous forces are at work, and choices are being made which will not, I believe, be reversed by the year 2000.

In the first place, the trend toward greater freedom in sexual relationships, in adolescents and adults, is likely to continue, whether this direction frightens us or not. Many elements have conspired together to bring about a change in such behavior, and the advent of "the Pill" is only one of these. It seems probable that sexual intimacy will be a part of "going steady" or of any continuing special interest in a member of the opposite sex. The attitude of prurience is fast dying out, and sexual activity is seen as a potentially joyful and enriching part of a relationship. The attitude of possessiveness—of owning another person, which historically has dominated sexual unions—is likely to be greatly diminished. It is certain that there will be enormous variations in the quality of these sexual relationships—from those where sex is a purely physical contact which has almost the same solitary quality as masturbation to those in which the sexual aspect is an expression of an increasing sharing of feelings, of experiences, of interests, of each other.

By the year 2000 it will be quite feasible to ensure that there will be no children in a union. By one of the several means currently under study, each individual will be assured of lasting infertility in early adolescence. It will take positive action, permissible only after a thoughtful decision, to reestablish fertility. This will reverse the present situation where only by positive action can one *prevent* conception. Also, by that time, computerized matching of prospective partners will be far more sophisticated than it is today and will be of great help to an individual in finding a congenial companion of the opposite sex.

Some of the temporary unions thus formed may be legalized as a type of marriage—with no permanent commitment, with no children (by mutual agreement), and, if the union breaks up, no legal accusations, no necessity for showing legal cause, and no alimony.

It is becoming increasingly clear that a man-woman relationship will have *permanence* only in the degree in which it satisfies the emotional, psychological, intellectual, and physical needs of the partners. This means that the *permanent* marriage of the future will be even better than marriage in the present, because the ideals and goals for that marriage will be of a higher order. The partners will be demanding more of the relationship than they do today.

If a couple feel deeply committed to each other and mutually wish to remain together to raise a family, then this will be a new and more binding type of marriage. Each will accept the obligations involved in having and rearing children. There may be a mutual agreement as to whether or not the marriage includes sexual faithfulness to one's mate. Perhaps by the year 2000 we shall have reached the point where, through education and social pressure, a couple will decide to have children only when they have shown evidence of a mature commitment to each other, of a sort which is likely to have permanence.

What I am describing is a whole continuum of man-woman relationships, from the most casual dating and casual sex relationship to a rich and fulfilling partnership in which communication is open and real, where each is concerned with promoting the personal growth of the partner, and where there is a long-range commitment to each other which will form a sound basis for having and rearing children in an environment of love. Some parts of this continuum will exist within a legal framework; some will not.

One may say, with a large measure of truth, that much of this continuum already exists. But an awareness of, and an open acceptance of, this continuum by society will change its whole quality. Suppose it were openly accepted that some "marriages" are no more than ill-mated and transitory unions and that they will be broken. If children are not permitted in such marriages, then one divorce in every two marriages (the current rate in California) is no longer seen as a tragedy. The dissolving of the union may be painful, but it is not a *social* catastrophe, and the experience may be a necessary step in the personal growth of the two individuals toward greater maturity.

Parents and Children

What of the relationships between parents and their children? Here it is terribly difficult to foresee the future. If parents in general hold to the static views which have served reasonably well through the centuries of little change—"I know the values that are important in life," "I am wiser than my child in knowing the direction his life should take"—then the generation gap will grow so large that our culture will literally be split wide open. This may be the course of future events.

But there are straws in the wind which point in another way. Some parents wish to be *persons*—growing, changing persons—living in person-to-person relationships with the youngsters in their families. So we see the development of family encounter groups (still in their infancy) in which parents learn about themselves from their own and others' children, and children learn about themselves from their own and others' parents. Here the self-insights, the awareness of how one comes across to the other generation, bring changes in behavior and new ways of relating based on an open respect for oneself, out of which can grow a genuine respect for the other.

A new type of parent education is also developing in which there is respect for the parent as a person with feelings and rights as well as for the child and his feelings and rights. We find family groups where parent and child each *listen* to the other, where honest, open expression is also mutual. Parental authority and childhood submission give way before a realness which confronts realness. Such family relationships are not necessarily smooth, and the problems of process living are as perplexing as the problems brought on by static views; but there is communication, and there is respect—and the generation gap becomes simply the communication gap which, in some degree, separates all individuals.

It may be hard for us to realize that some help from this new type of family relationship may come from industry. Some corporations, realizing that to start to educate a child at six is much too late, are beginning to dream up learning activities, learning "packages," which will not only be fun for the children but which will involve the whole family in mutually pleasurable and communicative activities.

Everyone will have a good time learning—together.

Let me turn to quite a different facet of the relations of parents and children. What will the future hold for children from broken homes—[children] who will continue to exist even if my most optimistic speculations come true? I trust there will be widespread experimentation in dealing with these youngsters. Perhaps we should take a lesson from the *kibbutzim,* where the child is cared for and gains his security from workers who love children and are trained to care for them, and where the contacts with parents, though relatively brief, tend to be full of love and fun. Perhaps some of the "hippie" groups are showing the way in their small, close communities where the child is, ideally at least, cared for by all. We are in desperate need of creative approaches to this problem. Almost anything would be better than the present situation. Now the child is often fought over in court. He learns that one parent is bad, the other good. He is often exposed to the attempts of each parent to win him away, emotionally, from the other. He is often experienced as a burden by the mother, who is attempting to reestablish herself in a job and a new life. Or he is the sole focus of the mother's affections, which may be even worse. *He* is the one who suffers from divorce, and we have been most unimaginative in trying to promote his welfare. Hence my hope is that there will be many types of experimentation three decades from now, in helping the child of divorced parents to grow in the most favorable possible environment.

Learning in Interpersonal Relationships

What of education in the year 2000, especially as it involves interpersonal relationships?

It is possible that education will continue much as it is—concerned only with words, symbols, rational concepts based on the authoritative role of the teacher, further dehumanized by teaching machines, computerized knowledge, and increased use of tests and examinations. This is possible, because educators are showing greater resistance to change than any other institutional group. Yet I regard it as unlikely, because a revolution in education is long overdue, and the unrest of students is only one sign of this. So that I am going to speculate on some of the other possibilities.

It seems likely that schools will be greatly deemphasized in favor of a much broader, thoughtfully devised *environment for learning,* where the experiences of the student will be challenging, rewarding, affirmative, and pleasurable.

The teacher or professor will have largely disappeared. His place will be taken by a facilitator of learning, chosen for his facilitative attitudes as much as for his knowledge. He will be skilled in stimulating individual and group initiative in learning, skilled in facilitating discussions -in-depth of the *meaning* to the student of what is being learned, skilled in fostering creativity, skilled in providing the resources for learning. Among these resources will be much in the way of programmed learning, to be used as the student finds these learnings appropriate; much in the way of audiovisual aids such as filmed lectures and demonstrations by experts in each field; much in the way of computerized knowledge on which the student can draw. But these "hardware" possibilities are not my main concern.

We shall, I believe, see the facilitator focusing his major attention on the prime period for learning—from infancy to age six or eight. Among the most important learnings will be the personal and interpersonal. Every child will develop confidence in his own ability to learn, since he will be rewarded for learning at his own pace. Each child will learn that he is a person of worth, because he has unique and worthwhile capacities. He will learn how to be himself in a group—to listen, but also to speak, to learn about himself,

but also to confront and give feedback to others. He will learn to be an individual, not a faceless conformist. He will learn, through simulations and computerized games, to meet many of the life problems he will face. He will find it permissible to engage in fantasy and daydreams, to think creative thoughts, to capture these in words or paints or constructions. He will find that learning, even difficult learning, is fun, both as an individual activity and in cooperation with others. His discipline will be self-discipline.

His learning will not be confined to the ancient intellectual concepts and specializations. It will not be a *preparation* for living. It will be, in itself, an *experience* in living. Feelings of inadequacy, hatred, a desire for power, feelings of love and awe and respect, feelings of fear and dread, unhappiness with parents or with other children—all these will be an open part of his curriculum, as worthy of exploration as history or mathematics. In fact, this openness to feelings will enable him to learn content material more readily. His will be an education in becoming a whole human being, and the learnings will involve him deeply, openly, exploringly, in an awareness of his relationship to himself, an awareness of his relationships to the world of others, as well as in an awareness of the world of abstract knowledge.

Because learning has been exciting, because he has participated heavily and responsibly in choosing the directions of his learning, because he has discovered the world to be a fantastically changing place, he will wish to continue his learning into adult life. Thus, communities will set up centers which are rich environments for learning, and the student will *never be graduated.* He will always be a part of a "commencement."

Persons in Industry

In view of my past prejudices I find it somewhat difficult but necessary to say that of all of the institutions of present-day American life, industry is perhaps best prepared to meet the year 2000. I am not speaking of its technical ability. I am speaking of the vision it is acquiring in regard to the importance of persons, of interpersonal relationships, and of open communication. That vision, to be sure, is often unrealized, but it does exist.

Let me speculate briefly on the interpersonal aspect of industrial functioning. It is becoming increasingly clear to the leaders of any complex modern industry that the old hierarchical system of boss and employees is obsolete. If a factory is turning out one simple product, such a system may still work. But if it is in the business of producing vehicles for space or elaborate electronic devices, it is definitely inadequate. What takes its place? The only road to true efficiency seems to be that of persons communicating freely with persons—from below to above, from peer to peer, from above to below, from a member of one division to a member of another division. It is only through this elaborate, individually initiated network of open human communication that the essential information and know-how can pervade the organization. No one individual can possibly "direct" such complexity.

Thus, if I were to hazard a guess in regard to industry in the year 2000, it would be something different from the predictions about increasing technical skill, increasing automation, increasing management by computers, and the like. All of those predictions will doubtless come true, but the interpersonal aspect is less often discussed. I see many industries, by the year 2000, giving as much attention to the quality of interpersonal relationships and the quality of communication as they currently do to the technological aspects of their business. They will come to value persons as persons, and to recognize that only out of the *communicated* knowledge of all members of the organization can innovation and progress come. They will pay more attention to breakdowns in personal communication

than to breakdowns of the circuitry in their computers. They will be forced to recognize that only as they are promoting the growth and fulfillment of the individuals on the payroll will they be promoting the growth and development of the organization.

What I have said will apply, I believe, not only to persons in management but to persons classed as "labor." The distinction grows less with every technological advance. It also applies, obviously, to the increasingly direct and personal communication between persons in management and persons in the labor force, if an industry is to become and remain healthily productive.

Religion as Interpersonal Living

Historically, much of man's life has revolved around his relationship to his God or gods and around his relationship to others who share his religious views. What will be the situation three decades from now?

It is definitely conceivable that out of a deep fear of the rapidly changing world he is creating, man may seek refuge in a sure dogma, a simplistic answer to life's complexities, a religion which will serve him as a security blanket. This seems unlikely, but I can imagine the circumstances under which it might occur.

The more likely possibility—or so it appears to me—is that by the year 2000, *institutionalized* religion, already on the wane as a significant factor in everyday life, will have faded to a point where it is of only slight importance in the community. Theology may still exist as a scholastic exercise, but in reality the God of authoritative answers will be not only dead but buried.

This does not mean at all that the concerns which have been the basis of religion will have vanished. The mysterious process of life, the mystery of the universe and how it came to be, the tragedy of man's alienation from himself and from others, the puzzle of the meaning of individual life—these mysteries will all be very much present. There may, indeed, be a *greater appreciation* of mystery as our knowledge increases (just as theoretical physicists now marvel at the true *mystery* of what they have discovered).

But religion, to the extent that the term is used, will consist of tentatively held hypotheses which are lived out and corrected in the interpersonal world. Groups, probably much smaller than present-day congregations, will wrestle with the ethical and moral and philosophical questions which are posed by the rapidly changing world. The individual will forge, with the support of the group, the stance he will take in the universe—a stance which he cannot regard as final because more data will continually be coming in.

In the open questioning and honest struggle to face reality which exist in such a group, it is likely that a sense of true community will develop—a community based not on a common creed nor an unchanging ritual but on the personal ties of individuals who have become deeply related to one another as they attempt to comprehend and to face, as living men, the mysteries of existence. The religion of the future will be man's existential choice of his way of living in an unknown tomorrow, a choice made more bearable because [it will have been] formed in a community of individuals who are likeminded, but like-minded only in their searching.

In line with the thread which runs through all of my remarks, it may well be that out of these many searching groups there may emerge a more unitary view of man, a view which might bind us together. Man as a creature with ability to remember the past and foresee the future, a creature with the capacity for choosing among alternatives, a creature whose deepest urges are for harmonious and loving relationships with his fellows, a creature with the capacity to understand the reasons for his destructive behaviors, man as a person who has at least limited powers to form himself and to shape his future in the way he desires—this might

be a crude sketch of the unifying view which could give us hope in a universe we cannot understand.

The Relationship with the Slum Dweller

I have left until the last the most difficult area: the relationship between the persons in the urban ghettos (Negroes and other minority groups) and the persons outside the ghetto.

Our inability to accept the changing nature of this anguished struggle is one of the deepest reasons for pessimism regarding the future. The more favored community seems, thus far, unwilling and unable to understand the effects upon individuals of a lifetime of defeat, frustration, and rejection. It seems thus far, unable to comprehend that rebellion is *most* likely, not least likely, to occur in the very cities and situations in which there is, at last, some hope. We seem reluctant to give the ghetto dweller responsibility, the one thing which might restore his human dignity—because he will make mistakes. We seem to have no recognition that learning from mistakes is the only true way to independence. And, most tragically of all, we appear—on both sides—to have lost the belief that communication is possible. Thus I cannot deny the possibility that the next decades will see a growing rebellion, a bloody guerrilla warfare in our cities, with concentration camps, with military government, with fear and hatred in the heart of every citizen. It took a century for the hatreds between the North and the South to diminish to manageable proportions. How many centuries will it take for the hatreds of this new war to die down, a war which it may be too late to prevent?

What makes it, from my point of view, incredibly tragic is that the deepest, most basic issues revolve around communication. Distrust, suspicion, disillusionment have grown to such mammoth proportions on both sides—though perhaps especially on the part of the ghetto dweller—that it is taken for granted that communication is no longer possible. Yet funds, however great, and vocational retraining and housing projects and all the rest can do little without free, direct, honest communication between persons.

Is it impossible? It is my contention that if we mounted a massive effort to reestablish communication, in groups ranging from militant blacks through liberals of both colors to conservative whites; if we drew into this effort dedicated individuals, from the ghetto and outside, who were desirous of improving relationships; if we drew on the expert knowledge available in the social and behavioral sciences; if we backed this effort with a sum at least equivalent to the cost of all our B-52 bombers—then there might be a chance of preventing the bloody tragedy which faces us.

I should not want to be understood as saying that improved communication, improved interpersonal relationships, would *resolve* the situation. What I am saying is that if, in small groups or large, the hatreds and the disillusionments could be accepted and *understood;* if suspicion and despair could be fully voiced and met with respect; then out of such groups might slowly grow a mutual respect in which responsible decisions could be taken and realistic solutions worked out. In these decisions the ghetto dweller would be a fully involved participant, as would the person from outside. Leadership in the ghetto would meet on a fully equal basis with leadership in the "establishment." Both would bear responsibility, through black power and white power, for seeing that the decisions were *carried out.* Idealistic, you say? But we have the

knowledge and the wealth which would make such a massive effort possible. And if we choose to follow the present trend, we have in South Vietnam a full color picture of how guerrilla warfare not only sacrifices lives but brutalizes the minds and hearts of the living. Shall we permit it to happen here? Or shall we choose to make a great and concerted effort to behave as persons with persons? On this issue I dare not even speculate.

Conclusion

Perhaps it is just as well that I conclude on this somberly precarious note. I hope I have made it clear the potentialities for change and enrichment in the interpersonal world of the year 2000 most assuredly exist. There can be more of intimacy, less of loneliness, an infusion of emotional and intellectual learning in our relationships, better ways of resolving conflicts openly, man-woman relationships which are enriching, family relationships which are real, a sense of community which enables us to face the unknown. All of this is possible if as a people we choose to move into the new mode of living openly as a continually changing process.

References and Notes

1. This paper was part of a symposium entitled "U.S.A. 2000," sponsored by the Esalen Institute and held in San Francisco, Calif., January 10, 1968.
2. J. B. Calhoun, "Population Density and Social Pathology," *Scientific American* 206, no. 2 (1962): 139–50.

HUMANISTIC ELEMENTS IN GROUP GROWTH

Jack R. and Lorraine M. Gibb

Some groups seem to grow. They appear healthy—and seem to get more healthy as time goes on. In such groups the human being seems to emerge as having great worth and great potential. It is difficult to separate feelings of personal growth and well-being from feelings of membership and interdependent fulfillment. Members of the group feel free, emergent, and creative.

Some groups appear to stagnate. They seem unhealthy. Members may speak defensively about their membership. In such groups the human being may appear as less than he is, as having little worth and little potential. Members may wonder whether the group is ever really going to amount to much or whether it will ever accomplish its aims. Members may feel restricted by the demands of the group. Persons may feel that they give more to the group than they get from it.

What distinguishes sick from healthy groups is a significant question. For most of us, groups are important elements in the structure of our culture. Some groups grow, and become, in a sense, actualized. Other groups progress slowly or fail to develop in meaningful dimensions. Therapy groups can provide a setting for therapy and remedial help, or they can be useless to the members. Classroom groups can be environments where growth and learning are easy, or they can be of little help and actually inhibit such growth. YMCA clubs can be climates which foster healthy spirituality and character formation, or they can hamper such formation. Families, regardless of such variables as economic welfare or presence or absence of fathers, can foster healthy growth in parents and children, or they can be festering grounds for juvenile delinquency, neurotic habits, or unhappiness. Research teams can be creative atmospheres for innovation and productivity, or they can lead to mediocrity, stagnation, and low productivity.

Research Base of Observation

In our research on group growth,[1] we have obtained a revealing and even inspiring view of man as he might become, and we have had occasional glimpses of groups in peak experiences of sustained creativity and trust, i.e., group actualization. These group experiences have occurred most often (1) when groups have been in sensitivity training in semiweekly sessions for eight or nine consecutive months; (2) when groups have been in around-the-clock "marathon" sessions for 90 to 120 hours with little or no sleep, or (3) when groups have been in twelve-hour sessions daily for twelve or thirteen consecutive days. In our experience, this optimal growth occurs most frequently in groups which have no professional leader present and in which emergent and interdependent strength is maximized.

Under these conditions, the groups are qualitatively different from the groups usually met in natural settings. The groups attain and often maintain states of creativity, depth of communication, and trust that are impressive and memorable, both to those participating and to those observing. We have seen this state of affairs in occasional natural groups in organizational settings, usually after the group has undergone a training experience of appropriate duration and intensity.

Group and Person Potentials

Research from several different disciplines has indicated that man grows at a fraction of his potential growth rate. This underdevelopment is even more startling when one examines the growth rate of groups in our culture. In our research program, we made systematic observations of groups in natural settings—YMCA clubs, management teams, national boards, therapy groups, work groups, and families. We made use of a number of methods in comparing the groups under depth training with natural groups: group interviews, individual depth interviews, coded group observations, questionnaires, expert opinions, and analysis of taped recordings (Gibb, 1955; Gibb, 1963; Gibb, 1964).

In this chapter, we shall present informal summaries of our general impressions from the longitudinal research and of our conclusions about a humanistic theory of personal and group growth.

Our impression is that man's capacity for creativity, happiness, and personal growth is greatly underrated, both by himself and by many scientists who study man. Behavioral scientists, in evaluating potential, have looked at persons and groups in the natural setting and judged what they might become. It is as if, wishing to determine how well men could hit golf balls, we lined up fifty average adult males at a golf tee, had each hit two balls, measured the distances, and concluded that the average man's driving potential was 30 yards. After practice and effort, perhaps the average man could hit the ball 155 yards. However, after experiencing a refined instruction process, the average person could possibly be trained to hit the ball 225 yards. The above analogy is relevant to the testing of the group's capability for creative growth. There is a qualitative difference between the average management team in the usual organizational setting and the same group after it receives the kind of training that is now possible. This significant fact has led to a new look at human potential in persons and groups, to new organizational theories, and to new theories of individual and group development.[2]

Basic Dimensions of Group Life

The process aspects of the group, *qua* group, are a relatively recent object of scientific study. Knowing little about groups and often fearing them, man has sometimes felt that they were a hindrance to human growth. It now seems likely that man can reach new satisfactions and significant functional levels of living in group action.

Our research indicates four significant dimensions in which groups differ. These dimensions are interdependent, and as yet we have no clear comprehension of that interdependence, but we do have some convincing evidence of the relevance of each of these factors in group growth, health, or actualization.

Groups differ in (1) the degree of *reciprocal trust* among members; (2) the *validity, depth, and quality of the feedback system;* (3) the degree of *directionality toward group-determined goals,* and (4) the degree of *real interdependence in the system.* A schematic picture of these four variables is given in Table 1. Let us examine each of these factors in some detail.

The Formation of Trust

Trust is the pacemaker variable in group growth. From it stem all the other significant variables of health. That is, to the extent that trust develops, people are able to communicate genuine feelings and perceptions on relevant issues to all members of the system. To the degree that trust is present, people are able to communicate with themselves and others to form consensual goals. To the degree that trust is present, people can be truly interdependent. Each of the four group-growth variables is dependent upon the prior variable in the hierarchy. Feedback is dependent upon trust. Goal formation is dependent upon feedback and trust. Interdependence is dependent upon goal formation, feedback, and trust.

As is indicated in Table 1, the four factors in group growth are related to parallel factors in personal growth. There is some agreement among psychologists on the criteria of mental health in personal growth.[3] There is considerably less agree-

Table 1 Personal and Group Growth

Key Areas of Social Behavior	Directions of Personal Growth	Directions of Group Growth
Climate (membership)	Acceptance of self; acceptance of others	Climate of trust; climate of support
Data flow (decision-making)	Awareness (input); openness (output)	Valid feedback system; consensual decision-making
Goal formation (productivity)	Goal integration in self; self-determination; self-assessment	Goal integration in group; group determination and assessment of goals
Control (organization)	Interdependence (inner, emergent control and value system)	Interdependence (inner, emergent control and norm system)

ment among group scientists on the criteria of group health and development. The schema outlined here provides a framework for analyzing group actualization.

The Dynamic of Fear

The most impressive dynamic of early group life is the presence of fear. Fear grows out of distrust. We tend to fear events, people, and stimuli for which we feel we have no adequate response. Many factors in the new or immature group increase the normal residual fear that all people share. Great uncertainty increases fear, and individuals have many ways of trying to reduce this uncertainty. They put other people into categories which they feel they can understand and predict. "If I know she is a nurse, then I know what nurses are like and can respond to what I know they will do." They get the group to agree upon some ground rules. "If we take turns talking around the circle, then I know when my turn comes." Individuals also try to find out what the other members think of them and about the world.

Some of these efforts to lessen uncertainty are unsuccessful, while others are fairly effective. Even if I can reduce the ambiguity in my own perceptual world, this gets shattered when I realize that growth in me and in the group can come only with ambiguity, tension, conflict, and unfreezing. I cannot truly become safe from my fears by building my perceptual world into safe and predictable categories.

Growth turns out to be something more.

The group in its early stages will attempt to cling to and create fragile structural stabilities to reduce fear. These apparently secure structures turn out to be made of sand. A group may assign a timekeeper so that one person will not monopolize the group; it may appoint a chairman, or it may decide in what order people will speak. This supposedly "rules in" order and control and "rules out" chaos and threatening situations.

For some people, moving quickly lessens fear by reducing the tension and turmoil of decisionmaking in depth. "Let's do anything," "Let's get something done," "We are wasting time," and other impatient expressions aimed at speeding up direct movement are common in the early stages of group development. Later observations show that these frantic demands for movement are fear-based.

Other Group Evidences of Fear

Politeness and formality are early indications of fear. Politeness prevents retaliation, keeps people at a safe distance, makes it unnecessary to face members in such a way that intimidating negative feelings would be revealed, discourages the other person from giving negative feedback, and in general serves the unanalyzed needs of the fearful person.

Another response to fear in early stages of group life is the use of humor. It is ambiguous enough to serve as a presumably safe camouflage for hostile feedback to another person. Humor tends to encourage people to keep things from getting too sentimental, too intimate, and too close to embarrassing or painful exposure or confrontation. By using humor, a person can "hedge his bets" and deny the hostile intent if the listener accuses him of being unfriendly.

In its early stages, the group is sometimes work-addicted. The group can avoid fearsome confrontation, interpersonal conflict, and exposure by hard, safe work upon a seemingly legitimate task. Groups can make long lists, engage in routine tasks, and attempt to look busy to themselves and others, in order to avoid depth relationships. A group may engage in an unending warm-up session, talking in an apparently serious, work-oriented vein about the factors determining today's weather. Of course, all the defense mechanisms are relevant here.

People who are afraid distrust the motivations of other members and tend to step in and try to control the situation in order to prevent those whom they fear from exerting prior influence. This is often done in subtle ways, such as nominating a less feared person to be chairman. This apparent cleanly motivated act can hopefully be seen as selfless and group-oriented rather than as a disguised manipulation for control.

Signs of Group Growth

Thus, fear and distrust characterize behavior in the early stages of group development. As groups grow, these fears gradually become reduced. Trust grows. People learn to tolerate greater degrees of ambiguity. They become more spontaneous and less cautious. Members make allowances for greater differences, both in themselves and in others. People are allowed to hold a wider variety of opinions. They are permitted to be themselves—to dress differently, to be unpredictable, and perhaps even to be disloyal. The boundaries of acceptance widen. Whereas in the early stages of development, the group boxes in or punishes persons who deviate from the group norms, in the later stages, nonconformists are encouraged. Radical ideas are used to test reality or to create new solutions. Deviation is perhaps even welcomed as a creative contribution to possible group productivity.

Fear reduction allows people to feel and to express publicly the warmth that wells up. People are able to show affection in a number of spontaneous, often gestural, ways without the need for exaggerated or showy expressions. There is a great deal of warmth in the group. In addition, there is an easy expression of "I feel this way," on the assumption that other members will permit the voicing of individualistic feelings. It is also common to hear people spontaneously say and feel "we," rather than "you." (The use of "you" in referring to the group is a sign of membership denial.)

The problem of trust formation is the problem of attaining membership. One achieves genuine belonging by trusting himself and the group. The critical index of group health is trust development. As the group grows, fear decreases and trust increases. Thus, group actualization is a process of attaining increasingly higher levels of trust.

Communication and Decisionmaking

In the early stages of group development, the customary fear and distrust make it difficult for a valid feedback system to occur, for people to talk honestly with one another, and for the group to integrate these feelings and perception data into appropriate decisions for the group.

The processes of ambiguity, strategy, facade building, and gamesmanship, mentioned in the earlier paragraph as resulting from fears, also tend to reduce the effectiveness of the communication system. With the presence of fear and the lack of trust, there is little encouragement for open exploration of one's own inner world of motivations and attitudes. People give off mixed messages: There is a difference between facial expression and verbal content, between tone of voice and what one says, between what one has courage enough to say in a subgroup and what one says publicly in the total group, and between what one says the first time and what one says when challenged to repeat or clarify the message. Thus, such differences further increase the distortion of data.

In low trust, a great number of concealing skills develop. People become adept at consciously or unconsciously withholding feelings. Especially in situations of actual or supposed power differences, the weaker person, the person lower in the hierarchy, or the person with the lowest status may deliberately treat a disliked person with great friendliness in order to cover his real negative feelings. Secretaries may develop complicated strategies for seeming busy. Using facades, bosses may camouflage favoritism or degrees of differential feelings about employees.

People spread rumors in order to test reactions. This feedback distortion is used to hurt others or to explore the depth of feeling. There are elaborate skills for learning one's way in the maze of distortion in the usual organization.

A common process which suppresses relevant information in the group is the ignoring of known or suspected experts. People are jealous of those with knowledge and are suspicious of their motives. The expert is frequently articulate and persuasive, so he overstates his case in an imposing manner and rebreeds resentment and resistance. Thus, there are many reasons why people with information are discouraged from sharing it.

Another source of distortion occurs because of inadequate methods of problem solving. In its early stages, the group seldom adequately defines the problem, and because problem definition may cause conflict, the participants find it safer to philosophize about nonpersonal items.

As the group develops, the members learn that it is possible to deal with many deep-seated feelings and concerns without undue fear and anxiety about being hurt. The participants discover that, although long-withheld feelings are sometimes disturbing to everyone present, the alternative of holding back the feelings has even worse consequences for the group. It becomes clear to the group that feelings can, in a genuine sense, be integrated into work, creativity, and problem solving.

Effective groups, with development, are able to develop consensual decision-making about significant problems that the group faces. This is the payoff of data processing and the feedback system of the group.

Goal Formation and Productivity

Group health is related to the integration of group goals. Unhealthy groups are unable to decide what they want to be or want to do. Lacking an adequate system of communication, members may not know that they, as a group, are not doing what they want to do. The difficulties in goal formation arise rather directly from partial data processing, which in turn grows out of fear and distrust. When members distrust the motivations of other members, it is difficult to share goals in a meaningful way. The problem that the group faces is somehow to create out of the available data a satisfying goal which would adequately include the real goals of the members and which would be more fulfilling than any of the half-verbalized goals that the individuals have.

One of the early errors that groups make is to force the expression of a few goals that come "off the top of the head," separate these into some alternatives, and then vote on a goal. This process necessitates a compromise, so that participants often feel that they are now doing something less satisfying than they would have done alone. They say that they are going along to satisfy others, to appear flexible, to avoid being seen as stubborn or rebellious, and to please authorities. In our early research, we found a high "reservation score" in early stages of group growth; that is, a large number of members were seen by the rest of the group as consenting, but were found (when data were later gathered by better means such as depth interviews) to have a number of unverbalized reservations about the decisions that had been made by the group (Gibb, 1963).

Coercion and Resistance

One error made by unhealthy groups is the attempt to impose control mechanisms and to verbalize public goals before the group has worked through its fears and data-processing problems. Verbal, anxious, or dominant people are prone to do this. For various reasons, weak, uninterested, or nonverbal individuals often go along with these coercive members. Members combat persuasion by using various forms of resistance, often little understood by the high persuaders. Thus, members, consciously or not, will be withdrawn and apathetic and will show a low commitment to verbalize any goals. Then, too, there are those who really do not know what they want to do. Perhaps because they have so often gone along with persuasive or dynamic leadership, they have never developed the capacity to examine their own goals and plan life activities that will accomplish these aims.

One of the first tasks in training groups or teams in natural situations is to learn to examine the motivations of individuals. This may be a lengthy task, calling for long-dormant skills and feelings. The general stagnation of self and the lack of personal identity in our withdrawn culture are evident in immature groups. In the developing group, members can seek their identity; they can learn to explore previously half-formulated desires, repressed wishes, and formerly unrealizable goals in an atmosphere of trust and listening. Sharpening of this inner quest takes place in the caring group.

The apparent reverse of apathy is a condition of frenetic work of tasks that the group uses to respond to duty motivations, loyalty to the organization, compulsive needs, and the desire to prove to themselves and to others that they can work hard. This busywork can easily be misunderstood and seen as productive or creative work.

Public Goals and Real Goals

A common error is the declaring of public "motherhood-and-the-flag" kinds of goals. There is no real commitment to these goals, and they are used as a cover-up. Learning groups, for instance, will set up as a goal a two-hour discussion of foremen training because this seems like something that the company would want or that the group should be interested in. In reality, though, the people come to the meeting to complain about the company, air personal grudges, or get a vacation, or because of a whole variety of motivations that are unrelated to the public statement.

When a group of people have worked through the fear, trust, and data-flow problems to the point where they can communicate in high trust or "speak the truth in love," it is possible to work to a reasonable consensus on major problems of goal formation and decisionmaking.

The members integrate tasks, groups, and individual goals. (We are assuming that all people are achievement-motivated and that work, when self-determined, is intrinsically satisfying.) In order for personal and group needs to be met, the group must select a task and make some kind of visible progress toward accomplishing it. In effective groups, esprit de corps, individual satisfaction over group achievement, and commitment to the group are vital. Group members must also feel some sense of belonging, fulfillment, self-worth, influence, and linkage to whatever goals are currently important to them as individuals. As high trust and a valid communication system develop, it becomes possible to mesh these needs in satisfying ways without undue group pressures to conform for the sake of conformity. The creation of this state of affairs gives people a sense of freedom.

A well-known vice-president of one of America's largest corporations once said, after observing a T-group in a highly cooperative session, that he had never seen a group in which people listened to one another so deeply and were so well able to integrate what they said into a creative and satisfying discussion. He was so impressed that he had a deep emotional experience just observing the session! A minister stated, after spending a day in such a group, "This is the first time that I have ever really had a religious experience!" When the average organization works at from 20 to 40 percent effectiveness, it is a dramatic and memorable occasion to see a group working at a 70 percent efficiency level. Those of us who have seen participative groups in action, both in training and in the natural organizational setting, are aware of the exciting and awesome potential of people who are engaged in creative interaction on group-initiated tasks. Group actualization occurs with the productive integration of deeply personal needs into a genuine consensus on goals. The group continues to form goals that are a creative synthesis of personal goals—new, exciting, and fulfilling (Gibb, 1961a; Gibb, 1965).

Control Systems and Organization

Most all of us in the process of socialization develop authority and influence problems that stem from our early relations with our parents and teachers. When a group of people meets in the early stages, problems of mutual influence become immediately visible to the observer and to the more sensitive members. This is true of all groups, whether their purpose is work or recreation. Distrust, distorted communication, and imposed or ambiguous goals tend to make these feelings more severe and to limit growth.

One of our T-groups, composed of upper-middle management people from governmental, industrial, educational, and religious organizations, was discussing what seemed to be an innocent problem of whether or not to take a coffee break. The issue was brought up by a member in the first three minutes of the opening session as an apparently harmless and minor goal. The member's proposal was followed by a few, apparently frivolous, comments about the absence of cream, some mild

wishes for tea, some weak resistance to taking time from the group for an unnecessary break, a few jokes, and laughter. This then led a few of the more vigorous members to try to push for a quick decision. These tactics snowballed into a mild resistance, and a long conversation developed. The discussion became more heated and continued for two hours and twenty minutes, until the group was actually late for lunch and yet still deadlocked about whether to waste time taking a morning coffee break! People shouted, developed hurt feelings, withdrew occasionally to sulk, and argued violently about apparently trivial issues. The group broke up at someone's suggestion and went to lunch. After lunch, one of the observers interpreted the discussion as a power struggle. This meaning was violently rejected by those engaged in the fight, but three days later, the group laughed together in recognition that it had been just that.

In undeveloped groups we often see such camouflaged and displaced battles for power and authority. Members are aware to various degrees of these interpersonal feelings in themselves and others. When communication and trust are low and facades are high, people pretend that there is no struggle, that the argument is "purely intellectual," that mixed feelings toward powerful members are inevitable and nonintrusive, and that there is nothing they can do about the matter.

Feelings of Impotence

A sense of powerlessness or impotence is a dominant characteristic of the early life of groups. Because people seldom listen, because the group has a difficult time finding a satisfying direction, and for a number of other reasons explored above, individuals in the group feel that it is very difficult to influence other individuals or "the group." Both the quiet and the talkative people have these feelings.

Resistance to induction takes many forms. The aggressive, high initiators are responded to with apathy or passive listening. Persuasion leads to resistance. Quiet, low-status, mild people are often ignored and thought to be idealists or un-interested in initiation. A recent study in-dicated that, in general, during the early stages of group life, members thought that unusually restrained people were stupid, uninterested, afraid, or lazy! Another fac-tor that leads to the feeling of powerless-ness is the tendency of people, especially during the early fear and distrust stages, to be suspicious of the motivations of other people. Thus, our study indicated that quiet members thought that the ag-gressive members were insecure, manipu-lative, domineering, and showing off their knowledge! It is also true that some of the noninitiators saw the initiators as helpful, full of ideas, and courageous. Some of the talkative members saw quiet individuals as good listeners, flexible, and courteous. As people trust and communicate better, the initiators are more apt to be seen as wanting to help, and the quiet members are more apt to be seen as receptive lis-teners. Ironically, in early stages the same behavior is viewed as dominance, manipu-lation, or uninterested resistance (Gibb, 1959; Gibb, 1961b; Gibb, 1964).

When people are afraid and feel power-less to influence their own important de-velopment or goal setting, they try to sway the group in a number of ways. People may not wish to admit to themselves or to the other members of the group that they do desire to influence, because this unrelieved need for power, as such, is looked down on in our aspiring-to-be-democratic society. Direct influence ef-forts are fairly easy to deal with, but cam-ouflaged or devious attempts are more difficult for the group to examine and handle. Covert strategies are used by in-dividuals with varying degrees of con-sciousness. Some may deliberately try to use strategies and manipulative gimmicks. Others may unconsciously use tricky means of getting their way (Gibb, 1961a).

Sometimes the opposition may be con-scious and take the form of strategies such as appointing committees, using par-liamentary maneuvers, calling for a sum-mary, or apparently innocent or useful list making, in order to prevent an impending decision that is being pushed by a person who is thought to be seeking power.

Desires to influence are apparently characteristic of all of us. These needs are troublesome only when they are covered up and are thus difficult for the group to handle or when they are denied (although overpowering because of fear and anx-iety), so that the group cannot deal with the behavior for what it is. The wish to influence and be influenced is a produc-tive and creative one and is necessary for group growth.

The Fear of Uncontrolled Groups

Groups in early stages of development seem unmanageable. This gives rise to the feeling that special procedures are neces-sary to control the group. The organiza-tion tries rules, regulations, appointed leaders, span of control, parliamentary procedure, channels of communication, tight organization, and "articles of war" formally to control the behavior of people in groups. It seems to members that it would be unthinkable for the group to operate without strong formal leadership and regulations. Thus, tight controls arise which tend to be self-deceiving. People resist the rules by various forms of dis-placed rebellion, by apathy, or by a kind of unimaginative obedience. Conflict, spontaneity, and vigorous interplay are all productive in a high-trust and high-feedback situation. These factors, how-ever, produce disruptions and unproduc-tive organizations in a low-trust and low-feedback condition.

Another state of affairs characteristic of the early stages of group life and related to control and organization may be the calm of the orderly, obedient, peace-at-any-price atmosphere. The deadly polite-ness may be interpreted by members or observers as productive work. "Sweetness and light" can be a cover-up for the group's uncertainty about the handling of the control and authority problems.

Permissiveness is another uncertain

concept in this connection. What is called "permissiveness" may be many things. In low-trust and low-communication groups, it may be a kind of unrelated, undigestible disorder in which people look as if they are doing what they want to do, but are in fact responding to impulse, play, and resistance. Lacking formal leadership, the group is thus confused and structureless. Permissiveness in high-trust, high-feedback groups can be realized in exciting, spontaneous, and playful integration of creative efforts in the group. Opponents of permissiveness are thinking about low-trust groups, while the advocates of permissiveness are thinking about the high-trust situation that occurs in the relatively well-developed group.

It has been our observation that developed groups can operate in a leaderless situation without formal, prepared agenda, without organizational coercion in the formal sense, and without the parliamentary procedures which are thought to make decisionmaking easier.

Extrinsic Solutions to Group Problems

Because of low trust and low communication, groups have invented mechanisms for solving the problems on these four dimensions. A legal system of formal laws has been invented to solve the fear and distrust problem. Membership requirements such as college entrance examinations and racial and religious codes for housing, clubs, and jobs have been developed.

A great many mechanisms have been produced to solve the low-communication, poor-data-flow problems. Communication channels are organized. Parliamentary procedures which guarantee minimal opportunity for people to talk are set up. Formal rules for making decisions by majority votes are used. Company newspapers, written memoranda, multiple copy systems, and many tools of the communications and public relations profession have arisen.

Various mechanisms are devised during the early stages of group development to solve the passivity toward the goal-formation dimension. Most of these involve the artificial creation of motivation by extrinsic reward systems: competition, grades, piecework, and praise and merit systems.

All these mechanisms are control systems which arise as a result of recognition of membership, decision, and motivation problems. Mechanisms for handling control problems, of course, are also used. Rules of way, bargaining contracts, codes of gentlemen, punishments for nonconformity, formal job prescriptions, and tables of organizations are all examples. As groups grow, the necessity for these formal control systems disappears.

Conflict

Conflicts will occur in living and in active and creative people. Resolving the conflict, by finding alternatives that are creative solutions rather than deadening compromises, can be a productive process. The motivation to build something new can come from the dissatisfaction revealed by the discord. The deliberate creation of conflict is likely to occur in the early stages of group development, when frantic leaders have no other way for creating excitement or when playful members are bored. However, when conflict does exist, the best way to handle it is to look at it and resolve it. The mature group is able to do this. A process analysis of the way the conflict arose and was solved is potentially meaningful and is likely to be cathartic. The aftermath of conflict can also be productive. People can learn about themselves, about the group, and about the reality of the world by the way that they, as individuals or as a group, have handled the discord.

Conclusion

Groups are often unhealthy and add little to the lives of their members. Such groups might well be discontinued or certainly changed. Grouping can become a fetish, and many groups are preserved long beyond their day. As we have seen, signs of ill health include undue fear and distrust, inadequate and distorted communication, undigested and dysfunctional goal systems, and unresolved dependency problems.

Groups *can* be healthy. Groups can be creative, fulfilling, and satisfying to all their members. We have seen groups that can be appropriately described as actualizing. Such groups develop a high degree of trust, valid communication in depth, a consensual goal system, and a genuine interdependence. Our research has shown promising data that provide a way for therapists, parents, managers, and teachers to aid in the process of creating groups which are in themselves healthy organisms and which provide a climate for member growth and fulfillment (Gibb, 1964; Gibb, 1965). It is such groups that can provide the framework for a better world.

References

J. R. Gibb, "Factors Producing Defensive Behavior Within Groups, II," *Annual Technical Report, Office of Naval Research,* Contract Nonr–1147(03), NR 170–226, 1955.

J. R. Gibb, "Factors Producing Defensive Behavior Within Groups, VI," *Final Technical Report, Office of Naval Research,* Contract Nonr–2285(01), 1959.

J. R. Gibb, "Defensive Communication," *Journal of Communication* 11 (1961): 141–48. (a)

J. R. Gibb, "Defense Level and Influence Potential in Small Groups." In L. Petrullo and B. M. Bass, eds., *Leadership and Interpersonal Behavior* (New York: Holt, Rinehart & Winston, Inc., 1961), pp. 66–81. (b)

J. R. Gibb, "Factors Producing Defensive Behavior Within Groups, VII," *Final Technical Report, Office of Naval Research,* Contract Nonr–3088(00), 1963.

J. R. Gibb, "Climate for Trust Formation." In L. P. Bradford, J. R. Gibb, and K. D. Benne, eds., *T-Group Theory and Laboratory Method* (New York: John Wiley & Sons, Inc., 1964), pp. 279–309.

J. R. Gibb, "Fear and Facade: Defensive Management." In R. E. Farson, ed., *Science and Human Affairs* (Palo Alto, Calif.: Science & Behavior Books, Inc., 1965), pp. 197–214.

Marie Jahoda, *Current Concepts of Positive Mental Health,* a report by the Joint Commission on Mental Illness and Health (New York: Basic Books, Inc., Publishers, 1958).

Notes

1. Since 1951, the authors have conducted a series of experimental and field studies designed to investigate longitudinal changes in small groups, particularly as these changes are associated with the arousal and maintenance of defensive or productive behavior. These studies were financed mainly by a series of grants from the Group Psychology Branch of the Office of Naval Research.
2. The burgeoning area of group life is dealt with from several perspectives in . . . [the] book: See Haigh (Chapter 22), Thomas (Chapter 23), Shapiro (Chapter 24), Clark (Chapter 27), and Rogers (Chapter 28).
3. See a helpful analysis of contemporary agreement and disagreement on criteria of personal growth in Jahoda (1958).

Chapter 5   Organizational Environments and Adaptation

THE CAUSAL TEXTURE
OF ORGANIZATIONAL ENVIRONMENTS[1]

F. E. Emery and E. L. Trist

Identification of the Problem

A main problem in the study of organizational change is that the environmental contexts in which organizations exist are themselves changing, at an increasing rate, and towards increasing complexity. This point, in itself, scarcely needs laboring. Nevertheless, the characteristics of organizational environments demand consideration for their own sake, if there is to be an advancement of understanding in the behavioral sciences of a great deal that is taking place under the impact of technological change, especially at the present time. This paper is offered as a brief attempt to open up some of the problems, and stems from a belief that progress will be quicker if a certain extension can be made to current thinking about systems.

In a general way, it may be said that to think in terms of systems seems the most appropriate conceptual response so far available when the phenomena under study—at any level and in any domain—display the character of being organized, and when understanding the nature of the interdependencies constitutes the research task. In the behavioral sciences, the first steps in building a systems theory were taken in connection with the analysis of internal processes in organisms, or organizations, when the parts had to be related to the whole. Examples include the organismic biology of Jennings, Cannon, and Henderson; early Gestalt theory and its later derivatives such as balance theory; and the classical theories of social structure. Many of these problems could be represented in closed-system models. The next steps were taken when wholes had to be related to their environments. This led to open-system models.

A great deal of the thinking here has been influenced by cybernetics and information theory, though this has been used as much to extend the scope of closed-system as to improve the sophistication of open-system formulations. It was von Bertalanffy (1950) who, in terms of the general transport equation which he introduced, first fully disclosed the importance of openness or closedness to the environment as a means of distinguishing living organisms from inanimate objects. In contradistinction to physical objects, any living entity survives by importing into itself certain types of material from its environment, transforming these in accordance with its own system characteristics, and exporting other types back into the environment. By this process the organism obtains the additional energy that renders it "negentropic"; it becomes capable of attaining stability in a time-independent steady state—a necessary condition of adaptability to environmental variance.

Such steady states are very different affairs from the equilibrium states described in classical physics, which have far too often been taken as models for representing biological and social transactions. Equilibrium states follow the second law of thermodynamics, so that no work can

141

be done when equilibrium is reached, whereas the openness to the environment of a steady state maintains the capacity of the organism for work, without which adaptability, and hence survival, would be impossible.

Many corollaries follow as regards the properties of open systems, such as equifinality, growth through internal elaboration, self-regulation, constancy of direction with change of position, etc.—and by no means all of these have yet been worked out. But though von Bertalanffy's formulation enables exchange processes between the organism, or organization, and elements in its environment to be dealt with in a new perspective, it does not deal at all with those processes in the environment itself which are among the determining conditions of the exchanges. To analyze these an additional concept is needed—*the causal texture of the environment*—if we may reintroduce, at a social level of analysis, a term suggested by Tolman and Brunswik (1935) and drawn from S. C. Pepper (1934).

With this addition, we may now state the following general proposition: that a comprehensive understanding of organizational behavior requires some knowledge of each member of the following set, where L indicates some potentially lawful connection, and the suffix 1 refers to the organization and the suffix 2 to the environment:

$$L_{1\,1}, \ L_{1\,2}$$
$$L_{2\,1}, \ L_{2\,2}$$

$L_{1\,1}$ here refers to processes within the organization—the area of internal interdependencies; $L_{1\,2}$ and $L_{2\,1}$ to exchanges between the organization and its environment—the area of transactional interdependencies, from either direction; and $L_{2\,2}$ to processes through which parts of the environment become related to each other—in other words, its causal texture—the area of interdependencies that belong within the environment itself.

In considering environmental interdependencies, the first point to which we wish to draw attention is that the laws connecting parts of the environment to each other are often incommensurate with those connecting parts of the organization to each other, or even with those which govern the exchanges. It is not possible, for example, always to reduce organization-environment relations to the form of "being included in"; boundaries are also "break" points. As Barker and Wright (1949), following Lewin (1936), have pointed out in their analysis of this problem as it affects psychological ecology, we may lawfully connect the actions of a javelin thrower in sighting and throwing his weapon; but we cannot describe in the same concepts the course of the javelin as this is affected by variables lawfully linked by meteorological and other systems.

The Development of Environmental Connectedness (Case 1)

A case history, taken from the industrial field, may serve to illustrate what is meant by the environment becoming organized at the social level. It will show how a greater degree of system-connectedness, of crucial relevance to the organization, may develop in the environment, which is yet not directly a function either of the organization's own characteristics or of its immediate relations. Both of these, of course, once again become crucial when the response of the organization to what has been happening is considered.

The company concerned was the foremost in its particular market in the food-canning industry in the United Kingdom and belonged to a large parent group. Its main product—a canned vegetable—had some 65 percent of this market, a situation which had been relatively stable since before the war. Believing it would continue to hold this position, the company persuaded the group board to invest several million pounds sterling in erecting a new, automated factory, which, however, based its economies on an inbuilt rigidity—it was set up exclusively for the long runs expected from the traditional market.

The character of the environment, however, began to change while the factory was being built. A number of small canning firms appeared, not dealing with this product nor indeed with others in the company's range, but with imported fruits. These firms arose because the last of the postwar controls had been removed from steel strip and tin, and cheaper cans could now be obtained in any numbers— while at the same time a larger market was developing in imported fruits. This trade being seasonal, the firms were anxious to find a way of using their machinery and retaining their labor in winter. They became able to do so through a curious side effect of the development of quick-frozen foods, when the company's staple was produced by others in this form. The quick-freezing process demanded great constancy at the growing end. It was not possible to control this beyond a certain point, so that quite large crops unsuitable for quick freezing but suitable for canning became available— originally from another country (the United States) where a large market for quick-frozen foods had been established. These surplus crops had been sold at a very low price for animal feed. They were now imported by the small canners—at a better but still comparatively low price, and additional cheap supplies soon began to be procurable from underdeveloped countries.

Before the introduction of the quick-freezing form, the company's own canned product—whose raw material had been specially grown at additional cost—had been the premier brand, superior to other varieties and charged at a higher price. But its position in the product spectrum now changed. With the increasing affluence of the society, more people were able to afford the quick-frozen form. Moreover, there was competition from a great many other vegetable products which could substitute for the staple, and people preferred this greater variety. The advantage of being the premier line among canned forms diminished, and demand increased both for the not-so-expensive varieties among them and for the quick-frozen forms. At the same time, major changes were taking place in retailing; supermarkets were developing, and more and more large grocery chains were coming into existence. These establishments wanted to sell certain types of goods under their own house names, and began to place bulk orders with the small canners for their own varieties of the company's staple that fell within this class. As the small canners provided an extremely cheap article (having no marketing expenses and a cheaper raw material), they could undercut the manufacturers' branded product, and within three years they captured over 50 percent of the market. Previously, retailers' varieties had accounted for less than 1 percent.

The new automatic factory could not be adapted to the new situation until alternative products with a big sales volume could be developed, and the scale of research and development, based on the type of market analysis required to identify these, was beyond the scope of the existing resources of the company either in people or in funds.

The changed texture of the environment was not recognized by an able but traditional management until it was too late. They failed entirely to appreciate that a number of outside events were becoming connected with each other in a way that was leading up to irreversible general change. Their first reaction was to make a herculean effort to defend the traditional product, then the board split on whether or not to make entry into the cheaper unbranded market in a supplier role. Group H.Q. now felt they had no option but to step in, and many upheavals and changes in management took place until a "redefinition of mission" was agreed, and slowly and painfully the company reemerged with a very much altered product mix and something of a new identity.

Four Types of Causal Texture

It was this experience, and a number of others not dissimilar, by no means all of them industrial (and including studies of change problems in hospitals, in prisons, and in educational and political organizations), that gradually led us to feel a need for redirecting conceptual attention to the causal texture of the environment, considered as a quasi-independent domain. We have now isolated four "ideal types" of causal texture, approximations to which may be thought of as existing simultaneously in the "real world" of most organizations—though, of course, their weighting will vary enormously from case to case.

The first three of these types have already, and indeed repeatedly, been described—in a large variety of terms and with the emphasis on an equally bewildering variety of special aspects—in the literature of a number of disciplines, ranging from biology to economics and including military theory as well as psychology and sociology. The fourth type, however, is new, at least to us, and is the one that for some time we have been endeavoring to identify. About the first three, therefore, we can be brief, but the fourth is scarcely understandable without reference to them. Together, the four types may be said to form a series in which the degree of causal texturing is increased, in a new and significant way, as each step is taken. We leave as an open question the need for further steps.

Step One

The simplest type of environmental texture is that in which goals and noxiants ("goods" and "bads") are relatively unchanging in themselves and randomly distributed. This may be called the *placid, randomized environment.* It corresponds to Simon's idea of a surface over which an organism can locomote: Most of this is bare, but at isolated, widely scattered points there are little heaps of food (1957, p.137). It also corresponds to Ashby's limiting case of no connection between the environmental parts (1960, S15/4); and to Schutzenberger's random field (1954, p.

100). The economist's classical market also corresponds to this type.

A critical property of organizational response under random conditions has been stated by Schutzenberger: that there is no distinction between tactics and strategy, "the optimal strategy is just the simple tactic of attempting to do one's best on a purely local basis" (1954, p. 101). The best tactic, moreover, can be learned only by trial and error and only for a particular class of local environmental variances (Ashby, 1960, p. 197). While organizations under these conditions can exist adaptively as single and indeed quite small units, this becomes progressively more difficult under the other types.

Step Two

More complicated, but still a placid environment, is that which can be characterized in terms of clustering: Goals and noxiants are not randomly distributed but hang together in certain ways. This may be called the *placid, clustered environment,* and is the case with which Tolman and Brunswik were concerned; it corresponds to Ashby's "serial system" and to the economist's "imperfect competition." The clustering enables some parts to take on roles as signs of other parts or become means-objects with respect to approaching or avoiding. Survival, however, becomes precarious if an organization attempts to deal tactically with each environmental variance as it occurs.

The new feature of organizational response to this kind of environment is the emergence of strategy as distinct from tactics. Survival becomes critically linked with what an organization knows of its environment. To pursue a goal under its nose may lead it into parts of the field fraught with danger, while avoidance of an immediately difficult issue may lead it away from potentially rewarding areas. In the clustered environment the relevant objective is that of "optimal location," some positions being discernible as potentially richer than others.

To reach these requires concentration

of resources, subordination to the main plan, and the development of a "distinctive competence," to use Selznick's (1957) term, in reaching the strategic objective. Organizations under these conditions, therefore, tend to grow in size and also to become hierarchical, with a tendency towards centralized control and coordination.

Step Three

The next level of causal texturing we have called the *disturbed-reactive environment*. It may be compared with Ashby's ultrastable system or the economist's oligopolic market. It is a type 2 environment in which there is more than one organization of the same kind; indeed, the existence of a number of similar organizations now becomes the dominant characteristic of the environmental field. Each organization does not simply have to take account of the others when they meet at random, but has also to consider that what it knows can also be known by the others. The part of the environment to which it wishes to move itself in the long run is also the part to which the others seek to move. Knowing this, each will wish to improve its own chances by hindering the others, and each will know that the others must not only wish to do likewise, but also know that each knows this. The presence of similar others creates an imbrication, to use a term of Chein's (1943), of some of the causal strands in the environment.

If strategy is a matter of selecting the "strategic objective"—where one wishes to be at a future time—and tactics a matter of selecting an immediate action from one's available repertoire, then there appears in type 3 environments to be an intermediate level of organizational response—that of the *operation*—to use the term adopted by German and Soviet military theorists, who formally distinguish tactics, operations, and strategy. One has now not only to make sequential choices, but to choose actions that will draw off the other organizations. The new element

is that of deciding which of someone else's possible tactics one wishes to take place, while ensuring that others of them do not. An operation consists of a campaign involving a planned series of tactical initiatives, calculated reactions by others, and counteractions. The flexibility required encourages a certain decentralization and also puts a premium on quality and speed of decision at various peripheral points (Heyworth, 1955).

It now becomes necessary to define the organizational objective in terms not so much of location as of capacity or power to move more or less at will, in other words, to be able to make and meet competitive challenge. This gives particular relevance to strategies of absorption and parasitism. It can also give rise to situations in which stability can be obtained only by a certain coming-to-terms between competitors, whether enterprises, interest groups, or governments. One has to know when not to fight to the death.

Step Four

Yet more complex are the environments we have called *turbulent fields*. In these, dynamic processes, which create significant variances for the component organizations, arise from the field itself. Like type 3 and unlike the static types 1 and 2, they are dynamic. Unlike type 3, the dynamic properties arise not simply from the interaction of the component organizations, but also from the field itself. The "ground" is in motion.

Three trends contribute to the emergence of these dynamic field forces:

1) The growth to meet type 3 conditions of organizations, and linked sets of organizations, so large that their actions are both persistent and strong enough to induce autochthonous processes in the environment. An analogous effect would be that of a company of soldiers marching in step over a bridge.

2) The deepening interdependence between the economic and the other

facets of the society. This means that economic organizations are increasingly enmeshed in legislation and public regulation.

3) The increasing reliance on research and development to achieve the capacity to meet competitive challenge. This leads to a situation in which a change gradient is continuously present in the environmental field.

For organizations, these trends mean a gross increase in their area of *relevant uncertainty*. The consequences which flow from their actions lead off in ways that become increasingly unpredictable: They do not necessarily fall off with distance, but may at any point be amplified beyond all expectation; similarly, lines of action that are strongly pursued may find themselves attenuated by emergent field forces.

The Salience of Type 4 Characteristics (Case 2)

Some of these effects are apparent in what happened to the canning company of case 1, whose situation represents a transition from an environment largely composed of type 2 and type 3 characteristics to one where those of type 4 began to gain in salience. The case now to be presented illustrates the combined operation of the three trends described above in an altogether larger environmental field involving a total industry and its relations with the wider society.

The organization concerned is the National Farmers Union of Great Britain to which more than 200,000 of the 250,000 farmers of England and Wales belong. The presenting problem brought to us for investigation was that of communications. Headquarters felt, and was deemed to be, out of touch with county branches, and these with local branches. The farmer had looked to the N.F.U. very largely to protect him against market fluctuations by negotiating a comprehensive deal with the government at annual reviews concerned with the level of price support. These re-

views had enabled home agriculture to maintain a steady state during two decades when the threat, or existence, of war in relation to the type of military technology then in being had made it imperative to maintain a high level of homegrown food without increasing prices to the consumer. This policy, however, was becoming obsolete as the conditions of thermonuclear stalemate established themselves. A level of support could no longer be counted upon which would keep in existence small and inefficient farmers—often on marginal land and dependent on family labor—compared with efficient medium-size farms, to say nothing of large and highly mechanized undertakings.

Yet it was the former situation which had produced N.F.U. cohesion. As this situation receded, not only were farmers becoming exposed to more competition from each other, as well as from Commonwealth and European farmers, but the effects were being felt of very great changes which had been taking place on both the supply and marketing sides of the industry. On the supply side, a small number of giant firms now supplied almost all the requirements in fertilizer, machinery, seeds, veterinary products, etc. As efficient farming depended upon ever greater utilization of these resources, their controllers exerted correspondingly greater power over the farmers. Even more dramatic were the changes in the marketing of farm produce. Highly organized food processing and distributing industries had grown up dominated again by a few large firms, on contracts from which (fashioned to suit their rather than his interests) the farmer was becoming increasingly dependent. From both sides deep inroads were being made on his autonomy.

It became clear that the source of the felt difficulty about communications lay in radical environmental changes which were confronting the organization with problems it was ill-adapted to meet. Communications about these changes were being interpreted or acted upon as if they referred to the "traditional" situation. Only through a parallel analysis of the environment and the N.F.U. was provress made towards developing understanding on the basis of which attempts to devise adaptive organizational policies and forms could be made. Not least among the problems was that of creating a bureaucratic elite that could cope with the highly technical long-range planning now required and yet remain loyal to the democratic values of the N.F.U. Equally difficult was that of developing mediating institutions—agencies that would effectively mediate the relations between agriculture and other economic sectors without triggering off massive competitive processes.

These environmental changes and the organizational crisis they induced were fully apparent two or three years before the question of Britain's possible entry into the Common Market first appeared on the political agenda—which, of course, further complicated every issue.

A workable solution needed to preserve reasonable autonomy for the farmers as an occupational group, while meeting the interests of other sections of the community. Any such possibility depended on securing the consent of the large majority of farmers to placing under some degree of N.F.U. control matters that hitherto had remained within their own power of decision. These included what they produced, how and to what standard, and how most of it should be marketed. Such thoughts were anathema, for however dependent the farmer had grown on the N.F.U. he also remained intensely individualistic. He was being asked, he now felt, to redefine his indentity, reverse his basic values, and refashion his organization—all at the same time. It is scarcely surprising that progress has been, and remains, both fitful and slow, and hidden with conflict.

Values and Relevant Uncertainty

What becomes precarious under type 4 conditions is how organizational stability can be achieved. In these environments individual organizations, however large, cannot expect to adapt successfully simply through their own direct actions—as is evident in the case of the N.F.U. Nevertheless, there are some indications of a solution that may have the same general significance for these environments as have strategy and operations for types 2 and 3. This is the emergence of *values that have overriding significance for all members of the field.* Social values are here regarded as coping mechanisms that make it possible to deal with persisting areas of relevant uncertainty. Unable to trace out the consequences of their actions as these are amplified and resonated through their extended social fields, men in all societies have sought rules, sometimes categorical, such as the ten commandments, to provide them with a guide and ready calculus. Values are not strategies or tactics; as Lewin (1936) has pointed out, they have the conceptual character of "power fields" and act as injunctions.

So far as effective values emerge, the character of richly joined, turbulent fields changes in a most striking fashion. The relevance of large classes of events no longer has to be sought in an intricate mesh of diverging causal strands, but is given directly in the ethical code. By this transformation a field is created which is no longer richly joined and turbulent but simplified and relatively static. Such a transformation will be regressive, or constructively adaptative, according to how far the emergent values adequately represent the new environmental requirements.

Ashby, as a biologist, has stated his view, on the one hand, that examples of environments that are both large and richly connected are not common, for our terrestrial environment is widely characterized by being highly subdivided (1960, p. 205); and, on the other, that, so far as they are encountered, they may well be beyond the limits of human adaptation, the brain being an ultrastable system. By contrast the role here attributed to social values suggests that this sort of environment may in fact be not only one to which adaptation is possible, however difficult, but one that has been increasingly characteristic of the human condition since the beginning of settled communities. Also, let us not forget that values can be rational as well as irrational and that the rationality of their rationale is likely to become more powerful as the scientific ethos takes greater hold in a society.

Matrix Organization And Institutional Success

Nevertheless, turbulent fields demand some overall form of organization that is essentially different from the hierarchically structured forms to which we are accustomed. Whereas type 3 environments require one or an other form of accomodation between like, but competitive, organizations whose fates are to a degree negatively correlated, turbulent environments require some relationship between dissimilar organizations whose fates are, basically, positively correlated. This means relationships that will maximize cooperation and which recognize that no one organization can take over the role of "the other" and become paramount. We are inclined to speak of this type of relationship as an *organizational matrix.* Such a matrix acts in the first place by delimiting on value criteria the character of what may be included in the field specified— and therefore who. This selectivity then enables some definable shape to be worked out without recourse to much in the way of formal hierarchy among members. Professional associations provide one model of which there has been long experience.

We do not suggest that in other fields than the professional the requisite sanctioning can be provided only by state-controlled bodies. Indeed, the reverse is far more likely. Nor do we suggest that organizational matrices will function so as to eliminate the need for other measures to achieve stability. As with values, matrix organizations, even if successful, will only help to transform turbulent environ-

ments into the kinds of environment we have discussed as "clustered" and "disturbed-reactive." Though, with these transformations, an organization could hope to achieve a degree of stability through its strategies, operation, and tactics, the transformations would not provide environments identical with the originals. The strategic objective in the transformed cases could no longer be stated simply in terms of optimal location (as in type 2) or capabilities (as in type 3). It must now rather be formulated in terms of *institutionalization.* According to Selznick (1957) organizations become institutions through the embodiment of organizational values which relate them to the wider society.[2] As Selznick has stated in his analysis of leadership in the modern American corporation, "the default of leadership shows itself in an acute form when *organizational* achievement or survival is confounded with *institutional success"* (1957, p. 27). " . . . the executive becomes a statesman as he makes the transition from administrative management to institutional leadership" (1957, p. 154).

The processes of strategic planning now also become modified. In so far as institutionalization becomes a prerequisite for stability, the determination of policy will necessitate not only a bias towards goals that are congruent with the organization's own character, but also a selection of goal-paths that offer maximum convergence as regards the interests of other parties. This became a central issue for the N.F.U. and is becoming one now for an organization such as the National Economic Development Council, which has the task of creating a matrix in which the British economy can function at something better than the stop-go level.

Such organizations arise from the need to meet problems emanating from type 4 environments. Unless this is recognized, they will only too easily be construed in type 3 terms, and attempts will be made to secure for them a degree of monolithic power that will be resisted overtly in democratic societies and covertly in others. In the one case they may be prevented from ever undertaking their missions; in the other one may wonder how long they can succeed in maintaining them.

An organizational matrix implies what McGregor (1960) has called Theory Y. This in turn implies a new set of values. But values are psychosocial commodities that come into existence only rather slowly. Very little systematic work has yet been done on the establishment of new systems of values, or on the type of critera that might be adduced to allow their effectiveness to be empirically tested. A pioneer attempt is that of Churchman and Ackoff (1950). Likert (1961) has suggested that, in the large corporation or government establishment, it may well take some ten to fifteen years before the new type of group values with which he is concerned could permeate the total organization. For a new set to permeate a whole modern society the time required must be much longer—at least a generation, according to the common saying—and this, indeed, must be a minimum. One may ask if this is fast enough, given the rate at which type 4 environments are becoming salient. A compelling task for social scientists is to direct more research onto these problems.

Summary

(a) A main problem in the study of organizational change is that the environmental contexts in which organizations exist are themselves changing—at an increasing rate, under the impact of technological change. This means that they demand consideration for their own sake. Towards this end a redefinition is offered, at a social level of analysis, of the causal texture of the environment, a concept introduced in 1935 by Tolman and Brunswik.

(b) This requires an extension of systems theory. The first steps in systems theory were taken in connection with the analysis of internal processes in organisms, or organizations, which involved relating parts to the whole. Most of these problems could be dealt with through closed-system models. The next steps were taken when wholes had to be related to their environments. This led to open-system models, such as that introduced by Bertalanffy, involving a general transport equation. Though this enables exchange processes between the organism, or organization, and elements in its environment to be dealt with, it does not deal with those processes in the environment itself which are the determining conditions of the exchanges. To analyze these an additional concept—the causal texture of the environment—is needed.

(c) The laws connecting parts of the environment to each other are often incommensurate with those connecting parts of the organization to each other, or even those which govern exchanges. Case history 1 illustrates this and shows the dangers and difficulties that arise when there is a rapid and gross increase in the area of relevant uncertainty, a characteristic feature of many contemporary environments.

(d) Organizational environments differ in their causal texture, both as regards degree of uncertainty and in many other important respects. A typology is suggested which identifies four "ideal types," approximations to which exist simultaneously in the "real world" of most organizations, though the weighting varies enormously:

1) In the simplest type, goals and noxiants are relatively unchanging in themselves and randomly distributed. This may be called the placid, randomized environment. A critical property from the organization's viewpoint is that there is no difference between tactics and strategy, and organizations can exist adaptively as single, and indeed quite small, units.

2) The next type is also static, but goals

and noxiants are not randomly distributed; they hang together in certain ways. This may be called the placid, clustered environment. Now the need arises for strategy as distinct from tactics. Under these conditions organizations grow in size, becoming multiple and tending towards centralized control and co-ordination.

3) The third type is dynamic rather than static. We call it the disturbed-reactive environment. It consists of a clustered environment in which there is more than one system of the same kind, in other words, the objects of one organization are the same as, or relevant to, others like it. Such competitors seek to improve their own changes by hindering each other, each knowing the others are playing the same game. Between strategy and tactics there emerges an intermediate type of organizational response—what military theorists refer to as operations. Control becomes more decentralized to allow these to be conducted. On the other hand, stability may require a certain coming-to-terms between competitors.

4) The fourth type is dynamic in a second respect, the dynamic properties arising not simply from the interaction of identifiable component systems but from the field itself (the "ground"). We call these environments turbulent fields. The turbulence results from the complexity and multiple character of the causal interconnections. individual organizations, however large, cannot adapt successfully simply through their direct interactions. An examination is made of the enhanced importance of values, regarded as a basic response to persisting areas of relevant uncertainty, as providing a control mechanism, when commonly held by all members in a field. This raises the question of organizational

forms based on the characteristics of a matrix.

(e) Case history 2 is presented to illustrate problems of the transition from type 3 to type 4. The perspective of the four environmental types is used to clarify the role of Theory X and Theory Y as representing a trend in value change. The establishment of a new set of values is a slow social process requiring something like a generation—unless new means can be developed.

References

W. Ross Ashby, *Design for a Brain* (London: Chapman & Hall, 1960).

R. G. Barker and H. F. Wright, "Psychological Ecology and the Problem of Psychosocial Development," *Child Development* 20 (1949): 131–43.

L. von Bertalanffy, "The Theory of Open Systems in Physics and Biology," *Science* 111 (1950): 23–29.

I. Chein, "Personality and Typology," *Journal of Social Psychology* 18 (1943): 89–101.

C. W. Churchman and R. L. Ackoff, *Methods of Inquiry* (Chicago: Educational Publishers, Inc., 1950).

C. W. Churchman and F. E. Emery, "On Various Approaches to the Study of Organizations," *Proceedings of the International Conference on Operational Research and the Social Sciences* (Cambridge, England: September 14–18, 1964). [Originally scheduled for publication] in book form as *Operational Research and the Social Sciences* (London: Tavistock Publications, 1965).

Lord Heyworth, *The Organization of Unilever* (London: Unilever Limited, 1955).

K. Lewin, *Principles of Topological Psychology* (New York: McGraw-Hill Book Company, 1936).

K. Lewin, *Field Theory in Social Science* (New York: Harper & Row, Publishers, 1951).

R. Likert, *New Patterns of Management* (New York: McGraw-Hill Book Company, 1961).

D. McGregor, *The Human Side of Enterprise* (New York: McGraw-Hill Book Company, 1960).

S. C. Pepper, "The Conceptual Framework of Tolman's Purposive Behaviorism," *Psychological Review* 41 (1934): 108–33.

M. P. Schutzenberger, "A Tentative Classification of Goal-Seeking Behaviors," *Journal of Mental Science* 100 (1954): 97–102.

P. Selznick, *Leadership in Administration* (New York: Harper & Row, Publishers, 1957).

H. A. Simon, *Models of Man* (New York: John Wiley & Sons, Inc., 1957).

E. C. Tolman and E. Brunswik, "The Organism and

the Causal Texture of the Environment," *Psychological Review* 42 (1935): 43–77.

Notes

1. A paper read at the 17th International Congress of Psychology, Washington, D.C., U.S.A., August 20–26, 1963. A French translation appeared in *Sociologie du Travail* (April 1964).

2. Since the present paper was presented, this line of thought has been further developed by Churchman and Emery (1964) in their discussion of the relation of the statistical aggregate of individuals to structured role sets: Like other values, organizational values emerge to cope with relevant uncertainties and gain their authority from their reference to the requirements of larger systems within which people's interests are largely concordant.

ORGANIZATION-ENVIRONMENT INTERFACE

Paul R. Lawrence and Jay W. Lorsch

It is no mystery that organizations must carry on transactions with their environment simply to survive, and, even more importantly, to grow. In the first chapter, we identified the quality of these transactions as posing one of the fundamental developmental problems of any organization. Other analysts of organizational affairs have consistently mentioned transactions with the environment as a crucial, if not the most crucial issue. It is an issue that has been dealt with extensively by economists and by specialists in business policy and strategy. They have dealt primarily with the content of these relationships—the actual kind and amount of goods, services, and funds that are part of these transactions. But the issue has not been extensively studied by specialists in the application of behavioral sciences, and attention has not been focused on such human aspects affecting the quality of these transactions as: What is the quality of the information exchanged across the organizational boundaries? What are the major determinants of the quality? What are its consequences?[1] Such questions have been asked many times of the relations between individuals and groups within the organization, but the boundary-spanning relations have simply not

been subjected to comparable scrutiny. It is not surprising therefore, that systematic efforts to diagnose and improve the quality of these organization-environment relations have also lagged behind the effort applied to improving internal relations. It is worth speculating about the reasons for this lack of attention.

Perhaps the focus has been placed on internal transactions because both parties to a faulty relation, being within the institution, tend to bring their troubles to a single source—their shared superior up the chain of command. This focuses attention on the costs of unsatisfactory work relations and triggers corrective action. There is less likelihood that this will happen in connection with boundary transactions. It is, moreover, not so easy to collect information about the status of the boundary-spanning relation since the outside participants may feel no obligation to cooperate. The relative neglect may also be due to the traditional division of labor between academic disciplines. It may be automatically assumed that economists are the experts on boundary transactions while the psychologist and the sociologist are expected to confine their efforts to internal relations. Even within business schools, it is traditional for the functional specialties, such as marketing and finance, to have exclusive concern with the quality of sales-man-customer and treasurer-banker relationships. Only recently have such specialists drawn on behavioral disciplines to aid them in the study of these matters.

The authors themselves became involved in the study and improvement of relations at this interface by approaching the topic through the back door. We had been concerned for some years with the quality of intergroup relations in organizations. This interest led us to the observation that major groups in industry displayed some distinctive characteristics that persisted in spite of efforts from top management toward consistency. We came to the conclusion that this persistence could be accounted for if these groups needed these characteristics to conduct favorable transactions with the segment of the firm's environment with which they were especially involved. So, in order to account for some important sources of intergroup conflict, we began to study each group's relations with its special segment of the environment. Our research findings tended strongly to confirm our theory. This, in turn, led us into a new interest not only in understanding these transactions from a behavioral standpoint, but also in helping organizations and their managers diagnose the quality of these relations and improve them.

The Certainty-Uncertainty Continuum

Our research findings with specific relevance to this interface can be quickly summarized. . . . We started our inquiry with the simple notion that the characteristics of an organizational unit would in some way need to match up with those of its segment of the environment if healthy transactional relations were to prevail. We were particularly interested in information flows across these boundaries. It seemed to us that if the sector of the environment

involved was a fairly steady, unchanging state, the amount and complexity of the information needed would be much less than if the opposite were true—namely, if there existed a high degree of uncertainty and change in the relevant part of the environment. As the environment varies along this certainty-uncertainty continuum, we expected to find matching differences in the organizational unit concerned if the transactions were to be sound. We identified four measurable features of groups that we thought might vary with the certainty-uncertainty of their parts of the environment. These were:

1) the degree of reliance on formalized rules and formal communication channels within the unit;
2) the time horizon of managers and professionals in the groups;
3) their orientation toward goals, either diffuse or concentrated; and
4 their interpersonal style, either relationship-or task-oriented.

Using measures of these four characteristics, we made a study of high-and low-performing companies in three different industries, and arrived at the specific conclusion that there was a closer fit in the high-performing organizations than in the low performers between the attributes of each unit and the demands of its relevant part of the environment.[2]

One way to visualize the meanings of these findings is to think again in terms of information flows. In order to relate effectively to its environment, any organization must have reasonably accurate and timely information about the environment and especially about environmental changes. This is clearly an easier job if the environment is relatively stable. The job can be specified in a predetermined set of operating rules. The necessary messages can be handled through the traditional superior-subordinate channels, which may be few and constricted but are probably less subject to error and relatively inexpensive. Fairly short time horizons are usually adequate to take account of the reactions of such an environment to the firm's actions. This makes it sensible to use a straightforward, task-oriented approach in managerial style.

On the other hand, life in an organizational unit must become more complex in order to deal adequately with an uncertain and rapidly changing sector of the environment. To have more points of contact with the environment, a flatter organization is employed. Formal rules cannot be formulated that will be suitable for any appreciable time period, so it seems better not to rely heavily on them. More of an all-to-all communications pattern is indicated, which can keep environmental clues moving throughout the unit for interpretation at all points instead of just through superior-subordinate channels. A longer time orientation is usually needed. The growth of this necessarily more complex and sophisticated (as well as more costly) communication network is fostered by an interpersonal style that emphasizes building strong relationships rather than just accomplishing the task, per se.

Stability Versus Change in the Environment

Securing and processing relevant information from the environment, while highly critical, is not the only requirement for high-quality transactions at the organization-environment interface. In addition to exchanging information, people at these interfaces must frequently negotiate the terms of exchange of tangible goods and less-tangible services of many kinds. These bargaining and/or problem-solving kinds of relationships can also be analyzed in terms of the findings of research. Fouraker has used his findings from experimental research to develop the idea that orgainzational units with different internal features are more or less effective depending upon whether their environment is characterized by harsh competition for scarce resources or by more beneficient circumstances.[3] In a relatively

unchanging environment, it is likely that time has brought more competitors into the struggle and that therefore resources are scarce. In this circumstance, he argues that the organizations which can conduct more favorable transactions will operate with tighter internal controls, more rules, and simpler channels of communication. In short, they will have closed ranks and geared up for a competitive fight. Again, it is a matching process.

At the other extreme is an organization unit dealing with a rapidly changing environment. The resources are plentiful and diverse, but the organization must be capable of creative and flexible problem-solving to discover potential opportunities for conducting more favorable transactions. Here again that unit will thrive which relies not on rules but on a more complex and flatter communication network which serves to stimulate new ideas. Such a unit would be oriented to a longer time perspective. It would thus be matched with the features of its environment as it works at solving the problem of defining and continually redefining the terms of its environmental transactions.

These, then, are the highlights of current research on the matching of organizational units with their respective sectors of the environment. Good matching seems to foster sound transactions at this organization-environment interface. In our research we studied this interface only for the important functions of sales, research, and production; but Table 1 (see p. 154) indicates how many additional interfaces of this type are relevant to most business organizations. Similar lists could be drawn for other types of organizations.

One of the ways of evolving an overall strategy for any organization is to develop within the organization the capacity to carry on fully adequate transactions at each of these important interfaces, with some special advantages in regard to one or two of them where a favorable exchange is possible. These are areas of "distinctive competence," to use Selznick's term.[4] An organization in which each of its boundary-spanning units is well matched

Table 1

Organizational Unit	Relevant Environmental Sector
Sales	Customers and competitors
Research	Science and technology
Production and engineering	Technology and equipment suppliers
Purchasing	Suppliers
Finance	Financial institutions
Personnel	Labor and professional markets
Public relations	The press and legislative bodies
Legal	Governmental regulatory agencies

with its corresponding environmental sector is in a desirable position to detect opportunities for new kinds of favorable transactions with the environment and to anticipate newly developing hazards in the environment. This matching process is a highly flexible way to maintain the kind of continuous search that is recommended by a pioneering study recently conducted by Aguilar on how business firms scan their relevant environments.[5]

As the relevant environment changes, however, organizations not only need suitable matched units, but on occasion also need to establish new units to address newly emerging environmental facts and to regroup old units. For instance, the emergence of the computer as a new environmental fact has led many firms to create a new unit such as management-information services; and the development of newly relevant mathematical techniques has led to the emergence of operations-research groups and long-range planning groups. Such new groups not only draw together people with different technical skills, but also they often need different orientations, structures, and styles to transact their business successfully.

In addition, as firms grow in terms of product variety and geographical coverage, a need frequently arises to switch the first big structural division of work in the company from the traditional functional

basis, implicit in our discussion so far, to some other basis. Valid arguments can be mustered for various choices of first-level structural division, but the soundest arguments will be based on environmental facts. For instance, if different geographical areas require quite different ways of marketing, while the products of a firm are quite similar technically, a first-level split *by geography* is usually indicated, and vice versa. If, on the other hand, the products and the geographical conditions are relatively homogeneous, an initial division *by function* is probably the soundest basis.

This analysis of differences and similarities needs to be complemented by an analysis of the intensity of the interdependencies between various units to find the best possible trade-off. Once the primary basis for structurally dividing work is selected, secondary means can be provided not only at lower levels but also by staff groups. In some instances where two factors, such as functions and products, are both highly different and critical, some firms, as in the aerospace industry, are turning to a matrix organization. In such an organization two bases are used simultaneously as a first-level division of labor.

We have seen that whether we view the environmental transaction primarily as a problem of information exchange or as one of bargaining and problem solving, we are pointed toward a matching of organizational traits and orientations with environmental features. We are now in a position to explain how we use this method of analysis as a practical tool in helping specific organizations improve the quality of their environmental transactions. We will do this by examining several specific cases.

The first set of cases involves situations where mismatches could be directly addressed by making adjustments in the internal arrangements of the unit concerned. A second set of cases will also be examined where other types of adjustments were needed to improve the matching process:

1) by releasing counterpressures in the organization for consistency among all units;
2) by adjusting units to accommodate shifts in the environment;
3) by creating new units to meet newly important environmental conditions; and
4) by realigning units to cope with the increased scope of the business.

In reviewing these cases emphasis will be given to the variety of variables in the organizational systems that were selected as the initial means of implementing planned change.

Before turning to the cases, however, we need to get a feel for the way problems at this interface are likely to first present themselves to managers and in turn to behaviorally-oriented consultants. Problems at the environment-organization interface are likely to manifest themselves eventually through economic results. For example, at the sales-customer interface, it is in a loss of sales volume; in research and development, it is in a drop in the flow of new products, etc. However, these indicators of interface trouble are fairly slow to show up, and managers learn to be sensitive to earlier clues of difficulty. These often take the form of complaints from the outside—letters from customers, a private word dropped at lunch by a banker, an important move by a competitor that caught everyone flatfooted. The customer may be saying that your organization is unresponsive, that you cannot seem to tailor your products to his needs, that he is getting tired of fighting his way through your red tape. In other cases, the concern will develop because a competitor seems too frequently to be first with a new-product introduction, or a new marketing technique. Perhaps in the production area it is a failure to realize economies through process innovation or falling behind in the race with rising wages and salaries. Another clue might be that the best specialists are not staying in the company—there is a worrisome amount of turnover among the more

promising professionals in the physical or managerial sciences. These are the clues that might well be traced back to human problems at the environment-organization interface.

Examples of Organization-Environment Mismatches

Our first case of an organizational development problem at this interface was initially identified by worrisome symptoms of an economic nature. During our research activity in an organization developing, marketing, and manufacturing plastics products, we heard numerous complaints that the basic research laboratory was not turning out new process and product ideas. An analysis of the data we had collected on organizational practices in this laboratory revealed that the laboratory had a highly peaked management hierarchy, with most of the decisions being made exclusively by higher management. This was clearly inconsistent with the uncertainty and complexity of the information with which these scientists were expected to deal. The scientists complained that they did not have enough autonomy to follow research leads which seemed highly important to them. As one lower-level research administrator put it:

When one project gets killed, we get another one. This is a sore point with me because we aren't given a chance to look around ourselves for new projects. We are given a project and told to work on it. My objection is that we don't give the group leader and the bench chemist the time to investigate different problems before they are being thrust into a [management-defined] program. . . .

This high degree of formalized decision-making made it difficult for these scientists to carry on meaningful transactions with the dynamic environment confronting them. It was difficult for them to freely respond to new information from the scientific environment. In addition, they had neither the authority to make decisions about research activities nor direct access to persons with market information, which could have enabled them to make effective decisions. In addition to constraining and confusing the flow of environmental information into this unit, this inappropriate structure undoubtedly also affected the motivation of these scientists. We will develop this theme in some detail in the fifth chapter.

The remedy for this sort of problem is not hard to see. Find ways of getting lower-level scientists and managers more involved in decision-making, and, in general, loosen up the structure. While we were involved only as researchers, and thus were not expected to propose such actions, it is interesting to note that individual laboratory members were already finding ways out of these constraints. As one research manager put it:

The individual chemist can initiate a program to a greater degree than the research manager would like to believe. It isn't always possible to get the control [the managers want] because what's going on in a certain project is always linked somewhat to the influence of the man who is working on it.

This kind of sub rosa response probably improves matters to some extent, but it is suboptimal as compared with forthright mutual decisionmaking between junior and senior people.

A more complicated problem at the organization-environment interface is illustrated by a situation which one of the authors encountered in his consulting activities. The organization in question was a unit of a major chemical company which had as its assigned mission the development, manufacture, and marketing of entirely new and unique products which did not fall within the realm of existing product divisions. Once this division, which we shall label the New Products Division (NPD), had demonstrated that a product

was commercially successful, the product was transferred to an existing division, or a new division was established for it. The NPD thus dealt with products for only a limited time and during the most uncertain phase of their existence, when both markets and technology were ill-defined. In sum, the parts of the environment confronting this organization were highly uncertain.

The NPD had sales, development, and research units and drew upon various manufacturing facilities within the company, depending upon the nature of the particular product. The division general manager was aware of what he considered to be an unhealthy amount of conflict among all of these functional units, but particularly between sales and development. As a result, he asked that we help him define the nature and causes of these conflicts and then help him develop solutions to these problems. Accordingly, a diagnostic study was undertaken.

The study confirmed that the organization was achieving relatively poor integration between the functional units, and that certain conflict-management practices were not as effective as they might be. But, central to the issues we are considering here, the diagnosis also revealed that the differentiation within the organization was not in tune with its environmental demands. While the research and the development units both had structure and member orientations that were consistent with their task requirements, the sales unit did not. Whereas members of the sales unit needed to have a relatively short-term time orientation and a strong marketing-goal orientation, they actually had a long-term time horizon and were oriented toward a balance of technical and market goals. In fact, along these two dimensions, the sales unit was almost identical to the development unit. What seemed to be happening was that the two units were trying to perform the same task, and, in essence, were competing with each other for control of this task. This competition was one important source of the poor integration and unresolved conflict about which the general manager was concerned.[6]

The reason that the sales unit had drifted into the sphere of the development group was not difficult to explain. At the time of our involvement, the NPD had not yet brought many products to the stage where an active test-marketing program was required. As a result, the kind of information with which the managers in the sales unit were accustomed to dealing just did not exist. However, these managers wanted something to do, so they began taking a longer-range look at potential markets. As a consequence, they were dealing with information which was the legitimate concern of developmental personnel. This threatened the position of the latter group, and hostility developed between the groups, making it difficult for them to cooperate.

With this data and this explanation in hand, we made a feedback presentation to the general manager and his chief subordinates. The data and their implications were accepted without too much difficulty by the general manager, the research manager, and even the development manager. The sales manager, however, showed a great deal of resistance to this interpretation. The chief reason for this was that accepting this interpretation brought into serious question the role of his unit in the organization for the immediate future. He had brought together a group of five experienced sales managers, and had gotten them involved in identifying market opportunities, since there was very little to be done in marketing with the few new products already available. Accepting our interpretation meant either finding a more appropriate activity for these managers, which was not possible without something to sell, or having them reassigned to another division. The latter obviously would involve a loss of face for the sales manager.

Because of this resistance from the sales manager, several sessions of this management group were held with and without the consultant present. Ultimately, even though some limited progress was made in working through this problem, the general manager concluded that the most viable solution, given the bind in which the sales manager was caught, was to have him reassigned to another job of equal status and responsibility. This was accomplished, and his replacement reduced the size of the sales unit and limited its activity to dealing with more immediate market issues. As a result, much of the tension between the marketing and development groups was relieved. With each unit having orientations fitting the information requirements of its task, the organization seemed to function more effectively.

As a final brief example of a rather unusual form of mismatching at the environment-organization interface, we cite a particular unit of a large electronics manufacturing firm which was charged with doing research, development, and manufacturing of some esoteric types of semiconductors. It put a heavy emphasis on participatory management, with an extensive use of product teams for decision purposes. There was also careful planning of physical arrangements so as to facilitate necessary interactions between groups. Management officials hoped to secure high involvement from all levels and a working climate that induced creative work. In many ways their experiment succeeded, but they were troubled by serious complaints from many of the specialized engineering and technical people who had critical positions. The comments below from some of these people indicate the nature of their concerns:

In a way, the [unit] is not a satisfying place for the [technical] professional. You seem to have to go through a lot of red tape and coordination to get something technical done.

The technical guy is principally interested in technical things and the business team in economic problems. There's a certain type of research-oriented person who would be completely frustrated in the team. He's not interested in business or human relations unless they have a direct bearing on what he's doing.

I'm basically a scientist. Scientists are individualists, and you appreciate freedom in your thoughts and action. And this basically goes across the grain of the business team.

The complaints stand in sharp contrast to the highly favorable responses of almost all of the nontechnical personnel. This contrast became apparent to one of the authors in the course of research in preparing a teaching case. The senior officials of the unit, upon seeing the pattern, concluded that the heavy emphasis being placed on securing integration through the use of group methods had not allowed the technical people enough of an opportunity to differentiate their role and orientation. A careful internal study was made of the issue, and a modification of the group procedures was adopted. This seemed to correct the situation. In essence, the engineering personnel were freed from involvement in business activity, and an integrator was provided to link them to these activities. Thus technical personel were freer to develop orientations related to their major task.

Other Varieties of Organization-Environment Problems

Not all of the issues involving transactions between the environment and organizational units appear as the kind of mismatch situations that can be directly addressed in the manner we have been reviewing. The examples presented below indicate the range and variety of other problems that can now be more systematically analyzed at this interface and moved through the entire development cycle on a more predictable basis.

The first example involves the relation between headquarters and field units and the impact these had on environmental

transactions. One of the authors had the opportunity to take part in the efforts of a large "heavy industry" firm to make adjustments in their geographically dispersed production units that would improve the match with their respective environments. This issue had been addressed under a number of different headings in this company and in a number of ways, but the key issue had remained the same. At one time or another, it had been called a line-staff problem, a headquarters-field problem, and a centralization-vs-decentralization problem. In a variety of ways, the company had been working repeatedly through the diagnosis, planning, action, and evaluation cycle of change. The trend over several years had been away from an earlier insistence on company-wide consistency and toward greater local autonomy in order to foster better matching with environmental conditions. It is revealing to review the history of these change efforts and, in particular, a recent major educational intervention.

This company had gone through an earlier period of rapid expansion as it exploited an advantage it enjoyed in securing one of its basic raw materials at a significantly lower cost than its competitors. During this period, it was not crucial that each and every one of its major plants be optimally matched with its respective local environmental conditions. But as the company gradually lost its original unique advantage, these matching issues became important. However, a tradition had become well established that the various aspects of the business were largely controlled from headquarters, with each central functional department dominating its respective affairs throughout the organization. For instance, the central engineering group had the dominant voice not only in new construction but also in new-equipment decisions and production-process modifications. The same largely held for other functions such as accounting, purchasing, quality control, transportation, and personnel. This affected a set of widely scattered plants that roughly did one of two types of work—basic bulk manufacturing or secondary fabrication work. The managers in these outlying locations began to perceive that many opportunities for performance improvement in their local environments were being lost because of the demand for consistency from the center.

With this issue as one of its principal objectives, the company decided to undertake an extensive educational program. A considerable number of managers were sponsored in attending sensitivity-training sessions. This was later followed up by conducting "family" work-planning conferences of three or four days' duration for members of a managerial group. A few laboratory-training sessions were organized on an intergroup basis that brought together such pairs of groups as managers at headquarters from some one functional speciality. At about this time, the company decided to make a formal structural separation of the management of the basic material plants from the management of the fabricating units. A major reason for the decision was that the fabricating plants were in need of a shorter-term and more market-oriented management in contrast to the longer-term and cost-oriented management customary in the basic plants. The structural step was designed to foster the needed differentiation, but it was initially not well understood by middle management.

At this point, one of the authors became involved in the further planning and implementing of this company's push toward fitting its units with environmental requisites. A small planning group of senior company managers and outside consultants undertook to further diagnose the company situation. In spite of progress being made by earlier change efforts, this top group was not satisfied with the quality of the intergroup relations and the responsiveness of major units to changes in the environment. When this planning group found they were in agreement in their size-up of the situation, they decided to proceed with a major additional educational effort rather than undertaking a

more systematic diagnostic study. Plans were developed for bringing together the general managers of all the major plants and the heads of all the headquarters departments in a training design that called for three one-week sessions spaced three to four months apart. The theme of the sessions was the managing of corporate change.

The training group, when assembled, decided to focus its efforts on assessing environmental changes and identifying shared company problems. Two issues emerged as being of paramount importance. One was the repercussions in the company of the recent structural separation of the basic and fabricating units. This change was seen as threatening the sense of overall unity in the company or what might be called "the one big family" feeling. This change needed to be assimilated on both a cognitive and an emotional basis. At the cognitive level, the participants were exposed to the logic of the move in terms of environmental demands and the concepts of differentiation and integration. The representatives of the various units then described to the total group the typical problems and issues they faced in their respective environments. Striking differences became apparent that they had not fully appreciated before.[7] As these realities were clarified, the structural split met with more emotional acceptance without the loss of mutual respect.

The second major issue that emerged was the relation between the headquarters departments and the basic manufacturing plants. The central departments felt under pressure to permit more of their functions to be performed under plant control. They were becoming very uncomfortable with this trend, and tended to ascribe it simply to a fad for decentralization. Meanwhile the plant people were still feeling unnecessarily constricted by the rules and regulations of at least some of the central units. Once again, these issues were directly faced both by examining in detail their specifics on a function-by-function basis and by drawing on the general concept of differentiation and integration to provide a framework for systematic thinking. The net effect of these sessions was to see:

1) the very real business need for further relaxation of some of the rules designed to enforce consistency;
2) the need for a careful sorting of functions between the center and the plants in terms of the locus of relevant skills and pertinent information; and
3) the need for more open communication channels for the continuing adjustment of mutual problems between the center and the field.

The thrust was toward greater differentiation without losing integration; and, of course, the greater differentiation was designed to further the matching of the outlying units with their changing environmental circumstances.

At the end of the third residential session, the participants undertook to do their own evaluation of the program. Some of the program values they emphasized as having been realized were: "design of work procedures for examining and defining service unit role," "construction of a cross-company network of good will, communication, and trust for future problem solving," and "greater insight into company's overall operations and problems." In addition, they arranged to have their group act as a resource panel to work on the detailed review of the division of work between headquarters and the field plants on a function-by-function basis.

This program in toto can be characterized by emphasizing an educational type of intervention to improve the matching at the environmental-organizational interface. In effect, it approached the problem obliquely by releasing the constraining pressures from the headquarters departments rather than by driving directly toward the matching of environmental demands with unit characteristics. When the

problem is defined as seeking a change in a field of forces, as suggested by Kurt Lewin, this emphasis on relaxing a constraining force can be fully as effective as a more direct approach. This theoretical conclusion is supported by the available facts in this instance. This case also put an emphasis on education as the major lever of change, with only a sketchy use of systematic diagnosis. Much of the diagnosis was done by drawing from the perceptions of the managers during the early part of the training sessions. This method tended to increase the sense of involvement by these men, but at some cost in the specificity of the diagnosis. It should also not be ignored that one important part of the change was the structural shift of formally splitting the basic and fabricating units. In our judgment, this formal differentiation was needed to better match the environmental requirements, but the education effort was also needed to assimilate this change.

To turn to another case, the authors have been involved over a period of several years in working with a major company in the consumer packaged-food industry, which faced a major problem in realigning itself with its market environment. This company had been highly successful in conducting a decentralized business, with geographically dispersed sales units performing the final packaging and marketing functions. The market environment had been relatively stable for more than a generation. Few changes were needed in product or marketing methods to build upon an earlier innovative period. As a result, the outlying units had evolved some highly detailed routines for handling the products.

In recent years, this market environment had become much more turbulent. New products and packages were being sought by customers. New sales outlets were coming into being. The company had, of course, been responding to these changes, but rather sluggishly, and seldom as the innovator. The field units that performed so well under stable conditions were faced with an environment where change was becoming a steady pattern rather than an occasional event. Some more fundamental changes in the units were needed to secure responses that went beyond firefighting and counter punching.

As this diagnosis emerged, the company undertook a major and continuing educational program directed toward these decentralized units. The program has addressed various topics but with a consistent method. The method has been to expose the managers concerned to the facts of relevant environmental change around a given topic and then to push them into struggling with the implications of these changes for their own organizations. There has been a heavy reliance on the use of teaching cases as materials for discussion and analysis. Different aspects of the business were reviewed in this manner. The managers had not been told how to respond but have been helped to develop more appropriate problem-solving methods.

As this effort has proceeded, there has been a clearly noticeable change in the behavior of these managers. They consistently testify to the improvement of their general ability to tackle new problems. Their enhanced sense of competence has made them willing to search their environments more thoroughly for early signs of opportunities or threats. The speed of response of their organizations seems to have improved considerably. In short, they are on the road to learning to exist successfully in a more dynamic environment.

The final two examples involve situations where formal structural change was the key element in the change process. In the first situation the R & D units of a large petrochemical organization were diagnosed as having become so heavily development-oriented that long-term basic research was relatively neglected. The company decided to create an essentially new unit that would be carefully tailored to perform the desired research job. In this situation, the authors were asked to provide assistance in the analysis of the relevant scientific environment in order to specify roughly how the new unit should be organized to improve the probabilities of success of this organization-environment interface. This included consideration of recruitment criteria, formal structure, internal departmental procedures, physical layout, and communication linkages with other company units. It is much too early to assess results in this instance, but it is clear that the managers involved have already achieved a much clearer sense of where they are going and how they are going to get there than is the usual pattern. They have been able to obtain a higher level of agreement on the specific points of their organization plan and on its overall integrity.

In another quite different application a general manager in a consumer-goods field was being pressed by his superior to restructure his major division from a functional basis of first-order differentiation to a product basis. The manager agreed with the argument that the rapid state of proliferation of new products in his unit would eventually warrant such a reorganization. The question was "when?" He felt that the recent success of his unit stemmed principally from a higher creative development group that not only worked together effectively as a total group, but had also managed to develop some fairly strong working links with both the marketing and manufacturing units. He feared that a premature reorganization would disrupt this innovative combination. A procedure was developed by which he could secure periodic readings on his organization to improve the timing of the inevitable reorganization. In effect, differentiation and integration measurements were devised to answer the following question: When would the loss of effectiveness because of the simultaneous handling of multiple products exceed the gain of keeping a close interchange going between all the development specialists? This application indicated that more substantive data can be a useful guide on this kind of complex timing issue.

Conclusion

The examples cited above all present some variant of an organization-environment interface problem. Taken together, they illustrate the considerable range of practical issues that are becoming amenable to more systematic study and action, using concepts and methods adapted from the behavioral sciences. In these situations, it has not always been appropriate or possible to put equal emphasis on all phases of the change cycle. Flexibility is needed; for instance, the diagnostic phase varied from highly specific and quantified work to more qualitative studies based upon the shared observations of managers.

We should particularly note that the goals of change have been sought in these cases by using a wide variety of methods. Specifically designed educational programs have been employed that used various pedagogical techniques. Shifts in the formal structure have been employed ranging from major reorganization to shifts in the content of particular roles and their incumbents. The wide range of variables used might suggest a more chaotic rather than a more systematic approach to improvement of organization-environment transactions if it were not for a consistent set of concepts and diagnostic methods that were applied in each case. Clarity of conceptualization has fostered flexibility in the choice of change methods.

The use of behavioral methods to seek improvement in the fit between organiza-tional units and their sectors of the environment is a relatively new field of application. The early steps in this direction which the authors report here are suggestive of a much wider array of possible future applications.

References and Notes

1. One notable exception has been the work on boundary transactions reported in Kahn et. al., *Organizational Stress* (New York: John Wiley and Sons, Inc., 1964).
2. P. R. Lawrence and J. W. Lorsch, *Organization and Environment: Managing Differentiation and Integration* (Boston: Division of Research, Harvard Business School, 1967).
3. L. E. Fouraker, unpublished manuscript.
4. P. Selznick, *Leadership Administration* (New York: Harper & Row, Publishers, 1957), pp. 8–42.
5. F. J. Aguilar, *Scanning the Business Environment* (New York: The Macmillan Company, 1967).
6. The reader will recognize that poor integration with low differentiation is contrary to the basic antagonism between these two states. . . .
   Although this is the only case of such low differentiation the authors have found (and it is therefore dangerous to generalize), it does suggest that the inverse relationship between differentiation and integration may not be a straight line. Instead, it may be curvilinear, with both high and low differentiation being associated with poor integration. High differentiation leads to problems of communication between units and makes integration difficult to achieve. Extremely low differentiation means the units have begun to deal with the same parts of the environment and are basically in competition.
7. An associated program, conducting an exchange of plant visitations by contrasting pairs during the interval between sessions, served to reinforce these perceptions of differences and the necessity for them.

Chapter 6   Breakthroughs in Change and Innovation

CHANGE BY DESIGN, NOT BY DEFAULT

Robert R. Blake and Jane Srygley Mouton

Men who have studied organization processes over the past ten years have shuffled and shifted the labels applied to their subject. Not only scholars but industrial men as well began in the late fifties to study and discuss what now has emerged as a science in itself. They first referred to it merely as "organization change," then "organization improvement," and eventually "organization development."

What they seem to have been seeking, and what has finally emerged may more appropriately be described as "systematic development." This title reflects the fact that much has been learned about changing, improving, and developing an organization. The dynamics of change are now far better understood than ever before.

Men can at last act deliberately to take systematic steps to achieve specifically planned change within their organizations. There are proven ways to move an organization from where it stands to where it *should* stand to be a model organization. This suggests the surface meaning of systematic development, but it is far deeper and more meaningful for the businessman of the future. What underlies systematic development?

The Dilemma of Change

Change is thought of in various ways. This poses a major dilemma. It may be that processes of change are limited to evolutionary modifications or revolutionary churnings. Or change may be a process which can be engineered according to specifications of systematic development. If one thinks in an evolutionary or revolutionary way, his strategy and tactics of change are quite different from those he would have if he thought according to a systematic development approach.

Creeping Change by Evolution

Evolutionary adjustments occur when change is small and within broader status quo expectations. Evolutionary accommodation rarely violates the traditions or customary practices of those involved in it or affected by it. An underlying assumption is that progress is possible if each problem is dealt with as it arises. Changes are usually piecemeal, taking place one by one. Because they are adjustments within the status quo, they seldom promote great enthusiasm, arouse deep resistance, or have dramatic results. Solutions that prove sound are repeated and reinforced. Those that are unsound simply disappear. They are based on the belief that beyond survival, growth and development are most probable for the company that is most successful at finding solutions to each specific problem as it arises, situation by situation.

Acceptance of evolutionary concepts is widespread by many managers and scholars of behavioral science for several reasons. The changes often represent forward progress. They rarely constitute significant departures from past practices. They are reasonably easy to understand and accept. They are unlikely to provoke resistance.

But there are limitations to expecting significant change or development from evolutionary ways. Only those problems that force themselves into the limelight are likely to be solved and these are not necessarily the most important for the good of the organization. The very fact that an evolutionary approach accepts the status quo arrangements of the system as a whole poses what may be the real barriers to progress. Prevailing values often constitute rigidities which prevent deeper problems from being seen, or, if a brief awareness does occur, organization norms make the problem harder to tackle.

Evolutionary processes are likely to be so slow that, even though change is occurring, its tempo does not prevent the organization from falling ever farther behind. They may be little more than accommodations, adjustments, and compromises involving matters of style and technique only, not the deeper and more significant aspects of the organization. The evolutionary approach on the whole, and despite its limitations, is highly characteristic of American corporate life.

Revolutionary Upheaval

Processes of change can be viewed as revolutionary when the shift results in overturning status quo arrangements. Revolutionary change causes violations, rejections, or suppression of old expectations. It compels acceptance of new ones. Revolutionary changes are more likely to be effected through the exercise of power and authority which can compel compliance.

Revolutionary change rarely is resorted to except where situations have become so intolerable that evolutionary modifications are seen as insufficient, and, if there are other possibilities, they go unrecognized. Revolutionary change is likely to be championed by those who feel deeply frustrated by the status quo although the same status quo is resented just as much by those adhering to it.

Another motivation to revolutionary methods is the desire for speedy change. When traditional assumptions and rules of conduct are overthrown, revolution brings about a new situation very rapidly. The underlying tensions may extend back over a long period of suffering, and the relief gained from taking a new action is often better than either the standing still or pursuing an evolutionary course, despite the risks that are involved in revolution.

These changes may have dramatic results, and they may be either positive or negative. Long-standing problems may be fundamentally resolved one way or another. Negative side effects are often produced, such as underground resistance, a building up of resentment, and sabotage as opposed to involvement, commitment, or dedication—particularly among those from whom compliance is extracted.

Both evolutionary and revolutionary methods are as old as history. Both are deeply ingrained in the assumptions by which men are guided. This, however, does not mean that they are sound approaches to change.

Systematic Development—The New Scientific Way to Change

Systematic development is a new alternative to evolution or revolution. It starts neither with acceptance nor with rejection of status quo. Rather it begins with an intellectual model of what might be ideal, or what "should be." The properties of the model are specified according to theory, logic, and fact. The model is pretested against probable circumstances projected over defined periods of time. The model is a blueprint, not of what *is,* but of what *should be.*

The use of such a strategic model is not the same as planning or as management by objectives. Both of these methods are undertaken within the status quo constraints and often entail little more than extrapolations from the past projected into the future, rarely improving an active process of learning to reject the outmoded properties of the status quo. Both planning and management by objectives, however, are invaluable conceptual tools in implementation of such a model.

Here are the important specifications for an approach based on systematic development.[1]

Designing a Model of What Should Be

Clear-cut objectives are a prerequisite to the kind of development that takes place under the systematic approach. An ideal model specifies what the results should be at a designated time. To be systematic, the model must be based on theory, fact, and logic, uncontaminated either by assumptions embedded in the status quo or by extrapolations from the past.

The model must be understood to represent the *ideal,* not the *idealistic.* Ideal thinking can identify what is possible according to theory, logic, and fact. Ideal thinking can be tested against objective criteria to assess its practicality. Idealistic thinking, on the other hand, would have an unreal quality, probably rooted in self-deception and expressing what is desired or what is wanted without having been tested against theory, logic, or fact.

Idealistic thinking is subjective and is based on criteria having little or nothing to do with the facts of the situation. Ideal thinking has sometimes been suspect and rejected as idealistic. Yet through history, some of what might qualify as among the world's greatest change projects—the Magna Charta, the Constitution of the United States—have probably come about through ideal-type formulations.

Objective Appraisal of the "As-Is" Situation

The status quo cannot be taken for granted. It is as necessary to learn what the status quo is as to describe what it should be. The *as is* is formulated in a way which permits point-by-point parallel-

ing between what *is* and what *should be* to be implemented under the ideal model. Weaknesses and strengths of the present situation can become clearer.

When the ideal is used as a spotlight to see the actual, objectivity about what *is* can more readily be attained. Without an ideal model for comparison, rationalization, self-deception, and ingrained habits operate to obscure the true properties of the situation. To change a situation, then, those responsible for operating it must learn to reject it. This is not "unlearning." It is new learning through which insight is acquired into deficiencies of arrangements that exist. From a technical point of view, it is a strategy of escape from corporate ethnocentrism.

This step of learning to reject the status quo is most difficult. It is a fact usually left undone. As an ideal model, the Constitution was insufficient because it did not reflect active learning to reject the status quo which contained deep injustices in the American cultural scheme. Amendments and court interpretations attest to this. We continue to identify and reject some of these deep-lying contradictions.

Discrepancies Between Actual and Ideal

The gaps between actual and ideal are motivators. Closing gaps gives organization development and changes its direction. When conditions that should be rejected and replaced are identified, steps of development can then be planned and programmed for implementation.

A deeper significance than appears on the surface comes sharply into focus when development is built upon producing and closing gaps as a method of motivating change. There are two concepts of motivation here—tension reduction and financial and status rewards. Much industrial thinking is based on acceptance of the idea that financial and status rewards are important motivators. But these alone appear insufficient to provoke the tensions that motivate men to search for solutions to problems. They may in fact even do precisely the opposite.

Many organizations give salary increases and promotions to those who best fit into an outmoded *status quo*. Here the reward system is unlikely to motivate actions to change. But there are psychological factors in all problem situations that appear to be important for stimulating creativity and innovative problem solving. When men recognize a clear-cut discrepancy between what *is* and what *should be,* tensions arise that focus their thoughts, efforts, and feelings on how to resolve the matter to eliminate the contradiction.

Such tensions provide a motivational force that compels men to solve those problems that pose barriers to corporate performance. They may arise independently of financial or status rewards, and they appear to be highly critical in the achievement of the solutions to problems. Through understanding the force of these tensions, leaders can make deliberate use of them, harnessing energy toward orderly production of change. This energy is only partially tapped in the conduct of industry today.

The contrast of motivational forces of tension reduction with those of financial and status rewards is clear. But this should not imply that they work in opposition, though they can do so. Money and status do contribute to a person's feeling fairly and justly remunerated and accepted by the organization. When such feelings are present, men tend to become involved in the organization and committed to its objectives, thereby experiencing the kinds that are associated with discrepancies and call forth action.

The Complete Ideal Model
and Organization Subsystems

The ideal model is complete only when it takes into consideration all identifiable forces bearing on each subsystem of the corporation. This includes not only the forces that are directly controlled by the organization but also the outside environ-

ment within which the organization is embedded and under the influence of which it must operate.

Steering, Correction, and Control
Mechanisms

Merely setting processes in motion does not necessarily insure that the action needed for converting from the actual to the ideal will take place. Steering, correction, and control mechanisms and retro-learning techniques are indispensable for guiding development. Ideally, the situation should be measured before development is initiated, at various points during the development activity, and at the end of it. Then information is available to steer action as well as to determine results. The organization can identify factors in the situation impeding progress and unsuspected weaknesses or limitations in the model. Signs of drag and drift can be anticipated and corrected.

Systematic development has several advantages. One is that it relies upon theory, logic, and facts. It, therefore, arouses enthusiasm for bringing about change rather than resistance to it. There is only one real limit on the magnitude of change that is possible through systematic development and that is in the capacity of men to reason and analyze their problems. Risk is reduced because the changes which are projected can be tested beforehand for their probable consequences before implementation is started.

There are also disadvantages. The depth of intellectual endeavor calls for rigorous thinking which is most demanding and time consuming. Many managers prefer the excitement of fire fighting to the conceptual activity and brainwork that systematic development calls for.

These three possible methods of change underlie understanding of how it occurs. Evolution and revolution take place "naturally." They have emerged through history. Systematic development, by comparison, has properties in common with the scientific methods that are used in designing experiments and verifying results.

Systematic development as an alternative to evolution and revolution is an example of the wider movement of society from a prescientific to a scientific age.

Tomorrow's Changes

What is this scientific approach to change going to mean for organizations of the future? What implications does it have for industry?

Many new steps and increasingly more rapid progress can be expected through the deliberate design and management of change for the future. A look at the past readily suggests simple examples of the kinds of change involved.

Imagine a group of railroad men at the turn of the century and what might have happened had they recognized their business as the transportation business instead of railroading, set growth and financial objectives for an ideal transportation business of the future, set the model for achieving these objectives, then concentrated their energies on systematically implementing the model rather than "saving" the railroad.

Imagine the strides that might have been made by unions of working men for their memberships had their leaders, back in the days when they were embroiled in pushing for various sections of the Wagner Act or again fighting Taft-Hartley, designed specific models of ideal union management relationships and had their management counterparts recognized the soundness of the ideal model approach. Something far better and more valuable for working men might well have been achieved than has been through revolutionary strike tactics or the chipping away at "management prerogatives" through grievance procedures.

The possibilities of progress through the systematic design of change are bounded only by the imagination—progress not only for industrial and other organizations but even for world society as a whole.

Note

1. A more detailed presentation of the theory, techniques, and results of systematic development is contained in a book by the authors entitled *Corporate Excellence Through Grid Organization Development: A Systems Approach* (Houston: Gulf Publishing Company, 1968)

BUREAUCRACY AND INNOVATION

Victor A. Thompson

It has become a commonplace among behavioral scientists that the bureaucratic form of organization is characterized by high productive efficiency but low innovative capacity. There is a growing feeling that modern organizations, and particularly the large, bureaucratic business and government organizations, need to increase their capacity to innovate. This feeling stems in part from the obvious fact of the increased rate of change, especially technological change, but also from a rejection of the older process of innovation through the birth of new organizations and the death or failure of old ones. It seems difficult to contemplate the extinction of existing and well-known organizational giants, for too many interests become vested in their continued existence. Consequently, many behavioral scientists feel that innovation must increasingly occur within the bureaucratic organizations. Also technical innovation is becoming costlier, and financing it may be easier through healthy, existing, organizations than through newly created ones.

This paper considers the obstacles to innovation within the modern bureaucratic organization and makes some suggestions for changes that would facilitate innovation. No attempt is made to answer the question as to whether innovation is desirable or not. By innovation is meant the generation, acceptance, and implementation of new ideas, processes, products, or services. Innovation therefore implies the capacity to change or adapt. An adaptive organization may not be innovative (because it does not generate many new ideas), but an innovative organization will be adaptive (because it is able to implement many new ideas).

For a group of people to act as an entity, an ideology is required. This ideology explains what the group is doing, what it ought to do, and legitimizes the coercion of the individual by the group. For the modern bureaucratic organization, this body of doctrine could be called a production ideology. The organization is conceived as having an owner who has a goal to be maximized by means of the organization.[1] The organization is a tool (or weapon) for reaching this objective. The various participants are given money in return for the use of their time and effort as means of achieving the owner's goal. As Henry Ford said, "All that we ask of the men is that they do the work which is set before them." Management consists of functions and processes for perfecting the tool for this purpose—that is, controlling intraorganizational behaviors so that they become completely reliable and predictable like any good tool. From the standpoint of this production ideology, innovative behavior would only be interpreted as unreliability.

The production ideology leads to rapid and detailed specification and commitment of resources. Of especial interest is the detailed specification of human resources. Adam Smith's advice to reduce the job of pin making to that of making a part of the pin has been generally followed. This response will be termed the "Smith's pins" effect. It has been said that the detailed specification of human resources reduces investment costs per unit of program execution.[2] The production ideology results in jobs which typically require only a small part of the worker's training or knowledge. Consequently, this detailed specification of resources will be called "overspecification" of resources, somewhat argumentatively, no doubt.

Monocratic Social Structure and Innovation

Large, modern bureaucratic organizations dominated by production ideology are framed around a powerful organization stereotype, which following Max Weber, will be called the monocratic organization. This stereotype reflects conditions prevalent in the past, two being important because they no longer hold (1) great inequality among organization members in social standing and abilities and a corresponding inequality in contributions and rewards, and (2) a technology simple enough to be within the grasp of an individual.

In this stereotype, the organization is a great hierarchy of superior-subordinate relations in which the person at the top, assumed to be omniscient, gives the general order that initiates all activity. His immediate subordinates make the order more specific for their subordinates; the latter do the same for theirs, etc., until specific individuals are carrying out specific commands. All authority and initiation are cascaded down in this way by successive delegations. There is complete discipline enforced from the top down to assure that these commands are faithfully obeyed. Responsibility is owed from the bottom up. To assure predictability and accountability, each position is narrowly defined as to duties and jurisdiction, without overlapping or duplication. Problems that fall outside the narrow limits of the job are referred upward until they come to a person with sufficient authority to make a decision. Each person is to receive orders from and be responsible to only one other person—his superior.

Such a system is monocratic because there is only *one* point or source of legitimacy. Conflict cannot be legitimate (although it may occur because of the weakness and immorality of human beings). Therefore, the organization does not need formal, legitimate, bargaining devices. Thus, although it might be considered empirically more fruitful to conceive of the organization as a coalition,[3] according to the monocratic stereotype, the organization as a moral or normative entity is the tool of an owner, not a coalition. Coalitional and other conflict-settling activities therefore, take place in a penumbra of illegitimacy.

The inability to legitimize conflict depresses creativity. Conflict generates problems and uncertainties and diffuses ideas. Conflict implies pluralism and forces coping and search for solutions, whereas concentrated authority can simply ignore obstacles and objections. Conflict, therefore, encourages innovations. Other things being equal, the less bureaucratized (monocratic) the organization, the more conflict and uncertainty and the more innovation.[4]

The monocratic stereotype dictates centralized control over all resources. It can control only through extrinsic rewards such as money, power, and status, because it demands the undifferentiated time of its members in the interests of the owner's goals. Even as the organization is a tool, so are all of its participants. There can be no right to "joy in work." To admit such a right would be to admit an interest other than the owner's and to lose some control over the participants.

The necessity of relying upon such extrinsic rewards forces the organization to make its hierarchical positions rewards for compliance. Such a reward system depends upon the organization's ability to find enough people who are willing to exchange their time for a chance at a small group of status positions. It is doubtful

that this would have been possible without help from other social institutions, including religious ones. The general belief that work is not supposed to be enjoyable has helped, as has the social definition of success as moving up a managerial hierarchy. The further belief that the good man is the successful one has closed the system.

With education as a criterion of social class, the blue-collar group and a large part of the lower white-collar group have been eliminated from the competition for these scarce status prizes. Furthermore, highly educated people are increasingly seeking basic need satisfaction outside of the organization—in hobbies, community activities, their families.[5] Consequently, organizations have become sorely pressed to find rewards sufficient to induce the needed docility. Although the use of money alone has raised the price of goods, it does not seem to have been very successful in promoting production interests.[6]

With the enormous expansion of knowledge flooding the organization with specialists of all kinds and with the organization increasingly dependent upon them, this reward system is facing a crisis. With all his pre-entry training, the specialist finds that he can "succeed" only by giving up work for which he is trained and entering management—work for which he has had no training.[7]

The extrinsic reward system, administered by the hierarchy of authority, stimulates conformity rather than innovation. Creativity is promoted by an internal commitment, by intrinsic rewards for the most part. The extrinsic rewards of esteem by colleagues, and the benevolent competition through which it is distributed, are largely foreign to the monocratic, production-oriented organization. Hierarchical competition is highly individualistic and malevolent. It does not contribute to cooperation and group problem solving.

For those committed to this concept of success, the normal psychological state is one of more or less anxiety. This kind of success is dispensed by hierarchical superiors. Furthermore, the more success one attains, the higher he goes, the more vague and subjective become the standards by which he is judged. Eventually, the only safe posture is conformity. Innovation is not likely under these conditions. To gain the independence, freedom, and security required for creativity, the normal individual has to reject this concept of success. But even those who have adopted a different life pattern and measure their personal worth in terms of professional growth and the esteem of professional peers must feel a great deal of insecurity within these monocratic structures, because the opportunity for growth is under the control of the organization, and especially the work they are asked to perform.

One further aspect of monocratic structure needs to be briefly described before we proceed to assess the implications of these structural variables for innovation within the organization. The hierarchy of authority is a procedure whereby organizationally directed proposals from within are affirmed or vetoed. It is a procedure which gives advantage to the veto because monocratic systems do not provide for appeals. An appeal implies conflicting rights which must be adjudicated, but the superior's veto of a subordinate's proposal legitimately rejects the proposal. An approval must usually go higher, where it is again subject to a veto. Thus, even if the monocratic organization allows new ideas to be generated, it is very apt to veto them.

Because production interests lead to overspecification of human resources, organizations in the past were composed largely of unskilled or semiskilled employees who carried out more or less simple procedures devised within the particular organization without previous special preparation. The white-collar unskilled or semiskilled have been conveniently labeled the "desk classes."[8] The work of the desk classes, as distinguished from scientific and technical workers, is determined by the organization rather than by

extensive pre-entry preparation. Deprived of intrinsic rewards related to the work or the rewards of growing esteem of professional peers, they become largely dependent upon the extrinsic rewards distributed by the hierarchy of authority, thereby greatly reinforcing that institution. Their dependence upon organizational programs and procedures for whatever function they acquire induces a conservative attitude with regard to these programs and procedures.

Except for the successful few, the morale of the desk classes is one of chronic, though not necessarily acute, dissatisfaction.[9] Overspecification plus dependence upon extrinsic rewards of promotion result in vast overrequirement of qualifications. The individual often becomes qualified for the minor incremental increase in difficulty of the next higher job years before it becomes available. The resulting, easily recognized, mental and emotional condition has been called the bureaucratic orientation.[10]

The bureaucratic orientation is conservative. Novel solutions, using resources in a new way, are likely to appear threatening. Those having a bureaucratic orientation are more concerned with the internal distribution of power and status than with organizational goal accomplishment. This converts the organization into a political system concerned with the distribution of these extrinsic rewards.[11] The first reaction to new ideas and suggested changes is most likely to be, "How does it affect us?" Some observations of the decisionmaking process in business organizations suggest that search in these organizations is largely an attempt by the groupings in this political system to find answers to that question: "How does it affect us?" They also suggest that the expectations of consequences upon which these organizations base their decisions are heavily biased by these same political interests.[12]

If new activities cannot be blocked entirely they can at least be segregated and eventually blocked from the communication system if necessary. Typically, the introduction of technical innovative activities into modern organizations is by means of segregated units, often called research and development units. Segregating such activities prevents them from affecting the status quo to any great extent. The organization does not have to change.[13]

We should add that it is not only the organizational political system which causes the segregation of new problems. There is often no place in the existing structure into which they can be fitted. When a new problem appears, the monocratic production-oriented organization is likely to find that the resources of authority, skills, and material needed to cope with it have already been fully specified and committed to other organization units. Since no existing unit has the uncommitted resources to deal with the new problem, a new organization unit is established.

An organization runs into a great deal of trouble trying to stimulate innovativeness within these segregated units. Since it cannot use the extrinsic reward system upon which the political system is based, it must fumble toward a reward system alien to the monocratic organization. It must establish conditions entirely foreign to the conditions of production upon which the monocratic organization is based. Two milieus, two sets of conditions, two systems of rewards, must be established, the one for innovation, the other for the rest of the organization's activities. This duality is divisive and upsetting to the existing distribution of satisfactions.

Beyond the political interests in the distribution of extrinsic rewards, there are other factors which strengthen tendencies toward parochialism. The organization seems to factor its activities into narrow, single-purpose, exclusive categories and to assign these to subunits composed of a superior and subordinates. Very often strong subunit and subgoal identifications arise from this pattern so that members of any unit know and care little about what other units are doing.[14] The organization tends to become a collection of small entities with boundaries and frontiers. When work is completed in one entity, it is handed over to another, and interest in it is dropped. Interest tends to be in protecting the records and protocols of the hand-over transaction so that blame can always be placed on another unit. Although the narrow-mission assignments are justified as needed "to pinpoint responsibility," they actually encourage irresponsibility as far as new problems are concerned because they facilitate dodging responsibility for them.[15]

The production-oriented overspecification and commitment of resources prevent the accumulation of free resources needed for innovative projects, including time, and deprives participants of the diversity of input so important in the generation of new ideas. Thus, even when people are hired to *innovate* they may be treated as though they were hired to *produce* and kept tied to their work. Diversity of input is also lost because of the tendency to assign each activity to a separate unit, which concentrates whatever diversity of input there is at one or a few local points. Thus, there may be stimulating ideas and information discussed within a planning unit or a research unit, but it does not extend to the rest of the organization. The research unit may be very creative, but the organization cannot innovate.

In monocratic responsibility, praise and blame attach to jurisdictions. People are to be punished for mistakes as well as wrongdoing, and they are to be punished for failures which occur within their jurisdictions whether due to their activities or not. ("He should have prevented it. It was his responsibility.")[16] Although this theory is not strictly applied any more, it is still feared. Thus, an individual may hesitate to advise an organization to take a particular action though he has good reason to believe that the probabilities for a satisfactory outcome are good. Should the project fail in this instance, he may be a personal failure. It is difficult to apply the concept of probability to personal failure.

One feels, rightly or wrongly, that he can only fail once. Therefore, what would be rational from the standpoint of the organization's goal may appear irrational from the standpoint of the individual's personal goals.[17]

New ideas are speculative and hence particularly dangerous to personal goals and especially the goals of power and status. Consequently, the monocratic organization, structured around such extrinsic goals and explicitly committed to this stringent theory of responsibility, is not likely to be highly innovative.

A monocratic variant which is highly innovative should be mentioned. New organizations are sometimes begun by highly creative individuals who attract like-minded people, maintain an atmosphere conducive to innovation, build up a powerful esprit de corps and achieve a very high level of organizational creativity. Often these are small engineering or research organizations started by an engineer or scientist assisted by a small group of able and personally loyal peers. The organization is new and small and not yet bureaucratized. Many able young people may be attracted to it because of the opportunity provided for professional growth. As these organizations grow larger and, particularly after the charismatic originator is no longer there, the monocratic stereotype reasserts itself and they become bureaucratized. This phenomenon is an old one, discussed by Weber as the "institutionalization of charisma." It is seen in one form in the post-revolutionary bureaucratization of successful revolutionary organizations.

The Innovative Organization

In summarizing the scattered suggestions for an organization with a high capacity to innovate, first the qualities and conditions needed will be discussed, then the structures or structural changes that will facilitate or create the required qualities and conditions.

General Requirements

First are needed resources for innovation—uncommitted money, time, skills, and good will. In human resources this means upgraded work and workers, optimally a person who has developed himself thoroughly in some area, about to the limits of his capacities, so that he has that richness of experience and self-confidence upon which creativity thrives —a professional. Complex technology requires the administration of "technical generalists," or professionals. A technology is incorporated into an organization through individuals. To incorporate it through overspecification or task specialization requires enormous coordination. Furthermore, coordinating the elements of a technology is part of the technology itself, as the current technical emphasis on systems design, systems engineering, etc., testify. The technology deals not only with simple relationships, but with the relationships between relationships as well. Hence, coordination is not a different, non-technical process, such as management, but part of the complex technology itself. Although production interests may be well served by employing a few technical professionals to coordinate the many over-specified workers, the innovative potential of the technology can hardly be realized in this way.

The innovative organization will allow the diversity of inputs needed for the creative generation of ideas. Long periods of pre-entry, professional training, and wide diffusion of ideas within the organization, including a wide diffusion of problems and suggested solutions, will provide the variety and richness of experience required. Included should be a wide diffusion of uncertainty so that the whole organization is stimulated to search, rather than just a few professional researchers. Involving larger parts of the organization in the search process also increases chances of acceptance and implementation. This wide diffusion, in turn, will depend upon ease and freedom of communication and a low level of parochialism.

Complete commitment to the organization will not promote innovation, as we have seen; neither will complete alienation from the organization. The relationship between personal and organizational goals, ideally, would seem to be where individuals perceive the organization as an avenue for professional growth. The interest in professional growth provides the rising aspiration level needed to stimulate search beyond the first-found satisfactory solution, and the perception of the organization as a vehicle for professional growth harnesses this powerful motivation to the interests of the organization in a partial fusion of goals, personal and organizational.[18]

Instead of the usual extrinsic organizational rewards of income, power, and status, satisfactions come from the search process, professional growth, and the esteem of knowledgeable peers—rewards most conducive to innovation. Benevolent intellectual competition rather than malevolent status and power competition is needed. For these reasons, creative work, the process of search and discovery, needs to be highly visible to respected peers. Dedication to creative work cannot be expected if positional status continues to be defined as the principal sign of personal worth. But reduction of status-striving is also important because it is inescapably associated with personal insecurity,[19] which is hardly compatible with creativity. What is needed is a certain level of problem insecurity and challenge, but a high level of personal security.

The creative atmosphere should be free from external pressure. A person is not likely to be creative if too much hangs on a successful outcome of his search activities, for he will have a strong tendency to accept the first satisfactory solution whether or not it seems novel or the best possible. Thus, he needs indulgence in time and resources, and particularly in organizational evaluations of his activities.

He needs freedom to innovate. He also needs considerable, but not complete, autonomy and self-direction and a large voice in deciding at what he will work.[20]

In summary, the innovative organization will be much more professional than most existing ones. Work will be much less determined by production-oriented planners on the Smith's pins model and more determined by the extended periods of pre-entry training. The desk classes will decline in number and importance relative to professional, scientific, and technical workers. There will be a great increase in interorganizational mobility and a corresponding decline in organizational chauvinism. The concept of organizations as organic entities with some claim to survive will tend to be replaced by the concept of organizations as opportunities for professional growth. In the innovative organization, professional orientations and loyalties will be stronger relative to organizational or bureaucratic ones. Esteem striving will tend to replace status striving. There will be less control by superiors and more by self and peers. Power and influence will be much more broadly dispersed.

The dispersal of power is important because concentrated power often prevents imaginative solutions of problems. When power meets power, problem solving is necessarily called into play. The power of unions has undoubtedly stimulated managerial innovations.[21] Dispersed power, paradoxically, can make resources more readily available to support innovative projects because it makes possible a larger number and variety of subcoalitions. It expands the number and kinds of possible supporters and sponsors.

Structural Requirements

The innovative organization will be characterized by structural looseness generally, with less emphasis on narrow, nonduplicating, nonoverlapping definitions of duties and responsibilities. Job descriptions will be of the professional type rather than the duties type. Communications will be freer and legitimate in all directions. Assignment and resource decisions will be much more decentralized than is customary.

The innovative organization will not be as highly stratified as existing ones. This is implied in the freedom of communication, but the decline in the importance of the extrinsic rewards of positional status and the growth of interest in professional esteem would bring this about anyway. Salary scales will be adjusted accordingly and no longer reflect chiefly awesome status differences.

Group processes will be more, and more openly, used than at present. The freer communication system, the broader work assignments, the lack of preoccupation with overlap and duplication, the lessened emphasis upon authority will all work in the direction of a greater amount of interpersonal communication and multiple group membership. Multiple group membership will facilitate innovation by increasing the amount and diversity of input of ideas and stimulation, and by acting as a discipline of the hierarchical veto. When a new idea is known and supported by groupings beyond the authority grouping, it is not easy to veto it. Multiple-group membership helps to overcome the absence of a formal appeal by providing an informal appeal to a free constituency of peers.

In an atmosphere which encourages and legitimizes multiple group membership, the malignant peer competition of the authority grouping (of fellow subordinates) will no longer exercise the powerful constrainings against "showing-up" with new ideas.[22] The greater ease of acquiring group memberships and the greater legitimacy of groups will reduce the risk of innovation to the individual. Responsibility for new ideas can be shared as can the onus of promoting them. Wide participation in the generation process will greatly facilitate acceptance and implementation.

Present methods of departmentalization encourage parochialism with its great re-

sistance to new ideas from outside. Often it is not goals that are assigned, actually, but jurisdictions. (For example, although 98 percent of the farms are electrified, the Rural Electrification Administration has not been abolished.) It is not a group of interdependent skills brought together to carry out some project, but a conference of sovereignty. At the simple unit level (superior and subordinates), it is often, but not always, an aggregative grouping—a number of people with the same skills doing the same thing. Lacking the stimulation of different skills, views, and perspectives, and the rewards of project completion and success, such groupings are likely to seek extrinsic rewards and to seek them through the organizational political system.

Other simple units, even though not composed of aggregations of people doing the same thing, are very often composed of overspecified desk classes carrying out some continuing program—getting out the house organ, or managing the budget, or recruiting, or keeping stores. In such an integrative grouping there may be more interpersonal stimulation, but overspecification—the sheer subprofessional simplicity of the jobs—prevents the diversity and richness required for anything but very minor innovations.

The aggregative grouping has neither interdependence nor goal. Group innovation is therefore impossible. Individual innovation in the interest of the organization is hardly likely, unless the organization offers rewards for it. Sometimes organizations reward individual innovative suggestions through suggestion-box systems. Such systems are rarely successful. As far as aggregative units are concerned, the lack of input diversity prevents any important innovative insights. For integrative units, suggestion boxes are frequently disruptive because the true authorship of the suggestion is likely to be in dispute, and the group will often feel that the idea should have been presented to the group rather than individually presented for an award.[23]

In the innovative organization, departmentalization must be arranged so as to keep parochialism to a minimum. Some overlapping and duplication, some vagueness about jurisdictions, make a good deal of communication necessary. People have to define and redefine their responsibilities continually, case after case. They have to probe and seek for help. New problems cannot with certainty be rejected as ultra vires.[24]

The simple unit should be an integrative grouping of various professionals and subprofessionals engaged upon an integrative task requiring a high degree of technical interdependence and group problem solving. Or else the simple unit should be merely a housekeeping unit. Project teams could be drawn from such housekeeping units. Ideally, individuals would have project rather than continuing assignments. If project organization is not feasible, individuals should be rotated occasionally. Even if continuing assignments, or jurisdictions, seem to be technically necessary, organization units can probably convert a large part of their activities into successive projects, or have a number of projects going on at the same time, so that individuals can be constantly renewing themselves in new and challenging problems and experiencing a maximum input of diverse stimulation and ideas. It might even be possible for individual and unit jurisdictions and responsibilities to be exchanged occasionally.

If formal structures could be sufficiently loosened, it might be possible for organizations and units to restructure themselves continually in the light of the problem at hand. Thus, for generating ideas, for planning and problem solving, the organization or unit would "unstructure" itself into a freely communicating body of equals. When it came time for implementation, requiring a higher degree of coordination of action (as opposed to stimulation of novel or correct ideas), the organization could then restructure itself into the more usual hierarchical form, tightening up its lines somewhat.

Empirical evidence that different kinds of structure are optimal for different kinds of problems is compelling.[25] Almost equally compelling is the evidence that leadership role assignments need to be changed as the situation changes.[26] Bureaucratic rigidity makes such rational structural alterations almost impossible. It is hard to escape the conclusion that current organization structures are *not* the most rational adaptations for *some* kinds of problem solving. Although experimental groups have been successfully restructured from bureaucratic to collegial by means of verbal redefinitions of roles along lines perceived to be more appropriate to the task at hand,[27] such restructuring is probably impossible in real-live "traditionated" organizations as presently constituted.

The abandonment of the use of hierarchical positions as prizes or rewards, however, and the decline in the importance of extrinsic rewards generally, would render organizational structure much more amenable to manipulation. The personal appropriation of administrative resources (such as position and authority), almost universal in modern bureaucratic organizations and reminiscent of primitive agrarian cultures, could decline considerably.[28] If it should prove impossible for organizations to become flexible enough to allow restructuring themselves in the light of the problem at hand, it would be preferable to retain a loose structure in the interest of generating new ideas and suffer from some fumbling in the attempt to coordinate action for the purpose of carrying them out. After all, thought and action cannot be sharply distinguished, and a good deal of problem solving occurs during implementation. The thinking is then tested and completed.

Integrative departmentalization, combined with freedom of communication, interunit projects, and lessened subunit chauvinism, will create extradepartmental professional ties and interests, resulting in an increase in the diversity and richness of inputs and in their diffusion, thereby stimulating creativity. Intellectual competition is more likely to be provided by this broader milieu. It is more likely to be the generating area than the smaller authority grouping or the larger organization.

We need to think in terms of innovative areas rather than formal departments, in terms of the conditions for generating new and good ideas rather than of jurisdiction. In the innovative organization, innovation will not be assigned to an isolated or segregated jurisdiction such as research and development. The innovative contributions of everyone, including the man at the machine, are needed. Characteristically, the innovative area will be larger than the formal unit and smaller than the organization. Resource control should be sufficiently decentralized so that appropriate resource accumulation through subcoalition would be possible within the innovative area. In effect, the formal distribution of jurisdictions should be just a skeleton to be used when an arbitrary decision was required.

In the physical aspect of organizations, the architecture and furnishings of today's bureaucratic organizations seem to be departing further and further from the needs of the innovative organization. The majestic, quiet halls and closed, windowless office doors are not designed to encourage communication. They fill a potential communicator with fear. "Will I be disturbing him?" he wonders. It is doubtful that deep blue rugs have anything to do with discovery and invention. We all remember where the first atomic chain reaction took place. Modern bureaucratic architecture and furnishings seem to reflect an increased concern with the extrinsic reward system. We seem to be in the midst of a new primitivism; the means of administration seem to be increasingly appropriated by the officials. This may reflect an attempt by the monocratic organization to attract innovative technical and scientific talent. With success available to only a few and the organization increasingly dependent upon large numbers of highly trained professionals and subprofessionals, it is hoped that richness of surroundings will do what an inappropriate reward system cannot do.

The purchase of motivation with extrinsic rewards is becoming more and more costly, and innovation cannot be purchased in this way at all. What is needed is both much less expensive and much more costly—the devaluation of authority and positional status and the recognized, official sharing of power and influence.

Implications for Administrative Practice

Associated with all of these structural changes there will need to be many changes in administrative practices. Only a few of the most obvious ones will be mentioned. The present common practice of annual performance ratings by superiors would probably have to be dropped. Many believe that this practice is hostile even to production interests. It is clearly inconsistent with increasing professionalism, since professional standing is not determined by a hierarchical superior. Rather than a single system of ranks, with corresponding salaries, there will be a multiple ranking system and multiple salary scales. The managerial or hierarchical ranking system will be only one among many. Presumably, it will not carry the highest ranks. The American public has for a long time ranked several occupations above management.[29]

Job descriptions and classifications will have to accommodate an increasing proportion of professionals. The duties and responsibilities approach to job descriptions was designed for a desk-class age. It does not accommodate professional work easily.

Peer evaluations will become more important in recruitment and placement, and it is possible that a kind of election process will be used to fill authority positions. At any rate, the wishes of subordinates will probably be considered a good deal more than is present practice. One would expect considerable modification in procedures relating to secrecy and loyalty. The innovative organization will be more indulgent with regard to patents, publications, and so on. The relationship between visibility and professional growth will require this, and increased interorganizational mobility will enforce it. Present fringe benefit devices that tend to restrict mobility will have to be altered.

Administrative innovation requires the same conditions and structures as technical innovation. Professionalization in this area also requires the elimination of overspecified resources. The unskilled administrative worker should go along with his blue-collar counterpart. Many administrative technologies are poorly accredited, and some are perhaps spurious pseudoskills in handling some more or less complex procedure. If the procedure is changed, these "skills" will no longer be needed. It is doubtful that the rapid expansion of administrative overhead in recent years has contributed to productivity, suggesting that some of this expansion may not have been technically justified and that it represents organizational slack made possible by increased productivity resulting from other causes.[30]

Administrative activities should be dispersed and decentralized down to the level of the innovative area, allowing administrative personnel to become part of integrative problem-solving groups rather than resentful onlookers sharpshooting from the outside. The innovative organization is innovative throughout and the innovative insights of the engineer, the research scientist, the machine tender, the administrative expert are all needed. If responsibilities and jurisdictions are occasionally exchanged, as suggested above, administrative responsibilities should be included in such exchanges. To paraphrase a famous expression, administrative work is too important to be left entirely to administrators.

Resistance to suggestions of this kind will be especially strong in the monocratic organization oriented to production and control. The reevaluation of the relative importance of managerial and nonmanagerial activities and the declining emphasis on extrinsic rewards, both implied in increasing professionalization of organiza-

tions, will reduce this resistance. The "need to control" is an almost inevitable psychological product of the structured field which the modern bureaucratic organization constitutes. Altering the field alters the product.

The emphasis on the need for free resources, time, indulgence with regard to controls, decentralization, and many more, all suggest on the surface that the innovative organization will be a costly one. Perhaps a high level of innovation is too costly, but the available knowledge is not adequate to reach a conclusion. We do not know the value of the novel ideas, processes, and products which might be produced by the innovative organization, and we do not know that our present methods of costing and control are the best approach to achieving low-cost production. Likert's arguments that present methods of cost reduction are superficial and actually increase costs in the long run by impairing the health of the social organism are impressive.[31] It would seem that the overspecification of work would automatically create the need for a costly administrative overhead apparatus to plan, schedule, coordinate and control so that all the overspecified parts are kept fully meshed and fully occupied. The problem is like that of keeping inventory. We cannot say that the organizational structure outlined will be either more or less costly, more or less beneficial to society, but it will be more innovative. We also suspect that it may be a fair projection of the organization of the future.

References and Notes

1. See Richard M. Cyert and James G. March, *A Behavioral Theory of the Firm* (Englewood Cliffs, N.J.: Prentice-Hall, Inc., 1963), pp. 27–28.
2. James G. March and Herbert A. Simon, *Organizations* (New York: John Wiley & Sons, Inc., 1958), p. 158; and Herbert A. Simon, *The New Science of Management Decision* (New York: Harper & Row, Publishers, 1960), p. 7.
3. Cyert and March, *Behavioral Theory*.
4. See Tom Burns and G. M. Stalker, *The Management of Innovation* (London: Tavistock Publications, 1959); and Gerald Gordon and Selwyn Becker,

"Changes in Medical Practice Bring Shifts in the Patterns of Power," *The Modern Hospital* 102 (Feb. 1964): 89.

5. See Robert V. Presthus, *The Organizational Society* (New York: Alfred A. Knopf, Inc., 1962).

6. Recent investigations of work motivation indicate quite strongly that a poorly administered wage and salary system can make for dissatisfaction, but that a well-administered one has little power to motivate to high performance. See Frederick Herzberg, Bernard Mausner, and Barbara Snyderman, *The Motivation to Work* (New York: John Wiley & Sons, Inc., 1959) and M. Scott Meyers' unpublished report on recent motivation research at the Texas Instrument Company, "The Management of Motivation to Work."

7. See Lewis C. Mainzer, "The Scientist as Public Administrator," *Western Political Quarterly* 16 (1963): 814–29. Of the Federal executives in grades GS–14 and above, only about one in forty-five has had college training in public administration (derived from Table 42B, p. 361, in W. Lloyd Warner, Paul P. Van Riper, Norman H. Martin, and Orvis F. Collins, *The American Federal Executive* [New Haven, Conn.: Yale University, 1963]).

8. Nigel Walker, *Morale in the Civil Service: A Study of the Desk Worker* (Edinburgh: Edinburgh University, 1960).

9. Ibid.

10. The contrast between the professional and the bureaucratic orientation has been studied and discussed by many people. A few references are: Alvin W. Gouldner, "Cosmopolitans and Locals," *Administrative Science Quarterly* 2 (1957–1958): 281–306, and 444–80; Leonard Reissman, "A Study of Role Conceptions in a Bureaucracy," *Social Forces* 27 (1949): 305–10; and Harold L. Wilensky, *Intellectuals in Labor Unions* (New York: Free Press, Div. of The Macmillan Company, 1956), 129–44.

11. Burns and Stalker, *The Management of Innovation,* and Melville Dalton, "Conflict Between Line and Staff Managerial Officers," *American Sociological Review* 15 (1950): 342–51.

12. See R. M. Cyert, W. R. Dill, and J. G. March, "The Role of Expectations in Business Decision-making," *Administrative Science Quarterly* 3 (1958): 307–40; and Cyert and March, *Behavioral Theory,* chap. iv.

13. Burns and Stalker, *The Management of Innovation.*

14. See Eliot O. Chapple and Leonard R. Sayles, *The Measure of Management* (New York: The Macmillan Company, 1961), pp. 18–40; March and Simon, *Organizations,* pp. 150–54; Victor A. Thompson, *The Regulatory Process in OPA Rationing* (New York: King's Crown Press, 1950), pt. II; and James R. Bright, ed., *Technological Planning on the Corporate Level* (Boston: Harvard University Graduate School of Business Administration, 1962), passim.

15. Burns and Stalker, *The Management of Innovation.*

16. See Victor A. Thompson, *Modern Organization* (New York: Alfred A. Knopf, Inc., 1961), pp. 129–37.

17. Derived from Kurt W. Back's discussion of non-rational choice. See "Decisions under Uncertainty," *American Behavioral Scientist* 4 (1961): 14–19.

18. See Peter M. Blau and W. Richard Scott, *Formal Organizations* (San Francisco: Chandler Publishing Company, 1962), pp. 60–74.

19. Rollo May, *The Meaning of Anxiety* (New York: Ronald Press Company, 1950), especially pp. 181–89.

20. A good part of the literature on individual creativity is summarized in Morris I. Stein and Shirley J. Heinze, *Creativity and the Individual* (New York: Free Press, Div. of The Macmillan Company, 1960).

21. See Eric Hoffer, *The Ordeal of Change* (New York: Harper & Row, Publishers, 1964), pp. 81–82; and Seymour Melman, *Decisionmaking and Productivity* (Oxford: Oxford University, 1958).

22. See William H. Whyte, Jr., *The Organization Man* (Garden City, N.Y.: Doubleday & Company, Inc., 1957), chaps. x and xvi.

23. See Norman J. Powell, *Personnel Administration in Government* (Englewood Cliffs, N.J.: Prentice-Hall, Inc., 1956), pp. 438–44. Powell believes that suggestion-box systems are better than no communication with the rank and file at all. Because of disputed authorship of suggestions, the TVA decided to give only group (noncash) awards.

24. Burns and Stalker, *The Management of Innovation.* See also B. Klein, "A Radical Proposal for R and D," *Fortune* 57 (May 1958): 112; B. Klein and W. Meckling, "Application of Operations Research to Development Decisions," *Operations Research* 6 (1958): 352–63; Albert O. Hirshman, *The Strategy of Economic Development* (New Haven, Conn.: Yale University, 1958); Albert O. Hirshman and Charles E. Lindblom, "Economic Development, Research and Development, Policy Making: Some Converging Views," *Behavioral Science* 7 (1962): 211–22; and David Braybrooke and Charles E. Lindblom, *A Strategy of Decision* (New York: Free Press, Div. of The Macmillan Company, 1963).

25. Some of this evidence is reviewed in Blau and Scott, *Formal Organizations,* chap. v.

26. The evidence is reviewed in Cecil A. Gibb, "Leadership," in Gardner Lindzey, ed., *Handbook of Social Psychology* (Reading, Mass.: Addison-Wesley Publishing Company, Inc., 1954), vol. 2, pp. 877–917.

27. André L. Delbecq, *Leadership in Business Decision Conferences* (unpublished Ph.D. dissertation, Indiana University, 1963).

28. See Victor A. Thompson, "Bureaucracy in a Democracy," in Roscoe Martin, ed., *Public Adminis-*

tration and Democracy (Syracuse, N.Y.: Syracuse University, forthcoming).

29. Alex Inkeles and Peter H. Rossi, "National Comparisons of Occupational Prestige," in Seymour Martin Lipset and Neil J. Smelser, eds., *Sociology: The Progress of a Decade* (Englewood Cliffs, N.J.: Prentice-Hall, Inc., 1961), pp. 506–16.

30. See Seymour Melman, "The Rise of Administrative Overhead in the Manufacturing Industries of the United States, 1899–1947," *Oxford Economic Papers* 3 (1951): 62–93 and *Dynamic Factors in Industrial Productivity* (New York: John Wiley & Sons, Inc., 1956).

31. Rensis Likert and Stanley E. Seashore, "Making Cost Control Work," *Harvard Business Review* 41 (November-December 1963): 96–108.

INNOVATION-RESISTING AND INNOVATION-PRODUCING ORGANIZATIONS

Herbert A. Shepard

When an organization learns to do something it did not know how to do before, and then proceeds to do it in a sustained way, a process of innovation has occurred. Similarly, it is an innovation if an organization learns not to do something it formerly did, and proceeds to not do it in a sustained way—for example, when a large mail-order house decided to stop keeping a mass of records that it formerly kept.

Three stages are often distinguished in the innovative process: idea generation, adoption, and implementation. The phases may overlap or merge into each other. For example, participation in the phase of generation is likely to accomplish the adoption phase for the participants. But since there is a limit to the number of subunits that can be brought into the generation phase, there must usually be a separate phase of co-option, persuasion, demonstration, and command before the organization can be said to have adopted the idea. In some cases, adoption is tantamount to implementation; in others, implementation may be the most difficult part of the process, and require more creative problem solving than did the generation phase. For example, a government agency adopted the idea of building a professional, consultant-client relationship between its personnel and the public, but failed to provide an adequate retraining program for its personnel. As a result, the achievement of the agency's mission began to suffer, and the innovation was abandoned.

An organization is itself an innovation, but most organizations of the past have been designed to be innovation resisting. Like fully automated factories, organizations that contain people have customarily been designed to do a narrowly prescribed assortment of things and to do them reliably. To insure reliable repetition of prescribed operations, the organization requires strong defenses against innovation. Efforts to innovate must be relegated to the categories of error, irresponsibility, and insubordination, and appropriate corrective action taken to bring the would-be innovators "back in line." Any change is likely to run counter to certain vested interests and to violate certain territorial rights. Sentiments of vested interest and territorial rights are sanctified as delegations of legitimate authority in traditional organizations, thus guaranteeing quick and effective counteraction against disturbances. In theory, the innovation-resisting organization is not resistant to innovations issuing from the top of its authority structure. In the Preface to one of the first Operations Research books, its authors stressed the importance of having the Operations Research team report directly to the chief executive, recognizing that the military organization can learn only at the top; changes in operations at lower levels occur by instruction from higher levels. But even the power of command is not always equal to the power of resistance, especially as society puts ever greater limitations on the power of command in civilian life.

For these reasons, exploration of the innovative process in organizations can conveniently proceed along two paths; first, how innovation is induced in settings which are resistant to innovation; and second, how to design an organization which is productive of innovations rather than resistant to them. A third path emerges out of an examination of the first two, namely, the exploration of a particular class of innovations, those which change an innnovation-resisting organization into an innovation-producing one, or vice versa.

The Process of Innovation in Innovation-Resisting Organizations

Innovative ideas are most likely to occur to persons who have some familiarity with the situation to which the ideas would apply. Hence, most novel ideas are likely to be generated at some distance from the power center of the organization. Since new ideas are disturbances, they are efficiently screened out of the stream of upward communication. But because power is centralized at the top, top support for an idea is almost a necessity if it is to move toward becoming an innovation. What strategies are available for breaking out of this system?

One alternative is to conceal the innovation from the rest of the organization. Almost all policing systems have loopholes. Perhaps the commonest example of concealment is the machine opera-

tor who develops a device to simplify his work but does not use it when the industrial engineers are setting standards for his job. Similarly, salesmen often use methods and procedures that increase their effectiveness but are unknown to their superiors and even explicitly contrary to company rules. Most organizations possess an underworld of technique and technology, some of which is simply used to gain some freedom from the impositions of higher levels of authority and some of which contributes to the achievement of corporate goals. Within the underworld, the innovations may or may not be circulated. A worker who invents a jig to help him perform a particular operation may tell no one else, or he may have his co-workers act as sentinels to insure that he is not found out.

Most concealed innovations must take the form of local conspiracies if they are to be of real significance. Perhaps the most general formula for effective innovation is: "An idea; initiative; and a few friends." Sometimes large segments of organizations conspire in this way. One vice-president speaks of "holding an umbrella" over certain of his subordinate organizations so that they are free to innovate. Another speaks of "surrounding the president with a moving framework" so that new developments can occur in the organization. An important weapon system was developed by a small group in a government laboratory over a five-year period in continuous violation of directives from headquarters to discontinue work. The entire laboratory gave support to the innovators in concealing their assignments and the costs of development. Two of our largest corporations now do over a third of their business in areas which the board of directors explicitly decided not to enter, only to find that the company was already obligated by contracts negotiated at lower levels. A manufacturing vice-president successfully concealed from his superiors an experiment in union-management cooperation in one of his plants.

Evidently, the innovator or the innovating group must be prepared to take some risks. The subjective side of these risks deserves attention. For the dependent person who is "a good soldier," responsive to the formal structure of authority, the risks have to do with job security and the threat to his chances of a raise and advancement in the structure. He avoids innovation and checks innovators. The less simple-minded executive (as described by Vance Packard or William H. Whyte, Jr.), oriented primarily toward achievement, avoids only major innovations, since recognition by superiors requires the appearance of innovativeness. He risks advancement if he wanders toward the extremes of appearing to be just a good soldier or appearing to lack mature judgment. As Jennings puts it:

Anyone who takes long chances will find that the averages are against him. This we found to be an axiom of political experience. Major changes set loose unknown forces that gather a momentum of their own and smash through to results unwanted by anyone, including the executive. Consequently, it is far wiser to sponsor many minor changes that only appear to be tests of ability. . . . [1]

The innovator who fails is likely to be motivated by rebelliousness against authority. For him the risk is in *not innovating* [Italics added.]—in having to confront feelings of inferiority or subordination.

For the successful innovator, too, the subjective risk lies in not innovating. He risks his sense of self-worth if he must settle for compromises or for less than full personal effectiveness and contribution. The "objective" risk, in terms of the organization's logics [sic][, is to his job security or chances for advancement, but this does not mean that he is subjectively taking the risk in the hope of a large payoff in terms of personal advancement. In this sense, successful innovators are often marginal to the organization; that is, their basis for self-esteem is somewhat independent of organizational values as expressed in its reward and punishment system. They are also, perhaps for the same reason, often marginal in the sense that they are more able than others to cross some traditional boundaries in the organization—to gain personal acceptance farther up and down the line than others or among a larger number of peers across the organization.

To insure that his idea becomes an innovation, the innovator must take steps to insure the maintenance and advancement of his own influence, even though this may not be his motive in innovating. Often it appears that he has sufficient personal conviction about the potential value of his innovation that he is willing to "bet his job and reputation on it." The key innovator in the weapons system development referred to earlier was convinced that, if he could get it to the point of demonstration, top military officials would find it irresistible, despite the fact that it had been produced in violation of direct orders, accounting rules, etc. He was correct, and was named head of the laboratory. In a somewhat similar way, the persons who negotiated contracts which obligated their companies to enter new businesses were indispensable to the successful conduct of the new business.

Outside as well as inside sources of support are often used by the successful innovator in acquiring a critical mass of support. A group of staff engineers in one company designed a process plant containing a number of radical innovations, then arranged to have a distinguished chemical engineer employed as consultant to evaluate their work. A comparison of two approaches within a university, both by men whose motivation was that of successful innovators, is instructive. Each was given an opportunity to develop an interdisciplinary research institute. One concentrated on building collaborative relations with key members of the departments involved; the other concentrated on raising research funds from outside the university, which required the collaboration of only a few other members of the staff. Deducing which institute succeeded is left as an exercise for the reader.

As some of the above examples imply, respectability is an innovator's best friend, and, since innovation is not a respectable undertaking in innovation-resisting organizations, he should choose respectable friends to support him. If he can find none in the organization, then he may seek them outside and help them find ways they can help him. But highly respected executives inside the firm are in a better position to serve as promoters and protectors, midwives and nurses.

Although top management support is always necessary for the adoption of an innovative idea, it is by no means sufficient to insure its implementation. The skill with which the career civil service staff of a government agency can frustrate the innovative efforts of a newly appointed chief from industry is often dramatic. Similarly, the university president who seeks to reform the college is met with resistance tactics that the use of the power of his office cannot thwart. In industry, a new chief executive entering the organization from outside finds it easier to remove subordinate executives who stand in the way of his innovative efforts, and even a chief executive promoted from within is able to rearrange the power structure with greater ease than can be done in government or in a university.

Radical innovations are most readily adopted and implemented in times of organizational crisis. Earlier it was noted that the innovator must find a way of breaking out of the closed organizational system that is resistant to innovation. During a crisis there is an external threat to the survival of that system; for a moment it is open and searching for new solutions to the basic problem of survival.

A state of crisis does not itself generate good innovative ideas. But the uncertainty and anxiety generated by the crisis make organization members eager to adopt new structures that promise to relieve the anxi-

ety. Thus, in an early crisis in the automobile industry, a new leader brought into one corporation had a ready-made plan for reorganization that made it possible for the firm to recover quickly and take the lead. In another company in the same industry, the crisis brought panic innovations—for example, most of the telephones were removed—instead of innovations rationally designed to solve the problems.

Innovators may even help to generate a crisis in order to create conditions favorable to the adoption and implementation of their innovation. One man in charge of manufacturing a number of product lines in a large corporation saw that one of them was suffering severely in the competition in its industry. He developed a plan for radically altering the financial, marketing, engineering, and production organization behind this product line, although he was aware that higher levels of management would reject it. He then waited two years until the product line was losing so badly that it came to the attention of top management to decide whether it should be dropped. At that time, the innovator produced his plan for reorganization and asked for a year to try the experiment. He got it.

So much for innovation in innovation-resisting organizations. It requires an unusual combination of qualities: a creative but pragmatic imagination; psychological security and an autonomous nature; an ability to trust others and to earn the trust of others; great energy and determination; a sense of timing; skill in organizing; and a willingness and ability to be Machiavellian where that is what the situation requires.

Innovation in Innovation-Producing Organizations

An innovation-producing organization is one which is continuously learning, adapting to changes within itself and in its environment, and successfully innovating in that environment. What can we say about the organizational form, values and norms, decisionmaking processes, rewards, punishments, structures of authority, power, influence and status, and the mentality and character structure of members in successful innovation-producing organizations?

The nature of the problem confronting modern organizations has been changing rapidly. In the past, the major problem has appeared to be how to get and coordinate reliable, efficient repetitive responses from specialized individuals: how to do complex, programmable tasks with people as the doers. But the direction of modern technology is to eliminate people from the doing of programmable tasks. What must be done many times can, in general, be automated. Principles of human organization developed to serve that end are almost certain to be misleading when the major problem becomes finding ways in which people can organize for innovative, unprogrammable activities. Yet manufacturing, command, mechanistic, and bureaucratic principles are so pervasive in our society that all activities tend to be forced into this mold even when it prevents the achievement of announced objectives. The schools stand in the way of learning; the research organization stands in the way of research; the sales and service organizations stand in the way of sales and service.

Yet there are some organizations and parts of organizations whose principles of operation are different from the bureaucratic norm and whose output is innovative. From observations of such organizational inventions, some tentative principles can be inferred.

One of the most prominent of these is periodicity—or a number of kinds of alternation associated with innovating groups. One kind consists of adapting organizational form to suit the requirements of the task at a given phase of innovation. For the generation phase of an innovation, the organization needs a quality of openness so that diverse and heterogeneous persons can contribute, and so that many alternatives can be explored. For implementation, a quite different quality may be needed: singleness of purpose, functional division of labor, responsibility and authority, discipline, the drawing of internal communication boundaries, and so on. For example, a military raiding unit in the Pacific during World War II made use of alternating organizational forms. The planning before a raid was done jointly by the entire unit—the private having as much opportunity to contribute to the planning as the colonel. During the raid, the group operated under a strict military command system. Following each raid, the unit returned to the open system used in planning for purposes of evaluating and maximizing learning from each raid.

A similar periodicity has been noted in the precontract and postcontract phases of development projects in the industries serving space and weapons systems needs of the government. Before the contract, in exploring alternatives and preparing a proposal, an open system is often used. After the contract, or in the implementation phase, a discipline is imposed. External controls imposed on development groups are often dysfunctional, of course, but even in organizations where these are de-emphasized, groups acquire a singleness of purpose, a system of role differentiation, and a discipline which is lacking during the exploratory phase.

Some industries are provided with natural periodicities, either seasonal or through such industrial traditions as an annual model change. These rhythms permit an opportunity for alternation of periods of action, involvement, experience, and discipline with periods of evaluation, revitalization, reflection, and planning (though the opportunities may not be grasped). In industries not provided with natural alternation, opportunities for periods of evaluation, revitalization, reflection, and planning have to be created. There is an increasing use of executive "retreats" for these purposes.

Other types of periodicity which seem

to be stimulating to the innovative process have been noted. One is to have two groups working in parallel on the same problem, with periodic opportunities for intergroup communication. The use of special task forces or a modified project form[2] of organization provides another kind of periodicity, so that members are regrouped and provided with novel challenges periodically.

Returning to the example of the military raiding unit, it seems clear that the interpersonal relationships and group norms of this unit were at variance with those of an innovation-resisting organization, even though at times the unit operated as a command system in accord with military regulations. It was as though they chose to operate as a command system by consensus, rather than operating at other times as an open system by command. Presumably, their close interdependence for physical survival helped to create a climate of sufficient mutual trust and respect that rank could be cast aside and the private could feel free to criticize his superiors. The same qualities of trust, mutual respect, openness, and ability to confront conflict appear to characterize innovative groups in other contexts. This was the quality of relationships in some of the ad hoc project teams of distinguished scientists and engineers created by the government shortly after World War II to appraise certain key issues in national defense. The same was true of "Blackett's Circus," the pioneering operational research team in England during World War II. The boundaries of each individual's scientific territory were freely crossed, and symbols of differential status in the scientific community were thrown aside in favor of joint problem solving.

It is significant that the examples that come to mind are in temporary systems created by national emergencies. They are in fact only further examples of the point already made with respect to the readiness of innovation-resisting organizations for innovation during a period of survival crisis. At such times, men are readier to give up their boring and petty struggles for status—scientific politics—to become less alienated from one another and from themselves.

Yet we know that simply putting one group against another under win-lose conditions does not lead to the best use of its resources. As noted earlier, it is more likely to lead to panic innovation, closing off of communication lines, closed system operation, and punishment of nonconformity. The common factor in the above examples is that the groups operated as open systems; the national emergency provided a common cause, challenge, or superordinate goal, rather than a source of panic.

Under these conditions then—superordinate goals held in common, and a temporary system in which status struggles can for the moment be set aside—the members of the system all evidence, to greater or lesser degree, the "unusual" qualities earlier attributed to the innovator: a creative but pragmatic imagination; psychological security and an autonomous nature; an ability to trust others and to earn the trust of others, great energy and determination; skill in organizing; and a willingness and ability to be Machiavellian (in these cases, the group's mission called for just that).

Can equivalent conditions be attained in an organization whose task is to produce innovations? The character structure of the innovator in innovation-resisting organizations corresponds to what the existential psychologists call the "self-actualizing" person. He is his own man rather than the organization's man; his behavior and sense of self-worth are not blindly determined by the organization's reward and punishment system (either in the form of submission to it or rebellion against it); if he cannot transform his situation into one in which he and others can be both autonomous and interdependent, he feels free to fight it or to leave it.

Such men are rare because the institutions of our society do not provide the conditions under which many persons are able to grow to this degree of human maturity. The innovation-producing organization must aim to provide an environment in which this kind of growth can occur. This means a climate in which members can view one another as resources rather than competitive threats or judges; a climate of openness and mutual support in which differences can be confronted and worked through, and in which feedback on performance is a mutual responsibility among members so that all can learn to contribute more. Such an environment is difficult to provide, since it is at variance with traditional management doctrine. A case will illustrate its importance for innovation-producing organizations and also the difficulties of maintaining it.

By direction of a governmental sponsor, a prime contractor awarded two subcontracts for prototype development of a complex and highly sophisticated subsystem. The contract for advanced development, engineering, and production of the subsystem would then be awarded to the subcontractor producing the better prototype. The working environment in Subcontractor A's establishment was a close approximation of an ideal innovation-producing environment. The members of this project team in Subcontractor A's establishment set about building with the prime contractor the same climate of openness and problem solving as they experienced with one another and with other groups in A. They encountered and solved creatively many problems in developing the prototype. The prime contractor was kept fully informed of their problems as well as their methods of tackling them, and was extremely pleased by their ingenuity and the rapid progress they were making toward a satisfactory prototype.

Subcontractor B's establishment proceeded to relate in a more traditional manner. They provided the prime contractor with glowing accounts of their progress and discussed no problems. The prime contractor also operated in a traditional way with B, and through unofficial espionage learned that Subcontractor B was in fact doing very badly, in contradiction of his reports.

About halfway through the period set for prototype development, political pressures on the governmental sponsoring agency caused it to put pressure on the prime contractor for progress reports on development of this subsystem. The prime contractor then asked Subcontractor A to desist from telling the truth and begin to provide reports which reflected no problems. The prime contractor felt that it would be damaging to both his own and A's position if he officially knew of problems in A's work, but officially knew of no problems in B's work. Thereafter, Subcontractor A worked with the prime contractor in the traditional manner.

Innovations Which Help an Innovation-Resisting Organization Become an Innovation-Producing Organization

If the foregoing analysis has some validity, there are many organizations attempting to become innovation producers within a framework of managerial assumptions and practices which are appropriate for innovation-resisting organizations. For them, the innovative processes which should be of greatest interest are ones which would help them to adopt and implement a framework more appropriate for the task.

The analysis strongly implies that this movement requires something more basic than structural change: decentralization, the use of a project form of organizations, or the creation of a class of senior scientists who have freedom of mobility in the organization. Such structural inventions can help, but if the major preoccupation of members of the organization is with status, with controlling others, and getting a larger slice of an unexpanding pie, these devices will not produce the desired results. The adaptability and creative application which are sought require a different outlook on life, on oneself, and on others.

The impact of traditional methods of education, child rearing, and organizational experience has been to develop rather complex skills for competing with others in a variety of games with a variety of first prizes and booby prizes, and requiring a variety of facades. Viewed from the standpoint of the lofty humanistic ideals that we proclaim from time to time, our practice is a theater of the absurd. At the same time, our capacities for collaboration, confrontation of ourselves and others, or for developing in ourselves and one another our full human potential have received little attention; the rules of our organizational games discourage the development and use of these capacities.

In sum, movement toward innovation-producing organization requires processes of personal and interpersonal reeducation so that more of us develop the qualities of independence and capacity for autonomous interdependence earlier attributed to the ideal innovator.

References and Notes

1. E. E. Jennings, "The Anatomy of Leadership," *Management of Personnel Quarterly,* Autumn 1961, pp. 2–9.
2. By a project form of organization is meant one in which a temporary organizational unit is created for each task containing all the skills necessary for performing the task.

Part Three
New Perspectives in Organizational Theory

INTRODUCTION TO PART THREE

The necessity for building new theories for tomorrow's organizations has been emphasized in the introductions to previous sections of this volume, but possible new theories have not always been supplied. Part Three directs attention to many new theoretical perspectives, including open-systems theory, cybernetics, the decisionmaking approach, exchange theory, motivation, and role analysis. In addition, we offer phenomenology as a useful perspective for integrating macro and micro theories. We anticipate that this will offer readers the wherewithal to participate in the theory-building process.

The bureaucratic model has been substantially modified by these and other organizational theories. For the student to develop new perspectives which he may used to understand contemporary and future organizations, he must make himself familiar with existing theories. The use of such new theories becomes significant for the dual process of integrating properties of whole systems into human elements and vice versa. Further, different theories at the macro and the micro levels may be complementary; a new theory developed on one of those levels may

supply precious knowledge for relating the other level into the total situation. The microscopic view of an organization allows administrators to initiate the dynamics of change in the organization, while the macroscopic view provides a means to manage change both internally and externally. The integrated approach we propose here represents an attempt to synthesize different perspectives with which to study organizational and social phenomena. A similar attempt has been accomplished through the open-systems approaches used by Katz and Kahn as well as Schein.[1] Before we address ourselves to the need for multiple theories and their use in the process of changing, we will, in the following sections, briefly consider major features of different theoretical developments.

The Morphogenic Process in Complex Organizations

Generally speaking, the so-called systems approach implies a "complex whole" made up of complex subsystems. In order to study the modern organization as an open system, one must observe not only complex structure but also processes—input, throughput, output, and feedback. These processes involve a continuous energy exchange between the organization and its environment. In this context, feedback offers a vital control process; system output supplies the basis for feedback to the input, thus affecting the control of subsequent outputs.[2] As the process becomes self-regulating, it represents the essence of cybernetic theory in operation.

Stressing the concept of feedback and cybernetics in open systems, Walter Buckley declines to accept a neat input-throughput-output model of open systems. He introduces the terms *morphostasis* and *morphogenesis* to explain major alternative processes which may characterize modern sociocultural systems. The former term refers to those processes in complex system-environment exchanges which tend to preserve or maintain a system's given form, organization, or state (thereby suggesting an innovative character such as "self-regulating," "self-directing," or "self-organizing"); the latter term refers to processes which tend to elaborate or *change* a system's given form, structure, or state (thus suggesting an adaptive character). As an open system adapts to its environment, system goals tend to be reformulated and changed, rather than to maintain equilibrium. Unlike the equilibrium orientation implicit in Parsonian structural-functional theory (and other input-output systems), Buckley's sociocultural system recognizes organizational conflict, deviant behavior, collective behavior, coercive power, and social exchange as vital sources of inputs into open systems. In other words, he attempts to relate such micro theories as exchange theory and role theory (as well as psychological properties) to complex social systems. His "morphogenic model" is designed to offer means to continual adaptive changing rather than scheduled change. It is both real-time and reality oriented; it accounts and uses the various disruptive forces in the organizational world rather than disregarding them or attempting to control them by organizational formalisms.

Mixed Scanning in the Active Decisionmaking Process

One of the most important theories of modern organization extends and refines the decisionmaking approach first introduced by Herbert Simon.[3] Amitai Etzioni introduces a contemporary, integrated approach to decisionmaking which he calls the "mixed-scanning model." Mixed scanning is characterized as a reasonable combination of rationalistic and incremental approaches to decisionmaking. The rationalistic decision model assumes that the variables pertinent to the decision can be identified and fairly appraised, thereby assuring a decision which takes appropriate account of all relevant factors. The incremental approach assumes that the decision environment is too complex and the surrounding force field too powerful to justify the rational model. Incremental theory assumes that decisions—and changes—are achieved through a succession of "partisan mutual adjustments," wherein few, if any, of the elements in the force field are seriously jeopardized, and only a limited amount of information is available. Etzioni summarizes these two views in his article and shows the value of integrating them. His approach draws upon the advantage of these theories to develop the broader, presumably more operationally useful, perspective of mixed scanning. Mixed scanning requires two sets of data in the process of active decisionmaking:

1) The set of information necessary to make fundamental decisions and hence guide the total situation. One must know about a

changing environment to be pro-active in decisionmaking.

2) Data related to analysis of activities and to measurement of coordination and consensus among decision makers. These data serve as a basis for incremental decisions.

The most significant possibility offered by the mixed-scanning approach seems to be the continuous development of short-term and long-term goals. Short-term goals (represented by incremental decisions) are established within the context of long-term goals (long-term planning for social change based on rational decision processes). Effective scanning for development of these goals depends, of course, upon organizational capacity, or "morphological factors," in Etzioni's terms. Students familiar with the increasingly evident limitations of "rational" decision processes as well as the growing critique of pluralism in the policy (decision) process may find in mixed scanning a viable means to improve complex policy decisions in both public and private organizations.

Exchange Processes in Maintaining Stability

Understanding complex human behavior inevitably leads us to a consideration of social exchange processes. Marcel Mauss, a French sociologist, introduced the principle of reciprocity in primitive exchange in which one person, A, contributes something to another person, B, then B becomes obligated to return the favor when it is needed.[4] Means of reciprocal reinforcement can be either in goods or services. If B does not reciprocate the exchange in the future, their interpersonal relationship tends to be jeopardized. Homans, Blau, Skinner, Emerson, Burgess, and many other contemporary scholars have developed further the notion of reciprocity in their exchange theories of interpersonal relationships, small group interaction, complex social structures, and culture.

Homans, applying the analogy of economic transactions to his theory of exchange, has developed the properties of larger groups from the properties of dyads; if the dyad is inadequately analyzed, something will be missing from the theory of the larger group.[5] He considers human interaction as exchange in which each participant of a group seeks fair value from value given. According to Homans, human interaction involves two basic elements—activities and sentiments. Activity includes the reciprocal exchange of goods and services, while sentiments involve the psychological feelings of a person toward other participants. Homans emphasizes the exchange concepts of profit, reward, and penalty. The small group or large-scale organization must provide more rewards than penalties in order to survive. These concepts are similar to the notion of inducement-contribution initially suggested by Chester I. Barnard.[6]

Blau's articles in Chapter 8 describes the complexity of social transactions (exchange of both extrinsic and intrinsic rewards) in social interaction. Blau argues that the elements of exchange are the prerequisites of social power and the complex structures of communities and societies. Thus the elements of power and social structure (integration, differentiation, organization, and opposition) can be explained from exchange processes characteristic of human interaction among individuals, in group behavior, in the search for social approval, and so forth. Blau argues, too, that the dialectical processes of disequilibrating reequilibrating forces are vital in bringing social change. Exchange theory clearly offers a means both for understanding micro and macro aspects of complex organizations and for building organizations more skillfully so they take better account of the real variables pertinent to their performance.

Individual Motivations

There is great concern among organizational theorists about the motivation of individuals in organizations. When an organization fails to accomplish its intended goals, critics often speak of the lack of motivation among participants. Success or failure of organizational goals and activities apparently relates in part to the level of achievement motivation of people. Achievement motivation is considered to be "the striving to increase, or keep as high as possible, one's own capability in all activities in which a standard of excellence is thought to apply and where the execution of such activities can, therefore, either succeed or fail."[7] McClelland's essay introduces two major hypotheses in his motivation theory of n-Achievement: (1) The economic growth rate of a country is a function of the value placed on need-achievement; and (2) Men with high need-achievement more often become entrepreneurs and managers then do those low in need-achievement, and they are more successful in those roles. McClelland has completed many studies measuring administrators' desire for success and their fear of failure in performing organizational activities. His concept of achievement motivation focuses around either the possibility of arriving at success or of avoiding failure.

Motivation theory is closely related to the theory of personality. An individual's motivation is significantly related to his personal growth and development. While McClelland may underestimate the potentiality of motivation in the need to achieve, Maslow recognizes the great importance of individual motivation.[8] Maslow considers an individual's motivations not in terms of a series of drives, but rather as part of a hierarchy of needs, certain higher needs becoming activated to the extent that lower ones have been satisfied. In the hierarchy of human needs, physiological needs are placed at the lowest level, followed by safety needs, love, self-esteem (ego needs), and finally the need for self-actualization (self-fulfillment needs). Maslow suggests that these levels are interdependent and overlapping, each higher need level emerging before the lower needs have been satisfied completely.

Integrating the Organization Through Role Relationships

To analyze the complex interrelationships which attend organizational behavior requires understanding role concepts. The concept of role is both simple and complex. When one attempts to analyze an individual or an organization member's rights, duties, and obligations according to the organization chart, procedure manual, and prescribed power and authority pattern, the individual role is easy to interpret and to understand. However, role analysis becomes a complex task when one considers the behavioral patterns of people in the process of interaction. The former approach is objective; the latter subjective. The two may or may not exist together.

The concept of role has been useful as both a descriptive and explanatory tool in several disciplines. The sociologist has approached role as a set of social constraints; the psychologist approaches it as an individual's concept of himself. The social psychologist views role in terms of its reciprocal and normative nature. In organizational contexts, the concept of role provides us with a linkage between the behaviors and expectations of individuals, dyads, groups, the whole organization, and, in a broad sense, with the social system. A role can be considered as a set of expected behaviors of the individual in a defined social position that is perceptually shared in at least certain aspects by all persons in that social situation. This role definition includes three central concepts: (1) a set of behaviors perceived by an individual toward himself; (2) the set perceived toward others, and (3) the shared expectations of others toward him, not as an individual, but as an occupant of a position within a social system or as a member of a team.

Gross, Mason and McEachern[9] introduced the concept of position as one of role theory's basic terms—a term that refers to the location of an actor in a system of social relationships. The social relationship may be a formal one existing in a total social system, or it may be an informal one in a social context. Any position in social relationships may be described either relationally in terms of the other positions with which it is related or situationally in terms of the boundaries of the situation within which the position occurs. Hage and Marwell, in Chapter 8, go beyond the positional analysis in arguing the use of the role relationship as the unit of analysis to comprehend the position, the individual, the interpersonal relationship, and the interpositional relationship. The organization consists of different roles associated with these units and many role relationships as well. A role relationship (or "role set") includes a set of expected behaviors and each role relationship involves occupants, activities, locations, occurrences, and goals.

People are likely to behave differently in different social situations because of the different expectations those situations present. Organizational and social phenomena involve complex patterns of role behavior associated with positions, interpersonal relationships, and other activities. This suggests the need for further analysis of the interdependence of multiple role relationships and their integration. Hage and Marwell, in their essay, suggest ways of understanding and integrating such relationships.

Integration Through Organizational Cybernetics

Cybernetics is proving to be a useful tool for helping to integrate the individual and the organization. The cybernetic organization aims at fusion of personal and organizational needs and values as well as personal and managerial perceptions. Key elements of cybernetic-oriented organizations are decisionmaking based on continuous feedback, information control and self-regulation. This implies an organization which is capable of real-time response that accounts those behavioral, attitudinal, and situational variables which are pertinent to its program. Complex human organizations require more extensive means for self-regulating and self-correcting adjustments to internal and external change. Through the cybernetic model we can relate a variety of human values and motivations to total organizational phenomena. Shibutani notes that:

The cybernetic model is more comprehensive than the other approaches. It shows the place of tension reduction, response to stimulation, and conscious intent within a larger unit and the manner in which these components are related to each other. Cybernetics deals with the organization of processes within any assembly treated as a whole. It is an approach that emphasizes time, information, and feedback. Although this scheme may be of limited utility to psychologists concerned with the microscopic details of perception and learning, social psychologists studying macroscopic matters—such as the relationship of self-conceptions to certain types of decisions—will find it far more useful than other models. . . . [10]

Ericson, in Chapter 7, stresses the relevance of the cybernetic approach to new organizational design, the design of self-actualizing organizations which will assure, to the maximum extent possible, the transcendence of human values. Ericson points out that the non-cybernetic organization pursues its goals in terms of special behavioral standards and management objectives—an arrangement which minimizes the need for effective use of communication processes. On the other hand, the cybernetic organization assumes full awareness of the virtue of effective managerial and interpersonal communication. Cybernetically-oriented organizations are not only able to evaluate organizational outputs and their effectiveness, but they also have great potential for meeting human needs and values. Ericson's article suggest that cybernetically-oriented organizations tend to have a greater capacity to improve in the following areas:

1) Motivation of development
2) Tolerance of ambiguity
3) Participative problem solving
4) Search for "optimum instability" for the system
5) Rationality
6) Greater self-actualization via a "collegial" milleu
7) More freedom and autonomy
8) Modification of organization goals and values
9) Increased organizational viability
10) Reflect social values through environmental interactions
11) The potential for greater value-realization
12) Meeting demands for different leadership styles
13) Capacity to forecast future challenges.

Phenomenology: A New Perspective

The concept of phenomenology is sufficiently new in organizational study to require more discussion than has been accorded the relatively familiar theories included in this section of the book. Since Edmund Husserl introduced phenomenology, his thoughts have penetrated a number of academic fields, appearing under such labels as phenomenology, the new existentialism, existential phenomenology, ontology, phenomenological anthropology, and various other designations. Tiryakian's article in Chapter 9 attempts to establish a meaningful linkage between Husserl's phenomenological method and existential analysis as a broad, recognizable perspective for integrating sociological knowledge. Tiryakian suggests that the complementarity of existential phenomenology and sociology offers the possibility of a future general theory of social existence. From the standpoint of organization theory, the understanding of phenomenology (or existential phenomenology)[11] offers man increased capability to search for new perspectives for using new knowledge. Phenomenology does not provide a neat conceptual model for integrating existing theories into a fully-articulated new theory, nor does it cover all possibilities in explaining the complexity of the modern organization at the present stage of development. Rather, the phenomenological approach offers a frame of reference with which to view organizational and social phenomena. As Lauer argues in Chapter 9, phenomenology is, as well as a philosophy, a method "which must be taken in order to arrive at the pure phenomenon." In any case, the central ideas of phenomenology are worthy of exploration and application in the study of organizational behavior. They offer a framework for understanding the subjective meanings in individual consciousness associated with the "phenomenal world," in other words, the world around us. In the study of organizations, phenomenology may illuminate policy choices through the construction of various reality situations.

In this introduction, we can penetrate only a small way into phenomenology. In order to have a complete understanding of what phenomenology has accomplished in the social sciences, one would have to make an extensive survey of the literature, ranging from the many works of Husserl to more contemporary contributions by such writers as Schutz, Gurvitch, Zaner, Lauer, Merleau-Ponty, Giorgi, Berger and Luckmann, and others. Only a few aspects relating to organizational study are considered here.

Most phenomenological concepts aim at the reconstruction of social reality. Karl Mannheim, who was a distinguished German sociologist, introduced an integration of social knowledge through the fusion of functional and substantial rationalities in constructing a responsible democratic system.[12] Mannheim's idea suggests that administrative activities associated with coordination of action to achieve a goal cannot reflect the real meaning of a social situation without consideration of the "intelligent act of thought" which reveals intelligent intuition as part of the complex, interrelated events in the situation. To Tiryakian, social reality is not an objective reality transcending individuals, but instead it is a "subjective existential reality." He also stresses the intersubjective nature of social reality. These arguments imply that the existence of individuals in organizations and in society should not be considered separately. Moreover, individual reality is coexistent with other multiple realities in daily human life.

The total of social phenomena includes not only many realities but also the multiple meanings implied by inter-subjectivity: a personal meaning for the individual, a social meaning for the community, a worldliness for the world community and, in a broader context, a spiritual meaning for mankind. According to Alfred Schutz, man acts in the context of an intersubjective reality which is shared by other people.[13] Thus, phenomenology is concerned with the phenomena of the social world and offers a method for comprehending human actions in the social world.

Emphasizing the macrosociological view of social reality, Gurvitch introduces the levels of social reality to reveal their different depths:[14] (1) the surface level of morphology and ecology; (2) social organization; (3) the stratum of social patterns; (4) unorganized collective behavior; (5) the web of social roles; (6) collective attitudes; (7) social symbols; (8) creative collective behavior; (9) collective ideas and values, and (10) the collective mind. These ten dimensions of reality supply a framework for Gurvitch to look at social reality, in other words, the total collection of social phenomena. Each social phenomenon includes these various levels, while different social phenomena are related dynamically and dialectically. The study of multiple social phenomena implies the categorization of social relationships and the social involvements of people. Thus, the total social phenomenon is supposed to explain human interactions and their results. An organization in social context is related to a complex web of realities—the reality of identification, symbolism, behavior, and motivation; the temporal, physical, interpersonal, and group realities, etc. These are not mutually exclusive phenomena; such multiple realities add up to the total organizational reality. Thus, the organizational phenomenon not only describes daily human life but also how the individual sees his situation and how he incorporates whatever has meaning for him. It is a dynamic process wherein the meaning of reality is constantly being modified and transformed as people interact with each other, learn, and experience their worlds.

The idea of consciousness of self in phenomenology provides another insightful conceptual foundation. Man's consciousness of himself and others affects his attitude toward the assessment of reality. Consciousness of his own objectives and goals and those of his organization affects the results of his relationships with both people and programs. His awareness of the multiple realities around his situation can

Figure 1   Organizational Theories for Changing

Theoretical Perspectives	Analytical Problems	Units
Open Systems Approach (Buckley)	Maintaining morphogenetic and morphostatic processes at the same time	Macro-micro units; total system, subsystems, individuals
Cybernetics	Regulation of information	Communication channels
Decisionmaking: Mixed Scanning (Etzioni)	A synthesis of rational and incremental decision processes	Macro-micro-macro: process of integrating decision units
Exchange (Blau)	Maintaining a balance of interests and an exchange of powers	Micro-macro: individual interactions related to organization and society
Motivation (McClelland and Maslow)	Developing n-Achievement; Drive arousal; hierarchy of needs	Micro-macro: personality pattern, intrinsic needs, individual-environment relationship
Role analysis (Hage and Marwell)	Analyzing multiple role relationships	Micro-macro: positions, interpersonal, interpositional relationships
Phenomenology	Meaning of realities; Analysis of self-consciousness and intentionality	Self-concept, intersubjectivity; the phenomenal world

provide new possibilities in making choices and solving complex problems. Man's self-consciousness may also stimulate a new look at his temporal reality. As man interacts with other people, he develops an "inner cognitive map or frame of reference" which shapes his future actions.[15] This offers many possibilities for change and self-improvement; man becomes aware that his life is worthwhile for him and that it has meaning; he seeks for alternative possibilities whereby he may change his situation. To plan for "the different future" for human society requires the broadest possible consciousness of the implications of our value judgments and the way we exercise responsibility through various policies. In this respect, phenomenology adds philosophical thinking to the study of organizations. It substantially broadens the viewpoint offered by rational, technocratic schools of thought.

In summary, phenomenological thinking includes certain advantages over other organizational theories. Perhaps the most important of these is the philosophical orientation phenomenology offers the study of organizations. Phenomenology suggests a means of introducing a philosophical way of thinking or a frame of reference for considering *reality*—both in organizational matters in particular and the social sciences in general. It introduces a fundamental conceptual scheme for analyzing the complex interrelationships between the needs and values of man and his "intentional consciousness" toward the social world. Phenomenological thinking introduces new parameters which administrators may employ in their efforts to construct social reality; it assumes that responsibility for making policy choices must be executed within a context of "complex reality" rather than a simplex, un-

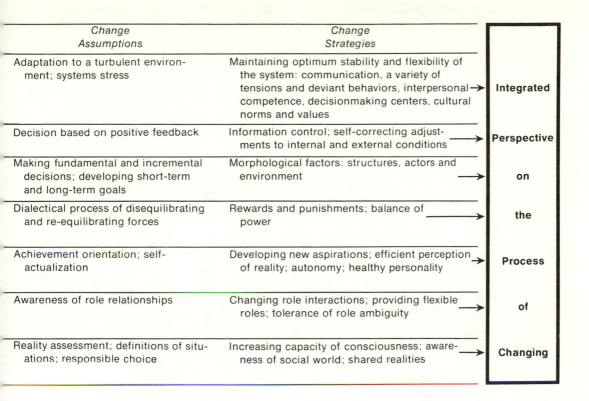

Change Assumptions	Change Strategies	
Adaptation to a turbulent environment; systems stress	Maintaining optimum stability and flexibility of the system: communication, a variety of tensions and deviant behaviors, interpersonal competence, decisionmaking centers, cultural norms and values	→ Integrated
Decision based on positive feedback	Information control; self-correcting adjustments to internal and external conditions	→ Perspective
Making fundamental and incremental decisions; developing short-term and long-term goals	Morphological factors: structures, actors and environment	→ on
Dialectical process of disequilibrating and re-equilibrating forces	Rewards and punishments; balance of power	→ the
Achievement orientation; self-actualization	Developing new aspirations; efficient perception of reality; autonomy; healthy personality	→ Process
Awareness of role relationships	Changing role interactions; providing flexible roles; tolerance of role ambiguity	→ of
Reality assessment; definitions of situations; responsible choice	Increasing capacity of consciousness; awareness of social world; shared realities	→ Changing

cluttered environment which everyone will perceive in the same way.

An Integrated Perspective on the Process of Changing

In order to predict and explain various social phenomena relevant to organizational contexts, it is necessary to organize these phenomena into some kind of logical framework which can be applied to organizational or social settings. Such a framework is generally called a theory, which, in order to explain social phenomena, must have applicability. One may apply several theories to interpret any particular set of phenomena—for example, the simultaneous existence of wave and particle theories of light in physics. This is Gurvitch's argument of "contextualism." He says:

The toleration of one person by another requires some sort of complementary understanding. How could differing views exist side by side unless this were so in everyday life? It is logical to believe that if one were to examine certain phenomena from several perspectives or positions, the data accumulated and the generalizations coming from such observation would be more accurate and valid. Contradiction is part of social life and this contradiction, when it is included in analysis, makes the study much more relevant and authentic. . . . [16]

The values of multiple theory also apply to organization study, where, as we have shown, there are a number of theoretical models. Each theory attempts to explain the complex organizational phenomenon. Figure 1 indicates how the different theories may be related to organizational change, the listed points being selected, of course, from among many aspects of each author's theoretical position. Each theory has evident limitations in providing an adequate framework to explain the *total* range of problems relating to organizational phenomena in general or organizational *changing* in particular, yet each makes a distinct, valuable contribution. Clearly, a comprehensive organization theory does not exist as yet; the study of modern complex organizations requires that we draw from this variety of theories, that from this we may be able to develop a position on which a "theory of changing" can reasonably be based.

The integrated approach assumes a "theory of changing" as opposed to a "theory of change." Robert Chin expresses this as follows:

The social scientist generally prefers not to change the system, but to study how it works and to predict what would happen if some new factor were introduced. So we find his attention focused on a "theory of change," or how the system achieves change. In contrast, the practitioner is concerned with diagnosis: how to achieve understanding in order to engage in change. The practitioner, therefore, has some additional interests; he wants to know how to change the system, he needs a "theory of changing" the system. . . . [17]

The changing organization includes various processes which take place continuously in the turbulent environment, in human interaction, and in complex men. The process of *changing* requires the adoption of a great deal of new knowledge about the total organization and its social phenomena, including new organizational environments, various functional processes, more information for decisionmaking, the exchange concept, motivational problems, more flexible roles, men's potential for self-conscious awareness,

the range of complex realities, the dynamics of cybernetics, and so forth. The perception and comprehension of tomorrow's organizations as representing "a state of changing" thus demands a broad range of new theory applications to establish the conditions of changing.

In general, scholars have explored their theory at extremely micro levels, focusing on the dynamics of individual behavior; at other times they have probed either with a macro perspective, stressing systems and the organizational point of view or with a mixture of micro and macro perspectives. These differing orientations suggest that scholars have: (1) applied different conceptual frameworks around such matters as systems, structures, roles, exchanges, personality, motivation, etc.; (2) used mutually exclusive methodologies for data gathering to develop information prerequisites for structural-functional analysis, group observations, laboratory techniques, interviews, etc.; (3) controlled different variables in order to predict theory, decisions, rewards and punishments, consciousness, etc., and (4) tended to generalize organizational and social phenomena based on limited empirical evidence. While this appears to indict the scholars involved, it is more realistic to perceive these as almost inevitable developments as research takes form in a new field. The differences now evident in method and product constitute the very richness upon which integrated new theory may properly be based.

Some micro theorists tend to have a deterministic orientation in their theory construction. For example, McClelland's theory of n-achievement suggests the overriding importance of individual success in the economic development of a society; all behavior is strongly motivated by need-achievement, in this theory. Maslow's self-actualization theory suggests that individual survival and development are factors involved in the need for higher levels of achievement. We may learn, however, that the total mix of individual and social development represents a far more complex process than can be explained simply by understanding need-achievement.

Exchange theory and role theory also assume that organizational phenomena can be understood only by analysis of individual or small group interactions or role behaviors directed toward other people or groups. From an organizational point of view, we must expect a certain amount of system stability in the process of changing—at least this is the tendency in organizations today. In this regard, exchange concepts provide a way of balancing the interests of individual and organization, thus enabling organizations to maintain their equilibrium. However, the changing organization cannot properly be regarded as being "in equilibrium," since the organization's environment as well as its human elements are also changing, and they are changing continuously. This is, perhaps, the main dilemma of administrators today. The deterministic view appears less evident in the open-systems or cybernetic approaches or in the mixed-scanning model.

We anticipate that in this volume we have demonstrated that application of but one of the many theories which are being considered today is not enough for understanding our unique organizational problems. The complexities of social relationships, which arise from human behavior, require many theoretical perspectives. New theories have made available a rich variety of suggestive insights and ways of thinking about organizational problems.

References and Notes

1. Daniel Katz and Robert L. Kahn, *Social Psychology of Organizations* (New York: John Wiley and Sons, Inc., 1966), and Edgar H. Schein, *Organizational Psychology* (Englewood Cliffs, N.J.: Prentice-Hall, Inc., 1965).

2. Katz and Kahn, *Social Psychology of Organizations,* chap. 1 and 2.

3. See Herbert A. Simon, *Administrative Behavior* (New York: Free Press, Div. of The Macmillan Company, 1945, 1957) for the initial statement on the use of the decisionmaking process as the basic perspective for studying organizations.

4. Marcel Mauss, *Essay on the Gift* (New York: Free Press, Div. of The Macmillan Company, 1954).

5. George C. Homans, *Social Behavior: Its Elementary Forms* (New York: Harcourt Brace Jovanovich, Inc., 1961).

6. Chester I. Barnard, *The Functions of the Executive* (Cambridge, Mass.: Harvard University Press, 1938, 1953).

7. Heinz Heckhausen, *The Anatomy of Achievement Motivation,* trans., Kay F. Butler, R. C. Birney, and David C. McClelland (New York: Academic Press, 1967).

8. Abraham H. Maslow, *Motivation and Personality* (New York: Harper & Row, Publishers, 1954) and *Toward a Psychology of Being,* 2d ed. (New York: Van Nostrand Reinhold Company, Inc., 1968).

9. Neal Gross, Ward S. Mason, and Alexander W. McEachern, *Explorations in Role Analysis: Studies of the School Superintendency Role* (New York: John Wiley & Sons, Inc., 1958), pp. 48 and 58.

10. Tamitsu Shibutani, "A Cybernetic Approach to Motivation," in Walter Buckley, ed., *Modern Systems Research for the Behavioral Scientist* (Chicago: Aldine-Atherton, Inc., 1968), p. 335. Shibutani's essay contributes to the following list of areas benefited by cybernetics.

11. The complementarity between phenomenology and existentialism is also discussed in Tiryakian's reply to Kolaja and Berger on the criticism of existential phenomenology. See *American Sociological Review* 31, no. 2 (April 1966), 258–64; Adrian Van Kaam, "The Impact of Existential Phenomenology, *Review of Existential Psychology and Psychiatry* 1 (1961), 63–83.

12. Karl Mannheim, *Man and Society in an Age of Reconstruction* (New York: Harcourt Brace Jovanovich, Inc., 1940).

13. Alfred Schutz, *The Phenomenology of the Social World,* trans. by George Walsh and Frederick Lehnert (Evanston, Illinois: Northwestern University Press, 1967).

14. Phillip Bosserman, *Dialectical Sociology: An Analysis of the Sociology of George Gurvitch* (Boston: Porter Sargent, Inc., 1968), pp. 110–40.

15. James C. Coleman, *Psychology and Effective Behavior* (Glenview, Ill.: Scott, Foresman and Company, 1969), p. 65.

16. Phillip Bosserman, *Dialectical Sociology,* p. 234.

17. Robert Chin, "The Utility of System Models and Developmental Models for Practitioners," in W. G. Bennis, R. Chin, and K. Benne, eds., *Planning of Change,* 2d ed. (New York: Holt, Rinehart & Winston, Inc., 1969), p. 308.

Chapter 7   Open Systems, Cybernetics, and Decisions

SOCIETY AS A COMPLEX ADAPTIVE SYSTEM

Walter Buckley

We have argued at some length in another place[1] that the mechanical equilibrium model and the organismic homeostasis models of society that have underlain most modern sociological theory have outlived their usefulness. A more viable model, one much more faithful to the *kind* of system that society is more and more recognized to be, is in process of developing out of, or is in keeping with, the modern systems perspective (which we use loosely here to refer to general systems research, cybernetics, information and communication theory, and related fields). Society, or the sociocultural system, is not, then, principally an equilibrium system or a homeostatic system, but what we shall simply refer to as a complex adaptive system.

To summarize the argument in overly simplified form: Equilibrial systems are relatively *closed* and *entropic*. In going to equilibrium they typically *lose structure* and have a *minimum of free energy;* they are affected only by external "disturbances" and have *no internal or endogenous sources of change;* their component elements are *relatively simple* and *linked directly via energy exchange* (rather than information interchange); and, since they are relatively closed, they have no feedback or other systematic self-regulating or adaptive capabilities. The homeostatic system (for example, the organism, apart from higher cortical functioning) is open and negentropic, maintaining a moderate energy level within controlled limits. But for our purposes here, the system's main characteristic is its functioning to *maintain the given structure of the system* within pre-established limits. It involves feedback loops with its environment, and possibly information as well as pure energy interchanges, but these are geared principally to *self-regulations* (structure maintenance) rather than adaptation (*change* of system structure). The complex adaptive systems (species, psychological and sociocultural systems) are also open and negentropic. But they are *open "internally" as well as externally* in that the interchanges among their components may result in *significant changes in the nature of the components themselves* with important consequences for the system as a whole. And the energy level that may be mobilized by the system is subject to relatively wide fluctuation. Internal as well as external interchanges are mediated characteristically by *information flows* (via chemical, cortical, or cultural encoding and decoding), although pure energy interchange occurs also. True feedback control loops make possible not only self-regulation, but self-direction or at least adaptation to a changing environment, such that the system may *change or elaborate its structure* as a condition of survival or viability.

We argue, then, that the sociocultural system is fundamentally of the latter type, and requires for analysis a theoretical model or perspective built on the kinds of characteristics mentioned. . . . It is further argued that a number of recent sociological and social psychological theories and theoretical orientations articulate well with this modern systems perspective, and we outline some of these to suggest in addition that modern systems research is not as remote from the social scientists' interests and endeavors as many appear to believe.

Complex Adaptive Systems: A Paradigm

A feature of current general systems research is the gradual development of a general paradigm of the basic mechanisms underlying the evolution of complex adaptive systems. The terminology of this paradigm derives particularly from information theory and cybernetics. We shall review these concepts briefly. The *environment,* however else it may be characterized, can be seen at bottom as a set or ensemble of more or less distinguishable elements, states, or events, whether the discriminations are made in terms of spatial or temporal relations, or properties. Such distinguishable differences in an ensemble may be most generally referred to as *"variety."* The relatively stable "causal," spatial and/or temporal relations between these distinguishable elements or events may be generally referred to as *"constraint."* If the elements are so "loosely" related that there is equal probability of any element or state being associated with any other, we speak of "chaos" or complete randomness, and hence, lack of "constraint." But our more typical natural environment is characterized by a relatively high degree of constraint, without which the development and elaboration of adaptive systems (as well as "science") would not have been possible. When the internal organization of an adaptive system acquires features that permit it to discriminate, act upon, and respond to aspects of the environmental variety and its constraints, we might generally say that the system has *"mapped"* parts of the environmental variety and constraints into its organization as structure and/or "information." Thus, a subset of the ensemble of constrained variety in the environment is coded and transmitted in some way via various channels to result in a change in the structure of the receiving system which is isomorphic in certain respects to the original variety. The system thus becomes selectively matched to its environment both physiologically and psychologically. It should be added that two or more adaptive systems, as well as an adaptive system and its natural environment, may be said to be selectively interrelated by a mapping process in the same terms. This becomes especially important for the evolution of social systems.

In these terms, then, the paradigm underlying the evolution of more and more complex adaptive systems begins with the fact of a potentially changing environment characterized by variety with constraints, and an existing adaptive system or organization whose persistence and elaboration to higher levels depends upon a successful mapping of some of the environmental variety and constraints into its own organization on at least a semipermanent basis. This means that our adaptive system—whether on the biological, psychological, or sociocultural level—must manifest (1) some degree of *"plasticity"* and *"irritability"* vis-à-vis its environment such that it carries on a constant interchange with environmental events, acting on and reacting to it; (2) some source or mechanism for *variety,* to act as a potential pool of adaptive variability to meet the problem of mapping new or more detailed variety and constraints in a changeable environment; (3) a set of *selective* criteria or mechanisms against which the "variety pool" may be sifted into those variations in the organization or system that more closely map the environment and those that do not, and (4) an arrangement for *preserving and/or propagating* these "successful" mappings.[2]

It should be noted, as suggested above, that this is a *relational* perspective, and the question of "substance" is quite secondary here. (We might also note that it is this kind of thinking that gives such great significance to the rapidly developing relational logic that is becoming more and more important as a technical tool of analysis.) Also, as suggested, this formulation corresponds closely with the current conception of "information" viewed as the process of selection—from an ensemble of variety—of a subset which, to have "meaning," must match another subset taken from a similar ensemble.[3] Communication is the process by which this constrained variety is transmitted in one form or another between such ensembles, and involves coding and decoding such that the original variety and its constraints remains relatively invariant at the receiving end. If the source of the "communication" is the causally constrained variety of the natural environment, and the destination is the biological adaptive system, we refer to the Darwinian process of natural selection whereby the information encoded in the chromosomal material (for example, the DNA) reflects or is a mapping of the environmental variety, and makes possible a continuous and more or less successful adaptation of the former system to the latter. If the adaptive system in question is a (relatively high-level) psychological or cortical system, we refer to "leaning," whereby the significant environmental variety is transmitted via sensory and perceptual channels and decodings to the cortical centers where, by selective criteria (for example, "reward" and "punishment") related to physiological and/or other "needs" or "drives," relevant parts of it are encoded and preserved as "experience" for varying periods of time and may promote adaptation. Or, on the level of the symbol-based sociocultural adaptive system, where the more or less patterned actions of persons and groups are as crucial a part of the environment of other persons and groups as the nonsocial environment, the gestural variety and its more or less normatively defined constraints is encoded, transmitted, and decoded at the receiving end by way of the various familiar channels with varying degrees of fidelity. Over time, and again by a selective process—now much more complex, tentative, and less easily specified—there is a selective elaboration

and more or less temporary preservation of some of this complex social as well as nonsocial constrained variety in the form of "culture," social organization," and "personality structure."

On the basis of such a continuum of evolving, elaborating levels of adaptive system (and we have only pointed to three points along this continuum), we could add to and refine our typology of systems. Thus, we note that as adaptive systems develop from the lower biological levels through the higher psychological and sociocultural levels we can distinguish: (1) the *varying time span* required for exemplars of the adaptive system to map or encode within themselves changes in the variety and constraints of the environment; phylogenetic time scales for organic systems and for tropistic or instinctual neural systems; ontogenetic time scales for higher psychological or cortical systems; and, in the sociocultural case, the time span may be very short—days— or very long; but complicated by the fact that the relevant environment includes both intra and intersocietal variety and constraints as well as natural environment variety (the latter becoming progressively less determinant); (2) the greatly *varying degrees of fidelity of mapping* of the environment into the adaptive system, from the lower unicellular organisms with a very simple repertoire of actions on and reactions to the environment, through the complex of instinctual and learned repertoire, to the ever-proliferating, more refined, and veridical accumulations of a sociocultural system; (3) the progressively greater separation and independence of the more refined "stored information" from purely biological processes as genetic information is gradually augmented by cortically imprinted information, and finally by entirely extrasomatic cultural depositories. The implications of these shifts, and others that could be included, are obviously far-reaching.

One point that will require more discussion may be briefly mentioned here. This is the *relative* discontinuity we note in the transition from the nonhuman adaptive system to the sociocultural system. (The insect society and the rudimentary higher animal society make for much less than a complete discontinuity). As we progress from lower to higher biological adaptive systems we note, as a general rule, the gradually increasing role of other biological units of the same as well as different species making up part of the significant environment. The variety and constraints represented by the behavior of these units must be mapped along with that of the physical environment. With the transition represented by the higher primate social organization through to full-blown human, symbolically mediated, sociocultural adaptive systems, the mapping of the variety and constraints characterizing the subtle behaviors, gestures, and intentions of the individuals and groups making up the effective social organization become increasingly central, and eventually equal if not overshadow the requirements for mapping the physical environment.[4]

It was these newly demanding requirements of coordination, anticipation, expectation, and the like within a more and more complex *social* environment of interacting and interdependent others— where genetic mappings were absent or inadequate—that prompted the fairly rapid elaboration of relatively new system features. These included, of course: the ever-greater conventionalizing of gestures into true symbols; the resulting development of a "self," self-awareness, or self-consciousness out of the symbolically mediated, continuous mirroring and mapping of each unit's behaviors and gesturings in those of ever-present others (a process well described by Dewey, Mead, Cooley, and others); and the resulting ability to deal in the present with future as well as past mappings and hence to manifest goal-seeking, evaluating, self-other relating, norm-referring behavior. In cybernetic terminology, this higher level sociocultural system became possible through the development of higher order feedbacks such that the component individual subsystems became able to map, store, and selectively act toward, not only

the external variety and constraints of the social and nonsocial environment, but also their own internal states. To speak of self-consciousness, internalization, expectations, choice, certainty and uncertainty, and the like, is to elaborate this basic point. This transition, then, gave rise to the newest adaptive system level we refer to as sociocultural. . . .

The Sociocultural Adaptive System

From the perspective sketched above, the following principles underlying the sociocultural adaptive system can be derived:

(1) The principle of the "irritability of protoplasm" carried through to all the higher level adaptive systems. "Tension" in the broad sense—in which stress and strain are manifestations under conditions of felt blockage—is ever-present in one form or another throughout the sociocultural system—now as diffuse, socially unstructured strivings, frustrations, enthusiasms, aggressions, neurotic or psychotic or normative deviation; sometimes as clustered and minimally structured crowd or quasi-group processes, normatively supportive as well as destructive; and now as socioculturally structured creativity and production, conflict and competition, or upheaval and destruction. As Thelen and colleagues put it:

> Man is always trying to live beyond his means. Life is a sequence of reactions to stress: Man is continually meeting situations with which he cannot quite cope.
> In stress situations, energy is mobilized and a state of tension is produced.
> The state of tensions tends to be disturbing, and Man seeks to reduce the tension.
> He has direct impulses to take action. . . . [5]

(2) Only closed systems running down to their most probable states, that is, losing organization and available energy, can be profitably treated in equilibrium terms.

Outside this context the concept of equilibrium would seem quite inappropriate and only deceptively helpful. On the other side, only open, tensionful, adaptive systems can elaborate and proliferate organization. Cannon coined the term "homeostatis" for biological systems to avoid the connotations of equilibrium, and to bring out the dynamic, processual, potential-maintaining properties of *basically unstable* physiological systems.[6] In dealing with the sociocultural system, however, we need yet a new concept to express not only the *structure-maintaining* feature, but also the *structure-elaborating and changing* feature of the inherently unstable system. The notion of "steady state," now often used, approaches the meaning we seek if it is understood that the "state" that tends to remain "steady" is *not to be identified with the particular structure* of the system. That is, as we shall argue in a moment, in order to maintain a steady state the system may change its particular structure. For this reason, the term "morphogenesis" is more descriptive. . . . [7]

(3) We define a system in general as a complex of elements or components directly or indirectly related in a causal network, such that at least some of the components are related to some others in a more or less stable way *at any one time.* The interrelations may be mutual or unidirectional, linear, nonlinear or intermittent, and varying in degrees of causal efficacy or priority. The particular kinds of more or less stable interrelationships of components that become established at any time constitute the particular *structure* of the system at that time.

Thus, the complex, adaptive system as a continuing entity is not to be confused with the structure which that system may manifest at any time. Making this distinction allows us to state a fundamental principle of open, adaptive systems: *Persistence or continuity of an adaptive system may require, as a necessary condition, change in its structure*—the degree of change being a complex function of the internal state of the system, the state of its relevant environment, and the nature of the interchange between the two. Thus, animal species develop and persist or are continuously transformed (or become extinct) in terms of a change (or failure of change) of structure—sometimes extremely slow, sometimes very rapid. The higher individual organism capable of learning by experience maintains itself as a viable system vis-à-vis its environment by a change of structure—in this case the neural structure of the cortex. It is through this principle that we can say that the "higher" organism represents a "higher" level of adaptive system capable, ontogenetically, of *mapping the environment more rapidly and extensively* and with *greater refinement and fidelity,* as compared to the topistic or instinct-based adaptive system which can change its structure only phylogenetically. The highest-level adaptive system—the sociocultural—is capable of an even more rapid and refined mapping of the environment (including the social and nonsocial environment, as well as at least some aspects of its own internal state) since sociocultural structures are partially independent of both ontogenetic and phylogenetic structures, and the mappings of many individuals are selectively pooled and stored extrasomatically and made available to the system units as they enter and develop within the system.

Such a perspective suggests that, instead of saying, as some do, that a prime requisite for persistence of a social system is "pattern maintenance," we can say, after Sommerhof and Ashby,[8] that persistence of an adaptive system requires as a necessary condition the maintenance of the system's "essential variables" within certain limits. Such essential variables and their limits may perhaps be specified in terms of what some have referred to as the "functional prerequisites" of any social system (for example, a minimal level of organismal sustenance, of reproduction, of patterned interactive relations, etc.). But the maintenance of the system's essential variables, we are emphasizing, may hinge on (as history and ethnography clearly show) *pattern reorganization or change*. It is true, but hardly helpful, to say that *some* minimal patterning or stability of relations, or integration of components, is necessary—by the very definition of "system" or adaptive organization. Nor can we be satisfied with the statement that persistence, continuity, or social "order" is promoted by the "institutionalization" of interactive relations via norms and values, simply because we can say with equal validity that discontinuity or social "disorder" is *also* promoted by certain kinds of "institutionalization."

To avoid the many difficulties of a one-sided perspective, it would seem essential to keep before us as a basic principle that the persistence and/or development of the complex sociocultural system depends upon structuring, destructuring, and restructuring—processes occurring at widely varying rates and degrees as a function of the external social and nonsocial environment. . . .

(4) The cybernetic perspective of control or self-regulation of adaptive systems emphasizes the crucial role of "deviation," seen in both negative and positive aspects. On the negative side, certain kinds of deviations of aspects of the system from its given structural state may be seen as "mismatch" or "negative feedback" signals *interpreted by certain organizing centers* as a failure of the system's operating processes or structures relative to a goal state sought, permitting—under certain conditions of adaptive structuring—a change of those operating processes or structures toward goal optimization. (Thus, one facet of the "political" process of sociocultural systems may be interpreted in this light, with the more "democratic" type of social organization providing the more extended and accurate assessment of the mismatch between goal attainment on the one hand, and current policy and existing social structuring on the other.)

On the positive side, the cybernetic perspective brings out the absolute necessity of deviation—or, more generally, "variety"—in providing a pool of potential new transformations of process or structure that the adaptive systems might adopt in responding to goal mismatch. On the lower, biological levels we recognize here the principle of genetic variety and the role of gene pools in the process of adaptive response to organismic mismatch with a changed environment. (And in regard to the other major facet of the "political" process, the more democratic type of social organization makes available a broader range of variety, or "deviation," from which to select new orientations.)

Thus, the concept of requisite deviation needs to be proffered as a high-level principle that can lead us to theorize: A requisite of sociocultural systems is the development and maintenance of a significant level of nonpathological deviance manifest as a pool of alternate ideas and behaviors with respect to the traditional, institutionalized ideologies and role behaviors. Rigidification of any given institutional structure must eventually lead to disruption or dissolution of the society by way of internal upheaval or ineffectiveness against external challenge. The student of society must thus pose the question—What "mechanisms" of non-pathological deviance production and maintenance can be found in any society, and what "mechanisms" of conformity operate to counteract these and possibly lessen the viability of the system?

Attempts to analyze a society from such a perspective make possible a more balanced analysis of such processes as socialization, education, mass communication, and economic and political conflict and debate. We are then encouraged to build squarely into our theory and research designs the full sociological significance of such informally well-recognized conceptions as socialization for "self-reliance" and relative "autonomy," education for "creativity," ideational flexibility and the "open mind," communications presenting the "full spectrum" of viewpoints, etc., instead of smuggling them in unsystematically as if they were only residual considerations or ill-concealed value judgments.

(5) Given the necessary presence of variety or deviance in an adaptive system, the general systems model then poses the problem of the *selection* and more or less permanent *preservation* or systemic structuring of some of this variety. On the biological level, we have the process of "natural selection" of some of the genetic variety existing within the interfertile species and subspecies gene pool, and the preservation for various lengths of time of this variety through the reproductive process. On the level of higher order psychological adaptive systems, we have trial-and-error selection, by way of the so-called law of effect, from the variety of environmental events and the potential behavioral repertoire to form learned and remembered experience and motor skills more or less permanently preserved by way of cortical structuring.[9] As symbolic mapping or decoding and encoding of the environment and one's self becomes possible,[10] the selection criteria lean less heavily on direct and simple physiological reward and more heavily on "meanings" or "significance" as manifested in existing self-group structural relations. In the process, selection from the full range of available variety becomes more and more refined and often more restricted, and emerges as one or another kind of "personality" system or "group character" structure. On the sociocultural level, social selection and relative stabilization or institutionalization of normatively interpreted role relations and value patterns occurs through the variety of processes usually studied under the headings of conflict, competition, accommodation, and such; power, authority and compliance; and "collective behavior," from mob behavior through opinion formation processes and social movements to organized war. More strictly "rational" processes are of course involved, but often seem to play a relatively minor role as far as larger total outcomes are concerned.

It is clearly in the area of "social selection" that we meet the knottiest problems. For the sociocultural system, as for the biological adaptive system, analysis must focus on both the potentialities of the system's structure at a given time and the environment changes that might occur and put particular demands on whatever structure has evolved. In both areas the complexities are compounded for the sociocultural system. In developing a typology of systems and their internal linkages we have noted that, as we proceed from the mechanical or physical through the biological, psychic and sociocultural, the system becomes "looser," the interrelations among parts more tenuous, less rigid, and especially less directly tied to physical events as energy relations and transformations are overshadowed by symbolic relations and information transfers. Feedback loops between operating sociocultural structures and the surrounding reality are often long and tortuous, so much so that knowledge of results or goal mismatch, when forthcoming at all, may easily be interpreted in nonveridical ways (as the history of magic, superstition, and ideologies from primitive to present amply indicate). The higher adaptive systems have not been attained without paying their price, as the widespread existence of illusion and delusions on the personality and cultural levels attest. On the biological level, the component parts have relatively few degrees of freedom, and changes in the environment are relatively directly and inexorably reacted to by selective structural changes in the species.

Sociocultural systems are capable of persisting within a wide range of degrees of freedom of the components, and are often able to "muddle through" environmental changes that are not too demanding. But of course this is part of the genius of this level of adaptive system: It is capable of temporary shifts in structure to meet exigencies. The matter is greatly complicated for the social scientist, however, by this system's outstanding ability to act on and partially control the environment of which a major determining part is made up of other equally loose-knit, more or less flexible, illusion-ridden, sociocultural adaptive systems. Thus, although the minimal integration required for a viable system does set limits on the kinds of structures that can persist, these limits seem relatively broad compared to a biological system.[11] And given the relatively greater degrees of freedom of internal structuring (structural alternatives, as some call them) and the *potentially* great speed with which restructuring may occur under certain conditions, it becomes difficult to predict the reactions of such a system to environmental changes or internal elaboration. Considering the full complexities of the problem we must wonder at the facility with which the functionalist sociologist has pronounced upon the ultimate functions of social structures, especially when—as seems so often the case—very little consideration is given either to the often feedback-starved social selective processes that have led to the given structures, or to the environmental conditions under which they may be presumed to be functional.

Although the problem is difficult, something can be said about more ultimate adaptive criteria against which sociocultural structures can be assessed. Consideration of the grand trends of evolution provides clues to the very general criteria. These trends point in the direction of: (1) greater and greater flexibility of structure, as error-controlled mechanisms (cybernetic processes of control) replace more rigid, traditionalistic means of meeting problems and seeking goals; (2) ever more refined, accurate, and systematic mapping, decoding and encoding of the external environment and the system's own internal milieu (via science), along with greater independence from the physical environment; (3) and thereby a greater elaboration of self-regulating substructures in order—not merely to restore a given equilibrium or homeostatic level—but to purposefully restructure the system without tearing up the lawn in the process.[12]

With these and perhaps other general criteria, we might then drop to lower levels of generality by asking what restrictions these place on a sociocultural adaptive system if it is to remain optimally viable in these terms. It is possible that

this might provide a value-free basis for discussing the important roles, for example, of a vigorous and independent science in all fields; the broad and deep dissemination of its codified findings; the absence of significant or long-lasting subcultural cleavages, power centers and vested interests, whether on a class or ethnic basis, to break or hinder the flow of information or feedback concerning the internal states of the system; and the promotion of a large "variety pool" by maintaining a certain number of degrees of freedom in the relations of the component parts—for example, providing a number of real choices of behaviors and goals. Thus we can at least entertain the feasibility of developing an objective rationale for the sociocultural "democracy" we shy from discussing in value terms.

(6) Further discussion of the intricacies of the problem of *sociocultural selection processes* leading to more or less stable system *structures* may best be incorporated into the frame of discussion of the problem of *"structure versus process."* This is another of those perennial issues of the social (and other) sciences, which the modern systems perspective may illuminate.

Our argument may be outlined as follows:

Much of modern sociology has analyzed society in terms of largely structural concepts: institutions, culture, norms, roles, groups, etc. These are often reified, and make for a rather static, overly deterministic, and elliptical view of societal workings.

But for the sociocultural system, "structure" is only a relative stability of underlying, ongoing micro-processes. Only when we focus on these can we begin to get at the selection process whereby certain interactive relationships become relatively and temporarily stabilized into social and cultural structures.

The unit of dynamic analysis thus becomes the systemic *matrix* of interacting, goal-seeking, deciding individuals and subgroups—whether this matrix is part of a formal organization or only a loose collectivity. Seen in this light, society becomes a continuous morphogenic process, through which we may come to understand in a unified conceptual manner the development of structures, their maintenance, and their change. And it is important to recognize that out of this matrix is generated, not only *social* structure, but also *personality* structure, and *meaning* structure. All, of course, are intimately interrelated in the morphogenic process, and are only analytically separable.

Structure, Process, and Decision Theory

Though the problem calls for a lengthy methodological discussion, we shall here simply recall the viewpoint that sees the sociocultural system in comparative perspective against lower-level mechanical, organic, and other types of systems. As we proceed upward along such a typology we noted that the ties linking components become less and less rigid and concrete, less direct, simple and stable within themselves. Translation of energy along unchanging and physically continuous links gives way in importance to transmission of information via internally varying, discontinuous components with many more degrees of freedom. Thus for mechanical systems, and parts of organic systems, the "structure" has a representation that is concrete and directly observable—such that when the system ceases to operate much of the structure remains directly observable for a time. For the sociocultural system, "structure" becomes a theoretical construct whose referent is only indirectly observable (or only inferable) by way of series of events along a time dimension; when the system ceases to operate, the links maintaining the sociocultural structure are no longer observable.[13] "Process," then points to the actions and interactions of the components of an ongoing system, in which varying degrees of structuring arise, persist, dissolve, or change. (Thus "process" should not be made synonymous simply with "change,"

as it tended to be for many earlier sociologists.)

.   .   .

We can take only brief note of a few of the more recent arguments for the process viewpoint. The anthropologists, for example, have become acutely concerned in the last few years with this issue. G. P. Murdock seems to be echoing Small when he says, "All in all, the static view of social structure which seeks explanations exclusively within the existing framework of a social system on the highly dubious assumption of cultural stability and nearly perfect functional integration seems clearly to be giving way, in this country at least, to a dynamic orientation which focuses attention on the processes by which such systems come into being and succeed one another over time."[14] At about the same time, Raymond Firth was stating: "The air of enchantment which for the last two decades has surrounded the 'structuralist' point of view has now begun to be dispelled. Now that this is so, the basic value of the concept of social structure as an heuristic tool rather than a substantial social entity has come to be more clearly recognized."[15]

.   .   .

Among sociologists, a perennial critic of the overly-structural conception of the group is Herbert Blumer. Blumer has argued that it is from the process of ongoing interaction itself that group life gets its main features, which cannot be adequately analyzed in terms of fixed attitudes, "culture," or social structure—nor can it be conceptualized in terms of mechanical structure, the functioning of an organism, or a system seeking equilibrium, " . . . in view of the formative and explorative character of interaction as the participants *judge* each other and *guide* their own acts by that judgment."

The human being is not swept along as a neutral and indifferent unit by the operation of a system. As an organism capable of self-interaction he forges his actions out of a process of definition involving choice, appraisal, *and* decision. . . . *Cultural norms, status positions and role relationships are only* frameworks *inside of which that process* [*of formative transaction*] *goes on.*[16]

Highly structured human association is relatively infrequent and cannot be taken as a prototype of a human group life. In sum, institutionalized patterns constitute only one conceptual aspect of society, and they point to only a part of the ongoing process (and, we might add, they must be seen to include deviant and dysfunctional patterns: For conceptual clarity and empirical relevance, "institutionalization" cannot be taken to imply only "legitimacy," "consent," and ultimately adaptive values).

.   .   .

It can be argued, then, that a refocusing is occurring via "decision theory," whether elaborated in terms of "role-strain" theory; theories of cognitive dissonance, congruence, balance, or concept formation; exchange, bargaining, or conflict theories, or the mathematical theory of games. The basic problem is the same: How do interacting personalities and groups define, assess, interpret, "verstehen," and act on the situation? Or, from the broader perspective of our earlier discussion, how do the processes of "social selection" operate in the "struggle" for sociocultural structure? Instead of asking how structure affects, determines, channels actions and interactions, we ask how structure is created, maintained and recreated.

Thus we move down from structure to social interrelations and from social relations to social actions and interaction processes—to a matrix of "dynamic assessments" and intercommunication of meanings, to evaluating, emoting, deciding, and choosing. To avoid anthropomorphism and gain the advantages of a broader and more rigorously specified conceptual system, we arrive at the language of modern systems theory.

Basic ingredients of the decisionmaking focus include, then: (1) a *process* approach; (2) a conception of *tension* as inherent in the process, and (3) a renewed concern with the role and workings of man's enlarged cortex seen as a complex adaptive subsystem operating within an *interaction matrix* characterized by *uncertainty conflict,* and other dissociative (as well as associative) processes *underlying the structuring and restructuring of the large psychosocial system.*

Process Focus

The process focus points to information-processing individuals and groups linked by different types of communication nets to form varying types of interaction matrices that may be characterized by "competition," "cooperation," "conflict," and the like. Newer analytical tools being explored to handle such processes include treatment of the interaction matrix over time as a succession of states described in terms of transition probabilities, Markoff chains, or stochastic processes in general. The Dewey-Mead "transactions" are now discussed in terms of information and codings and decodings, with the essential "reflexivity" of behavior now treated in terms of negative and positive feedback loops linking via the communication process the intrapersonal, interpersonal, and intergroup subsystems and making possible varying degrees of matching and mismatching of Mead's "self and others," the elaboration of Boulding's "Image,"[17] and the execution of Miller's "Plans" (Chapter 45 [Walter Buckley, ed., *Modern Systems Research for the Behavioral Scientist;* Chicago, Aldine-Atherton, Inc., 1968]). And herein we find the great significance for sociology of many of the conceptual tools (though not, at least as yet, the mathematics) of information and communication theory, cybernetics, or general systems research, along with the rapidly developing techniques of *relational* mathematics such as the several branches of set theory—topology, group theory, graphy theory, symbolic logic, etc.

Conception of Tension

Tension is seen as an inherent and essential feature of complex adaptive systems; it provides the "go" of the system, the "force" behind the elaboration and maintenance of structure. There is no "law of social inertia" operating here, nor can we count on "automatic" re-equilibrating forces counteracting system "disturbances" or "deviance," for, whereas we do find deviance-reducing negative feedback loops in operation we *also* find deviance-maintaining and deviance-amplifying *positive* feedback processes often referred to as the vicious circle or spiral, or "escalation."[18] It is not at all certain whether the resultant will maintain, change, or destroy the given system or its particular structure. The concepts of "stress" or "strain" we take to refer only to the greater mobilization of normal tension under conditions of more than usual blockage. And instead of a system's seeking to manage *tension,* it would seem more apt to speak of a system's seeking to manage *situations* interpreted as responsible for the production of greater than normal tension.

The "role strain" theory of William J. Goode is an illustrative attack on assumptions of the widely current structural approach, using a process and tension emphasis and contributing to the decision-theory approach. Goode analyzes social structure or institutions into role relations, and role relations into role transactions. "Role relations are seen as a sequence of 'role bargains' and as a continuing process of selection among alternative role behaviors, in which each individual seeks to reduce his role strain."[19] Contrary to the current stability view, which sees social system continuity as based primarily on normative consensus and normative integration, Goode thus sees "dissensus, nonconformity, and conflicts among norms and roles as the usual state of affairs. . . . The individual cannot satisfy fully all demands, and must move through a continuous sequence of role decision and bargains . . . in which he seeks to reduce his role strain, his felt difficulty in carrying out his obligations"[20]

.   .   .

It should be noted, however, that Goode accepts unnecessarily a vestige of the equilibrium or stability model when he states, "The total role structure functions so as to reduce role strain."[21] He is thus led to reiterate a proposition that—when matched against our knowledge of the empirical world—is patently false. Or, more precisely, not false, but a half-truth: It recognizes deviance-reducing negative feedback processes, but not deviance-amplifying positive feedback processes. . . .

Study of Cognitive Processes

A more concerted study of cognitive processes, especially under conditions of *uncertainty* and *conflict,* goes hand in hand, of course, with a focus on decisionmaking and role transactions. Despite the evolutionary implications of man's enlarged cortex, much social (and psychological) theory seems predicated on the assumption that men are decorticated. Cognitive processes, as they are coming to be viewed today, are not to be simply equated with the traditional, ill-defined, concept of the "rational." That the data-processing system—whether socio-psychological or electromechanical—is seen as inherently "rational" tells us little about its outputs in concrete cases. Depending on the adequacy and accuracy of the effectively available information, the total internal organization or "Image," the character of the "Plans" or program, and the nature of the significant environment, the output of either "machine" may be sense or nonsense, symbolic logic or psychologic, goal-attainment or oscillation.

.   .   .

Fortunately, however, there are recent statements that rally to the side of the sociological interactionist theorists, whose perspective continues to be ignored or little understood by so many personality theorists who are nevertheless gradually rediscovering and duplicating its basic principles. A good beginning to a truly interpersonal approach to personality theory and the problem of stability and change in behavior is the statement of Paul F. Secord and Carl W. Backman, which remarkably parallels Goode's theory of stability and change in social systems discussed earlier. Pointing to the assumptions of several personality theorists that when stability of behavior occurs it is solely a function of stability in personality structure, and that this latter structure has, inherently, a strong resistance to change except when special change-inducing forces occur, Secord and Backman see as consequences the same kinds of theoretical inadequacies we found for the stability view of social systems:

The first is that continuity in individual behavior is not a problem to be solved; it is simply a natural outcome of the formation of stable structure. The second is that either behavioral change is not given systematic attention, or change is explained independently of stability. Whereas behavioral stability is explained by constancy of structure, change tends to be explained by environmental forces and fortuitous circumstances.[22]

Their own theoretical view abandons these assumptions and "places the locus of stability and change in the interaction process rather than in intrapersonal structures." Recognizing the traditional two classes of behavioral determinants, the cultural-normative and the intrapersonal, their conceptualization

attempts to identify a third class of determinants, which have their locus neither in the individual nor the culture, but in the interaction process itself. In a general sense this third class may be characterized as the tendencies of the individual and the persons with whom he interacts to shape the interaction process according to certain requirements, i.e., they strive to produce certain patterned relations. As will be seen, the principles governing this activity are truly interpersonal; they require as much attention to the behavior of the other as they do to the behavior of the individual, and it cannot be said that one or the other is the sole locus of cause.[23]

They go on to analyze the "interpersonal matrix" into three components: an aspect of the self-concept of a person, his interpretation of those elements of his behavior related to that aspect, and his perception of related aspects of the other with whom he is interacting. "An interpersonal matrix is a recurring functional relation between these three components."

In these terms, Secord and Backman attempt to specify the conditions and forces leading to or threatening congruency or incongruency, and hence stability or change, in the matrix. Thus, four types of incongruency, and two general classes of resolution of incongruency, are discussed. One of these latter classes "results in restoration of the original matrix, leaving self and behavior unchanged (although cognitive distortions may occur), and the other leads to a new matrix in which self or behavior are changed."[24] In sum, contrary to previous approaches, theirs emphasizes that "the individual strives to maintain interpersonal relations characterized by congruent matrices, rather than to maintain a self, habits, or traits."

Maintenance of intrapersonal structure occurs only when such maintenance is consistent with an ongoing interaction process which is in a state of congruency. That most individuals do maintain intrapersonal structure is a function of the fact that the behavior of others toward the individuals in question is normally overwhelmingly consistent with such maintenance.[25]

And this conception also, as most approaches do not (or do inadequately), predicts or accounts for the fact that, should the interpersonal environment cease to be stable and familiar, undergoing great change such that others behave uniformly toward the individual in new ways, the individual "would rapidly modify his own behavior and internal structure to produce a new set of congruent matrices. As a result, he would be a radically changed person."[26]

Further Examples

Ralph Turner has addressed himself to the elaboration of this perspective in that conceptual area fundamental to the analysis of institutions—roles and role-taking.[27] The many valid criticisms of the more static and overdetermining conception of roles is due, he believes, to the dominance of the Linton view of role and the use of an oversimplified model of role functioning. Viewing role-playing and role-taking, however, as a process (as implied in Meadian theory), Turner shows that there is more to it than just "an extension of normative or cultural deterministic theory" and that a process view of role adds novel elements to the notion of social interaction.

The morphogenic nature of role behavior is emphasized at the start in the concept of *"role-making."* Instead of postulating the initial existence of distinct, identifiable roles, Turner posits "a tendency to create and modify conceptions of self- and other-roles" as the interactive orienting process. Since actors behave *as if* there were roles, although the latter actually exist only in varying degrees of definitiveness and consistency, the actors attempt to define them and make them explicit—thereby in effect creating and modifying them as they proceed. The key to role-taking, then, is the morphogenic propensity "to shape the phenomenal world into roles"; formal organizational regulation restricting this process is not to be taken as the prototype, but rather as a "distorted instance" of the wider class of role-taking phenomena. To the extent that the bureaucratic setting blocks the role-

making process, organization is maximal, actors are cogs in a rigid machine, and the morphogenic process underlying the viability of complex adaptive systems is frustrated.

Role interaction is a tentative process of reciprocal responding of self and other, challenging or reinforcing one's conception of the role of the other, and consequently stabilizing or modifying one's own role as a product of this essentially feedback-testing transaction. The conventional view of role emphasizing a prescribed complementarity of expectations thus gives way to a view of role-taking as a process of "devising a performance on the basis of an imputed other-role," with an important part being played by cognitive processes of inference testing. In a manner consistent with models of the basic interaction process suggested by Goode and by Secord and Backman, Turner views as a central feature of role-taking "the process of discovering and creating 'consistent' wholes out of behavior," of "devising a pattern" that will both cope effectively with various types of relevant others and meet some recognizable criteria of consistency. Such a conception generates empirically testable hypotheses of relevance to our concern here with institutional morphogenesis, such as: "Whenever the social structure is such that many individuals characteristically act from the perspective of two given roles simultaneously, there tends to emerge a single role which encompasses the action."[28]

.   .   .

An example is provided by the study by Gross et al. of the school-superintendent role. It is found that incumbency in this role (1) actually involved a great deal of choice behavior in selecting among the alternative interpretations and behaviors deemed possible and appropriate, and that (2) consistency and coherence of an incumbent's behavior could be seen only in terms of the total role as an accommodation with correlative other-roles of school board member, teacher, and parent, with which the superintendent was required to interact simultaneously. As Gross puts it, a "system model" as against a "position-centric" model involves an important addition by including the interrelations among the counter positions. "A position can be completely described only by describing the total system of positions and relationships of which it is a part. In other words, in a system of interdependent parts, a change in any relationship will have an effect on all other relationships, and the positions can be described only by the relationships."[29]

In sum, "institutions" may provide a normative framework prescribing roles to be played and thus assuring the required division of labor and minimizing the costs of general exploratory role-setting behavior, but the actual role transactions that occur generate a more or less coherent and stable working compromise between ideal set prescriptions and a flexible role-making process, between the structured demands of others and the requirements of one's own purposes and sentiments. This conception of role relations as "fully interactive," rather than merely conforming, contributes to the recent trends "to subordinate normative to functional processes in accounting for societal integration"[30] by emphasizing the complex adaptive interdependence of actors and actions in what we see as an essentially morphogenic process—as against a merely equilibrial or homeostatic process.

Organization as a Negotiated Order

Next we shall look at a recently reported empirical study of a formal organization that concretely illustrates many facets of the above conceptualization of Turner and contributes further to our thesis. In their study of the hospital and its interactive order, Anselm Strauss and colleagues develop a model of organizational process that bears directly on the basic sociological problem of "how a measure of order is maintained in the face of inevitable changes (derivable from sources both external and internal to the organization)."[31] Rejecting an overly structural view, it is assumed that social order is not simply normatively specified and automatically maintained but is something that must be "worked at," continually reconstituted. Shared agreements, underlying orderliness, are not binding and shared indefinitely but involve a temporal dimension implying eventual review, and consequent renewal or rejection. On the basis of such considerations, Strauss and colleagues develop their conception of organizational order as a "negotiated order."

The hospital, like any organization, can be visualized as a hierarchy of status and power, of rules, roles, and organizational goals. But it is also a locale for an ongoing complex of transactions among differentiated types of actors: professionals such as psychiatrists, residents, nurses and nursing students, psychologists, occupational therapists and social workers; and nonprofessionals such as various levels of staff, the patients themselves, and their families. The individuals involved are at various stages in their careers, have their own particular goals, sentiments, reference groups, and ideologies, command various degrees of prestige, esteem, and power, and invest the hospital situation with differential significance.

The rules supposed to govern the actions of the professionals were found to be far from extensive, clearly stated, or binding; hardly anyone knew all the extant rules or the applicable situations and sanctions. Some rules previously administered would fall into disuse, receive administrative reiteration, or be created anew in a crisis situation. As in any organization, rules were selectively evoked, broken, and/or ignored to suit the defined needs of personnel. Upper administrative levels especially avoided periodic attempts to have the rules codified and formalized, for fear of restricting the innovation and improvisation believed necessary to the care of patients. Also, the multiplicity of professional ideologies, theories, and purposes would never tolerate such rigidification.

In sum, the area of action covered by clearly defined rules was very small, constituting a few general "house rules" based on long-standing shared understandings. The basis of organizational order was the generalized mandate, the single ambiguous goal, of returning patients to the outside world in better condition. Beyond this, the rules ordering actions to this end were the subject of continual negotiations—being argued, stretched, ignored, or lowered as the occasion seemed to demand. As elsewhere, rules failed to act as universal prescriptions, but retired judgment as to their applicability to the specific case.

References and Notes

1. Many of the ideas expressed here appear in more extended form in the author's *Sociology and Modern Systems Theory* (Englewood Cliffs, N.J.: Prentice-Hall, Inc., 1967).
2. See Pringle, Chapter 33 [in Buckley, op. cit.]; and Donald T. Campbell, "Methodological Suggestions from a Comparative Psychology of Knowledge Processes," *Inquiry* 2 (1959): 152–67.
3. See, for example, Rapoport and MacKay selections, Chapter 16 and 24 [in Buckley, op. cit.].
4. For an excellent recent overview of this transition, see A. Irving Halowell, "Personality, Culture, and Society in Behavioral Evolution," in Sigmund Koch, ed., *Psychology: A Study of a Science,* vol. 6: Investigations of Man as Socius (New York: McGraw-Hill Book Company, 1963), 429–509.
5. Herbert A. Thelen, "Emotionality and Work in Groups," in Leonard D. White, ed., *The State of the Social Sciences* (Chicago: University of Chicago Press, 1956), pp. 184–86.
6. See Cannon selection, Chapter 32 [in Buckley, op. cit.].
7. Or perhaps we might take Cadwallader's suggestion (Chapter 52 [in Buckley, op. cit.]) and use Ashby's term "ultrastability." I dislike, however, the connotative overemphasis on "stability," which is sure to be misunderstood by many.

I prefer the term "morphogenesis" at best expressing the characteristic feature of the adaptive system. (See, for one, Maruyama's usage in Chapter 36 [of Buckley, op. cit.]. Thus, we might say that physical systems are typically equilibrial; physiological systems are typically homeostatic; and psychological, sociocultural, or ecological systems are typically morphogenic. From this view, our paradigm of the mechanisms underlying the complex system becomes a basic paradigm of the morphogenic process, perhaps embracing as special cases even the structuring process below the complex adaptive system level.
8. See Chapters 34 and 35 [of Buckley, op. cit.].
9. See Campbell, "Methodological Suggestions", and Pringle, Chapter 33 [in Buckley, op. cit.].
10. Recall Osgood's interpretation in Chapter 23 [in Buckley, op. cit.]. Also, see Charles E. Osgood, "Psycholinguistics," in S. Koch, ed., *Psychology,* loc. cit., pp. 244–316; O. Hobart Mowrer, *Learning Theory and the Symbolic Processes* (New York: John Wiley & Sons, Inc., 1960), esp. Chapter 7: "Learning Theory, Cybernetics, and the Concept of Consciousness." For less behavioristic and more genetic and emergent views see, for example, George H. Mead, *Mind, Self and Society* (Chicago: University of Chicago Press, 1934), and more recently, Heinz Werner and Bernard Kaplan, *Symbol Formation* (New York: John Wiley & Sons, Inc., 1963).
11. See, for example, Marshall D. Sahlins, "Culture and Environment: The Study of Cultural Ecology," in Sol Tax, ed., *Horizons of Anthropology* (Chicago: Aldine-Atherton, Inc., 1964), pp. 132–47.
12. See especially the selections . . . from Nett (Chapter 48), Deutsch (Chapter 46), Hardin (Chapter 55) and Vickers (Chapter 56). [Selections appear in Buckley, op. cit.].
13. However, we should not deemphasize the important structuring role of concrete artifacts, for example, the structure of physical communication nets, road nets, cities, interior layouts for buildings, etc., as limiting and channeling factors for sociocultural action and interaction.
14. George P. Murdock, "Changing Emphasis in Social Structure," *Southwestern Journal of Anthropology* 11 (1955): 336.
15. Raymond Firth, "Some Principles of Social Organization," *Journal of the Royal Anthropological Institute* 85 (1955): 366.
16. Herbert Blumer, "Psychological Import of the Human Group, in Muzafer Sherif and M. O. Wilson, eds., *Group Relations at the Crossroads* (New York: Harper & Row, Publishers, 1953), pp. 199–201. Emphasis added.
17. Kenneth E. Boulding, *The Image* (Ann Arbor: University of Michigan Press, 1956).
18. . . . Maruyama's discussion in Chapter 36 [of Buckley, op. cit.].
19. William J. Goode, "A Theory of Role Strain," *American Sociological Review* 25 (August 1960): 483.
20. Ibid., 495.
21. Ibid., 487.
22. Paul F. Secord and Carl W. Backman, "Personality Theory and the Problem of Stability and Change in Individual Behavior: An Interpersonal Approach," *Psychological Review* 68 (1961): 22.
23. Ibid.

24. Ibid., 26.
25. Ibid., 28.
26. Ibid.
27. Ralph H. Turner, "Role-Taking: Process Versus Conformity," in Arnold M. Rose, ed., *Human Behavior and Social Processes* (Boston: Houghton Mifflin Company, 1962), Chapter 2.
28. Ibid., 26.

29. Neal Gross *et al., Explorations in Role Analysis* (New York: John Wiley & Sons, Inc., 1958), p. 53.
30. Ibid., p. 38.
31. Anselm Strauss et al., "The Hospital and Its Negotiated Order," in Eliot Freidson, ed., *The Hospital in Modern Society* (New York: The Free Press, Div. of the Macmillan Company, 1963), p. 148.

ORGANIZATIONAL CYBERNETICS AND HUMAN VALUES

Richard F. Ericson

Introduction: Science and the Human Condition

The essential method of modern science is analysis. Reductionism and incrementalism have given us deep insight into the nature of matter and energy. We have built a techno-industrial society structured mainly so as to maximize the power of these understandings in order to give us leverage in our age-old struggle with nature. Thus, some would conjecture that at long last we may be at that point where there can truly be a "human use of human beings." But only the most extreme optimist would hold that such an outcome is as yet more than a vision.

The fact is that, in this decade of the 1960s, we may trace the locus of another exponential curve in man's experiences. To a large degree it is a curve which measures a countervailing inclination in man's nature. It measures man's desire to synthesize—to find meaning and purpose—from man's point of view.

This drive, in and of itself, is not new. It is the essence of religion. Much of philosophy concerns man's search for holistic concepts which will help him see a meaningful pattern in the complexity with which his perceptual world confronts him. What *is* new is the rapidly growing intensity of the quest, and the modern context of the search. Plato's *Republic* is from a world quite different from that of Boguslaw's *The New Utopians.*

The essence of modern science has recently been epitomized as follows:

1) Science is constantly, systematically and inexorably revisionary. It is a self-correcting process and one that is self-destroying of its own errors. . . .

2) A related trait of science is its destruction of idols, destruction of the gods men live by . . . Science has no absolute right or absolute justice . . . To live comfortably with science, it is necessary to live with a dynamically changing system of concepts . . . it has a way of weakening old and respected bonds. . . .

3) Not only are the tenets of science constantly subject to challenge and revision, but its prophets are under challenge too. . . .

4) Further, the findings of science have an embarrassing way of turning out to be relevant to the customs and to the civil laws of men—requiring these customs and laws also to be revised. . . .

5) Certainly we have seen spectacular changes in the concept of private property and of national borders as we have moved into the space age. . . .

6) Moreover, the pace of technological advance gravely threatens the bountiful and restorative power of nature to resist modification. . . .

7) Another trait of science that leads to much hostility or misunderstanding by the nonscientist is the fact that science is practiced by a small elite . . . (which) has cultural patterns discernibly different from those of the rest of society . . .

8) The trait that to me seems the most socially important about science, however, is that it is a major source of man's discontent with the status quo. . . .[1]

Examination of the essence of this list of characteristics of modern science gives us a basis for appreciating Norbert Wiener's closing words in his assessment of the "Moral and Technical Consequences of Automation" made only a decade ago:

. . . we can still by no means always justify the naive assumption that the faster we rush ahead to employ the new powers for action which are opened up to us, the better it will be. We must always exert the full strength of our imagination to examine where the full use of our new modalities may lead us.[2]

Delineations of the highly exponential rate of change in the growth and application of human knowledge abound. Examples from many fields are readily at hand. That we live in an era of quantum jumps in science and technology seems patent and uncontestable, at least measured by any yardstick provided by man's experience to date. Yet, our full appreciation of the magnitude of what is happening to us is only slowly dawning. As one astute observer wrote a few years ago:

Within a decade or two it will be generally understood that the main challenge to U.S. society will turn not around the production of goods, but around the difficulties and opportunities involved in a world of accelerating change and ever-widening choices. Change has always been part of the human condition. What is different now is the pace of change, and the prospect that it will come faster and faster, affecting every part of life, including personal values, morality, and religion, which seem most remote from technology. . . . So swift is the acceleration, that trying to "make sense" of change will come to be our basic industry.[3]

And the urgency of contemporary circumstances has been well expressed recently by a biologist, who feels that:

. . . now the empirical evidence may be turning to support those who feel that science is in some sense in the grip of natural forces which it does not command. . . .

I am not really sure that we stand on the kind of watershed Luther stood on when he nailed his theses to the door of the cathedral, but we may make a serious mistake if we do not at least entertain that possibility. If we fail to recognize the average man's need to believe that he has some reasonable command over his own life, he is simply going to give up supporting those systematic elements in society which he sees as depriving him of this ability.[4]

This paper is concerned with man in organizations. The major hypothesis explored is that managers of large enterprises—public or private, in any context—have an increasingly urgent sociohumanistic responsibility to create self-actualizing organizations which will assure to the maximum extent possible the transcendence of human over technological values. The major thesis is that general systems insights, cybernetic science, and computer technology can, so to speak, be "turned upon themselves" and made to provide the basis for achievement of this paramount requirement of contemporary managers.

Human Values and Noncybernetic Technologies

Concern for the impact of technology upon human values is hardly a recent phenomenon. With varying degrees of explicitness, since Karl Marx at least, many have sought to call man's attention to the shift away from naturalistic values implicitly required by machine civilization. As man was released from nature's grasp by his power-multiplying and labor-extending artifacts, he came under a new yoke: The man/machine interface had its own set of action priorities and behavior imperatives.

Effective interaction with machines necessitated shifts in attitudes, change in values. Nowhere was this more evident than in the workplace.

The utilization of steam power, for example, clearly implied the clustering of workers about factories. The accompanying value shift requirements have been noted, for example, by Elton Mayo, in his contrast of the "established" and the "adaptive" society. Clearly, the attitudinal skill most valued by modern industrial society is adaptiveness. Where the only constant is change, ready accommodation to change is a valued behavior. Mayo agreed with Janet that, in modern circumstances, for most of us, "sanity is an achievement." To keep one's emotional equilibrium is not easy among the shifting patterns in which most of us live.

But just at the time that man was called upon to contrive stability in increasingly dynamic environments, he was also required to find his place in increasingly large-scale and monolithic bureaucratic structures. As industrial artifacts evolved to more complicated forms and interrelated processes, a correspondingly complex set of organizational modes was generated.

Thus, one strand of our concerns in this paper is with the impact of technologically induced organizational complexes upon the attitudes and values of the humans who populate them. The other strand is concerned with the larger questions deriving from the impacts of technology upon man's environment in general. The substance of our inquiry today may, perhaps, be encapsulated by this question: "Are we now again pursuing a witness decision path where the sole parameter is 'What is possible technologically?' as we yesterday appeared only to ask the question 'Does it make sense economically?' "

It would not be sufficiently useful for purposes here to describe in detail the growing demand for articulation, for integration, for synthesis, for a more cosmic understanding of the sociopolitical implications of man's econo-technological behavior during the past century. But perhaps it is worth illustrating the point. Let us consider the now familiar example of the pollution of our physical environment.

In classical economic doctrine, air is a commonly cited example of a "free" good. Economists are concerned only with the "optimally efficient allocation of economic resources," and "economic goods" are those which are in short supply, relative to demand.

But in recent times some of the most essential noneconomic resources have rapidly moved out of that category. Concern for the magnitude and rate of pollution—environmental, social, and others—has intensified. Air, water, quiet, privacy—rather suddenly, these are decidedly economic goods. We are finally beginning to comprehend the accumulation of enormous "hidden" costs of our econo-technological order, costs never reckoned in industrial or national accounts.

The dawning realization of the extent to which man has already fouled his nest brings us up short. Indeed, we fear that, in some compartments and, in some respects, "spaceship earth" may already have been irremediably damaged. What price unbridled technological progress? Increasingly, the urgent need for holistic assessment of applied science is manifest. Only if we are sufficiently aware of the full social ramifications of applied science will we be able to forestall the deleterious consequences of the "technological cornucopia" we have generated.

Thus, from society's standpoint, modern science and technology is Janus-faced: it has given us wealth in one sense, and poverty in another; it has harnessed nature to man's basic needs in ways and to extents undreamed-of only a few decades ago; but it has fostered a continuingly lowered "quality of life." Today's massive environmental pollution problems are largely a consequence of the nearly unchallenged primacy of econo-industrial values. (And, to compound the felony, economic values [have been] improperly costed, from a social system point of view, since implicit and opportunity costs of production were largely ignored.) Our essential concern grows from this historical trend. Will tomorrow's "human pollution" problems result from even more disastrous neglect of cybernetics applied to social constructs and human values? This is the haunting issue.

Some years ago the noted American educator Robert Maynard Hutchins opened an essay dealing with an assessment of the latent social impacts of cybernetics with the sanguine statement, "I assume 1985 can be anything we want it to be." Is this any longer a tenable assumption? How is it to be reconciled with the conviction recently expressed by the nuclear physicist Amost DiShalit when he predicted that the time has come for us to recognize that the *most* man can hope for is *parity* with the emerging "self-organizing" cybernetic computer complexes, apparently an increasingly inherent part of our organizational life?[5]

General Systems Theory, Cybernetics, and the Methods of Modern Science

Before turning to the development of the argument, however, we must take note of another view expressed by Norbert Wiener which has caused some concern among those of us working for the development of organizational cybernetics. It may be recalled that in (one of his last works) *God and Golem, Inc.* Wiener concluded that he had

. . . accomplished the task of showing many valid analogies between certain religious statements and the phenomena studies by cybernetics, and had gone reasonably far in showing how cybernetic ideas may be relevant to the moral problems of the individual.[6]

He rather tartly dismissed the idea that the social sciences could benefit by the application of cybernetics because, in his words, "cybernetics is nothing if it is not mathematical" and that he had "found mathematical sociology and mathematical economics, or econometrics, suffering under a misapprehension of what is the proper use of mathematics in the social sciences. . . . " Wiener's major concern was that, in the social sciences, we have not appreciated how much mathematical physics rests upon the ability accurately and validly to measure the data with which it deals. And there is, for Wiener, an inherent difficulty, because, for example:

. . . the economic game is a game where the rules are subject to important revisions, say, every ten years, and bears an uncomfortable resemblance to the Queen's croquet game in "Alice in Wonderland" . . . . Under the circumstances, it is hopeless to give too precise a measurement to the quantities occurring in it.[7]

We will not quibble that for Wiener not to have distinguished mathematical economics from econometrics may reveal his own lack of appreciation of the value of heuristic model building, as against inductive validation of mathematically deduced statements about nature. Be that as it may. We shall simply assert the social utility of speculatively considering the value impacts of "alternative futures," using concepts such as homeostasis, positive and negative feedback, isomorphic reasoning, and morphogenic systems. We shall certainly not pretend that the social sciences have, even yet, much prospect of completely rigorous application of cyber-

Figure 1 "Reality Analysis" of Organizational Behavior Processes

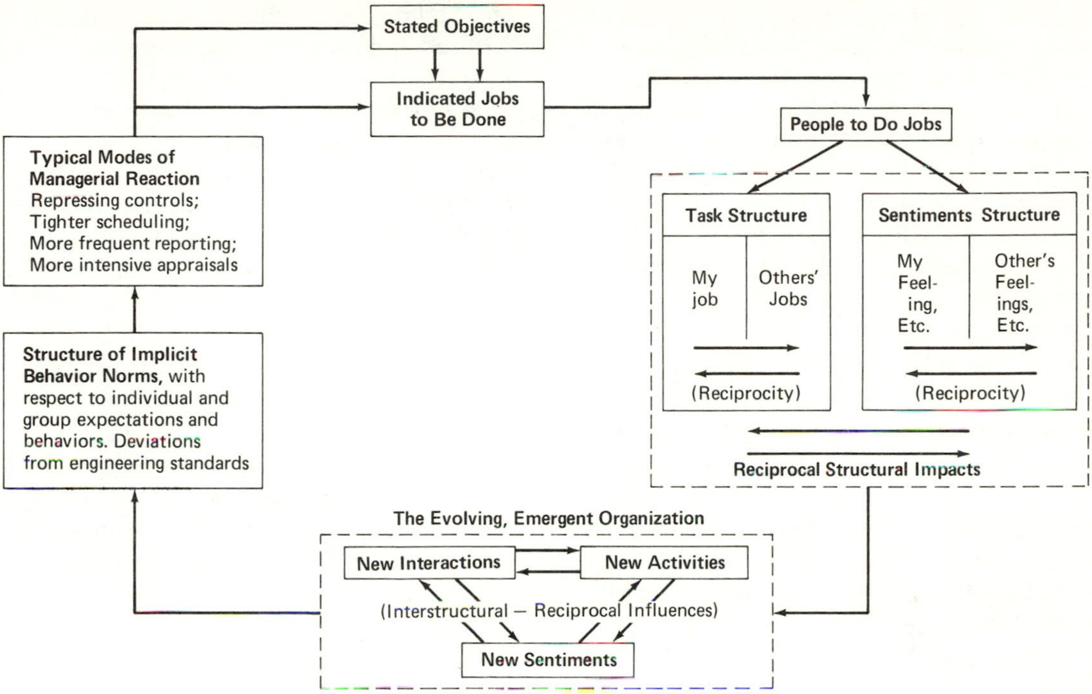

Stated Objectives

Indicated Jobs to Be Done

People to Do Jobs

Typical Modes of Managerial Reaction
Repressing controls;
Tighter scheduling;
More frequent reporting;
More intensive appraisals

Task Structure

My job | Others' Jobs

(Reciprocity)

Sentiments Structure

My Feeling, Etc. | Other's Feelings, Etc.

(Reciprocity)

Structure of Implicit Behavior Norms, with respect to individual and group expectations and behaviors. Deviations from engineering standards

Reciprocal Structural Impacts

The Evolving, Emergent Organization

New Interactions — New Activities

(Interstructural — Reciprocal Influences)

New Sentiments

netic science. But given the magnitude of and the urgency of the social need for fresh insight and imaginative outlook, general systems and cybernetic imagery such as found in the works of Kenneth Boulding, Anatol Rapoport, Ludwig von Bertalanffy and Stafford Beer are sorely needed. The identification of system isomorphies and the construction of homomorphic models is well worth whatever "pure science" rigor must be sacrificed when, in the words of Rapoport:

Once this logic is grasped, the system approach to the study of man can be appreciated as an effort to restore meaning (in terms of intuitively grasped understanding of wholes) while adhering to the principles of disciplined generalizations and rigorous deduction. It is, in short, an attempt to make the study of man both scientific and meaningful.[8]

A Contrast of Paradigms: Noncybernetic Vis-à-Vis Cybernetic Organizations

Early in his book *Cybernetics and Management* Stafford Beer says: "It is inevitable that the word 'control' must be used frequently in the forthcoming discussions. I wish to state explicitly at this point that henceforth it will be used in a special sense: It will never denote the repressive and mandatory type of system which customarily passes for control. . . ."[9] The accompanying paradigm illustrates what Beer probably had in mind when he spoke of such a "repressive and mandatory" control system. It also serves to bring into focus our concern for human values as affected by organizational processes. Let us interpret the (clockwise) progression on Figure 1.

At the outset, we assume the existence of more or less clearly stated organizational objectives, for we are dealing here with purposive organizations. On the basis of the application of the "principles of organization and management" as usually delineated in traditional texts, management thinks in terms of the logics of hierarchical authority structure and of rational modes of departmentation of the jobs to be done, as the organization is designed. Efficiency, coordination logics, "span of control" considerations: These are the bywords in terms of which organization charts are usually drawn.

But, unfortunately for such an approach, people are required to do the jobs; and, eventually, specific names have to be written into the boxes on the chart. But here, at this early stage in design, the usual approach begins to fail to take important parameters into account; for managements usually attend to only the "task" subsystem of the total system with which they should, in reality, be dealing. That is, management understands the necessity of organizational design which integrates each task into the total work flow; principles such as "scalar chain" are applied to assure, on paper at least, that each job will contribute to the organization's ultimate purposes. But historically it has only recently come to appreciate the other major subsystem with which it should deal: that of "sentiments," to use F. J. Roethlisberger's characterization. The argument is simply this: The effectiveness with which an organization functions is determined at least as much by who holds the positions which are delineated on the organization chart, as by the cleverness of the organization structure which defines and abstractly interrelates the "jobs to be done." Thus, the assumptions, feelings, perceptions, values, etc. which comprise the "personalities" of the specific people involved in the operation must somehow be taken into account if a systemic organizational model is to be achieved. And this is all the more so since, as the exhibit indicates, there is not only reciprocal influence exerted within each of the subsystems, but *between the subsystems themselves* as well.

Thus, the dynamics of organizations-

in-action should be viewed as an evolving social system, with management attention focused on the continually emergent system resulting from the reciprocal influences exerted by new activities (jobs), interactions (relationships), and sentiments (values)—to use Homans' terminology. Now, because historically management simply did not have the communication and control tools to deal adequately with such emergent phenomena on a "real-time" basis, we usually find that a subtle and intricate set of "implicit behavior norms" comprises the real essence of the actual control mechanism operative in large-scale organizations. That is, something is usually needed in order to "make the organization work" and to fill the behavior interstices left by the formalized statement of the system found in such paraphernalia as organization charts, manuals of operating procedure, and the like. Organizational cement is therefore manufactured by organizational participants within the framework of the inadequate formal control system specified. This cement comprises the behavior norms which are based upon the "evolving pattern of expectations" which organizational role-players develop. A sub rosa dynamic control system arises, most often in terms of the tacit pattern of agreements which evolves among interacting organizational participants, reflecting their needs and values, as well as the organization's.

Now, when management belatedly becomes aware that, for example, engineering standards are habitually not being met in work outputs, the usual reaction is for the activation of formal authority and control mechanisms. Unsatisfactory performance evaluations more often than not seem to lead directly to the imposition of explicit, formal, manifest control mechanisms. And, as subsequent events all too often show, such delayed and proscriptive reactions either merely trigger a search for new modes of behavior which will put management off for another period of time, or to a divergent cycling and organizational explosion which we usually refer to as a "positive feedback" phenomenon.

If things deteriorate sufficiently—and they usually do—the cycle depicted on the accompanying schematic is usually completed by someone in management concluding that "it's time we reorganize." Indeed, a favorite bureaucratic pathology seems to be "if in doubt, reorganize," either in terms of restructuring positions, or reshuffling people, or both. It is hypothesized here, however, that *an index of managerial quality* is to be found in the frequency with which managers have to resort to the instruments of formal control: The more the need for using explicit sanctions, the greater the likelihood is that the manager(s) in question does not adequately understand the nature of the problem(s) with which he seeks to deal. The cliché "Having lost sight of our objectives, we redouble our efforts" reflects this overanxious and erroneous managerial reaction. As the chart indicates, the fact may be that what really needs to be called into question is the organization's *stated objectives*.

Here then is a telescoped image of a behavior cycle which lead Chris Argyris over a decade ago to the conclusion that "there is a lack of congruency between the needs of healthy individuals and the demands of formation organization."[10] What is the alternative?

Perhaps the most important single characteristic of modern organizational cybernetics is this: That in addition to concern with the deleterious impacts of rigidly-imposed notions of what constitutes the application of good "principles of organization and management," the organization is viewed as a subsystem of larger system(s), and as comprised, itself, of functionally interdependent subsystems. Thus, the so-called "human relations movement" of the past quarter-century or so concentrates upon analysis of the internal dynamics of organizational life. The "fusion process" is its focus: Out of the individual's attempt to personalize the organization, and the organization's efforts to socialize the in-

dividual, comes an amalgam which hopefully enables each concurrently to fulfill its needs.

But at best, feedback in organizational concepts such as those delineated above depends upon a very high order of managerial perceptual sensitivity and interpersonal communications clarity. Even where such managers are to be found, in large-scale organizations the permutations and combinations of interaction dynamics soon exceed human channel capacities. Thus, it is only as we have moved into the world of general systems theory, cybernetic science, and computer technology have the on-line, real-time loops been adequately closed. Perhaps this can best be illustrated by considering how organizational cybernetics has the potential for substantially eliminating three kinds of communication and control lags usually found in management information systems.

Figure 2 indicates that, as the non-cybernetic organization pursues its goals along a chosen behavior path, from time to time the output indicators signal that the behavior tolerances have been violated. This requires positive managerial action to bring the output within prescribed limits. But we see that correction usually occurs only some time after the limits have been exceeded, and then only with a time lag.

Figure 2   Comparison of Surveillance, Reaction, and Correction Lags: Noncybernetic and Cybernetic Controls

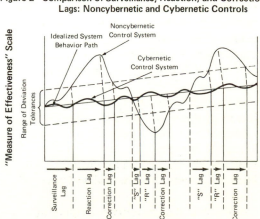

Analytically, what we see is that three kinds of lags are identifiable: the "surveillance" lag, the "reaction" lag and the "correction" lag. By the first is meant simply that, more often than not, days or weeks or months pass between the occurrence of an actual deviation and its report to management: This is the surveillance lag. But even after managers are aware of the need to do something, and actually set about corrective action, organizational inertia must be overcome. The firm may tend to persist for some time as it has been heading, before the redirection brakes take hold: This is the reaction lag. Finally, the correction lag occurs between the time the system begins to exhibit a reversal of inertia, and return to a path within the range of tolerance.

Now of course the slightly deviant behavior path which oscillates about the "ideal" path represents the situation after realization of on-line, real-time reporting and control capability. It may be noted in passing that, as the Forrester industrial dynamics model has shown,[11] immediately corrective and completely remedial managerial actions which will always instantaneously return organizational behavior to the idealized path are usually *not* desirable. Optimal lags often exist, as complex organizational subsystems interact. But here too, cybernetic approaches to organizational design will help reveal what these are. This is no small point. It bears upon Beer's concern for the complementary fallacies of composition and division.[12] And since Beer has admirably presented the technical case for organizational cybernetics in both his *Cybernetics and Management* and his more recent comprehensive volume *Decision and Control*,[13] I shall rest the argument at this point.

So we come at last to the essential question: How will all this promote the realization of human values?

Psychocybernetic Organizations, Human Needs, and Social Values

Louis Fried has recently provided an imaginative utilization of Kurt Lewin's topological and vector psychology and the associated force-field theory to describe how the man/machine (psychocybernetic) system may be integrated with questions of perceptions and values in human organizations.[14] Suffice it to say that this kind of analysis represents substantiation of the line of argument presented here, which may now be summarized as follows: (1) Really effective human organizations tend to be those which openly acknowledge usually implicit values, and assign them explicit priorities; (2) continuous discussion and modification of organizational values by participants will increase the likelihood of organization viability (homeostasis) and progress (heterostasis or morphogenesis), and (3) cybernetically-designed and managed organizations are not only most likely to realize their targeted levels of effectiveness, they also have greatest potential for fulfilling basic human needs and for realizing associated human values.

Let us be more specific in this linkage of human needs, social values, and organizational cybernetics. Clyde Kluckhohn has defined a value as a "conception, explicit or implicit, distinctive of an individual or characteristic of a group, or the desirable which influences the selection from available modes, means, and ends of action."[15] Another anthropologist concludes that: (1) values differ, but all people have values; (2) values appear as parts of patterns of behavior developed in coping with specific sorts of life circumstances; (3) the concepts we develop to think about human life are shaped by values; (4) it is very difficult for us human beings to treat the solution of human problems as a technical matter . . . , and (5) even though the doctrine of "cultural relativity," as once put forward, has failed to withstand more sophisticated examination, it will never again be possible for us to think in terms of ethical absolutions in the same way that our nineteenth-century forebears did.[16]

But values, in turn, are functionally related to kinds and levels of perceived needs. Of course, needs too are culturally determined in substantial measure—at least in the modes of their realization. But equally, it is possible to identify basic categories of human needs which transcend cultural contexts. Table 1 links six basic human needs to corresponding social values, frequently expressed in modern industrial societies.[17] The table is constructed on the basis of the following putative assertion: *Cybernetically-controlled organizations will be more likely to respond to the indicated social values, and therefore will more ably identify and more effectively meet human needs.*

Because cybernetically-oriented control systems give the organization far greater potential for articulation with larger systems of which they are a part (subsystem), the organization's values are likely to be highly responsive to those in the social environment. The cybernetic organization's value interpretations are also, reciprocally, very likely to influence substantially the general social values to an appreciably larger extent than in the case of traditional noncybernetically-managed entities. As I have elsewhere suggested, this cybernetic subsystem-system-suprasystem integration will tend to increase managerial value characteristics such as these: (1) moral sensitivity; (2) service motivation; (3) "extra-organizational" loyalties; (4) attitudes of tentativeness (tolerance); (5) democratic procedural orientations; (6) compassion; (7) search for "optimum instability" for the system; (8) rationality, and (9) greater self-actualization via "collegial" milieux.[18] The final column in Table 1 comprises items which are meant to be illustrative of the ways in which psychocybernetic organizations at least *have potential* for considerably enhancing the need-meeting, value-serving response modes typically found in traditionally-controlled organizations (see p. 222).

But we ascribe only the *potential* for greater value realization. Various images of cybernetically-oriented organizations have, for many years now, been speculatively and suspiciously viewed as bringing about, with at least an equal degree of potentiality, quite the opposite result. So in conclusion, we address the question: What ground do we have for projecting the far greater likelihood that cybernetically-managed organizations will in fact bring about—sooner or later—a more "human use of human beings?"

Our Sociocybernetic World: Man's New Basis for Consanguinity

The essential premise of this paper has been that we do indeed live in an era of "historical discontinuity," and of "radical change," where guidelines that have served man not too badly in the past have little relevance to present circumstances. Not that man has never before been thrust into eras which broke sharply with the past. Social revolutions and cultural cataclysms are an integral part of the human experience. But the present discontinuity is unique, for it is subtle, intangible, and extremely complex in its manifestations. It has at once an "either/or" quality, an Armeggedon and a Utopian feel to it.

Thus, man is no longer merely in a "game against nature." As never before, man is now in an "x-person" game, where the outcome is almost surely *not* of the zero-sum type. R. Buckminster Fuller's "World Game" is an imaginative expression of this viewpoint.[19] For these reasons there is, as never before, an urgent need to understand the forces at work, so as reasonably to assure their resolution in man's favor. More than this, the requirement is for man to control the *generation* of these science/technology vectors, in terms of sociocultural hierarchies of values upon which consensus has been reached. As the British historian E. H. Carr concluded several years ago:

. . . progress in human affairs, whether in science or in history or in society, has come mainly through the bold readiness of human beings not to confine themselves to seeking piecemeal improvements in the

Table 1 Types of Organizational Response to Human Needs and Social Values

Categories of Human Needs	Category Definitions	Corresponding Social Values	Typical Modes by which Noncybernetic Organizations respond (Satisfaction Modes)	Illustrative Enhancement Potentials in Cybernetic Organizations
Recognition-Status	Need to be considered competent or good in a professional, social, occupational, or play activity. Need to gain social or vocational position, i.e., to be more skilled or better than others.	Opportunity	—Merit advancement —Award systems —Incentive programs —Overt commendations by superiors —Status symbols	—Expanded range of rational choice —Fewer organizational rigidities —Easier to identify individual merit —Objectification of performance appraisal criteria —More peer-group selections
Protection-Dependency	Need to have another person or group of people prevent frustration or punishment, or to provide for satisfaction of other needs.	Security	—Job tenure (employment security) —Group solidarity (implicit group behavior norms) —Unions and formal associations —Informal cliques —Dyads; "Buddy" systems	—Greater intraorganizational mobility —More feelings of "belonging" because of greater total communication, etc. —Greater openness; deeper awareness of mutuality
Dominance	Need to direct or control the actions of other people, including members of family and friends. To have any action taken which he suggests.	Progress	—Hierarchical leadership roles —"Father figures" translated into bureaucratic structures —Formal, legalistically legitimized role structures —"Superior/subordinate" chains; political maneuvering	—More leadership roles filled on basis of genuine merit —Greater dynamism, therefore greater opportunity for morphogenesis —Greater release of creativity because of more amorphous structures; —"ad hoc" and task-directed leadership
Independence	Need to make own decisions, to rely on oneself, together with the need to develop skills for obtaining satisfactions directly without the mediation of other people.	Freedom	—Pseudo-and quasi-democratic processes —Grievance procedures —"Corporate devil's advocates;" "Ombudsmen" —Staff roles; specialized expertise	—More chance to "do one's thing" in terms of organizational needs —Objectivity a norm: release from bondage of unprovable assertions —Greater interorganizational mobility —Freedom to innovate and be creative because technological change is a norm
Love and Affection	Need for acceptance and indication of liking by other individuals. In contrast to recognition-status, not concerned with social or professional positions of friends, but seeks their warm regard.	Participation	—Supportive and "human-centered" management —Rapport developed by after-hours activities, company-sponsored diversions, etc. —"Coffee Klatsen" groups —Confidents; mutual "back-scratching"	—Greater professionalism leads to greater mutuality and sharing —More ad hoc groups, formed on a voluntary (sociometric) basis —Greater inclination and opportunity to test consensus —More opportunity for spontaneous collaboration.
Physical Comfort	Learned need for physical satisfaction that has become associated with the gaining of security.	Environmental Quality	—Provision of work-conducive surroundings —Equipment support and services —Sensory protection —Ancillary reinforcements, e.g., provision of parking space, etc.	—Earlier, clearer, and more focused evidence of dysfunctional circumstances —Greater chance for selectively providing for individual needs —More automation and robotizing of laborious tasks

way things are done, but to present funda-mental challenges in the name of reason to the current way of doing things and to the avowed or hidden assumptions on which it rests.[20]

Recent interpretative works in the United States such as Ferkiss' *Techno-logical Man,*[21] McHale's *The Future of the Future,*[22] and Boguslaw's *The New Utopians,*[23] speculations such as Kahn and Wiener's *The Year 2000,*[24] and the Daedalus volume *Toward the Year 2000*[25]; and institutionalizations of such ideas as are found in the recently-formed World Future Society and the Institute for the Future have their counterparts in Europe and other parts of the world. They sug-gest that there are conjunctive forces in modern high-technology societies which are bringing into sharp focus the necessity for man to recognize that he now has the possibility of "creating his own future" as never before.

But even more discomforting, in terms of old values and ancient premises, man is now meaningfully able to *design* his own future, not just choose from nature's al-ternatives. Thus, in the words of a promi-nent solar astronomer:

In our explosively changing world it is no longer sufficient to live with philosophies or religions simply handed down from an older generation. . . . Rather than simply fight for the preservation of the old things that are good, we must plan creatively also to shape the new. We must commit ourselves to dare to build the world we want, knowing that it is possible if we but demand it. . . . [26]

We have presented the argument that cybernetically-controlled organizations, when we learn sufficiently well how to de-sign and maintain them, have the potential for bringing about the kind of psychologi-cally maturing "reciprocation" between organization and individual of which the managerial psychiatrist Harry Levinson has so ardently written.[27] Moreover, the application of cybernetics has potential

for revolutionizing political processes, by providing for individualized responses to great questions arising in large-scale com-plex social systems. Within the past year, the British Minister of Technology has expressed the opinion that:

Carried to its logical conclusion, this (cybernetically-inspired) process of decentrali-zation could well provide a far greater role for the individual in the community than the 1984 pessimists about technology have ever realized. It is not only possible, but certain, that the evolution of modern management science will ultimately allow every single individual *to be taken into full account in the evolution of social planning, taxation, and social security policy. Through a system which took ac-count of the circumstances of each in-dividual, governments could get a feed-back so comprehensive as to allow policy to be really personalized . . . . Our discus-sion will become, more openly, arguments about value judgments . . . . (Italics sup-plied.)*[28]

In the United States, the "hippies" who want to "turn on, tune in, and drop out," the "yippies" who seem to prefer anarchy to the kind of rationalized social chaos they perceive, the campus malcontents, and the considerable number of those "over 30" oldsters who seem, in some measure, to share such views: All bespeak an extreme manifestation of what the re-spected motivational psychologist Ernest Dichter discerned many years ago—that the "Mr. Jones" who typifies urban Ameri-can society has himself been undergoing profound change.[29] In substance, we seem increasingly to be, in Riesman's nomen-clature, "inner directed" rather than "other directed." This represents a pro-found change in value sets and action pri-orities from those which prevailed only a rather short time ago when William Whyte discovered the "organization man." It is exemplified in the United States, of course, by Detroit's finally having to take cognizance of the increasing incursions of the VW "beetle" and now the Toyota into the domestic U.S. automobile market. Similar trends are currently evident in other consumption propensities.

In the early part of this decade I suggested that such value shifts, in conjunction with the emergent impacts of organizational cybernetics, would provide a new basis for consanguinity among the nations of man. The substance of the chain of argument was expressed as follows:

Scientific management was an early attempt to rationalize the management function. Now digital computers, epitomizing the new information technology, bid fair to automate the office as well as the factory. Cybernetic management, utilizing the information technology, evolves optimal logico-deductive patterns of industrial organization and procedure. As these technological imperatives impinge, nations will converge in terms of socio-industrial authority structures and behavioral modes. It seems most likely that there will be a universal tendency toward pluralistic industrialism.[30]

If or to the extent that such tendencies eventuate in the coming decade or two, we shall perhaps witness a general trend away from the "entrepreneurial ethic" to that which has been called "scientific humanism," having the following characteristics:

1) More effort will be organized around the problem to be solved, rather than around traditional functions such as production, marketing, etc.;
2) The leadership role will rotate within each mission or project, based on the nature of the problem and the sequence of knowledge required at various stages of its solution, and
3) Participation in the management process will become more widely distributed among all levels of the organization.[31]

Thus, "the frantic search for individualism in a society that increasingly demands interdependence from its members . . . (will create pressures) for production systems that are built around human needs rather than around conventional concepts of efficiency."[32] Warren Bennis' predictions of the "coming death of bureaucracy" gain credibility when viewed in terms of the emerging organizational cybernetics.

So, both from the standpoint of their likely impacts upon organizational structures and processes and from their projected potentials in creating new organizational environments, the trinity comprising (1) general systems concepts; (2) information theory and the associated cybernetic science, and (3) computer technology may prove holy or otherwise, depending upon man's implementing value priorities. "Who controls the controllers, and how?" is a question which assumes greater urgency now that the apparition which George Orwell conjured in 1949 looms as an ominous potential only fourteen years hence [as of 1970]. We conclude here as Boguslaw did in the final paragraph of his trenchant work:

Our own utopian renaissance receives its impetus from a desire to extend the mastery of man over nature. Its greatest vigor stems from a dissatisfaction with the limitations of man's existing control over his physical environment. Its greatest threat consists precisely in its potential as a means for extending the control of man over man.[33]

And while we are mindful of Ferkiss' warning that:

Man's destiny lies in continuing to exploit this "openness," rather than entering into a symbiotic relationship with the inorganic machine that, while it might bring immediate increments of power, would inhibit his development by chaining him to a system of lesser potentialities. . . . Man must stand above his physical technologies if he is to avoid their becoming his shell and the principle of their organization his anthill,[34] we share McHale's view that:

The future of cultural forms already has many more dimensions of rich diversity. The promise within the newer media is of a greater interpenetration and interaction of life-art-culture rather than the forms-objects-images that preserved and isolated social life.

   As for the larger communication and understanding implied in a shared planetary culture, it is more than obvious today that we must understand and cooperate on a truly global scale, or we perish.[35]

References and Notes

1. Walter Orr Roberts, "Science, A Wellspring of Our Discontent," *American Scholar* (1967), pp. 252–58.

2. *Science* (May 6, 1960), reprinted in Morris Philipson, *Automation: Implications For The Future* (New York: Vintage Books, Random House, Inc., 1962), p. 172.

3. Max Ways, "The Era of Radical Change," *Fortune* (May 1964), p. 113.

4. Robert S. Morison, "Science and Social Attitudes," *Science* (July 11, 1969), p. 154.

5. Dialogue recorded at the Center for the Study of Democratic Institutions, Santa Barbara, California, Tape No. 199 entitled "After Automation—What?"

6. The volume is subtitled, *A Comment on Certain Points Where Cybernetics Impinges on Religion* (Cambridge, Mass.: M.I.T. Press, March 1966), p. 90.

7. Ibid., p. 91.

8. Foreward to Walter Buckley, ed., *Modern Systems Research for The Behavioral Scientist* (Chicago, Ill.: Aldine-Atherton, Inc., 1968), p. 22.

9. Stafford Beer, *Cybernetics and Management* (New York: John Wiley & Sons, Inc., 1959).

10. Argyris first made this statement in "The Individual and Organization: Some Problems of Mutual Adjustment," *Administrative Science Quarterly* (June 1957), p. 9. (See also his book *Personality and Organization*).

11. See Jay W. Forrester, "Industrial Dynamics: A Major Breakthrough for Decision Makers," *Harvard Business Review* (July–August 1958), especially Exhibit X, "Effect of Correction Time on Inventories," p. 49. This article (as in the case of Argyris above) preceeded Forrester's book, *Industrial Dynamics*.

12. See especially Stafford Beer, "Below the Twilight Arch: A Mythology of Systems," *Yearbook of The Society For General Systems Research* 5 (1960): 17.

13. The book's subtitle, "The Meaning of Operational Research and Management Cybernetics," gives a clue to its orientation (New York: John Wiley & Sons, Inc., 1966).

14. "Psychocybernetics and the Organization," *Data Processing Magazine* (Nov. 1966), pp. 44–45.

15. Quoted in R. Tagiuri, "Value Orientations and the Relationship of Managers and Scientists," *Administrative Science Quarterly* (June 1965), p. 40.

16. L. R. Peattie, "Anthropology and the Search for Values," *The Journal of Applied Behavioral Science* 1, no. 4 (1965): 371–2.

17. The six "basic human needs" and the corresponding definitions (columns one and two of Table 1) are from J. B. Rotter, *Social Learning and Clinical Psychology* (Englewood Cliffs, N.J.: Prentice-Hall, Inc., 1954).

18. R. F. Ericson, "The Impact of Cybernetic Information Technology on Management Value Systems," prepared for the XV International Meeting of The Institute of Management Sciences (Cleveland, Ohio, Sept., 12, 1968). Published in the October 1969 issue of *Management Science,* and in vol. 14 (1969) of the *Society for General Systems Research Yearbook.*

19. Published in multilith as "World Game: How It Came About," April 21, 1968.

20. *What is History* (New York: Alfred A. Knopf, Inc., 1961), p. 207.

21. Victor C. Ferkiss, *Technological Man: The Myth and The Reality* (New York: George Braziller, 1969).

22. John McHale, *The Future of The Future* (New York: George Braziller, 1969).

23. Robert Boguslaw, *The New Utopians: A Study of System Design and Social Change* (Englewood Cliffs, N.J.: Prentice-Hall, Inc. 1965).

24. Herman Kahn and Anthony J. Wiener, *The Year 2000: A Framework for Speculation on The Next Thirty-Five Years* (New York: The Macmillan Company, 1967).

25. Summer issue, 1967.

26. W. O. Roberts, *Science, a Wellspring, p. 260.*

27. *Reciprocation: The Relationship Between Man and Organization,"* Administrative Science Quarterly (March 1965), p. 370 ff.

28. Anthony Wedgwood Benn, "Living with Technological Change," *New Statesman* (Dec. 12, 1968), p. 827.

29. "Discovering the 'Inner Jones,' " *Harvard Business Review (May-June 1965), p. 6 ff.*

30. "Toward a Universally Viable Philosophy of Management," *Management Science* (May 1962), p. 47–48.

31. E. J. Korprowski, "New Dimensions for Decision-making," *Management of Personnel Quarterly* (Winter 1968).

32. Ibid.

33. Robert Boguslaw, *New Utopians,* p. 204.

34. Robert Boguslaw, *New Utopians,* p. 255.

35. Robert Boguslaw, *New Utopians,* p. 300.

MIXED SCANNING: A "THIRD" APPROACH TO DECISIONMAKING

Amitai Etzioni

In the concept of social decisionmaking, vague commitments of a normative and political nature are translated into specific commitments to one or more specific courses of action. Since decisionmaking includes an element of choice, it is the most deliberate and voluntaristic aspect of social conduct. As such, it raises the question: To what extent can social actors decide what their course will be, and to what extent are they compelled to follow a course set by forces beyond their control? Three conceptions of decisionmaking are considered here with assumptions that give varying weights to the conscious choice of the decisionmakers.

Rationalistic models tend to posit a high degree of control over the decisionmaking situation on the part of the decisionmaker. The incrementalist approach presents an alternative model, referred to as the art of "muddling through," which assumes much less command over the environment. Finally, the article outlines a third approach to social decisionmaking which, in combining elements of both earlier approaches, is neither as utopian in its assumptions as the first model nor as conservative as the second. For reasons which will become evident, this third approach is referred to as mixed scanning.

The Rationalistic Approach

Rationalistic models are widely held conceptions about how decisions are and ought to be made. An actor becomes aware of a problem, posits a goal, carefully weighs alternative means, and chooses among them according to his estimates of their respective merit, with reference to the state of affairs he prefers. Incrementalists' criticism of this approach focuses on the disparity between the re-

quirements of the model and the capacities of decisionmakers.[1] Social decisionmaking centers, it is pointed out, frequently do not have a specific, agreed upon set of values that could provide the criteria for evaluating alternatives. Values, rather, are fluid and are affected by, as well as affect, the decisions made. Moreover, in actual practice, the rationalistic assumption that values and facts, means and ends, can be clearly distinguished seems inapplicable:

> . . . Public controversy . . . has surrounded the proposal to construct a branch of the Cook County Hospital on the South Side in or near the Negro area. Several questions of policy are involved in the matter, but the ones which have caused one of the few public *debates of an issue in the Negro community concern whether, or to what extent, building such a branch would result in an all-Negro or "Jim Crow" hospital and whether such a hospital is desirable as a means of providing added medical facilities for Negro patients. Involved are both an issue of* fact *(whether the hospital would be segregated, intentionally or unintentionally, as a result of the character of the neighborhood in which it would be located) and an issue of* value *(whether even an all-Negro hospital would be preferable to no hospital at all in the area). In reality, however, the factions have aligned themselves in such a way and the debate has proceeded in such a manner that the fact issue and the value issue have been collapsed into the single question of whether to build or not to build. Those in favor of the proposal will argue that the facts do not bear out the charge of "Jim Crowism"—"the proposed site . . . is not considered to be placed in a segregated area for the exclusive use of one racial or minority group"; or "no re-*

sponsible officials would try to develop a new hospital to further segregation"; or "establishing a branch hospital for the . . . more adequate care of the indigent patient load, from the facts thus presented, does not represent Jim Crowism." At the same time, these proponents argue that whatever the facts, the factual issue is secondary to the overriding consideration that "there is a here-and-now need for more hospital beds. . . . Integration may be the long-run goal, but in the short-run we need more facilities."[2]

In addition, information about consequences is, at best, fractional. Decisionmakers have neither the assets nor the time to collect the information required for rational choice. While knowledge technology, especially computers, does aid in the collection and processing of information, it cannot provide for the computation required by the rationalist model. (This holds even for chess playing, let alone "real-life" decisions.) Finally, rather than being confronted with a limited universe of relevant consequences, decisionmakers face an open system of variables, a world in which all consequences cannot be surveyed.[3] A decisionmaker, attempting to adhere to the tenets of a rationalistic model, will become frustrated, exhaust his resources without coming to a decision, and remain without an effective decisionmaking model to guide him. Rationalistic models are thus rejected as being at once unrealistic and undesirable.

The Incrementalist Approach

A less demanding model of decisionmaking has been outlined in the strategy of "disjointed incrementalism" advanced by Charles E. Lindblom and others.[4] Disjointed incrementalism seeks to adapt decisionmaking strategies to the limited cognitive capacities of decisionmakers and to reduce the scope and cost of information collection and computation. Lindblom

summarized the six primary requirements of the model in this way:[5]

1) Rather than attempting a comprehensive survey and evaluation of all alternatives, the decisionmaker focuses only on those policies which differ incrementally from existing policies.

2) Only a relatively small number of policy alternatives are considered.

3) For each policy alternative, only a restricted number of "important" consequences are evaluated.

4) The problem confronting the decisionmaker is continually redefined: Incrementalism allows for countless ends-means and means-ends adjustments which, in effect, make the problem more manageable.

5) Thus, there is no one decision or "right" solution but a "never-ending series of attacks" on the issues at hand through serial analyses and evaluation.

6) As such, incremental decisionmaking is described as remedial, geared more to the alleviation of present, concrete social imperfections than to the promotion of future social goals.

Morphological Assumptions of the Incremental Approach

Beyond a model and a strategy of decisionmaking, disjointed incrementalism also posits a structure model; it is presented as the typical decisionmaking process of pluralistic societies, as contrasted with the master planning of totalitarian societies. Influenced by the free competition model of economics, incrementalists reject the notion that policies can be guided in terms of central institutions of a society expressing the collective "good." Policies, rather, are the outcome of a give-and-take among numerous societal "partisans." The measure of a good decision is the decisionmakers' agreement about it. Poor decisions are those which exclude actors capable of affecting the projected course of action; decisions of this type tend to be blocked or modified later.

Partisan "mutual-adjustment" is held to provide for a measure of coordination of decisions among a multiplicity of decision-makers and, in effect, to compensate on the societal level for the inadequacies of the individual incremental decision-maker and for the society's inability to make decisions effectively from one center. Incremental decisionmaking is claimed to be both a realistic account of how the American polity and other modern democracies decide and the most effective approach to societal decision-making, i.e., both a descriptive and a normative model.

A Critique of the Incremental Approach as a Normative Model

Decisions by consent among partisans without a society-wide regulatory center and guiding institutions should not be viewed as the preferred approach to decisionmaking. In the first place, decisions so reached would, of necessity, reflect the interests of the most powerful, since partisans invariably differ in their respective power positions; demands of the under-privileged and politically unorganized would be underrepresented.

Secondly, incrementalism would tend to neglect *basic* societal innovations, as it focuses on the short-run and seeks no more than limited variations from past policies. While an accumulation of small steps could lead to a significant change, there is nothing in this approach to guide the accumulation; the steps may be circular—leading back to where they started, or dispersed—leading in many directions at once but leading nowhere. Boulding comments that, according to this approach, "we do stagger through history like a drunk putting one disjointed incremental foot after another."[6]

In addition, incrementalists seem to underestimate *their* impact on the decisionmakers. As Dror put it, "Although Lindblom's thesis includes a number of reservations, these are insufficient to alter

its main impact as an ideological rein-forcement of the pro-inertia and anti-innovation forces."[7]

A Conceptual and Empirical Critique of Incrementalism

Incrementalist strategy clearly recognizes one subset of situations to which it does not apply—namely, "large" or funda-mental decisions,[8] such as a declaration of war. While incremental decisions greatly outnumber fundamental ones, the latter's significance for societal decisionmaking is not commensurate with their number; it is thus a mistake to relegate nonincremental decisions to the category of exceptions. Moreover, it is often the fundamental de-cisions which set the context for the nu-merous incremental ones. Although funda-mental decisions are frequently "pre-pared" by incremental ones in order that the final decision will initiate a less abrupt change, these decisions may still be con-sidered relatively fundamental. The incre-mental steps which follow cannot be un-derstood without them, and the preceding steps are useless unless they lead to fun-damental decisions.

Thus, while the incrementalists hold that decisionmaking involves a choice be-tween the two kinds of decisionmaking models, it should be noted that (a) *most incremental decisions specify or anticipate fundamental decisions, and* (b) *the cumu-lative value of the incremental decisions is greatly affected by the related fundamental decisions.*

Thus, it is not enough to show, as Fenno did, that Congress makes primarily marginal changes in the federal budget (a comparison of one year's budget for a federal agency with that of the preceding year showed on many occasions only a 10 percent difference[9]), or that for long periods the defense budget does not change much in terms of its percentage of the federal budget, or that the federal budget changes little each year in terms of its percentage of the Gross National Prod-uct.[10] These incremental changes are often the unfolding of trends initiated at critical turning points at which fundamental decisions were made. The American defense budget jumped at the beginning of the Korean War in 1950 from 5 percent of the GNP to 10.3 percent in 1951. The fact that it stayed at about this level, ranging between 9 and 11.3 percent of the GNP after the war ended (1954–1960), did reflect incremental decisions, but these were made within the context of the decision to engage in the Korean War.[11] Fenno's own figures show almost an equal number of changes above the 20 percent level as below it; seven changes represented an increase of 100 percent or more and 24 changes increased 50 percent or more.[12]

It is clear that, while Congress or other societal decisionmaking bodies do make some cumulative incremental decisions without facing the fundamental one implied, many other decisions which appear to be a series of incremental ones are, in effect, the implementation or elaboration of a fundamental decision. For example, after Congress set up a national space agency in 1958 and consented to back President Kennedy's space goals, it made "incremental" additional commitments for several years. Initially, however, a fundamental decision had been made. Congress in 1958, drawing on past experiences and on an understanding of the dynamics of incremental processes, could not have been unaware that once a fundamental commitment is made it is difficult to reverse it. While the initial space budget was relatively small, the very act of setting up a space agency amounted to subscribing to additional budget increments in future years.[13]

Incrementalists argue that incremental decisions tend to be remedial; small steps are taken in the "right" direction, or, when it is evident the direction is "wrong," the course is altered. But if the decisionmaker evaluates his incremental decisions and small steps, which he must do if he is to decide whether or not the direction is right, his judgment will be greatly affected by the evaluative criteria he applies. Here, again, we have to go outside the incrementalist model to ascertain the ways in which these criteria are set.

Thus, while actors make both kinds of decisions, the number and role of fundamental decisions are significantly greater than incrementalists state, and when the fundamental ones are missing, incremental decisionmaking amounts to drifting—action without direction. A more active approach to societal decisionmaking requires two sets of mechanisms: (a) high-order, fundamental policymaking processes which set basic directions and (b) incremental processes which prepare for fundamental decisions and work them out after they have been reached. This is provided by mixed scanning.

The Mixed Scanning Approach

Mixed scanning provides both a realistic description of the strategy used by actors in a large variety of fields and the strategy for effective actors to follow. Let us first illustrate this approach in a simple situation and then explore its societal dimensions. Assume we are about to set up a worldwide weather observation system using weather satellites. The rationalistic approach would seek an exhaustive survey of weather conditions by using cameras capable of detailed observations and by scheduling reviews of the entire sky as often as possible. This would yield an avalanche of details, costly to analyze and likely to overwhelm our action capacities (e.g., "seeding" cloud formations that could develop into hurricanes or bring rain to arid areas). Incrementalism would focus on those areas in which similar patterns developed in the recent past and, perhaps, on a few nearby regions; it would thus ignore all formations which might deserve attention if they arose in unexpected areas.

A mixed scanning strategy would include elements of both approaches by employing two cameras: a broad-angle camera that would cover all parts of the sky but not in great detail, and a second one which would zero in on those areas revealed by the first camera to require a more in-depth examination. While mixed scanning might miss areas in which only a detailed camera could reveal trouble, it is less likely than incrementalism to miss obvious trouble spots in unfamiliar areas.

From an abstract viewpoint mixed scanning provides a particular procedure for the collection of information (e.g., the surveying or "scanning" of weather conditions), a strategy about the allocation of resources (e.g., "seeding"), and—we shall see—guidelines for the relations between the two. The strategy combines a detailed ("rationalistic") examination of some sectors—which, unlike the exhaustive examination of the entire area, is feasible—with a "truncated" review of other sectors. The relative investment in the two kinds of scanning—full detail and truncated —as well as in the very act of scanning, depends on how costly it would be to miss, for example, one hurricane; the cost of additional scanning; and the amount of time it would take.

Scanning may be divided into more than two levels; there can be several levels with varying degrees of detail and coverage, though it seems most effective to include an all-encompassing level (so that no major option will be left uncovered) and a highly detailed level (so that the option selected can be explored as fully as is feasible).

The decision on how the investment of assets and time it to be allocated among the levels of scanning is, in fact, part of the strategy. The actual amount of assets and time spent depends on the total amount available and on experimentation with various interlevel combinations. Also, the amount spent is best changed over time. Effective decisionmaking requires that sporadically, or at set intervals, investment in encompassing (high-coverage) scanning be increased to check for far removed but "obvious" dangers and to search for better lines of approach. Annual budget reviews and the State of the Union messages provide, in principle, such occasions.

An increase in investment of this type is also effective when the actor realizes that the environment radically changes or when he sees that the early chain of increments brings no improvement in the situation or brings even a "worsening." If, at this point, the actor decides to drop the course of action, the effectiveness of his decisionmaking is reduced, since, through some high-coverage scanning, he may discover that a continuation of the "loss" is about to lead to a solution. (An obvious example is the selling of a declining stock if a further review reveals that the corporation is expected to improve its earning next year, after several years of decline.) Reality cannot be assumed to be structured in straight lines where each step towards a goal leads directly to another and where the accumulation of small steps in effect solves the problem. Often what from an incremental viewpoint is a step away from the goal ("worsening") may from a broader perspective be a step in the right direction, as when the temperature of a patient is allowed to rise because this will hasten his recovery. Thus mixed scanning not only combines various levels of scanning but also provides a set of criteria for situations in which one level or another is to be emphasized.

In the exploration of mixed scanning, it is essential to differentiate fundamental decisions from incremental ones. Fundamental decisions are made by exploring the main alternatives the actor sees in view of his conception of his goals, but unlike what rationalism would indicate— details and specifications are omitted so that an overview is feasible. Incremental decisions are made but within the contexts set by fundamental decisions (and fundamental reviews). Thus, each of the two elements in mixed scanning helps to reduce the effects of the particular shortcomings of the other; incrementalism reduces the unrealistic aspects of rationalism by limiting the details required in fundamental decisions, and contextuating rationalism helps to overcome the conservative slant of incrementalism by exploring longer-run alternatives. Together, empirical tests and comparative study of decisionmakers would show that these elements make for a third approach which is at once more realistic and more effective than its components.

Can Decisions Be Evaluated?

The preceding discussion assumes that both the observer and the actor have a capacity to evaluate decisionmaking strategies and to determine which is the more effective. Incrementalists, however, argue that since values cannot be scaled and summarized, "good" decisions cannot be defined and, hence, evaluation is not possible. In contrast, it is reasonable to expect that the decisionmakers, as well as the observers, can summarize their values and rank them, at least in an ordinal scale.

For example, many societal projects have one primary goal such as increasing birth control, economically desalting sea water, or reducing price inflation by one-half over a two-year period. Other goals which are also served are secondary, e.g., increasing the country's R & D sector by investing in desalting. The actor, hence, may deal with the degree to which the *primary* goal was realized and make this the central evaluative measure for a "good" policy, while noting its effects on secondary goals. When he compares projects in these terms, he, in effect, weighs the primary goal as several times as important as all the secondary goals combined. This procedure amounts to saying, "As I care very much about one goal and little about the others, if the project does not serve the first goal, it is no good and I do not have to worry about measuring and totaling up whatever other gains it may be providing for my secondary values."

When there are two or even three primary goals (e.g., teaching, therapy, and research in a university hospital), the actor can still compare projects in terms of the extent to which they realize each primary goal. He can establish that project X is good for research but not for teaching while project Y is very good for teaching but not as good for research, etc., without having to raise the additional difficulties of combining the effectiveness measures into one numerical index. In effect, he proceeds as if they had identical weights.

Finally, an informal scaling of values is not as difficult as the incrementalists imagine. Most actors are able to rank their goals to some extent (e.g., faculty is more concerned about the quality of research than the quality of teaching).

One of the most imaginative attempts to evaluate the effectiveness of programs with hard-to-assess objectives is a method devised by David Osborn, Deputy Assistant Secretary of State for Educational and Cultural Affairs. . . . Osborn recommends a scheme of cross-multiplying the costs of the activities with a number representing the rank of its objectives on a scale. For instance, the exchange of Fulbright professors may contribute to "cultural prestige and mutual respect," "educational development," and gaining "entrée," which might be given scale numbers such as 8, 6, and 5, respectively. These numbers are then multiplied with the costs of the program, and the resulting figure is in turn multiplied with an ingenious figure called a "country number." The latter is an attempt to get a rough measure of the importance to the U.S. of the countries with which we have cultural relations. It is arrived at by putting together in complicated ways certain key data, weighed to reflect cultural and educational matters, such as the country's population, Gross National Product, number of college students, rate of illiteracy, and so forth. The resulting numbers are then revised in the light of working experience, as when, because of its high per capita income, a certain tiny middle-eastern country turns out to be more important to the U.S. than a large eastern European one. At this point, coun-

try numbers are revised on the basis of judgment and experience, as are other numbers at other points. But those who make such revisions have a basic framework to start with, a set of numbers arranged on the basis of many factors, rather than single arbitrary guesses.[14]

Thus, in evaluation as in decisionmaking itself, while full detailed rationalism may well be impossible, truncated reviews are feasible, and this approach may be expected to be more effective in terms of the actors' goals than "muddling through."

Morphological Factors

The structures within which interactions among actors take place become more significant the more we recognize that the bases of decisions neither are nor can be a fully ordered set of values and an exhaustive examination of reality. In part, the strategy followed is determined either by values nor by information but by the positions of and power relations among the decisionmakers. For example, the extent to which one element of mixed scanning is stressed as against the other is affected by the relationship between higher and lower organizational ranks. In some situations, the higher in rank, concerned only with the overall picture, are impatient with details, while lower ranks—especially experts—are more likely to focus on details. In other situations, the higher ranks, to avoid facing the overall picture, seek to bury themselves, their administration, and the public in details.

Next, the environment should be taken into account. For instance, a highly incremental approach would perhaps be adequate if the situation were more stable and the decisions made were effective from the start. This approach is expected to be less appropriate when conditions are rapidly changing and when the initial course was wrong. Thus, there seems to be no one effective decisionmaking strategy in the abstract, apart from the societal environment into which it is introduced.

Mixed scanning is flexible; changes in the relative investment in scanning in general as well as among the various levels of scanning permit it to adapt to the specific situation. For example, more encompassing scanning is called for when the environment is more malleable.

Another major consideration here is the capacities of the actor. This is illustrated with regard to interagency relations by the following statement: " . . . the State Department was hopelessly behind. Its cryptographic equipment was obsolescent, which slowed communications, and it had no central situation room at all."[15] The author goes on to show how as a consequence the State Department was less able to act than was the Defense Department.

An actor with a low capacity to mobilize power to implement his decisions may do better to rely less on encompassing scanning; even if remote outcomes are anticipated, he will be able to do little about them. More generally, the greater a unit's control capacities the more encompassing scanning it can undertake, and the more such scanning, the more effective its decisionmaking. This points to an interesting paradox: The developing nations, with much lower control capacities than the modern ones, tend to favor much more planning, although they may have to make do with a relatively high degree of incrementalism. Yet modern pluralistic societies —which are much more able to scan and, at least in some dimensions, are much more able to control—tend to plan less.

Two different factors are involved which highlight the difference in this regard among modern societies. While all have a higher capacity to scan and some control advantages as compared to nonmodern societies, they differ sharply in their capacity to build consensus. Democracies must accept a relatively high degree of incrementalism (though not as high as developing nations) because of their greater need to gain support for new decisions from many and conflicting subsocieties, a need which reduces their capacity to follow a long-run plan. It is easier to reach consensus under noncrisis situations, on increments similar to existing policies, than to gain support for a new policy. However, the role of crises is significant; in relatively less passive democracies, crises serve to build consensus for major changes of direction which are overdue (e.g., desegregation).

Totalitarian societies, more centralist and relying on powers which are less dependent on consensus, can plan more but they tend to overshoot the mark. Unlike democracies which first seek to build up a consensus and then proceed, often doing less than necessary later than necessary, totalitarian societies, lacking the capacity for consensus-building or even for assessing the various resistances, usually try for too much too early. They are then forced to adjust their plans after initiation, with the revised policies often scaled down and involving more "consensus" than the original one. While totalitarian gross misplanning constitutes a large waste of resources, some initial overplanning and later down-scaling is as much a decisionmaking strategy as is disjointed incrementalism, and is the one for which totalitarian societies may be best suited.

A society more able to effectively handle its problems (one referred to elsewhere as an *active society*)[16] would require:

1) A higher capacity to build consensus than even democracies command.
2) More effective though not necessarily more numerous means of control than totalitarian societies employ (which new knowledge technology and better analysis through the social sciences may make feasible).
3) A mixed-scanning strategy which is not as rationalistic as that which the totalitarian societies attempt to pursue and not as incremental as the strategy democracies advocate.

References and Notes

1. See David Braybrooke and Charles E. Lindblom, *A Strategy of Decision* (New York: Free Press, Div. of The Macmillan Company, 1963), pp. 48–50 and pp. 111–43; Charles E. Lindblom, *The Intelligence of Democracy* (New York: Free Press, Div. of The Macmillan Company, 1965), pp. 137–39. See also Jerome S. Bruner, Jacqueline J. Goodnow, and George A. Austin, *A Study of Thinking* (New York: John Wiley & Sons, Inc., 1956), chaps. 4–5.
2. James Q. Wilson, *Negro Politics* (New York: Free Press, Div. of The Macmillan Company, 1960), p. 189.
3. See review of *A Strategy of Decision* by Kenneth J. Arrow in *Political Science Quarterly* 79 (1964): 585. See also Herbert A. Simon, *Models of Man* (New York: John Wiley & Sons, Inc., 1957), p. 198, and Aaron Wildavsky, *The Politics of the Budgetary Process* (Boston: Little, Brown and Company, 1964), pp. 147–52.
4. Charles F. Lindblom, "The Science of 'Muddling Through,' " *Public Administration Review* 19 (1959): 79–99; Robert A. Dahl and Charles E. Lindblom, *Politics, Economics and Welfare* (New York: Harper & Row, Publishers, 1953); Braybrooke and Lindblom, *Strategy of Decision;* and Lindblom, *Intelligence of Democracy.*
5. Lindblom, *Intelligence of Democracy,* pp. 144–48.
6. Kenneth E. Boulding in a review of *A Strategy of Decision* in the *American Sociological Review* 29 (1964): 931.
7. Yehezkel Dror, "Muddling Through—'Science' or Inertia?" *Public Administration Review* 24 (1964): 155.
8. Braybrooke and Lindblom, *Strategy of Decision,* pp. 66–69.
9. Richard Fenno, Jr., *The Power of the Purse* (Boston: Little, Brown and Company, 1966), pp. 266ff. See also Otto A. Davis, M. A. H. Dempster, and Aaron Wildavsky, "A Theory of the Budgetary Process," *American Political Science Review* 60 (1966): esp. 530–31.
10. Samuel P. Huntington, quoted by Nelson E. Polsby, *Congress and the Presidency* (Englewood Cliffs, N.J.: Prentice-Hall, Inc., 1964), p. 86.
11. Ibid.
12. Fenno, *Power of the Purse.*
13. For an example involving the Supreme Court's decision on desegregation, see Martin Shapiro, "Stability and Change in Judicial Decisionmaking: Incrementalism or *Stare Decisis,*" *Law in Transition Quarterly* 2 (1965): 134–57. See also a commentary by Bruce L. R. Smith, *American Political Science Review* 61 (1967), esp. p. 151.
14. Virginia Held, "PPBS Comes to Washington," *The Public Interest* 4 (Summer 1966), pp. 102–15, quotation from pp. 112–13.
15. Roger Hilsman, *To Move a Nation: The Politics of Foreign Policy in the Administration of John F. Kennedy* (Garden City, N.Y.: Doubleday & Company, Inc., 1967), p. 27.
16. Amitai Etzioni, *The Active Society: A Theory of Societal and Political Processes* (New York: Free Press, Div. of The Macmillan Company, 1968).

Chapter 8 Exchange, Motivation, and Role Theory

DIALECTICAL FORCES

Peter M. Blau

Two fundamental questions can be asked in the analysis of interpersonal relations—what attracts individuals to the association and whether their transactions are symmetrical or not. The first distinction is that between associations that participants experience as intrinsically rewarding, as in love relations, and social interactions in which individuals engage to obtain some extrinsic benefits, as in instrumental cooperation. Extrinsic benefits are, in principle, detachable from their social source—that is, the persons who supply them—and thus furnish external criteria for choosing between associates, for example, for deciding which colleague to ask for advice. No such objective criteria of comparison exist when an association is an end-in-itself, since the fused rewards that make it intrinsically attractive cannot be separated from the association itself. The second distinction is that between reciprocal and unilateral social transactions. Cross classification of these two dimensions yields four types of associations between persons:

in terms of two underlying dimensions. In this case, the first question is whether particularistic or universalistic standards govern the pattern of social relations and orientations in a collectivity. That is, whether the structure of social relations reveals preferences among persons with similar status attributes or universal preferences throughout the collectivity for persons with given attributes. Particularistic standards refer to status attributes that are valued only by the ingroup, such as religious or political beliefs, whereas universalistic standards refer to attributes that are generally valued, by those who do not have them as well as by those who do, such as wealth or competence. The second question is whether the patterns of social interaction under consideration are the emergent aggregate result of the diverse endeavors of the members of the collectivity, or whether they are organized and explicitly focused on some common, immediate or ultimate, objectives. Cross classification of these two dimensions yields four facets of social structure:

	Intrinsic	Extrinsic
Reciprocal	Mutual attraction	Exchange
Unilateral	One-sided attachment	Power

	Particularism	Universalism
Emergent	Integration	Differentiation
Goal-focused	Opposition	Legitimation

The structures of social association in groups and societies can also be analyzed

These two schemas reflect the main topics discussed in this book. In short, two pairs of conceptual dimensions provide the framework for the analysis presented. A serious limitation of such typologies derived from underlying dimensions, however, is that they imply a static conception of social life and social structure. Although the explicit inclusion of opposition, a major generator of social change, as one of the types is an attempt to overcome this limitation, the schemas still fail to indicate the manifold conflicts between social forces and the dynamic processes of social change. The prime significance of the contrast between reciprocity and imbalance, for example, is not as a dimensions for classifying social associations but as a dynamic force that transforms simple [sic] into increasingly complex social processes and that serves as a catalyst of ubiquitous change in social structures. There is a strain toward reciprocity in social associations, but reciprocity on one level creates imbalances on others, giving rise to recurrent pressures for re-equilibration and social change. In complex social structures with many interdependent, and often interpenetrating, substructures, particularly, every movement toward equilibrium precipitates disturbances and disequilibria and thus new dynamic processes. The perennial adjustments and counteradjustments find expression in a dialectical pattern of social change.

In this . . . [selection], those points that pertain to the dialectical forces of social change will be reviewed. Dilemmas of social life and the conditions that produce them will be analyzed. The progressive differentiation of status in social structures and its implications will be examined. The dynamic interrelations between emergent exchange processes and the explicit organization of collectivities will be briefly investigated. Finally, a dialectical conception of structural change will be formulated.

Dilemmas

Social exchange is the basic concept in terms of which the associations between persons have been analyzed. The proto-type is the *reciprocal* exchange of *extrinsic* benefits. People often do favors for their associates, and by doing so they obligate them to return favors. The anticipation that an association will be a rewarding experience is what initially attracts individuals to it, and the exchange of various rewarding services cements the social bonds between associates. Either dimension of "pure" exchange can become modified, however, yielding the two special cases of intrinsic attraction and power based on unilateral services. When an association is intrinsically rewarding, as in love, the exchange of extrinsic benefits is merely a means to attain and sustain the ultimate reward of reciprocated attraction. The supply of recurrent unilateral services is a source of power, since it obliges those who cannot reciprocate in kind to discharge their obligations to the supplier by complying with his wishes.

There are a number of similarities between social exchange and economic exchange. Individuals who do favors for others expect a return, at the very least in the form of expressions of gratitude and appreciation, just as merchants expect repayment for economic services. Individuals must be compensated for social rewards lest they cease to supply them, because they incur costs by doing so, notably the cost of the alternatives foregone by devoting time to the association. The principle of the eventually diminishing marginal utility applies to social as well as economic commodities. Thus the social approval of the first few colleagues is usually more important to a newcomer in a work group than that of the last few after the rest have already accepted him. In addition to these similarities, however, there are also fundamental differences between social and strictly economic exchange.

In contrast to economic transactions, in which an explicit or implicit formal contract stipulates in advance the precise obligations incurred by both parties, social exchange entails unspecified obligations. There is no contract and there is no exact price. A person to whom others are indebted for favors performed has the general expectation that they will discharge their obligations by doing things for him, but he must leave the exact nature of the return up to them. He cannot bargain with them over how much his favors are worth, and he has no recourse if they fail to reciprocate altogether, except, of course, that he can, and probably will, discontinue to do favors for them. Since there is no contract that can be enforced, social exchange requires trust. But little trust is required for the minor transactions with which exchange relations typically start, and the gradual expansion of the exchange permits the partners to prove their trustworthiness to each other. Processes of social exchange, consequently, generate trust in social relations. The mutual trust between committed exchange partners encourages them to engage in a variety of transactions—to exchange advice, help, social support, and companionship—and these diffuse transactions give the partnership some intrinsic significance. Only impersonal economic exchange remains exclusively focused on specific extrinsic benefits, whereas in social exchange the association itself invariably assumes a minimum of intrinsic significance.

Exchange can be considered a mixed game, in which the partners have some common and some conflicting interests. This is this case for each transaction and for the enduring partnership. If both partners profit from a transaction, they have a common interest in effecting it, but their interests conflict concerning the ratio at which they exchange services. Moreover, both have a common interest in maintaining a stable exchange partnership. The more committed individuals are to an exchange relation, the more stable it is. The person who is less committed to the partnership gains a special advantage, since the other's commitment stabilizes the relationship, and since his lesser commitment permits him, more so than the other, to explore alternative opportunities. Hence, aside from their common interest in assuring that there is sufficient commitment, the two partners also have conflict-

ing interests, because each is interested in having the other make the greater commitment. This situation poses the dilemma for each partner that he must put pressure on the other to make the greater commitment by withholding his own commitment up to the point where it would endanger the relationships but not beyond this point.

Social life is full of dilemmas of this type and others. Whenever two individuals are attracted to one another, either is confronted by the dilemma of waiting until the other makes the greater commitment first, thereby possibly endangering the continuation of the relationship, or committing himself before the other, thereby worsening his position in the relationship. Another dilemma faces the individual seeking to become integrated into a group. For an individual's endeavors to impress the rest of the group with his outstanding qualities in order to prove himself attractive to them and gain their social acceptance simultaneously poses a status threat for these others that tends to antagonize them. The very outstanding qualities that make an individual differentially attractive as an associate also raise fears of dependence that inhibit easy sociability and thus make him unattractive as a sociable companion.

Social approval poses dilemmas, and so does love. People seek the approval of those they respect, and they also seek their help with improving their own performance. But the two are not compatible, inasmuch as supportive approval fails to furnish an instrumental basis for improvements and critical appraisals imply disapproval. By being supportive through his praise of others, a person gains their appreciation but fails to earn their respect, and by offering incisive criticisms, he earns their respect but often also their dislike, since they are predisposed to consider his criticism too severe. If others value a person's approval, moreover, he is under pressure to offer it, yet approval that is offered freely, not only for outstanding performances but also for mediocre ones, depreciates in value. The demand for approval and the need to with-hold it to protect its value create cross pressures. Lovers, too, are under cross pressure to furnish emotional support and express affection for one another, on the one hand, and to withhold excessive dem-onstrations of affection and premature commitments, on the other, because the free expression of affection and commit-ment depreciates their value.

The achievement of a position of leadership in a group entails a dilemma, since it requires that a person command power over others and receive their legiti-mating approval of this power, but many of the steps necessary to attain domi-nance tend to antagonize others and evoke their disapproval. To mobilize his power a leader must remain independent of his followers and husband his re-sources; to receive their legitimating ap-proval, however, he must acknowledge his dependence on them and freely use the resources available to him to furnish re-wards to followers as evidence of the ad-vantages that accrue to them from his leadership. Another dilemma confronts the members of emergent radical opposi-tion movements that fail to expand rapidly. Unless they modify their extremist ideol-ogy to increase its appeal, they have little chance to make new converts and achieve success, yet if they do modify it, they surrender in advance the very ideals they aspired to realize, and they alienate the most devoted members of the movement. The opposition to a growing opposition movement, too, is faced with a dilemma, because intolerant resistance is re-quired to suppress it, but such intolerance publicly acknowledges that the powerful threat of the opposition must be taken seriously and may create a bandwagon ef-fect that further strengthens it.

One source of the dilemmas of social associations is the conflict of interests in mixed-game situations. If two individuals are attracted to one another, the first choice of either is to have the other make the greater commitment, but each prefers to make the commitment himself rather than let the relationship perish. The di-

lemma is how far to go in putting pressure on the other to make his commitment first, inasmuch as withholding commit-ment too long in order to gain a superior position in the relationship may endanger the relationship itself. A second source of dilemmas is that two interdependent con-tradictory forces govern the impact of so-cial rewards on social interaction.

The abundance of social rewards depre-ciates their value, with the result that fur-nishing rewards has contradictory implica-tions for social conduct. The more gratifi-cation an individual experiences in a social association, for example, the more likely he is to become committed to it. His gratification is a function of both the actual rewards he receives in the relationship and the value he places on these rewards. The more of a certain reward he receives, however, the less value further incre-ments have for him, in accordance with the principles of eventually diminishing marginal utility. By furnishing an increas-ing amount of rewards to an individual to enhance his incentives to become commit-ted, therefore, one depreciates the value of these rewards and hence their impact as incentives for commitment. The dilemma is how much to offer—how much ap-proval, how much emotional support, how much help—before the deflated value of the rewards outweighs the significance of their increasing volume.

The marginal principle reflects different forces in social life.[1] There is not only the psychological process that, as individuals reach higher and higher levels of expecta-tions and aspirations, the significance of further attainments declines, but there are also social forces that deflate the value of abundant social rewards. The value of most rewards rests not so much on their inherent utility as on the social demand for them. Since goods in great demand tend to be scarce, scarcity itself becomes a symbol of social value.

.   .   .

A final important source of dilemmas is the existence of incompatible require-ments of goal states. Social actions have multiple consequences, and actions designed to attain one goal often have consequences that impede the attainment of another, or actions that meet one requirement for accomplishing a given objective interfere with meeting another requirement for accomplishing the same objective. Two prerequisites of leadership are a position of dominance and the legitimating approval of followers, but the practices through which a man achieves dominance over others frequently inspire more fear than love, that is, create obstacles to obtaining the approval of followers.[2]

.   .   .

The manifold interdependence between interpenetrating substructures on numerous levels in complex social structures produces many incompatibilities, that is, social conditions that have been established or have developed to meet some requirement of goal states become impediments for meeting others. For example, the effective achievement of social objectives in large societies requires formal organizations with committed and loyal members. It also requires that the members of these organizations have made investments in acquiring occupational skills and have become committed to occupational careers. To have incentives to make such investments, men must receive a fair return for them. Opportunity for mobility is a basic prerequisite for receiving a fair return for one's services, since without it individuals who do not receive a fair return cannot better their position. The attachments of men to occupations and organizations, however, which are necessary in modern societies, restrict the mobility that alone can assure that most men receive a fair return for their services. Another illustration of these incompatibilities is the dilemma between centralization and departmental autonomy in large organizations. The autonomy required for effective operations in the major segments of an organization and the centralized direction required for effective coordination of the various segments often come into conflict, and many practices instituted to further one impede

the other. The prototype is the perennial conflict between professional and administrative requirements in bureaucracies with professional personnel.

The dilemmas posed by incompatible requirements demand more than compromise. Each requirement must be attended to. Individuals confronted by such dilemmas generally shift their strategies from taking care of one horn to taking care of the other, so to speak. To become an integrated member of a group, for instance, requires that an individual demonstrate both his attractiveness and his approachability, but outstanding qualities that make him attractive also make him unapproachable. To overcome this dilemma and meet these incompatible requirements, individuals usually first seek to impress others to prove themselves attractive companions and then shift to expressions of self-depreciating modesty to counteract the status threat their impressive demeanor has created and prove themselves easily approachable sociable companions. Incompatible requirements in social structures lead to recurrent reorganizations. Thus, as professional problems become acute in an organization, the professional staff is given more autonomy to cope with them, and as this reorganization produces new administrative problems, administrative reforms are instituted in an attempt to meet them. In this manner, dilemmas that confront organized collectivities promote a dialectical pattern of change, which may entail fundamental transformations *of* the social structure itself as well as lesser adjustments *within* it.[3]

The differentiation of status that develops in groups and societies resolves some of the dilemmas of individuals which occur primarily in unstructured situations, but it simultaneously produces new dialectical forces of change. Once a man commands respect and compliance in a group and his superior status is generally acknowledged among the other members, integration no longer poses a serious dilemma for him. If there is social consensus in the rest of the group concerning the importance of his contributions and their indebtedness to him, moreover, this superior can afford to be generous and modest in his conduct, thereby earning the group's legitimating approval of his leadership. The differentiation in the group, however, which emerges to provide incentives for making significant contributions to its welfare and objectives, intensifies the need for integrative bonds to fortify group cohesion. Generally, integrative and differentiating processes come into conflict, as do legitimate organizations and the opposition provoked by the constraints they exert, and so do the diverse implications value standards have for the social structure and its component substructures. Such conflicting social forces give rise to alternating patterns of structural change.

Differentiation

Structural differentiation occurs along different lines in collectivities. Competition for scarce resources, whether it involves speaking time in discussion groups, material resources in communities, or superior status in collectivities of all kinds, leads to a differential allocation of these resources initially in accordance with the valued contributions the various members of the collectivity make or are expected to make. Differentiation in respect arises when individuals demonstrate variations in relevant abilities, and the high regard of his fellows gives an individual a competitive advantage in the subsequent differentiation of power and competition for dominance and leadership. As several aspects of status become successively differentiated, exchange relations also become differentiated from competitive ones, since only those successful in the earlier competition can continue to compete for dominant positions and leadership, whereas the unsuccessful become exchange partners of the successful in this competition. Role specialization develops as leaders use their authority to assign different tasks to followers and as other

members seek to gain status by making new kinds of contributions. The division of labor becomes the basis of further differentiation into subgroups of many different types in large collectivities.

Superior status securely rooted in the social structure leads to the expansion of power. With the exception of the special case of coercive force, power has its origin in unilateral exchange transactions. A person who has services or resources at his disposal that others need and who is independent of any with which the others could reciprocate can gain power over them by making the supply of his services or resources contingent on their compliance with his directives. People who become indebted to a person for essential benefits are obligated to accede to his wishes lest he cease to furnish these benefits. An individual who distributes gifts and services to others makes a claim to superiority over them. If they properly repay him or possibly even make excessive returns, they challenge this claim and invite him to enter into a peer relation of mutual exchange. If they are unable to reciprocate, however, they validate his claim to superiority. The continuing unilateral supply of needed services to others creates a backlog of obligations on which the supplier can draw at his discretion, and these accumulated obligations to accede to his demands give him power over the others.

The possession of resources enabling a person to satisfy important needs of others, however, is not a sufficient condition for achieving power over them. Four other conditions must also be met, that is, there are four conditions that make it possible for others to remain independent of a person or group with such resources. First, if others have resources that permit them to reciprocate for his services by furnishing him with benefits he needs, they remain his equals. Second, if there are many alternative suppliers in competition from whom others can obtain the needed services, they do not become dependent on any. Third, if they have the power to force the person to give them what they want, they maintain their independence of him. Fourth, if people learn to get along without the benefits they originally considered necessary, a person's ability to dispense these benefits no longer gives him power over them. Within the framework of these limiting conditions, however, the person who can supply essential benefits to others has an undeniable claim to power over them. Unless one of these four possibilities is open to them, individuals who want benefits at the disposal of another have no choice but to submit to his power as an incentive for him to provide these benefits.

Superior status, like capital, is an accumulated resource, which an individual can draw on to obtain advantages, which is expanded in use, and which can be invested at risk to increase it. A person to whom others are obligated can ask them to do things whenever it is to his advantage, but his making such requests gives them an opportunity to discharge their obligations. Once they are no longer indebted to him he has no more power over them, unless he has replenished his power by furnishing more services, thus keeping them under obligation. The sheer reminder that they owe him a service indicates that he is dependent on their doing things for him, just as they are dependent on his doing things for them, and this evidence of interdependence weakens his power over them. The man with great power, however, needs no reminders of this sort, because others are eager to discharge some of their obligations to him to maintain his good will without ever being able to discharge all of them. Power over an entire group, moreover, enables a man to live on his interests, as it were, benefiting from his power without using it up, because a man in such a position can coordinate the activities of group members to further the achievement of common objectives and thereby continually renew their indebtedness to him for his effective guidance. Assuming responsibility for coordination involves a risk, since unsuccessful direction of the activities of others typically entails the loss of power over

them. The rewards that accrue to group members from successful guidance, however, increase their obligations to the leader and fortify his position of leadership. In addition, the compliance the leader commands among his followers extends his power over outsiders.

Two factors secure a person's superior status and create a basis for additional improvements in it—multiple supports in the social structure and joint support by subordinates. The multiple supports of the power of a man who has the resources to command the compliance of one hundred others make his power not only one hundred times as great but also immeasurably more secure than is the power of a man who only commands the compliance of one other. The basic reason is that power over many others enables a man to spread the risk of defections from his rule by taking into account the cost of such defections and insuring himself against their disadvantageous consequences, in accordance with the principles of eliminating uncertainty through insurance as advanced by Knight.[4] The employer of a single employee depends on his services, just as the employee depends on the employer's wages, the degree of dependence of each being contingent on the alternative opportunities available to him for obtaining as good a worker or as a good a job, respectively. The employer of one thousand employees, in contrast, is not dependent on any of them, although they are dependent on his wages, since he can calculate on the basis of past experience the amount of turnover expected and insure himself against it by taking into account the cost of regularly having to replace a certain proportion of employees.[5]

. . .

The significance of multiple and joint supports is not confined to power but extends to other aspects of status. A man who is not known in a group can only impress others by telling them about his achievements and abilities, whereas the one whose achievements are generally known and acknowledged can modestly belittle his accomplishments and thereby be the more impressive. The individual who accepts gifts or services from others without reciprocating becomes subordinate to them, but the chief whose institutional authority is firmly established can accept tributes from his subjects without in the least endangering his position.

.   .   .

Superior status secured by multiple structural supports makes men relatively independent of others. It is this independence that is the source of the tolerance of powerful men, but the same independence also makes it possible for them intolerantly to exploit and oppress others when they have reason for doing so. Great power is more likely than little power to be ample for the purposes of the individuals or groups who have it, which allows them to be moderate and permissive in exercising control over others. Should, however, their power, regardless of how great it is in absolute terms, fall short of their needs, that is, be insufficient to accomplish the objectives to which they aspire, they are likely to exploit all the power they have fully, and their very independence of the members of inferior social strata enables them to exercise their power oppressively without fear of retaliation. But this independence of the very powerful is only relative and not irrevocable. Excessive exploitation and oppression provoke opposition movements that, if they spread and are successful, may overthrow existing powers. For a successful opposition, by uniting the different groups of oppressed in a common endeavor, deprives the ruling group of the multiple supports on which their independence and power rests, inasmuch as such alternative supports persist only as long as subordinates act independently and collapse once they act in unison.

Opposition forces have paradoxical implications. The strong can afford to tolerate some opposition; the weak cannot for fear that it crush them. By tolerating an opposition movement, and possibly even laughing it off, people demonstrate that their own strength is immune to it, and this social evidence that the opposition does not have to be taken seriously undermines its strength by discouraging potential supporters from joining such a movement presumably doomed to failure. An opposition that poses a serious threat, however, must be taken seriously, which means that it will be intolerantly opposed. But intolerant resistance against the opposition and unrelenting endeavors to fight it publicly acknowledge that it constitutes an important force and grave danger. They thus may actually reinforce the opposition by encouraging individuals to join it for fear of its power or in anticipation of its victory. In short, the intolerance directed against it may strengthen the opposition, and the clash between opposition forces intensifies intolerance on both sides. The typical result of fierce battles between two hostile camps is the suppression of the vanquished by the victor. The toleration of opposition is difficult, but it is essential in a democracy, for it dulls the edge of opposition forces and thereby prevents fights to the finish that lead to the suppression of opposition and to the end of democratic institutions.

Dynamics

Four facets of social structures have been distinguished—integration, differentiation, organization, and opposition. The first two emerge in the course of social transactions without any explicit design, whereas the last two are the result of organized efforts focused on some collective objectives or ideals. Integration and opposition rest on particularistic values that unite ingroups and divide them from outgroups. Differentiation and legitimation are governed by universalistic standards that specify the achievements and qualities that are generally valued within the compass of the collectivity under consideration and that bestow superior status on those who exhibit them. Two of these four facets of social structure can be directly derived from an analysis of exchange, and the other two, more indirectly.

Social exchange has been defined by two criteria—assocations oriented largely to extrinsic rather than purely intrinsic rewards and reciprocal rather than unilateral transactions. In the course of recurrent reciprocal exchange of extrinsic benefits, partnerships of mutual trust develop that assume some intrinsic significance for the partners, introjecting an intrinsic element into social interaction. At the same time, some individuals can supply important services to others for which the latter cannot appropriately reciprocate, and the unilateral transactions that consequently take place give rise to differentiation of status. Exchange processes, therefore, lead to the emergence of bonds of intrinsic attraction and social integration, on the one hand, and of unilateral services and social differentiation, on the other.

The development of social integration and differentiation in a collectivity creates a fertile soil for the establishment of an organization designed to coordinate endeavors in the pursuit of common objectives. Integrative bonds provide opportunities for communication about common problems, some of which can only be solved through concerted action, and in these social communications agreement on collective goals tends to arise. In the process of social differentiation, some individuals have demonstrated their ability to make outstanding contributions to the welfare of the rest, and these become apparent candidates for directing collective endeavors, that is, for leadership. Agreement on social objectives is a prerequisite for organization and leadership in a collectivity, because common objectives are the incentives for organizing and coordinating the activities of various members, and because they provide the conditions that permit leaders to arise. For a leader to be able to guide the activities in a collectivity, all or most members must be obliged to comply with his directives. A common purpose makes it possible for a man, by making crucial contributions to

its achievement, to obligate all members simultaneously and thus command the compliance of all of them. In groups without a common purpose, a man commands the compliance of others by contributing to their individual ends, and this makes it impossible, except in very small groups, for leadership to evolve, since no man has the time to furnish services to a large number of men singly.[6]

Formal organizations are explicitly instituted to achieve given objectives. Their full establishment requires that the objectives they are intended to serve and the authority of their leadership become legitimated by social values. The contributions effective leadership makes to the welfare of the rest create joint obligations and social approval, which give rise to social norms among followers that demand compliance with the orders of leaders and effectuate their authority. The enforcement of compliance with the directives of superiors *by the collectivity of subordinates* is the distinctive characteristic of legitimate authority.

.   .   .

Within the organization, indirect exchange processes become substituted for direct ones, although direct ones persist in interstitial areas, such as informal cooperation among colleagues. The development of authority illustrates the transformation of direct into indirect exchange transactions. As long as subordinates obey the orders of a superior primarily because they are obligated to him for services he has rendered and favors he has done for them individually, he does not actually exercise authority over the subordinates, and there is a direct exchange between him and them, of the type involving unilateral services. . . .

Indirect transactions are characteristic of the complex structures in large collectivities generally. Since direct contact between most members in a large collectivity is not possible, the interrelations between them uniting them in a social structure are primarily indirect, and social values serve as the media of these indirect links and transactions. Particularistic values create a common solidarity and integrative ties that unify the members of the collectivity and divide them from other collectivities, functioning both as substitutes for the personal bonds of attraction that solidify face-to-face groups and as a basis for such bonds in the collectivity and its subgroups. Universalistic standards define achievements and qualifications that are generally acknowledged as valuable, making indirect exchange transactions possible, notably in the form of enabling individuals and groups to accumulate social status and power in one setting and gain advantages from them in another. Legitimating values expand the scope of social control beyond the limits of personal influence by establishing authority that commands willing compliance enforced by the subordinates themselves, and these values become the foundation for organizing collective effort on a large scale. Opposition ideals serve as rallying points of opposition movements and as catalysts of social change and reorganization. These four types of value standards constitute media of social associations and transactions; they are the social context that molds social relations, and they act as mediating links for indirect connections in the social structure.

One characteristic that distinguishes macrostructures from microstructures is that social processes in the macrostructures are mediated by prevailing values. Another differentiating criterion is that macrostructures are composed of interrelated social structures, whereas the constituent elements of microstructures are interrelated individuals in direct social contact. Furthermore, parts of the complex social structures in societies assume enduring form as institutions. Institutionalization involves two complementary social mechanisms through which social patterns are perpetuated from generation to generation. On the one hand, external social arrangements are historically transmitted, partly through written documents that circumscribe and preserve them, as exemplified by the form of government in a society resting on its constitution and laws. On the other hand, internalized cultural values are transmitted in processes of socialization and give the traditional external manifestations of institutions continuing meaning and significance. These institutional mechanisms are implemented by the power structure, since the powerful groups in a society tend to use their power to preserve the traditional institutions.

Once organized collectivities have developed, social transactions occur between them. A basic distinction can be made between two major types of processes that characterize the transactions of organized collectivities—as well as those of individuals, for that matter—competitive processes reflecting endeavors to maximize scarce resources and exchange processes reflecting some form of interdependence. Competition occurs only among like social units that have the same objective and not among unlike units with different objectives—among political parties and among business concerns but not between a party and a firm—whereas exchange occurs only between unlike units—between a political party and various interest groups but not among the different parties(except when two form a coalition and thus cease to be two independent political units). Competition promotes hierarchical differentiation between the more and the less successful organizations, and exchange promotes horizontal differentiation between specialized organizations of diverse sorts. Extensive hierarchical differentiation, however, makes formerly alike units unlike in important respects and unlike ones alike in their power and opportunity to attain a dominant position. Hence, exchange relations may develop between units that once were alike as the result of differential success in competition, and competition for dominance may develop among unlike units made alike by their success. . . .

The interdependent organizations in a society engage in exchange and various related transactions.[7] Formal organizations often exchange services. For example, welfare and health organizations refer clients to each other,[8] parties adopt programs that serve the interests of various groups in exchange for political support, and, of course, firms exchange a large variety of products and services for a price. Many organizational exchanges are mediated through the community. Thus, the police provide protection to the members of the community, schools furnish training for the young, universities supply research knowledge, hospitals render health services, and they all receive support from the community in exchange for their services. Organizations sometimes form coalitions committing them to joint decisions and actions. Small parties unite forces in a political campaign, for instance, several unions agree to carry out a strike together, and churches join in an ecumenical council. Coalitions among organizations may become mergers that destroy the former boundaries between them. But even without complete mergers, transactions between organized collectivities often lead to their interpenetration and obscure their boundaries. A political party that is primarily supported by two occupational groupings, for example, cannot be said to constitute a social entity distinct from these groups that engages in exchange relations with them. Rather, representative segments of these occupational groups are constituent elements of the party, and competition and bargaining occur between them within the party as each seeks to influence its political program and course of action.

Transactions among organized collectivities, then, may give rise to social ties that unite them, just as social exchange among individuals tends to produce integrative bonds. These transactions also differentiate competing organizations and may result in the elimination or absorption of competitors and the dominance of one or a few organizations—a few giant corporations, two major parties, a universal church—just as unilateral transactions and competition among individuals generate hierarchical differentiation and may result

in the dominance of one or a few leaders in a group. The existence of a differentiated structure of relations among organized collectivities creates the conditions for its formalization and the explicit establishment of an overall political organization in order to maintain order and protect the power of the organizations and ruling groups, which rests on the distribution of needed benefits, against being overthrown by violence, which is the major threat to it. For a political organization to become instituted in a society, however, requires that social values legitimate its objectives and invest it with authority. This process is again analogous to the development of a single organization when the emergent social integration and differentiation in a collectivity are complemented by social values that legitimate common endeavors and the authority to pursue them. No claim is made that the conception outlined represents the actual historical evolution of social organization. It is merely a theoretical model, in which political organization is analytically derived from transactions among organized collectivities and these organizations, in turn, are traced back to simpler processes of social exchange. This model can be schematically presented in the following form:

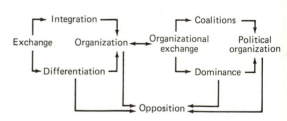

The dynamics of organized social life has its source in opposition forces. The dominant power of individuals, groups, or organizations over others makes it possible for them to establish legitimate authority by exercising their power fairly and with moderation and by making it profitable for others to remain under their protective influence. Dominant power, however, also makes it possible to exploit others and thereby gain advantages, and it consequently is often exercised oppressively. Serious deprivations caused by the unfair exercise of power tend to engender a desire for retaliation. If the exploitation is experienced in a group situation, particularly in a group comparatively isolated from the rest of the community, communication among the oppressed socially justifies and reinforces their feeling of hostility against existing powers by giving rise to an opposition ideology that transforms this hostility from a selfish expression of revenge into a noble cause pursued to further the welfare of one's fellow men. While oppression is not the sole reason for opposition, ideological identification with a cause is essential for the support of radical movements, inasmuch as existing powers have the sanctions to assure that such support harms a man's self-interest and thus is not warranted on purely rational grounds. Opposition ideals create a surplus of resources, since devotion to them frees social energies by making men willing to sacrifice material welfare for their sake, and the opposition movement they inspire constitutes a new social investment that brings about social change and reorganization.

. . .

Dialectic

There is a dialectic in social life, for it is governed by many contradictory forces. The dilemmas of social associations reflect this dialectic, and so does the character of social change.[9] To conceive of change in social structures as dialectical implies that it involves neither evolutionary progress in a straight line nor recurring cycles but alternating patterns of intermittent social reorganization along different lines. The analysis of the relationship between reciprocity and imbalance illustrates the underlying conception.

Reciprocity is an equilibrating force, the assumption being that every social action is balanced by some appropriate counteraction. Individuals who receive needed benefits from others are obligated, lest the supply of benefits cease, to reciprocate in some form, whether through expressions of gratitude, approval, material rewards, services, or compliance. Reciprocity on one level, however, entails imbalances on others. If persons are obligated to accede to another's wishes because he renders essential services to them for which they cannot otherwise compensate him, their compliance reciprocates for the unilateral services they obtain and in this sense restores balance, but it also creates an imbalance of power. The reactions to the exercise of power superimpose a secondary exchange upon the primary one. The exercise of power with fairness and moderation earns a man social approval, whereas the oppressive use of power evokes disapproval. The social approval that rewards rulers for not taking full advantage of their power and the social disapproval that penalizes them for taking excessive advantage of it equilibrate the scales, so to speak. Simultaneously, however, the collective approval of subordinates legitimates the governing group's authority over them and thus reinforces the imbalance of power, and the collective disapproval of the oppressed tends to give rise to opposition forces that disturb social equilibrium and stimulate reorganizations in the social structure. Every social process restoring equilibrium engenders some new imbalances.

Social forces often have contradictory implications. One reason for this is that the conditions produced by a social force may provoke the emergence of another force in the opposite direction. Processes of social integration, in which group members impress each other with their outstanding qualities, give rise to differentiation of status, and social differentiation reinforces the need for processes that effect social integration. Inelastic supply of advice that is in high demand in a work group intensifies status differences, since experts gain much status in exchange for their counsel, but the high price of advice encourages the formation of mutual partnerships of consultation, which lessen the status differences in the group. The very increase in rewards intended to elicit greater contributions depreciates the value of these rewards as incentives for making contributions. By increasing the number of promotions in a company, for example, the level of expectations is raised, with the result that the same promotion no longer creates the same satisfaction as before. The deprivation of the underprivileged prompts them to organize unions and leftist opposition parties in order to improve their conditions, and the relative deprivation of the lower-middle class consequent to success in these endeavors fosters the development of rightist opposition movements.

The multiple consequences of a social force are another reason it may have contradictory repercussions in the social structure. The forces set in motion to restore equilibrium in one respect, or in one segment of the social structure, are typically disequilibrating forces in other respects, in other segments. For supply and demand to reach an equilibrium, established exchange relations must be upset. The equilibrium in an organization is disturbed by membership turnover and promoted by a stable membership committed to the organization and their occupational careers in it, but these organizational attachments impede the mobility of individuals that is necessary for occupational investments and the returns received for them to attain a state of equilibrium. The success of some organized collectivities in competition, which produces optimum conditions for meeting internal requirements, spells the failure of others, with consequent internal disruptions and possible failure to survive altogether. Conditions established to further centralized planning and coordination in an organization interfere with the departmental autonomy required for effective operations. Many incompatible requirements exist in complex social structures, and given the interdependence between substructures, social processes that meet some requirements frequently create impediments for meeting others, stimulating the emergence of different social processes to meet these other requirements.

There is much resistance to social change in societies. Vested interests and powers, established practices and organizations, traditional values and institutions, and other kinds of social investments are forces of stability and resistance to basic social innovations and reorganizations. New problems and social needs continually arise, but they often persist for long periods of time before the adjustments necessary to meet them occur, since due to these forces of resistance considerable pressure toward change must build up before it is realized. Changes in major social institutions supported by interested powers as well as traditional values, in particular, require strenuous and prolonged struggles by strong opposition movements. Oppression and hardships must be severe and widespread for men to be likely to make social investments in a radical opposition movement and for the movement to have the wide appeal required for its ultimate success. The lesser opposition forces that crisscross complex social structures, overlapping and going in diverse directions, must also gather some momentum before they can produce readjustments. The existence of conflicting forces that pull in different directions itself would be reflected in social change in the direction of the resultant force, but in combination with the need for a latency period before opposition forces can realize their potential, it leads to structural change characterized not so much by continuous adjustments as by intermittent reorganizations.

Structural change, therefore, assumes a dialectical pattern. While social structures are governed by equilibrating forces, given the complex interdependence and incompatible requirements of intersecting substructures in a society, virtually every equilibrating force generates disequilibrium on other levels. In the process of creating readjustments in one respect, other dislocations are typically produced that necessitate further readjustments. Social imbalances may persist for prolonged periods, and social equilibrium is not constantly maintained, because a latency period intervenes before opposition forces have mobilized sufficient strength to effect adjustments. The recurrent disequilibrating and re-equilibrating forces on many levels of social structure are reflected in the dialectical nature of structural change.

References and Notes

1. The marginal principle in economics also reflects different underlying forces. The principle of the eventually diminishing marginal utility of increasing possessions of a commodity rests either on satiation or on the fact that rewards necessary to meet expectations and aspirations are more significant than further increments in rewards. The so-called law of diminishing returns, that is, the principle of the eventually diminishing marginal physical productivity, on the other hand, is due to the fact that it takes a combination of inputs to produce a certain output. Increases in a single input without corresponding increases in others fail to raise the output proportionately. See Kenneth E. Boulding, *Economic Analysis,* 3d ed. (New York: Harper & Row, Publishers, 1955), pp. 682-83, 588-90.

2. The dilemma is revealed in Niccolo Machiavelli's famous phrase that a prince "ought to be both feared and loved, but as it is difficult for the two to go together, it is much safer to be feared than loved, if one of the two has to be wanting." *The Prince and the Discourses* (New York: Modern Library, Inc., Div. of Random House, Inc., 1940), p. 61 (from *The Prince*).

3. Talcott Parsons and Neil J. Smelser, *Economy and Society* (New York: Free Press, Div. of The Macmillan Company, 1956), pp. 247–49, distinguish between processes of change *in* a structure and processes of equilibrium *within* it, but the distinction is one of degree rather than a clear dichotomy, since hardly any adjustments merely restore a pre-existing equilibrium.

4. Frank H. Knight, *Risk, Uncertainty, and Profit,* 2d ed. (Boston: Houghton Mifflin Company, 1933), esp. chapter viii.

5. Concerted action by employees, notably in the form of collective bargaining through unions, makes large employers as dependent on employees as small ones are, since it deprives the large employers of independent alternatives.

6. Reference here is to direct services rendered by a person to others. The situation is different if a man has the resources to pay wages to many others. Such financial resources are a major source of extensive power over large numbers of men, since money as a general medium of exchange makes indirect transactions on a large scale possible.

7. For a typology of relations among organizations, see James D. Thompson and William J. McEwen, "Organization Goals and Environment," *American Sociological Review* 23 (1958): 23–31.

8. See Sol Levine and Paul E. White, "Exchange as a Conceptual Framework for the Study of Interorganizational Relationships," *Administrative Science Quarterly* 5 (1961): 583–601.

9. For a theoretical conception of dialectical change, which has similarities with the one presented, but which unfortunately was published too late for full discussion here, see Pierre L. van der Berghe, "Dialectic and Functionalism," *American Sociological Review* 28 (1963): 695–705.

TOWARD A THEORY OF MOTIVE ACQUISITION[1]

David C. McClelland

Too little is known about the processes of personality change at relatively complex levels. The empirical study of the problem has been hampered by both practical and theoretical difficulties. On the practical side it is very expensive both in time and effort to set up systematically controlled educational programs designed to develop some complex personality characteristic like a motive, and to follow the effects of the education over a number of years. It also presents ethical problems since it is not always clear that it is as proper to teach a person a new motive as it is a new skill like learning to play the piano. For both reasons, most of what we know about personality change has come from studying psychotherapy where both ethical and practical difficulties are overcome by the pressing need to help someone in real trouble. Yet, this source of information leaves much to be desired: It has so far proven difficult to identify and systematically vary the "inputs" in psychotherapy and to measure their specific effects on subsequent behavior, except in very general ways (cf. Rogers & Dymond, 1954).

On the theoretical side, the dominant views of personality formation suggest anyway that acquisition or change of any complex characteristic like a motive in adulthood would be extremely difficult. Both behavior theory and psychoanalysis agree that stable personality characteristics like motives are laid down in childhood. Behavior theory arrives at this conclusion by arguing that social motives are learned by close association with reduction in certain basic biological drives like hunger, thirst, and physical discomfort which loom much larger in childhood than adulthood. Psychoanalysis, for its part, pictures adult motives as stable resolutions of basic conflicts occurring in early childhood. Neither theory would provide much support for the notion that motives could be developed in adulthood without somehow re-creating the childhood conditions under which they were originally formed. Furthermore, psychologists have been hard put to it to find objective evidence that even prolonged, serious, and expensive attempts to introduce personality change through psychotherapy have really proven successful (Eysenck, 1952). What hope is there that a program to introduce personality change would end up producing a big enough effect to study?

Despite these difficulties, a program of research has been under way for some time which is attempting to develop the achievement motive in adults. It was undertaken in an attempt to fill some of the gaps in our knowledge about personality change or the acquisition of complex human characteristics. Working with n-Achievement has proved to have some important advantages for this type of research: The practical and ethical problems do not loom especially large because previous research (McClelland, 1961) has demonstrated the importance of high n-Achievement for entrepreneurial behavior, and it is easy to find businessmen, particularly in underdeveloped countries, who are interested in trying any means of improving their entrepreneurial performance. Furthermore, a great deal is known about the origins of n-Achievement in childhood and its specific effects on behavior so that educational programs can be systematically planned and their effects evaluated in terms of this knowledge. Pilot attempts to develop n-Achievement have gradually led to the formulation of some theoretical notions of what motive acquisition involves and how it can be effectively promoted in adults. These notions have been summarized in the form of 12 propositions which it is the ultimate purpose of the research program to test. The propositions are anchored so far as possible in experiences with pilot courses, in supporting research findings from other studies, and in theory.

Before the propositions are presented, it is necessary to explain more of the theoretical and practical background on which they are based. To begin with, some basis for believing that motives could be acquired in adulthood had to be found in view of the widespread pessimism on the subject among theoretically oriented psychologists. Oddly enough, we were encouraged by the successful efforts of two quite different groups of "change agents"—operant conditioners and missionaries. Both groups have been "naïve" in the sense of being unimpressed by or ignorant of the state of psychological knowledge in the field. The operant conditioners have not been encumbered by any elaborate theoretical apparatus; they do not believe motives exist anyway, and continue demonstrating vigorously that if you want a person to make a response, all you have to do is elicit it and reward it (cf. Bandura & Walters, 1963, pp. 238 ff.). They retain a simple faith in the infinite plasticity of human behavior in which one response is just like any other and any one can be "shaped up" (strengthened by reward)—presumably even an "achievement" response as produced by a subject in a fantasy test. In fact, it was the naïve optimism of one such researcher (Burris, 1958) that had a lot to do with getting the present research under way. He undertook a counseling program in which an attempt to elicit and reinforce achievement-related fantasies proved to be successful in motivating college students to get better grades. Like operant conditioners, the missionaries have gone ahead changing people because they have believed it possible. While the evidence is not scientifically impeccable, common-sense observation yields dozens of cases of adults whose motivational structure has seemed to be quite radically and permanently altered by the educational efforts of Communist Party, Mormon, or other devout missionaries.

A man from Mars might be led to observe that personality change appears to be very difficult for those who think it is very difficult, if not impossible, and much easier for those who think it can be done. He would certainly be oversimplifying the picture, but at the very least his observation suggests that some theoretical revision is desirable in the prevailing views of social motives which link them so decisively to early childhood. Such a revision has been attempted in connection with the research on n-Achievement (McClelland, Atkinson, Clark, and Lowell, 1953) and while it has not been widely accepted (cf. Berelson & Steiner, 1964), it needs to be briefly summarized here to provide a theoretical underpinning for the attempts at motive change to be described. It starts with the proposition that all motives are learned, that not even biological discomforts (as from hunger) or pleasures (as from sexual stimulation) are "urges" or "drives" until they are linked to cues that can signify their presence or absence. In time, clusters of expectancies or associa-

tions grow up around affective experiences, not all of which are connected by any means with biological needs (McClelland et al., 1953, chap. 2), which we label motives. More formally, motives are "affectively toned associative networks" arranged in a hierarchy of strength or importance within a given individual. Obviously, the definition fits closely the operations used to measure a motive: "an affectively toned associative cluster" is exactly what is coded in a subject's fantasies to obtain an n-Achievement score. The strength of the motive (its position in the individual's hierarchy of motives) is measured essentially by counting the number of associations belonging to this cluster as compared to others that an individual produces in a given number of opportunities. If one thinks of a motive as an associative network, it is easier to imagine how one might go about changing it: The problem becomes one of moving its position up on the hierarchy by increasing its salience compared to other clusters. It should be possible to accomplish this end by such tactics as: (a) setting up the network—discovering what associations, for example, exist in the achievement area and then extending, strengthening, or otherwise "improving" the network they form; (b) conceptualizing the network—forming a clear and conscious construct that labels the network; (c) tying the network to as many cues as possible in everyday life, especially those preceding and following action, to insure that the network will be regularly re-aroused once formed, and (d) working out the relation of the network to superordinate associative clusters, like the self-concept, so that these dominant schemata do not block the train of achievement thoughts—for example, through a chain of interfering associations (e.g., "I am not really the achieving type").

This very brief summary is not intended as a full exposition of the theoretical viewpoint underlying the research, but it should suffice to give a rough idea of how the motive was conceived that we set out to change. This concept helped define the goals of the techniques of change, such as reducing the effects of associative interference from superordinate associate clusters. But what about the techniques themselves? What could we do that would produce effective learning of this sort? Broadly speaking, there are four types of empirical information to draw on. From the animal learning experiments, we know that such factors as repetition, optimal time intervals between stimulus, response, and reward, and the schedule of rewards are very important for effective learning. From human learning experiments, we know that such factors as distribution of practice, repetitions, meaningfulness, and recitation are important. From experiences with psychotherapy (cf. Rogers, 1961), we learn that warmth, honesty, nondirectiveness, and the ability to recode associations in line with psychoanalytic or other personality theories are important. And, from the attitude-change research literature, we learn that such variables as presenting one side or two, using reason or prestige to support an argument, or affiliating with a new reference group are crucial for developing new attitudes (cf. Hovland, Janis, and Kelley, 1953). Despite the fact that many of these variables seem limited in application to the learning situation in which they were studied, we have tried to make use of information from all these sources in designing our "motive acquisition" program and in finding support for the general propositions that have emerged from our study so far. For our purpose has been above all to produce an effect large enough to be measured. Thus we have tried to profit by all that is known about how to facilitate learning or produce personality or attitude change. For, if we could not obtain a substantial effect with all factors working to produce it, there would be no point to studying the effects of each factor taken one at a time. Such a strategy also has the practical advantage that we are in the position of doing our best to "deliver the goods" to our course participants since they were giving us their time and attention to take part in a largely untried educational experience.[2]

Our overall research strategy, therefore is "subtractive" rather than "additive." After we have demonstrated a substantial effect with some 10–12 factors working to produce it, our plan is to subtract that part of the program that deals with each of the factors to discover if there is a significant decline in the effect. It should also be possible to omit several factors in various combinations to at interactional effects. This will obviously require giving a fairly large number of courses in a standard institutional setting for the same kinds of businessmen with follow-up evaluation of their performance extending over a number of years. So obviously it will be some time before each of the factors incorporated into the propositions which follow can be properly evaluated so far as its effect on producing motive change is concerned.

The overall research strategy also determined the way the attempts to develop the achievement motive have been organized. That is to say, in order to process enough subjects to permit testing the effectiveness of various "inputs" in a reasonable number of years, the training had to be both of *short duration* (lasting one to three weeks) and *designed for groups* rather than for individuals as in person-to-person counseling. Fortunately these requirements coincide with normal practice in providing short courses for business executives. To conform further with that practice, the training has usually also been *residential* and *voluntary*. The design problems introduced by the last characteristic we have tried to handle in the usual ways by putting half the volunteers on a waiting list or giving them a different, technique-oriented course, etc. So far we have given the course to develop n-Achievement in some form or another some eight times to over 140 managers or teachers of management in groups of 9–25 in the United States, Mexico, and India. For the most part the course has been offered by a group of two to four consultant psychologists either to executives in a single company as a company training program, or to executives from several different companies as a self-improvement program, or as part of the program of an institute or school devoted to training managers. The theoretical propositions which follow have evolved gradually from these pilot attempts to be effective in developing n-Achievement among businessmen of various cultural backgrounds.

The first step in a motive development program is to create confidence that it will work. Our initial efforts in this area were dictated by the simple practical consideration that we had to "sell" our course or nobody would take it. We were not in the position of an animal psychologist who can order a dozen rats, or an academic psychologist who has captive subjects in his classes, or even a psychotherapist who has sick people knocking at his door every day. So we explained to all who would listen that we had every reason to believe from previous research that high n-Achievement is related to effective entrepreneurship and that therefore business executives could expect to profit from taking a course designed to understand and develop this important human characteristic. What started as a necessity led to the first proposition dealing with how to bring about motive change.

Proposition 1. The more reasons an individual has in advance to believe that he can, will, or should develop a motive, the more educational attempts designed to develop that motive are likely to succeed. The empirical support for this proposition from other studies is quite impressive. It consists of *(a)* the prestige-suggestion studies showing that people will believe or do what prestigeful sources suggest (cf. Hovland et al., 1953); *(b)* the so-called "Hawthorne effect" showing that people who feel they are especially selected to show an effect will tend to show it (Roethlisberger & Dickson, 1947); *(c)* the "Hello-Goodbye" effect in psychotherapy showing that patients who merely have contact with a prestigeful medical authority improve significantly over waiting list controls and almost as much as those who get prolonged therapy (Frank, 1961); *(d)* the "experimenter bias" studies which show that subjects will often do what an experimenter wants them to do, even though neither he nor they know he is trying to influence them (Rosenthal, 1963); *(e)* the goal-setting studies which show that setting goals for a person particularly in the name of prestigeful authorities like "science" or "research" improves performance (Kausler, 1959; Mierke, 1955); *(f)* the parent-child interaction studies which show that parents who set higher standards of excellence for their sons are more likely to have sons with high n-Achievement (Rosen & D'Andrade, 1959). The common factor in all these studies seems to be that goals are being set for the individual by sources he respects—goals which imply that his behavior should change for a variety of reasons and that it *can* change. In common-sense terms, belief in the possibility and desirability of change are tremendously influential in changing a person.

So we have used a variety of means to create this belief: the authority of research findings on the relationship of n-Achievement to entrepreneurial success, the suggestive power of membership in an experimental group designed to show an effect, the prestige of a great university, our own genuine enthusiasm for the course and our conviction that it would work, as expressed privately and in public speeches. In short, we were trying to make every use possible of what is sometimes regarded as an "error" in such research—namely, the Hawthorne effect, experimenter bias, etc., because we believe it to be one of the most powerful sources of change.

Why? What is the effect on the person, theoretically speaking, of all this goal setting for him? Its primary function is probably to arouse what exists of an associative network in the achievement area for each person affected. That is, many studies have shown that talk of achievement or affiliation or power tends to increase the frequency with which individuals think about achievement or affiliation or power (cf. Atkinson, 1958). And the stronger the talk, the more the relevant associative networks are aroused (McClelland et al., 1953). Such an arousal has several possible effects which would facilitate learning: *(a)* It elicits what exists in the person of a "response" thus making it easier to strengthen that response in subsequent learning; *(b)* It creates a discrepancy between a goal (a "Soll-lage" in Heckhausen's—1963—theory of motivation) and a present state ("Ist-lage") which represents a cognitive dissonance the person tries to reduce (cf. Festinger, 1957); in common-sense terms he has an image clearly presented to him of something he is not but should be; *(c)* It tends to block out by simple interference other associations which would inhibit change—such as, "I'm too old to learn," "I never learned much from going to school anyway," "What do these academics know about everyday life?," or "I hope they don't get personal about all this."

After the course has been "sold" sufficiently to get a group together for training, the first step in the course itself is to present the research findings in some detail on exactly how n-Achievement is related to certain types of successful entrepreneurial performance. That is, the argument of *The Achieving Society* (McClelland, 1961) is presented carefully with tables, charts and diagrams, usually in lecture form at the outset and with the help of an educational TV film entitled the *Need to Achieve.* This is followed by discussion to clear up any ambiguities that remain in their minds as far as the central argument is concerned. It is especially necessary to stress that not all high achievement is caused by high n-Achievement—that we have no evidence that high n-Achievement is an essential ingredient in success as a research scientist, professional, accountant, office or personnel manager, etc., that, on the contrary, it seems rather narrowly related to entrepreneurial, sales, or promotional

success, and therefore should be of particular interest to them because they hold jobs which either have or could have an entrepreneurial component. We rationalize this activity in terms of the following proposition.

Proposition 2. The more an individual perceives that developing a motive is consistent with the demands of reality (and reason), the more educational attempts designed to develop that motive are likely to succeed. In a century in which psychologists and social theorists have been impressed by the power of unreason, it is well to remember that research has shown that rational arguments do sway opinions, particularly among the doubtful or the uncommitted (cf. Hovland et al., 1953). Reality in the form of legal, military, or housing rules does modify white prejudice against Negroes (cf. Berelson & Steiner, 1964, p. 512). In being surprised at Asch's discovery that many people will go along with a group in calling a shorter line longer than it is, we sometimes forget that under most conditions their judgments conform with reality. The associative network which organizes "reality"—which places the person correctly in time, place, space, family, job, etc.—is one of the most dominant in the personality. It is the last to go in psychosis. It should be of great assistance to tie any proposed change in an associative network in with this dominant schema in such a way as to make the change consistent with reality demands or *"reasonable"* extensions of them. The word "reasonable" here simply means extensions arrived at by the thought processes of proof, logic, etc., which in adults have achieved a certain dominance of their own.

The next step in the course is to teach the participants the n-Achievement coding system. By this time, they are a little confused anyway as to exactly what we mean by the term. So we tell them they can find out for themselves by learning to code stories written by others or by themselves. They take the test for n-Achievement before this session and then find out what their own score is by scoring this record. However, we point out that if they think their score is too low, that can be easily remedied, since we teach them how to code and how to write stories saturated with n-Achievement; in fact, that is one of the basic purposes of the course: to teach them to think constantly in n-Achievement terms. Another aspect of the learning is discriminating achievement thinking from thinking in terms of power or affiliation. So usually the elements of these other two coding schemes are also taught.

Proposition 3. The more thoroughly an individual develops and clearly conceptualizes the associative network defining the motive, the more likely he is to develop the motive. The original empirical support for this proposition came from the radical behaviorist Skinnerian viewpoint: If the associative responses are the motive (by definition), to strengthen them one should elicit them and reinforce them, as one would shape up any response by reinforcement (cf. Skinner, 1953). But, support for this proposition also derives from other sources, particularly the "set" experiments. For decades laboratory psychologists have known that one of the easiest and most effective ways to change behavior is to change the subject's set. If he is responding to stimulus words with the names of animals, tell him to respond with the names of vegetables, or with words meaning the opposite, and he changes his behavior immediately and efficiently without a mistake. At a more complex level Orne (1962) had pointed out how powerful a set like "This is an experiment" can be. He points out that if you were to go up to a stranger and say something like "Lie down!" he would in all probability either laugh or escape as soon as possible. But, if you say, "This is an experiment. Lie down!" more often than not, if there are other supporting cues, the person will do so. Orne has demonstrated how subjects will perform nonsensical and fatiguing tasks for very long periods of time under the set that "This is an experiment." At an even more complex level, sociologists have demonstrated

often how quickly a person will change his behavior as he adopts a new role set (as a parent, a teacher, a public official, etc.). In all these cases an associative network exists usually with a label conveniently attached which we call set and which, when it is aroused or becomes salient, proceeds to control behavior very effectively. The purpose of this part of our course is to give the subjects a set or a carefully worked out associative network with appropriate words or labels to describe all its various aspects (the coding label for parts of the n-Achievement scoring system like Ga^+, I^+, etc.; cf. Atkinson, 1958). The power of words on controlling behavior has also been well documented (cf. Brown, 1958).

It is important to stress that it is not just the label (n-Achievement) which is taught. The person must be able to produce easily and often the new associative network itself. It is here that our research comes closest to traditional therapy which could be understood as the prolonged and laborious formation of new associative networks to replace anxiety-laden ones. That is, the person over time comes to form a new associative network covering his relations, for example, to his father and mother, which still later he may label an "unresolved Oedipus complex." When cues arise that formerly would have produced anxiety-laden associations, they now evoke this new complex instead, blocking out the "bad" associations by associative interference. But all therapists, whether Freudian or Rogerian, insist that the person must learn to produce these associations in their new form, that teaching the label is not enough. In fact, this is probably why so-called directive therapy is ineffective: It tries to substitute new constructs ("You should become an achiever") for old neurotic or ineffective ones ("rather than being such a slob") without changing the associative networks which underlie these surface labels. A change in set such as "Respond with names of vegetables" will not work unless the person has a whole associative network which defines the meaning of the set. The relation of this argument is obviously both to Kelley's (1955) insistence on the importance of personal constructs and to the general semanticists' complaints about the neurotic effects of mislabeling or overabstraction (Korzybski, 1941).

But, theoretically speaking, why should a change in set as an associative network be so influential in controlling thought and action? The explanation lies in part in its symbolic character. Learned acts have limited influence because they often depend on reality supports (as in typewriting), but learned thoughts (symbolic acts) can occur any time, any place, in any connection, and be applied to whatever the person is doing. They are more generalizable. Acts can also be inhibited more easily than thoughts. Isak Dinesen tells the story of the oracle who told the king he would get his wish so long as he never thought of the left eye of a camel. Needless to say, the king did not get his wish, but he could easily have obeyed her prohibition if it had been to avoid *looking* at the left eye of a camel. Thoughts once acquired gain more control over thoughts and actions than acquired acts do because they are harder to inhibit. But why do they gain control over actions? Are not thoughts substitutes for actions? Cannot a man learn to think achievement thoughts and still not act like an achiever in any way? The question is taken up again under the next proposition, but it is well to remember here that thoughts are symbolic acts and that practice of symbolic acts facilitates performing the real acts (cf. Hovland, 1951, p. 644).

The next step in the course is to tie thought to action. Research has shown that individuals high in n-Achievement tend to act in certain ways. For example, they prefer work situations where there is a challenge (moderate risk), concrete feedback on how well they are doing, and opportunity to take personal responsibility for achieving the work goals. The participants in the course are therefore introduced to a "work" situation in the form of a business game in which they will have an opportunity to show these characteristics in action or more specifically to develop them through practice and through observing others play it. The game is designed to mimic real life: They must order parts to make certain objects (e.g., a Tinker Toy model bridge) after having estimated how many they think they can construct in the time allotted. They have a real chance to take over, plan the whole game, learn from how well they are doing (use of feedback), and show a paper profit or loss at the end. While they are surprised often that they should have to display their real action characteristics in this way in public, they usually get emotionally involved in observing how they behave under pressure of a more or less "real" work situation.

Proposition 4. The more an individual can link the newly developed network to related actions, the more the change in both thought and action is likely to occur and endure. The evidence for the importance of action for producing change consists of such diverse findings as *(a)* the importance of recitation for human learning; *(b)* the repeated finding that over commitment and participation in action changes attitudes effectively (cf. Berelson and Steiner, 1964, p. 576), and *(c)* early studies by Carr (cf. McGeoch and Irion, 1952) showing that simply to expose an organism to what is to be learned (e.g., trundling a rat through a maze) is nowhere near as effective as letting him explore it for himself in action.

Theoretically, the action is represented in the associative network by what associations precede, accompany, and follow it. So including the acts in what is learned *enlarges* the associative network or the achievement construct to include action. Thus, the number of cues likely to trip off the n-Achievement network is increased. In common-sense terms, whenever he works he now evaluates what he is doing in achievement terms, and whenever he thinks about achievement he tends to think of its action consequences.

So far, the course instruction has remained fairly abstract and removed from the everyday experiences of businessmen.

So, the next step is to apply what has been learned to everyday business activities through the medium of the well-known case-study method popularized by the Harvard Business School. Actual examples of the development of the careers or firms of business leaders or entrepreneurs are written up in disguised form and assigned for discussion to the participants. Ordinarily, the instructor is not interested in illustrating "good" or "bad" managerial behavior—that is left to participants to discuss—but in our use of the material, we do try to label the various types of behavior as illustrating either n-Achievement and various aspects of the achievement sequence (instrumental activity, blocks, etc.), or n-Power, n-Affiliation, etc. The participants are also encouraged to bring in examples of managerial behavior from their own experience to evaluate in motivational terms.

Proposition 5. The more an individual can link the newly conceptualized association-action complex (or motive) to events in his everyday life, the more likely the motive complex is to influence his thoughts and actions in situations outside the training experience. The transfer-of-training research literature is not very explicit on this point, though it seems self-evident. Certainly, this is the proposition that underlies the practice of most therapy when it involves working through or clarifying, usually in terms of a new, partially formed construct system, old memories, events from the last 24 hours, dreams, and hopes of the future. Again, theoretically, this should serve to enlarge and clarify the associative network and increase the number of cues in everyday life which will re-arouse it. The principle of symbolic practice can also be invoked to support its effectiveness in promoting transfer outside the learning experience.

For some time, most course participants have been wondering what all this has to do with them personally. That is to say, the material is introduced originally on a "take it or leave it" objective basis as something that ought to be of interest to them. But sooner or later, they must confront the issue as to what meaning n-Achievement has in their own personal lives. We do not force this choice on them, nor do we think we are brainwashing them to believe in n-Achievement. We believe, and we tell them we believe in the "obstinate audience" (cf. Bauer, 1964), in the ultimate capacity of people to resist persuasion or to do in the end what they really want to do. In fact, we had one case in an early session of a man who at this point decided he was not an achievement-minded person and did not want to become one. He subsequently retired and became a chicken farmer to the relief of the business in which he had been an ineffective manager. We respected that decision and mention it in the course as a good example of honest self-evaluation. Nevertheless, we do provide them with all kinds of information as to their own achievement-related behavior in the fantasy tests, in the business game, in occasional group dynamic session—and ample opportunity and encouragement to think through what this information implies so far as their self-concept is concerned and their responsibilities to their jobs. Various devices such as the "Who am I?" test, silent group meditation, or individual counseling have been introduced to facilitate this self-confrontation.

Proposition 6. The more an individual can perceive and experience the newly conceptualized motive as an improvement in the self-image, the more the motive is likely to influence his future thoughts and actions. Evidence on the importance of the ego or the self-image on controlling behavior has been summarized by Allport (1943). In recent years, Rogers and his group (Rogers, 1961; Rogers and Dymond, 1954) have measured improvement in psychotherapy largely in terms of improvement of the self-concept in relation to the ideal self. Indirect evidence of the importance of the self-schema comes from the discussion over whether a person can be made to do things under hypnosis that are inconsistent with his self-concept or values. All investigators agree that the hypnotist can be most successful in getting the subject to do what might normally be a disapproved action if he makes the subject perceive the action as consistent with his self-image or values (cf. Berelson and Steiner, 1963, p. 124).

The same logic supports this proposition. It seems unlikely that a newly formed associative network like n-Achievement could persist and influence behavior much unless it had somehow "come to terms" with the pervasive superordinate network of associations defining the self. The logic is the same as for Proposition 2 dealing with the reality construct system. The n-Achievement associations must come to be experienced as related to or consistent with the ideal self-image; otherwise associations from the self-system will constantly block thoughts of achievement. The person might be thinking, for example: "I am not that kind of person; achievement means judging people in terms of how well they perform and I don't like to hurt people's feelings."

Closely allied to the self-system is a whole series of networks only half conscious (i.e., correctly labeled) summarizing the values by which the person lives which derive from his culture and social milieu. These values can also interfere if they are inconsistent with n-Achievement as a newly acquired way of thinking. Therefore, it has been customary at this point in the course to introduce a value analysis of the participants' culture based on an analysis of children's stories, myths, popular religion, comparative attitude surveys, customs, etc., more or less in line with traditional, cultural anthropological practice (cf. Benedict, 1946; McClelland, 1964). For example, in America we have to work through the problem of how being achievement oriented seems to interfere with being popular or liked by others which is highly valued by Americans. In Mexico a central issue is the highly valued "male dominance" pattern reflected in the patriarchal family and in the *macho* complex (being extremely masculine). Since data shows that dominant

fathers have sons with low n-Achievement and authoritarian bosses do not encourage n-Achievement in their top executives (Andrews, 1965), there is obviously a problem here to be worked through if n-Achievement is to survive among thoughts centered on dominance. The problem is not only rationally discussed. It is acted out in role-playing sessions where Mexicans try, and often to their own surprise fail, to act like the democratic father with high standards in the classic Rosen and D'Andrade (1959) study on parental behavior which develops high n-Achievement. Any technique is used which will serve to draw attention to possible conflicts between n-Achievement and popular or traditional cultural values. In the end it may come to discussing parts of the *Bhagavad Gita* in India, or the *Koran* in Arab countries, that seem to oppose achievement striving or entrepreneurial behavior.

Proposition 7. The more an individual can perceive and experience the newly conceptualized motive as an improvement on prevailing cultural values, the more the motive is likely to influence his future thoughts and actions. The cultural anthropologists for years have argued how important it is to understand one's own cultural values to overcome prejudices, adopt more flexible attitudes, etc., but there is little hard evidence that doing so changes a person's behavior. What exists comes indirectly from studies that show prejudice can be decreased a little by information about ethnic groups (Berelson and Steiner, 1963, p. 517), or that repeatedly show an unconscious link between attitudes and the reference group (or subculture to which one belongs—a link which presumably can be broken more easily by full information about it, especially when coupled with role-playing new attitudes (cf. Berelson and Steiner, 1963, pp. 566 ff.).

The theoretical explanation of this presumed effect is the same as for Propositions 2 and 6. The newly learned associative complex to influence thought and action effectively must somehow be adjusted to three superordinate networks that may set off regularly interfering associations—namely, the networks associated with reality, the self, and the social reference group or subculture.

The course normally ends with each participant preparing a written document outlining his goals and life plans for the next two years. These plans may or may not include references to the achievement motive; they can be very tentative, but they are supposed to be quite specific and realistic; that is to say, they should represent moderate levels of aspiration following the practice established in learning about n-Achievement of choosing the moderately risky or challenging alternative. The purpose of this document is in part to formulate for oneself the practical implications of the course before leaving it, but even more to provide a basis for the evaluation of their progress in the months after the course. For it is explained to the participants that they are to regard themselves as "in training" for the next two years, that 10–14 days is obviously too short a time to do more than conceive a new way of life: It represents the residential portion of the training only. Our role over the next two years will be to remind them every six months of the tasks they have set themselves by sending them a questionnaire to fill out which will serve to rearouse many of the issues discussed in the course and to give them information on how far they have progressed towards achieving their goals.

Proposition 8. The more an individual commits himself to achieving concrete goals in life related to the newly formed motive, the more the motive is likely to influence his future thoughts and actions.

Proposition 9. The more an individual keeps a record of his progress toward achieving goals to which he is committed, the more the newly formed motive is likely to influence his future thoughts and actions. These propositions are both related to what was called "pacing" in early studies of the psychology of work. That is, committing oneself to a specific goal and then comparing one's performance to that

goal has been found to facilitate learning (cf. Kausler, 1959), though most studies of levels of aspiration have dealt with goal setting as a result rather than as a "cause" of performance. At any rate, the beneficial effect of concrete feedback on learning has been amply demonstrated by psychologists from Thorndike to Skinner. Among humans the feedback on performance is especially effective if they have high n-Achievement (French, 1958), a fact which makes the relevance of our request for feedback obvious to the course participants.

The theoretical justification for these propositions is that in this way we are managing to keep the newly acquired associative network salient over the next two years. We are providing cues that will regularly re-arouse it since he knows he is still part of an experimental training group which is supposed to show a certain type of behavior (Proposition 1 again). If the complex is re-aroused sufficiently often back in the real world, we believe it is more likely to influence thought and action than if it is not aroused.

As described so far, the course appears to be devoted almost wholly to cognitive learning. Yet this is only part of the story. The "teachers" are all clinically oriented psychologists who also try to practice whatever has been learned about the type of human relationship that most facilitates emotional learning. Both for practical and theoretical reasons this relationship is structured as warm, honest, and nonevaluative, somewhat in the manner described by Rogers (1961) and recommended by distinguished therapists from St. Ignatius[3] to Freud. That is to say, we insist that the only kind of change that can last or mean anything is what the person decides on and works out by himself, that we are there not to criticize his past behavior or direct his future choices, but to provide him with all sorts of information and emotional support that will help him in his self-confrontation. Since we recognize that self-study may be quite difficult and unsettling, we try to create an optimistic relaxed atmosphere in which the person is warmly encouraged in his efforts and given the opportunity for personal counseling if he asks for it.

Proposition 10. Changes in motives are more likely to occur in an interpersonal atmosphere in which the individual feels warmly but honestly supported and respected by others as a person capable of guiding and directing his own future behavior. Despite the widespread belief in this proposition among therapists (except for operant conditioners), one of the few studies that directly supports it has been conducted by Ends and Page (1957) who found that an objective learning-theory approach was less successful in treating chronic alcoholics than a person-oriented, client-centered approach. Rogers (1961) also summarizes other evidence that therapists who are warmer, more emphatic, and genuine are more successful in their work. Hovland et al. (1953) report that the less manipulative the intent of a communicator, the greater the tendency to accept his conclusions. There is also the direct evidence that parents of boys with high n-Achievement are warmer, more encouraging, and less directive (fathers only) than parents of boys with low n-Achievement (Rosen and D'Andrade, 1959). We tried to model ourselves after those parents on the theory that what is associated with high n-Achievement in children might be most likely to encourage its development in adulthood. This does not mean permissiveness or promiscuous reinforcement of all kinds of behavior; it also means setting high standards as the parents of the boys with high n-Achievement did but having the relaxed faith that the participants can achieve them.

The theoretical justification for this proposition can take two lines: Either one argues that this degree of challenge to the self-schema produces anxiety which needs to be reduced by warm support of the person for effective learning to take place, or one interprets the warmth as a form of direct reinforcement for change following the operant-conditioning model. Perhaps both factors are operating. Certainly there is ample evidence to support the view that anxiety interferes with learning (cf. Sarason, 1960) and that reward shapes behavior (see Bandura & Walters, 1963, pp. 283 ff.).

One other characteristic of the course leads to two further propositions. Efforts are made so far as possible to define it as an "experience apart," "an opportunity for self-study," or even a "spiritual retreat" (though the term can be used more acceptably in India than in the United States). So far as possible it is held in an isolated resort hotel or a hostel where there will be few distractions from the outside world and few other guests. This permits an atmosphere of total concentration on the objectives of the course including much informal talk outside the sessions about Ga^+, Ga^+, I^+, and other categories in the coding definition. It still comes as a surprise to us to hear these terms suddenly in an informal group of participants talking away in Spanish or Telugu. The effect of this retreat from everyday life into a special and specially labeled experience appears to be twofold: It dramatizes or increases the salience of the new associative network and it tends to create a new reference group.

Proposition 11. Change in motives are more likely to occur the more the setting dramatizes the importance of self-study and lifts it out of the routine of everyday life. So far as we know there is no scientific evidence to support this proposition, though again if one regards Jesuits as successful examples of personality change, the Order has frequently followed the advice of St. Ignatius to the effect that "the progress made in the Exercizes will be greater, the more the exercitant withdraws from all friends and acquaintances, and from all worldly cares." Theory supports the proposition in two respects: Removing the person from everyday routine *(a)* should decrease interfering associations (to say nothing of interfering appointments and social obligations), and *(b)* should heighten the salience of the experience by contrast with everyday life and make it harder to handle with the usual defenses ("just one more course," etc.). That is to say, the network of achievement-related associations can be more strongly and distinctly aroused in contrast to everyday life, making cognitive dissonance greater and therefore more in need of reduction by new learning. By the same token we have found that the dramatic quality of the experience cannot be sustained very long in a 12–18 hour-a-day schedule without a new routine attitude developing. Thus, we have found that a period somewhere between 6 to 14 days is optimal for this kind of "spiritual retreat." St. Ignatius sets an outside limit of 30 days, but this is when the schedule is less intensive (as ours has sometimes been), consisting of only a few hours a day over a longer period.

Proposition 12. Changes in motives are more likely to occur and persist if the new motive is a sign of membership in a new reference group. No principle of change has stronger empirical or historical support than this one. Endless studies have shown that people's opinions, attitudes, and beliefs are a function of their reference group and that different attitudes are likely to arise and be sustained primarily when the person moves into or affiliates with a new reference group (cf. Berelson and Steiner, 1963, pp. 580 ff.). Many theorists argue that the success of groups like Alcoholics Anonymous depends on the effectiveness with which the group is organized so that each person demonstrates his membership in it by "saving" another alcoholic. Political experience has demonstrated that membership in small groups like Communist or Nazi Party Cells is one of the most effective ways to sustain changed attitudes and behavior.

Our course attempts to achieve this result *(a)* by the group experience in isolation—creating the feeling of alumni who all went through it together; *(b)* by certain signs of identification with the group, particularly the language of the coding system, but also including a certificate of membership, and *(c)* by arranging where possible to have participants come from the same community so that they can form a "cell" when they return that will serve as an immediate reference group to prevent gradual undermining of the new network by other pressures.

In theoretical terms a reference group should be effective because its members constantly provide cues to each other to re-arouse the associative network, because they will also reward each other for achievement-related thoughts and acts, and because this constant mutual stimulation, and reinforcement, plus the labeling of the group, will prevent assimilation of the network to bigger, older, and stronger networks (such as those associated with traditional cultural values).

In summary, we have described an influence process which may be conceived in terms of "input," "intervening," and "output" variables as in Table 1. The propositions relate variables in Column A via their effect on the intervening variables in Column B to as yet loosely specified behavior in Column C, which may be taken as evidence that "development" of n-Achievement has "really" taken place. The problems involved in evaluation of effects are as great and as complicated as those involved in designing the treatment, but they cannot be spelled out here, partly for lack of space, partly because we are in an even earlier stage of examining and classifying the effects of our training one and two years later preparatory to conceptualizing more clearly what happens. It will have to suffice to point out that we plan extensive comparisons over a two-year period of the behaviors of our trained subjects compared with matched controls along the lines suggested in Column C.

What the table does is to give a brief overall view of how we conceptualize the educational or treatment process. What is particularly important is that the propositions refer to *operationally defined* and *separable* treatment variables. Thus, after having demonstrated hopefully a large effect of the total program, we can subtract a variable and see how much that decreases the impact of the course. That is to say, the course is designed so that it

Table 1   Variables Conceived as Entering into the Motive Change Process

A Input or independent variables	B Intervening variables	C Output or dependent variables
1. Goal setting for the person (P1, P11)	Arousal of associative network (salience)	Duration and/or extensiveness of changes in:
2. Acquisition of n-Achievement associative network (P2, P3, P4, P5)	Experiencing and labeling the associative network	1. n-Achievement associative network
3. Relating new network to superordinate networks	Variety of cues to which network is linked	2. Related actions: use of feedback, moderate risk taking, etc.

reality   (P2)
    the self   (P6)
    cultural values (P7)
	Interfering associations assimilated or bypassed by reproductive interference	3. Innovations (job improvements)
		4. Use of time and money
		5. Entrepreneurial success as defined by nature of job held and its rewards

4. Personal goal setting (P8)		
5. Knowledge of progress (P3, P4, P9)		
6. Personal warmth and support (P10)	Positive effect associated with network	
7. Support of reference group (P11, P12)		

Note: P1, P11, etc., refer to the numbered propositions in the text.

could go ahead perfectly reasonably with very little advanced goal setting (P1), with an objective rather than a warm personal atmosphere (P11), without the business game tying thought to action (P9), without learning to code n-Achievement and write achievement-related stories (P3), without cultural value analysis (P7), or an isolated residential setting (P1, P11, P12). The study units are designed in a way that they can be omitted without destroying the viability of the treatment which has never been true of other studies of the psychotherapeutic process (cf. Rogers & Dymond, 1954).

But is there any basis for thinking the program works in practice? As yet, not enough time has elapsed to enable us to collect much data on long-term changes in personality and business activity. However, we do know that businessmen can learn to write stories scoring high in n-Achievement, that they retain this skill over one year or two, and that they like the course—but the same kinds of things can be said about many unevaluated management training courses. In two instances we have more objective data. Three courses were given to some 34 men from the Bombay area in early 1963. It proved pos-

sible to develop a crude but objective and reliable coding system to record whether each one had shown *unusual* entrepreneurial activity in the two years prior to the course or in the two years after course. "Unusual" here means essentially an unusual promotion or salary raise or starting a new business venture of some kind. Of the 30 on whom information was available in 1965, 27 percent had been unusually active before the course, 67 percent after the course ($x^2 = 11.2$, $p < 0.01$). In a control group chosen at random from those who applied for the course in 1963, out of 11 on whom information has so far been obtained, 18 percent were active before 1963, 27 percent since 1963.

In a second case, four courses were given throughout 1964 to a total of 52 small businessmen from the small city of Kakinada in Andhra Pradesh, India. Of these men, 25 percent had been unusually active in the two-year period before the course, and 65 percent were unusually active immediately afterwards ($x^2 = 17.1$, $p < 0.01$). More control data and more refined measures are needed, but it looks very much as if, in India at least, we will be dealing with a spontaneous "activation" rate of only 25 percent—35 percent among entrepreneurs. Thus we have a distinct advantage over psychotherapists who are trying to demonstrate an improvement over a two-thirds spontaneous recovery rate. Our own data suggest that we will be unlikely to get an improvement or "activation" rate much above the two-thirds level commonly reported in therapy studies. That is, about one-third of the people in our courses have remained relatively unaffected. Nevertheless the two-thirds activated after the course represent a doubling of the normal rate of unusual entrepreneurial activity—no mean achievement in the light of the current pessimism among psychologists as to their ability to induce lasting personality change among adults.

One case will illustrate how the course seems to affect people in practice. A short time after participating in one of our courses in India, a 47-year-old businessman rather suddenly and dramatically decided to quit his excellent job and go into the construction business on his own in a big way. A man with some means of his own, he had had a very successful career as employee-relations manager for a large oil firm. His job involved adjusting management-employee difficulties, negotiating union contracts, etc. He was well-to-do, well thought of in his company, and admired in the community, but he was restless because he found his job increasingly boring. At the time of the course his original n-Achievement score was not very high and he was thinking of retiring and living in England where his son was studying. In an interview, eight months later, he said the course had served not so much to "motivate" him but to "crystallize" a lot of ideas he had vaguely or half-consciously picked up about work and achievement all through his life. It provided him with a new language (he still talked in terms of standards of excellence, blocks, moderate risk, goal anticipation, etc.), a new construct which served to organize those ideas and explain to him why he was bored with his job, despite his obvious success. He decided he wanted to be an n-Achievement-oriented person,

that he would be unhappy in retirement, and that he should take a risk, quit his job, and start in business on his own. He acted on his decision and in six months had drawn plans and raised over £ 1,000,000 to build the tallest building in his large city to be called the "Everest Apartments." He is extremely happy in his new activity because it means selling, promoting, trying to wangle scarce materials, etc. His first building is partway up and he is planning two more.

Even a case as dramatic as this one does not prove that the course produced the effect, despite his repeated use of the constructs he had learned, but what is especially interesting about it is that he described what had happened to him in exactly the terms the theory requires. He spoke not about a new motive force but about how existing ideas had been crystallized into a new associative network, and it is this new network which *is* the new "motivating" force according to the theory.

How generalizable are the propositions? They have purposely been stated generally so that some term like "attitude" or "personality characteristic" could be substituted for the term "motive" throughout, because we believe the propositions will hold for other personality variables. In fact, most of the supporting experimental evidence cited comes from attempts to change other characteristics. Nevertheless, the propositions should hold best more narrowly for motives and especially the achievement motive. One of the biggest difficulties in the way of testing them more generally is that not nearly as much is known about other human characteristics or their specific relevance for success in a certain type of work. For example, next to nothing is known about the need for power, its relation to success, let us say, in politics or bargaining situations, and its origins and course of development in the life history of individuals. It is precisely the knowledge we have about such matters for the achievement motive that puts us in a position to shape it for limited, socially and individually desirable ends. In the future, it seems to us, research in psychotherapy ought to follow a similar course. That is to say, rather than developing "all purpose" treatments, good for any person and any purpose, it should aim to develop specific treatments or educational programs built on laboriously accumulated detailed knowledge of the characteristic to be changed. It is in this spirit that the present research program in motive acquisition has been designed and is being tested out.

References

G. W. Allport, "The Ego in Contemporary Psychology," *Psychological Review* 50 (1943): 451–78.

J. D. W. Andrews, "The Achievement Motive in Two Types of Organizations," *Journal of Personality and Social Psychology* (1965, in press).

J. W. Atkinson, ed., *Motives in Fantasy Action and Society* (New York: Van Nostrand Reinhold Company, 1958).

A. Bandura and R. H. Walters, *Social Learning and Personality Development* (New York: Holt, Rinehart & Winston, Inc., 1963).

R. A. Bauer, "The Obstinate Audience: The Influence Process From the Point of View of Social Communication," *American Psychologist* 19 (1964): 319–29.

Ruth Benedict, *The Chrysanthemum and the Sword* (Boston: Houghton Mifflin Company, 1946).

B. Berelson and G. A. Steiner, *Human Behavior: An Inventory of Scientific Findings* (New York: Harcourt Brace Jovanovich, Inc., 1964).

R. W. Brown, *Words and Things* (New York: Free Press, Div. of The Macmillan Company, 1958).

R. W. Burris, *The Effect of Counseling on Achievement Motivation* (Unpublished doctoral dissertation, Indiana University, 1958).

E. J. Ends and C. W. Page, "A Study of Three Types of Group Psychotherapy with Hospitalized Male Inebriates," *Quarterly Journal on Alcohol* 18 (1957): 263–77.

H. J. Eynsenck, "The Effects of Psychotherapy: An Evaluation," *Journal of Consulting Psychology* 16 (1952): 319–24.

L. Festinger, *A Theory of Cognitive Dissonance* (New York: Harper & Row, Publishers, 1957).

J. Frank, *Persuasion and Healing* (Baltimore: Johns Hopkins Press, 1961).

E. G. French, "Effects of the Interaction of Motivation and Feedback on Task Performance." In J. W. Atkinson, ed., *Motives in Fantasy, Action and Society* (New York: Van Nostrand Reinhold Company, 1958), pp. 400–08.

H. Heckhausen, "Eine Rehmentheorie der Motivation in zehn Thesen," *Zeitschrift für experimentelle und angewandte Psychologie* X/4, (1963): 604–26.

C. I. Hovland, "Human Learning and Retention." In S. S. Stevens, ed., *Handbook of Experimental Psychology* (New York: John Wiley & Sons, Inc., 1951).

C. I. Hovland, I. L. Janis, and H. H. Kelley, *Communication and Persuasion: Psychological Studies of Opinion Change* (New Haven: Yale University Press, 1953).

D. H. Kausler, "Aspiration Level as a Determinant of Performance," *Journal of Personality* 27 (1959): 346–51.

G. A. Kelley, *The Psychology of Personal Constructs* (New York: W. W. Norton & Company, Inc., 1955).

A. Korzybski, *Science and Sanity* (Lancaster Pa.: Science Press, 1941).

D. C. McClelland, *The Achieving Society* (New York: Van Nostrand Reinhold Company, 1961).

D. C. McClelland, *The Roots of Consciousness* (New York: Van Nostrand Reinhold Company, 1964).

D. C. McClelland, J. W. Atkinson, R. A. Clark, and E. L. Lowell, *The Achievement Motive* (New York: Appleton-Century-Crofts, 1953).

J. A. McGeoch and A. L. Irion, *The Psychology of Human Learning,* 2d ed. (London: Longmans, Green & Company, Ltd., 1952).

K. Mierke, *Wille und Leistung* (Göttingen: Verlag für Psychologie, 1955).

M. Orne, "On the Social Psychology of the Psychological Experiment: With Particular Reference to Demand Characteristics and their Implications," *American Psychologist* 17 (1962): 776–83.

F. J. Roethlisberger and W. J. Dickson, *Management and the Worker* (Cambridge: Harvard University Press, 1947).

C. R. Rogers, *On Becoming a Person* (Boston: Houghton Mifflin Company, 1961).

C. R. Rogers and R. F. Dymond, eds., *Psychotherapy and Personality Change* (Chicago: University of Chicago Press, 1954).

B. C. Rosen and R. G. D'Andrade, "The Psychosocial Origins of Achievement Motivation," *Sociometry* 22 (1959): 185–218.

R. Rosenthal, "On the Social Psychology of the Psychological Experiment: The Experimenter's Hypothesis As Unintended Determinant of Experimental Results," *American Scientist* 51 (1963): 268–83.

I. Sarason, "Empirical Findings and Theoretical Problems in the Use of Anxiety Scales," *Psychological Bulletin* 57 (1960): 403–15.

B. F. Skinner, *Science and Human Behavior* (New York: The Macmillan Company, 1953).

Notes

1. "I am greatly indebted to the Carnegie Corporation of New York for its financial support of the

research on which this paper is based, and to my collaborators who have helped plan and run the courses designed to develop the achievement motive—chiefly George Litwin, Elliott Danzig, David Kolb, Winthrop Adkins, David Winter, and John Andrews. The statements made and views expressed are solely the responsibility of the author."

2. Parenthetically, we have found several times that our stated desire to evaluate the effectiveness of our course created doubts in the minds of our sponsors that they did not feel about many popular courses for managers that no one has ever evaluated or plans to evaluate. An attitude of inquiry is not always an asset in education. It suggests one is not sure of his ground.

3. In his famous spiritual exercises which have played a key role in producing and sustaining personality change in the Jesuit Order, St. Ignatius states: "The director of the Exercizes ought not to urge the exercitant more to poverty or any promise than to the contrary, not to one state of life or way of living more than another . . . [while it is proper to urge people outside the Exercizes] the director of the Exercizes . . . without leaning to one side or the other, should permit the Creator to deal directly with the creature, and the creature directly with his Creator and Lord."

TOWARD THE DEVELOPMENT OF AN EMPIRICALLY BASED THEORY OF ROLE RELATIONSHIPS[1]

Jerald Hage and Gerald Marwell

The object of this paper is to present a programmatic approach to the development of a theory of role relationships. Such a theory is not itself presented below. Instead, we are concerned with delineating the series of choices concerning variables, definitions, and assumptions, upon which a network of testable propositions about role relationships might be based. It should be understood that we are here discussing only one aspect of a broader category of concern which has been loosely titled "role theory." As indicated by a recent volume on this topic (Biddle and Thomas, 1966), theories of interpersonal perception, theories of organizational conflict, theories of individual behavior, theories of legislatures, etc., may all involve the concept of role in their explanatory processes, and thus be considered "role theories." Although each of these is a legitimate enterprise, we are here seeking something else—a theory of roles, or, more specifically, role relationships.

A theory of role relationships may be defined by a set of empirically interrelated, verifiable propositions (see, for example, Zetterberg, 1963). In its simplest form, any one of these propositions would state, for example, that role relationships that are high on variable X tend to be high (or low) on variable Y. Paraphrasing Homans (1950) this form may be filled with content by demonstrating that role relationships within which there is a high frequency of interaction are also role relationships within which there is a high degree of sentiment.

Our concern is not only that there appear to be few verified propositions about differences and similarities among role relationships, but that the literature contains few statements of such propositions even in the form of verifiable hypotheses to be tested. It is our belief that the delineation of an approach that aids in the statement of such hypotheses is the first necessary step in the development of an empirically based theory.

An Approach

Different research approaches may be characterized in terms of a series of choices that must be made. Three of these choices are particularly important in this

Table 1

Type of Unit	Examples
Individual	George Cukor, David Niven, David Lean, Marlon Brando, Talcott Parsons, Neil Smelser, Hans Gerth, C. Wright Mills
Interpersonal Relationship	George Cukor-David Niven, David Lean-Marlon Brando, David Niven-Marlon Brando, Talcott Parsons-Neil Smelser, Hans Gerth-C. Wright Mills, Talcott Parsons-Hans Gerth
Position	Movie Director, Movie Star (actor), Professor, Graduate Student
Role (Interpositional) Relationship	Movie Director-Movie Actor, Professor-Graduate Student, Co-Star (actor)-Co-Star, Professor-Professor

analysis: (1) the definition of the unit of analysis for research; (2) the selection of the sample of units, and (3) the selection of the kind of variables.[2] In the sections that follow, we suggest that certain choices rather than others are more likely to promote the development of an empirically based theory. If the choices are the role relationship for the unit of analysis rather than the position or the individual, a large rather than small number of role relationships, and general rather than content or role-specific variables, we feel that testable propositions are much more likely to emerge. In our review of the role literature, we have not been able to find any research that has used this particular combination of choices, although one or two of these three suggested options have been selected at some times. For example, Hemphill (1960) and Stogdill and Shartle (1960) have considered a large number of positions; Kahn et al. (1964) and Gross et al. (1958) have examined several general variables (as well as role-specific variables) for a number of positions. We hope to demonstrate, however, that unique advantages accrue from a combination of all three of these choices.

The Choice of the Unit of Analysis: The Role Relationships Versus the Position

A major problem which must be faced in any research concerned with the concept of role is the definition of this frequently used term. Several reviews have indicated the many different usages and meanings of the concept that exist within even the same discipline (Thomas and Biddle, 1966; Gross et al., 1958). For the purposes of this paper, our definition focuses on the interaction or relationship that exists between two social positions. This tradition is exemplified by the theoretical work of Merton (1957) and the empirical research of Gross et al. (1958).

The role relationship as a unit of analysis may be distinguished from three particularly relevant alternatives for research: the individual, the inter*personal* relationship, and the position. Table 1 gives examples of each of these units.

Of course, each of these units (as well as others, such as the organization) is important for social science to consider. In the role literature, however, the particular salience of the *position* has been stressed as an alternative to the individual actor. Oeser and Harary's (1966) discussion is a recent example. As Merton (1957) has pointed out, however, each position may have several counterpositions within its role set. Thus, the movie star has a director *and* a co-star *and* a dresser *and* a fan, etc. The behavior of the position occupant often varies radically, depending upon which counter position is involved in the interaction. For example, an important aspect of the definition of the position fore-man might be that he gives orders. Never-theless, he should limit this activity to his relationships with workers, and only those in his department. By giving orders to the superintendent, his supervisor, to sales-men in the company, etc., he would be behaving in a decidedly unusual manner. In other words, the behaviors and ex-pectations associated with a position are often, although not always, directed to-ward specific other positions. Thus, a focus on the relationship corresponds more immediately to the organization of behavior, much of which, although "at-tached" to particular positions, is speci-fied in terms of relevant relationships.

Since few studies have started with a *dyadic* conceptualization of roles, the fact that relationships do exist between posi-tions has been obscured. Yet, it is the *net-work* of such relationships which may be viewed as most relevant to the classic problem of sociology, the Hobbesian prob-lem of order. It is the linking of posi-tions that defines the organization of the system, not the presence of the positions themselves.

Finally, it appears to us that the role relationship as the unit of analysis also has the advantage of emphasizing contex-tual and temporal variables. Because it focuses on interaction it leads to a series of interesting questions, such as: How long does interaction last? How durable is the relationship? Althouth these questions might be rephrased for positions, the transformation seems difficult and strained.

The Choice of the Sample of Units: A Small Versus a Large Number of Role Relationships

In formulating a concrete research pro-gram the researcher is often confronted with a large number of role relationships (or positions), enacted by a large number of individuals, who behave in many dif-ferent ways. Since most researchers con-sider their ultimate task the traditional problem of predicting behavior, and have

studied positions, they have tended to look at variance in behavior among a large number of individuals enacting the same position or, at best, to compare the actions of several persons in one position with individuals in another.

We believe that this approach reduces the ability of the analyst to see similarities and differences between broad classes of either role relationships or positions. Con-centration on a small number of positions or role relationships may sensitize the analyst to differences of particular sali-ence for the units he is studying but is of secondary value for uncovering general concepts that will be useful across a broad spectrum of units. Thus, we pro-pose that there is a need for research that defines as its population all role relation-ships within a given society, or, for the more ambitious, across societies. To put it another way, we advocate the importance of comparative analysis versus the case study. The arguments for the comparative approach to organizations, to politics, to economics, and to societies all apply to the study of role relationships as well.

The task of the research procedures would be to assign each role relationship a score on each variable being considered. It is, of course, understood that there may be great variance among inter*personal* re-lationships as to how a given role rela-tionship is "played." Not all doctor-nurse dyads interact in exactly the same way. This makes the task of abstracting the common element difficult. Nevertheless, we assume that in general there is some "norm," some central tendency for per-formance in each role relationship, which is common through the society. We fur-ther assume that this norm acts as a model, setting the expectations of participants in and observers of the role relationship.

It is against this backdrop of societally defined "norms" that variations among specific actor dyads may best be under-stood. An illuminating example of this oc-curs in a study by Jones et al. (1966). Their research indicates that people "get to know" something about an actor as an individual from observing his behavior only when that behavior *varies* from that which would be predicted by the role (position) the individual is enacting. Furthermore, individual variance in performance of role relationships may itself be an important variable at the level of analysis we are suggesting. Thus, each role relationship may be scored for the permitted within-relationship variance on each variable as well as for its point of central tendency. For example, it may not be as important for different "brother-brother" dyads to interact about as often as the "typical" "brother-brother" as it is for a given "boyfriend—girl friend" dyad to approximate the norm.

The Choice of Variables: Specific Versus General

Research with social roles has generally attempted description in terms of the specific behaviors involved. Thus, dentists are defined by the fact that they drill on teeth, pilots by the fact that they fly planes and are in command of their crews, mothers by the fact that they raise children, etc. The work of Gross et al. (1958) is typical of this approach. Their research instruments emphasize statements such as whether or not school superintendents should "carry out decisions of the school committee which (they) believe to be unsound," or "consult with staff members about filling vacant teaching positions."

It is our belief that these specific descriptions have extremely limited usefulness as variables for describing a large number of role relationships. They do not apply to mother-son or friend-friend interactions, for example. In addition, the number of such specific variables appears to be almost limitless.

As an alternative approach, we feel that the development of general properties of role relationships represents a surer path for the creation of theory (as suggested by Cassirer, 1953). General properties are universal quantities; they apply to each unit of analysis, regardless of its specific content, and without resorting to what

may be described as a kind of "dummy-variable," either-or technique. Within a population of role relationships this latter type of variable tends to produce highly skewed distributions, often to the point where only one unit would be scored "yes." For example, the variable "drills teeth" applies to dentists but to few (no) other roles. Such distributions are not useful for delineating classes of units and therefore do not aid in the production of the kinds of propositions of interest here.

It is somewhat paradoxical, perhaps, that George Homans (1964), who has been outspokenly critical of the concept of role, provides some of the best examples of the kinds of general variables we would suggest. Frequency of interaction and number of different activities are examples of variables that may be measured for all social relationships, either interpersonal or at the level of role, in any society and at any point in time. Similarly, Morris' (1966) typology of norms is based upon variables that can be applied not only to economic or political or scientific norms, as he suggests, but to norms that no longer exist or have yet to emerge. Hage (1965) has developed a list of eight general variables in a theory of organizations. Parsons' (1951) five pattern variables for the analysis of roles and/or role relationships are also general in character. Each of these examples represents general variables that can be applied across all units of a particular type.

In looking for variables which apply across all role relationships we may find that we uncover variables which apply across times and cultures as well. The advantages of such properties are many. For example, Durkheim's (1951) comparison of suicide rates among Catholics, Protestants, and Jews tells us little about cultures in which these religions do not exist unless some general variable, such as "the degree of regulation," is conceptualized as underlying the findings.[3] By being independent of time general variables may also make the evolution of specific role relationships amenable to study. Changing technology alters the behavior between the doctor and patient, between the mother and the child, or between the farmer and his helper, but the frequency of interaction, the duration of interaction, the relative choice of activities and other variables such as these can always be applied to these relationships. We can compare the scores on these variables for doctors and patients in Boston in 1760, 1860, and 1960 if the data are available.

The Choice of Variables II:
An Illustrative List
of General Variables

Although it is easy to say that the variables used in research aimed at developing a theory of role relationships should be "general" some might feel that it would be difficult to generate such variables. As we have specified our suggested unit of analysis (the role relationship) and population for sampling, we here suggest a provisional list of those general variables that we expect at this time will be most useful in developing a theory of role relationships. These variables were generated by considering a system of coordinates which we have called "elements" and "quantities." The elements are defined in a manner similar to the system advanced by Dodd (summarized by Lundberg, 1956)—in terms of who, what, where, when, and why. These seemed to us to be five fundamental elements of all relationships, and, therefore, a useful beginning point for the selection of general variables. Each role relationship involves occupants, activities, locations, occurrences (times), and goals, and therefore the general variables must refer to characteristics of these elements.

Our next step was to look for inherent aspects of these elements, or basic quantities, which could be used to generate general variables. In Table 2, we have used the basic quantities of scope, intensity, integration, independence, and value. This is by no means an exhaustive list of quantities, but it does represent a starting point for the generation of variables. These quantities also have the advantage of re-

ferring to some basic concepts in the sociological literature.[4]

Scope refers to how many while intensity represents how much of each element is present in a given relationship. For example, how many occupants, or the uniqueness of the occupants, can be measured independently of how much intensity, or compartmentalization. Thus, most individuals participate in few mother-son relationships (i.e., the relationship has few occupants on the average in society), and there is also very low compartmentalization. An uncle-nephew relationship also has relatively few occupants, but, depending on the society, may be quite compartmentalized.

The integration of the relationship refers to the articulation of the relationship vis-à-vis other relationships while the independence represents the amount of choice that is allowed by society. Again, while these two quantities may be highly correlated, it is possible to measure them separately. For example, we may have considerable dovetailing between our activities in some relationships with many other relationships and at the same time exercise some choice in what activities we perform in the role. Thus, the activities of the judge-defense lawyer dovetail significantly with the activities of at least three counterpositions attached to this relationship, defendant or client, jury member, district attorney. At the same time, the defense lawyer has considerable choice over what he does in the courtroom. Some work relationships are highly formalized in industrial societies, e.g., insurance salesman-client, worker-foreman, while other relationships such as therapist-client, and dean-president of the university are not likely to be formalized.

In Table 2 one of the elements, goals (why), and one of the quantities, value, are given special treatment, and are placed in a somewhat isolated location. This reflects our own discomfort with their inclusion in the classification system. Although we did not find it difficult to generate general variables using these characteristics it did seem to us that these

Table 2 The General Variables of Role Relationships

Quantities	Elements				
	Occupants	Activities	Locations	Occurrences	Goals
Scope of the relationship	Average number of occupants (uniqueness)	Average number of activities (specificity)	Average number of locations (availability)	Average number of occurrences (frequency)	Average number of goals (purposiveness)
Intensity of the relationship	Average distance between occupants (compartmentalization)	Average act effort	Average location compactness	Average duration of occurrences	Average goal drive
Integration of the relationship	Average occupant overlap (common role sets)	Average act dovetailing (articulation)	Average communality of locations	Average simultaneity of occurrences	Average goal compatability (legitimacy)
Independence of the relationship	Average degree of occupant choice (replaceability)	Average degree of activity choice (formalization)	Average degree of location choice (movability)	Average degree of occurrence choice	Average degree of goal choice (freedom)
Value of the relationship	Average value of partners (sentiment)	Average value of activities (pleasure)	Average value of locations	Average value of occurrences	Average value of goals (importance)
	(who-whom)	(what)	(where)	(when)	(why)

properties were on a less "objective" level than the others in the system. In order to ascertain what goals are relevant to a given relationship, it is necessary to enter into the feelings of the participants. Similarly, one must make important psychological inferences to determine the various "values" involved. On the other hand, a sensitive observer may more or less ascertain the appropriate scores on each of the other variables without entering into the thoughts and feelings of the participants. Perhaps the question of "why" in the scientific sense is best asked only in terms of relationships among variables at this more objective level, and the "subjective" column and row should not be included in the system at all.

The cross-classification of five quantities and five elements generates 25 general variables. In some cases they correspond to familiar concepts, e.g., the number of occurrences is the frequency of interaction, the value of the occupants is the degree of sentiment. In some cases, the general variables appear to us to represent new concepts, at least new within the context of the role literature. The degree of occupant choice or replaceability, and the number of locations or availability, intuitively appear to be important variables and yet they do not seem to be prominent in the literature. Similarly, some of the concepts of the human ecologists which appear in Table 2, specifically duration, scheduling, and compactness, have not normally been applied in the context of role theory.

Finally, we wish to reemphasize that we have no reason to believe that Table 2 exhausts the list of possibly useful general variables. We have not continued to search for additional variables because we feel that 25 is sufficient to begin the development of a theory and because we believe that we have isolated some central variables.

The Prospective Utility of a New Approach

There are at least three criteria by which an approach can be evaluated: (a) the general fruitfulness of the approach; (b) the generality or contribution to parsimony of the approach, and (c) the relevance of the approach to major problems in the area. Let us consider each of these as they apply to the approach outlined above.

The Criterion of Fruitfulness

Essentially, this criterion concerns the generation of insights and hypotheses and the further specification of existing hypotheses so as to set the limits under which they operate. In the case of the evaluation of an approach (as opposed to a "theory") such generation stems from what might be described as a "cuing" function. Does the approach "bring to mind"—the mind of the investigator—new questions? Some of our own thinking may serve to illustrate the prospective fruitfulness of this particular approach:

(1) Although Homans has pointed to the frequency of occurrence of interaction as a major variable, other aspects of time seem to us to have been neglected. For example, it seems plausible that there is an important relationship between the average duration of occurrences and the average distance between partners. As role occupants spend longer periods of time together, they should reduce the compartmental nature of the role relationship and expose more and more of themselves. The classic stories of the intimate revelations of persons seated together on long train or plane trips—a one-shot, but long duration relationship—fit here particularly well.

Similarly, we can develop propositions relating properties of space or locations. Even if we cannot here give the answer, we can at least ask what consequences availability has for the compactness and communality of locations.

(2) The juxtaposition of spatial and temporal variables, most often used by ecologists, with occupant and activity variables, more typical of role analysis, suggests several ideas. For example, the extent to which activities within a given relation-

ship dovetail into activities within other relationships might place considerable pressure on the generation of locations in which multiple relationships may be enacted at once. It may also mean a greater need for the scheduling of occurrences so that the multiple role-playing involved in "articulated" activities may be systematically pursued.

(3) Consider Homan's hypothesis that the greater the sentiment the greater the frequency of interaction. Several other variables may be introduced to further specify this hypothesis. For example, the degree of occupant choice may affect the strength of the association. Where there is little choice, the hypothesis might not hold. The slave-master relationship is perhaps the extreme example. It might also be argued that high formalization of activities would have the same effect. The relationship between ticket taker and commuter is a case in point. Where the number of different kinds of acts (specificity) is small, we might not expect high frequency to lead to high sentiment—if this is the causal direction of the original hypothesis. The single act, purchase of a newspaper in a customer-newspaper vendor relationship is an example. If location compactness is high, on the other hand, this might be conducive towards greater sentiment. Similarly, private locations might strengthen the association between frequency of interaction and degree of sentiment. In short, each of the variables in the system may be examined, specifying the conditions under which Homan's major postulate is most likely to be correct.

It should also be noted that hypotheses can be generated by using other sociological and psychological variables. For example, individuals with particular personality characteristics may tend to have certain patterns of social relationships. Organizations that have certain characteristics of power or rules may have certain patterns of social relationships. We do not mean to imply that our system of variables is self-contained, only that the specification of the properties of role rela-

tionships allows for the development of a theory of roles and, for that matter, the development of many other kinds of sociological and social-psychological propositions.

The Criterion of Generality
A second major consideration in evaluating approaches is whether or not they are applicable to a broad range of problems and phenomena within the field. The approach limited to one or two small problems or phenomena is limited in its ultimate utility, regardless of how well it helps explain its specific focus. We have already noted that it is our feeling that general variables have distinct advantages in the role area because they are applicable across all role relationships. We also feel that our approach has an advantage in its potential for applicability to other intellectual problems. Most of the variables can be easily applied to an analysis of interaction between individuals on the interpersonal level. Thus, in analyzing concrete cases of interaction we may specify how much act effort was involved, how long it lasted, how scheduled it was, how much choice the actors had in selecting the other to interact with, etc. We can then compare the differences between individuals in either similar or different role relationships, and relate these to personality variables. Similarly, interactions between organizations or even societies, can be analyzed with the same set of variables.

We have already suggested that the study of relationships does not preclude the analysis of positions, the unit of analysis most frequently employed in role research. A position can be conceptualized as a set of relationships that can be scored on these variables. Different positions not only have different numbers of relationships attached to them but the averages for any of the scope, intensity, integrations, and independence variables can be different as well.

For those who prefer the approach of expectations to that of interaction, it is still possible to use the same variables, substituting the term expectation. Individuals can have expectations about the frequency of interaction or the amount of disclosure or the amount of effort. Is this not the meaning of statements such as individual X doesn't come to see us very often; or he never says much about himself; or he isn't trying to make the relationship work? Each of these statements represents a violation of an expectation but of an important expectation that in different degrees can be applied to any role relationship.

The Criterion of Relevance to Major Problems

As Underwood (1957: p. 185) has commented, "the fact that the theory suggests research does not mean that it is automatically significant research." A similar question should be raised about any "approach." Unfortunately, we have few useful indicators for predicting significance. One of these might be whether or not the research is aimed at intellectual problems which have interested several students in the field. In the area of sociology, these problems tend to be defined by specific dependent variables, with the hypotheses for research phrased in terms of prediction through the use of various independent variables.

In a sense, our approach suffers by this criterion. As we claim that no previous analyst has specifically used the variables we suggest at the role relationship level the questions with some history in the field are currently phrased in very different ways than we would phrase them. Nevertheless, as in the case of Homans' hypotheses, we feel that our approach has definite relevance if considered in other than a routine manner.

For example, much of the recent research in the role area has concentrated on questions of role strain, conflict, dissensus, or ambiguity (Kahn et al., 1964; Gross et al., 1958). We feel that a focus on the general properties of role relationships may bring to light new perspectives on even these questions. Thus, role conflict is often thought to occur when two partners of an individual playing a given role expect different behavior. A relational scheme can add to this conception. Can the person in the focal role "compartmentalize" his relationship with each of the partners, keeping each from knowing what he does vis-à-vis the other, and thus meet the different expectations of both? Or is compartmentalization deviant in these role relationships as defined by society? Is the contested behavior visible in time and space to both partners or is some kind of deception possible? Is not one major type of role conflict defined, to a great extent, by our concept of "independence?"

Another set of problems concerns the basic question of integration. Our scheme of general variables suggests five ways in which integration of relationships may occur, and thus allows an extension of some or Durkheim's ideas. For example, for Durkheim integration is defined either in terms of values, or of number of social relationships or of functional interdependence. Our concepts of role set overlap and communality of locations suggest additional ways in which integration can occur. It should be noted that the general variables allow the development of many hypotheses about when each type of integration might occur.

Finally, we might note that the reader may object that we have not developed a theory in this paper, and that this is the main function of even integrative "think-pieces." It is only theory, he might feel, which leads to meaningful research. It is our feeling that the variables and units of analysis in terms of which the student thinks are the structure upon which substantive theory must be built. In "underdeveloped" areas of science, those without substantiated relationships between variables, the cuing functions of a systematic approach may prove more fruitful than any "premature" theory.

References

Bruce Biddle and Edwin Thomas, eds., *Role Theory: Concepts and Research* (New York: John Wiley & Sons, Inc., 1966).

Peter M. Blau, *Exchange and Power in Social Life* (New York: John Wiley & Sons, Inc., 1964).

Ernest Cassirer, *Substance and Function* (New York: Dover Publications, 1953).

Emile Durkheim, *Suicide* (New York: Free Press, Div. of The Macmillan Company, 1951).

Eric Fromm, *Escape from Freedom* (New York: Holt, Rinehart & Winston, Inc., 1941).

Neal Gross, Ward Mason, and Alexander McEachern, *Explorations in Role Analysis* (New York: John Wiley & Sons, Inc., 1958).

Jerald Hage, "An Axiomatic Theory of Organizations," *Administrative Science Quarterly* 10 (December 1965): 289–321.

John K. Hemphill, *Dimensions of Executive Positions* (Columbus, Ohio: Bureau of Business Research, The Ohio State University, 1960).

George Homans, *The Human Group* (New York: Harcourt Brace Jovanovich, Inc., 1950).

George Homans, "Bringing Men Back In," *American Sociological Review* 29 (December 1964): 809–18.

Edward E. Jones, Keith E. Davis, and Kenneth J. Gergen," Role-Playing Variations and Their Informational Value for Person Perception," pp. 171–79 in Biddle and Thomas (1966).

Robert L. Kahn, Donald M. Wolfe, Robert P. Quinn, J. Diedrick Snoek, and Robert A. Rosenthal, *Organizational Stress* (New York: John Wiley & Sons, Inc., 1964).

George A. Lundberg, "Some Convergences in Sociological Theory," *American Journal of Sociology* 62 (July 1956): 21–27.

Robert K. Merton, *Social Theory and Social Structure* (New York: Free Press, Div. of The Macmillan Company, 1957).

Richard T. Morris, "A Typology of Norms," pp. 110–12 in Biddle and Thomas (1966).

Theodore M. Newcomb, "Foreward," pp. v–vi in Biddle and Thomas (1966).

Oscar A. Oeser and Frank Harary, "Role Structures: A Description in Terms of Graph Theory," pp. 92–102 in Biddle and Thomas (1966).

Talcott Parsons, *The Social System* (New York: Free Press, Div. of The Macmillan Company, 1951).

Ralph M. Stogdill and L. Shartle, *Patterns of Administrative Performance* (Columbus, Ohio: Bureau of Business Research, The Ohio State University, 1960).

Edwin Thomas and Bruce Biddle, "The Nature and History of Role Theory," pp. 3–19 in Biddle and Thomas (1966).

Benton J. Underwood, *Psychological Research* (New York: Appleton-Century Crofts, 1957).

Hans Zetterberg, *On Theory and Verification in Sociology* (Totowa, N.J.: Bedminster Press, 1963).

Notes

1 This work was supported by the United States Air Force Office of Scientific Research, grant AFOSR-926-65. This is a revised version of a paper titled "Research Toward the Development of Role Theory: A New Approach," given at the annual meetings of the American Sociological Association, Chicago, 1965.

2 It might be noted that these three choices apply to many different kinds of theoretical inquiries and not just to the study of role relationships.

3 Durkheim seems to have recognized this problem to some extent, as he ends his discussion by saying that the content of the religious dogmas did not make a difference, but, instead, the number of such dogmas or beliefs was the key.

4 Integration is a classical concept, dating from the work of Durkehim. Intensity was implicitly involved in the work of Toennies and Simmel in their discussions of the movement of societies from blood relationships to economic ones. Value has been most widely used recently, e.g., Blau (1964) and Homans (1961). Scope and independence are less frequently mentioned. The latter is implied in the work of Eric Fromm (1941).

Chapter 9 Phenomenology: The Search for New Perspectives

WHAT IS PHENOMENOLOGY?

Quentin Lauer

With the passage of time it becomes more and more difficult to determine what the words "phenomenology" and "phenomenological" are supposed to mean in the contexts in which they are used. Like the terms "existentialism" and "existential" it has become fashionable to designate thereby some sort of profound, recondite, and very up-to-date approach to philosophy or science, without it being entirely clear in what sense the terms are being applied. There is a sense, of course, in which this vague use is justified, since every attempt to get away from speculative construc- tionism and to limit oneself to the data which are presented in consciousness— describing rather than explaining them—is to that extent phenomenological, at least in method. Still, the sort of vagueness which goes with modishness leads to con- fusion and makes for a terminology al- most empty of meaning. In recent years, for example, phenomenology has in some minds become so intimately bound up with existentialism that the two terms are used almost indiscriminately, despite sig- nificant differences in the attitudes repre- sented by the two titles. The reason for this may be that the thought of Jean-Paul Sartre, which is both phenomenological and existential, it taken as typical. Many thinkers, such as Martin Heidegger and Gabriel Marcel, who consider their own approach to philosophy as phenomeno- logical, have expressly indicated their de- sire not to be identified with the direction represented by Sartre. Others, such as Jean Hering or Dietrich von Hildebrand, would see no sense in referring to their thought as in any way "existential."

In whatever context the term phenome- nology is used, however, it refers back to the distinction introduced by Kant be- tween the *phenomenon* or appearance of reality in consciousness, and the *nou- menon,* or being of reality in itself. Kant himself did not develop a phenomenology as such, but since his *Critique of Pure Reason* recognizes scientific knowledge only of *phenomena* and not at all of *nou- mena,* his critique can be considered a sort of phenomenology. According to this position, whatever is known is phenome- non, precisely because to be known means to appear to consciousness in a special way, so that what does not in any way appear is not known —at least not by speculative reason. Still, according to Kant, it is possible to *think* what is not *known,* and this we think of as a "thing- in-itself" or *noumenon,* of which the *phe- nomenon* is the known aspect. This sort of phenomenology, which will restrict scientific knowledge to appearances, is di- rected both against the rationalism of Descartes, which seeks a rational knowl- edge of all reality, and against the phe- nomenism of Hume, which will accept no scientific knowledge at all except that of mathematics. Kant insists that there can be true scientific knowledge which is not mathematical, but he denies that there can be such a knowledge in metaphysics.

The first philosopher to characterize his own approach to philosophy as phenome- nology was Hegel. Like Kant he con- tended that phenomena are all we have to go on, but unlike Kant he was convinced that they afforded a sufficient basis for a universal science of being. He saw no need of even thinking of an unknown thing-in-itself. Phenomena, according to Hegel, reveal all that is to be revealed—not simply in themselves but through the medium of the dialectical process, which is the necessary process of human thought. Beginning with the simplest form of consciousness, which is immediate sense perception, he brings us through consciousness of self (in a series of dialectics which reveal the social and historical nature of knowledge) to reason, wherein reality is reduced to unity, ultimately to that of the Absolute Idea, Absolute Spirit, which *is* all reality. To be *fully* conscious of self is to be fully conscious of all reality, since the ultimate self is all reality. In all this Hegel sees no departure from the original phenomenon, since the dialectical process constitutes an unbreakable chain which has never lost contact with the first experience.

With the positivism of Ernst Mach and of the Vienna Circle, which drew its inspiration from Mach, we find another kind of phenomenology, which is not ordinarily characterized as such. In spirit these men were closer to Kant than they were to Hegel, since they preferred Kant's rejection of metaphysics (at least from the point of view of speculative reason) to Hegel's affirmation of it. They would ask no questions at all with regard to reality, convinced as they were that to such questions there were no answers; they were simply satisfied with describing consciousness, the data of which are susceptible only of description, not of explanation. And in this description they found no grounds for affirming a reality, whether it be the "substance" of Spinoza or the "thing-in-itself" of Kant. An approach so exclusively descriptive as this is obviously completely nonmetaphysical. Unfortunately, however, many particular positivist interpretations have a tendency not only to eliminate reality as an object of scientific inquiry but to reject any reality whatever, a position which in its negative way is just as metaphysical as its op-

posite. When Freud in his clinical work confines himself to a pure description of the behaviors he has observed, his approach, too, can be called phenomenological, at least to the extent that any description of what is observed will always be phenomenological.[1] It is, of course, problematical just how successful one can be in completely avoiding any metaphysics whatever—unless one confines oneself to a pure analysis of meaning, which is what the logical positivists of the Vienna Circle do. This results in a sort of mathematics of language, which is probably more purely descriptive than even the most completely conscious phenomenology.

When the term "phenomenology" is used today, it usually refers to the philosophy of Edmund Husserl or of someone of those who have drawn their inspiration from him. From the beginning of his philosophical career, Husserl was opposed to what he called the "dualism" of Kant, the "constructionism" of Hegel, and the "naturalism" or "psychologism" of the positivists. He agrees with them in asserting that only phenomena are *given,* but he will claim that *in* them is given the very *essence* of that which is. Here there is no concern with reality as existing, since existence is at best contingent and, as such, can add to reality nothing which would be the object of scientific knowledge. If one has described phenomena, one has described all that can be described, but in the very constant elements of that description is revealed the *essence* of what is described. Such a description can say nothing regarding the existence of what is described, but the phenomenological "intuition" in which the description terminates tells us *what* its object *necessarily* is. To know this is to have an "essential" and hence a "scientific" knowledge of being. Contemporary phenomenologists usually follow the development elaborated by Husserl—at least in its methodological aspects—though many of them have rejected the idealistic and metaphysical implications of Husserl's own position. They consider as phenomenology's distinctive mark its capacity to reveal essences, not its refusal to come to terms with "existing" reality. Unlike the investigations of Husserl, those of his followers range over a very wide field, so that there is scarcely an aspect of philosophy or of science which has not been investigated phenomenologically. To mention but a few: We find that Heidegger, Jaspers, Sartre, Marcel, and Conrad-Martius are developing the phenomenological method in its ontological implications; Pfänder, Geiger, Merleau-Ponty, Ricoeur, and Binswanger apply it to psychology; Scheler, Von Hildebrand, and Hartmann have developed a phenomenological ethics and general theory of values; Otto, Hering, and Van der Leeuw have studied religion in the same way; while in esthetics Simmel, Ingarden, Malraux, Duffrenne, and Lipps have been conspicuously successful. Among these same authors we find contributions to epistemological, sociological, linguistic, and logical developments. All are in one way or another concerned with the *essences* of the concepts employed in these disciplines.

Though there is a certain unity of purpose discernible in all these efforts, still there is a certain disadvantage in speaking of the phenomenological method or of phenomenology, without further qualification. The disadvantage is twofold. First of all, the genius of Kant has been so influential that one almost inevitably thinks of phenomena in terms of the Kantian dichotomy of *phenomenon* and *noumenon,* thus giving rise to the opinion that a phenomenology must either be a phenomenism a la Hume, which simply refuses to go beyond sensible appearances, or else an introductory stage to a sort of noumenology, which would be some kind of modified Scholasticism, wherein the being which is sought would be something "behind" the phenomenon. The second disadvantage is that, even where the distinction between phenomenology and phenomenism is recognized, there is a tendency to group all phenomenologists together, without attention to the really great differences between the phenomenologies of Scheler, Husserl, Marcel, and

Heidegger—to mention a few. It is true, of course, that Husserl provided the impetus for what might loosely be termed "the phenomenological movement," but in so doing he evolved a philosophy which is peculiarly his own, in which no one of his disciples followed him to the limit. Still, if we are to understand what phenomenology means as a contemporary philosophical attitude, we must first understand what it meant in the mind of its founder, Edmund Husserl.

.   .   .

The problem of reconciling reality and thought about reality is as old as philosophy—we might say, as old as thought itself. The problem is complicated by the obvious fact that we cannot know reality independently of consciousness, and we cannot know consciousness independently of reality—to do so would be to meet the one and the other in isolation, which is an impossibility. We meet consciousness only as consciousness of something; and we meet reality only as a reality of which we are conscious. It seems reasonable to assume that the normal individual will, without reflection, see a certain duality in his experiences of the world about him: In them there is a world which he experiences, and which he assumes to be independently [*sic*] of himself pretty much as he experiences it; and there is also the experience wherein he grasps this world, which he assumes to be distinct from the world. It is also reasonable to assume that he has never been able to analyze his experiences to such an extent that he can isolate—the way one does in analyzing water into hydrogen and oxygen (if even that is possible)—the "elements" which belong to the "independent" world of reality and those which have been contributed by the very act of experiencing this reality. Finally, it seems reasonable to assume that he will not be too much concerned.

The philosopher, however, is committed to penetrating this mystery—for mystery it is—and to coming up with some sort of consistent reconciliation of the two worlds, if he is to continue plying his trade. In a certain sense, the history of philosophy is the record of a series of attempts to make this reconciliation. The problem as it faces us, and as it has faced philosophers from the beginning of philosophizing—apart from the accuracy of the original judgment which the "normal" individual makes—offers a limited number of approaches to a solution. One can approach it from the side of the reality of which we are conscious, from that of the consciousness we have of reality, or from the point of view of a contact between the two. Despite the limited number of approaches, however, there seems to be no limit to the explanations which have been and will continue to be attempted.

The phenomenologist is no exception in this almost universal quest for a solution.[2] Whatever may be his particular position, he seeks to reduce the problem to its simplest terms and *in* them, rather than *from* them, to find a solution, or at least, the approach to a solution. According to the phenomenologist, if there is a solution at all, it must be contained in the *data* of the problem—although, of course, there is a disagreement as to what the data are. The point of agreement, however—and this is what makes each a phenomenologist—is that only phenomena are *given* and that therefore, if an answer is to be found, it must be sought in phenomena. There will be a disagreement as to just what are to be considered as phenomena and as to what can be discovered in them, but there will be agreement that we cannot enlist the aid of the nonphenomenal in seeking our solution. As Maurice Merleau-Ponty, one of the most coherent of the phenomenologists, has expressed it, "Phenomenology is an inventory of consciousness as of that wherein a universe resides."[3] If we are to know what anything is—and this the phenomenologist will do—we must examine the consciousness we have of it; if this does not give us an answer, nothing will.

The consciousness with which the phenomenologist is here concerned, is not consciousness as a psychic function, in the way it is, for example, to the experimental psychologist. He is concerned with consciousness as a kind of being which things exercise, the only kind of being directly available to the investigator. Thus, for him, consciousness is best expressed by the German word *Bewusstsein,* which means the kind of being an object of knowledge has in being known. This is not necessarily an identification of being and being-known, but it is an assertion that the only key we have to being is in examining its being-known. Now, even a superficial examination of any act of consciousness will reveal two inescapable facts: (1) It cannot be isolated from other acts of consciousness, but belongs to a whole life of consciousness, is conditioned by all the dispositions of which a subject is capable, is prepared for and colored by the whole series of conscious acts which have preceded it; (2) it is never completely arbitrary, in the sense of being conditioned only subjectively; it is what it is because it is consciousness of this or that object, which, precisely as an object, is in some sense independent of the individual act wherein it is grasped; there is some similarity between the experiences of one subject and another when faced with a similar situation, no matter what the previous experiences of the two may have been.

The attempts to reduce the problem to its simplest terms, however, is not so simple after all. If the only approach we have is through consciousness, and, if every act of consciousness is a complex of inseparable elements, some objective and some subjective, the analysis of consciousness which will reveal to us the very meaning of being is a complex affair. The phenomenologist, however, is convinced that this analysis can be made and that in making it he can return to the very origin of consciousness, distinguishing what is pure consciousness from all the accretions which custom, prejudice, assumption, and tradition have built around it. When he has uncovered consciousness in this pure form, he is convinced that he will have arrived at an understanding of the only being which can have significance for him.

In speaking thus of phenomenology we have admittedly come to treat exclusively of the kind of phenomenology advocated by Edmund Husserl and by those who follow him more or less closely. In this sense phenomenology is both a method and a philosophy. As a method it outlines the steps which must be taken in order to arrive at the pure phenomenon, wherein is revealed the very essence not only of appearances but also of that which appears.[4] As a philosophy it claims to give necessary, essential knowledge of that which is,[5] since contingent existence cannot change what reason has recognized as the very essence of its object.[6] In the course of its investigations, therefore, it discovers (or claims to discover) that the quasi infinity of objects which go to make up an experienced world can be described in terms of the consciousness wherein they are experienced. Phenomenology is conceived as a return to "things," as opposed to illusions, verbalisms, or mental constructions, precisely because a "thing" *is* the direct object of consciousness in its purified form. The color "red" is no less a thing than is a horse, since each has an "essence" which is entirely independent of any concrete, contingent existence it may have. It is sufficient that the experience of red can be as clearly distinguished from the experience of green as can the experience of horse from that of man. The dispute as to whether colors are "primary" or "secondary" qualities is entirely without significance; each color has an essence which can be grasped in consciousness, precisely because the essence of any color is contained in the experience of that color. The fact that the content of this experience is an essence is manifest from the fact that it can be clearly distinguished from whatever is essentially something else.[7] In this sense an imaginary object has its distinct *essence* just as truly as does a "real" object. Whether an object is *real* or *fictitious* can be determined by an analysis of the act of which it is object.

All this, however, would be without significance if it were not aimed at discovering "objective" essences, which are what they are not only independently of contingent existence but also independently of any arbitrary meaning which a subject *wants* to give them. Though it is of the essence of an object to be related to a subject, the phenomenologist will deny that "things" act upon subjects in such a way as to engender this relation or that subjects simply "produce" objects. He will insist that by investigating pure consciousness he can discover a relationship which is truly objective, in the sense that its validity is not derived from the conscious act wherein the relationship resides, and is necessary, in the sense that it could not be otherwise, no matter who the subject grasping the object may be. Husserl's own phenomenological investigations were, it is true, chiefly logical, epistemological, and to a certain extent ontological. Still, phenomenology even as he conceived it is at its persuasive best in the realm of values.

Realistic systems of philosophy have always found the question of moral, religious, esthetic, and social values a particularly difficult hurdle to clear since the subjective elements in all value judgments are too obvious to be ignored. One can, of course, explain evaluations in terms of the objective values which are being judged and then describe objective values in terms of their relationship to an evaluating subject; but this sort of thing looks suspiciously like going around in a circle. It is perhaps for this reason that there were no consistent attempts to evolve theories of value, until the days when idealism was enjoying widespread triumph. Idealistic theories, however, have always run the risk of becoming so subjective that the very concept of value loses any communicable significance. Husserl himself was not particularly successful—we might even say that he was eminently unsuccessful—in coming to terms with the complicated problems of value,[8] but his theories, particularly in their ontological aspects, inspired others to look for a world of values which are *what* they are independently of any particular or general judgments regarding them. According to Scheler, Hartmann, Von Hildebrand, and others such values are to be *discovered in* things and not to be *imposed on* things by an observing—and evaluating—subject. And the techniques for discovering them are to be the phenomenological techniques of objective analysis and description, resulting in an *"intuition"* of value essences (essential values).

.   .   .

Phenomenology, as we have pointed out, is a study of consciousness. It is not, however, a psychological study of consciousness. Rather, it is an attempt to examine each act of consciousness as a "pure" act of consciousness, seeking to discover in each its essence. Now in 1900, while writing his *Logical Investigations,* Husserl submitted consciousness itself to a phenomenological investigation. He came to the conclusion that it is the very essence of consciousness to be "consciousness of" something. Thirty years later, in the *Cartesian Meditations,* which was to be the last of Husserl's major works published during his lifetime, he expressed the same insight by saying that the essence of the Cartesian *cogito* contained the *cogitatum* as immediately as the *cogito* itself. In both expressions Husserl was saying that an act of consciousness and its object are inseparable or, as he said in *Ideas 1,* published in 1913, they are but the subjective and objective aspects of the same thing. Thus, to know an act of consciousness adequately, which is to say essentially, is to know its object. What is more, it is to know the object absolutely, in a state of isolation from the contingent conditions of its existence, which is at best always subject to doubt. To know, then, the essence of any conscious act is to know the essence of its object, and that is to have scientific knowledge of its object.

Now, objects of consciousness are many and varied. They may be things or thoughts, persons or events, categories or states of affairs, or they may be mental constructs such as numbers or geometrical figures. Each of these objects has an essence which can be "seen" immediately in an adequate view of the act of consciousness wherein it is contained. The last two, however, differ from all the rest in being entirely products of consciousness itself and therefore not subject to the conditions which progressive experience imposes on all other objects. Mathematical essences are static and changeless; they can be fixed once and for all and described with perfect exactitude. Of other essences it is possible to have strict knowledge, but it must be a knowledge conformed to the types of essence with which it is concerned. Here, too, a distinction must be made. If the object in question is a physical thing it is experienced constantly as identical, which is to say that it has a "nature," which along broad lines at least can be determined with exactitude. Where, however, it is the essence of the phenomenon itself which has to be determined, there is no fixity of nature, there is only the mobility of the vital flow of consciousness, which will cease to be what it is if it is immobilized. Of the phenomenon no exact knowledge is possible, but this is not to say that its essence is not scientifically knowable. If the phenomenon has an essence at all, this essence is scientifically knowable and within somewhat broader limits describable, at least sufficiently to distinguish it from other essences. This is scientific knowledge of essences, since it is knowledge of essences *as they are,* which is to say, as nonfixed, morphological essences, which can be described in terms of "types," though not in terms of exactly determinable "classes."

In all this it may seem that the whole basis of phenomenology has been undermined, since no object can be known except in the appearance whereby it is present to consciousness, which appearance cannot be described with any degree of exactitude. Husserl's point, however, is that it can be described in a manner adequate to the essence in question. To describe this sort of essence *exactly* would be to falsify it, whereas to describe it in the way which the phenomenological method permits is to describe it within limits which are sufficiently narrow to permit that the knowledge based on it be called "scientific."

Instead, then, of undermining the basis of phenomenology, we might say that the modification introduced with the notion of a "morphological" essence has saved it from an impossible situation. Rather than the sort of science which is quite obviously not achievable in philosophy, phenomenology advocates an attempt to understand being in terms of essence, while recognizing that there must be a certain latitude in the conception of *what* essences are. Coupled with a real attempt at intersubjective understanding, the sort of essential insight which Husserl describes might well provide a basis for the dialogue whereby Plato sought to approach the essences of things. Though Husserl himself may have conceived it in a too-narrowly scientific sense, it is significant that phenomenology has provided a basis for tendencies as diverse as the personalism of Max Scheler, Martin Heidegger's philosophy of existence, Gabriel Marcel's Christian existentialism, and Maurice Merleau-Ponty's dialectical philosophy of form . . . .

References and Notes

1. Martin Heidegger, *Sein und Zeit,* 7th ed., (Tübingen, Germany: Max Niemeyer, Verlag, 1953), p. 35, says that the expression "descriptive phenomenology" is tautological—the two terms are inseparable.
2. We say "almost universal" because the positivist *claims,* at least, to be utterly unconcerned with the *what* of reality or of consciousness. His only objection to any "explanation" which may be given should be that he cannot understand what the explanation means, which is fair enough, if he remains there.
3. *La Structure du Comportement,* 3d ed., (Paris: Presses Universitaires de France, 1953), p. 215.
4. According to Husserl, there is no essence other than that discoverable in appearances.
5. "Phenomenology, which will be nothing less than a theory of essence contained in pure intuition," from *Ideen 1* edited by Walter Biemel on the basis of the author's own marginal notations to the 1922 edition (The Hague: Martinus Nijhoff, 1950), p. 154. "With regard to phenomenology, it wants to be a *descriptive* theory of essences," *ibid.,* p. 171. Among the followers of Husserl there is considerable divergence of emphasis, some stressing the *description* of phenomena, others stressing the discovery of *essences* in phenomena. As is so frequently the case, the differences seem to be traceable to the predispositions which each has brought with him in his approach to phenomenology.
   For a complete Bibliography of significant Husserliana, consult the author's *La Phénoménologie de Husserl* (Paris: Presses Universitaires de France, 1954).
6. If there is any difference at all between phenomenon and reality, it cannot be other than accidental, since the essence of that which is remains absolutely identical. "Immanent being, then, is undoubtedly absolute being, in the sense that, in principle, *nulla 're' indiget ad existendum,"* ibid., p. 115; cf. *Nachwort zu meinen Ideen* (Halle: Max Niemeyer, Verlag, 1930), p. 14.
7. Moritz Schlick has objected that phenomenology has labored hard to produce some very inconsequential distinctions, which distinctions are ultimately nothing more than the distinctions one chooses to assign to terms: cf. "Is there a Factual a Priori?", *Readings in Philosophical Analysis,* Feigl and Sellars, eds., (New York: Appleton-Century-Crofts, 1949) pp. 277–85. There is, it is true, in the works of the phenomenologists a suspicion that the distinctions they make are derived from convictions which antecede the use of the phenomenological method.
8. In a sort of diary, Husserl recounted, in September, 1916, his decision to pursue theoretical truth as a value in preference to other values in life. Neither here nor anywhere else, however, does he justify the objectivity of the value judgment itself. Cf. "Philosophie als strenge Wissenschaft," *Logos,* 1 (1911): 289–341, 338.

EXISTENTIAL PHENOMENOLOGY AND THE SOCIOLOGICAL TRADITION

Edward A. Tiryakian

A recent article observes that general theory in sociology is characterized by "a perplexing multivariety of basic orientations" and that the lack of a fundamental unity bars the "integration of all or even most of the existing sociological knowledge."[1] The purpose of the present paper is to reexamine the mainstream of sociology's theoretical tradition, placing in relief the elements for a general theory whose philosophical grounding is consonant with the broad movement of existential phenomenology.[2] At the conclusion I shall suggest the heuristic significance of this perspective and some of its methodological implications.

I shall not attempt to formulate a general theory of social existence, for this would be entirely premature, but so far as it demonstrates major areas of convergence in the sociological tradition which have not been explicitly recognized, this paper represents an important step in the direction of such a theory.

The Phenomenological School in Sociology

Although the history of sociology includes no accepted "existential sociology," various writers of texts on theory[3] have shown an awareness of the phenomenological approach. Figures in this "school," however, are usually treated as peripheral to the major sociological currents underlying contemporary sociology. The original phenomenological school of sociology flourished in German-speaking areas of Europe in the interwar period; moreover, phenomenological sociology was directly under the philosophical influence of Edmund Husserl and Martin Heidegger. Underlying both German sociology and phenomenology was a concern for the cultural crisis of European society that had manifested itself in the upheavals of World War I.

The person most clearly recognized as a figure in phenomenological sociology is Alfred Vierkandt (1867–1952), who saw sociology as a radically formal study of social phenomena. Quite in keeping with the phenomenological method, he stressed the necessity of grasping directly the "essential types," "ultimate facts" (including sentiments), and "meaningful wholes" in the inner life of social interaction and social groups. The pure description of intersubjective bonds, of the "spiritual" elements of collective life does not rely on an inductive approach to grasp the essence (*eidos* in Husserl's terminology) of the social phenomenon being considered. Because the direct apprehension of social essences cannot be achieved by means of analysis (in the sense of seeking to arrive at a whole by means of investigating component parts), Vierkandt gave primacy to understanding directly the integral wholeness of each society and social group, a wholeness manifested in the specific ethos, spirit, or way of life of distinct social systems.

Vierkandt hardly ranks as a major theorist today. Yet, his perspective on social phenomena as totalities in their formal structure is directly related to Gestalt psychology (also influenced by Husserl), on the one hand, and to the anthropological tradition of functionalism, which in its radical aspect stressed the total integration of culture as a unified whole, on the other. Ruth Benedict's well-known *Patterns of Culture,* which seeks to grasp the "essence" of the cultural ethos of certain non-Western societies, has a distinct affinity with Vierkandt's methodological stand. Thus, formal sociology, Gestalt psychology, and functionalism share as a basic point of departure the acceptance of structural wholes as the fundamental units of investigation.

Better-known figures in the phenomenological school are Max Scheler and Karl Mannheim, though they have not always been recognized primarily as phenomenologists. Spiegelberg in his excellent historical study of phenomenology[4] discusses the relation between Scheler and Husserl but omits Mannheim, while Timasheff in his survey of sociological theories[5] talks of the "isolated" Mannheim in the philosophical school but leaves out Scheler in discussing phenomenological sociology. Mannheim and Scheler are usually identified as major writers in the sociology of knowledge, but their *"Wissenssoziologie"* is not widely understood as an integral part of their phenomenological approach to sociology. Their common concern in this endeavor was with the cultural crisis of their age, characterized in part by the fragmentation and relativization of knowledge. I shall discuss Mannheim and Scheler at some length in this context, since their contributions to sociological theory have not been given the attention they deserve.

Mannheim's studies of *Weltanschauung* (a global perception of social reality) reflect in part the influence of Wilhelm Dilthey on German sociology. Dilthey had raised the significance for the social sciences *(Geisteswissenschaften)* of grasping the integral perception of a culture's life situation and world view. Taking his lead from this suggestion, Mannheim made thorough empirical investigations of the social basis of *Weltanschauungen,* which as collective mental products or collective representations of reality (in Durkheim's sense) are among the cultural products found in human society. Mannheim's approach is distinctly phenomenological, as may be seen in his important "On the Interpretation of 'Weltanschauung.'"[6] This is not surprising, for the notion of *Weltanschauung* implies the notion of *intentionality,* which plays a cardinal role in the doctrines of Husserl and his mentor, Franz Brentano.[7] Intentionali-

ty as an act of consciousness which directs the subject outward (i.e., consciousness is always relational, directed to something outside itself or as the phenomenologists state it, consciousness is always "consciousness of" something) is a crucial tenet of the existential-phenomenological movement. Mannheim's studies of world views represents a sociological extension of this notion, for a *Weltanschauung* is an intentional psychological act of a collectivity of subjects, the apprehension of their collective world of lived experience perceived as a totality.

Mannheim's approach is phenomenological in other related aspects. His careful attention to the types of meanings[8] given in the phenomenal presentation of cultural objects reflects very much Husserl's stress on the "meaningful" aspect of the intentional act: reduction to the essentials of a phenomenon involves unveiling successive layers of meaning, from the externally manifest to the core latent "noematic" content.[9] For Mannheim the notion of "structure" is cardinal and denotes the immanent unity of the social whole, a unity resting on the complementarity of conflicting social relationships and hence not fixed or "static." Not only is "structure" akin to "Gestalt" in psychology, but it is also very much related to Husserl's notion of the "constitution" of the objective field of consciousness. "Structure" is not an empirical social object any more than "constitution" is; yet it is a real object of the observer's perception. Without the presence of structure we could not perceive a meaningful region but only a disconnected series of unrelated (social) objects. It is the structure of things that gives us their meaning as wholes, and, since there are various layers of structure, various strata of meaning, any phenomenon has a certain ambiguity in its relation to its ground. For the sake of brevity I shall not develop Mannheim's ideas further along this line, but it should be realized by now that this phenomenological approach to "meaning" and "structure" is at the heart of functional analysis, particularly as formulated by Merton in his distinction between "manifest" and "latent" functions.[10]

Mannheim's "The Problem of Generations"[11] is also relevant, not so much as a seminal sociological study of structural sources of social change, but more, in this context, because it shows that Mannheim treated the spatial-temporal existence and historicity of social groups very much in the existential-phenomenological perspective. Inherent in this approach is the awareness that the existential space-time location of men and cultural objects does not coincide with an absolute space-time location; the latter is a construct derived from the world of experience (*Lebenswelt*). In this essay Mannheim refers to Heidegger, whose *Being and Time,* first published in 1927, has been a decisive influence in modern existential thought. He gives even more attention to Heidegger in "Competition as a Cultural Phenomenon,"[12] where, after discussing Heidegger's description of the everyday world and the impersonal *"das Man"* or "they" who act as the ubiquitous socializing agencies and manipulators of public knowledge, Mannehein comments,

The philosopher looks at this "They," this secretive Something, but he is not interested to find out how it arose; and it is just at this point, where the philosopher stops, that the work of the sociologist begins.[13]

This remark indicates the grounds of a fruitful collaboration between existential phenomenology and sociological research; far from entangling sociology in the cobwebs of metaphysics, phenomenology can sensitize it to major aspects of social reality. But perhaps I should reserve the "moral" of this article for the end, rather than making it in the middle.

For Mannheim, the sociology of knowledge as related to the study of *Weltanschauung* is not an abstract pursuit but an existential one, and this in a double sense. First, the methodology of the physical sciences is inappropriate for the sociology of knowledge because important items of knowledge are existentially determined in concrete historical situations, hence incapable of being measured quantitatively and interpreted on an absolute scale. We cannot assume that sociocultural units are constant in space and time, and this raises the methodological problem of measurement (e.g., how can we quantitatively compare a conservative American *Weltanschauung* in 1965 with a conservative German *Weltanschauung* in 1865?). The phenomenological method, which is more appropriate than that of the physical sciences in studying problems of this sort, signifies that

. . . certain insights concerning some qualitative aspect of the living process of history are available to consciousness only as formed by certain historical and social circumstances, so that the historico-social formation of the thinking and knowing subject assumes epistemological importance.[14]

Second, not only does the sociology of knowledge uncover the existential relations of knowledge to social structure but also the task of *Wissensoziologie* is itself an existential one, that of overcoming the relativism of the modern age. If knowledge is not absolute but rather determined by socio-historical processes, and, if social groups presently have opposed world views, can a phenomenologically based sociology overcome this fragmentation and thus prevent the dissolution of the modern world? Mannheim attempts to answer this existential question via his ideas of "relationism" and "socially unattached" intellectuals who can transcend conflicting perspectives.[15]

In this brief overview it is impossible to do justice to the richness of Max Scheler's phenomenological sociology[16] but some of its aspects may be rapidly indicated. Scheler's achievements of significance for sociology were (a) relating the intentionality of consciousness to specific forms of interaction; (b) phenomenological reductions of primary interpersonal psychological states, and (c) his attempt to arrive at ultimate, nonrelative values. As a sociologist, Scheler is probably best known for his sociology of values, but his grounding affective intentionality in social structure is an important link in the development of existential phenomenology and the sociology of knowledge as well. An important theme of the existential-phenomenological tradition (from Kierkegaard to Sartre, Jaspers, and other recent figures) is that human existence is disclosed in affective states: Our existential self *(Dasein)* is always a sentient self (even indifference is a feeling), and the structure of our orientation to our situation is a spatial-temporal one of emotiveness. "Rational man" is a useful construct, but it is an abstraction from the integral self. Scheler deepened this insight into the affective nature of experience by suggesting the interdependence between affect and social structure (i.e., social bonds and roles have an affective structural basis reflected in personality). Scheler's phenomenological approach, therefore, uncovered a significant link between personality and social structure.

The phenomenologists Vierkandt, Mannheim, and Scheler have not had many followers as such among contemporary sociologists. George Gurvitch, the foremost theorist in France, came in contact early with the phenomenological movement. Although his "sociology in depth"[17] also reflects the influence of such sources as von Wiese and Mauss, and, although Gurvitch has dissociated himself from formal phenomenology, his approach to social reality is very much an expression of existential phenomenology. His view of social structures as dynamic intersubjective realities is akin to Mannheim's notion of structure (and at odds with a notion of structure as a fixed entity that exists apart from a socio-historical process). Moreover, Gurvitch's rejection of social determinism and causality operating in social phenomena, his emphasis on the multiplicity of social times reflecting the multiplicity of social structures,[18] and his notion of the communal "we" as a

primary factor in the intentionality of consciousness (man experiences social reality as a part of a "we" no less directly than as an individual "I")—all these reflect his early formative contacts with phenomenology.

To round out the contemporary scene, mention should be made of Chambard's article on the social experiential meanings of religious symbols in India,[19] which also contains an excellent general discussion of the relation of phenomenology to sociology. Though little explicit attention has been given to phenomenology in American sociology, contacts with Scheler did influence the late Howard Becker.[20] Perhaps the sociologist who has been most active in developing phenomenological sociology is Harold Garfinkel. His doctoral dissertation[21] investigated the significance of a person's imputing motives to others; it is a phenomenological study of the changing intentionality of social objects, including others as personalities given as "wholes" in perception. In this work Garfinkel acknowledges the influence of both Husserl and Alfred Schutz, and the affinity with Scheler is also apparent. A later article[22] deals with the phenomenology of moral indignation as social affect, and more recently Garfinkel has presented data disclosing how individuals implicitly structure their situation vis-à-vis others.[23]

Existential Phenomenology in the Sociological Mainstream

The phenomenological tradition in sociology is not limited to the above recognized figures, for much of the theory of sociologists who are not identified with the existential-phenomenological movement is in keeping with its presuppositions. In this section, therefore, I shall argue that a meaningful methodological convergence exists in the works of Max Weber, Georg Simmel, Emile Durkheim, William I. Thomas, Pitirim Sorokin and Talcott Parsons, and that this convergence points to a more comprehensive theory of social existence.

In relating Max Weber to phenomenology, mention must be made of the intellectual ferment in Germany in his formative years concerning the nature of investigation into "cultural" phenomena. Wilhelm Dilthey had posited that the disciplines dealing with cultural phenomena or "spiritual products" *(the Geisteswissenschaften)* were to be sharply differentiated from those dealing with physical matter (the *Naturwissenschaften*): The logical status of the cultural sciences was of a different order due to the nature of their objects of inquiry (that is, their objects are mental products of human consciousness). Thus, a causal interpretation along the lines of a mechanistic model is precluded in historical studies: The human spirit transcends any cadre of classification which enables the physical sciences to study their objects with precision, and, furthermore, human behavior is permeated with value orientations. The methodology of the natural sciences treats values as irrelevant for an "objective" study of things and the dismissal of values limits the generality of positivistic methodology. Moreover, since the meaning we perceive in the world around us is grounded in the values we explicitly hold, social scientists and their studies are value laden, which does away with an "objective" interpretation of human events. Thus, runs Dilthey's argument, the precise, accurate measurements necessary to establish causal connections in the natural sciences are unavailable to the cultural disciplines. The latter, however, have a distinct methodological feature: Since the observer is a human being studying other human beings, he has access to their inner world of experience. This direct access is "sympathetic understanding" and "intuition" by means of which the observer can view cultural phenomena "from within."

Weber was ambivalent concerning Dilthey's famous dichotomy. On the one hand, he felt that there is but one scientific logic, which applies equally to natural and cultural phenomena.[24] The construc-tion of concepts is required for the empirical validation of statements concerning cultural as well as natural phenomena, and nothing in the nature of "cultural" objects prevents one from constructing general concepts. The observer's values affect his sociological observations (e.g., in the selection of his theoretical problem), but he can make them explicit and go on to treat objectively the role of values in the sociocultural phenomena he observes. Sociology should not accept the belief that the "irrational" basis of human life manifests itself in the unique and thus assume the uniqueness of a cultural phenomenon. On the contrary, the initial presupposition should be that human behavior may be interpreted by means of a "rationally consistent system of theoretical concepts."[25] We first begin the analysis of specific historical phenomena, argued Weber, by constructing logical "ideal types" on the assumption that actions are rational. Only when these ideal types qua categories of analysis are insufficient for the comprehension of an empirical course of events do we go on to look for "irrational" factors, but even then we do not assume that there are noumenal "things-in-themselves" which cannot be incorporated in a consistent theoretical framework.

On the other hand, Weber did accept important notions of the *Geisteswissen schaften,* notably the legitimacy of *"intuition"* and "understanding" *(Verstehen)* as modes of comprehending cultural phenomena which are in their nature irreducible to physical phenomena. Weber rejected a materialistic causal interpretation of history in terms of an economic determinism; he saw clearly that human behavior cannot be comprehended without reference to the motivation of human agents and to the subjective meanings they impute to their action.[26] This stress on the subjective meanings of the social situation is at the heart of Weber's sociology,[27] and it establishes a significant link between Weber and existential phenomenology.

Weber considered the intentionality of

social action crucial for sociological analysis,[28] and this is entirely in keeping with the basic tenet of existential thought, originating with Kierkegaard, that "subjectivity is truth" (namely, truth is always an experienced truth for the existent self). The latter proposition does *not* mean that the meaning a situation has for the subject cannot be communicated to others (which would make it truly "irrational"). Certainly, as Weber forcefully stated in his well-known means-end schema, "all interpretation of meanings, like all scientific observation, strives for clarity and verifiable accuracy of insight and comprehension."[29] Thus, seemingly irrational conduct, which may be a significant causal agent in social change, as in the case of charisma, may nevertheless be emotionally understood and intellectually interpreted by the observer in terms of its meaning to the actors and its influence on subsequent social action.

Weber's methodology of *Verstehen*, thus, turns out to be upon closer examination an expression of existential phenomenology. It requires the sociological observer to uncover the subjective meanings manifested in historical phenomena and to relate one set of meanings to another (e.g., relating economic action to religious motivation). The major task of sociological investigation is to elucidate the dimensions of historical social structures; this is very different from trying to formulate causal social laws, which would imply a deterministic view of the social world.

Georg Simmel also reflects the influence of Dilthey in accepting the distinctness of sociocultural phenomena. Simmel was as much a philosopher as a sociologist and wrote equally in both fields.[30] It is difficult to locate him in the history of sociology, though his is commonly taken to be a "formal sociology."[31] This is perhaps misleading, since Simmel did not take a "formal" and distant approach to social phenomena but rather considered the description of pure "social forms" as that which differentiates sociology from other disciplines. His analysis of specific structures of social life and the

psychological processes they reflect (e.g., competition, subordination) is not germane here. It is important to note, however, the ties between Simmel and phenomenology.[32]

First, an important parallel exists between his distinction between the *form* and the *content* of social behavior, on the one hand, and Husserl's distinction between the *quality* of an intentional act and its *material* (or content). Second, although he diverged from Husserl in some respects, Simmel's study of social life may be viewed as an *eidetic one,* in the sense that he sought to reduce manifestly different concrete forms of social phenomena to their underlying essential characteristics ("forms"). Forms are revealed by means of an "insightful look" at social life, grasping its essential psychological meanings as wholes; apparently heterogeneous contents may thus be shown to have a common form. The logic behind this is that the motivational factors in social life are emotional (affective psychological dispositions) which are adapted to specific types of social setting. A common nuclear "meaning" underlies the repetitive aspects, the uniformities of social activity, and once the observer has grasped and described it (e.g., the meaning of the triad, the stranger, the cocktail party), its structural aspects will manifest themselves irrespective of the specific contents or occasions of the particular "sociation" in question.

The affinity of Simmel's approach to phenomenological analysis is evident in the following interrelated elements of his sociology: (a) a pure description of social phenomena which (b) reduces them to their essential characteristics in terms of (c) meaningful core components of a nonsocial nature. Simmel was not interested in an empiricist, positivistic approach in which generalizations can only be made after carefully controlled experiments, but rather in a sophisticated direct "understanding" of the forms underlying a variety of seemingly diverse phenomena. His investigations were mainly ahistorical; yet his methodology overlaps with Weber's, for both gave primary emphasis to the subjective category of *Verstehen*.

Emile Durkheim seems, at first glance, at odds with an existential-phenomenological perspective, since his explicit methodology is that of "positivism." The latter is commonly viewed as a repudiation not only of the "subjective" perspective of existential phenomenology but also of the distinction between the physical and the sociocultural sciences. Durkheim's positivism is indicated in his famous methodological dictum, to "consider social facts as things."[33]

Taken out of context, this statement might appear to make Durkheim antithetical to an existential-phenomenological viewpoint, but such a conclusion is unwarranted. On the contrary, "consider social facts as things" has for Durkheim the same import and meaning as Husserl's dictum "to the things themselves" (*"zu den Sachen"*). For Husserl,[34] valid phenomenological knowledge can be obtained by an initial reduction from the "natural attitude," by bracketing the judgements about reality we make in our unreflective, everyday attitude of accepting things as they are perceived without questioning their foundation. But this phenomenological precept is exactly the counterpart of Durkheim's sociological rule!

Durkheim's positivism is grounded in accepting social facts as sui generis phenomena of intersubjective consciousness, as products of social interaction, which cannot properly be understood if reduced to a lower order of phenomena (physical or organic). They must be approached *naïvely*, that is, without preconceptions as to their nature or functions; this implies a suspension of the causal framework within which the positivism of the physical sciences operates. Since Durkheim's sociological analysis is really phenomenological, his studies owe their richness to a *radical description* of the interdependence of social phenomena rather than to the demonstration of causal principles operative in society. Indeed, I suggest that the spirit of Durkheimian sociology is profoundly akin to Heidegger's notion of

truth as the discovery of being; namely, sociology must discover what social facts really are and not what they are taken to be in the uncritical set of assumptions used by the public.

Durkheim's implicitly phenomenological approach, used to uncover successive layers of social reality from its overt manifestations to its covert essential characteristics,[35] is clearly illustrated in his famous study, *Suicide.* The "surface" manifestations of suicide establish its presence as a social phenomenon; these objective, quantitative factors are then "reduced" phenomenologically to underlying layers of the social structure in which the act of suicide occurs, and ultimately the meaning of the act is grounded in the psychological nexus between the individual and his social milieu (which is a subjective one). The "depth" analysis leads Durkheim to perceive that sharp historical fluctuations in suicide rates are phenomenal "surface" manifestations of much deeper, societal currents of a psychological nature, which presently lie outside the scope of scientific research. Thus, Durkheim casts sociological "light" on what may initially appear to be an individual, irrational action.

I have treated Durkheim's relation to existential thought (as differentiated from phenomenology as a method) elsewhere,[36] but some summarizing remarks are appropriate here. In exactly the same spirit as the existential movement, Durkheim was primarily preoccupied with the moral crisis of modern society. Like the existentialist philosophers, he views man's existence as a "coexistence," as a "being-in-the-world." His analysis may logically be seen as an extension and enrichment of Heidegger's idea that the existential self (*Dasein*) is also a *"Mitsein,"* a "being-with." Durkheim always stressed that personality is constituted in society,[37] so that one's existence as "being-in-the-world" may be said to be ontologically "being-solidary-in-the-world-with-others." Existence, then, is first and foremost social existence, grounded in solidarity. Hence, the breakdown in the normative consensus fundamental to social structure and in the consequent primacy of social obligations is, in Durkheim's eyes, the salient pathological feature . . . of the modern world, and if left unattended it will injure both individual and society. The moral fragmentation of society (Durkheim's notion of *anomie* is the equivalent of today's "pluralistic" society) and the fragmentation of personality are thus necessarily interrelated.

Existentialism and Durkehim's sociology are in spirit complementary, not polar, if Durkheim's perspective is seen as leading to "social existentialism" and away from a narrower "individual existentialism" from which no general theory of social order could be constructed. Durkheim's concern was the existential situation of modern society, and, in particular, how its moral dissolution was attended by a pathological weakening of the bonds of solidarity. His concern with modern society as an integral whole complements the existentialists' concern with man as an integral being. It is true that the existentialist ethic of Heidegger, Jaspers, and especially Sartre contains an individualistic bias: To fulfill his potentialities the individual must liberate himself from the yoke of impersonal society. But this does not mean that sociology and existential phenomenology are not complementary disciplines, for at the heart of the existentialist analysis of modern man is the idea that *freedom entails responsibility,* and that the liberation of the self from the routinized, banal, impersonal social world whose very appearance of objectivity and solidity conceals its existential ground, is a call not to anarchy or self-pity but to authentic intersubjective social participation.

Recall that Durkheim emphasized that "organic" society offers more potential freedom of action than "mechanical" society, since it evaluates the individual in terms of personal achievement rather than by ascriptive status; the possibilities for freedom of action have historically been enlarged with the development of a differentiated but normatively integrated soci-

ety. Yet, Durkheim also went on to criticize modern society *because* the normative or moral nexus between individuals has been so severely strained. What I wish to suggest is that Durkheim's critique of *anomic* society is highly congruent with the existential analysis of the *depersonalizing* effect of mass society; both have as their focal concern *inauthentic* social existence and its consequences.

In brief, Durkheim's sociology is no more "anti-individual" than existential thought is "antisocial," and only a gross misreading could warrant such a conclusion. Durkheim, in spite of his Cartesian rationalism, always made a significant place for nonrational elements in his descriptions of social reality as well as in the process by which he arrived at such descriptions.[38]

Turning to American sociology, the problem is to select what should be taken for the mainstream of the American tradition. We have had various schools, but I suggest that the tradition represented until the present generation by Cooley, Mead, and W. I. Thomas has had the most lasting impact on sociological theory. Before seeing how Thomas' work in particular is related to existential phenomenology, I would like to point out very briefly a key link between American social thought and the existential-phenomenological tradition. John Wild has recently pointed out that phenomenology owes much to the direct influence of William James, in particular to his stress on "the relational structure of our lived experience."[39] James treated the concrete experiences of life as a continuous process of becoming; his work, then, is an important bridge between the American pragmatic tradition and the European existential-phenomenological tradition. (Moreover, James acknowledged his major influence to be Charles Renouvier, the same French thinker who was Durkheim's teacher of philosophy!)

William I. Thomas was perhaps the major source of pressure to take sociology and social psychology out of the academic walls and into "the field." This impulse to see what is going on "outside" and its rejection of academic abstractions is a major aspect of existential phenomenology. Thomas is well known, of course, as the author of the "self-fulfilling prophecy," but it is not so clearly realized that his theorem is a sociological formulation of the existential tenet that "subjectivity is truth."

Thomas' major works point out the subjective meanings of social action as basic reference points for sociological investigation. Objective social conditions have to be seen in the light of subjective components of social actors: their attitudes, their basic wishes, their definitions of the situation. Without an awareness of these subjective meanings, objective correlations are incomplete descriptions of reality.

Equally relevant is Thomas' more general perspective on the sociological endeavor, one which reveals a profound affinity with phenomenology. His conception of man is that he is meaningfully related to society, culture, and social others, and that in his activities he has an important element of conscious control. That is, the social actor is capable of organizing his social stage; he is capable of meaningfully relating himself in his consciousness to his social environment, though sudden changes in the environment (e.g., immigration) bring about disruptive crises. As Martindale points out, Thomas quite early held that the sociological endeavor should have as its object "the phenomena [sic] of attention—'the mental attitude which takes note of the outside world and manipulates it.'"[40] Although Martindale does not relate Thomas to phenomenology, the notion of "attention" in the quoted passage is equivalent to the phenomenological notion of "intention."

If Thomas is a representative spokesman for the "second generation," Sorokin and Parsons are probably the most eminent contributors in the contemporary generation of theorists. Sorokin's sociology expresses a rapprochement to existential phenomenology more explicitly, perhaps, than any other discussed in this essay. First, he accepts the *Naturwissenschaften-Geisteswissenschaften* distinction, holding that sociocultural phenomena have properties not accounted by psychological or biophysical models of explanation.[41] Sorokin has repeatedly stressed that sociocultural phenomena are interrelated by a realm of *meanings* imputed by social actors to these phenomena; such meanings (values, norms, esthetics) transform the natural properties of objects.[42] The explanation of such phenomena involves a statement of interrelations at the level of meaningful wholes, which presupposes a sociocultural space-time reality of a more fundamental nature than the physical sciences' abstract geometrical space and absolute time. Consequently, seemingly diverse sociocultural phenomena may permit the sociological uncovering of integrated macro-sociocultural systems, characterized by fundamental premises that provide the basic orientation of these systems to reality.

Now, Sorokin's methodological approach is not only a more precise statement of the presuppositions underlying structural-functional analysis, but it also is phenomenological in spirit: His emphasis on uncovering meanings and "reducing" macro-sociocultural systems to their essential characteristics parallel Husserl's stress on intentionality and the reduction of phenomena to their core meanings *(noemata).* Sorokin's emphasis on an existential realm of sociocultural reality apart from a physical conception of the universe is of fundamental importance for this paper. *This is one of the major foci of convergence in the sociological tradition being considered.*

The acceptance of a social reality qualitatively distinct from and more primary in experience than physical reality is the foundation of a general theory of social existence and an expression of *social realism.* Sorokin's approach is thus very similar to that of the Durkheimian school, and both may be regarded as part of an enlarged existential-phenomenological perspective. Durkheim, Mauss, and others of the "sociologistic" school found that social space has properties different from physical space; moreover, Durkheim argued in *The Elementary Forms of Religious Life* that the scientific conceptions of space, time, and logical classes are derivatives of a primordial set of social existentials. This is a remarkable convergence with Heidegger's argument that the space-time continuum of modern science is not in itself reality "out there" but rather a derivative of our existential being-in-the-world. Translated into the sociological tradition, Heidegger's notion of *Dasein,* the existential self as a being-in-the-world, should be treated as *intersubjective consciousness.* Sorokin and Durkheim implicitly concur with the existential stress on truth as a subjective reality, if this is extended to signify that sociocultural systems and social groups perceive truth in the light of their existential social situations. The sociological tradition converges in the relational (but not relativistic) view that truth is an existential relation between the social actor and his situation; seen phenomenologically, truth and reality are binding for the actor who is always *engaged* in his situation. It is only for the *detached* observer that social truth appears to be an arbitrary or relative matter.

Sorokin's conception of sociology and social reality is congruent with existential phenomenology in two other major respects. First, his "integralist" model is linked with the existential (and Gestalt) perspective of being-in-the-world as an integral whole. Just as phenomenal reality as a total process of *becoming* cannot be represented adequately, therefore, by a simplistic reduction to mechanistic models, for Sorokin (and Durkheim, Weber, Scheler, Mead, Thomas and the others discussed here), sociocultural reality cannot be reduced to any form of material causation because a dialectic interaction takes place, in the world of experiences, between moral phenomena (ideas, values, beliefs) and physical phenomena. The world is *symbolically perceived* and not simply responded to physically, as

empiricism and behaviorism would have us believe. Second, Sorokin shares a common agreement that modern society has lost sight of its moral basis, that the dissolution of the moral structure of the social world creates a normative crisis externally manifested in seemingly different symptoms, ranging from a crisis in epistemology to attacks on norms governing sexual behavior.

The work of Talcott Parsons is the hardest test case of this argument, for his general theory of action is in some major respects at odds with an existential-phenomenological perspective. Since I think that an action orientation is essentially congruent with such a perspective, I shall suggest briefly what the deviations are and what accounts for the divergence. First, unlike the basic existentialist evaluation that modern society is in a state of profound moral crisis (resulting in "depersonalization," "objectification" and other features of mass society), Parsons' implicit orientation is much more one of "rational optimism." In his sociological writings, even the more recent ones, he gives very little attention to social problems as reflections of an underlying societal crisis;[43] this seems to indicate that he is unaware of the saliency of social conflict as a problematic structural feature of modern society. The "equilibrium" model suggests that the ship of American society can be kept on its main course mechanically by means of an automatic pilot.

Second, and much more fundamental, Parsons makes implicit use of two quite different and basically antithetical models of human action. One of these models is based on a phenomenological perspective, but the other belongs to quite another tradition: broadly, that of utilitarianism, rationalism, nominalism, and behaviorism (the latter implying material determinism). This second model represents a later development in Parsons' approach to the action scheme, as Scott has cogently shown.[44] It is manifest in the hedonistic image of the individual actor in *Toward a General Theory of Action,* in the notion of "need-disposition" and the statement that "the personality may . . . be conceived as a system with a persistent tendency toward the optimum level of gratification."[45] Grafted onto this Tolman-influenced behavioristic-psychological view of the individual as an organism is the Freudian model of personality; the notions of "internalization," "cathexis," and "mechanisms of defense" in *Toward a General Theory of Action* reflect the postwar influence of Freud on Parsons. The net effect of "adopting" a Freudian model (and with it a deterministic, biologistic, object-relation psychology) is, as Scott has pointed out,[46] to undermine Parsons' own earlier voluntaristic scheme! The view of individual actions as the result of either primary libidinal drives or passive receptivity to socialization (via the unreflective mechanism of superego internalization), on the one hand, is basically incompatible with an emphasis on the individual's volitional organization of the situation and the omnipresent possibility of choice in selecting its configuration.

Since the voluntaristic perspective is basic to a theory of action and is clearly articulated with an existential-phenomenological *Weltanschauung,* it is important to examine Parsons' earlier *The Structure of Social Action.*[47] In this seminal study, Parsons noted a convergence in sociological theory which may be termed "subjective realism." Ends (goals, values) are not random or arbitrary; they are real, nonempirical (that is, not given by sensory perception), and extra-individual. Social action has a normative base and cannot be seen only as overt behavior; it is essentially the actor's subjective orientation to his situation in the light of his knowledge of the past, present and anticipated future.[48] Hence, scientifically valid (or positivistic, "objective") knowledge of the situation does not exhaust all its significant elements, for these include subjective ones not accountable merely by reference to "ignorance and error." The action frame of reference stresses the unfolding continuity of the actor's acts.

"Action is a temporal process,"[50] states Parsons, and he adds that the conceptual schema for analyzing this process "is inherently subjective . . . the normative elements can be conceived of as 'existing' only in the mind of the actor."[51] that the conceptual schema for analyzing this process "is inherently subjective . . . the normative elements can be conceived of as 'existing' only in the mind of the actor."[51]

This begins to suggest how closely the action frame of reference is consistent with a phenomenological perspective. Not only does it assume a *Naturwissenschaft Geisteswissenschaft* distinction, in opposition to radical positivism,[52] but also, as Parsons explicitly acknowledges,

. . . the action frame of reference may be said to have what many, following Husserl, have called a "phenomenological" status.[53]

As in Husserl's approach, emphasis is given to the *description* of the personality as a totality of unit acts. In going beyond description to a *causal* interpretation of acts by reference to motivational factors, Parsons' action perspective

. . . becomes, in Husserl's sense 'psychological.' But its phenomenological aspect, as a frame of reference, does not disappear; it remains implicit in any use of the action schema.[54]

This early and fundamental formulation of Parsonian "action theory" is also very much in keeping with the existential side of phenomenology, with its stress on the actor's *freedom* and *becoming* as integral aspects of his social existence. As a recent reviewer of Parsons' sociological theory points out, action theory rests on an indeterminate element of voluntarism in the actor's orientation to his situation:

Without this crucial element of freedom, denied in any closed, determinate system, action becomes mere behavior.[55]

"Mere behavior" involves no element

of volition on the part of the subject, no symbolic organization of the *environmental* elements into an existential *situation* which is a subjective reality and not just a set of physical objects. "Action" implies interaction, or "intersubjective consciousness." This further implies that the subject is not passively socialized as an assembly-line product but that the actor (either individual or collectivity) is actively involved in the socialization process; the dialectic between individual and collective volitions suggests that "there always remains some lack of congruence between individual and societal goals."[56] The very conception of socialization as a continuous process of adjustment to social life is basic not only to an action frame of reference and to the sociological tradition noted here, but also to the existential perspective on reality as a *becoming* and not as fixed *being*. A Freudian model of personality development, however, is quite incompatible with such a notion of the socialization process, no matter how sociologically respectable one tries to render it.

In dealing with the personality as a system in the totality of action, Parsons has leaned heavily in recent years on the behavioristic-Freudian model. This model is so at odds with the earlier and more basic model that the term "voluntarism" seems to have been shelved from the action theory vocabulary in recent formulations. And yet, when he analyzes the real world of experience, Parsons is far from having divorced himself from the mainstream under consideration. Thus, the "pattern variables"[57] have a subjective reference, for they are a structural elaboration of Thomas' notion of the "definition of the situation," which is only meaningful from a subjective perspective. Moreover, one of the pattern variables, "affectivity-affective neutrality" as a role dilemma, may be seen as an important refinement of Scheler's insight that affect is grounded in intersubjective consciousness; this and the other pattern variables are certainly significant heuristic devices

for any phenomenological investigation of social situations. The basic affinity between Parsons and existential phenomenology creates other continuities worth noting. As a feature of the American value system, for instance, Parsons includes "instrumental activism" which is closely related to "institutionalized individualism"; this, he notes,[58] must be sharply differentiated from a "utilitarian" version of individualism. Why? Because the former stresses a moral obligation to achievement "rather than an orientation to hedonistic enjoyment."[59]

Here, then, is a very important return to the voluntaristic model of *The Structure of Social Action.* The voluntaristic model *is* one of "instrumental individualism," that is, its implicit view is that of socially given goals that each member of the social order is morally bound to implement; the actor's self-realization in a situation is instrumental to the self-realization of the community to which he belongs. Voluntarism, in other words, presupposes that the individual actor's situation is always defined in terms of a moral community, that the social world is not just cognitively but also morally ordered (and thus all social acts are to some degree morally evaluated). The world of the actor qua subject of action is a moral constituion that grounds the meaning of particular situations and particular objects (including social objects).

Parsons' phenomenological approach is also evident in his discussion of culture as a relational system of "meanings" which are not properties of physical objects but rather a function of perception.[60] In its underlying form, then, the action frame of reference is a model of social existence emphasizing intersubjectivity, self-realization via an institutional moral order, the "openness" of the actor to the world, the actor as a sentient being (and not a rationalistic creation). It is entirely consonant, therefore, with a conception of existential phenomenology as the philosophical underpinning of general sociological theory.

Conclusion

I have sought to show, in the course of this paper, that at the heart of the major intellectual sources of the sociological tradition is an underlying consensus which may be called "subjective realism," and that this view of the individual and society has a marked affinity with existential phenomenology. Subjective realism approaches social reality as it is phenomenally experienced by actors; it thereby avoids the pitfalls of both materialism and idealism. In the sociological tradition subjective realism manifests itself in various labels such as "voluntarism" (related to "personalism"[61]), "pragmatism," "integralism," and "sociologism." The convergence with existential phenomenology leads to the possibility of a general theory of social existence. I have previously[62] suggested ways in which recognition of its affinity with existential thought may be fruitful for the development of sociology, but at that time I did not clearly realize the links with phenomenology. Consequently, I should like to expand these suggestions very briefly.

Sociologists will find very profitable the writings that provide significant bridges between existential phenomenology and the social sciences, in particular those of Maurice Merleau-Ponty[63] and Alfred Schutz.[64] From these and other sources may be gathered a number of "sensitizing concepts" (to use Blumer's phrase), such as "alienation," "care," "guilt," "authenticity," "horizon," which can fruitfully be used to formulate new conceptions of empirical research that would make accessible social phenomena not amenable to a quantitative, external, object approach.

Existential phenomenology complements rather than entirely replaces the present typically positivistic approach to research; that is, it validates objective techniques of describing social phenomena, just as highly reliable quantitative propositions may be used to validate phenomenologically derived insights and interpretations of social reality. The methodology appropriate for the subjective realist frame of reference in sociology may be termed *transobjectivity,* to indicate that explanation goes beyond the object to a complex elucidation of the multiple perspectives and the social spatial-temporal dimensions of the social phenomenon. This methodology is, after all, at the heart of what Marcel Mauss proposed in his notion of the "total social fact."[65] The "global" approach to social phenomena sees them as an actualizing (or in Heidegger's terminology, a "temporalizing") set of events, since historicity is the ground of social actions; stated differently, social existence unfolds in social time.

Moreover, not only does sociological knowledge require both subjective understanding and objective cognizance[66] of the social situation (which should always be considered as a phenomenon of inter subjective consciousness), but it should also be seen as an essentially *radical description* of social reality. Existential phenomenology applied to sociology seeks the *roots* of social existence. This implies that it seeks to elucidate the existential nature of social structures by uncovering the surface institutional phenomena of the everyday "accepted" world; by probing the "subterranean," noninstitutional social depths concealed from public gaze, by interpreting the dialectic between the institutional and the noninstitutional (e.g., the relation of charisma to the secular).[67]

At present, sociological theory is not doing justice to this unexplored realm of social existence; we are in a position roughly comparable to rationalistic psychology before the advent of depth psychology. Yet, the sociological tradition sketched out in this paper has already paved the way for a meaningful interplay between sociological theory and the existential-phenomenological perspective developed in modern philosophy (and spread in clinical psychology).[68] Sociological theory can remain true to itself and yet renovate its formulations by focusing on the existential horizon of social life. We know much more about the physical *uni-*

verse than about the social *world(s)* and its (their) elastic properties; we still have to investigate rigorously the interrelations of the two (e.g., the physical consequences of movement in social space), and this will in turn enable sociological theory to treat meaningfully the dialectic between the quantitative and the qualitative. In broad outline, these are the directions to which the sociological tradition points.

Finally, an existential awareness translated into empirical research will enable sociology better to appreciate and thereby cope with the seemingly "irrational" discontinuities and large-scale upheavals of modern society. Far from abandoning sociology as a science, this is to restore its heritage, grounded in the sociological tradition, of utilizing its global knowledge for socially responsible ends.

References and Notes

1. Helmut R. Wagner, "Types of Sociological Theory: Toward a System of Classification," *American Sociological Review* 28 (1963): 735–36.
2. Space limitation obviates the explication of the philosophical background and central notions of existential thought and the phenomenological method; for purposes of the present discussion these will be treated as given. Good introductions to the major concepts, problems, and figures in this general philosophical movement are: John Wild, *The Challenge of Existentialism* (Bloomington: Indiana University Press, 1955); Pierre Thévenaz, *What is Phenomenology?* (Chicago: Quadrangle Books Inc., 1962); Anna-Teresa Tymieniecka, *Phenomenology and Science in Contemporary European Thought* (New York: Noonday Press, 1962).
3. Theodore Abel, *Systematic Sociology in Germany* (New York: Columbia University Press, 1929); Nicholas S. Timasheff, *Sociological Theory, Its Nature and Growth,* rev. ed. (New York: Random House, Inc., 1957); Don Martindale, *The Nature and Types of Sociological Theory* (Boston: Houghton Mifflin Company, 1960).
4. Herbert Spiegelberg, *The Phenomenological Movement,* 2 vols. (The Hague: Martinus Nijhoff, 1960).
5. Nicholas Timasheff, op. cit.
6. In his *Essays on the Sociology of Knowledge,* edited by Paul Kecskemeti (London: Routledge & Kegan Paul, Ltd., 1952), pp. 33–83.
7. See Franz Brentano, "The Distinction between Mental and Physical Phenomena," in Roderick M. Chisholm, ed., *Realism and the Background of Phenomenology* (New York: Free Press, Div. of The Macmillan Company, 1960), pp. 39–61.
8. Mannheim, op. cit., pp. 43–63.
9. Edmund Husserl, *Ideas* (New York: P. F. Collier, Inc., 1962).
10. Robert Merton, "Manifest and Latent Functions," in *Social Theory and Social Structure* (New York: Free Press, Div. of The Macmillan Company, 1949), esp. pp. 61–65.
11. Mannheim, op. cit., pp. 276–320.
12. Ibid., pp. 191–229.
13. Ibid., p. 199.
14. Ibid., p. 194.
15. The convergence between Durkheim and Mannheim on some key points of their sociological perspective is striking. Durkheim's final perspective on morality *Le Pragmatisme et Sociologie,* edited by Armand Cuvillier (Paris: Vrin Librarie Philosophique, 1955); partially translated in Kurt H. Wolff, ed., *Emile Durkheim 1858–1917* (Columbus: Ohio State University Press, 1960), pp. 386–436) is essentially one of relationism. Furthermore, Durkheim saw the role of the intellectuals and of education in the reconstruction of the moral basis of modern society in very much the same fashion as Mannheim. Both also felt that sociology must accept a role of social responsibility as its ultimate justification.
16. See Georges Gurvitch, *Les Tendances Actuelles de la Philosophie Allemande,* 2d printing (Paris: Vrin Librarie Philosophique, 1949), pp. 67–152; also the introduction by Werner Stark to Max Scheler's *The Nature of Sympathy* (London: Routledge & Kegan Paul, Ltd., 1954).
17. Timashaff, op. cit., p. 268.
18. Georges Gurvitch, *The Spectrum of Social Time* (Dordrecht, Holland: D. Reidel Publishing Company, 1964); also "Social Structure and the Multiplicity of Times," in Edward A. Tiryakian, ed., *Sociological Theory, Values and Sociocultural Change: Essays in Honor of Pitirim A. Sorokin* (New York: Free Press, Div. of The Macmillan Company, 1963), pp. 171–84.
19. Jean-Luc Chambard, "Pour une Sociologie Phénoménologique de l'Inde," *Cahiers Internationaux de Sociologie* 25 (1958): pp. 152–76.
20. Howard Becker, "Current Sacred-Secular Theory and Its Development," in Howard Becker and Alvin Boskoff, eds., *Modern Sociological Theory in Continuity and Change* (New York: The Dryden Press, 1957), p. 179.
21. "The Perception of the Other: A Study in Social Order," (Cambridge, Mass.: Harvard University, unpublished Ph.D. thesis, 1952).
22. "Conditions of Successful Degradation Ceremonies," *American Journal of Sociology* 61 (1956): pp. 420–24.
23. "Studies of the Routine Grounds of Everyday Activities," *Social Problems* 11 (1964): pp. 225–50. Garfinkel's imaginative research contains suggestive applications of Husserl's notion of *epoché* as

a heuristic device, i.e., the "bracketing" of the natural attitude to accept the world as solidly given. See Husserl, op. cit., pp. 91–100 for a crucial chapter on the foundations of the phenomenological method.

24. For a comprehensive discussion of Weber's methodology and its relation to Dilthey's thesis, see Talcott Parsons, *The Structure of Social Action* (New York: Free Press, Div. of The Macmillan Company, 1949), pp. 579–639.

25. Ibid., p. 589.

26. This is reflected in his familiar definition of social action: "In 'action' is included all human behavior when and in so far as the acting individual attaches a subjective meaning to it." Max Weber, *The Theory of Social and Economic Organization*, ed. and trans. by Talcott Parsons and A. M. Henderson (New York: Oxford University Press, 1947), pp. 88.

27. Abel, op. cit., p. 124.

28. Ibid., p. 123.

29. Weber, op. cit., p. 90.

30. For a general study of Simmel as a philosopher, see Rudolph H. Weingartner, *Experience and Culture* (Middletown, Conn.: Wesleyan University Press, 1962).

31. This is the perspective on Simmel adopted by Abel, op. cit., Martindale, op. cit., and Raymond Aron, *German Sociology* (New York: Free Press, Div. of The Macmillan Company, 1957).

32. For a discussion of the contacts between Simmel and Husserl, see Weingartner, op. cit., p. 23 ff.

33. *The Rules of Sociological Method* (New York: Free Press, Div. of The Macmillan Company, 1950), p. 14.

34. Supra, footnote 23.

35. Durkheim stops short of a "transcendental reduction," in phenomenological terms, in that he does not seek to establish the universal essence of society. Either this would lead sociology into metaphysics, or else by its very generality such an essence would have no sociologically meaningful content.

36. *Sociologism and Existentialism: Two Perspectives on the Individual and Society* (Englewood Cliffs, N.J.: Prentice-Hall, Inc., 1962).

37. See in particular his "Le dualisme de la nature humaine et ses conditions sociales," *Scientia* 15 (1914): 206–21, translated as "The Dualism of Human Nature" in Wolff, op. cit., pp. 325–40.

38. In his study of religion, for example, he does not arrive inductively at its essential characteristics as a social phenomenon but rather reaches them in a phenomenological "intuitive" or "insightful" manner (which, of course, is neither introspective nor arbitrary).

39. John Wild, *Existence and the World of Freedom* (Englewood Cliffs: Prentice-Hall, Inc., 1963), p. 31.

40. Martindale, op. cit., p. 348.

41. *Sociocultural Causality, Space, Time* (Durham, N. C.: Duke University Press, 1942). This methodological standpoint, so explicit in the European so-ciological mainstream (including Weber and Durkheim), is also characteristic of the American tradition under consideration. Note, for example, the dualism implied in the following statement by George H. Mead: "The physical object is found to be that object to which there is no social response which calls out again a social response in the individual. The objects with which we cannot carry on social intercourse are the physical objects of the world." *The Philosophy of the Act* (Chicago: University of Chicago Press, 1938), p. 292.

42. *Society, Culture, and Personality: Their Structure and Dynamics* (New York: Harper & Row, Publishers, 1947), p. 49. Durkheim, of course, had opened up this sociological perspective in *The Elementary Forms of Religious Life* (New York: P.F. Collier, Inc., 1961), p. 364 and passim.

43. Thus, in "Social Strains in America," in Daniel Bell, ed., *The Radical Right* (Garden City, N.Y.: Doubleday & Company, Inc., 1963), pp. 175–99 he views the reactions of the political right as a temporary phenomenon in American society and not as a surface manifestation of a deeper social malaise and polarization of society. Whether such a malaise "objectively" exists in American society is beside the point, which is that, unlike the Continental tradition, Parsons' perspective is not a crisis-oriented one.

44. John Finley Scott, "The Changing Foundations of the Parsonian Action Scheme," *American Sociological Review* 28 (1963): pp. 716–35.

45. Talcott Parsons and Edward A. Shils, eds., *Toward a General Theory of Action* (Cambridge, Mass.: Harvard University, 1951), p. 121.

46. Scott, op. cit., pp. 725 and 730.

47. *The Structure of Social Action* (New York: Free Press, Div. of The Macmillan Company, 1949 [first published in 1937, New York: McGraw-Hill Book Company]).

48. Ibid., p. 79.

49. Ibid., p. 81.

50. Ibid., p. 732.

51. Ibid., p. 733.

52. Radical positivism, empiricism, behaviorism, and materialism all are opposed to any dualistic view of reality.

53. Ibid., p. 733.

54. Ibid., p. 750f.

55. Edward C. Devereux, Jr., "Parsons' Sociological Theory," in Max Black, ed., *Social Theories of Talcott Parsons* (Englewood Cliffs, N.J.: Prentice-Hall, Inc., 1961), p. 13.

56. Ibid., p. 25.

57. *Toward a General Theory of Action*, pp. 76–91.

58. Talcott Parsons and Winston White, "The Link Between Character and Society," in Talcott Parsons *Social Structure and Personality* (New York: Free Press, Div. of The Macmillan Company, 1964), p. 197 [first published in Seymour M. Lipset and Leo Lowenthal, eds., *Culture and Social Character* (New York: Free Press, Div. of The Macmillan Company, 1961)].

59. Loc. cit.

60. See his "Introduction" to Part Four, "Culture and the Social System," in Talcott Parsons, Edward Shils, Kaspar D. Naegele, and Jesse R. Pitts, eds., *Theories of Society,* vol. 2 (New York: Free Press, Div. of The Macmillan Company, 1961), p. 964. This, of course, is in direct agreement with Durkheim and Sorokin, supra, fn. 42.

61. See Albert C. Knudson, *The Philosophy of Personalism* (Nashville, Tenn.: Abingdon Press, 1927); also Emmanuel Mounier, *Le Personalisme* (Paris: Presses Universitaires de France, 1962); Paul Ricoeur, "Une philosophie personnaliste," *Esprit* (December 1950), pp. 860–87; Edward A. Tiryakian, "The Person as Existential Self," in Chad Gordon and Kenneth J. Gergen, eds., *The Self in Social Interaction* (New York: John Wiley & Sons, Inc., 1968).

62. *Sociologism and Existentialism,* pp. 164–69.

63. *The Structure of Behavior* (Boston: Beacon Press, 1963); *Phenomenology of Perception* (New York: Humanities Press, 1962); *Signs* (Evanston, Ill.: Northwestern University Press, 1964).

64. *Collected Papers I: The Problem of Social Reality,* Maurice Natanson, ed. (The Hague: Martinus Nijhoff, 1962).

65. In the crucial conclusion of his "Essai sur le Don" (English translation: *The Gift: Forms and Functions of Exchange in Archaic Societies* (New York: Free Press, Div. of The Macmillan Company, 1954); see the perceptive comments by Claude Levi-Strauss in his introduction to Marcel Mauss, *Sociologie et Anthropologie* (Paris: Presses Universitaires de France, 1960), pp. xxiii–xxx.

66. The intended distinction is reflected in the French *connaitre* and *savoir,* or in the German *kennen* and *wissen.*

67. This depth analysis of the multilayered meanings of social reality is, after all, in the spirit of structural-functional analysis. The reification of "structure" has led its critics to assume that structural analysis is "static," whereas in fact the existential reality of social structures renders their analysis more "dynamic" than anything else.

68. Following the lead of Durkheim and Weber, the sociological formulation of a theory of social existence also requires codification of the comparative data in *space* provided by ethology and those in *time* offered by historical studies. Such a background in the fundamental symbolic forms and historical processes of social experience (viz., the existential structure of societies) is of the utmost relevance to a sophisticated sociological understanding of nonrandom trends in contemporary large-scale societies. I am preparing a lengthy study of the modernization of sub-Sahara Africa which will seek, in part, to demonstrate the applicability of a social existential frame of reference to the sociological analysis of a concrete historical situation and type of society, namely "colonial Africa."

Part Four Strategies for Integrated Change

INTRODUCTION TO PART FOUR

In introducing this book we said that tomorrow's organizations will require many strategies different from those generally used today to solve complex social and organizational problems. In Part Four we present a selection of alternatives for achieving *change capability,* a matter especially pertinent to future organizations. Our purpose is to suggest means to achieve that objective in an integrated manner.

In order to initiate planned organizational change, management should be aware that it has both opportunity and responsibility to *select* the proper strategy to achieve organizational change and development. Chin and Benne, in Chapter 10, present a typology of ways for changing organizations, including empirical-rational, normative-re-educative and power-coercive means. In their overview of organizational change they emphasize that these general categories include more specific strategies which are situational and which are based on both a knowledge of human qualities and a knowledge of the non-human elements of the environment.

We suggest five specific strategies for change which we believe to be operational. We argue for an integrated approach which draws upon those five alternatives in any combination ap-propriate to the given needs. The five include: (1) Deliberate alteration of the organization's structure; (2) forcing change by technological inputs; (3) achieving organizational change through behavioral change; (4) creating new roles for proactive administrators, and (5) achieving change through organization research and policy development. In Part Four we develop the background of these alternatives, which we believe must be understood and properly applied to achieve organizations capable of functioning in "the different future."

Interdependence Among Multiple Change Strategies

The interdependence of the various dimensions of change is the feature of organizational change which is emphasized in this book. Figure 1 illustrates this, showing how all internal change strategies—structural behavioral, and technological—are subject to inputs from forces in the external environment. To illustrate the resultant interdependence, we will, in this section, limit our consideration to three broad strategies which are more or less common in the literature—change as a result of external conditions, change through structural alterations, and change to increase the capacity for technological adaptation.

Internal organizational change is affected not only by theoretical knowledge but also by various changes taking place in the sociocultural, economic, political, and technological environments. As in the case of integration of organization theories, the integration of change implies making use of an interdisciplinary approach to select the most appropriate strategies. Figure 1 also shows the interrelatedness of the structural, behavioral, and technological strategies. The behavior of manager, work group, or individual is best analyzed in conjunction with problems and constraints accompanying structural or technological change; new technological adaptation may limit possibilities available to the existing organizational structure, and so forth. The significance of such interrelation-

ships among the several approaches to change is well stated by Harold Leavitt:[1]

. . . Most efforts to effect change, whether they begin with people, technology structure, or task, soon must deal with the others. Students of human relations must cope with the intrusions of technological innovations. They must evaluate alternative structures, classing some as consonant and some as dissonant with their views of the world. Structuralists must take stands on the kinds of human interaction that are supportive of their position and the kinds that threaten or undermine it.

The strategy of achieving change through structural alterations may be considered from various perspectives. One, for example, involves changing organizational structure vis-à-vis the job

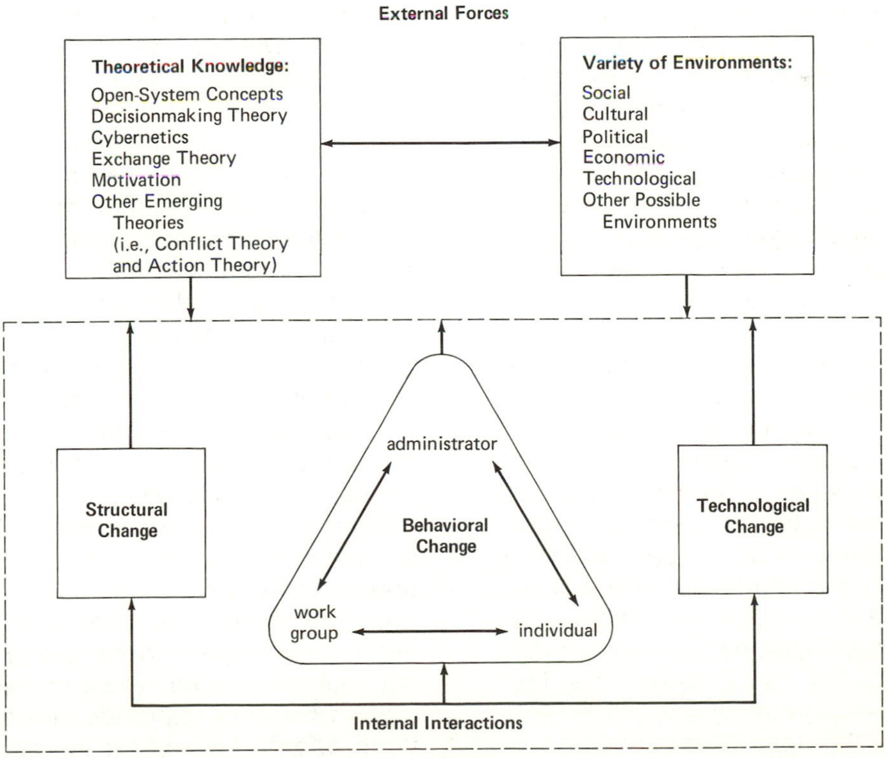

Figure 1   An Analytical Framework for Understanding Interrelations Among Change Strategies

tasks and activities of people in the organization. Through such change, management hopes to improve relationships among job tasks and to achieve not only better coordination of hierarchical authority but also a more precise sense of member responsibilities. This perspective is well illustrated by classical organization theory. A second, more contemporary approach to structural change takes into consideration psychological and social aspects of the situation. Here the objective is to change the structure to fit more adequately the characteristics of organization members. For example, a research-type organization may adopt such variant organizational conditions as increased autonomy and discretion for members, more emphasis on innovation, and less on hierarchy, etc., because of its unusual objectives and needs. We present Bell's article in Chapter 11 to show the relationship between structural flexibility and professional behavior in complex organizations.

As a third perspective, management may change for the purpose of strengthening a system's capacity for adaptation to a changing environment. The idea of the "turbulent field" suggested by Emery and Trist and the "organization-environment interface" described by Lorsh and Lawrence (both in Chapter 5) are examples of this position. Another contemporary—and very stimulating—way of looking at structural change involves what is termed the *self-management structure,* an approach which is discussed in more detail later in this introduction and illustrated in Chapter 11.

The behavioral approach to change is very attractive to management scholars today. A behavioral approach based on laboratory training techniques and emphasizing changes in individual behavior was developed by Kurt Lewin many years ago. The contemporary manifestation of this, beginning in the early 1960's, is the trend toward what is termed "organization development," an approach stressing integration of knowledge and method from the behavioral sciences in problem-solving processes among management, work groups, and individual employees to achieve planned change and total organizational growth and development. This subject is presented in Chapter 12.

The work of Frederick W. Taylor, founder of the scientific management school, was a major breakthrough in industrial management. Taylor applied technological means to achieve change in various industries. He developed scientific and engineering methods for measuring work, including time and motion studies, standardization of work, piece rates, and other similar procedures. Operations research and management science, both of which employ mathematical and computer tools, are the current form whereby technology is utilized to achieve change in industrial organizations.

Another stimulating trend which is exciting both American and British scholars in the area of organizational change is the new emphasis on socio-technical systems which was originated by the Tavistock Institute of Human Relations in London.[2] This approach assumes that industrial organizations must consider the human or social aspects of organization (job satisfaction, motivation, individual needs, group norms, informal leadership, etc.) as well as technological elements (machines, tools, the collection of plants, and other production facilities), investing their efforts to assure that these two sides of the organizational equation are related to each other in the most complementary way possible.

There are many empirical studies of sociotechnical systems. Of these, two appear to have special importance. The first derives from the study which Trist and his colleagues conducted in a British coal mine. Their research revealed that, in certain organizational situations, effective use of technology can markedly increase group participation and job satisfaction.[3]

Another important research has been developed by Joan Woodward and her research team at the Imperial College of Science and Technology. Her project has focused since 1962 on one hundred industrial firms in South Essex.[4] One of the major assumptions of the project is that, through technological changes, an organization may improve its productivity as well as the socio-psychological health of its workers. Moreover, technological change and the use of production hardware will limit the organizational structure as well as individual behavior to a greater or lesser degree. The article by James Taylor in Chapter 11 shows some of the significant relationships between technology and organization behavior in a large petroleum refinery, and the article supports the above tenets.

In summary, there is still some doubt as to whether technological change must precede change in the human-social system whether the opposite is in reality the case. We have learned that behavioral change is related to the successful accomplishment of structural and technological change, but, at this point in time, we are not fully aware of the best means to utilize that knowledge. In any event, we may generalize that integrated change must include a consideration of changes in both the social and the technical systems. More empirical analysis of multifaceted changes is needed to understand how the change methods affect each other. Integrated organizational change can be accelerated by increased management effort to understand how the above three change strategies are implemented—and how well they work out—in large, complex organizations.

Structural Flexibility and Professional Behavior

Administrators and change agents often find themselves in situations where overall structural change is needed to facilitate behavioral change. This problem has been most keenly described by Argyris in his training experience with the foreign service officers of the United States Department of State.[5] His research supplies a very important signal to officials in the federal government. To set the stage for much-needed behavioral change among State Department officers, fundamental structural changes must be made. These include changes in the promotion system, seniority structure, job assignment procedures, personnel development practices, and many other elements of the system. Argyris found that officials in the system were afraid of risk-taking and experimentation, showed very little openness with others, and lacked the skills and initiative necessary for innovation and creativity. Obviously, under State's rigid organizational environment, one can hardly expect to find much in the way of creative experimentation and innovation in U. S. foreign policy as initiated at the level of the Bureaucracy.

Argyris' insights into the U. S. State Department suggest that the management of organizational change assumes two dimensions: the management of structural change, on the one hand, and the management of behavioral change on the other. Both of these, of course, involve significant new strategies within the realm of the administrator's responsibility; the effectiveness of the administrator's role lies in understanding these challenges, facing up to them, and developing the skills needed to handle both sides of the change-equation in a positive manner.

A structural overhauling will be even more necessary for the so-called "knowledge organization"—the professional organization—to handle properly the increasing numbers of knowledgeable men and to maintain a climate for achievement (such as McGregor's "Theory-Y" environment offers). Zand[6] emphasizes that structural flexibility is essential for the following processes:

1) Collecting and disseminating knowledge that already exists in the organization
2) Acquiring and creating new knowledge
3) Converting knowledge to profitable products and service
4) Managing people who work with knowledge

The knowledge organization (for example, a research and development organization) depends upon effective interaction between professionals, research managers, and management executives. In spite of organizational charts, lines of authority, job assignments, and so forth, the management of knowledge organizations can no longer, in practice, be a one-man job. The process of determining organizational goals and objectives is more and more being shared with a group (or a whole team) of knowledgeable men. Certainly, the gray flannel suit is being replaced by a variety of colors and fabrics in knowledge organizations. What has been added to new organizations are new men and a diversity of human knowledge. Increased knowledge in science and technology is opening up management acceptance of change and developing a variety of new attitudes. The article by Gerald Bell stresses the structural flexibility of professional organizations—a flexibility which will allow more freedom and autonomy, more discretion and power, and more free communication and participation.

As the knowledge organization has grown, however, it has revealed a lamentable tendency to adopt the rigid organizational form common to bureaucracies in order to do the work more "efficiently" with tighter control. This has usually stifled professional discretion and knowledge processing in the knowledgeable society, a disadvantage which has had the effect of system reinforcement being imposed by management to the further detriment of the knowledge organization. Tomorrow's administrator must be aware of this tendency and its weaknesses for the knowledge-processing organization. Thompson's article above (Chapter 6) suggests that bringing scientific sophistication to organizational decisionmaking may create more problems than it solves, i.e., overcentralization with concomitant negative implications. This appears especially likely in knowledge organizations, with their heavy emphasis on individual performance. Where purely mathematical and "rational" models are involved, results may include alternatives unrelated to societal, human, or even organizational needs. On the other hand, making better decisions requires use of knowledge that is available. Where centralizing effects are offset through such means as extensive communication among affected groups, policymaking and problem solving may continue to be handled well despite centralization of other organizational processes.

Approaches to Planned Organizational Change

The strategy of achieving organizational change through behavioral change is central to the papers presented in Chapter 12. Many means to achieve this purpose have been developed by behavioral scientists; in general, the schemes emphasize "planned organizational change."[7] Based on literature in the field, we may characterize two approaches to planned organizational change:[8] individual attitude change and systemic, integrated change. The assumption behind individual attitude change is that we may increase individual performance and organizational effectiveness by changing the individual's attitudes and by increasing his ability to be aware of organizational problems.

Buchanan's essay, based on an extensive literature survey, describes the significant impact of laboratory training upon behavioral changes in the individual and the improvement of organizational performance. However, he admits that the laboratory method is not a magic tool which will cure all organizational and individual problems; laboratory training is one method of a multiphased change program. Schein and Bennis assert that "laboratory training is an educational strategy which is based primarily on the experience generated in various social encounters by the learners themselves, and which aims to influence attitudes and develop conpetencies toward learning about human interactions."[9] They admit that laboratory training is still young, immature, and incomplete. Much experimentation is being done on structures in order to find the most effective model within which such training may best be used. Jack and Lorraine Gibb pointed out in Chapter 4 that some problems occur when the recipient of sensitivity training comes back to his organization; his increased empathy and suddenly changed behavior may not be acceptable to the members of his organization. Obviously, this consequence is derived from the discrepancy between his changed behavior and the behaviors of unchanged others.

For all of the apparent limitations of such training, there are some general characteristics of it which should be mentioned. The focus is on the individual's behavior. Individuals attending the training sessions learn not only about themselves but also about others, groups, organizations, social systems, and, most important, about the emotional learning process. Schein and Bennis admit in their analysis that this type of training is not a cure-all for problems of change in organizations but that it has a positive bearing on the process.[10]

The second, or systemic, integrated approach to planned organizational change, recognizes the existence both of organizational values (i.e., pyramidal values such as hierarchy, productivity, authority, and power, etc.) and of human values in organizational development programs. French, after reviewing the objectives and assumptions of organizational development, suggests various strategies for different phases of development. He sees organization development as a total-system effort, a continuous effort to develop the organization's internal systems and human resources for effective change in the future.

By using knowledge of the behavioral sciences and by adopting an appropriate change program, organization development may bring about an effective integration of the individuals and the organization. Chris Argyris suggests increasing interpersonal competence to achieve group problem solving and organizational innovation. In his book *Organization and Innovation,* Argyris concluded that the individual who holds highly pyramidal values will be incompetent in transactions with others because he emphasizes overwhelmingly task-oriented behavior and puts too much effort into selling his ideas.[11] As a member of an encounter group perceiving that he really does have trouble effectively relating and working with other people—especially other organization members—he begins to undergo a learning process that enhances his interpersonal competence. During this period of change, the individual receives help initially from the consultant (or change agent) and then from his fellow workers. According to Argyris, people who increase their interpersonal ability tend to show innovativeness, willingness to take risks, and problem-solving effectiveness.

Although this book does not include the training technique developed by Blake and Mouton,[12] their change model deserves special attention as an example of integrated behavioral change. The *managerial grid model* includes the concept of encounter groups. The primary goal of the grid method is to exchange ineffective relationships between people in the organization—be it in groups or person-to-person—for effective relationships, so that problem solving will be smoother and more efficient and so that greater production effort may occur throughout the organization. The Blake and Mouton method is based upon their framework of managerial styles. The managerial grid identifies many variations of managerial behavior and classifies them into five different styles:[13] (1) country-club management (1,9); (2) impoverished management (1, 1); (3) middle-of-the-road management (5,5); (4) task management (9,1), and (5) team management (9,9). The whole attempt of the organization development program is to change the organization to a team management (9,9) style, wherein organizational productivity, the human elements, and individual and organizational goals are integrated.

The training method utilized in Grid team training is not the same as that commonly employed in the T-group laboratory. One important difference is the laboratory instructor. Whereas Schein and Bennis posited the professional behavioral scientist as the ultimate change agent, the Grid method uses line personnel. The purpose of using this type of instructor is to make organizational members more aware of the importance of the change method and to provide an emotional feeling of increased responsibility among participants.

There are several other methods in planned organizational change. The above two processes illustrate means which may bring integrated changes into organizational contexts. The individual approach and the systemic, integrated approach both attempt to change human behavior but use different training methods. How useful the relatively academic change programs are depends upon an administrator's willingness to experiment with new methods for training members and for

changing organizations. If organizations, especially strict bureaucratic ones, are unable or unwilling to change, then other methods will have to be used—such as the "power-coercive approach" mentioned by Chin and Benne.

Technology, Change, and Self-Management

The influence of technological change on individual behavior is a subject of which we know very little. Research into the relationship between technology, structure, and individual behavior is rather new. One of the aims considered in studies by the Tavistock Institute has been to see whether technical changes can bring more contributions from the employees and work groups. One of the important results is a study of self-regulation of shift and job rotation.[14] Through the self-governing system of rotating workers from shift to shift, the work group was able to share the "good" day shift. Furthermore, this form of job rotation provided flexibility to workers' role assignments and increased their sense of responsibility for their shared job tasks. A similar study has been done recently by the Saab-Scania Company in Sweden. Greiner points out that:[15]

Currently there are a number of experiments taking place in Swedish industry concerned with motivational problems on the assembly line. These experiments are far more profound than the simple application of "job enrichment." Probably the most notable is the Saab-Scania Company which has built a new truck factory organized around work teams on the assembly line. The members of each team are expected to learn the jobs of everyone else, as well as how to put an entire unit together, such as an engine. In addition, one team is always off from the line learning about new techniques.

The essay by Taylor included in Chapter 11 was focused on a large petroleum refinery in the United States. His study shows that technological change can facilitate organizational change toward greater autonomy and participation by workers. Under higher-technology conditions, work groups generally tend to generate a more favorable evaluation of supervisory and peer leadership. According to the work of Taylor and other researchers, studies of technology and organization behavior indicate the likelihood that technological change will have the most positive impact on production organizations and impose more significant behavioral constraints upon blue-collar than white-collar workers.[16]

Technological development in the "postindustrial society" apears likely to continue, resulting quite possibly in the interjection of external technology into the organization and thereby influencing organizational behavior and productivity. Understanding the potential of external technology to affect an organization either positively or negatively will help administrators to make better selections of strategies for bringing technological change into their organizations. We may anticipate that, through increased use of technological means to facilitate change, management will expand the opportunity for more decentralization, more group processes, and increased individual participation, role flexibility, and self-management derived from improved individual and management responsibility.

In Chapter 11 we present a paper in which Elizabeth Borgese reviews the status of self-management and estimates the possibilities for such an approach in the future. Self-management stems partly from structural adaptation and partly from possibilities implicit in technological development. The concept stresses individual participation in the working organization, with direct involvement of the workers at all levels of decisionmaking. During the past twenty years the workers of Yugoslavia have developed an example of self-management which has proven to be successful in reversing the traditional centralization of the decision process. Experiments in self-management have been conducted by a Norwegian research institute and additional investigation of this concept is now being undertaken elsewhere. Research evidence currently available suggests that, in certain situations, the self-management method can increase productivity and job satisfaction among workers. Self-management depends upon characteristics of the external environment. Since the organization is considered a subsystem of the total social system, development of a self-management structure requires that the administrator must receive positive external support. In addition, there is the internal factor of management's willingness to change and redefine existing ways of doing things, including decentralization, shared power, redefinition of goals, introduction of small, autonomous work teams and task forces, and so on. Apparently among the advantages of such change and redefinition is the psychological values derived from the individual member's appreciation of his contribution to the organizational processes.

The Need for Proactive Administrators

Just as tomorrow's organizations will be different from today's, tomorrow's administrators will perform new roles and manifest new behaviors. Peter Drucker and Donald Michael, among others, argue that tomorrow's organizations will have to be led by a new brand of administrator, many of whom must now be studying in colleges and universities. According to those writers, the young, potential administrators will be making all kinds of new decisions and

Figure 2   The Complex Role Environment of the Administrator

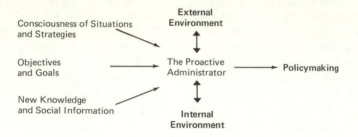

doing all kinds of new things long before the year 2000; therefore, their training should focus on making them more perceptive to changing environments and more able to change their behavior. This new generation has less invested in the old values, is less socialized to traditional thoughtways and behaviors, and is not imbued with old theories of organization and management. Accordingly, the young are changeable and adaptable with respect to new ideas. Tomorrow's organizations must be administered by today's students; today's students must become people of vision who can manage technological change and who can alter their organizations to cope with a rapidly changing environment. In turn, administrators already working for organizations must learn to learn, to subject themselves to the process of continual reeducation. If they cannot do this, they can no longer hope for continuing success in tomorrow's organization.[17]

Thus, integrated organizational change puts a strong emphasis on the administrator's responsibility. The complexity of his role environment is illustrated in Figure 2. The broad, double-headed arrows connecting internal and external environments indicate the administrator's responsibility for integrating member and management needs as well as management and client needs. The administrator in this complex role situation becomes a "linking pin," tying together into an integrated system individuals, groups, the organization, outside client groups, and so forth.[18]

An administrator's policymaking and problem solving skill is influenced by his consciousness of objectives and goals, his awareness of the situation, and his capacity to change his strategy to fit his perceptions. Thus, the study of phenomenology as well as existentialism will aid the proactive administrator to enhance his capability in the areas of consciousness and freedom of choice. In order to further his skill, he must expose himself to new knowledge as a stimulus for the new ideas he needs to generate in considering possibilities. Richter asserts that "the existentialist executive must be prepared to alter his choices as he receives fresh information from his environment." As the rate of societal change increases, new situations will present a broader range of possibilities by which an administrator may influence his internal and external environment.

The underlying purpose in this discussion is to emphasize that we need a "new administrator" for tomorrow's organizations; we label this man the "proactive administrator" and attempt, in Chapter 13, to convey an impression of him. Hubert Bonner argues that all men are proactive to some degree. He says that " . . . like intelligence, proaction can be modified by circumstances and by the individual's effort to transform himself in the light of his abilities and social conditions."[19] According to Bonner, proactive man tends to have a different personality orientation. We cite some major characteristics of the proactive personality:[20]

1) Freedom and anxiety. Freedom of choice involves the fear of unpredictable consequences. Both the proactive and the less forward-directed individuals experience anxiety in the face of freedom and an unstructured life situation. But the proactive individual, by virtue of his strong desire for new experience and his capacity to assimilate and control anxiety, becomes anxiety's master instead of its slave.

   Freedom is a powerful psychological incentive of the proactive individual, in making his own choices and reaching his own decisions regarding the person he wants to become.

2) Esthetic view of life. The proactive individual approaches life with a marked sense of form and symmetry, beauty, and harmony. His esthetic style of life refers to his seeking of a perfection which is becoming, but never achieved.

3) Idealization. Proactive idealization is the envisioning of ourselves as being different from what we are. Rather than being an act of self-deception and self-falsification, idealization is the process through which the healthy person generally and the proactive person in particular become authentic persons.

4) Creativity. In his approach to life, the proactive man is essentially creative.

a) The proactive man is moved by a strong need for individuation for being himself as a person.

b) The proactive man is constantly in pursuit of new values or a fresh recognition of the old ones. Transcendence of past accomplishments, both in others and in himself, is therefore another characteristic of the creative, proactive human being.

c) The creative individual, almost without exception, has a high degree of intellectual and emotional turbulence.

5) Self-transformation. Being essentially forward thrusting, future oriented, and broadly creative, the proactive individual is constantly engaged in the task of making of himself a "better" human being. [Editor's note: Bonner argues that proactive man strives constantly to make himself literally "a work of art."]

Utilizing Bonner's ideas in the organizational process, we emphasize that the proactive administrator will be aware of and use his freedom of choice (within appropriate limits); he will show willingness to discover the possibilities of man, to pursue new values in the various forms of organization, to be self-actualized, and to advocate future-oriented activities. Thus, the proactive administrator will initiate future changes rather than simply react to the forces of immediate change. Furthermore, he will anticipate change forces in order to plan and manage change for the future.

The proactive administrator will also have a less structured, more imaginative capacity to deal with complex, changing situations and to develop flexible policies for the members and for the whole organization. As a result of the complex role requirement illustrated in Figure 2, he will have to possess both research knowledge and a substantial intellectual capability in order to appraise the information he is receiving and to make judgments about the relation of variables to the complex system with which he is involved.

Perhaps his ability to deal with people (interpersonal competence) will prove to be the critical element in the role of the future administrator. Interpersonal competence depends upon an awareness of self as well as an awareness of others. Interpersonal competence also implies an awareness of the effects of one's own behavior on others and how one's personality shapes his own particular leadership style.[21] Emphasis on interpersonal competence further implies that the future administrator will manifest a human bias in his leadership approach. He will be concerned primarily with people in order to make better organizational policy.

Tomorrow's organizations will have to be increasingly "open" systems in order to achieve the level of adaptive capability upon which their survival will depend. Although the importance of achieving an open system is clear, the means to that end are less obvious. In part, at least, the permeability will depend upon the openness of our future administrator: his willingness to communicate with people, his receptivity to both new ideas and criticism, and his awareness of the "phenomenal world." These qualities will prove indispensable to him in formulating and implementing policies as well as in meeting future social needs. Tomorrow's administrator will clearly be different from those of the past and present. He will be a flexible integrator (or "synchronizer") and an individual highly adaptive to many responsibilities, able to learn readily from new experiences, able to conceptualize broad new philosophies of organization, capable of imagination and creativity—and able to translate his vision into operations. Moreover, he will be adept at the management of ideas, as discussed in Anshen's article.

As Roher and his colleagues note, tomorrow's management will involve itself with developing personal growth, organizational innovation, and creativity. Management has always had the responsibility for creating a favorable organizational climate, but, in the past, this has been interpreted in terms of control. Tomorrow the climate will have to be favorable for adaptiveness, innovation, human development, and self-actualization.

To recapitulate, the essays in Chapter 13 emphasize how important it is to consider the need for new roles for proactive administrators in the future. The managers of today's organizations must understand the probable future responsibilities of tomorrow's administrators so that we may begin *now* to train these men for tomorrow's challenges. Training and preparing new administrators for more complex roles, equipping them with new knowledge and behaviors, and socializing them to perceive new possibilities is a viable means to achieve change capability and increased effectiveness in the organizations of tomorrow.

Why Organization Research?

The human being can shape his physical environment by research and by redefining situations based on his selective perception, experience, information, and ability. In the same fashion, the human organization may conduct various research activities, both to change the organization itself and to cope with needs. Organization research serves many purposes for tomorrow's organization.

In the first place, information derived from research activity can improve the process of policymaking (formulation, implementation, evaluation, and revision phases) while, at the same time, it can help managers to avoid the risk of *unintended consequences* which are always possible when new alternatives are being tested. The late Hadley Cantril, who has demonstrated how psychological dimensions may be applied at the national and international levels of policymaking, has described his attempts, made over many years, to induce consideration of *psychological* factors affecting crucial government decisions. The concluding chapter of one of his last books explains the procedures statesmen should follow to achieve the best possible policy.[22] His major point is that top U.S. policymakers should take on the perspectives of the peoples of the world by means of a consistent, systematic use of the techniques he has devised. This view of policymaking is based on the idea that policymakers should have a genuine understanding of the people that policy is designed to affect. Cantril strongly believed that if the United States follows this vital research information, particularly as related to psychological dimensions of the policy process, we would avoid such disastrous pitfalls as the Bay of Pigs invasion and perhaps even the war in Southeast Asia.

According to Kahn and Wiener, the undesirable consequences which often accompany social processes may be based on any of the following hazards:

1) Criteria for decisions are often too narrow.
2) Decisions are made at inappropriate points in the structure. A closely related common error is the mistaken assumption that a prescription, for macrobehavior is one that will affect microbehavior, or vice versa.
3) Inadequate thought by administrators
4) Bad luck: unknown issues that could not be assessed due to insufficient information
5) Bad luck: unlikely events
6) Changes in actors: a lack of continuity in effective actors
7) Inappropriate models: technically wrong model; someone has made a mistake

8) Inappropriate values: misgivings about future values
9) Overdiscounting or underdiscounting of uncertainty or of the future
10) The best may be the enemy of the good (and sometimes vice versa): excessive or utopian objectives prevent incremental progress.

A second advantage of organization research is that it may provide better social information through societal feedback in the process of policymaking. As a new problem situation emerges, the organization is faced with many uncertain, ambiguous variables pertinent to the problem; old methods may not offer applicable means for solving the new problem. Under this circumstance, policymakers or administrators find themselves aware of a pressing need for new information, new ideas, new knowledge, and new methods. Organization research offers access to all of those. Greer asserts in Chapter 14 that social science can indeed contribute new knowledge to assist in making policy choices. The uncertainty factor is more of a problem when the organization attempts to do long-term policy planning, according to Bauer's article. Planning and control require continuous integration of new knowledge about the rapidly changing environment and the increasing interrelatedness of society. Computer-based information systems offer opportunities to develop large masses of data into social indicators, to forecast manpower requirements, to refine simulation techniques, to project changes in human values, and so forth.

A third advantage of organization research is as follows: Using new knowledge derived from research, management can deal more effectively with both human development and organizational productivity. There is the possibility, too, of using research methods as a preface to reorganization or change by evaluating experiments which have been undertaken.[23] All of these alternatives reflect typical problems which are faced by organizations today; through organization research, possible solutions may be developed. Moreover, future-oriented research is necessary for forecasting "the different future" and for discovering different goals for better organizational life. Kahn and Wiener suggest the following objectives for future-oriented policy research:[24]

1) To stimulate and stretch the imagination and to improve perspectives
2) To clarify, define, expound, and argue major issues
3) To design and study alternative policy "packages" and contexts
4) To create propaedeutic and heuristic expositions, methodologies, paradigms, and frameworks
5) To improve intellectual communication and cooperation, particularly by the use of historical analogies, scenarios, metaphors, analytic models, precise concepts, and suitable language
6) To increase ability to identify new patterns and crises and to understand their character and significance
7) To furnish specific knowledge and to generate and document conclusions, recommendations, and suggestions
8) To clarify currently realistic policy choices, with emphasis on those that retain efficiency and flexibility over a broad range of contingencies
9) To improve the "administrative" ability of decisionmakers and their staff to react appropriately to the new and unfamiliar

Considering the above objectives, tomorrow's organizations may open up new opportunities and possibilities for development. Furthermore, organizations may improve or modify existing policies related to future goals. Studying the future environment from many different perspectives offers a means for bringing about better human life in the not-too-distant future. The proactive administrator must be aware of the need for continuous research to develop broad social indicators which will show the changing nature of human values, the developments relevant to organizational structure and technology, the variety of environments, and the status of social change in the world. Sophisticated measurements of these and other matters will be a central dimension of survival for tomorrow's organizations.

References and Notes

1. Harold J. Leavitt, "Applied Organization Change in Industry: Structural, Technological, and Humanistic Approaches," in James G. March, ed., *Handbook of Organizations* (Chicago: Rand-McNally & Co., 1965), p. 1145.
2. E. L. Trist, "Sociotechnical Systems," *Tavistock Institute of Human Relations,* Document No. 572 (November 1959).
3. E. L. Trist, *et al., Organizational Choice* (London: Tavistock Publications, 1963).
4. Joan Woodward, *Industrial Organization: Theory and Practice* (London: Oxford University Press, 1965) and Joan Woodward, ed., *Industrial Organization: Behavior and Control* (London: Oxford University Press, 1970).
5. Chris Argyris, *Some Causes of Organizational Ineffectiveness Within the Department of State,* Occasional Papers No. 2 (Washington, D.C.: Center for International Systems Research, Department of State).
6. Dale Zand, "Managing the Knowledge Organization," in Peter F. Drucker, ed., *Preparing Tomorrow's Business Leaders Today* (Englewood Cliffs, N.J.: Prentice-Hall, Inc., 1969), pp. 112–36.
7. Planned organization change is termed a movement from one state of organizational affairs to another state through a devised or projected course of action. Garth Jones, *Planned Organizational Change: A Study in Change Dynamics* (New York: Praeger Publishers, Inc., 1969), p. 5.
8. Similar distinctions are introduced by Peter A. Clark and Janet R. Ford, "Methodological and Theoretical Problems in the Investigation of Planned Organizational Change," *The Sociological Review* 18, no. 1 (March 1970), pp. 29–52. See also Daniel Katz and Robert Kahn, *Social Psychology of Organizations* (New York: John Wiley & Sons, 1965).

9. Edgar H. Schein and Warren G. Bennis, *Personal and Organizational Change Through Group Methods: The Laboratory Approach* (New York: John Wiley & Sons, Inc.; 1965), p. 4.

10. Schein and Bennis, *op. cit.,* p. 309.

11. Chris Argyris, *Organization and Innovation* (Homewood: Richard D. Irwin Inc., 1965).

12. Robert R. Blake and Jane S. Mouton, *The Managerial Grid* (Houston: Gulf Publishing Company, 1964) and *Corporate Excellence Through Grid Organizational Development* (Houston: Gulf Publishing Company, 1968).

13. The parenthetical numbers refer to locations on the grid. The initial number indicates commitment to system goals, while the second measures humanistic orientation. On each scale, a 9 is high while 1 is low.

14. Eric L. Trist, et al., *op. cit.,* 1963; see also H. A. Clegg, *New Approach to Indusrial Democracy* (London: Oxford University Press, 1960).

15. Larry E. Greiner, "Conceptions of Organization Development in Sweden," paper presented at the 33rd Annual Conference of the American Society for Public Administration, New York City, April, 1972, p. 1. We note in passing that early in 1972 the Saab and Volvo automobile companies apparently began application of the sociotechnical approach, using autonomous work teams to assemble complete automobiles. How this is faring is not known at this writing. Something of the possible effect of the experiment may be seen in the reaction of a young General Motors worker on strike in Lordstown, Ohio, in the spring of 1972 (as quoted in the *New York Times):* "It's going to take something . . . where a guy can take an interest in the job. GM can say to us 'You're crazy,' but a guy can't do the same thing eight hours a day year after year. And it's got to be more than just saying to a guy 'Okay instead of six spots on the weld you'll do five spots.' I was reading about Sweden where they're going to bring parts together and then have a team of 20 guys put the whole car together. That's the kind of thing I'm talking about." Quoted in Roy W. Walters & Associates, Inc., *Job Enrichment Newsletter* (March 1972).

16. See also F. C. and L. R. Hoffman, *Automation and the Worker* (New York: Holt, Rinehart & Winston, Inc., 1960).

17. Donald N. Michael, *The Unprepared Society: Planning for a Precarious Future* (New York: Basic Books, Inc., Publishers, 1968).

18. Rensis Likert, *The Human Organization: Its Management and Value* (New York: McGraw-Hill Book Company, Inc., 1967).

19. Hubert Bonner, "The Proactive Personality," in James F. T. Bugental, ed., *Challenges of Humanistic Psychology* (New York: McGraw-Hill Book Company, 1967).

20. *Ibid.,* pp. 63–66.

21. Warren G. Bennis, "Postbureaucratic Leadership," *Transaction* (July-August 1969), pp. 44–51, 61.

22. Hadley Cantril, "The Psychological Dimensions of Policy," *The Human Dimension: Experiences in Policy Research* (New Brunswick: Rutgers University Press, 1967).

23. Donald T. Campbell, "Reforms as Experiments," *American Psychologist* (1969), pp. 409–29. Along with considering the strategic values of treating reforms as experiments, Campbell explores appropriate research methods for evaluating results.

24. Kahn and Wiener, *op. cit.,* pp. 398–409.

Chapter 10 General Strategies for a Changing Organization

GENERAL STRATEGIES FOR EFFECTING
CHANGES IN HUMAN SYSTEMS

Robert Chin and Kenneth D. Benne

Discussing general strategies and procedures for effecting change requires that
we set limits to the discussion. For, under
a liberal interpretation of the title, we
would need to deal with much of the literature of contemporary social and behavioral science, basic and applied.

Therefore, we shall limit our discussion
to those changes which are planned
changes—in which attempts to bring
about changes are conscious, deliberate,
and intended, at least on the part of one
or more agents related to the change attempt. We shall also attempt to categorize
strategies and procedures which have a
few important elements in common but
which, in fact, differ widely in other respects. And we shall neglect many of
these differences. In addition, we shall
look beyond the description of procedures
in common-sense terms and seek some
genotypic characteristics of change strategies. We shall seek the roots of the main
strategies discussed, including their variants, in ideas and idea systems prominent
in contemporary and recent social and
psychological thought.

One element in all approaches to
planned changes is the conscious utilization and application of knowledge as an
instrument or tool for modifying patterns
and institutions of practice. The knowledge or related technology to be applied
may be knowledge of the nonhuman environment in which practice goes on or of
some knowledge-based "thing technology" for controlling one or another feature
of the practice environment. In education-

al practice, for example, technologies of
communication and calculation, based
upon new knowledge of electronics—
audiovisual devices, television, computers,
teaching machines—loom large among the
knowledges and technologies that promise
greater efficiency and economy in handling various practices in formal education. As attempts are made to introduce
these new thing technologies into school
situations, the change problem shifts to
the human problems of dealing with the
resistances, anxieties, threats to morale,
conflicts, disrupted interpersonal communications, and so on, which prospective
changes in patterns of practice evoke in
the people affected by the change. So the
change agent, even though focally and initially concerned with modifications in the
thing technology of education, finds himself in need of more adequate knowledge
of human behavior, individual and social,
and in need of developed "people technologies," based on behavioral knowledge, for dealing effectively with the
human aspects of deliberate change.

The knowledge which suggests improvements in educational practice may,
on the other hand, be behavioral knowledge in the first instance—knowledge
about participative learning, about attitude
change, about family disruption in inner-
city communities, about the cognitive and
skill requirements of new careers, and so
forth. Such knowledge may suggest
changes in school grouping, in the relations between teachers and students, in
the relations of teachers and principals to

310

parents, and in counseling practices. Here change agents, initially focused on application of behavioral knowledge and the improvement of people technologies in school settings, must face the problems of using people technologies in planning, installing, and evaluating such changes in educational practice. The new people technologies must be experienced, understood, and accepted by teachers and administrators before they can be used effectively with students.

This line of reasoning suggests that, whether the focus of planned change is in the introduction of more effective thing technologies or people technologies into institutionalized practice, processes of introducing such changes must be based on behavioral knowledge of change and must utilize people technologies based on such knowledge.

Types of Strategies for Changing

Our further analysis is based on three types or groups of strategies [See Figure 1]. The first of these, and probably the most frequently employed by men of knowledge in America and Western Europe, are those we call empirical-rational strategies. One fundamental assumption underlying these strategies is that men are rational. Another assumption is that men will follow their rational self-interest once this is revealed to them. A change is proposed by some person or group which knows of a situation that is desirable, effective, and in line with the self-interest of the person, group, organization, or community which will be affected by the change. Because the person (or group) is assumed to be rational and moved by self-interest, it is assumed that he (or they) will adopt the proposed change if it can be rationally justified and if it can be shown by the proposer(s) that he (or they) will gain by the change.

A second group of strategies we call normative–re-educative. These strategies build upon assumptions about human motivation different from those underlying

the first. The rationality and intelligence of men are not denied. Patterns of action and practice are supported by sociocultural norms and by commitments on the part of individuals to these norms. Sociocultural norms are supported by the attitude and value systems of individuals— normative outlooks which undergird their commitments. Change in a pattern of practice or action, according to this view, will occur only as the persons involved are brought to change their normative orientations to old patterns and develop commitments to new ones. And changes in normative orientations involve changes in attitudes, values, skills, and significant relationships, not just changes in knowledge, information, or intellectual rationales for action and practice.

The third group of strategies is based on the application of power in some form, political or otherwise. The influence process involved is basically that of compliance of those with less power to the plans, directions, and leadership of those with greater power. Often the power to be applied is legitimate power or authority. Thus the strategy may involve getting the authority of law or administrative policy behind the change to be effected. Some power strategies may appeal less to the use of authoritative power to effect change than to the massing of coercive power, legitimate or not, in support of the change sought.[1] (See Figure 1, p. 312.)

Empirical-Rational Strategies

A variety of specific strategies are included in what we are calling the empirical-rational approach to effecting change. As we have already pointed out, the rationale underlying most of these is an assumption that men are guided by reason and that they will utilize some rational calculus of self-interest in determining needed changes in behavior.

It is difficult to point to any one person whose ideas express or articulate the orientation underlying commitment to empirical-rational strategies of changing. In

Figure 1   Strategies of Deliberate Changing

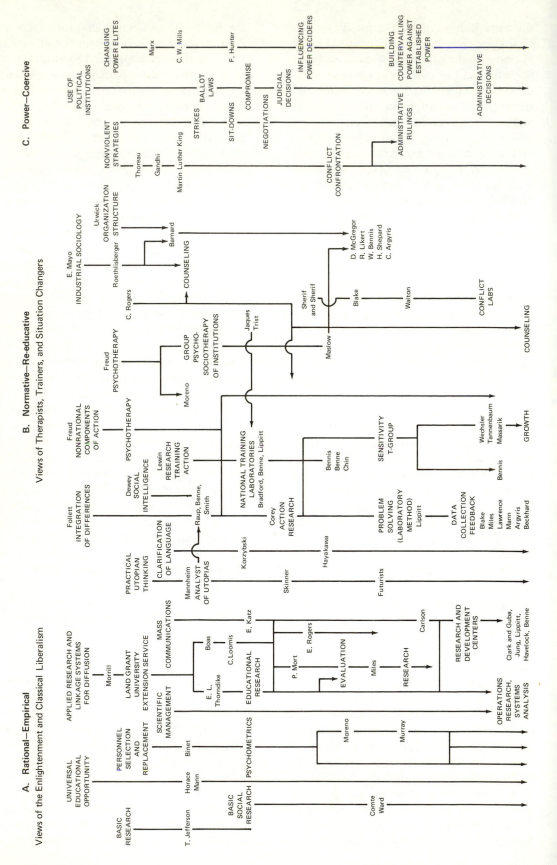

Western Europe and America, this orientation might be better identified with the general social orientation of the Enlightenment and of classical liberalism than with the ideas of any one man. On this view, the chief foes to human rationality and to change or progress based on rationality were ignorance and superstition. Scientific investigation and research represented the chief ways of extending knowledge and reducing the limitations of ignorance. A corollary of this optimistic view of man and his future was an advocacy of education as a way of disseminating scientific knowledge and of freeing men and women from the shackles of superstition. Although elitist notions played a part in the thinking of many classic liberals, the increasing trend during the nineteenth century was toward the universalization of educational opportunity. The common and universal school, open to all men and women, was the principal instrument by which knowledge would replace ignorance and superstition in the minds of people and become a principal agent in the spread of reason, knowledge, and knowledge-based action and practice (progress) in human society. In American experience, Jefferson may be taken as a principal, early advocate of research and of education as agencies of human progress. And Horace Mann may be taken as the prophet of progress through the institutionalization of universal educational opportunity through the common school.[2]

Basic Research and Dissemination of Knowledge through General Education

The strategy of encouraging basic knowledge building and of depending on general education to diffuse the results of research into the minds and thinking of men and women is still by far the most appealing strategy of change to most academic men of knowledge and to large segments of the American population as well. Basic researchers are quite likely to appeal for time for further research when confronted by some unmet need. And many people find this appeal convincing. Both of these

facts are well illustrated by difficulties with diseases for which no adequate control measures or cures are available—poliomyelitis, for example. Medical researchers asked for more time and funds for research and people responded with funds for research, both through voluntary channels and through legislative appropriations. And the control measures were forthcoming. The educational problem then shifted to inducing people to comply with immunization procedures based on research findings.

This appeal to a combination of research and education of the public has worked in many areas of new knowledge-based thing technologies where almost universal readiness for accepting the new technology was already present in the population. Where such readiness is not available, as in the case of fluoridation technologies in the management of dental caries, general strategy of basic research plus educational (informational) campaigns to spread knowledge of the findings do not work well. The cases of its inadequacy as a single strategy of change have multiplied, especially where "engineering" problems, which involve a divided and conflicting public or deep resistances due to the threat by the new technology to traditional attitudes and values, have thwarted its effectiveness. But these cases, while they demand attention to other strategies of changing, do not disprove the importance of basic research and of general educational opportunity as elements in a progressive and self-renewing society.

We have noted that the strategy under discussion has worked best in grounding and diffusing generally acceptable thing technologies in society. Some have argued that the main reason the strategy has not worked in the area of people technologies is a relative lack of basic research on people and their behavior, relationships, and institutions and a corresponding lack of emphasis upon social and psychological knowledges in school and college curricula. It would follow in this view that increased basic research on human affairs and relationships and increased efforts to diffuse the results of such research through public education are the ways of making the general strategy work better. Auguste Comte with his emphasis on positivistic sociology in the reorganization of society and Lester F. Ward in America may be taken as late nineteenth-century representatives of this view. And the spirit of Comte and Ward is by no means dead in American academia or in influential segments of the American public.

Personnel Selection and Replacement

Difficulties in getting knowledge effectively into practice may be seen as lying primarily in the lack of fitness of persons occupying positions with job responsibilities for improving practice. The argument goes that we need the right person in the right position, if knowledge is to be optimally applied and if rationally based changes are to become the expectation in organizational and societal affairs. This fits with the liberal reformers' frequently voiced and enacted plea to drive the unfit from office and to replace them with those more fit as a condition of social progress.

That reformers' programs have so often failed has sobered but by no means destroyed the zeal of those who regard personnel selection, assessment, and replacement as a major key to program improvement in education or in other enterprises as well. This strategy was given a scientific boost by the development of scientific testing of potentialities and aptitudes. We will use Binet as a prototype of psychological testing and Moreno as a prototype in sociometric testing, while recognizing the extensive differentiation and elaboration which have occurred in psychometrics and sociometrics since their original work. We recognize too the elaborated modes of practice in personnel work which have been built around psychometric and sociometric tools and techniques. We do not discount their limited value as actual and potential tools for change, while making two observations on the way they have often been used. First,

they have been used more often in the interest of system maintenance rather than of system change, since the job descriptions personnel workers seek to fill are defined in terms of system requirements as established. Second, by focusing on the role occupant as the principal barrier to improvement, personnel selection and replacement strategies have tended not to reveal the social and cultural system difficulties which may be in need of change if improvement is to take place.

Systems Analysts as Staff and Consultants

Personnel workers in government, industry, and education have typically worked in staff relations to line management, reflecting the bureaucratic, line-staff form of organization which has flourished in the large-scale organization of effort and enterprise in the twentieth century. And other expert workers—systems analysts—more attuned to system difficulties than to the adequacies or inadequacies of persons as role occupants within the system, have found their way into the staff resources of line management in contemporary organizations.

There is no reason why the expert resources of personnel workers and systems analysts might not be used in nonbureaucratic organizations or in processes of moving bureaucratic organizations toward nonbureaucratic forms. But the fact remains that their use has been shaped, for the most part, in the image of the scientific management of bureaucratically organized enterprises. So we have placed the systems analysts in our chart under Frederick Taylor, the father of scientific management in America.

The line management of an enterprise seeks to organize human and technical effort toward the most efficient service of organizational goals. And these goals are defined in terms of the production of some mandated product, whether a tangible product or a less tangible good or service. In pursuing this quest for efficiency, line management employs experts in the analysis of sociotechnical systems and in the laying out of more efficient systems. The experts employed may work as external consultants or as an internal staff unit. Behavioral scientists have recently found their way, along with mathematicians and engineers, into systems analysis work.

It is interesting to note that the role of these experts is becoming embroiled in discussions of whether or not behavioral science research should be used to sensitize administrators to new organizational possibilities, to new goals, or primarily to implement efficient operation within perspectives and goals as currently defined. Jean Hills has raised the question of whether behavioral science when applied to organizational problems tends to perpetuate established ideology and system relations because of blinders imposed by their being "problem centered" and by their limited definition of what is "a problem."[3]

We see an emerging strategy, in the use of behavioral scientists as systems analysts and engineers, toward viewing the problem of organizational change and changing as a wide-angled problem, one in which all the input and output features and components of a large-scale system are considered. It is foreseeable that with the use of high-speed and high-capacity computers, and with the growth of substantial theories and hypotheses about how parts of an educational system operate, we shall find more and more applications for systems analysis and operations research in programs of educational change. In fact, it is precisely the quasi-mathematical character of these modes of research that will make possible the rational analysis of qualitatively different aspects of educational work and will bring them into the range of rational planning—masses of students, massive problems of poverty and educational and cultural deprivation, and so on. We see no necessary incompatibility between an ideology which emphasizes the individuality of the student and the use of systems analysis and computers in strategizing the problems of the total system. The actual incompatibilities may lie in the limited uses to which existing organizers and administrators of educational efforts put these technical resources.

Applied Research and Linkage Systems for Diffusion of Research Results

The American development of applied research and of a planned system for linking applied researchers with professional practitioners and both of these with centers for basic research and with organized consumers of applied research has been strongly influenced by two distinctive American inventions—the land-grant university and the agricultural extension system. We, therefore, have put the name of Justin Morrill, author of the land-grant college act and of the act which established the cooperative agricultural extension system, on our chart. The land-grant colleges or universities were dedicated to doing applied research in the service of agriculture and the mechanic arts. These colleges and universities developed research programs in basic sciences as well and experimental stations for the development and refinement of knowledge-based technologies for use in engineering and agriculture. As the extension services developed, county agents—practitioners— were attached to the state land-grant college or university that received financial support from both state and federal governments. The county agent and his staff developed local organizations of adult farm men and women of farm youth to provide both a channel toward informing consumers concerning new and better agricultural practices and toward getting awareness of unmet consumer needs and unsolved problems back to centers of knowledge and research. Garth Jones has made one of the more comprehensive studies of the strategies of changing involved in large-scale demonstration.[4]

All applied research has not occurred within a planned system for knowledge discovery, development, and utilization like the one briefly described above. The system has worked better in developing and diffusing people technologies, though the development of rural sociology and of agricultural economics shows that extension workers were by no means unaware of the behavioral dimensions of change problems. But the large-scale demonstration, through the land-grant university cooperative extension service, of the stupendous changes which can result from a planned approach to knowledge discovery, development, diffusion, and utilization is a part of the consciousness of all Americans concerned with planned change.[5]

1) Applied research and development is an honored part of the tradition of engineering approaches to problem identification and solution. The pioneering work of E. L. Thorndike in applied research in education should be noted on our chart. The processes and slow tempo of diffusion and utilization of research findings and inventions in public education is well illustrated in studies by Paul Mort and his students.[6] More recently, applied research in its product development aspect, has been utilized in a massive way to contribute curriculum materials and designs for science instruction (as well as in other subjects). When we assess this situation to find reasons why such researches have not been more effective in producing changes in instruction, the answers seem to lie both in the plans of the studies which produced the materials and designs and in the potential users of the findings. Adequate linkage between consumers and researchers was frequently not established. Planned and evaluated demonstrations and experimentations connected with the use of materials were frequently slighted. And training of consumer teachers to use the new materials adaptively and creatively was frequently missing.

Such observations have led to a fresh spurt of interest in evaluation research addressed to educational programs. The fear persists that this too may lead to disappointment if it is not focused for two-way communication between researchers and teachers and if it does not involve collaboratively the ultimate consumers of the results of such research—the students. Evaluation researches conducted in the spirit of justifying a program developed by expert applied researchers will not help to guide teachers and students in their quest for improved practices of teaching and learning, if the concerns of the latter have not been taken centrally into account in the evaluation process.[7]

2) Recently, attempts have been made to link applied research activities in education with basic researchers on the one hand and with persons in action and practice settings on the other through some system of interlocking roles similar to those suggested in the description of the land grant–extension systems in agriculture or in other fields where applied and development researches have flourished.

The linking of research development efforts with diffusion-innovation efforts has been gaining headway in the field of education with the emergence of federally supported Research and Development Centers based in universities, Regional Laboratories connected with state departments of education, colleges and universities in a geographic area, and with various consortia and institutes confronting problems of educational change and changing. The strategy of change here usually includes a well-researched innovation which seems feasible to install in practice settings. Attention is directed to the question of whether or not the innovation will bring about a desired result, and with what it can accomplish, if given a trial in one or more practice settings. The questions of *how* to get a fair trial and *how* to install an innovation in an already going and crowded school system are ordinarily not built centrally into the strategy. The rationalistic assumption usually precludes research attention to these questions. For, if the invention can be rationally shown to have achieved desirable results in some situations, it is assumed that people in other situations will adopt it once they know these results and the rationale behind them. The neglect of the above questions has led to a wastage of much applied research effort in the past.

Attention has been given recently to the roles, communication mechanisms, and processes necessary for innovation and diffusion of improved educational practices.[8] Clark and Guba have formulated very specific processes related to and necessary for change in educational practice following upon research. For them, the necessary processes are: *development,* including invention and design; *diffusion,* including dissemination and demonstration; *adoption,* including trial, installation, and institutionalization. Clark's earnest conviction is summed up in this statement: "In a sense, the educational research community will be the educational community, and the route to educational progress will self-evidently be research and development."[9]

The approach of Havelock and Benne is concerned with the intersystem relationships between basic researchers, applied researchers, practitioners, and consumers in an evolved and evolving organization for knowledge utilization. They are concerned especially with the communication difficulties and role conflicts that occur at points of intersystem exchange. These conflicts are important because they illuminate the normative issues at stake between basic researchers and applied researchers, between applied researchers and practitioners (teachers and administrators), between practitioners and consumers (students). The lines of strategy suggested by their analysis for solving role conflicts and communication difficulties call for transactional and collaborative exchanges across the lines of varied organized interests and orientations within the process of utilization. This brings their

analysis into the range of normative–re-educative strategies to be discussed later.

The concepts from the behavioral sciences upon which these strategies of diffusion rest come mainly from two traditions. The first is from studies of the diffusion of traits of culture from one cultural system to another, initiated by the American anthropologist, Franz Boas. This type of study has been carried on by Rogers in his work on innovation and diffusion of innovations in contemporary culture and is reflected in a number of recent writers such as Katz and Carlson.[10] The second scientific tradition is in studies of influence in mass communication associated with Carl Hovland and his students.[11] Both traditions have assumed a *relatively passive recipient of input* in diffusion situations. And actions within the process of diffusion are interpreted from the standpoint of an observer of the process. Bauer has pointed out that scientific studies have exaggerated the effectiveness of mass persuasion since they have compared the total number in the audience to the communications with the much smaller proportion of the audience persuaded by the communication.[12] A clearer view of processes of diffusion must include the actions of the receiver as well as those of the transmitter in the transactional events which are the units of diffusion process. And strategies for making diffusion processes more effective must be transactional and collaborative by design.

Utopian Thinking as a Strategy of Changing

It may seem strange to include the projection of utopias as a rational-empirical strategy of changing. Yet inventing and designing the shape of the future by extrapolating what we know of in the present is to envision a direction for planning and action in the present. If the image of a potential future is convincing and rationally persuasive to men in the present, the image may become part of the dynamics and motivation of present action. The liberal tradition is not devoid of its utopias. When we think of utopias quickened by an effort to extrapolate from the sciences of man to a future vision of society, the utopia of B. F. Skinner comes to mind.[13] The title of the Eight State Project, "Designing Education for the Future" for which this paper was prepared, reveals a utopian intent and aspiration and illustrates an attempt to employ utopian thinking for practical purposes.[14]

Yet it may be somewhat disheartening to others as it is to us to note the absence of rousing and beckoning normative statements of what both can and ought to be in man's future in most current liberal-democratic utopias, whether these be based on psychological, sociological, political, or philosophical findings and assumptions. The absence of utopias in current society, in this sense, and in the sense that Mannheim studied them in his now classical study,[15] tends to make the forecasting of future directions a problem of technical prediction, rather than equally a process of projecting value orientations and preferences into the shaping of a better future.

Perceptual and Conceptual Reorganization through the Clarification of Language

In classical liberalism, one perceived foe of rational change and progress was superstition. And superstitions are carried from man to man and from generation to generation through the agency of unclear and mythical language. British utilitarianism was one important strand of classical liberalism, and one of utilitarianism's important figures, Jeremy Bentham, sought to purify language of its dangerous mystique through his study of fictions.

More recently, Alfred Korzybski and S. I. Hayakawa, in the general semantics movement, have sought a way of clarifying and rectifying the names of things and processes.[16] While their main applied concern was with personal therapy, both, and especially Hayakawa, were also concerned to bring about changes in social systems as well. People disciplined in general semantics, it was hoped, would see more correctly, communicate more adequately, and reason more effectively and thus lay a realistic common basis for action and changing. The strategies of changing associated with general semantics overlap with our next family of strategies, the normative–re-educative, because of their emphasis upon the importance of interpersonal relationships and social contexts within the communication process.

Normative–Re-Educative Strategies of Changing

We have already suggested that this family of strategies rests on assumptions and hypotheses about man and his motivation which contrast significantly at points with the assumptions and hypotheses of those committed to what we have called rational-empirical strategies. Men are seen as inherently active, in quest of impulse and need satisfaction. The relation between man and his environment is essentially transactional, as Dewey[17] made clear in his famous article on "The Reflex-Arc-Concept." Man, the organism, does not passively await given stimuli from his environment in order to respond. He takes stimuli as furthering or thwarting the goals of his ongoing action. Intelligence arises in the process of shaping organism-environmental relations toward more adequate fitting and joining of organismic demands and environmental resources.

Intelligence is social, rather than narrowly individual. Men are guided in their actions by socially funded and communicated meanings, norms, and institutions, in brief by a normative culture. At the personal level, men are guided by internalized meanings, habits, and values. Changes in patterns of action or practice are, therefore, changes, not alone in the rational informational equipment of men, but at the personal level, in habits and values as well and, at the sociocultural level, changes are alterations in normative structures and in institutionalized roles and relationships, as well as in cognitive and perceptual orientations.

For Dewey, the prototype of intelligence in action is the scientific method. And he saw a broadened and humanized scientific method as man's best hope for progress if men could learn to utilize such a method in facing all of the problematic situations of their lives. *Intelligence,* so conceived, rather than *Reason* as defined in classical liberalism, was the key to Dewey's hope for the invention, development, and testing of adequate strategies of changing in human affairs.

Lewin's contribution to normative–re-educative strategies of changing stemmed from his vision of required interrelations between research, training, and action (and, for him, this meant collaborative relationships, often now lacking, between researchers, educators, and activists) in the solution of human problems, in the identification of needs for change, and in the working out of improved knowledge, technology, and patterns of action in meeting these needs. Man must participate in his own re-education if he is to be re-educated at all. And re-education is a normative change as well as a cognitive and perceptual change. These convictions led Lewin[18] to emphasize action research as a strategy of changing, and participation in groups as a medium of re-education.

Freud's main contributions to normative–re-educative strategies of changing are two. First, he sought to demonstrate the unconscious and preconscious bases of man's actions. Only as a man finds ways of becoming aware of these nonconscious wellsprings of his attitudes and actions will he be able to bring them into conscious self-control. And Freud devoted much of his magnificent genius to developing ways of helping men to become [both] conscious of the main springs of their actions and so capable of freedom. Second, in developing therapeutic methods, he discovered and developed ways of Zilizing the relationship between change agent (therapist) and client (patient) as a major tool in re-educating the client toward expanded self-awareness, self-understanding, and self-control. Emphasis upon the collaborative relationship in therapeutic change was a major contribution by Freud and his students and colleagues to normative–re-educative strategies of changing in human affairs.[19]

Normative–re-educative approaches to effecting change bring direct interventions by change agents, interventions based on a consciously worked out theory of change and of changing, into the life of a client system, be that system a person, a small group, an organization, or a community. The theory of changing is still crude, but it is probably as explicitly stated as possible, granted our present state of knowledge about planned change.[20]

Some of the common elements among variants within this family of change strategies are the following. First, all emphasize the client system and his (or its) involvement in working out programs of change and improvement for himself (or itself). The way the client sees himself and his problem must be brought into dialogic relationship with the way in which he and his problem are seen by the change agent, whether the latter is functioning as researcher, consultant, trainer, therapist, or friend in relation to the client. Second, the problem confronting the client is not assumed *a priori* to be one which can be met by more adequate technical information, though this possibility is not ruled out. The problem may lie rather in the attitudes, values, norms, and the external and internal relationships of the client system and may require alteration or re-education of these as a condition of its solution. Third, the change agent must learn to intervene mutually and collaboratively along with the client into efforts to define and solve the client's problem(s). The here and now experience of the two provide[s] an important basis for diagnosing the problem and for locating needs for re-education in the interest of solving it. Fourth, nonconscious elements which impede problem solution must be brought into consciousness and publicly examined and reconstructed. Fifth, the methods and concepts of the behavioral sciences are resources which change agent and client learn to use selectively, relevantly, and appropriately in learning to deal with problems of a similar kind in the future.

These approaches center in the notion that people technology is just as necessary as thing technology in working out desirable changes in human affairs. Put in this bold fashion, it is obvious that for the normative–re-educative change agent, clarification and reconstruction of values is of pivotal importance in changing. By getting the values of various parts of the client system, along with his own, openly into the arena of change and by working through value conflicts responsibly, the change agent seeks to avoid manipulation and indoctrination of the client—in the morally reprehensible meanings of these terms.

We may use the organization of the National Training Laboratories in 1947 as a milestone in the development of normative–re-educative approaches to changing in America. The first summer laboratory program grew out of earlier collaborations among Kurt Lewin, Ronald Lippitt, Leland Bradford, and Kenneth Benne. The idea behind the laboratory was that participants, staff, and students would learn about themselves and their back-home problems by collaboratively building a laboratory in which participants would become both experimenters and subjects in the study of their own developing interpersonal and group behavior within the laboratory setting. It seems evident that the five conditions of a normative–re-educative approach to changing were met in the conception of the training laboratory. Kurt Lewin died before the 1947 session of the training laboratory opened. Ronald Lippitt was a student of Lewin's and carried many of Lewin's orientations with him into the laboratory staff. Leland Bradford and Kenneth Benne were both students of John Dewey's philosophy of education. Bradford had invented several technologies for participative learning and self-study in his work in WPA adult education programs and as training officer in several agencies of the federal government. Benne came out of a background in educational philosophy and had collaborated with colleagues prior to 1943 in developing a methodology for policy and decisionmaking and for the reconstruction of normative orientations—a methodology which sought to fuse democratic and scientific values and to translate these into principles for resolving conflicting and problematic situations at personal and community levels of human organization.[21] Benne and his colleagues had been much influenced by the work of Mary Follett,[22] her studies of integrative solutions to conflicts in settings of public and business administration, and by the work of Karl Mannheim[23] on the ideology and methodology of planning changes in human affairs, as well as by the work of John Dewey and his colleagues.

The work of the National Training Laboratories has encompassed development and testing of various approaches to changing in institutional settings, in America and abroad, since its beginning. One parallel development in England which grew out of Freud's thinking should be noted. This work developed in efforts at Tavistock Clinic to apply therapeutic approaches to problems of change in industrial organizations and in communities. This work is reported in statements by Elliot Jaques[24] and . . . by Eric Trist. Another parallel development is represented by the efforts of Roethlisberger and Dickson to use personal counseling in industry as a strategy of organizational change.[25] Roethlisberger and Dickson had been strongly influenced by the pioneer work of Elton Mayo in industrial sociology[26] as well as by the counseling theories and methodologies of Carl Rogers.

Various refinements of methodologies for changing have been developed and tested since the establishment of the National Training Laboratories in 1947, both under its auspices and under other auspices as well. For us, the model developments are worthy of further discussion here. One set of approaches is oriented focally to the improvement of the problem-solving processes utilized by a client system. The other set focuses on helping members of client systems to become aware of their attitude and value orientations and relationship difficulties through a probing of feelings, manifest and latent, involved in the functioning and operation of the client system.[27] Both approaches use the development of "temporary systems" as a medium of re-education of persons and of role occupants in various ongoing social systems.[28]

Improving the Problem-Solving Capabilities of a System

This family of approaches to changing rests on several assumptions about change in human systems. Changes in a system, when they are reality oriented, take the form of problem solving. A system to achieve optimum reality orientation in its adaptations to its changing internal and external environments must develop and institutionalize its own problem-solving structures and processes. These structures and processes must be tuned both to human problems of relationship and morale and to technical problems of meeting the system's task requirements set by its goals of production, distribution, and so on.[29] System problems are typically not social *or* technical but actually sociotechnical.[30] The problem-solving structures and processes of a human system must be developed to deal with a range of sociotechnical difficulties, converting them into problems, and organizing the relevant processes of data collection, planning, invention, and tryout of solutions, evaluation, and feedback of results, replanning, and so forth, which are required for the solution of the problems.

The human parts of the system must learn to function collaboratively in these processes of problem identification and solution, and the system must develop institutionalized support and mechanisms for maintaining and improving these pro-

cesses. Actually, the model of changing in these approaches is a cooperative, action-research model. This model was suggested by Lewin and developed most elaborately for use in educational settings by Stephen M. Corey.[31]

The range of interventions by outside change agents in implementing this approach to changing is rather wide. It has been most fully elaborated in relation to organizational development programs. Within such programs, intervention methods have been most comprehensively tested in industrial settings. Some of these more or less tested intervention methods are listed below. A design for any organizational development program, of course, normally uses a number of these in succession or combination.

1) Collection of data about organizational functioning and feedback of data into processes of data interpretation and of planning ways of correcting revealed dysfunctions by system managers and data collectors in collaboration.[32]

2) Training of managers and working organizational units in methods of problem solving through self-examination of present ways of dealing with difficulties and through development and tryout of better ways with consultation by outside and/or inside change agents. Usually, the working unit leaves its working place for parts of its training. These laboratory sessions are ordinarily interspersed with on-the-job consultations.

3) Developing acceptance of feedback (research and development) roles and functions within the organization, training persons to fill these roles, and relating such roles strategically to the ongoing management of the organization.

4) Training internal change agents to function within the organization in carrying on needed applied research, consultation, and training.[33]

Whatever specific strategies of intervention may be employed in developing the system's capabilities for problem solving, change efforts are designed to help the system in developing ways of scanning its operations to detect problems, of diagnosing these problems to determine relevant changeable factors in them, and of moving toward collaboratively determined solutions to the problems.

Releasing and Fostering Growth in the Persons Who Make Up the System to be Changed

Those committed to this family of approaches to changing tend to see the person as the basic unit of social organization. Persons, it is believed, are capable of creative, life-affirming, self- and other-regarding and respecting responses, choices, and actions, if conditions which thwart these kinds of responses are removed and other supporting conditions developed. Rogers has formulated these latter conditions in his analysis of the therapist-client relationship—trustworthiness, empathy, caring, and others.[34] Maslow has worked out a similar idea in his analysis of the hierarchy of needs in persons.[35] If lower needs are met, higher need-meeting actions will take place. McGregor[36] has formulated the ways in which existing organizations operate to fixate persons in lower levels of motivation and has sought to envision an organization designed to release and support the growth of persons in fulfilling their higher motivations as they function within the organization.

Various intervention methods have been designed to help people discover themselves as persons and commit themselves to continuing personal growth in the various relationships of their lives.

1) One early effort to install personal counseling widely and strategically in an organization has been reported by Roethisberger and Dickson.[37]
2) Training groups designed to facilitate personal confrontation and growth of members in an open, trusting, and accepting atmosphere have been conducted for individuals from various back-home situations and for persons from the same back-home setting. The processes of these groups have sometimes been described as "therapy for normals."[38]
3) Groups and laboratories designed to stimulate and support personal growth have been designed to utilize the resources of nonverbal exchange and communication among members along with verbal dialogue in inducing personal confrontation, discovery, and commitment to continuing growth.
4) Many psychotherapists, building on the work of Freud and Adler, have come to use groups, as well as two-person situations, as media of personal re-education and growth. Such efforts are prominent in mental health approaches to changing and have been conducted in educational, religious, community, industrial, and hospital settings. While these efforts focus primarily upon helping individuals to change themselves toward greater self-clarity and fuller self-actualization, they are frequently designed and conducted in the hope that personal changes will lead to changes in organizations, institutions, and communities as well.

We have presented the two variants of normative–re-educative approaches to changing in a way to emphasize their differences. Actually, there are many similarities between them as well, which justify placing both under the same general heading. We have already mentioned one of these similarities. Both frequently use temporary systems—a residential laboratory or workshop, a temporary group with special resources built in, an ongoing system which incorporates a change agent (trainer, consultant, counselor, or therapist) temporarily—as an aid to growth in the system and/or in its members.

More fundamentally, both approaches emphasize experience-based learning as an ingredient of all enduring changes in human systems. Yet both accept the principle that people must learn to learn from their experiences if self-directed change is to be maintained and continued. Frequently, people have learned to defend against the potential lessons of experience when these threaten existing equilibria, whether in the person or in the social system. How can these defenses be lowered to let the data of experience get into processes of perceiving the situation, of constructing new and better ways to define it, of inventing new and more appropriate ways of responding to the situation as redefined, of becoming more fully aware of the consequences of actions, and so forth? Learning to learn from ongoing experience is a major objective in both approaches to changing. Neither denies the relevance or importance of the non-cognitive determinants of behavior—feelings, attitudes, norms, and relationships—along with cognitive-perceptual determinants, in effecting behavioral change. The problem-solving approaches emphasize the cognitive determinants more than personal growth approaches do. But exponents of the former do not accept the rationalistic biases of the rational-empirical family of change strategies, already discussed. Since exponents of both problem-solving and personal growth approaches are committed to re-education of persons as integral to effective change in human systems, both emphasize norms of openness of communication, trust between persons, lowering of status barriers between parts of the system, and mutuality between parts as necessary conditions of the re-educative process.

Great emphasis has been placed recently upon the releasing of creativity in persons, groups, and organizations as requisite to coping adaptively with accelerated changes in the conditions of modern living. We have already stressed the emphasis which personal growth approaches put upon the release of creative responses in persons being re-educated. Problem-solving approaches also value creativity, though they focus more upon the group and organizational conditions which increase the probability of creative responses by persons functioning within those conditions than upon persons directly. The approaches do differ in their strategies for releasing creative responses within human systems. But both believe that creative adaptations to changing conditions may arise *within* human systems and do not have to be imported from *outside* them as in innovation-diffusion approaches already discussed and the power-compliance models still to be dealt with.

One developing variant of normative–re-educative approaches to changing, not already noted, focuses upon effective conflict management. It is, of course, common knowledge that differences within a society which demand interaccommodation often manifest themselves as conflicts. In the process of managing such conflicts, changes in the norms, policies, and relationships of the society occur. Can conflict management be brought into the ambit of planned change as defined in . . . [*The Planning of Change*, 2nd ed. (1969)]? Stemming from the work of the Sherifs in creating intergroup conflict and seeking to resolve it in a field-laboratory situation,[39] training in intergroup conflict and conflict resolution found its way into training laboratories through the efforts of Blake and others. Since that time, laboratories for conflict management have been developed under NTL and other auspices and methodologies for conflict resolution and management, in keeping with the values of planned change, have been devised. Blake's and Walton's work represent some of the findings from these pioneering efforts.[40]

Thus, without denying their differences in assumption and strategy, we believe that the differing approaches discussed in this section can be seen together within the framework of normative–re-educative approaches to changing. Two efforts to conceptualize planned change in a way to reveal the similarities in assumptions about changing and in value orientations toward change underlying these variant approaches are those by Lippitt, Watson, and Westley and by Bennis, Benne, and Chin.[41]

Another aspect of changing in human organizations is represented by efforts to conceive human organization in forms that go beyond the bureaucratic form which captured the imagination and fixed the contours of thinking and practice of organizational theorists and practitioners from the latter part of the nineteenth through the early part of the twentieth century. The bureaucratic form of organization was conceptualized by Max Weber and carried into American thinking by such students of administration as Urwick.[42] On this view, effective organization of human effort followed the lines of effective division of labor and effective establishment of lines of reporting, control, and supervision from the mass base of the organization up through various levels of control to the top of the pyramidal organization from which legitimate authority and responsibility stemmed.

The work of industrial sociologists like Mayo threw doubt upon the adequacy of such a model of formal organization to deal with the realities of organizational life by revealing the informal organization which grows up within the formal structure to satisfy personal and interpersonal needs not encompassed by or integrated into the goals of the formal organization. Chester Barnard may be seen as a transitional figure who, in discussing the functions of the organizational executive, gave equal emphasis to his responsibilities for task effectiveness and organizational efficiency (optimally meeting the human needs of persons in the organization).[43] Much of the development of subsequent organizational theory and practice has centered on problems of integrating the actualities, criteria, and concepts of organizational effectiveness and of organizational efficiency.

A growing group of thinkers and researchers have sought to move beyond the bureaucratic model toward some new model of organization which might set directions and limits for change efforts in organizational life. Out of many thinkers, we choose four who have theorized out of an orientation consistent with what we have called a normative–re-educative approach to changing.

Rensis Likert has presented an intergroup model of organization. Each working unit strives to develop and function as a group. The group's efforts are linked to other units of the organization by the overlapping membership of supervisors or managers in vertically or horizontally adjacent groups. This view of organization throws problems of delegation, supervision, and internal communication into a new light and emphasizes the importance of linking persons as targets of change and re-education in processes of organizational development.[44]

We have already stressed McGregor's efforts to conceive a form of organization more in keeping with new and more valid views of human nature and motivation (Theory Y) than the limited and false views of human nature and motivation (Theory X) upon which traditional bureaucratic organization has rested. In his work he sought to move thinking and practice relevant to organization and organizational change beyond the limits of traditional forms. "The essential task of management is to arrange organizational conditions and methods of operation so that people can achieve their own goals best by directing their own efforts toward organizational objectives."[45]

Bennis has consciously sought to move beyond bureaucracy in tracing the contours of the organization of the future.[46] And Shephard has described an organizational form consistent with support for continual changing and self-renewal, rather than with a primary mission of maintenance and control.[47]

Power-Coercive Approaches To Effecting Change

It is not the use of power, in the sense of influence by one person upon another or by one group upon another, which distinguishes this family of strategies from those already discussed. Power is an ingredient of all human action. The differences lie rather in the ingredients of power upon which the strategies of changing depend and the ways in which power is generated and applied in processes of effecting change. Thus, what we have called rational-empirical approaches depend on knowledge as a major ingredient of power. In this view, men of knowledge are legitimate sources of Mower, and the desirable flow of influence or power is from men who know to men who don't know through processes of education and of dissemination of valid information.

Normative–re-educative strategies of changing do not deny the importance of knowledge as a source of power, especially in the form of knowledge-based technology. Exponents of this approach to changing are committed to redressing the imbalance between the limited use of behavioral knowledge and people technologies and the widespread use of physical-biological knowledge and related thing technologies in effecting changes in human affairs. In addition, exponents of normative–re-educative approaches recognize the importance of noncognitive determinants of behavior as resistances or supports to changing—values, attitudes, and feelings at the personal level and norms and relationships at the social level. Influence must extend to these noncognitive determinants of behavior if voluntary commitments and reliance upon social intelligence are to be maintained and extended in our changing society. Influence of noncognitive determinants of behavior must be exercised in mutual processes of persuasion within collaborative relationships. These strategies are oriented against coercive and nonreciprocal influence, both on moral and on pragmatic grounds.

What ingredients of power do power-coercive strategies emphasize? In general, emphasis is upon political and economic sanctions in the exercise of power. But other coercive strategies emphasize the utilization of moral power, playing upon sentiments of guilt and shame. Political power carries with it legitimacy and the sanctions which accrue to those who break the law. Thus getting a law passed against racial imbalance in the schools brings legitimate coercive power behind efforts to desegregate the schools, threatening those who resist with sanctions under the law and reducing the resistance of others who are morally oriented against breaking the law. Economic power exerts coercive influence over the decisions of those to whom it is applied. Thus federal appropriations granting funds to local schools for increased emphasis upon science instruction tends to exercise coercive influence over the decisions of local school officials concerning the emphasis of the school curriculum. In general, power-coercive strategies of changing seek to mass political and economic power behind the change goals which the strategists of change have decided are desirable. Those who oppose these goals, if they adopt the same strategy, seek to mass political and economic power in opposition. The strategy thus tends to divide the society when there is anything like a division of opinion and of power in that society.

When a person or group is entrenched in power in a social system, in command of political legitimacy and of political and economic sanctions, that person or group can use power-coercive strategies in effecting changes, which they consider desirable, without much awareness on the part of those out of power in the system that such strategies are being employed. A power-coercive way of making decisions is accepted as in the nature of things. The use of such strategies by those in legitimate control of various social systems in our society is much more widespread than most of us might at first be willing or able to admit. This is true in educational systems as well as in other social systems.

When any part of a social system becomes aware that its interests are not being served by those in control of the system, the coercive power of those in control can be challenged. If the minority is committed to power-coercive strategies or is aware of no alternatives to such strategies, how can they make headway against existing power relations within the system? They may organize discontent against the present controls of the system and achieve power outside the legitimate channels of authority in the system. Thus teachers' unions may develop power against coercive controls by the central administrative group and the school board in a school system. They may threaten concerted resistance to or disregard of administrative rulings and board policies, or they may threaten work stoppage or a strike. Those in control may get legislation against teachers' strikes. If the political power of organized teachers grows, they may get legislation requiring collective bargaining between organized teachers and the school board on some range of educational issues. The power struggle then shifts to the negotiation table, and compromise between competing interests may become the expected goal of the intergroup exchange. Whether the augmented power of new, relevant knowledge or the generation of common power through joint collaboration and deliberation are lost in the process will depend on the degree of commitment by all parties to the conflict to a continuation and maintenance of power-coercive strategies for effecting change.

What general varieties of power-coercive strategies to be exercised either by those in control as they seek to maintain their power or to be used by those now outside a position of control and seeking to enlarge their power can be identified?

Strategies of Nonviolence

Mahatma Gandhi may be seen as the most prominent recent theorist and practitioner of nonviolent strategies for effecting change, although the strategies did not originate with him in the history of mankind, either in idea or in practice. Gandhi spoke of Thoreau's *Essay on Civil Disobedience* as one important influence in his own approach to nonviolent coercive action. Martin Luther King was perhaps America's most distinguished exponent of nonviolent coercion in effecting social change. A minority (or majority) confronted with what they see as an unfair, unjust, or cruel system of coercive social control may dramatize their rejection of the system by publicly and nonviolently witnessing and demonstrating against it. Part of the ingredients of the power of the civilly disobedient is in the guilt which their demonstration of injustice, unfairness, or cruelty of the existing system of control arouses in those exercising control or in others previously committed to the present system of control. The opposition to the disobedient group may be demoralized and may waver in their exercise of control, if they profess the moral values to which the dissidents are appealing.

Weakening or dividing the opposition through moral coercion may be combined with economic sanctions—like Gandhi's refusal to buy salt and other British manufactured commodities in India or like the desegregationists' economic boycott of the products of racially discriminating factories and businesses.

The use of nonviolent strategies for opening up conflicts in values and demonstrating against injustices or inequities in existing patterns of social control has become familiar to educational leaders in the demonstrations and sit-ins of college students in various universities and in the demonstrations of desegregationists against *de facto* segregation of schools. And the widened use of such strategies may be confidently predicted. Whether such strategies will be used to extend collaborative ways of developing policies and normative–re-educative strategies of changing or whether they will be used to augment power struggles as the only practical way of settling conflicts, will depend in some large part upon the strategy commitments of those now in positions of power in educational systems.

Use of Political Institutions to Achieve Change

Political power has traditionally played an important part in achieving changes in our institutional life. And political power will continue to play an important part in shaping and reshaping our institutions of education as well as other institutions. Changes enforced by political coercion need not be oppressive if the quality of our democratic processes can be maintained and improved.

Changes in policies with respect to education have come from various departments of government. By far the most of these have come through legislation on the state level. Under legislation, school administrators have various degrees of discretionary powers, and policy and program changes are frequently put into effect by administrative rulings. Judicial decisions have played an important part in shaping educational policies, none more dramatically than the Supreme Court decision declaring laws and policies supporting school segregation illegal. And the federal courts have played a central part in seeking to implement and enforce this decision.

Some of the difficulty with the use of political institutions to effect changes arises from an overestimation by change agents of the capability of political action to effect changes in practice. When the law is passed, the administrative ruling announced, or the judicial decision handed down legitimizing some new policy or program or illegitimizing some traditional practice, change agents who have worked hard for the law, ruling, or decision frequently assume that the desired changed has been made.

Actually, all that has been done is to bring the force of legitimacy behind some envisioned change. The processes of re-education of persons who are to conduct themselves in new ways still have to be carried out. And the new conduct often requires new knowledge, new skills, new attitudes, and new value orientations.

And, on the social level, new conduct may require changes in the norms, the roles, and the relationship structures of the institutions involved. This is not to discount the importance of political actions in legitimizing changed policies and practices in educational institutions and in other institutions as well. It is rather to emphasize that normative–re-educative strategies must be combined with political coercion, both before and after the political action, if the public is to be adequately informed and desirable and commonly acceptable changes in practice are to be achieved.

Changing through the Recomposition and Manipulation of Power Elites

The idea or practice of a ruling class or of a power elite in social control was by no means original with Karl Marx. What was original with him was his way of relating these concepts to a process and strategy of fundamental social change. The composition of the ruling class was, of course, for Marx those who owned and controlled the means and processes of production of goods and services in a society. Since, for Marx, the ideology of the ruling class set limits to the thinking of most intellectuals and of those in charge of educational processes and of communicating, rationales for the existing state of affairs, including its concentration of political and economic power, is provided and disseminated by intellectuals and educators and communicators within the system.

Since Marx was morally committed to a classless society in which political coercion would disappear because there would be no vested private interests to rationalize and defend, he looked for a counterforce in society to challenge and eventually to overcome the power of the ruling class. And this he found in the economically dispossessed and alienated workers of hand and brain. As this new class gained consciousness of its historic mission and its power increased, the class struggle could be effectively joined. The outcome of this struggle was victory for those best able to organize and maximize the productive power of the instruments of production—for Marx this victory belonged to the now dispossessed workers.

Many of Marx's values would have put him behind what we have called normative–re-educative strategies of changing. And he recognized that such strategies would have to be used after the accession of the workers to state power in order to usher in the classless society. He doubted if the ruling class could be re-educated, since re-education would mean loss of their privileges and coercive power in society. He recognized that the power elite could, within limits, accommodate new interests as these gained articulation and power. But these accommodations must fall short of a radical transfer of power to a class more capable of wielding it. Meanwhile, he remained committed to a power-coercive strategy of changing until the revolutionary transfer of power had been effected.

Marxian concepts have affected the thinking of contemporary men about social change both inside and outside nations in which Marxism has become the official orientation. His concepts have tended to bolster assumptions of the necessity of power-coercive strategies in achieving fundamental redistributions of socioeconomic power or in recomposing or manipulating power elites in a society. Democratic, re-educative methods of changing have a place only after such changes in power allocation have been achieved by power-coercive methods. Non-Marxians as well as Marxians are often committed to this Marxian dictum.

In contemporary America, C. Wright Mills has identified a power elite, essentially composed of industrial, military, and governmental leaders, who direct and limit processes of social change and accommodation in our society. And President Eisenhower warned of the dangerous concentration of power in substantially the same groups in his farewell message to the American people. Educators committed to democratic values

should not be blinded to the limitations to advancement of those values, which are set by the less than democratic ideology of our power elites. And normative–re-educative strategists of changing must include power elites among their targets of changing as they seek to diffuse their ways of progress within contemporary society. And they must take seriously Marx's questions about the re-educability of members of the power elites, as they deal with problems and projects of social change.

The operation of a power elite in social units smaller than a nation was revealed in Floyd Hunter's study of decisionmaking in an American city. Hunter's small group of deciders, with their satellite groups of intellectuals, front men, and implementers, is in a real sense a power elite. The most common reaction of educational leaders to Hunter's "discovery" has been to seek ways in which to persuade and manipulate the deciders toward support of educational ends which educational leaders consider desirable—whether bond issues, building programs, or anything else. This is non-Marxian in its acceptance of power relations in a city or community as fixed. It would be Marxian if it sought to build counter power to offset and reduce the power of the presently deciding group where this power interfered with the achievement of desirable educational goals. This latter strategy, though not usually Marxian inspired in the propaganda sense of that term, has been more characteristic of organized teacher effort in pressing for collective bargaining or of some student demonstrations and sit-ins. In the poverty program, the federal government in its insistence on participation of the poor in making policies for the program has at least played with a strategy of building countervailing power to offset the existing concentration of power in people not identified with the interests of the poor in reducing their poverty.

Those committed to the advancement of normative–re-educative strategies of changing must take account of present actual concentrations of power wherever they work. This does *not* mean that they must develop a commitment to power-coercive strategies to change the distribution of power except when these may be necessary to effect the spread of their own democratically and scientifically oriented methods of changing within society.

References and Notes

1. Throughout our discussion of strategies and procedures, we will not differentiate these according to the size of the target of change. We assume that there are similarities in processes of changing, whether the change affects an individual, a small group, an organization, a community, or a culture. In addition, we are not attending to differences among the aspects of a system, let us say an educational system, which is being changed—curriculum, audiovisual methods, team teaching, pupil grouping, and so on. Furthermore, because many changes in communities or organizations start with an individual or some small membership group, our general focus will be upon those strategies which lead to and involve individual changes.

   We will sidestep the issue of defining change in this paper. As further conceptual work progresses in the study of planned change, we shall eventually have to examine how different definitions of change relate to strategies and procedures for effecting change. But we are not dealing with these issues here.

2. We have indicated the main roots of ideas and idea systems underlying the principal strategies of changing and their subvariants on a chart which appears as Figure 1. It may be useful in seeing both the distinctions and the relationships between various strategies of changing in time perspective. We have emphasized developments of the past twenty-five years more than earlier developments. This makes for historical foreshortening. We hope this is a pardonable distortion, considering our present limited purpose.

3. Jean Hills, "Social Science, Ideology and the Purposes of Educational Administration," *Education Administration Quarterly* 1 (Autumn 1965): 23–40.

4. Garth Jones, "Planned Organizational Change, a Set of Working Documents," Center for Research in Public Organization, School of Public Administration (Los Angeles: University of Southern California, 1964).

5. For a review, see Ronald G. Havelock and Kenneth D. Benne, "An Exploratory Study of Knowledge Utilization," in *The Planning of Change,* 2d ed. (New York: Holt, Rinehart & Winston, Inc., 1969), Chapter 3, p. 124.

6. Paul R. Mort and Donald R. Ross, *Principles of School Administration* (New York: McGraw-Hill Book Company, 1957). Paul R. Mort and Francis G. Cornell, *American Schools in Transition: How our Schools Adapt their Practices to Changing Needs* (New York: Bureau of Publications, Teachers College, Columbia University Press, 1941).

7. Robert Chin, "Research Approaches to the Problem of Civic Training," in F. Patterson, ed., *The Adolescent Citizen* (New York: Free Press, Div. of The Macmillan Company, 1960).

8. Matthew B. Miles, *Some Propositions in Research Utilization in Education* (March 1965), in press. Kenneth Wiles, unpublished paper for seminar on Strategies for Curriculum Change (Columbus, Ohio: Ohio State University). Charles Jung and Ronald Lippitt, "Utilization of Scientific Knowledge for Change in Education," in *Concepts for Social Change* (Washington, D.C.: National Educational Association, National Training Laboratories, 1967). Ronald G. Havelock and Kenneth D. Benne, "An Exploratory Study of Knowledge Utilization," op. cit. David Clark and Egon Guba, "An Examination of Potential Change Roles in Education," seminar on Innovation in Planning School Curricula (Columbus, Ohio: Ohio State University, 1965).

9. David Clark, "Educational Research and Development: The Next Decade," in *Implications for Education of Prospective Changes in Society,* a publication of "Designing Education for the Future—an Eight State Project" (Denver, Colo., 1967).

10. Elihu Katz, "The Social Itinerary of Technical Change: Two Studies on the Diffusion of Innovation," in *The Planning of Change,* 2d ed., op. cit., Chapter 5, p. 230. Richard Carlson, "Some Needed Research on the Diffusion of Innovations," paper at the Washington Conference on Educational Change (Columbus, Ohio: Ohio State University). Everett Rogers, "What are Innovators Like?" in *Change Processes in the Public Schools,* Center for the Advanced Study of Educational Administration (Eugene, Oregon: University of Oregon, 1965). Everett Rogers, *Diffusion of Innovations* (New York: Free Press, Div. of The Macmillan Company, 1962).

11. Carl Hovland, Irving Janis, and Harold Kelley, *Communication and Persuasion* (New Haven: Yale University Press, 1953).

12. Raymond Bauer, "The Obstinate Audience: The Influence Process from the Point of View of Social Communication," in *The Planning of Change,* 2d ed., op. cit., Chapter 9, p. 507.

13. B. F. Skinner, *Walden Two* (New York: Crowell Collier & Macmillan, Inc., 1948).

14. "Designing Education for the Future—an Eight State Project" (Denver, Colo., 1967).

15. Karl Mannheim, *Ideology and Utopia* (New York: Harcourt Brace Jovanovich, Inc., 1946)

16. Alfred Korzybski, *Science and Sanity*, 3d ed., (Lakeville, Conn.: International Non-Aristotelian Library Publishing Company, 1948). S. I. Hayakawa, *Language in Thought and Action* (New York: Harcourt Brace Jovanovich, Inc., 1941).

17. John Dewey, *Philosophy, Psychology and Social Practice*, Joseph Ratner, ed., (New York: Capricorn Books, Div. of G. P. Putnam's Sons, 1967).

18. Kurt Lewin, *Resolving Social Conflicts* (New York: Harper & Row Publishers, 1948). Kurt Lewin, *Field Theory in Social Science* (New York: Harper & Row Publishers, 1951).

19. For Freud, an interesting summary is contained in Otto Fenichel, *Problems of Psychoanalytic Technique* (Albany: NT Psychoanalytic Quarterly Inc., 1941).

20. W. Bennis, K. Benne, and R. Chin, *The Planning of Change*, lst ed. (New York: Holt, Rinehart & Winston, Inc., 1961). R. Lippitt, J. Watson, and B. Westley, *The Dynamics of Planned Change* (New York: Harcourt, Brace Jovanovich, Inc., 1958). W. Bennis, *Changing Organizations* (New York: McGraw-Hill Book Company, 1966).

21. Raup, Benne, Smith, and Axtelle, *The Discipline of Practical Judgment in a Democratic Society*, Yearbook No. 28 of the National Society of College Teachers of Education (Chicago: University of Chicago Press, 1943).

22. Mary Follett, *Creative Experience and Dynamic Administration* (New York: David McKay Company, Inc., 1924).

23. Karl Mannheim, *Man and Society in an Age of Reconstruction* (New York: Harcourt Brace Jovanovich, Inc., 1940).

24. Elliot Jaques, *The Changing Culture of a Factory* (New York: Holt, Rinehart & Winston, Inc., 1952).

25. William J. Dickson and F. J. Roethlisberger, *Personal Counseling in an Organization: A Sequel to the Hawthorne Researches* (Boston: Harvard Business School, 1966).

26. Elton Mayo, *The Social Problems of an Industrial Civilization* (Cambridge, Mass.: Harvard University Press, 1945).

27. Leland Bradford, Jack R. Gibb, and Kenneth D. Benne, *T-Group Theory and Laboratory Method* (New York: John Wiley & Sons, Inc., 1964).

28. Matthew B. Miles, "On Temporary Systems," in M. B. Miles, ed., *Innovation in Education* (New York: Bureau of Publications, Teachers College, Columbia University Press, 1964), pp. 437–92.

29. Robert R. Blake and Jane S. Mouton, *The Managerial Grid* (Houston: Gulf Publishing Company, 1961).

30. Jay W. Lorsch and Paul Lawrence, "The Diagnosis of Organizational Problems," in *The Planning of Change*, 2d ed., op. cit., Chapter 8, p. 468.

31. Stephen M. Corey, *Action Research to Improve School Practices* (New York: Bureau of Publications, Teachers College, Columbia University Press, 1953).

32. See contributions by Miles et al., "Data Feedback and Organizational Change in a School System," in *The Planning of Change*, 2d ed., op. cit., Chapter 8, p. 457, and Jay W. Lorsch, and Paul Lawrence, "The Diagnosis of Organizational Problems," in *The Planning of Change*, 2d ed., op. cit., Chapter 8, p. 468.

33. C. Argyris, "Explorations in Consulting-Client Relationships," in *The Planning of Change*, 2d ed., op. cit., Chapter 8, p. 434. See also Richard Beckhard, "The Confrontation Meeting," in Chapter 8, p. 478.

34. Carl Rogers, "The Characteristics of a Helping Relationship," in *The Planning of Change*, 2d ed., op. cit., Chapter 4, p. 153.

35. Abraham Maslow, *Motivation and Personality* (New York: Harper & Row, Publishers, 1954).

36. Douglas M. McGregor, "The Human Side of Enterprise," in W. Bennis, K. Benne, and R. Chin *The Planning of Change* lst ed., (New York: Holt, Rinehart & Winston, Inc., 1961), pp. 422–31.

37. Dickson and Roethisberger, op. cit.

38. James V. Clark "A Healthy Organization," in *The Planning of Change*, 2d ed., op. cit., Chapter 6, p. 282. Irving Weschler, Fred Massarik, and Robert Tannenbaum, "The Self in Process: A Sensitivity Training Emphasis," in I. R. Weschler and E. Schein, eds., *Issues in Training*, Selected Reading Series No. 5 (Washington, D.C., National Training Laboratories).

39. Muzafer and Carolyn Sherif, *Groups in Harmony and Tension* (New York: Harper & Row, Publishers, 1953).

40. Robert Blake et al., "The Union Management Inter-Group Laboratory," in *The Planning of Change*, 2d ed., op. cit., Chapter 4, p. 176. Richard Walton, "Two Strategies of Social Change and Their Dilemmas," in *The Planning of Change*, 2d ed., op. cit., Chapter 4, p. 167.

41. R. Lippitt, J. Watson, and B. Westley, *Dynamics of Planned Change* (New York: Harcourt, Brace Jovanovich, Inc., 1958). W. Bennis, K. Benne, R. Chin, *The Planning of Change*, 1st ed., (New York: Holt, Rinehart & Winston, Inc., 1961).

42. Lyndall Urwick, *The Pattern of Management* (Minneapolis: University of Minnesota Press, 1956).

43. Chester I. Barnard, *The Functions of the Executive* (Cambridge, Mass.: Harvard University Press, 1938).

44. Rensis Likert, *New Patterns of Management* (New York: McGraw-Hill Book Company, 1961).

45. McGregor, pp. 422–31.

46. W. G. Bennis, "Changing Organizations," in *The Planning of Change*, 2d ed., op. cit., Chapter 10, p. 568.

47. H. A. Shephard, "Innovation-Resisting and Innovation-Producing Organizations," in *The Planning of Change*, 2d ed., op. cit., Chapter 9, p. 519.

Chapter 11 Structural Change, Technology, and Self-Management

FORMALITY VERSUS FLEXIBILITY IN COMPLEX ORGANIZATIONS[1]

Gerald D. Bell

Although there has been much research on organization in the past decade, for the most part it is segmented and loosely interrelated. There is an absence of theoretical formulations which tie current findings into a systematic framework. The stage has been attained, therefore, at which a middle-range theory might be beneficial in gaining a perspective on where our findings have brought us and in which direction we might aim.[2] As Robert V. Presthus comments, "An explicit synthesis between conceptual theory and empirical field research" is required at the present time in the study of organizations.[3]

We attempt here to formulate strategic, interrelated sets of hypotheses based on current research. Our attention is directed toward one, if not the most, significant topic with which recent investigations have been concerned. This is the problem of formal versus flexible patterns of organization.

We will analyze why contemporary research suggests that flexible, loosely structured enterprises are more efficient for given situations than more formally arranged systems. We first review early "formalistic investigations" to ascertain productive factors which are assumed to cause efficiency in work performance. Then, we compare these causal assumptions to those reported in recent "flexible studies." Following this analysis we attempt to trace consequences of these productive variables upon specific aspects of organization.

Formalized structures and processes refer to the degree to which role expectations and behavior are explicitly established and regulated by the administrative apparatus. An organization is formally structured when there is extensive regulation and control of behavior. Flexible structures and processes characterize those institutions in which the majority of tasks are not governed by explicitly stated regulations and policies and in which employees are not strictly governed by a rigid, clearly specified authority structure.

Theoretical Foundations

Early research viewed industrial research and service enterprises as formally and rationally structured units. Production activities were assumed to be clearly defined, well coordinated, and performed in a rigid, impersonal manner.[4] The "formalized theories" were given their most elaborate development, of course, in Max Weber's organizational precepts.[5]

We find evidence of widespread influence of these doctrines in the fact that much research in the past several decades has clustered around three problems arising from formal theories. First, the "human-relations school" attacked assumptions of formalized theories concerning workers' psychological dispositions and motivational orientations.[6] Second, researchers have been concerned with dysfunctional aspects of formalized modes of organization.[7] Finally, and of most significance for the present study, recent investigations have been in the direction of "structural alterations or quali-fications" of the formalistic model.[8] For the most part these efforts, which we have tentatively labeled the "flexible school," suggest that in many cases organizations with structures opposite to those prescribed by Weber exist and are conducive to a high degree of efficiency.

Examples of "flexible studies" are Alvin Gouldner's research on the sub-surface division of a gypsum plant.[9] Morris Janowitz's investigation of the changing structures of the military,[10] James Thompson and Arthur Tuden's analysis of formal and flexible tendencies which result from the extent of agreement that exists on decisions concerning both causative issues and preferences among alternatives,[11] Arthur Stinchcombe's formulations on "craft bureaucracies,"[12] and, finally, in Eugene Litwak's research on "human-relations" types of organization.[13] In general, these investigations suggest that authority structures are at a minimum, interaction is on a personal basis, and there is little rule usage.

Although the points of departure and variables considered are somewhat different, the flexible studies have proposed quite divergent patterns of organization than those expounded in the formalistic design; however, the causes for these differences are by no means clear. Let us attempt to explain, then, the causal assumptions upon which these two divergent theories stand.

Lack of Discretion in the Formal Theories

The causal notions of formalistic theorists —as exemplified by F. W. Taylor, Luther Gulick, and Max Weber—are revealed in their special emphasis upon subdivision of tasks, strict delimitation of duties, and reliability and calculability of behavior. These notions imply that duties to be performed by an individual are susceptible to easy specification and preplanning. They hold the idea, furthermore, that work demands performed in the productive system are highly predictable and repetitive. And finally, they make the all-important assumption that workers carry out their tasks by exercising only a small degree of discretion or decisionmaking effort.

Presence of Discretion in the Flexible Theories

Flexible investigations have been based upon notions quite contrary to the causal assumptions of formal theorists. Flexible studies have assumed, although somewhat implicitly, that the work environment is relatively nonpredictable and encourages much discretion on the part of the workers. And, a careful analysis of the assumptions implied in the "flexible theories" suggests that the amount of discretion workers exercise is a key feature which is causally related to the degree of formality of organizational structures. It is not, as is suggested in the flexible studies, improvisation, lack of rule usage, lack of close supervision, variation in work load, professionalization, or social skills per se which directly cause differences in organizational design. More precisely (l) we hypothesize that several of these variables are *important causes of the discretion a worker exercises in performing his tasks, and (2) discretion, in turn, has a significant influence on the flexibility of formalistic tendencies of organizational structure.* We will now direct our attention to these two postulates in their respective order.

Discretion

For each task a worker performs he is confronted with the opportunity, or sometimes the necessity, to exert a certain degree of discretion—that is, judgment, choice, or selection among alternatives in order to carry out his tasks. Furthermore, the total amount of discretion he exercises is directed toward one or some combinations of three main aspects of task performance: (1) *which tasks* he performs during a given period of time; (2) *how or by which methods,* and (3) *in which sequence* he performs his tasks.

Determinants of Discretion

Discretion on the part of the employee is brought into play when the character of the work itself and the routines governing how the work is done do not automatically determine for the employee doing the job the best way to do it in every respect. Discretion and judgment are necessary when there are more ways than one to go about doing a task. When causes of a problem are not clearly defined and when the solution is lacking acceptable alternatives, the final answer must rely on judgment.[14] And when there are many such situations, it is likely that an individual will learn to exercise his discretion, since there is a certain point at which it is uneconomical for the supervisor to make decisions for him. Beyond this point, the supervisor might as well be doing the job himself. An analysis of the flexible studies previously mentioned suggests that discretion taken as the dependent variable is caused by the following independent variables: (a) predictability of work demands; (b) management control, and (c) professionalization.

Predictability

Predictability of work demands refers to the extent to which unexpected events confront an individual while he is performing his job. Stinchcombe's "unstable work situations,"[15] Litwak's "nonuniform tasks,"[16] and Janowitz's "changing elements of battle technology"[17] all seem to cluster around the predictability category.

When situational demands are unpredictable, they present the worker with novel events toward which he has the opportunity to utilize his judgment in completing his tasks. When a surgeon, for example, opens a patient's stomach and finds an unexpected object inside he will be encouraged, presumably, to alter his activities (or to utilize his discretion) to meet the exigencies of the situation. In the same manner, if a stockbroker meets a new customer and begins his sales talk by presenting a "front region" of an intel-

lectual and then perceives that he is presenting the wrong front because the customer sympathizes with anti-intellectuals, he will be encouraged to change his behavior, that is, to use his judgment in order to come up with a new "self" which will enable him to carry out his tasks more effectively. This assumes, of course, that the worker is motivated to perform his tasks adequately.[18]

In addition to the direct effect of predictability upon discretion, predictability also indirectly influences discretion via two intervening variables. These are the degree of closeness of supervision and, in turn, rule usage, both taken as components of management control.

Management Control and Discretion

Management has the opportunity and ability to determine the exact degree of discretion a worker exercises regardless of the extent of predictability of job demands. For example, a supervisor of a research department (a fairly unpredictable unit) might normally expect that he would have much opportunity to exert his judgment in completing his tasks; however, if management decided, for whatever reason, to establish a very rigid, encompassing set of rules for this supervisor to follow, then he would not exert high discretion even though he still was faced with many unpredictable events on his job. New problems would continue to arise, new solutions would appear; however, the supervisor would not exert his judgment in meeting these unexpected events—rather, he would follow management's directives.

The point to be made here is that even though predictability might significantly affect discretion, discretion can also be influenced by management's control. But we hypothesize that management will perceive that if they control very tightly the tasks of workers who are faced with unpredictable work situations, then the rate of efficiency will be decreased. Consequently, we expect management to encourage workers who have unpredictable jobs to utilize their discretion.[19] Hence, in this case predictability is an independent variable influencing management control, and management control is an intervening variable causally related to workers' discretion.

Professionalization

Professionalization here means that workers have received a technical training to achieve a recognized occupational competence. The more professional training an employee has acquired, the more he will possess and demand skills which require discretion. In Stinchcombe's terms, craft administration differs from mass-production administration " . . . by substituting professional training of manual workers for detailed centralized planning of work."[20] In a similar light, Thompson and F. L. Bates rehearse the idea that the university must allow its personnel to exercise much discretion, since "knowledge" is given recognition as the basis of authority.[21] Simon Marcson also suggests that discretion and flexibility are important aspects of professional ranks of scientific research firms.[22]

Professional training improves technical competence; in a sense it creates technical and discretionary skills and at the same time produces expectations of freedom from supervisory control in the work setting. We hypothesize, then, that the higher the professional training, the higher the discretion. Correspondingly, professionalization indirectly affects discretion through the intervening variable of management control. In this latter instance, the higher the professional training, the lower will be the degree of management control over a worker's behavior, and thus the higher will be an individual's discretion.

In summary, predictability, management control, and professionalization act as important determinants of employees' discretion.

Problem in Past Assumptions

There are several problems associated with past theories which state that some of the above variables which we assume to affect discretion act independently to cause flexible or formalistic characteristics of work arrangement.

For example, in one of the first illuminating approaches to the general flexibility-formalistic dilemma, Litwak offered a provacative first step in attempting to explain why organizations had quite varying structures. He concluded, following Weber, that jobs (1) which stress uniform situations, that is, " . . . the task to be dealt with is recurrent (in time as well as among many people) and important, exemplified in such occupations as that of research scientist or developmental engineer, as opposed to supervisor of an assembly line";[23] and (2) which stress traditional areas of knowledge, such as knowledge of engineering, chemistry, economics, law, company rules, and the like, are those which bring about a rational, Weberian type of organization. On the other hand nonuniform jobs and those which require social skills tend to create organizations which stress primary relations and organizational goals.[24]

Litwak, indeed, has made a major contribution to the solution of the dilemma of formalistic-flexibilistic work patterns; however, we must carry his analysis further, and this necessitates some modifications in his causal assumptions. It is possible, for example, that such categories as social skills and traditional areas of knowledge can be somewhat misleading if, as has been proposed in this paper, the degree of discretion initiated by the worker is one of the key dimensions producing varying patterns of organization; for it is possible that jobs which require social skills (Litwak suggests jobs such as salesmen's, psychiatric social workers', and politicians') due to various circumstances may in fact allow the job incumbent only a small degree of discretion and, therefore, tend to produce a formalistic work structure, which is opposite to that expected in Litwak's interpretation. Similarly, jobs which stress traditional areas of knowledge (economics, law), contrary to what is implied by Litwak, might be nonpredictable and require a very high degree of discretion. Again, in this latter case, we would have quite different consequences for traditional, yet high-discretion, jobs than are proposed by Litwak. Work would tend toward flexible patterns of organization rather than toward the Weberian model as Litwak proposed.

Furthermore, Litwak's concept of uniform work tasks evidently refers to the activities *actually performed* by the employee, whereas predictability as developed here refers to the *work demands* which confront an individual. These are two distinct variables. A worker might be confronted by many unique and unexpected situations while carrying out his job; however, he might meet these unique events by performing tasks in a very repetitive, routine, or—in Litwak's terms—uniform way. In this situation unexpected events would continue to occur, but the worker would in a sense ignore these situational demands and perform his tasks in a routine manner. And in this case he would be making few decisions in performing his job. Consequently, his job

would fit rather easily into a formalistic work structure.

It would appear that the general categories mentioned by Litwak and others might profitably be modified by considering predictability of work demands and discretion. What Litwak and several of the other "flexible theorists" were exploring, in essence, was something similar to these two variables, but their causal assumptions were too broad to be able to generalize to precise causal relationships concerning organizational structure. Let us view now how discretion influences organizational design.

The Discretionary Model of Organization

It is hypothesized that the relationships portrayed in Figure 1 will prevail in organizations in which the productive systems are high on discretion. If these hypotheses are valid, then high discretion units may be characterized as having more flexible structures and processes. On

Figure 1   The Discretionary Model of Organization*

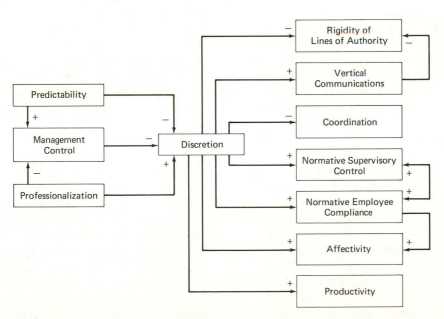

*The arrowed lines in the chart indicate the assumed causal direction of the relationships; and the plus and minus signs represent positive and negative associations, respectively. For example, when predictability is high, discretion is low.

the other hand, in the less discretionary units the direction of each of the hypotheses will be reversed, and, . . . [consequently], there firms will be more formal and rigid in their patterns of work arrangement. In other words, the more predictable the work demands and the fewer the decisions which must be made in the productive process to attain organization goals, the more formalized will be the patterns of administrative activities, communication, and coordination; and more flexible patterns of organization will result from unpredictable and highly discretionary productive processes.

The following set of hypotheses is in no way purported to be exhaustive; rather, it is a first attempt to build organizational theory from existing research. Limits must be placed upon each of these propositions, since there are many factors in addition to discretion which enter into the predicted relationships. The notation of "other things being equal" should be placed behind each hypothesis. We will begin our analysis by discussing relationships between discretion and the authority structure.

Discretion and the Authority Structure

We are concerned here with the extent to which lines of authority are clearly defined and rigidly adhered to. When tasks are unpredictable and encourage employees to make decisions frequently, lines of authority will be very ambiguous and flexible. Subordinates will not be expected to report to a specific superior for each action they take, rather they will tend to scatter their consultations among several different combinations of supervisors. Similarly, since demands placed upon workers' efforts are assumed to encourage them to utilize their ability in solving work problems and to call forth fairly unique solutions to their tasks, it would not appear likely that a rigid, carefully delineated authority system would be created in unpredictable, high-discretion systems.

On the contrary, in low-judgmental units employees' tasks will be easily specified and controlled, since work demands are highly predictable and require little decisionmaking effort. Correspondingly, superiors will be able to plan for and to establish rigid lines of authority more easily, and the predictability of situational demands will enable subordinate-superior relationships to be handled adequately through formalized channels. As Thompson and Bates have said, since standardization is high, deviations can be measured readily and thus responsibility accurately assigned to specific individuals.[25]

Vertical Communication

A survey of literature relevant to this variable suggests a rather interesting pattern between predictability, discretion, and vertical communications. There appears to be a positive relationship between vertical communications (any verbal, written, or symbolic exchange of information between members of different levels of authority) and discretion and, thus, predictability.[26]

In high-predictability–low discretion organizations, administrators are able to determine fairly accurately the tasks, methods, and sequence in which employees are to perform their tasks, and employees make few decisions. This enables managers to coordinate and train employees easily in their routine decisionmaking activities and consequently requires less control of their performance.[27] Furthermore, since communication and training partially substitute for each other, the better trained a person is for a job, the less becomes the need to communicate with him about his work.[28]

On the other hand, in high-discretion units, there will be much vertical communication. But instead of work demands being so predictable and involving so few decisions that close supervision and training are facilitated, work demands are unpredictable, and employees are highly skilled and competent . . . exercising much discretion. These factors encourage supervisors and subordinates to communicate frequently about work-related problems. The uniqueness and complexities involved in unpredictable and high-discretion demanding activities create a great need for exchange of ideas and information between workers and superiors concerning the solution of unique events.[29] The content of supervision in the latter case will be more on an equal "give-and-take" basis than on one in which supervisors closely regulate subordinates' activities. It would be a two-way, rather than merely a downward, communication as in the former case. Topics of exchange would in both cases probably be concerned with work activities—the solution of task-related problems, grievances, and so forth. However, the type of communication in the latter case might differ in being somewhat more complex, unique, and abstract than in the former.

Coordination of Activities

There is less need to coordinate activities between departments which involve unpredictable demands and high discretion than between those with high predictability and low discretion. Departments in which decisionmaking ability has been decentralized appear to be more self-contained than are less discretionary units. For instance, one might compare the amount of coordination which takes place between two divisions on an assembly line in an automated production plant with two departments, such as history and sociology, in the relatively discretionary organization—the university. The reason for differences in coordination is that high-discretion units are arranged in parallel department specialization, whereas low-discretion units are more functionally interdependent in Peter M. Blau and W. Richard Scott's terms.[30] In parallel specialization, work activities of one department are different from but not highly dependent on actions of others. In contrast, interdependent specialization exists when the activities of one unit are dependent upon the performance of tasks in other departments. The latter case makes coordination a fundamental managerial problem.

Why are nonpredictable, high-discretion departments specialized in a parallel manner, and why are predictable, low-discretion units interdependently specialized? The answer appears to be that when work demands are predictable and routine they can be subdivided and controlled fairly easily. Thus, more specialization can be obtained. And the more that tasks can be subdivided, the more they can be effectively planned for and coordinated by management's efforts. And thus, the more likely it is that they will be interdependently specialized.

Normative Supervisory Control

When an employee's superior attempts to motivate him to work by appealing to service norms and professional ideologies as opposed to such monetary rewards as pay, bonuses, or promotions, the supervisor, in Etzioni's terms, is using normative control attempts.[31] In departments in which tasks, methods, and sequence of performance are not clearly specified, and thus in which responsibility for the performance of each task is not clearly definable, administrators cannot easily direct the completion of each task. Correspondingly, rewards and responsibility cannot easily be assigned to tasks which are nonpredictable and which involve a high degree of discretion.

In these cases normative control attempts will provide incentives for members to perform necessary tasks on their own, since manipulation of pay does not lead to internalization of values but produces only superficial, expedient, and overt commitment.[32] In this connection Marcson points out that in large scientific organizations there is a necessity for a shift to less arbitrary, less direct, and less dominating control practices. In research organizations the utilization of direct and calculative control not only evokes resentment but also resistance to such control attempts.[33] Thus, we theorize that when work demands are nonpredictable and involve much discretion, normative and/or somewhat more informal constraints will appear.

Employee Compliance Structure

Employees meet and adjust to control attempts by management in particular patterns and intensities of compliance. Job incumbents in high-discretion and unpredictable organizations will be oriented toward administrative control more in terms of normative and ideological commitment to work than by monetary or calculative involvement. Employees will make many decisions, have a relatively high degree of self-investment and responsibility, and consequently will be highly involved in their work. When an individual exercises his judgment and initiative in solving problems, he invests a good portion of his "self" in their outcome. Research scientists, for example, often indicate a need for an authority system based on persuasion and normative encouragements.[34]

Furthermore, the coterminous presence of professionalization of jobs and normative control attempts by supervisors directed toward discretionary jobs exerts important pressures toward a congruent normative control–normative compliance structure. The internalization by workers of professional ideologies and codes of conduct partially eliminates administrators' needs to motivate and to control employees. Professional-technical socialization acts as an arm of management in the sense that it "builds" motivation into workers and at the same time acts as a continuing motivational reference group for them.

In predictable, low-discretion jobs, however, a worker invests little of his "self" in the outcome of his productive efforts. In fact, he seldom sees how his activities contribute to the final product on which he is working. Similarly, responsibilities and rewards can be more clearly assigned. Therefore, managers can revert

more easily to monetary and manipulative control attempts. In turn, employees will possess a calculative orientation toward their work and the organization.

Donald I. Warren has reported tentative evidence which indirectly supports these notions. He also introduces another dimension into the relationship between predictability, discretion, and normative involvement. He points out, following Rose Coser, that when visibility of formal authority agents is low (as is presumably the case in nonpredictable, high-discretion units) then attitudinal commitment to one's work and informal constraints are more likely to be conducive to effectiveness.[35]

Affectivity in Interpersonal Relations

In high-discretion and unpredictable organizations, workers are considered to not only have a high degree of responsibility and investment of "self" in their work, but they also are thought to have more freedom in expressing their opinions and beliefs. They are given more leeway and encouragement to display their emotions, and thus there is a high degree of affectivity in the relationships between workers in these organizations. In his pioneering study of the operating room (a high-discretion unit) in the hospital setting, Wilson reports that doctors and nurses frequently maintain close personal relationships and share many experiences.[36] Similarly, Blau suggests that in a government unemployment agency the counseling role which employees performed was often carried out with highly affective personal relationships.[37]

Productivity

Finally, in enterprises which entail highly discretionary productive units if the above variables take on the directions predicted, we assume they will obtain optimum levels of efficiency. That is, if departments in which jobs are unpredictable and involve much discretion on the part of workers are (1) left relatively unattended by members in authority; (2) entail high vertical communications; (3) have a low degree of coordination with other departments; (4) are sanctioned and rewarded by normative control attempts; (5) and, correspondingly, normatively committed to on the part of the employees, and (6) are associated with affectivity in interpersonal work relationships, then we expect this type of flexible work arrangement to be conducive to an (7) optimum level of efficiency.

Similarly, if the hypotheses are reversed for nondiscretionary firms, efficiency will also be at a high level. In other words, we are maintaining that efficiency can best be reached by two separate patterns of organization for the two ideal extremes of the discretionary predictability productive systems. On the one extreme, Weber's rational model appears to be efficient for those enterprises which encompass nondiscretionary productive tasks. On the opposite pole, more flexible patterns of work arrangement are considered to be most conducive to efficiency when productive tasks are nonpredictable and high on discretion demands.

Summary and Conclusions

We have attempted to formulate tentative hypotheses which partially explain why contemporary research has reported quite varying findings from Weber's early formulations. It is assumed that in organizations in which employees exert a high degree of discretion there will be: (1) less rigid lines of authority; (2) high vertical communications; (3) low coordination; (4) high normative control by supervisors; (5) high normative commitment by employees; (6) high affectivity in interpersonal relationships, and finally (7) relatively high productivity.

It is further theorized that discretion is determined by predictability, management control, and extent of professionalization of jobs. These postulates are tentative and, of course, assume that "other things

are held equal." Hopefully, this "discretionary model" will offer suggestions to some of the provocative questions concerning formal and flexible patterns of work arrangement raised in recent works and will suggest new avenues of research.

References and Notes

1. The author is greatly indebted to Stanley H. Udy, Jr., Elton F. Jackson, and Richard L. Simpson, who throughout the formulation of the investigation provided keen analytical critiques of the notions presented in this paper. Part of the research is based on the author's dissertation, Gerald D. Bell, "Formality Versus Flexibility in Complex Organizations: A Comparative Investigation within a Hospital" (Unpublished doctoral dissertation, Yale University, Department of Sociology, 1964).
2. Alvin Gouldner, "Organizational Analysis," in *Sociology Today,* Robert Merton et al., eds. (New York: Basic Books, Inc., Publishers, 1959), p. 404; James D. Thompson et al., *Comparative Studies in Administration* (Pittsburgh: University of Pittsburgh Press, 1959), p. 200; Amitai Etzioni, *A Comparative Analysis of Complex Organizations* (New York: Free Press, Div. of The Macmillan Company, 1960), p. xiii; Simon Marcson, *The Scientist in American Industry* (Princeton, N. J.: Princeton University Press, 1960), p. 122; M. D. Field, "Information and Authority: The Structure of Military Organization," *American Sociological Review* 24 (February 1959): 17; Stanley H. Udy, Jr., *Organization of Work* (New Haven, Connecticut: Human Relations Area Files Press, 1959).
3. Robert V. Presthus, "Behavior and Bureaucracy in Many Cultures," *Public Administration Review* 19 (1959): 25; See also, James March and Herbert Simon, *Organizations* (New York: John Wiley & Sons, Inc., 1958), p. 17–26, especially their discussion of Merton, Selznick, and Gouldner; Chris Argyris, "The Fusion of an Individual with the Organization." *American Sociological Review* 14 (June 1954), p. 272; Peter M. Blau and W. Richard Scott, *Formal Organizations* (San Francisco: Chandler Publishing Company, 1962), p. 35.
4. March and Simon, op. cit., p. 13. The flexible model, it should be pointed out, is rational in the sense that ends are related to the means in possibly the most appropriate method available. F. W. Taylor, *Shop Management* (New York: Harper & Row, Publishers. Inc., 1912); Luther Gulick and L. Urwick, eds., *Papers on the Science of Administration* (New York: Institute of Public Administration, 1937).
5. Hans Gerth and C. Wright Mills, trans. and eds., *From Max Weber: Essays in Sociology* (New York: Oxford University Press, Inc., 1946), p. 214.
6. See William F. Whyte, *Man and Organization:*

Three Problems in Human Relations in Industry (Homewood, Illinois: Richard D. Irwin, Inc., 1959).

7. For an excellent review of these studies see March and Simon, op. cit., pp. 26–47.

8. We are using "model" to refer to a general theory. Included in this category are Gouldner, op. cit.; Arthur Stinchcombe, "Bureaucratic and Craft Administration of Production: A Comparative Study," *Administrative Science Quarterly* 4 (September 1959); Morris Janowitz, "Changing Patterns of Organizational Authority: The Military Establishment," *Administrative Science Quarterly* 3 (March 1959): 473–93; Eugene Litwak, "Models of Bureaucracy Which Permit Conflict," *American Journal of Sociology* 67 (September 1961): 177–84.

9. Gouldner, op. cit.; James D. Thompson and F. L. Bates, "Technology, Organization and Administration," *Administrative Science Quarterly* 11 (December 1957), pp. 325–43.

10. Janowitz, op. cit., p. 481.

11. James D. Thompson and Arthur Tudan, "Strategies, Structures, and Processes of Organizational Decision," in James D. Thompson et al., op. cit., pp. 195–213.

12. Stinchcombe, op. cit.

13. Litwak, op. cit., pp. 177–84.

14. Jaques, Elliot, *The Measurement of Responsibility* (Cambridge: Harvard University Press, 1956), p. 86; Thompson and Tuden, op. cit., p. 199.

15. Stinchcombe, op. cit.

16. Litwak, op. cit.

17. Janowitz, op. cit.

18. Finally, there is a fascinating sidelight which should be mentioned in this connection. This is the fact that if unpredictable situational demands take the form of a threat to the organization, it is possible that the hypothesized association between predictability and discretion will be reversed. Several studies have indicated that outside threats tend to cause centralization of decisionmaking. (Janowitz, op. cit.)

19. It should also be pointed out here that it is possible that management's control might, in turn, affect the degree of predictability of an employee's job.

20. Stinchcombe, op. cit., p. 175.

21. Thompson and Bates, op. cit., p. 333.

22. Marcson, op. cit., p. 44.

23. Litwak, op. cit., p. 178.

24. Ibid., p. 170. Social skills refer to the actual capacity to communicate with others, to motivate them to work, to cooperate with others, and to internalize the values of the organization.

25. Thompson and Bates, op. cit., p. 334.

26. On this point see Richard L. Simpson, "Vertical and Horizontal Communication in Formal Organizations," *Administrative Science Quarterly* 4 (September 1959), p. 196. Although the predicted directions differ from those reviewed in Simpson's research, it does not appear that the problem lies in the theory as much as it does in the difficulty of ascertaining what actually is a high level of discretion, or mechanization. This appears to be an important point for scholars of administration to consider in future research.

27. Edward Gross, "Some Functional Consequences of Primary Controls," *American Sociological Review* 18 (August 1953), p. 379.

28. Etzioni, op. cit., p. 138.

29. When specific vertical communication exchange networks are used repeatedly and therefore become relatively patterned and accepted paths for exchange of information, communication channels are said to exist. In high-discretion organizations, since there will be many and varied decisions which must be made at a variety of times and in numerous situations, it is possible that there will be less opportunity for vertical communications to become patterned, and workers will presumably be required to consult with many different supervisors in inconsistent and sporadic patterns. Stinchcombe's analysis of communication files is consistent with this notion. (Stinchcombe, op. cit.)

30. Blau and Scott, op. cit., p. 183.

31. Etzioni, op. cit., p. xv.

32. Ibid.; see also Andrew F. Henry and Edgar Borgatta, "A Comparison of Attitudes of Enlisted and Commissioned Air Force Personnel," *American Sociological Review* 18 (December 1953), p. 670.

33. Marcson, op. cit.

34. Ibid.

35. Donald I. Warren, "The Role of Professional Peer Relations in a Formal Organization Setting: Some Correlates of Administrative Style" (unpublished paper presented at the Annual Meeting of the American Sociological Association, Montreal, Canada, September, 1964).

36. Robert N. Wilson, "Teamwork in the Operating Room," *Human Organization* 12 (1954).

37. Blau and Scott, op. cit.

SOME EFFECTS OF TECHNOLOGY IN ORGANIZATIONAL CHANGE[1]

James C. Taylor

Advanced technology appears, in general, to elicit new forms of work group structure and behavior. These behavioral effects of automation seem to produce favorable attitudes which may, in turn, strengthen those behaviors. It cannot be expected that these effects result wholly from behavioral constraints of the technology, but are conditioned by management decisions which facilitate adaptation to that technology.

Technological Effects on Employee Behavior

A review of research literature over the past decade reveals that technology can affect organizational structure (Burns and Stalker, 1961; Blauner, 1964; Woodward, 1965; Harvey, 1968), work group behavior and productivity (Trist and Bamforth, 1951; Trist, Higgin, Murray, and Pollock, 1963; Rice, 1958; Walker, 1957; Mann and Hoffman, 1960; Mann and Williams, 1959, 1962; Marrow, Bowers, and Seashore, 1967), and group member attitudes as well (Mann and Hoffman, 1960; Turner and Lawrence, 1965; Walker, 1957). Further, much of this evidence supports the notion that sophisticated technology, or automation, influences group process in the direction of more democratic, autonomous, and responsible activities.

Specifically, evidence in the literature reveals that the effects of modern technology on the nature of the work group are less equivocal than technological effects on other variables, such as individual skill requirements, intrinsic job satisfaction, or intergroup communication patterns. These work-group effects are clearer in the case of blue-collar groups than in white-collar counterparts, although it will be maintained that this difference is probably more historically artifactual than qualitatively real. Detailed description in two cases of unplanned social change following technological change (Mann and Hoffman, 1960; Walker, 1957) shows that intragroup status differences in blue-collar settings were reduced, and work roles became more interdependent under advanced technology. Evidence that this kind of effect on the blue-collar work group is a useful sort of target of planned social change is presented by researchers at London's Tavistock Institute (Trist and Bamforth, 1951; Rice, 1958, 1963; Trist et al., 1963). The Tavistock people state that more sophisticated technology can lead to a number of antithetical supervisory and work group behaviors, but that autonomous group functioning (multiskilled workers, responsibility to allocate members to all roles, group mission and incentive, and task definition involving continuity) seems to have the best results and is a more natural outgrowth of the technological change itself. The Tavistock people make an important contribution in concluding that more sophisticated technology is a necessary condition in installing autonomous groups, but for best effect, that structure must be consciously installed (Trist et al., 1963, p. 293).

In discussing the autonomous group, and sociotechnical systems, the Tavistock researchers describe a different and broader role for the supervisor from what is traditionally held. What is required is that as the group comes to control the production process, the formal supervisor shifts to a control of boundary conditions such as liaison, maintenance, and supply (Emery, 1959; Rice, 1963, p. 8). This is similar to observations of emerging supervisory behaviors noted by Walker (1957), by Mann and Hoffman (1960), and by Marrow et al. (1967). The easier technology makes it for both group and supervisor to evaluate results, the easier it becomes to supervise on the basis of results and the less likely is the autocratic management of work activities (Herbst, 1962, p. 8; Woodward, 1965, p. 225). It seems apparent that even though the pattern of actual supervisory activities differs from one industry or plant to another, the trend with advanced technology is in the direction of supervisors doing less in the way of traditional supervision—i.e., supervising the behaviors of subordinates, and attending to selection and training functions—and more in the direction of either acting as a facilitator and communications link for the work group or becoming more technically skilled operators themselves.

The effects described above were reported in studies of blue-collar firms. Technologically induced job changes in white-collar work appears to have less effect on supervision or work-group structure. A plausible explanation of this difference might be that white-collar technology has simply not moved as far as current levels of automation in blue-collar technology. Simple changes in computer input form would drastically reduce the number of key-punch and program set-up jobs. Mann and Williams (1962) have shown that job responsibility and availability of impersonal worker feedback in white-collar jobs have already increased. This is evidence that white-collar work in data processing, and jobs in automated factories, is more similar than different when we exclude the greater number of repetitive, fractionated, transitional tasks in the white-collar work.

It would seem that automation does, in fact, provide the potential or opportunity for enhanced worker discretion, responsibility, intrawork group autonomy, interdependence and cooperation in both blue- and white-collar organizations. In fact, what seems to be happening is that lowest level jobs are taking over more of what are usually thought of as traditional supervisory tasks. These results are not unequivocal, however, especially in white-collar work, but this anomaly seems primarily a function of the somewhat lagging quantitative position of white-collar

automation and not of an intrinsic or qualitative difference.

Organizational Change and Subsystem Interdependence

It is reasonable to postulate that there is a systemic interdependence among the subsystems of an organization. Changes cannot be affected in the technical system without repercussions in the social system. Katz and Kahn's open system theory in organizations (1966) relies on the relatedness of subunits or parts of a system vis-à-vis the organization's environment (pp. 19–29). Parts of social systems, for example personal and role relationships within work groups, can be changed without prior change in technical systems or organizational structure, but (they maintain) the change in organizational behavior is only mild reform, not radical change (p. 424). By the same token, parts of technical systems can also be changed without undue stress on the other systems in the organization.

Katz and Kahn view systemic change as the most powerful approach to changing organizations. Systemic change involves change inputs from the environment which create internal strain and imbalance among system subunits. It is this internal strain which is the potent cause of the behavioral adaptation of subsystems indirectly connected with the change input (pp. 446–48). However, values and motivations of organizational members change in a more evolutionary way. Katz and Kahn maintain these elements are not as immediately amenable to the influence of changed inputs as is organizational behavior (p. 446).

Guest (1962, p. 55), Mann and Hoffman (1960, p. 193), Marrow et al. (1967, p. 229), and Woodward (1965, p. 239), among others, implicitly support the notion of interrelatedness of subsystems and the importance of considering the derivative effect on the social system of significant changes in technology. Yet they all conclude from their evidence that an improvement in the technical system was not sufficient in itself to assure good performance via the existing social system.

Order and Precedence of Subsystem Change

It seems established that when technological change is considerable, some effects on the social system must be recognized and planned for, but the question of coordination of change in these two systems is still unanswered. Is technical change the best way of achieving organizational change, or would it be more efficient to purposefully change the social system, following that by planned changes in the organizational technology, or to change both simultaneously?

Cultural anthropologists have long maintained that changes in technology historically lead to changes in attitudes, values, and philosophies (Ogburn, 1957, 1962; White, 1959, p. 27). Some direct evidence for this position is found in the studies reviewed here. Burns and Stalker, for example, concluded that mechanistic and organic management systems were dependent variables to the rate of environmental change (i.e., technology and market situation). Trist et al. (1963, p. 293) state that change conditions for installing autonomous groups were more favorable under greater mechanization and low group cohesiveness. Even here, however, these authors discovered that when new equipment was installed, the existing social system could create forces of resistance to the full potential of the technology. The technical outsiders supervising the change were frequently unaware of the operator's responsibilities to the rest of the work cycle, and tended to isolate the machine activity (p. 273). This had effects of unfavorably disrupting the existing social system and making subsequent change difficult. Planning for this contingency was necessary. Guest (1962, pp. 52–53), and Marrow et al. (1967, p. 237) attribute direct behavioral effects to

the relatively minor technological change made, but in both of these cases these changes were preceded by management succession. These can be considered cases of what Schon (1967) describes as "innovation by invasion"—the old borrows what it can of the new, the new introduces change into the old, or the new displaces the old. In the open system notion of Katz and Kahn, this is systemic change representing organizational social system change via new inputs from the environment. In both of these cases also, changes in interpersonal relations were modified at the top of the organization coincident with the technological change at the bottom.

Precedence and Hierarchical Level

Argyris (1962), like Anshen (1962), suggests that production technology has little effect on higher management. Argyris continues that effective organizational change comes about by improving interpersonal competence directly at the top of the organization, while improving it at the bottom more indirectly through changes in technology and control systems (p. 282). This implies that the sociotechnical system is the lower part of the whole organization unlike the total organization of Katz and Kahn's open system. The Tavistock group, although it makes excursions into the sociotechnical nature of management systems (Miller and Rice, 1967; Trist et al., 1963) is primarily concerned with the production system (e.g., crews of miners across shifts) as sociotechnical systems. It is implicitly clear in these particular studies, however, that effective introduction of technological change for ultimate organizational change involved the upper ranks, either in a commitment to plan adequately for social system effects (Trist et al.) or in a commitment to the technological change itself as a method of improving social relationships (Guest; Marrow et al.).

Implications of Sophisticated Technology Effects on Social System Change

Direct effect

The direct effects of modern technology on more satisfying and productive methods of working have been noted (Guest; Mann and Hoffman; Mann and Williams; Marrow et al.; Trist et al.; Turner and Lawrence; Walker). Although the evidence is not overwhelming it appears that a properly planned technical change can lead directly and without additional inputs, albeit slowly, to increased job complexity, autonomous and responsible work group processes, more helpful supervision, and high productivity. It was also found that, at least for some workers, these direct effects can lead to more positive job involvement, improved work group relations, more favorable attitudes toward supervision, and pride in high productivity. The implication here is that social change can proceed as a direct outcome of certain technological changes, but, if this were the only way social change was affected, the outcome would be slow and limited by chance factors.

Indirect effects

Several of the studies reviewed here consider social change not only resulting from the new technology itself, but resulting from a planned social change input made possible, at least in part, by the mere disruption created by the technological change (Marrow et al.; Rice; Trist et al.; Williams and Williams, 1964). This kind of disruption has been labeled "unfreezing" by Lewin (1951) or "internal system strain" by Katz and Kahn. In both cases, the dynamic created is that of a force toward total system restructuring to find a new equilibrium. It seems that social system changes are possible without technological change, but organizations may not be able in themselves to provide the force necessary. Williams and Williams, for example, state that such changes are not possible without a catalyst like expenditure on technological change which creates stresses forcing departments and units to compromise on objectives and abandon traditional routines and activities. Marrow et al. claim that their apparel factory was unable to unfreeze itself—heroic measures were needed to create enough disturbance to allow normal change processes to begin (1967, p. 232). Trist et al. maintains that even limited technological changes can create enough disruption if their potentiality for inducing social change is recognized (1963, p. 284).

The dynamic involved in the direct effect of technology on social system changes seems to be the constraints it applies to employee behavior. The dynamic of unfreezing, on the other hand, seems to be a freedom provided by the new technology to seek new ways of behaving. Internal system strain comes about then in the latter case in which employees' cognitive maps may not match managements' under these circumstances, or that the values of one department may not match those of another. Management awareness of such conditions, and planning for it, becomes important for the outcomes on the social system.

It seems clear that the combination of direct and indirect effects of technology on the social system provides the basis for concluding that technological change would best precede social change, if both were contemplated, in that it probably requires less time and elicits less resistance. This is true because technology not only disrupts or unfreezes, but imposes strict, nonhuman control on minimum behavior. Following the same logic, it would also seem that changes toward autonomous group structure would be facilitated where an advanced system of technology was already in place.

Technology, Role Constraints, and Permanence of Social Change

There is no evidence to prove that any change strategy provides permanent effects. Schein (1961), in describing change by "compliance" (where an individual's behavior changes because the situation forces him to change), suggests that coercion-compliance is only a method of changing behavior; attitudinal change need not follow. In fact, if acquisition of new attitudes is also via coercive-compliance, these attitudes will be temporary if they obtain at all. On the other hand, he continues, if behavioral changes are coerced at the same time as unfreezing operations are undertaken, actual influence can be facilitated if the individual finds himself having to learn new attitudes to justify the kinds of behavior he has been forced to exhibit. These new attitudes should act then to maintain the new behaviors. This is exactly the outcome that Festinger's dissonance theory of attitude change would predict (Cohen, 1964, p. 82; Festinger, 1957, pp. 94–95; Insko, 1967, p. 219)—that counterattitudinal role playing will result in consistency-producing attitude change and maintenance of coerced behaviors. Although the attitude change portion of this position has received consistent support in the psychological laboratory (Insko, pp. 219–23), there is no mention of it as an explanatory concept in field research around technological change, and no evidence for the predictions of behavioral maintenance. In fact, only two cases exist where attitudes in industrial work were found to change as a function of the relatively ambiguous condition of role change (Lieberman, 1956; Tannenbaum, 1957). As this coercion-compliance position has received little empirical support in the field so has the other generic strategy—that of conversion (Bennis, 1966, pp. 170–71). "Conversion"—the attempt by persuasion and influence to change the individual's cognitive or attitudinal set—is a more common strategy in affecting social system change in organizations (Sayles, 1962).

Thus, it appears that although the evidence exists for asserting that planning for social change should, where possible, take place around technological change, it is not unambiguous. It seems that when technological changes are undertaken first, especially when the social effects are considered, the noticeable effects of change behavior will be manifested earlier. It is not at all clear, however, whether one sort of change strategy will work better with people of varied backgrounds, or will have more permanent effects via changed attitudes and satisfactions acting to maintain new behaviors.

Implications from the Literature

It is not advanced here that the social system in an organization cannot be changed directly by appeals to members to alter the way they believe and behave, coupled with attempts to train members in the skills necessary to behave differently. In fact, it is assumed that such direct changes can be affected. An interesting question to ask, however, is what facilitating effects are manifest where the members affected by direct social change attempts exist in a modern system of production technology—where: (a) behavioral constraints may exist in the direction of greater worker discretion, responsibility, interdependence, and cooperation; (b) where some residual effects of "unfreezing" may still exist in the direction of search for new ways of behaving vis-à-vis the modern technology, and (c) where the permanence of the technological constraints on behavior and the unfreezing effects may combine to change attitudes as well as behavior. Such facilitating effects seem reasonable to hypothesize given the data reported in the literature described above. The question is not whether direct social change attempts can be effective, but rather, whether the existence of modern, sophisticated technology can enhance the results of such change efforts.

The Study

Hypotheses
The purpose of the present study was to test several notions of those described above regarding the effects of sophisticated technology, or automation, on job-related behaviors in work groups. It tested three specific hypotheses: *first,* that sophisticated technology, in and of itself, is

associated with more autonomous and participative group process; *second,* that sophisticated technology will facilitate planned change efforts directed toward increasing participative group process, and *third,* that the change toward participative group process will be more permanent when the change is facilitated by technology than when it is not.

The literature reviewed above implied that automation has within it, certain built-in constraints for lowered supervision, and increased intragroup communication and responsibility. If this is true, then the introduction of such technology should lead to such changes in member social behavior. If such a system is aided in social change by a consultant or change agent, he can help the change process if he urges those behaviors which turn out to be compatible with the new technological system. That the resultant organizational changes will be more permanent than those brought about by the exhortations of management or a consultant alone, can be explained in two ways. First, the technical system and its constraints are permanent. Second, as Festinger and others have shown, constrained counterattitudinal behavior is one of the most important precursors of attitude change, ultimately making the new behaviors even more resistant to fluctuation than they otherwise would be.

The studies of technological effects mentioned above, and others like them, are mostly case studies. They have not quantitatively measured the effects of technology on group process. In addition, no longitudinal or quantitative studies of the facilitating effects of technology on planned social change programs are recorded. The present study dealt with both of these aspects, plus some assessment of the causal strength of changed behaviors on attitudes as well.

Methodology

This study used the responses of over 1,000 persons in 140 nonsupervisory work groups employed by a large petroleum refinery.[2] Respondents completed paper and pencil questionnaires dealing with supervisory and peer leadership, work group behaviors, satisfactions, and other job-related matters. These questionnaires were completed by respondents on three separate occasions over a period of 12 months.

A planned change program aimed toward more participative management was introduced following the initial survey.

Finally, the judgements of some in-plant people were used to obtain evaluations of the sophistication of work-group production technology. These evaluations were obtained retroactively, using judgemental questionnaires with several in-plant judges who were familiar with the technological characteristics of the groups they evaluated.

The analytic design involved controlling for sophistication of technology, and examination of the survey results of group responses to questionnaire variables measuring participative leadership, group behavior, and satisfaction.

Independent variable
The planned social change program is an implicit independent variable in this study. This change program involved an attempted change in management values and behaviors in the direction of Likert's "System IV" (Likert, 1967). "System IV" relies on a theory of organization and management in which high value is placed on total organizational commitment to joint decisionmaking, participation, openness, trust and confidence, mutual influence, and the sharing of organizational goals and mission. These planned changes, it was felt, would be compatible with the assumed forces inherent in advanced technology.

Consultants from the University of Michigan introduced this planned change program. This effort began following the first questionnaire administration, and prior to the second one. It involved using the by-group results of the survey as a self-help diagnostic tool and specially developed training programs as well. Consultants made themselves available to individual supervisors who wished help in using the data with which they were provided. On the basis of the survey data, and other observations, the consultants proceeded to develop training programs for use with various levels and groups within the company. Since the consultants attempted uniform diffusion of inputs throughout the lower level ranks in the refinery, this independent force was assumed constant.

The measure of sophistication of technology was considered both an independent variable and a conditioning variable in this study. As an independent variable, the effects of technology on pre-change levels of leadership, group process, and satisfaction were examined. As a conditioning variable, the effects of technology on rate of change in these variables, and on causal priorities among them following the change program were examined.

Sophistication of technology was assessed using a questionnaire instrument constructed to measure the qualities of *standard materials input, throughput, mechanization,* and *output control* for each work group. These three technological constructs were measured using the following items:

Sophistication of input
Standardization of material or objects transformed by the work group.
Predictability of objects transformed in those characteristics important to the group.

Sophistication of throughput
The proportion of routine operations which are handled by machines.
Degree of nonhuman power, and automatic control of operations.
Extent to which machine is independent of the operator.

Sophistication of output-control
Absence of feedback by supervisor.
Degree supervisor provides feedback on request versus initiating feedback.

Speed of feedback.
Primary source of feedback (nonhuman versus human).

This instrument utilized the retrospective structured judgements of work groups on the nine scales by a smaller number of administrative people within the organization. These judges were asked to evaluate the groups for the time of the first survey, some 18 months earlier. Since few technological changes had occurred in the intervening period, the task was relatively simple. Using this instrument in other organizations has revealed reasonable inter-rater and internal consistency reliability and discriminant validity for it (Taylor, 1970).

Dependent variables
The survey instrument administered over time included over 100 items, some of which were used as single item estimates of constructs or concepts, others of which were combined into factorially derived mean score index variables and used as measures of other constructs. Five-unit Likert scale response alternatives were used in all questions. From this large set of variables, 10 were used in the analysis for the present study. These variables fall into four classes: 4 areas of supervisory leadership; 4 areas of work group or peer leadership; work group behaviors; and satisfaction with the work group. These variables were measured using the following component questions:

Supervisory Leadership

Measured by the following four mean score indices:

Support
Behavior which increases his subordinates' feeling of being worthwhile and important people. (Mean score index—three items.)
In the surveys this was measured by the following questions:
How friendly and easy to approach is your supervisor?

When you talk with your supervisor, to what extent does he pay attention to what you are saying?

To what extent is your supervisor willing to listen to your problems?

Goal emphasis

Behavior which stimulates an enthusiasm among subordinates for getting the work done. (Mean score index—two items.) The survey used these items to measure this aspect of his behavior:

How much does your supervisor encourage people to give their best effort?

To what extent does your supervisor maintain high standards of performance?

Work facilitation

Behavior which helps his subordinates actually get the work done by removing obstacles and roadblocks. (Mean score index—three items.) These items measured this form of behavior:

To what extent does your supervisor show you how to improve your performance?

To what extent does your supervisor provide the help you need so that you can schedule work ahead of time?

To what extent does your supervisor offer new ideas for solving job-related problems?

Interaction facilitation

Behavior which builds the subordinate group into a work team. (Mean score index—two items.) These items were used to measure behavior of this kind:

To what extent does your supervisor encourage the persons who work for him to work as a team?

To what extent does your supervisor encourage people who work for him to exchange opinions and ideas?

Peer (Work-Group) Leadership

This was measured by survey questions and indices usually identical to those used to measure the manager's leadership. In this case, however, the questions are worded, "To what extent are (do) persons in your work group. . . . "

Support

(Mean score index—three items.)

Friendly and easy to approach?

Pay attention to what you're saying when you talk with them?

Willing to listen to your problems?

Goal emphasis

(Mean score index—two items.)

Encourage each other to give their best effort?

Maintain high standards of performance?

Work facilitation

(Mean score index—three items.)

Help you find ways to do a better job?

Provide the help you need so that you can plan, organize, and schedule work ahead of time?

Offer each other new ideas for solving job-related problems?

Interaction facilitation

(Mean score index—two items.)

Encourage each other to work as a team?

Emphasize a team goal?

Work Group Activities

Work group team process

(Mean score index—three items.)

"In your work group to what extent is work time used efficiently because persons in the work group plan and coordinate their efforts?"

"To what extent does your work group make good decisions and solve problems well?"

"To what extent do you feel that you and the other persons in your work group belong to a team that works together?"

Satisfaction

With work group

"All in all, how satisfied are you with the persons in your work group?"

These items are similar to those used in other studies at the Institute for Social Research and over time have revealed reasonable reliability and validity. The eight leadership variables are described in greater detail elsewhere (Bowers and Seashore, 1966; Taylor, in press).

These measures formed the basis of the dependent variables in the present study—the degree to which groups were originally participative and autonomous, and the extent to which they responded over time to the planned change program directed toward these ends.

Results

The data were first checked for the possible confounding effects of age, education, tenure with the company, and rural-urban upbringing of the respondents. It was determined that these variables had no measurable effect on any of the survey variables. Education of respondents was, however, found negatively related to the judgements of some of the technological characteristics for their groups, and related positively to some others. These effects of education were not unexpected, and were not corrected for in subsequent analyses.

The existence of interaction effects between sophistication of technology and the relationships among the dependent variables over time was noted. This interaction obviated any analysis technique using multiple linear regression in the estimation of causal priorities, or the relative strength of conditioning effects. As a consequence, the analyses took the somewhat cruder form of controlling for high and low levels of technological sophistication and examining the dependent variables for differences in mean scores, and differences in cross-lagged zero-order longitudinal correlations.

In order to keep the analysis simple, the data bases were combined such that groups with high sophistication of technological input, throughput, and output scores could be compared with groups with low input, throughput, and output scores. This total technology high-low design reduced the number of groups in each category, but still maintained reasonable N's for statistical purposes. The original 140 groups were reduced to 68 using this design. Maximum N in the high category was 42 groups. Maximum N in the low category was 26 groups. Levels of education for the high group and the low group were not found significantly different from one another. What effects education had on the individual technological characteristics described earlier were effectively cancelled out using the total technology combination.

Table 1 presents data relevant to the first hypothesis—that advanced technology by itself can influence autonomous group process.

The differences between the mean scores for the high and low categories at time one clearly suggest that members of groups with high sophistication of production technology initially perceive higher levels of peer work facilitation, supervisory and peer interaction facilitation, and democratic group process in their groups, than did members of groups with low sophistication of technology. This is evidence that sophisticated technology in itself is associated with more autonomous group process.

Table 1 also presents evidence in support of the second hypothesis—that technology will facilitate planned change efforts directed toward greater autonomy and participation. Between time one, the first measure, and time three, the final measure, the high technology groups significantly increased their level of evaluation of supervisory and peer leadership in nearly all dimensions while groups in the low technology category did not. It is interesting to note the only exception to this pattern in the high technology category, aside from satisfaction with the work

Table 1   Mean Score Differences on Dependent Variables Between Groups in the Categories of High and Low Sophistication of Technology; and Within These Categories Over Time

Dependent variables	High technology			Low technology			Differences	
	Means		Diff.	Means		Diff.		
	$Time_3$	$Time_1$	t_3-t_1	$Time_3$	$Time_1$	t_3-t_1	$High_1$-Low_1	$High_3$-Low_3
Supervisory support	4.16	3.92	0.24*	4.10	4.14	−0.04	−0.22	0.06
Supervisory goal emphasis	4.08	3.94	0.14	3.85	3.75	0.10	0.19	0.23*
Supervisory work facilitation	3.66	3.45	0.21*	3.39	3.20	0.19	0.25	0.27*
Supervisory interaction facilitation	3.92	3.64	0.28*	3.43	3.23	0.20	0.41*	0.49†
Peer support	4.01	3.83	0.18*	3.94	4.03	−0.07	−0.20	0.07
Peer goal emphasis	3.74	3.55	0.19*	3.48	3.44	0.04	0.11	0.26†
Peer work facilitation	3.75	3.47	0.28†	3.19	3.11	0.08	0.36*	0.56†
Peer interaction facilitation	3.65	3.37	0.28†	2.87	2.68	0.19	0.69†	0.78†
Group process	3.84	3.68	0.16*	3.33	3.17	0.16	0.51†	0.51†
Satisfaction with work group	4.38	4.38	0.00	4.22	4.22	0.00	0.16	0.16

* $p > 0.05$.
† $p < 0.01$.

group, is that of supervisory goal emphasis. If in fact these groups are becoming more autonomous, then *we should not expect* supervisory goal emphasis to increase as much as peer goal emphasis.

Figure 1 and 2 provide summary information in support of the second hypothesis.

Figure 1 presents the average means for *all four of the peer leadership variables* for high and low technology categories, compared with the combined four variables for the whole refinery ($n = 2,200$, NGPs $= 350$). It is clear from this figure that the high technology groups start higher in peer leadership and increase faster than either the low technology groups, or the refinery as a whole.

Figure 2 uses the same data bases, but presents average means of *the four supervisory leadership variables*. Once again, it is clear that the high technology groups start higher and increase faster than either of the other comparison groups.

The data in the final figure, to follow, help in examining the third hypothesis— that permanence of the change toward autonomous group process is greater in the high technology condition. This was done by examining the degree to which atti-

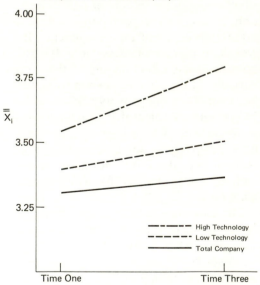

Figure 1 Combined Peer Leadership Mean Score Change Over Time for High and Low Technology Groups Compared with Total Company.

tudes toward the social system changed to conform with the new behavior. Partial assessment of these effects was obtained using cross-lagged analysis of average zero-order correlations, while controlling for high and low technology.

Cross-lagged analysis allows for an estimation of causal priorities of dependent variables measured early in the study on

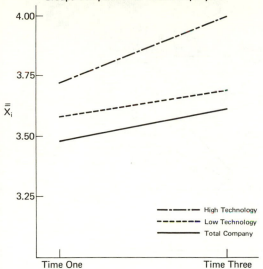

Figure 2 Combined Supervisory Leadership Mean Score Change Over Time for High and Low Technology Groups Compared with Total Company.

4.00

3.75

$\bar{\bar{X}}_i$

3.50

3.25

- - - - - High Technology
- - - - - Low Technology
———— Total Company

Time One   Time Three

those variables measured later. Since only general notions of causality were desired, average correlations among the major variables were used. This manipulation had the advantage of much simplifying an otherwise bewildering array of data. It also had the disadvantage of lower precision, and the inability to legitimately utilize tests of statistical significance. The advantage of clarity, however, was deemed to outweigh the disadvantages on both counts.

Figure 3 presents the dominant chains of causal priority among the dependent variables for the three measurement periods separately for high and low technology. In order to simplify the figure, cases of reciprocal causality are not shown in favor of presenting only recursive, or more intransitive causal chains.

Before reviewing Figure 3 for the effects on satisfaction with the work group, it should be recalled from Table 1 that satisfaction did not increase at all for either high or low technology over time. Original levels of satisfaction were quite high for both groups, and remained so during the period of the study. In spite of this, Figure 3 suggests that satisfaction

takes a key position in the causal matrix.

In the high-technology condition, peer leadership (probably our best indicator of autonomous group process) time two, is clearly the recipient of causal influence of the time one variables: group process, satisfaction, and, of course, itself. Nothing strongly influences satisfaction with the work group at time two. But by time three, consolidations in time two group process and peer leadership have led to realignments in satisfaction such that it is higher in groups which were more autonomous at time two. Thus, we may tentatively conclude that changes in group behavior, under the high technology condition, tend to maintain themselves via changes toward more consonant attitudes over time.

In the low technology condition, originally *lower* group process tends to lead to *higher* satisfaction at time two, and this, in turn, has a slight inverse causal influence on group process time three. It may be said that this situation reflects the less constraints on behavior for autonomous group process and little motivation for changing toward it. *Lower* group process time one produces *higher* satisfaction, which in turn has a slight perseverative effect on low group process time three, where technological sophistication is low.

Figure 3 also presents data in the high technology condition which suggests that supervisory leadership in this case had little effect on group process or group leadership. Rather, group process and satisfaction time one influence peer leadership time two, which in turn influenced group process and satisfaction time three. Originally, we might have speculated that groups in the high technology condition were supervised by foremen who were especially influential regarding the new behaviors, or especially active regarding the planned change program. Given these results in Figure 3, this effect seems unlikely. It would appear that behavioral constraints of sophisticated technology, operating before the change program was undertaken, had already set the autono-

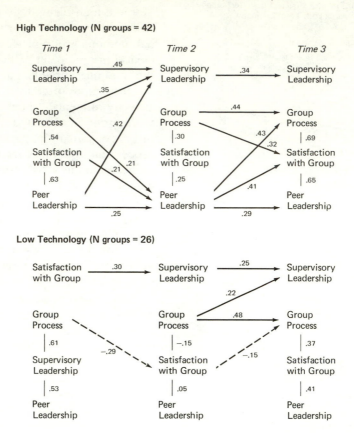

Figure 3   Results of Cross-lag Causal Analysis Refinery Data.

High Technology (N groups = 42)

Time 1	Time 2	Time 3

Supervisory Leadership —.45→ Supervisory Leadership —.34→ Supervisory Leadership

.35

Group Process —.44→ Group Process

|.54   .42 |.30   .43 |.69
                              .32

Satisfaction with Group   Satisfaction with Group   Satisfaction with Group

|.63   .21 .21 |.25   .41 |.65

Peer Leadership —.25→ Peer Leadership —.29→ Peer Leadership

Low Technology (N groups = 26)

Satisfaction with Group —.30→ Supervisory Leadership —.25→ Supervisory Leadership

.22

Group Process —.48→ Group Process

|.61   −.29 |−.15   −.15 |.37

Supervisory Leadership   Satisfaction with Group   Satisfaction with Group

|.53 |.05 |.41

Peer Leadership   Peer Leadership   Peer Leadership

---

mous group pattern which that program reinforced and more precisely directed.

Another possible confounding influence on these data might be the simple effect of initial level of dependent variables on their subsequent gain. Since, as we have seen from Figures 1 and 2, the high-technology condition was initially higher in peer and supervisory leadership, it might be claimed that this fact alone accounts for the subsequent increases in these variables for that category. This effect was examined directly by assessing level of time three leadership results, controlling for initial level (median-split over all nonsupervisory work groups) for these variables. This analysis revealed not a "gain effect" on the part of groups with high initial levels of leadership but rather a regression toward the mean for groups with initially high, and initially low leadership scores. Technology, it seems, by it-

self accounts for the greater gain over time in the high technology condition.

Conclusions and Implications

We may conclude, with respect to the first hypothesis tested here, that technological sophistication in this refinery does have a measurable association with democratic and autonomous group process. These static relationships do not inexorably lead to statements of causality, but it seems more likely that prechange levels of autonomous group process and peer leadership, were caused by, rather than caused, the advanced technology. This, of course, does not rule out a possible third variable leading to prechange levels in both technology and leadership. If it exists, however, its form is not evident in the data collected here; for example, age and tenure were found unrelated to either technology or the dependent variables.

In regard to the second hypothesis, the implications are less equivocal. It would appear quite undeniable that the social change program was facilitated in groups with more sophisticated technology. Although the present design was not balanced to test all possible alternatives in examining efficiency in *organizational change,* it was suitable to test the hypothesis as presented. We cannot conclude that in larger organizational change, which includes changes in *both* social and technical systems, that change will be faster or greater where technical change precedes social change than either a marked lack of sophistication in technology, or more average or moderate conditions of system technology would. This evidence, in addition to that presented in the introduction to the present paper, lends strength to the position that disruptive inputs from the organizational environment, in the service of social change, would more likely be technological than social in nature.

The results examined in the test of the third hypothesis in turn reinforce this conclusion. Traditionally, we have approached social change as an attempt to change attitudes directly—with varying degrees of success (subjectively assessed). Results in the present study strongly suggest that attitude change is better approached *indirectly* via more impersonal and compelling changes in behavior.

One final, and more general, implication may be drawn from the results of this study and others like it. These findings tend to suggest that the proposed management systems of such people as Argyris, Likert, McGregor, and others may reflect a zeitgeist stimulated by the advances in the industrial world. That is, the ideas advanced by these theorists may be most suitable for organizations in the present technological vanguard. As technology continues to advance, these ideas of participative management will have more meaning and application. The cultural-lag theories of anthropologists, such as Wil-liam Ogburn, form a suitable model in this regard. Such theories state that cultural values and philosophies are not the first to change in cultural development, but the last—invariably following changes in technology.

References

Anshen, M. (1962), "Managerial Decisions," in J. T. Dunlop, ed., *Automation and Technological Change* (New York: The American Assembly, Columbia University).

Argyris, C. (1962). *Interpersonal Competence and Organizational Effectiveness* (Homewood, Illinois: Richard D. Irwin, Inc.).

Bennis, W. G. (1966). *Changing Organizations* (New York: McGraw-Hill Book Company).

Blauner, R. (1964). *Alienation and Freedom* (Chicago: The University of Chicago Press).

Bowers, D. G. and Seashore, S. E. (1966). "Predicting Organizational Effectiveness—with a Four Factor Theory of Leadership," *Administrative Science Quarterly* 11: 238–63.

Burns, T. and Stalker, G. M. (1961). *The Management of Innovation* (London: Tavistock Publications).

Cohen, A. (1964). *Attitude Change and Social Influence* (New York: Basic Books, Inc.).

Emery, F. E. (1959)."Characteristics of Sociotechnical Systems," unpublished manuscript. (London: Tavistock Institute of Human Relations).

Festinger, L. (1957). *A Theory of Cognitive Dissonance* (Stanford: Stanford University Press).

Guest, R. H. (1962). *Organizational Change: The Effect of Successful Leadership* (Homewood, Illinois: Richard D. Irwin, Inc.).

Harvey, E. (1968). "Technology and the Structure of Organizations," *American Sociological Review* 33: 247–59.

Herbst, P. G. (1962). *Autonomous Group Functioning* (London: Tavistock Publications).

Insko, C. A. (1967). *Theories of Attitude Change* (New York: Appleton-Century-Crofts).

Katz, D. and Kahn, R. L. (1966). *The Social Psychology of Organizations* (New York: John Wiley & Sons, Inc.).

Lewin, K. (1951). *Field Theory in Social Science* (New York: Harper & Row, Publishers).

Lieberman, S. (1956). "The Effects of Changes in Role in the Attitudes of Role Occupants," *Human Relations* 9: 385–402.

Likert, R. (1967). *The Human Organization: Its Management and Value* (New York: McGraw-Hill Book Company).

Mann, F. C. and Hoffman, L. R. (1960). *Automation and the Worker* (New York: Holt, Rinehart & Winston, Inc.).

Mann, F. C. and Williams, L. K. (1959). "Organizational Impact of White-Collar Automation," *In-*

dustrial *Relations Research Association Proceedings.*

Mann, F. C. and Williams, L. K. (1962). "Some Effects of Changing Work Environment in the Office," *Journal of Social Issues* 18(3): 90–101.

Marrow, A. J. Bowers, D. G., and Seashore, S. E. (1967). *Management by Participation* (New York: Harper & Row, Publishers).

Miller, E. J. and Rice, A. K. (1967). *Systems of Organization.* (London: Tavistock Publications).

Ogburn, W. F. (1957). In Allen, F. R., Hart, H., Miller, D. C. and Ogburn, W. F., eds., *Technology and Social Change* (New York: Appleton-Century-Crofts).

Ogburn, W. F. (1962). "National Policy and Technology," in Walker, C. R., ed., *Modern Technology and Civilization* (New York: McGraw-Hill Book Company).

Rice, A. K. (1958). *Productivity and Social Organization: The Ahmedabad Experiment* (London: Tavistock Publications).

Rice, A. K. (1963). *The Enterprise and Its Environment: A System Theory of Management Organization* (London: Tavistock Publications).

Sayles, L. R. (1962). "The Change Process in Organizations: An Applied Anthropology Analysis," *Human Organization* 21(2): 62–67.

Schein, E. H. (1961). "Management Development As a Process of Influence," *Industrial Management Review* 2: 59–77.

Schon, D. A. (1967). *Technology and Change* (New York: Delta Books).

Tannenbaum, A. S. (1957). "Personality Change as a Result of an Experimental Change of Environmental Conditions," *Journal of Abnormal and Social Psychology* 55: 404–06.

Taylor, J. C. (1970). *The Conditioning Effects of Technology on Organizational Behavior in Planned Social Change,* doctoral dissertation, University of Michigan. (Ann Arbor: University Microfilms, No. 70–14659).

Taylor, J. C. (1971). "An Empirical Examination of a Four-Factor Theory of Leadership Using Smallest Space Analysis," *Organizational Behavior and Human Performance* (in press).

Trist, E. L. and Bamforth, K. W. (1951). "Some Social and Psychological Consequences of the Longwall Method of Coal Getting," *Human Relations* 4: 3–38.

Trist, E. L., Higgin, G. W., Murray, H., and Pollock, A. B. (1963). *Organizational Choice* (London: Tavistock Publications).

Turner, A. N. and Lawrence, P. R. (1965). *Industrial Jobs and the Worker* (Cambridge: Harvard University Press).

Walker, C. R. (1957). *Toward the Automatic Factory* (New Haven: Yale University Press).

White, L. A. (1959). *The Evolution of Culture* (New York: McGraw-Hill Book Company).

Williams, L. K. and Williams, B. C. (1964). "The Impact of Numerically Controlled Equipment on Factory Organization," *California Management Review,* 7(2): 25–34.

Woodward, J. (1965). *Industrial Organization: Theory and Practice.* (Oxford: Oxford University Press).

Notes

1. This paper is based upon the author's dissertation submitted in partial fulfilment of the requirements for the Ph.D. degree at the University of Michigan. The author gratefully acknowledges the helpful comments and suggestions of his committee: Stanley E. Seashore, Chairman; Frank M. Andrews, David G. Bowers, Edward O. Laumann, and Donald N. Michael. Financial support was provided from a basic research fund in the Business and Industry Group, Center for Research on Utilization of Scientific Knowledge and through an Office of Naval Research Grant (Contract No. N000 14–67–A–0181–0013).
2. The original study included a replication of the design using an insurance company. The insurance company experienced negative change overall, rather than positive change in the social system. These data, therefore, are not reported here because of the additional complexity they created. (Taylor, 1970, for complete report.)

THE PROMISE OF SELF-MANAGEMENT

Elisabeth Mann Borgese

The theory and practice of self-management is likely to catch the imagination and mobilize the activities of hundreds of millions of people all over the world during the last quarter of our century.

What is self-management? What are the

trends in contemporary history which may bring it into being, East, West, North, and South? And what are its chances of success in the postindustrial society of the twenty-first century?

The Center recently held a week's seminar to try to answer these questions. Experts from Chile, Germany, Israel, Malta, Norway, the United Kingdom, the United States, and Yugoslavia joined the staff for the discussions. What follows is largely inspired by the various papers and proceedings generated in that seminar.

Self-management is the kernel of Yugoslav political theory and constitutional law as it has been developing since the nineteen-fifties. The Yugoslavs must have written hundreds of thousands of pages on this subject. They have enacted self-management in their economic, social, cultural, and political organizations. They have built it into their constitution. They are enforcing it in their courts and tribunals. And they are experimenting, elaborating, adapting, developing, enlarging it, and amending their constitution accordingly.

Self-management politicizes the economic enterprise by transforming it into a community which is not bent on profit-making exclusively but on articulating the social and political as well as the economic decisionmaking processes of its members, workers, and managers alike.

Every enterprise has its workers council, elected by the total membership of the enterprise, on a one-man, one-vote basis. To prevent the professionalization of the workers councils, members are elected for a period not exceeding two years, and no one can be re-elected for a second consecutive term.

The workers council is an autonomous body that makes its own internal rules and decisions with regard to policies and plans, the sharing of revenues, the allocation of resources, and any other business, even including security (each enterprise has its own self-managed contingent of the Peoples Army).

Every enterprise also has its own executive committee whose members are elected from among the enterprise personnel. The executive committee is headed by a director who is the chief manager of the enterprise. He is elected either by the workers council or by the total membership and is responsible to the workers council and the membership. He may provisionally suspend decisions of the workers council if he finds them in conflict with the law. A municipal court of arbitration will then make the final decision on the case.

Self-management, at the same time, depoliticizes the state by transforming it into a community which articulates not only the political, but the economic, social, and cultural decisionmaking processes of its members. This happens through a multichamber assembly system. At the federal, republican, and municipal levels, the representatives of the political community share their decisionmaking power with representatives of economic enterprises, scientific institutions, public health institutions.

The microcommunity of the enterprise and the macrocommunity of what used to be the state thus look very much alike. Both are multidimensional or polyvalent (that is, embracing all dimensions of human activity), and both are organized from the bottom up, not from the top down. Both are interacting, and it is through this interaction and by participating in decisionmaking at the governmental level that the self-managing community really creates and asserts its autonomy.

This kind of order may sound utopian, impractical at the level of economic efficiency, too complex, and much too idealistic. But the facts do not bear out such a view. For while the Yugoslavs have undoubtedly run into all sorts of difficulties in the elaboration and enactment of their far-from-perfect system, twenty years of self-management have had the following results: Per-capita income has risen, from two hundred dollars in 1950, to seven hundred dollars in 1970. Industrial output has increased fivefold (a portion of the additional G.N.P. is invested in industrial development and for communal purposes); the nonagricultural sector of the economy, embracing only thirty percent of the working population in 1950, has grown to fifty-three percent. Exports of goods and services have risen from twelve percent of the gross national product in 1950 to twenty percent in 1969, with over fifty percent of these exports consisting of manufactured goods. The real standard of living of the population has risen three hundred percent during the last twelve years.

Self-management in Yugoslavia has deep autochthonous roots in the communal systems of Slavic society. It has intellectual roots in Marxist theory—or that part of it that the Yugoslav leaders could use to graft on the indigenous growth (there is a mixture of autochthonous and universal, existential, and intellectual factors in every revolution). And it has vigorous roots in the partisan movement that routed the fascist invaders in World War II and brought the new society into being.

War

There were hundreds of thousands of these partisans in the war. Bereft of means of communication, they received no orders. Lacking supplies of food, clothing, and arms, they had to rely on their own initiative and inventiveness and on the population around them. The partisan knew no distinction between soldier and civilian. He knew only people.

Partisan strategy, the Yugoslavs learned from this experience, cannot be made by top brass and imposed from above. It rises from the ranks. Each partisan is his own general. Partisan strategy is pragmatic and flexible, and thus hard to come by. Armies under a central command may win or lose. When they lose, it's over for them. But for every partisan contingent that goes down, a new one arises, as long as there are people. The partisan system, decentralized and enormously complex, turned out to be more stable than the relatively simple and highly centralized military system. The partisan system thrives on adversity and enhances a spirit of self-imposed sacrifice where the army system suffers demoralization. The partisan system is economical: There are no overhead expenses, no supervisory costs, there is no bureaucracy while the cost of military bureaucracy is skyrocketing.

One could continue, but it is clear that the partisan system was a self-management system applied to war—and it worked, in Yugoslavia as it later did in Algeria, in Israel as in Vietnam, and in Malaysia as in Latin America.

Since war as an institution is disintegrating, together with the war system of nation-states, two things are now happening: On the one hand, war is becoming a natural catastrophe of the highest magnitude, destroying soldiers, civilians, and obliterating any distinction between them, together with all the laws of war; on the other hand, and insofar as the absolute is rarely really absolute, this new type of soldier has been evolving on the rubble of the nation-state with its centralized army.

The centralized army, for its part, has developed the commando, a soldier displaying some of the characteristics of the partisan. The commando, however, is no match for the partisan. He is restricted by precise orders from above. His "self-management" is apparent only—like the "self-management" of a worker within the hierarchical structure of the big corporation.

But the pure type of partisan soldier is potentially a universal phenomenon as international wars are turning into transnational civil wars. Self-management, hence, has a universal potential.

. . . and Peace

The disintegration of war and its armies is largely due to technological developments. The impact of technology on the disintegration of work and its regiments is perhaps less dramatic but in the long run it is no less radical.

The beginning of this process lies in the past. Lewis Mumford was one of its earliest and most prophetic observers. In 1934, in *Technics and Civilization,* he described how, on the one hand, power production and automatic machines tend to eliminate the regiments of blue-collar workers. Two million workers were cast out between 1919 and 1929 in the United States while production itself actually increased. And the displacement of the work force from the primary sector of production to the tertiary (often pseudo) sector of services continues apace. On the other hand, advance in technology, as it decreases the number of human robots in the plant, increases the number of trained technicians in the laboratories. This Mumford called "the displacement of the proletariat."

The qualities of the new worker, as described by Mumford, are "alertness, responsiveness, an intelligent grasp of the operative parts: In short he must be an all-round mechanic rather than a specialized hand. . . . With complete automation, freedom of movement and initiative returns for that small part of the original working force now needed to operate the plant."

Mumford foresaw the "stimulation of invention and initiative within the industrial process, the reliance upon group activity and upon intimate forms of social approval, and the transformation of work into education, and of the social opportunities of factory production into effective forms of political action."

He predicted decentralization as a potential consequence of the new technologies: "Bigger no longer automatically means better: Flexibility of the power unit, closer adaptation of means to ends, nicer timing of operation, are the new marks of efficiency in industry." This process of decentralization, however, need not be anarchical or uncoordinated. "Small units of production can nevertheless be utilized by large units of administration, for efficient administration depends upon record-keeping, charting, routing, and communication, and not necessarily upon a local overseership."

But all these advances toward decentralization and a humanly controlled and effectively directed industrial production "await the formulation of noncapitalist modes of enterprise."

Mumford in fact predicted the abandonment of the concept of private ownership of natural resources. "The private monopoly of coal beds and oil wells is an intolerable anachronism—as intolerable as would be the monopoly of sun, air, running water . . . and the common ownership of the means of converting energy, from the wooded mountain regions where the streams have their sources down to the remotest petroleum well, is the sole safeguard to their effective use and conservation." Here are all the elements of the contemporary theories of self-management, including the concept of social ownership which is the basis of Yugoslav theory.

Social Ownership

In Yugoslavia, self-management took off from a socialist background, after a phase of expropriations and nationalizations. In other countries, this background does not exist. Must they go through socialism—Marxist or other—in order to get self-management, or can self-management be established in the context of private ownership and a capitalist production system?

Some of the participants at the Center conference, especially those from the United States and Great Britain, answered affirmitively. However, the experience from which they drew was more of a sociopsychological than a socioeconomic nature and was restricted to very small-scale and isolated systems of operation. Self-management, in fact, may be many things to many people. It may be a public-relations gimmick; it may be a means to get more out of the workers and to cut cost; it may be a mental-health medicine; it may be a research project, an experiment, a revolution.

One of the conference participants, Ichak Adizes, pointed out that far more important than ownership was the "sharing of managerial prerogatives." He went as far as to assert that "social ownership in Yugoslavia is a barrier to the future development of self-management rather than a basis for it, because it hampers the mobility of labor, and it hampers the mobility of capital."

Another participant, Einar Thorsrud, pointed out that in his country, Norway, self-management was introduced both in publicly and privately owned companies, and "when it comes to the mechanisms of workers' participation, the roles of people on the boards are exactly the same."

All these positions have one point in common: They indicate what is explicit also in Yugoslav theory, that self-management is a process that moves on a different plane from that of ownership. Self-management, in fact, articulates relations among people much more than relations between people and things. Therefore, what is important is not that the worker should own resources or the means of production but that nobody else should own them and thereby be placed in a position of hiring and firing and otherwise directing and manipulating the workers. If self-management need not be based on workers' ownership, it certainly excludes the possibility of ownership by others. The Yugoslav concept of social ownership in fact is a negative concept. It is the negation of ownership.

The Disintegration of Private Property

The disintegration of ownership is another one of the irresistible trends of contemporary history that moves modern societies in the direction of self-management.

I can distinguish three major developments tending to disintegrate our classical ownership concept. All three are interconnected.

Areas Beyond the Limits
of Ownership Rights

First, technology is opening up new areas which are presently beyond the limits of

ownership rights, whether of private individuals or of states (sovereignty), and to which the concept of ownership simply is not applicable. These include the limitless expanse of outer space and the depth of ocean space, which international law defines as "the common province of mankind" and "the common heritage of mankind" respectively. According to internationally accepted principles, these areas cannot be appropriated by any state or person, whether individual or corporate. They must be managed with the participation of all nations on equal terms and for the benefit of mankind as a whole, with particular regard to the needs of developing peoples (from everybody according to his ability, to everyone according to his need). Here is the principle of nonappropriability, the negation of ownership, the concept of social ownership writ large.

Environment

The second factor is the rise of environmental concern. This, again, has a strong technological component, but it also has a *Weltanschauung* component. It reflects a less anthropocentric view of man in his environment and a new reverence for nature, of which we are part.

Be this as it may, the social control of our environment and the improvement of its quality imposes restrictions on private-property rights which mankind, in the laissez-faire period of capitalist expansion, did not know and would not accept.

Now there is a clear and open conflict between unrestricted private ownership and social environmental control. You can have either one or the other. Political development during these last few years and the preparations for the Stockholm conference on the human environment seem to indicate that, with a heavy heart and many misgivings, mankind will be moving in the direction of a socially controlled environment and the disintegration of private ownership.

. . . and Resources

Resource management, of course, is the key to environmental control.

Current views on the earth's natural resources range from one extreme to the other. Whatever the position one takes, however, all resources must follow the way of ocean and outer-space resources: that is, they must be declared the common heritage of mankind.

If one accepts the position that resources are scarce, that heedless overexploitation and the goal of unlimited growth will, in the imminent future, exhaust all available energy sources, despoil mineral reserves, deforest continents, erode soils, deplete stocks, and drain water supplies, then the time has come, and is in fact overdue, when resources are too precious to be left to the whims of a market economy and the destructiveness of competitive private management. Rational resource management must be socially controlled—and this, certainly, undermines the concept of private ownership or resources as we know it. "The private monopoly of coal beds and oil wells is an intolerable anachronism—as intolerable as would be the monopoly of sun, air, running water . . . ."

If, on the other hand, one takes the position that the end of one phase of human economy is only the beginning of another; that the age of fossil fuel energy will be followed by the age of unlimited fusion energy; that the steel age will be followed by the magnesium age, that technology, through synthesis and mega-recycling, will produce resources unlimited, then natural resources lose their economic value. There is no more rent in them. To "own" them would be, not so much intolerable as meaningless—as meaningless as to own the water of the oceans or the light of the sun. Resources, in the postindustrial era, will become common property as they were in the pre-industrial and precapitalist era, in which they were (or appeared to be) equally unlimited.

Wealth-Producing Factors

The third development which is undermining our classical concept of ownership and property, then, is a shift that has been taking place in the weight of wealth-producing factors. Wealth is the product of resources, capital, and labor, with labor being divisible into manpower and skill. Skill used to be only one of the factors and by no means the most important, but technological advances keep increasing its significance. Skill, know-how, education, organization have displaced resources, capital, and manpower as wealth-producing factors. Needless to say, this displacement is not total. It is a trend, but an important one. Skill, know-how, education, and organization, however, are not "owned" by anybody. They are the common heritage of mankind.

The social order toward which we are moving therefore does not depend on expropriations. It does not transfer ownership rights from one group or class of people to another, nor from private owners to the state. It simply disintegrates and negates the concept of ownership. In such an order there are neither owners nor nonowners, therefore neither employers nor employees. There always will be more skilled and less skilled, better-educated and less-educated members in any working society. But in a social order not based on property but on self-management, this division need not be static. Such a working society is a learning society in which the unskilled worker is motivated to spend a great deal of his time on learning: learning to participate meaningfully in the making of decisions affecting his work and his environment. Every worker is a manager, and everyone who starts at the bottom may end, or, rather, have his turn, at the top. There is in fact no top and no bottom, self-management being a process that feeds back on itself.

A working society that is a learning society is also one that accelerates the process of development. This has been the experience in country after country. A recent seminar on profit-sharing and joint management which was held in Cairo, with delegates from nine developing nations, came to conclusions very similar to those reached by the Center seminar on self-management. "Many countries of the world are currently engaged in the task of promoting rapid economic development with a view to providing rising standards of living to their peoples," the Cairo seminar stated in its final report. "This task involves a revolutionary transformation of their social and economic institutions and a reorientation of the attitudes of their peoples. As a consequence, in the field of economic activities they are required to create new forms of organization and devise innovative methods of operating enterprises irrespective of the nature of their ownership."

Self-management building may conflict with nation building in the new and developing nations insofar as the nation is identified with the centralized state of modern European history and the thrust of self-management is decentralizing and de-etatizing. It is likely, however, that this identification of nation and centralized state will turn out to be at fault, not self-management. A self-managing, decentralized economy is likely to turn out to be more viable in the face of environmental stresses and the threat of penetration by more developed Western economies than is a centralized, state-controlled one.

"In this context and in the light of problems and practices examined by the delegates," the Cairo report concludes, "the seminar came to the view that there was an overwhelming necessity of developing a new approach to management of enterprises which recognizes the importance of achieving higher levels of productivity. The seminar regarded profit-sharing and joint management (self-management) as one of the most effective means of creating necessary conditions and motivations for this purpose . . . . "

World Organization and Self-Management

To sum up: The impact of technology on the organization of war and peace, the disintegration of ownership, due to our penetration of spaces beyond the limits of ownership rights, to environmental and resource pressures, and to a shift in the relative weight of wealth-producing factors, are facets of a universal experience of the late twentieth century. They make the Yugoslav experience with self-management potentially universal.

There is another universal experience, working in the same direction. This again has two dialectically complementary components. For there are two forces working within the human universe: one centrifugal, the other centripetal—integrative and disintegrative forces—and in this system, under the impact of these forces, a continuous regrouping and reclustering is taking place.

For a few hundred years, we have been living in an era of nation-states. We have been living in a hierarchical, vertical order; in a closed order, based on property, power, and sovereignty; in an order dominated by Western, Judeo-Grecian-Roman values.

Now we are regrouping. We are going to live in a postnational or transnational era in which nations will still exist, but they will no longer be the sole actors, or even the protagonists, on the scene of world history because other interests and other forms of organization—economic and cultural—are taking their place alongside and across the nation-state. We will live in a horizontal order, where men again participate in the decisions affecting them; we will live in an open order, with everybody being part of a number of overlapping subsystems organizing his work, leisure, economic life, cultural and spiritual life, and moving freely within these subsystems; and we will live in an order based no longer on property, nor on power, nor on sovereignty, for all these concepts are eroding under our eyes.

Finally, we will live in an order no longer dominated by Judeo-Grecian-Roman values. The new life-style will be infused with an admixture of Oriental values—symbolized by the great drama of the Chinese entry into the world organizations.

Owing to the working of the centrifugal force, there is today a remarkable tendency within nation-states to break up. This is a worldwide trend, affecting developed as well as developing nations, East, West, South, and North. I have only to mention Northern Ireland or Croatia, or Katanga or Nigeria, or East Bengal or Quebec, and it becomes clear what is meant. The black power movement in the United States should be viewed in the same context—as should, for that matter, student power, or even woman power.

What is remarkable is that the forces of law and order, sophisticated and formidable or even hypertrophized though they may be, are increasingly less capable of coping with these internal-disintegrative movements, just as, externally, they are impotent in the face of even weak and undeveloped antagonists, as in Vietnam.

Each of these movements has of course its own physiognomy, its own roots in its own history, and its own goals. What they have in common, however, is an urge toward self-determination, self-management, participation in decisionmaking on a scale that is comprehensible in human terms.

Self-management and self-governing communities, whether of a cultural, national, racial, economic, or other character, will be much more important as the infrastructure of world order than they have been in the era of the centralized nation-state.

If the centrifugal force thus undercuts the power of the nation-state, the centripetal overcuts it. I am thinking of such developments as the multinational corporations, the European Economic Com-

munities, the emerging ocean regime. Pressure comes from all those sectors of human activity which science and technology have so enlarged that they transcend the boundaries of the traditional nation-state. Resource and energy management, whether maritime or terrestrial; space technology; the management of the environment; weather control and modification; and transport and communications are cases in point. They have been dealt with in my previous studies, *The Ocean Regime* and *The World Communities.* For the purpose of the present discussion it may be enough to remember that:

The international institutions apt to cope with these problems are not primarily or directly based on nation-states nor are they an addition or merger of nation-states; they arise from transnational, nonterritorial functions.

Each one of these functions is polyvalent and involves new forms of decisionmaking in which industry, science, and government must share.

They are overlapping and interlocking.

The overall structure containing these functions will not be a superstate with the appanages of territoriality and sovereignty, but a network of communities partly functional and partly political; partly governmental and partly nongovernmental; partly international and partly intranational, with the traits of government, a business, an enterprise, a cooperative, and a union.

The impact of the forces of integration and disintegration, then, may shape a world order in which the macro organization of the interacting world communities, the median organization of the interacting self-governing nations (no longer states in the traditional sense), and the micro organization of the self-managing enterprise or other subnational system will be based on the same principles so that each part reflects the whole, and the whole reflects each part.

Human Nature

The forces of integration and disintegration acting on the human universe do not, however, stop at the level of the self-managing subsystems. They affect each individual; rather, our concept of human nature and our concept of world order are always based on the same principles and reflect each other.

Although we are by no means "beyond freedom and dignity," nor do we wish or expect to get there, it is clear that when we say we are free we are mostly kidding ourselves, such is the impact of our environment, the culture in which we live, our economic status, the kind of stimuli we are exposed to from the moment of conception onward, not to speak of our genetic heritage. Man is not really an individual, but a network of interacting forces, a shifting nodal point of influences. Statistically we really can whittle him down to nonexistence.

It is in his interaction with environmental forces and influences, though, that man gains his autonomy, he develops his responsibility, and creates a freedom that does not pre-exist and must be re-created continuously.

His self-awareness increases with his awareness of his environment, both physical and social. Increasing awareness engenders increasing interaction, which engenders new participational structures, which in turn reintegrate his own structure and render him autonomous, just as the self-managing subsystem creates and re-creates its autonomy by interacting in the participatory structures of the wider community, just as the nation creates and re-creates its sovereignty by interacting in the network of world communities.

A self-management theory, therefore, contains elements for an ideology for postindustrial man. It is an ideology which transcends the dualistic concept of man versus society; abolishes the dichotomy between owner and nonowner, manager and worker, manual work and intellectual work, work and learning, work and leisure. It is an ideology which adapts to change, enhances growth and development of the individual, the society, the economy. It is also an ideology which offers an alternative to the corporate structure, decreases the power of bureaucracy, and de-institutionalizes and humanizes. It is also a practical philosophy which is embodied and enacted in a growing number of countries whose experience is there for us to learn from.

Chapter 12 Behavioral Change and Organization Development

LABORATORY TRAINING AND ORGANIZATION DEVELOPMENT

Paul C. Buchanan

A systematic review of the literature on the effectiveness of laboratory training in industry (Buchanan, 1965) resulted in the following conclusions:

1) Laboratory training is effective as a means of facilitating specifiable changes in individuals in the industrial setting.
2) It has been used effectively in some programs of organizational development but not in others.
3) Behavioral scientists associated with the National Training Laboratories are actively engaged in subjecting their theories and methods to systematic analysis and in developing strategies for organization development.
4) Some of these strategies, now being studied systematically, are showing exciting results.

The purpose of this paper is to bring the earlier review up to date and to broaden the focus from industry to all types of organizations.

Interest in laboratory training in human relations has expanded significantly. For example, in 1968, National Training Laboratories were conducting 20 percent more sessions than in the previous year; sensitivity training has become a common activity in workshops and teacher institutes in the field of education; and the number of professionals in the National Training Laboratories has increased from 159 in 1963 to 289 in 1968.

Research on laboratory training has also expanded. There have been 68 technical articles or books which pertain to some aspect of laboratory training published since the earlier review (Buchanan, 1965). In a bibliography of research prepared by Durham and Gibb (1960), 49 studies were listed for the period 1947–1960, and 76 for the period 1960–1967. Undoubtedly the best single source of background information on the topic up to 1965 is the book by Schein and Bennis (1965).

Studies on laboratory training during the past four years deal with (1) the methodology of evaluation; (2) theory development; (3) kinds of learning brought about in the laboratories; (4) factors influencing learning in the laboratories; (5) types of individuals who learn from laboratory training, and (6) laboratory training in organization development.

Methodology of Evaluation

The methodology of evaluation continues to be a major problem, yet several recent studies indicate progress.

General Variables in Methodology

House (1967) classified the variables relevant to the problem of evaluation into four categories: objectives of the training, initial states of the learner, initial states of the organization, and methods of inducing change in the learner. Then, considering the methods as input variables, the objectives of the laboratory training as output variables, and the initial states of both the participants and the organization as moderators, he generated a paradigm of relationships that highlighted the issues in planning and assessing organizational development efforts and outlined a specific assessment design to illustrate the paradigm. The result is a clear presentation of relevant types of variables and their interconnectedness, a paradigm that is applicable to the design and assessment of any change in the "person dimension" (Leavitt, 1965) of organization performance. House's study also makes clear that neither the design nor the assessment of any training program is likely to be effective if it does not take into account variables in the *situation* as well as variables in the *person,* a finding highlighted earlier by Fleishman et al. (1955) but still often ignored. Equally important, House shows how theory can be used to make it possible for evaluation studies to contribute to a systematic body of knowledge. However, his paradigm is more adequate in providing for moderator than for output variables. As moderators he lists "the nature of the primary work group," "the formal authority system" of the organization, and "exercise of authority by superior"; yet he doesn't list these organization factors as output variables: He lists only changes in knowledge, skill, attitude, and job performance. But it is on the assumption that such changes in the participant will result in changes in the output of the work unit to which the learner belongs that organizations support training. As important as House's work is, therefore, it omits some important variables.

Problems of Design

While House dealt with general problems of design and evaluation, Harrison (1967) has made a thoughtful analysis of some specific issues. First, as he points out, it is seldom possible to assign participants randomly to the treatment and a control group. Usually participants are either self-selected, or are assigned for administrative or other organizational reasons (the personnel officer wants them to attend; they are part of a unit that is to participate; etc.) where control groups are used for assessment studies. They are usually selected *post hoc* and with little information available about their similarity to the treatment group. For example, in the studies of Bunker (1965) and Bunker and Knowles, (1967), control subjects were nominated by participants, and no data are given for the basis of this nomination, about the experiences the controls had during the period covered by the assessment, or the reasons why participants had attended the laboratory and the controls had not. Only two of the studies reviewed in this paper meet requirements for appropriate control groups (Deep, Bass, and Vaughan, 1967; Schmuck, 1968).

But there is an added difficulty in using a control group which Harrison discusses: The fact that being a member of a group influences expectations and thereby introduces bias, if perceptions of behavior are used as criteria. Because of these difficulties, Harrison encourages (and utilizes) assessment designs that examine the relation between (predicted) processes of training and outcomes from training.

A second problem is that of when assessment measures after laboratory training should be taken to obtain a valid evaluation of the impact of training. As Harrison points out, until one knows the pattern of the impact, he doesn't know what kinds of changes to look for and when. For example, the immediate effect on participants may be uncertainty, discomfort, and experimentation, which may then give way to confidence, new behavior patterns, and stabilization. If this were the case, then measures taken only at the end of the training would be very misleading.

Related to the issue of timing of evaluation is that of whether assessment should focus on predicted and/or desired outcomes (what Harrison calls a normative approach), or should be more like a net to catch whatever influences may be apparent. Harrison also discusses difficulties in assessing change on metagoals of laboratory training.

Because of variability in the designs of programs which are called laboratory training, it is difficult to specify and apply a design that can be replicated or meaningfully compared with other training methods. As Harrison (1967:6) says, " . . . we do not yet have adequate enough theory about the effects of different elements of training design even to permit us to classify laboratories according to design."

Miles (1965a, 1965b), for many years an innovator of evaluation designs, met many of the requirements of House's paradigm and Harrison's emphasis on examining process variables. More recently he and his associates have used theory in increasing the rigor of assessment designs (Miles et al., 1965 and 1966; Benedict et al., 1967). This method, which they called a "clinical-experimental approach," has five components: (1) It calls for a clear division of labor between the researcher responsible for assessment, and the change agents responsible for participants; (2) Data are collected both clinically (running account of events before, during, and following the interventions) and experimentally (by preplanned and periodic measurements of the treatment and a control group; (3) The investigators make theory-based general predictions about the impact that the training is likely to have on specific variables of the organization; (4) The change agent obtains information from the participants, and on this basis formulates specific training activities; then he makes short-range predictions about the variables which the intervention would affect; (5) Careful attention is given to the tactical assessment design. (Miles uses a design involving treatment and control groups and several post-training measurements.) In the study reporting their attempt to use this design (Benedict et al., 1967) were not completely successful in meeting their methodological prescriptions; problems arose around keeping the research members and change agents from influencing each other

(especially through the exchange of data); and there was questionable similarity between the treatment and the control groups. Even so, the approach of Miles and associates represents a significant improvement in evaluating change efforts.

The study by Marrow et al. (1967) is of special significance, partly because it exploited the availability of two large organizations with known similarity and with known "states of health." As in Miles' design, the change agents and the researchers constituted two separate teams. Measurements of human factors and management practices were repeated for both the treatment and the control organization. In addition, economic data were also obtained and systematically analyzed in relation to both short-range and longer-range impact on a number of variables. Further elaboration of the measure used is provided by Likert (1967).

Greiner's study of a grid-based organizational-development project was another methodological advance, in that in addition to the researchers' not being part of the change-agent team, information was obtained about conditions that preceded and in fact apparently led to, the intervention (Greiner, 1965); Blake et al., 1964).

Many of the studies reviewed have attempted, as Harrison and House suggest, to examine hypothesized relations among independent, intervening, and dependent variables (Rubin, 1967 a,b; Harrison, 1966; Kolb et al., 1968; French et al., 1966; Deep et al., 1967; and Friedlander, 1967); yet in many the basis on which the predicted connection between the training and the measured outcome is not specified (Bunker and Knowles, 1967; Byrd, 1967). Equally important, many do not provide theoretical links between the expected change and improvement in performance on the job.

The practice of assessing the extent of change attributed to a training program by asking participants and their associates to describe any changes they have noted during a specified time after the training (Bunker, 1965; Bunker and Knowles,

1967) has obvious weaknesses such as the demands it makes on memory. But comparisons of responses to questionnaires obtained before and after training also present difficulties. One problem is that the standard of reference used by the respondent may itself be influenced significantly by the training. For example, Blake and Mouton (1968) required participants to rank themselves as to grid styles before and at the end of the seminar, and one of the expected outcomes from the seminar was to to increase the use of the "9,9," style by participants. The data (Blake and Mouton, 1968:52) from measures before and after the seminar show a *decrease* of around 32 in the percentage of participants who saw themselves having 9,9 as their most characteristic style. And it is a common experience in groups where questionnaires are used to help the group diagnose and assess its progress on, say, openness, to find no increase or actually a decrease on ratings of openness at the same time that members state (and demonstrate) that they are becoming more open with each other.

There is also the problem of test sensitization, which can influence the responses of a control group. Friedlander (1967:305), in interpreting his data which revealed a decrease in effectiveness of the control group, noted:

The first administration of the [Group Behavior Inventory] queried comparison group members with blunt questions on sensitive issues which they were unprepared to confront at that time. But after six months of observing those inadequacies that did occur, expectations and standards of the leadership role became clearer. Since current leadership practice did not conform to these expectations, comparison group members now perceived significantly greater inadequacies in the rapport and approachability of their chairman.

To the extent that a decrease occurs in the responses of the comparison group after the laboratory training, statistically significant differences between the treatment and the control group will lead to inaccurate conclusions about the impact of the training upon the treatment group. (They will look better due to an apparent decrease in the control group.) It appears that any measurement scheme involving perceptions are [*sic*] subject to error; therefore, greater effort to devise other kinds are [*sic*] much needed.

Some additional shortcomings in the design of the assessment studies reviewed are:

1) In several evaluation procedures, changes noted were given equal weight, even though they appeared to vary greatly in importance (i.e., "listens more" was equivalent in the scoring system to "conducts more effective staff meetings").

2) Results from one study could not be compared with results from other studies, since the training programs evaluated varied in length, in the specific design, in the occupational mix of participants. Also, the studies varied in the variables examined, the instrument used to assess change in a given variable, and the time at which measures were gathered after the training period. Thus a body of self-consistent knowledge is slow to develop.

3) Where laboratory training was part of an organization development program (Blake and Mouton, 1968; Marrow et al., 1967; Miles et al., 1966), it was difficult to know how much any change effected was due to the laboratory training and how much to other circumstances (Greiner, 1965, 1967).

One must conclude, then, that even though much work has been done to devise more effective evaluation designs, the major shortcomings have not been overcome. This means that the findings summarized below are based on inadequate design and can only be tentative.

Theory Development

In 1964 eight fellows of the National Training Laboratories presented their views on what happens in a T-group. Several important theoretical papers dealing with this issue have appeared since that time.

Theories

Hampden-Turner (1966) developed "an existential learning theory" which he used to integrate findings from three empirical studies of T-group effectiveness. His theory involved a "developmental spiral," wherein he hypothesized that the participant's initial quality of cognition, clarity of identity, and extent of self-esteem would result in his ordering his experience. This ordering in the context of a T-group, leads the participant to risk his competence in interacting with another person; the reaction of the other person stimulates the participant to a new integration of his experiences. This in turn leads to changes in the quality of the participant's cognition, clarity of identity, and extent of self-esteem, and to a repetition of the cycle.

Harrison (1965) formulated a "cognitive model for interpersonal and group behavior" which was intended as a framework for research, and which he later used as a basis for forming training groups (Harrison and Lubin, 1965) and for designing laboratories (Harrison and Oshry, 1965). Harrison sees learning resulting when a participant's way of construing events is "up-ended" by confrontation with other participants who construe the same event differently, and when the participant also feels sufficiently supported by others that he is able to work through the consequences of the disturbing confrontation. This theory clearly has value as a basis for designing training experiences, and there is considerable support for the belief that the type of learning (change) it emphasizes is important. For example, Harvey (1966) has detected several differences in behavior of people who are high on abstract (versus concrete) thinking, a difference which appears to be compatible with Harrison's emphasis on cognitive structure.

Argyris (1965) stated a theory of individual learning from which he derived implications for designing laboratories. Criticism from several fellows of the National Training Laboratories (Argyris, 1967) should dispel any belief that the National Training Laboratories have become complaisant as a result of their present rapid growth and popularity. Argyris also utilized his theory to identify variables in terms of which change could be assessed, devised measures of these variables, and tested his theory (Argyris, 1965).

Clark and Culbert hypothesized that self-awareness develops as a function of mutually congruent therapeutic relations between participants and trainers (Clark and Culbert, 1965).

Schein and Bennis (1965) set forth a theory of learning through laboratory training which consists of a cyclical interplay of a dilemma or disconfirming experience, attitude change, new behavior, new information and awareness, leading to additional change, new behavior, etc.

Smith (1966) formulated and tested a complex theory of learning based on Kelman's model of influence. Bass (1967) made a critique of T-group theory and concluded that the kinds of learning emphasized can be dysfunctional to job performance. As partial evidence for this view, he cites a study (Deep et al. 1967) in which it was found that intact T-groups performed less effectively on a business game than groups composed of members from different T-groups. (In the study by Deep et al. (1967), the T-group met without trainers and were conducted in what is called "instrumented" laboratory training.)

Laboratory Training and the Improvement of Organizational Performance

Several people have formulated systematic theories about the use of laboratory training in improving the functioning of organizations. Perhaps the most important are those of Blake and Mouton (1964, 1968) in regard to industrial organizations, and Miles and associates (1966) in regard to schools. Blake and Mouton (1968) deal wholly with their plan for organizational development and with guidelines for implementing the plan. Although the basic concepts of planned change which they present are similar to those conceptualized by Lippitt, Watson, and Westley (1958) the value of the study lies in its technology: Blake and Mouton have devised and tested concrete and theoretically sound methods for implementing the concepts.

Miles and his associates (1966) built upon the survey-feedback strategy of planned change and made a special effort to determine empirically the way in which intervention (or input), intervening, and output variables were interrelated, especially in school systems.

Several other writers have formulated theories about organizations, which are congruent with the values of laboratory training and which emphasize laboratory training as a means of improving the functioning of organizations (Shepard, 1965; McGregor, 1967; Bennis, 1966; Davis, 1967; Schein and Bennis, 1965).

Greiner (1967) speculates systematically about "antecedents to planned change," asking why the Blake-Mouton interventions had the impact they did. He was able to identify "how the consultants made use of roots put down in the unplanned stages many years before [the beginning of the consultant-planned change] to build top management support for Managerial Grid training," and he relates specific events that occurred during the organization development program to these historic roots. His study thus integrates imaginative observation, survey findings, and theory derived from a variety of related fields into a coherent and nonpolemic theory of organization change. He emphasizes the importance of the historical development of an organization in attempts to change it, a conclusion

also reached by Sarason (1966) in his statement that the outcome of a *current* change effort is highly influenced by the outcome of *earlier* change efforts. Failure to cope effectively with the organization's earlier experiences with change also appeared to be one of the reasons for the limited impact of a change project in a recent study (Buchanan, 1968).

From this brief overview of recent theoretical developments, it appears that the primary focus has been on how an individual learns in T-groups, and on processes of planned organizational development. Much less attention has been given to the processes of *group* development. Only two studies (Lakin and Carlson, 1964; Psathas and Hardert, 1966) attempted to explore patterns of group development.

Kinds of Learning

Persistence of Learning

In summarizing findings from studies of laboratory training it seems appropriate, first, to consider whether the learning from laboratory training persists. Two studies bear on this question. Schutz and Allen (1966) gathered information on the FIRO-B (Fundamental Interpersonal Relations Orientation—Behavioral) questionnaire from participants (and a control group) at the beginning, the end, and six months after a two-week laboratory. They found that participants changed during the training and that the changes continued after the training. Harrison (1966) collected information from 76 participants at the beginning, a few weeks after, and a few months after they took part in a laboratory. He concluded that there was a change in the predicted direction at both follow-up periods, but that the difference became significant only between the end of the training and the second follow-up measure; thus the training appeared to be progressive. These findings are consistent with those of Bunker and Knowles (1967),

who found significant changes in participants (as compared with a control group)
10–12 months following training. Also,
Morton and Bass (1964), in a study of 97
participants, found a marked increase in
motivation to improve their performance
at the end of the laboratory and substantial changes in job performance in a follow-up 12 weeks later. French et al. (1966)
also found further changes in participants'
self-concepts following the laboratory.

Types of Learning

The next question to be explored concerns what is learned. Here it is difficult
to categorize the findings, since researchers rarely look for the same results; and
when they do, they typically use different
measures, except for the retrospective
"behavior change description questionnaire" developed by Miles (1965a) and
Bunker (1965) and used in at least three
studies.

Reduction of Extreme Behavior

Two studies produce findings, similar in
this respect to an earlier study by Boyd
and Ellis, which suggest that laboratory
training changes people selectively, depending upon their personality. Schutz
and Allen (1966) found that (as measured
by FIRO-B) very dominant participants
become less dominant, while very submissive participants become more assertive.
Using the same instrument, Smith (1964)
found that his experimental subjects (108
students in 11 training groups) changed
significantly more in the direction of a
better match between what they *expected*
and what they *wanted* on both the control
and the affection scales of FIRO-B. Some
of the findings of Bunker can also be interpreted as an indication that reduction
of abrasive or otherwise undesirable behaviors occurred. Such studies raise the
possibility that laboratory training produces other-directed behavior; but Kas-
sajian (1965) found no change in laboratory participants on an instrument which
purported to measure other-directedness.

*Openness, receptivity, awareness,
tolerance of differences*
Changes such as these are most consistently found following laboratory training
(and are, of course, among the most commonly stated objectives). Such changes
apparently result even from short laboratories. Bunker and Knowles (1967), Morton and Wight (1964), Rubin (1967), Morton and Bass (1964), Schutz and Allan
(1966), Smith (1966), and Kolb et al.
(1968) all report this kind of learning.
Such changes probably occurred in the
other studies also, but the measures used
did not relate to this kind of change.

Operational skills
This category includes behavior like listening, encouraging the participation of
others, use of new techniques, solicitation
of feedback, etc. Outcomes of this sort
were reported by Bunker and Knowles
(1967), Schutz and Allen (1966), Morton
and Wight (1964), Sikes (1964), De
Michele (1966), and Schmuck (1968).
    Because of its design, the study by
Schmuck is worth further comment. He
studied a four-week laboratory for 20
classroom teachers, where the design included T-groups, problem-solving exercises, and practice in using instruments
and procedures for diagnosing classroom
problems. Then before the laboratory
ended, each teacher formulated specific
plans for the following year, applying
what she had learned. Follow-up meetings
were held bimonthly from September
through December. He also met weekly
with another set of teachers from the
same large school system (and apparently
with random assignment of teachers to
the two groups), from September to December, covering the same material as in
the laboratory except for the T-group
work (and of course with much less total
time). He found marked differences in the
two groups as to the number of practices
the participants tried out in their classrooms (5 to 17 by laboratory participants
compared with 1 to 2 by the seminar participants), and in the esprit de corps
among the teachers as indicated by the

contacts they made with each other during the fall. What is more significant, he found improvement in the classrooms of the laboratory participants (as compared to both the seminar participants and a small control group), in that the students perceived themselves as having more influence in the class, as being better liked and an integral part of a friendship group in the class, and as being helpful to each other.

Cognitive style
Examples of this type of outcome are findings by Blake et al. (1965) that union and managerial participants reflected predicted differential shifts on a managerial grid questionnaire. Harrison (1966) found shifts on the Role Repertory Test from the use of concrete-instrumental toward inferential-expressive modes of thought. Oshry and Harrison (1966) found that many laboratory participants viewed their work environment more humanly and less impersonally, saw themselves more as a significant part of their work problems, and saw more connection between the meeting of interpersonal needs and the effectiveness of their work.

In some studies, however, changes that were expected were not found. Bowers and Soar (1961) found no differences between a group of 25 teachers who took part in half-day training sessions over a three-week period and a control group, with respect to their use of group processes in their classrooms during the following academic year. This contrasts with Schmuck's finding significant carry-over into the classrooms (but his intervention consisted of four weeks full time, with systematic follow-up during the fall). Bunker (1965) found no differences between his laboratory participants and controls in initiative and assertiveness. Sikes (1964) failed to find predicted differences between laboratory graduates and a control group in their accuracy in predicting the responses of other members in a discussion group. And Oshry and Harrison (1966) predicted, but did not find, significant changes in sensitivity to the interper-

sonal needs of others or in the importance attributed to the interpersonal needs of others, when participants returned to their jobs.

Where does laboratory training effect change? There is clear evidence that personal growth results for most participants—they feel better about themselves, have new insights, and consider the training one of the important experiences in their life. Furthermore, participants continually report improvement in their family relations as a result of the experience (Winn, 1966). The value of the laboratory experience for job performance, however, is less convincing: fewer extreme behaviors, greater openness and self-awareness, increased operational skills, and new alternatives for viewing situations. These seem small advances compared to the powerful forces that maintain a status quo in organizations. But what such change does represent is an increased readiness for "next steps."

Factors Influencing Learning

Several recent studies deal with factors that increase learning by participants in laboratory training; those dealing with the value of laboratory training for organizational development are discussed later.

Group Composition

Perhaps the most clear-cut results have emerged regarding the effects of group composition which have been examined in terms of personality and organizational membership of participants. Harrison (1965:418–19) theorizes about personality factors as follows:

The process of learning is best facilitated when the individual is placed in a learning situation where either the structure produces dissonance or a significant number of others will act, feel, and perceive in ways which create sharp, clear dissonance for the learner or are contrary to his values. The dissonance must, however, be meaningful to the learner in that the alternatives presented by the others have some anchoring points within his current cognitive systems regarding himself and his interpersonal relationships. . . . [W]e propose that a degree of polarization be created on important issues within the group. This polarization provides the battlefield on which learning by the explorations of opposites can take place. However, if the individual is exposed only to confrontation and dissonance, he is apt to react in extreme ways. . . . For our learning model to operate, the individual should find in the group some relationships which serve as a refuge and support. Persons with similar cognitive systems, values, and perceptions can provide this support and protection against the destructive efforts of a purely confronting experience. This supportive climate is the "castle" in our analogy.

After reviewing relevant literature, Harrison concluded that personality variables relevant to obtaining his conditions in the formation of groups were of three types: activity-passivity, high-low affect, and negative-positive affect. He found empirical confirmation of his theory, in that groups homogeneous or mixed on one or more of these variables differed predictably in the way the groups functioned and in the kind of learning. More specifically he concluded (1965:431):

1) Learning is facilitated by a group climate which provides support for one's cognitive, emotional, and behavioral orientation and, at the same time, confronts one with meaningful alternatives to those orientations.
2) Group climate can be manipulated by relatively crude selection procedures.
3) The models and the research findings reviewed here can be applied to the diagnosis of wide ranges of interpersonal learning difficulties and to the design of learning groups which will provide favorable conditions of support and confrontation.

A study by Smith (1966) seems to support Harrison's findings about the importance of personality mix of participants.

Morton and Wight (1964) studied differences in organizational membership. They conducted three instrumented laboratories within a company with groups composed so that participants in six of the D-groups (the designation for T-groups in instrumented laboratories) were all from one department, and all members had direct superior-subordinate relations with others in the group; whereas participants in the other six D-groups did not have direct superior-subordinate relationships, and were from separate units of the plant. The three laboratories were conducted according to the same design. On the basis of critical events (critical event was defined as "anything that has happened since the laboratory which would not have occurred had their been no training") obtained from 90 percent of the participants three months after the laboratories, they (1964:35–36) concluded that

Participants from the more homogeneous groups reported a significantly greater proportion of critical events. In areas of personal responsibility, such as supervisor responsibility for his subordinates, his responsibility for individual problem solving, for . . . listening . . . and sensitivity for what was taking place, there was no significant difference in the frequencies with which incidents were reported. When the problems exceeded the limits of the customary personal responsibility and involved the kind of responsibility that results in highly effective team working relations, the homogeneous . . . groups far exceeded the heterogeneous trained groups in the frequencies with which these critical incidents were reported. The post-training activities of the participants have led them into some difficulties. The nature of the difficulties have varied with the homogeneity of the groups. Those who trained in the less homogeneous groups are reporting less accomplished and more resistance of a personal nature. The members of the homogeneous groups, . . . are reporting the greatest number of organizational barriers to applying what they have learned. Whereas the heterogeneous trained groups found their greatest barriers within their primary work group, among those who have not been in the training, the homogeneous trained group report their greatest difficulty in problem solving with those outside their department who have not received training.

These findings must be considered tentative, however, since variables other than the D-group composition could account for the differences between the two types of groups. For example, the report does not make clear the circumstances under which so many members from one department participated in the laboratories; it may have been the supervisor's enthusiasm rather than the D-group composition which accounted for the change. It is also possible that the differences in outcome occurred because many people from the same department had a similar training experience (i.e., participating in a laboratory) rather than that they were in the same D-groups.

Duration of Laboratory

A third variable apparently making a difference in learning outcome is the duration of the laboratory training. Bunker and Knowles (1967) compared the outcomes from two three-week and two two-week summer sessions conducted by National Training Laboratories. They found that the three-week laboratories "fostered more behavioral changes" than the two-week ones; that is, more participants in the three-week ones made changes "toward more proactive and interactive behavior," while changes made by the two-week participants were in the area of increased receptiveness (i.e., listening, sensitivity, etc.) However, they noted that the laboratories were similar in the amount of time spent in T-groups, but differed greatly in the time devoted to

problems relating to their work; thus the differential impact could be due to the design, or interaction between the design and duration, rather than to duration alone. The question of duration merits more study since costs are closely related to duration, and almost every study indicates that the trained group shows change.

Trainer Behavior

Interaction effects between trainer and participant orientation on the FIRO-F questionnaire were found to have differential impact upon the "laboratory learning climate" (Powers, 1965) and upon kinds of learning (Smith, 1966). Bolman (1968) also studied the relation of trainer behavior-openness, congruence, and consistency (as judged by participants) to learning by participants. Although the results were inclusive, he succeeded in isolating dimensions of trainer behavior and a way of measuring them. Culbert examined the differential impact of "more" and "less" self-disclosing trainer behavior in two T-groups, and found that although trainer behavior differed as planned, the groups attained the same level of self-awareness (Culbert, 1968).

Goal-Setting and Feedback

Several studies have been conducted to examine the effects of goal-setting and feedback. Kolb et al. (1968) introduced a procedure in T-groups, by which each participant set a specific change goal for himself and was encouraged to work to meet his goal; then they varied the amount of feedback received during the training, and they attempted to heighten each participant's commitment to the goals he set. They found that differences in both the extent of commitment and in the amount of feedback influenced learning. French et al. (1966) also found that the greater the amount of feedback, the greater the extent of change on self-selected change goals. And Harrison (1966) found that the amount of change in cognitive orientation was significantly related to ratings by participants of how other participants reacted to and utilized feedback during T-group sessions. Those who made it easy for others to give feedback, and who tested the validity of feedback to seeking more, showed the most change. Thus it appears that provision for participants to obtain and utilize feedback is an important factor in laboratory design.

In summary, then, it appears that the climate which develops in the training group, and the kind and/or extent of learning which occurs, are influenced by the personality mix of the participants, the organizational relationships of the participants, and the way the design utilizes feedback. Studies regarding the effect of duration of the laboratory and of trainer behavior are inconclusive.

Type of Laboratory Training and Job Improvement

The question of whether the greatest improvement on the job results from laboratories which focus almost wholly on personal growth or from those which include personal growth, organizational problems, and planning for changes on the job has not been studied with sufficient rigor for meaningful conclusions to be drawn. Bunker and Knowles related their data to the issue; but since the laboratories that they studied varied in duration as well as in the proportion of time spent in T-groups, the differences they found cannot be attributed to the design alone.

Wilson et al. (1968) reported results from a follow-up on two 6-day "off-site" laboratories, one of which utilized "the traditional sensitivity approach described by Weschler" and the other Morton's version of an instrumented laboratory. Six months after the instrumented laboratory and 18 months after the "sensitivity" laboratory, a very high and similar proportion of participants of the two laboratories reported that the experience was of value to them as individuals; participants of the instrumented laboratory showed significantly greater improvement as managers, as members of a team, in building team effort in their organizations and in communicating with others in the work setting. Although the study design was a weak one, as the authors note, the findings were consistent with their predictions.

There are not studies comparing laboratory training with rational training (Ellis and Blum, 1967), "motive acquisition" training (McClelland, 1965), or other forms of training; yet there is certainly a need for such studies.

Types of Individual Influenced

Personality and Organization Variable

In one of the more thorough analyses of learning processes and outcomes, Miles (1965) explored 595 relations among criterion, home organization, treatment, and personal variables. He found significant relations between on-the-job change and sex (males change more), job security (as measured by years as a school principal, the more secure participant changed more), and power (as measured by number of teachers supervised, the more powerful changed more). He did not find significant differences between on-the-job change and age, ego strength (as measured by Barron's scale), flexibility (as measured by Barron's scale), need affiliation (as measured by French's test of insight), a combination of these personality variables, autonomy on the job (as measured by frequency of meetings with superior), perceived power in his work situation, perceived flexibility of his organization, and a combination of these three organizational variables. On the other hand, he found that several of these variables were significantly related to the participant's behavior during the training (specifically to the extent to which he became more communicative, and to the trainer's rating of the extent to which participants changed), and such behavior was in turn related to on-the-job changes.

Unfortunately, there are few replications of Miles' studies. No other study examines age or sex as a factor in learning from laboratories. With respect to personality, Rubin (1967) found that anomy (which as predicted was itself unaffected by laboratory training) significantly influenced the extent of change in self-awareness, which was a factor in the extent of change in acceptance of others. Harrison (1966) found no significant relation between prelaboratory scores on an instrument measuring concrete-instrumental versus inferential-expressive orientation and extent of change as indicated by comparing pretraining with posttraining scores on this instrument. He also found no relation between the prelaboratory scores on this instrument and the participants' reactions to feedback during the laboratory—a finding which seems surprising if Harrison's theory about the importance of cognitive orientation is accurate.

In a study of classroom teachers, Bowers and Soar (1961) found that an increase in the teachers' use of group processes in the classroom following training was greatest for teachers (a) who were well adjusted and (b) who used group methods before receiving the training. Harrison and Oshry (1965) found that people who were seen as changing most in a T-group were those who were described by colleagues as open to the ideas of others, were accepting of others, and listened well. These two studies suggest that laboratory training develops the participant's interpersonal style further rather than reversing it.

There is rather strong evidence that participants who become involved in the T-group learn more than those who are ranked low on involvement (Bunker, 1965; Harrison and Oshry, 1966). Although Miles did not find the relation between involvement and on-the-job change to be significant, he did find involvement significantly related to trainer ratings of the participants' effectiveness in the group, which was in turn significantly related to on-the-job change. Perhaps involvement in the training group is a function of the amount of dissonance produced—or of having "a castle and a battlefield," as Harrison suggests.

The direction that research should take, in the tradition of Miles' study, is exemplified by Smith (1966). Using a complex model of training based on Kelman's model of influence, and four separate measures of learning, Smith explored the relations among group climates (as indicated by the mix of participant orientation, trainer styles, and types of influence underlying the trainer-participant interaction process) and types of learning. He found support for his predictions that (1) the compliant learning pattern, found among groups with authority-oriented participants and trainers, showed highest learning in diagnostic ability, and (b) the internalizing learning pattern, found in groups with data-oriented participants and people-oriented trainers, showed the greatest favorable changes on FIRO scores and on interpersonal awareness. (This study was based on 31 T-groups, but since the laboratories varied in duration, and the participants in age and occupational background, it is difficult to know the extent to which extraneous factors clouded the findings.)

Influence of Background

Bunker and Knowles (1967) found that human relations laboratory participants from religious and governmental organizations showed significant change after a three-week laboratory but not after a two-week one; whereas participants from industry, education, and social service changed significantly after a two-week session, but the differences between the two-week and the three-week sessions were not significant. However, in this study the data on participants' background did not permit more than rough groupings; so, little confidence can be placed in the findings.

In summary, these studies provide some support for the prediction that sex, job security, organizational power, anomy of the participant, trainer-participant interaction patterns, the openness of the participant, and the participant's involvement in the T-group make a difference in how much the participant learns; but clearly this is a topic which merits much more systematic exploration.

Laboratory Training in Organization Development

The evidence rather clearly indicates that laboratory training has a predictable and significant impact on most participants; yet, it is also clear that from the standpoint of organizational improvement, laboratory training by itself is not enough. Several researchers have addressed themselves to facilitating "transfer of learning" (Winn, 1966; Bass, 1967; Oshry and Harrison, 1966). Bass has identified eight different approaches currently being tried as a means of increasing transfer. In varying degrees, these methods involve including in the training people and/or activities associated with participants on the job, while still retaining a focus on behavior in the laboratory. Laboratory training systematically undertakes throughout the company, using combinations of stranger, work, and interface groups, was a major intervention in the program at the Space Technology Laboratories (Davis, 1967), in Nonlinear Systems (Kuriloff and Atkins, 1966), and in a division of Alcan (Winn, 1966). And the indications are that in all three companies the development efforts were effective.

Laboratory Training as Part of a Development Program

In several strategies, however, laboratory training is one component of a multiphased program, as in Harwood Manufacturing Company's revitalization of Weldon (Marrow et al., 1967), in Beckhard's work (1966) with a large hotel company, in Blake's and Mouton's work (1968), and in several projects in school systems (Buchanan, 1968; Miles et al.,

1966). In all of these cases of organization development, it is difficult to assess how important the laboratory training was in the impact of the total program (and, of course, it is equally difficult to assess the effectiveness of the total program itself). In an attempt to learn (Buchanan, 1967) what characterized effective programs of organization development, eight successful programs and three unsuccessful ones were examined in the hope of finding some crucial variable. The use of laboratory training (or any other formal training) was not a crucial variable. Neither of the two cases (Guest, 1962; Jaques, 1951) where there was the clearest evidence of success involved formal training. One of the variables that did emerge as crucial was the introduction of new and more fruitful concepts for diagnosing current problems of the organization and setting improvement goals. Having new concepts for diagnosing current practices seemed to provide members of the organization with a means of getting from symptoms to variables which provided leverage for change; having new concepts for setting targets was important in working out clear ideas of potentiality and in developing dissonance and thus motivation for change. Information which has become available since that study was made is consistent with the conclusion about the development of new concepts as a crucial issue in organization development. In a project of organization development, analysis of the case reports on work done with two schools indicated that in the more effective of the two projects much more time was given to developing new concepts and the skills of key participants before diagnosis and planning for system change was undertaken (Buchanan, 1968). In the school system where there was more change, the superintendent had participated in a laboratory conducted by National Training Laboratories, and he and the key members of the system took part in a one-week laboratory of their own. In the other system, the superintendent did not have prior laboratory experience, and he and his key staff had a two-day laboratory of their own. In two other cases of organizational development where there was little evidence of effectiveness (Benedict et al., 1967; Miles et al., 1966), diagnosis of current conditions in the system was undertaken before any effort was made to develop new concepts. In contrast, Blake and Mouton (1968) continually stress the understanding of grid theory and the development of skills required in its application as an essential first step in each phase of their strategy. They begin by exposing the key person in the treatment organization to the managerial grid concept and to alternative styles of management and their implications. This is followed by familiarizing a representative sample of participants with the same concepts. Then all members of management are exposed to the same concepts, and only then are needs diagnosed and improvement goals set by individuals and teams for themselves and for the total organization. A case study recently reported by Bartlett (1967), in which the development effort appeared to be successful, also involved development of new concepts and skills as the first step in the program.

Cognitive Changes

Quite clearly, formal training is one effective means for developing cognitive changes as an opening step in organizational development. At the same time, it is also clear that there are other means of creating cognitive changes. The question, then, is whether laboratory training and, in fact, what *kind* of laboratory training provides the most useful concepts and skills for organizational development. Answers to this question can be sought from two sources: from theories about effective organization functioning, and from outcomes of organizational development programs that utilize different methods for introducing new concepts and skills. Although the latter method would be more convincing, at this time there is little such information available. One must therefore look to theory for support of the utility of laboratory training as a means of providing relevant cognitive changes in participants in programs of organizational development. Blake and Mouton have made a case for laboratory training based on grid theory; Shepard, Likert, Argyris, Bennis, and McGregor have provided relevant theory in the case of nongrid laboratory training; and Miles has systematically sought empirical data relevant to the question as it pertains to school systems.

One can summarize this review of the literature as to the value of laboratory training as follows:

1) It facilitates personal growth and development and thus can be of value to the individual who participates.
2) It accomplishes changes in individuals which according to several theories are important in effecting change in organizations and in effectively managing organizations.
3) One study, in which an instrumented laboratory was compared with sensitivity training, provides some indication that more organizational change resulted from the instrumented approach.
4) The findings from this literature search are compatible with the conclusions reached in a similar review made four years ago (Buchanan 1965).

References

Argyris, Chris
  1965 "Explorations in Interpersonal Competence—I and II," *Journal of Applied Behavioral Science* 1:58–83; 255–69.
  1967 "On the Future of Laboratory Education," *Journal of Applied Behavioral Science* 3:153–83.
Bartlett, Alton C.
  1967 "Changing Behavior As a Means to Increase Efficiency," *Journal of Applied Behavioral Science* 3:381–403.
Bass, Bernard M.
  1967 "The Anarchist Movement and the T-Group," *Journal of Applied Behavioral Science* 3:211–26.
Benedict, Barbara; Paula Calder; Daniel Callahan; Harvery Hornstein; and Matthew B. Miles

1967 "The Clinical-Experimental Approach to Assessing Organizational Change Efforts," *Journal of Applied Behavioral Science* 3:347–80.

Bennis, Warren G.
1966 *Changing Organizations* (New York: McGraw-Hill Book Company).

Beckhard, Richard
1966 "An Organization Improvement Program in a Decentralized Organization," *Journal of Applied Behavioral Science* 2:3–26.
1967 "The Confrontation Meeting," *Harvard Business Review* 45:149–55.

Blake, Robert R., and Jane S. Mouton
1964 *The Managerial Grid* (Houston: Gulf Publishing Company).
1966 "Some Effects of Managerial Grid Seminar Training on Union and Management Attitudes Toward Supervision," *Journal of Applied Behavioral Science* 2:387–400.
1968 *Corporate Excellence through Grid Organization Development* (Houston: Gulf Publishing Company).

Blake, Robert R.; Jane S. Mouton; Lewis B. Barnes; and Larry E. Greiner
1964 "Breakthrough in Organization Development," *Harvard Business Review* 42:133–55.

Blake, Robert R.; Jane S. Mouton; and Richard L. Sloma
1965 "The Union-Management Intergroup Laboratory: Strategy for Resolving Intergroup Conflict," *Journal of Applied Behavioral Science* 1:25–57.

Bolman, Lee
1968 *The Effects of Variations in Educator Behavior on the Learning Process in Laboratory Human Relations Education* (Doctoral dissertation, Yale University).

Bowers, N. D., and R. S. Soar
1961 "Evaluation of Laboratory Human Relations Training for Classroom Teachers," *Studies of Human Relations in the Teaching-Learning Process: V Final Report* (Columbia: University of South Carolina).

Buchanan, Paul C.
1965 "Evaluating the Effectiveness of Laboratory Training in Industry." In *Explorations in Human Relations Training and Research, Report No. 1* (Washington: National Training Laboratories).
1967 "Crucial Issues in Organizational Development." In Goodwin Watson, ed., *Change in School Systems* (Washington: National Training Laboratories).
1968 *Reflections on a Project in Self-Renewal in Two School Systems* (Washington: National Training Laboratories).

Bugental, James, and Robert Tannenbaum
1963 "Sensitivity Training and Being Motivation," *Journal of Humanistic Psychology* 3:76–85.

Bunker, Douglas R.
1965 "Individual Applications of Laboratory Training," *Journal of Applied Behavioral Sciences* 1:131–48.

Bunker, Douglas R., and Eric S. Knowles
1967 "Comparison of Behavioral Changes Resulting from Human Relations Training Laboratories of Different Lengths," *Journal of Applied Behavioral Science* 3:505–24.

Byrd, Richard E.
1967 "Training in a Nongroup," *Journal of Humanistic Psychology* 7:18–27.

Clark, James, and Samuel A. Culbert
1965 "Mutually Theraputic Perception and Self-Awareness in a T-Group" *Journal of Applied Behavioral Science* 1:180–94.

Culbert, Samuel A.
1968 "Trainer Self-Disclosure and Member Growth in Two T-Groups," *Journal of Applied Behavioral Science* 4:47–73.

Davis, Sheldon A.
1967 "An Organic Problem-Solving Method of Organizational Change," *Journal of Applied Behavioral Science* 3:3–21.

Deep, S.; Bernard Bass; and James Vaughan
1967 "Some Effects on Business Gaming of Previous Quasi-T-Group Affiliations," *Journal of Applied Psychology* 51:426–31.

De Michele, John H.
1966 *The Measurement of Rated Training Changes Resulting from a Sensitivity Training Laboratory of an Overall Program in Organization Development* (Doctoral dissertation, New York University).

Ellis, Albert, and Milton Blum
1967 "Rational Training: A New Method of Facilitating Management and Labor Relations," *Psychological Reports* 20:1267–84.

Fleishman, Edwin A.; E. F. Harris; and H. E. Burtt
1955 *Leadership and Supervision in Industry* (Columbus: Bureau of Educational Research, Ohio State University).

French, J. R. P.; J. J. Sherwood; and D. L. Bradford
1966 "Change in Self-Identity in a Management Training Conference," *Journal of Applied Behavioral Science,* 2:210–18.

Friedlander, Frank
1967 "The Impact of Organizational Training Laboratories upon the Effectiveness and Interaction of Ongoing Groups," *Personnel Psychology* 20:289–308.

Greiner, Larry E.
1965 *Organization Change and Development: A Study of Changing Values, Behavior, and Performance in a Large Industrial Plant* (Doctoral dissertation, Harvard Business School).
1967 "Antecedents of Planned Organization Change," *Journal of Applied Behavioral Science* 3:51–86.

Guest, Robert
1962 *Organizational Change* (Homewood, Ill.: Richard D. Irwin, Inc.).

Hampden-Turner, C. M.

1966 "An Existential 'Learning Theory' and the Integration of T-Group Research," *Journal of Applied Behavioral Science* 2:367–86.

Harrison, Roger
1965 "Group Composition Models for Laboratory Design," *Journal of Applied Behavioral Science* 1:409–32.
1966 "Cognitive Change and Participation in a Sensitivity Training Laboratory," *Journal of Consulting Psychology* 30:517–20.
1967 "Problems in the Design and Interpretation of Research on Human Relations Training." In *Explorations in Human Relations Training and Research, Report No. 1* (Washington: National Training Laboratories).

Harrison, Roger, and B. Lubin
1965 "Personal Style, Group Composition, and Learning," *Journal of Applied Behavioral Science* 1:286–301.

Harrison, Roger, and Barry Oshry
1965 "The Design of One-Week Laboratories." In E. H. Schein and W. G. Bennis, eds., *Personal and Organizational Growth through Group Methods* (New York: John Wiley & Sons, Inc.), pp. 98–106.
1966 *The Impact of Laboratory Training on Organizational Behavior: Methodology and Results* (Working paper, National Training Laboratories).

Harvey, O. J.
1966 *Experience, Structure, and Adaptability* (New York: Springer Publishing Company, Inc.).

House, Robert J.
1965 " 'T-Group' Training: Some Important Considerations for the Practicing Manager," *New York Personnel Management Association Bulletin* 21:4–10.
1967 "Manager Development: A Conceptual Model, Some Propositions, and a Research Strategy for Testing the Model." In *Management Development: Design, Evaluation and Implementation* (Ann Arbor: University of Michigan).

Jaques, E.
1951 *The Changing Culture of a Factory* (London: Tavistock Publications).

Kassarjian, H.
1965 "Social Character and Sensitivity Training," *Journal of Applied Behavioral Science* 1:433–40.

Knowles, Eric S.
1967 "A Bibliography of Research—Since 1960." In *Explorations in Human Relations Training and Research, Report No. 2* (Washington: National Training Laboratories).

Kolb, D. A.; S. K. Winter; and D. E. Berlew
1968 "Self-Directed Change: Two Studies," *Journal of Applied Behavioral Science* 4:453–71.

Kuriloff, A., and S. Atkins
1966 "T-Group for a Work Team," *Journal of Applied Behavioral Science* 2:63–93.

Lakin, M., and R. Carlson

1964 "Participant Perception of Group Process in Group Sensitivity Training," *International Journal of Group Psychotherapy* 14:116–22.

Leavitt, H.
1965 "Applied Organizational Change in Industry: Structural, Technological, and Humanities Approaches." In James G. March, ed., *Handbook of Organizations* (Chicago: Rand-McNally & Company), pp. 1144–70.

Likert, Rensis
1967 *The Human Organization* (New York: McGraw-Hill Book Company).

Lippitt, Ronald; Jeanne Watson; and Bruce Westley
1958 *The Dynamics of Planned Change* New York: Harcourt, Brace Jovanovich, Inc.).

McClelland, David C.
1965 "Toward a Theory of Motive Acquisition," *American Psychologist* 20:321–33.

McGregor, Douglas
1967 *The Professional Manager* (New York: McGraw-Hill Book Company).

Marrow, A; D. Bowers; and S. Seashore
1967 *Participative Management* (New York: Harper & Row, Publishers).

Medow, Herman
1967 "Sensible Nonsense," *Journal of Applied Behavioral Science* 3:202–3.

Miles, M. B.
1965a "Learning Processes and Outcomes in Human Relations Training: A Clinical-Experimental Study." In E. H. Schein and W. G. Bennis, eds., *Personal and Organizational Growth Through Group Methods* (New York: John Wiley & Sons, Inc.), pp. 244–54.
1965b *Methodological Problems in Evaluating Organizational Change: Two Illustrations* (Working paper, Columbia University).

Miles, M. B.; J. R. Milavsky; D. Lake; and R. Beckhard
1965 *Organizational Improvement: Effects of Management Team Training in Bankers Trust* (Unpublished monograph, Bankers Trust Company, New York).

Miles, M. B.; P. Calder; H. Hornstein; D. Callahan; and S. Schiavo
1966 *Data Feedback and Organizational Change in a School System* (Working paper, Columbia University).

Morton, R. B., and B. M. Bass
1964 "The Organizational Training Laboratory," *Training Directors Journal* 18:2–18.

Morton, R. B., and A. Wight
1964 *A Critical Incidents Evaluation of an Organizational Training Laboratory* (Working paper, Aerojet General Corporation).

Oshry, B., and R. Harrison
1966 "Transfer from 'Here-and-Now' to 'There-and-Then': Changes in Organizational Problem Diagnosis Stemming from T-Group Training," *Journal of Applied Behavioral Science* 2:185–98.

Powers, J. R.
1965 *Trainer Orientation and Group Composition in Laboratory Training* (Doctoral dissertation, Case Institute of Technology).

Psathas, G., and R. Hardert
1966 "Trainer Interventions and Normative Patterns in the T-Group," *Journal of Applied Behavioral Science* 2:149–69.

Rubin, I.
1967a "Increased Self-Acceptance: A Means of Reducing Prejudice," *Journal of Abnormal and Social Psychology* 5:233–38.
1967b "The Reduction of Prejudice Through Laboratory Training," *Journal of Applied Behavioral Science* 3:29–50.

Sarason, Seymour B.
1966 *The School Culture and Processes of Change* (College Park: College of Agriculture, University of Maryland).

Schein, E. H., and W. G. Bennis
1965 *Personal and Organizational Growth Through Group Methods* (New York: John Wiley & Sons, Inc.).

Schmuck, R. A.
1968 "Helping Teachers Improve Classroom Group Processes," *Journal of Applied Behavioral Science* 4:401–35.

Schutz, W. C.
1964 *An Approach to the Development of Human Potential* (Washington: National Training Laboratories, Subscription Service Report No. 6).
1967 *Joy* (New York: Grove Press, Inc.).

Schutz, W. C., and V. Allen
1966 "The Effects of a T-Group Laboratory on Interpersonal Behavior," *Journal of Applied Behavioral Science* 2:265–86.

Shepard, H. A.
1965 "Changing Relationships in Organizations." In James G. March, ed., *Handbook of Organizations* (Chicago: Rand-McNally & Company), pp. 1115–43.

Sikes, W.
1964 *A Study of Some Effects of a Human Relations Training Laboratory* (Doctoral dissertation, Purdue University).

Smith, P. B.
1964 "Attitude Changes Associated with Training in Human Relations," *British Journal of Social and Clinical Psychology* 3:104–12.
1966 *T-Group Climate, Trainer Style, and Some Tests of Learning* (Working paper, University of Sussex, England).

Tannenbaum, R., and James Bugental
1963 "Dyads, Clans, and Tribe: A New Design for Sensitivity Training," *NTL Training News* 7:1–3.

Wilson, J. E.; D. P. Mullen; and R. B. Morton
1968 "Sensitivity Training for Individual Growth—Team Training for Organization Development," *Training and Development Journal* 22:1–7.

Winn, A.
1966 "Social Change in Industry: From Insight to Implementation," *Journal of Applied Behavioral Science* 2:170–85.

ORGANIZATION DEVELOPMENT: OBJECTIVES, ASSUMPTIONS, AND STRATEGIES

Wendell French

Organization development refers to a long-range effort to improve an organization's problem-solving capabilities and its ability to cope with changes in its external environment with the help of external or internal behavioral-scientist consultants, or change agents, as they are sometimes called. Such efforts are relatively new but are becoming increasingly visible within the United States, England, Japan, Holland, Norway, Sweden, and perhaps in other countries. A few of the growing number of organizations which have embarked on organization development (OD) efforts to some degree are Union Carbide, Esso, TRW Systems, Humble Oil, Weyerhaeuser, and Imperial Chemical Industries Limited. Other kinds of institutions, including public school systems, churches, and hospitals, have also become involved.

Organization development activities appear to have originated about 1957 as an attempt to apply some of the values and insights of laboratory training to total organizations. The late Douglas McGregor, working with Union Carbide, is considered to have been one of the first behavioral scientists to talk systematically about and to implement an organization development program.[1] Other names associated with such early efforts are Herbert Shepard and Robert Blake who, in collaboration with the Employee Relations Department of the Esso Company, launched a program of laboratory training (sensitivity training) in the company's various refineries. This program emerged in 1957 after a headquarters human relations research division began to view itself as an internal consulting group offering services to field managers rather than as a research group developing reports for top management.[2]

Objectives of Typical OD Programs

Although the specific interpersonal and task objectives of organization development programs will vary according to each diagnosis of organizational problems, a number of objectives typically emerge. These objectives reflect problems which are very common in organizations:

1) To increase the level of trust and support among organizational members.
2) To increase the incidence of confrontation of organizational problems, both within groups and among groups, in contrast to "sweeping problems under the rug."
3) To create an environment in which authority of assigned role is augmented by authority based on knowledge and skill.
4) To increase the openness of communications laterally, vertically, and diagonally.
5) To increase the level of personal enthusiasm and satisfaction in the organization.
6) To find synergistic solutions[3] to problems with greater frequency. (Synergistic solutions are creative solutions in which 2 + 2 equals more than 4, and through which all parties gain more through cooperation than through conflict.)
7) To increase the level of self and group responsibility in planning and implementation.[4]

Difficulties in Categorizing

Before describing some of the basic assumptions and strategies of organization development, it would be well to point out that one of the difficulties in writing about such a "movement" is that a wide variety of activities can be and are subsumed under this label. These activities have varied all the way from inappropriate application of some "canned" management development program to highly responsive and skillful joint efforts between behavioral scientists and client systems.

Thus, while labels are useful, they may gloss over a wide range of phenomena. The "human relations movement," for example, has been widely written about as though it were all bad or all good. To illustrate, some of the critics of the movement have accused it of being "soft" and a "handmaiden of the Establishment," of ignoring the technical and power systems of organizations, and of being too naïvely participative. Such criticisms were no doubt warranted in some circumstances, but in other situations may not have been at all appropriate. Paradoxically, some of the major insights of the human relations movement, e.g., that the organization can be viewed as a social system and that subordinates have substantial control over productivity have been assimilated by its critics.

In short, the problem is to distinguish between appropriate and inappropriate programs, between effectiveness and ineffectiveness, and between relevancy and irrelevancy. The discussion which follows will attempt to describe the "ideal" circumstances for organization development programs, as well as to point out some pitfalls and common mistakes in organization change efforts.

Relevancy to Different Technologies and Organization Subunits

Research by Joan Woodward[5] suggests that organization development efforts might be more relevant to certain kinds of technologies and organizational levels, and perhaps to certain workforce characteristics, than to others. For example, OD efforts may be more appropriate for an organization devoted to prototype manufacturing than for an automobile assembly plant. However, experiments in an organization like Texas Instruments suggest that some manufacturing efforts which appear to be inherently mechanistic may lend themselves to a more participative, open management style than is often assumed possible.[6]

However, assuming the constraints of a fairly narrow job structure at the rank-and-file level, organization development efforts may inherently be more productive and relevant at the managerial levels of the organization. Certainly OD efforts are most effective when they start at the top. Research and development units—particularly those involving a high degree of interdependency and joint creativity among group members—also appear to be appropriate for organization development activities, if group members are currently experiencing problems in communicating or interpersonal relationships.

Basic Assumptions

Some of the basic assumptions about people which underlie organization development programs are similar to "Theory Y" assumptions[7] and will be repeated only briefly here. However, some of the assumptions about groups and total systems will be treated more extensively. The following assumptions appear to underlie organization development efforts.[8]

About People

1) Most individuals have drives toward personal growth and development, and these are most likely to be actualized in an environment which is both supportive and challenging.
2) Most people desire to make, and are capable of making, a much higher level of contribution to the attainment of organization goals than most organizational environments will permit.

About People in Groups

1) Most people wish to be accepted and to interact cooperatively with at least one small reference group, and usually with more than one group, e.g., the work group, the family group.
2) One of the most psychologically relevant reference groups for most people is the work group, including peers and the superior.
3) Most people are capable of greatly increasing their effectiveness in helping their reference groups solve problems and in working effectively together.
4) For a group to optimize its effectiveness, the formal leader cannot perform all of the leadership functions in all circumstances at all times, and all group members must assist each other with effective leadership and member behavior.

About People in Organizational Systems

1) Organizations tend to be characterized by overlapping, interdependent work groups, and the "linking pin" function of supervisors and others needs to be understood and facilitated.[9]
2) What happens in the broader organization affects the small work group and vice versa.

3) What happens to one subsystem (social, technological, or administrative) will affect and be influenced by other parts of the system.

4) The culture in most organizations tends to suppress the expression of feelings which people have about each other and about where they and their organizations are heading.

5) Suppressed feelings adversely affect problem solving, personal growth, and job satisfaction.

6) The level of interpersonal trust, support, and cooperation is much lower in most organizations than is either necessary or desirable.

7) "Win-lose" strategies between people and groups, while realistic and appropriate in some situations, are not optimal in the long run to the solution of most organizational problems.

8) Synergistic solutions can be achieved with a much higher frequency than is actually the case in most organizations.

9) Viewing feelings as data important to the organization tends to open up many avenues for improved goal setting, leadership, communications, problem solving, intergroup collaboration, and morale.

10) Improved performance stemming from organization development efforts needs to be sustained by appropriate changes in the appraisal, compensation, training, staffing, and task-specialization subsystem—in short, in the total personnel system.

Value and Belief Systems of Behavioral Scientist-Change Agents

While scientific inquiry, ideally, is value-free, the applications of science are not value-free. Applied behavioral scientist-organization development consultants tend to subscribe to a comparable set of values, although we should avoid the trap of assuming that they constitute a completely homogenous group. They do not.

One value, to which many behavioral scientist-change agents tend to give high priority, is that the needs and aspirations of human beings are the reasons for organized effort in society. They tend, therefore, to be developmental in their outlook and concerned with the long-range opportunities for the personal growth of people in organizations.

A second value is that work and life can become richer and more meaningful, and organized effort more effective and enjoyable, if feelings and sentiments are permitted to be a more legitimate part of the culture. A third value is a commitment to an action role, along with a commitment to research, in an effort to improve the effectiveness of organizations.[10] A fourth value—or perhaps a belief—is that improved competency in interpersonal and intergroup relationship will result in more effective organizations.[11] A fifth value is that behavioral science research and an examination of behavioral science assumptions and values are relevant and important in considering organizational effectiveness. While many change agents are perhaps overly action-oriented in terms of the utilization of their time, nevertheless, as a group they are paying more and more attention to research and to the examination of ideas.[12]

The value placed on research and inquiry raises the question as to whether the assumptions stated earlier are values, theory, or "facts." In my judgment, substantial body of knowledge, including research on leadership, suggests that there is considerable evidence for these assumptions. However, to conclude that these assumptions are facts, laws, or principles would be to contradict the value placed by behavioral scientists on continuous research and inquiry. Thus, I feel that they should be considered theoretical statements which are based on provisional data.

This also raises the paradox that the belief that people are important tends to result in their being important. The belief that people can grow and develop in terms of personal and organizational competency tends to produce this result. Thus, values and beliefs tend to be self-fulfilling, and the question becomes "What do you choose to want to believe?" While this position can become Pollyannaish in the sense of not seeing the real world, nevertheless, behavioral scientist-change agents, at least this one, tend to place a value on optimism. It is a kind of optimism that says people can do a better job of goal setting and facing up to and solving problems, not an optimism that says the number of problems is diminishing.

It should be added that it is important that the values and beliefs of each behavioral science-change agent be made visible both to himself and to the client. In the first place, neither can learn to adequately trust the other without such exposure—a hidden agenda handicaps both trust building and mutual learning. Second and perhaps more pragmatically, organizational change efforts tend to fail if a prescription is applied unilaterally and without proper diagnosis.

Strategy in Organization Development: An Action Research Model

A frequent strategy in organization development programs is based on what behavioral scientists refer to as an "action research model." This model involves extensive collaboration between the consultant (whether an external or an internal change agent) and the client group, data gathering, data discussion and planning. While descriptions of this model vary in detail and terminology from author to author, the dynamics are essentially the same.[13]

Figure 1 summarizes some of the essential phases of the action research model, using an emerging organization development program as an example. The key aspects of the model are diagnosis, data gathering, feedback to the client group, data discussion and work by the client group, action planning, and action. The sequence tends to be cyclical, with the focus on new or advanced problems as the client group learns to work more effectively together. Action research should also be considered a process, since, as

Figure 1   An Action Research Model for Organization Development

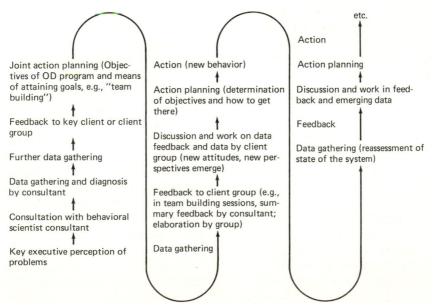

William Foote Whyte says, it involves " . . . a continuous gathering and analysis of human relations research data and the feeding of the findings into the organization in such a manner as to change behavior."[14] (Feedback we will define as non-judgmental observations of behavior.)

Ideally, initial objectives and strategies of organization development efforts stem from a careful diagnosis of such matters as interpersonal and intergroup problems, decisionmaking processes, and communication flow which are currently being experienced by the client organization. As a preliminary step, the behavioral scientist and the key client (the president of a company, the vice-president in charge of a division, the works manager or superintendent of a plant, a superintendent of schools, etc.), will make a joint initial assessment of the critical problems which need working on. Subordinates may also be interviewed in order to provide supplemental data. The diagnosis may very well indicate that the central problem is technological or that the key client is not at all willing or ready to examine the organization's problem-solving ability or his own managerial behavior.[15] Either could be a reason for postponing or moving slowly in the direction of organization development activities, although the technological problem may easily be related to deficiencies in interpersonal relationships or decision-making. The diagnosis might also indicate the desirability of one or more additional specialists (in engineering, finance, or electronic data processing, for example) to simultaneously work with the organization.

This initial diagnosis, which focuses on the expressed needs of the client, is extremely critical. As discussed earlier, in the absence of a skilled diagnosis, the behavioral scientist-change agent would be imposing a set of assumptions and a set of objectives which may be hopelessly out of joint with either the current problems of the people in the organization or their willingness to learn new modes of behavior. In this regard, it is extremely

important that the consultant hear and understand what the client is trying to tell him. This requires a high order of skill.[16]

Interviews are frequently used for data gathering in OD work for both initial diagnosis and subsequent planning sessions, since personal contact is important for building a cooperative relationship between the consultant and the client group. The interview is also important since the behavioral scientist-consultant is interested in spontaneity and in feelings that are expressed as well as cognitive matters. However, questionnaires are sometimes successfully used in the context of what is sometimes referred to as survey feedback, to supplement interview data.[17]

Data gathering typically goes through several phases. The first phase is related to diagnosing the state of the system and to making plans for organizational change. This phase may utilize a series of interviews between the consultant and the key client, or between a few key executives and the consultant. Subsequent phases focus on problems specific to the top executive team and to subordinate teams. (See Figure 2.)

Typical questions in data gathering or "problem sensing" would include: What problems do you see in your group, including problems between people, that are interfering with getting the job done the way you would like to see it done?; and what problems do you see in the broader organization? Such open-ended questions provide wide latitude on the part of the respondents and encourage a reporting of problems as the individual sees them. Such interviewing is usually conducted privately, with a commitment on the part of the consultant that the information will be used in such a way as to avoid unduly embarrassing anyone. The intent is to find out what common problems or themes emerge, with the data to be used constructively for both diagnostic and feedback purposes.

Two- or three-day offsite team-building or group problem-solving sessions typically become a major focal point in or-

Figure 2   Organization Development Phases in a Hypothetical Organization

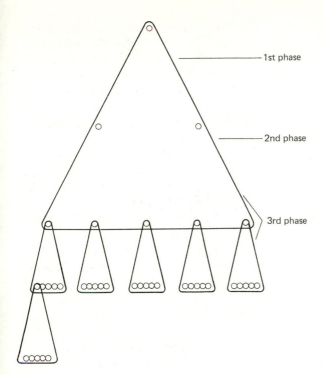

1st phase

2nd phase

3rd phase

1st phase. Data gathering, feedback and diagnosis—consultant and top executive only.

2nd phase. Data gathering, feedback, and revised diagnosis—consultant and two or more key staff or line people.

3rd phase. Data gathering and feedback to total top executive team in "team-building" laboratory, with or without key subordinates from level below.

4th and additional phases. Data gathering and team-building sessions with 2nd or 3rd level teams.

Subsequent phases. Data gathering, feedback, and interface problem-solving sessions across groups.

Simultaneous phases. Several managers may attend "stranger" T-groups; courses in the management development program may supplement this learning.

ganization development programs. During these meetings the behavioral scientist frequently provides feedback to the group in terms of the themes which emerged in the problem-sensing interviews.[18] He may also encourage the group to determine which items or themes should have priority in terms of maximum utilization of time. These themes usually provide substantial and meaningful data for the group to begin work on. One-to-one interpersonal matters, both positive and negative, tend to emerge spontaneously as the participants gain confidence from the level of support sensed in the group.

Different consultants will vary in their mode of behavior in such sessions, but will typically serve as "process" observers and as interpreters of the dynamics of the group interaction to the degree that the group expresses a readiness for such intervention. They also typically encourage people to take risks, a step at a time, and to experiment with new behav-

ior in the context of the level of support in the group. Thus, the trainer-consultant(s) serves as a stimulant to new behavior but also as a protector. The climate which I try to build, for example, is: "Let's not tear down any more than we can build back together."[19] Further, the trainer-consultant typically works with the group to assist team members in improving their skills in diagnosing and facilitating group progress.[20]

It should be noted, however, that different groups will have different needs along a task-process continuum. For example, some groups have a need for intensive work on clarifying objectives; others may have the greatest need in the area of personal relationships. Further, the consultant or the chief consultant in a team of consultants involved in an organization development program will play a much broader role than serving as a T-group or team-building trainer. He will also play an important role in periodic data gathering and diagnosis and in joint long-range planning of the change efforts.[21]

Laboratory Training and Organization Development

Since organization development programs have largely emerged from T-group experience, theory, and research, and since laboratory training in one form or another tends to be an integral part of most such programs, it is important to focus on laboratory training per se. As stated earlier, OD programs grew out of a perceived need to relate laboratory training to the problems of ongoing organizations and a recognition that optimum results could only occur if major parts of the total social system of an organization were involved.

Laboratory training essentially emerged around 1946, largely through a growing recognition by Leland Bradford, Ronald Lippitt, Kenneth Benne, and others, that human relations training which focused on the feelings and concerns of the participants was frequently a much more powerful and viable form of education than the lecture method. Some of the theoretical constructs and insights from which these laboratory training pioneers drew stemmed from earlier research by Lippitt, Kurt Lewin, and Ralph White. The term "T-group" emerged by 1949 as a shortened label for "Basic Skill Training Group"; these terms were used to identify the programs which began to emerge in the newly formed National Training Laboratory in Group Development (now NTL Institute for Applied Behavioral Science).[22] "Sensitivity Training" is also a term frequently applied to such training.

Ordinarily, laboratory training sessions have certain objectives in common. The following list, by two internationally known behavioral scientists,[23] is probably highly consistent with the objectives of most programs:

Self Objectives

1) Increased awareness of own feelings and reactions, and own impact on others.
2) Increased awareness of feelings and reactions of others, and their impact on self.
3) Increased awareness of dynamics of group action.
4) Changed attitudes toward self, others, and groups, i.e., more respect for, tolerance for, and faith in self, others, and groups.
5) Increased interpersonal competence, i.e., skill in handling interpersonal and group relationships toward more productive and satisfying relationships.

Role Objectives

1) Increased awareness of own organizational role, organizational dynamics, dynamics of larger social systems, and dynamics of the change process in self, small groups, and organizations.
2) Changed attitudes toward own role, role of others, and organizational relationships, i.e., more respect for and willingness to deal with others with whom one is interdependent, greater willingness to achieve collaborative relationships with others based on mutual trust.
3) Increased interpersonal competence in handling organizational role relationships with superiors, peers, and subordinates.

Organizational Objectives

1) Increased awareness of, changed attitudes toward, and increased interpersonal competence about specific organizational problems existing in groups or units which are interdependent.
2) Organizational improvement through

the training of relationships or groups rather than isolated individuals.

Over the years, experimentation with different laboratory designs has led to diverse criteria for the selection of laboratory participants. Probably a majority of NTL-IABS human relations laboratories are "stranger groups," i.e., involving participants who come from different organizations and who are not likely to have met earlier. However, as indicated by the organizational objectives above, the incidence of special labs designed to increase the effectiveness of persons already working together appears to be growing. Thus terms like "cousin labs," i.e., labs involving people from the same organization but not the same subunit, and "family labs" or "team-building" sessions, i.e., involving a manager and all of his subordinates, are becoming familiar. Participants in labs designed for organizational members not of the same unit may be selected from the same rank level ("horizontal slice") or selected so as to constitute a heterogeneous grouping by rank ("diagonal slice"). Further, NTL-IABS is now encouraging at least two members from the same organization to attend NTL Management Work Conferences and Key Executive Conferences in order to maximize the impact of the learning in the back-home situation.[24]

In general, experienced trainers recommend that persons with severe emotional illness should not participate in laboratory training, with the exception of programs designed specifically for group therapy. Designers of programs make the assumptions, as Argyris states them,[25] that T-group participants should have:

1) A relatively strong ego that is not overwhelmed by internal conflicts.
2) Defenses which are sufficiently low to allow the individual to hear what others say to him.
3) The ability to communicate thought and feelings with minimal distortion.

As a result of such screening, the incidence of breakdown during laboratory training is substantially less than that reported for organizations in general.[26] However, since the borderline between "normalcy" and illness is very indistinct, most professionally trained staff members are equipped to diagnose severe problems and to make referrals to psychiatrists and clinical psychologists when appropriate. Further, most are equipped to give adequate support and protection to participants whose ability to assimilate and learn from feedback is low. In addition, group members in T-group situations tend to be sensitive to the emotional needs of the members and to be supportive when they sense a person experiencing pain. Such support is explicitly fostered in laboratory training.

The duration of laboratory training programs varies widely. "Micro-labs," designed to give people a brief experience with sensitivity training, may last only one hour. Some labs are designed for a long weekend. Typically, however, basic human relations labs are of two weeks duration, with participants expected to meet mornings, afternoons, and evenings, with some time off for recreation. While NTL Management Work Conferences for middle managers and Key Executive Conferences run for one week, team-building labs, from my experience, typically are about three days in length. However, the latter are usually only a part of a broader organization development program involving problem sensing and diagnosis, and the planning of action steps and subsequent sessions. In addition, attendance at stranger labs for key managers is frequently a part of the total organization development effort.

Sensitivity training sessions typically start with the trainer making a few comments about his role—that he is there to be of help, that the group will have control of the agenda, that he will deliberately avoid a leadership role, but that he might become involved as both a leader and a member from time to time, etc. The following is an example of what the trainer might say:

This group will meet for many hours and will serve as a kind of laboratory where each individual can increase his understanding of the forces which influence individual behavior and the performance of groups and organizations. The data for learning will be our own behavior, feelings, and reactions. We begin with no definite structure or organization, no agreed-upon procedures, and no specific agenda. It will be up to us to fill the vacuum created by the lack of these familiar elements and to study our group as we evolve. My role will be to help the group to learn from its own experience, but not to act as a traditional chairman nor to suggest how we should organize, what our procedure should be, or exactly what our agenda will include. With these few comments, I think we are ready to begin in whatever way you feel will be most helpful.[27]

The trainer then lapses into silence. Group discomfort then precipitates a dialogue which, with skilled trainer assistance, is typically an intense but generally highly rewarding experience for group members. What goes on in the group becomes the data for the learning experience.

Interventions by the trainer will vary greatly depending upon the purpose of the lab and the state of learning on the part of the participants. A common intervention, however, is to encourage people to focus on and own up to their own feelings about what is going on in the group, rather than to make judgments about others. In this way, the participants begin to have more insight into their own feelings and to understand how their behavior affects the feelings of others.

While T-group work tends to be the focal point in human relations laboratories, laboratory training typically includes theory sessions and frequently includes exercises such as role playing or management games.[28] Further, family labs of subunits of organizations will ordinarily

devote more time to planning action steps for back on the job than will stranger labs.

Robert J. House has carefully reviewed the research literature on the impact of T-group training and has concluded that the research shows mixed results. In particular, research on changes as reflected in personality inventories is seen as inconclusive. However, studies which examine the behavior of participants upon returning to the job are generally more positive.[29] House cites six studies, all of which utilized control groups, and concludes:

All six studies revealed what appear to be important positive effects of T-group training. Two of the studies report negative effects as well . . . all of the evidence is based on observations of the behavior of the participants in the actual job situations. No reliance is placed on participant response; rather, evidence is collected from those having frequent contact with the participant in his normal work activities.[30]

John P. Campbell and Marvin D. Dunnette,[31] on the other hand, while conceding that the research shows that T-group training produces changes in behavior, point out that the usefulness of such training in terms of job performance has yet to be demonstrated. They urge research toward "forging the link between training-induced behavior changes and changes in job-performance effectiveness."[32] As a summary comment, they state:

. . . the assumption that T-group training has positive utility for organizations must necessarily rest on shaky ground. It has been neither confirmed nor disconfirmed. The authors wish to emphasize . . . that utility for the organization is not necessarily the same as utility for the individual.[33]

At least two major reasons may account for the inconclusiveness of research on the impact of T-group training on job performance. One reason is simply that little research has been done. The other reason may center around a factor of cultural isolation. To oversimplify, a major part of what one learns in laboratory training, in my opinion, is how to work more effectively with others in group situations, **particularly with others who have developed comparable skills.** Unfortunately, most participants return from T-group experiences to environments including colleagues and superiors who have not had the same affective (emotional, feeling) experiences, who are not familiar with the terminology and underlying theory, and who may have anxieties (usually unwarranted) about what might happen to them in a T-group situation.

This cultural distance which laboratory training can produce is one of the reasons why many behavioral scientists are currently encouraging more than one person from the same organization to undergo T-group training and, ideally, all of the members of a team and their superior to participate in some kind of laboratory training together. The latter assumes that a diagnosis of the organization indicates that the group is ready for such training and assumes such training is reasonably compatible with the broader culture of the total system.

Conditions and Techniques for Successful Organization Development Programs

Theory, research, and experience to date suggest to me that successful OD programs tend to evolve in the following way and that they have some of these characteristics (these statements should be considered highly tentative, however):

1) There is strong pressure for improvement from both outside the organization and from within.[34]

2) An outside behavioral scientist–consultant is brought in for consultation with the top executives and to diagnose organizational problems.

3) A preliminary diagnosis suggests that organization development efforts, designed in response to the expressed needs of the key executives, are warranted.

4) A collaborative decision is made between the key client group and the consultant to try to change the culture of the organization, at least at the top initially. The specific goals may be to improve communications, to secure more effective participation from subordinates in problem solving, and to move in the direction of more openness, more feedback, and more support. In short, a decision is made to change the culture to help the company meet its organizational goals and to provide better avenues for initiative, creativity, and self-actualization on the part of organization members.

5) Two or more top executives, including the chief executive, go to laboratory training sessions. (Frequently, attendance at labs is one of the facts which precipitates interest in bringing in the outside consultant.)

6) Attendance in T-group program is voluntary. While it is difficult to draw a line between persuasion and coercion, OD consultants and top management should be aware of the dysfunctional consequences of coercion (see the comments on authentic behavior below). While a major emphasis is on team-building laboratories, stranger labs are utilized both to supplement the training going on in the organization and to train managers new to the organization or those who are newly promoted.

7) Team-building sessions are held with the top executive group (or at the highest point where the program is started). Ideally, the program is started at the top of the organization, but it can start at levels below the president as long as there is significant support from the chief ex-

ecutive, and preferably from other members of the top power structure as well.

8) In a firm large enough to have a personnel executive, the personnel-industrial relations vice-president becomes heavily involved at the outset.

9) One of two organizational forms emerges to coordinate organization development efforts, either (a) a coordinator reporting to the personnel executive (the personnel executive himself may fill this role), or (b) a coordinator reporting to the chief executive. The management development director is frequently in an ideal position to coordinate OD activities with other management development activities.

10) Ultimately, it is essential that the personnel-industrial relations group, including people in salary administration, be an integral part of the organization development program. Since OD groups have such potential for acting as catalysts in rapid organizational change, the temptation is great to see themselves as "good guys" and the other personnel people as "bad guys" or simply ineffective. Any conflicts between a separate organization development group and the personnel and industrial relations groups should be faced and resolved. Such tensions can be the "Achilles heel" for either program. In particular, however, the change agents in the organization development program need the support of the other people who are heavily involved in human resources administration and vice versa; what is done in the OD program needs to be compatible with what is done in selection, promotion, salary administration, appraisal, and vice versa. In terms of systems theory, it would seem imperative that one aspect of the human resources function such as any organization development program must be highly interdependent with the other human resources activities including selection, salary administration, etc. (TRW Systems is an example of an organization which involves top executives plus making the total personnel and industrial relations group an integral part of the OD program.[35]

11) Team-building labs, at the request of the various respective executives, with laboratory designs based on careful data gathering and problem diagnosis, are conducted at successively lower levels of the organization with the help of outside consultants, plus the help of internal consultants whose expertise is gradually developed.

12) Ideally, as the program matures, both members of the personnel staff and a few line executives are trained to do some organization development work in conjunction with the external and internal professionally trained behavioral scientists. In a sense, then, the external change agent tries to work himself out of a job by developing internal resources.

13) The outside consultant(s) and the internal coordinator work very carefully together and periodically check on fears, threats, and anxieties which may be developing as the effort progresses. Issues need to be confronted as they emerge. Not only is the outside change agent needed for his skills, but the organization will need someone to act as a "governor"—to keep the program focused on real problems and to urge authenticity in contrast to gamesmanship. The danger always exists that the organization will begin to punish or reward involvement in T-group kinds of activities per se, rather than focus on performance.

14) The OD consultants constantly work on their own effectiveness in interpersonal relationships and their diagnostic skills so they are not in a position of "do as I say, but not as I do." Further, both consultant and client work together to optimize the consultant's knowledge of the organization's unique and evolving cul-

ture structure, and web of interpersonal relationships.

15) There needs to be continuous audit of the results, both in terms of checking on the evolution of attitudes about what is going on and in terms of the extent to which problems which were identified at the outset by the key clients are being solved through the program.

16) As implied above, the reward system and other personnel systems need to be readjusted to accommodate emerging changes in performance in the organization. Substantially improved performance on the part of individuals and groups is not likely to be sustained if financial and promotional rewards are not forthcoming. In short, management needs to have a "systems" point of view and to think through the interrelationships of the OD effort with the reward and staffing systems and the other aspects of the total human resources subsystem.

In the last analysis, the president and the "line" executive of the organization will evaluate the success of the OD effort in terms of the extent to which it assists the organization in meeting its human and economic objectives. For example, marked improvements on various indices from one plant, one division, one department, etc., will be important indicators of program success. While human resources administration indices are not yet perfected, some of the measuring devices being developed by Likert, Mann, and others show some promise.[36]

Summary Comments

Organization development efforts have emerged through attempts to apply laboratory training values and assumptions to total systems. Such efforts are organic in the sense that they emerge from and are guided by the problems being experienced by the people in the organization. The key to their viability (in contrast to becoming a passing fad) lies in an authentic focus on problems and concerns of the members of the organization and in their confrontation of issues and problems.

Organization development is based on assumptions and values similar to "Theory Y" assumptions and values but includes additional assumptions about total systems and the nature of the client–consultant relationship. Intervention strategies of the behavioral scientist-change agent tend to be based on an action-research model and tend to be focused more on helping the people in an organization learn to solve problems rather than on prescriptions of how things should be done differently.

Laboratory training (or "sensitivity training") or modifications of T-group seminars typically are a part of the organizational change efforts, but the extent and format of such training will depend upon the evolving needs of the organization. Team-building seminars involving a superior and subordinates are being utilized more and more as a way of changing social systems rapidly and avoiding the cultural-distance problems which frequently emerge when individuals return from stranger labs. However, stranger labs can play a key role in change efforts when they are used as part of a broader organization development effort.

Research has indicated that sensitivity training generally produces positive results in terms of changed behavior on the job, but has not demonstrated the link between behavior changes and improved performance. Maximum benefits are probably derived from laboratory training when the organizational culture supports and reinforces the use of new skills in ongoing team situations.

Successful organization development efforts require skillful behavioral scientist interventions, a systems view, and top management support and involvement. In addition, changes stemming from organization development must be linked to changes in the total personnel subsystem. The viability of organization development efforts lies in the degree to which they accurately reflect the aspirations and concerns of the participating members.

In conclusion, **successful organization development tends to be a total system effort; a process of planned change—not a program with a temporary quality; and aimed at developing the organization's internal resources for effective change in the future.**

References and Notes

This article is largely based on the forthcoming second edition of my *The Personnel Management Process: Human Resources Administration* (Boston: Houghton Mifflin Company, 1970), chapter 28.

1. Richard Beckhard, W. Warner Burke, and Fred I. Steele, "The Program for Specialists in Organization Training and Development," mimeographed, NTL Institute for Applied Behavioral Science, Dec. 1967, p. ii; and John Paul Jones, "What's Wrong With Work?" in *What's Wrong With Work?* (New York: National Association of Manufacturers, 1967), p. 8. For a history of NTL Institute for Applied Behavioral Science, with which Douglas McGregor was long associated in addition to his professiorial appointment at M.I.T. and which has been a major factor in the history of organization development, see Leland P. Bradford, "Biography of an Institution," *Journal of Applied Behavioral Science* 3, No. 2 (1967): 127–43. While we will use the word "program" from time to time, ideally organization development is a "process," not just another new program of temporary quality.

2. Harry D. Kolb, Introduction to *An Action Research Program for Organization Improvement* (Ann Arbor: Foundation for Research in Human Behavior, 1960), p. i.

3. Cattell defines synergy as "the sum total of the energy which a group can command." Daniel Katz and Robert L. Kahn, *The Social Psychology of Organizations* (New York: John Wiley & Sons, Inc., 1966), p. 33.

4. For a similar statement of objectives, see "What is OD?" *NTL Institute: News and Reports from NTL Institute for Applied Behavioral Science* 2 (June 1968): 1–2. Whether OD programs increase the overall level of authority in contrast to redistributing authority is a debatable point. My hypothesis is that both a redistribution and an overall increase occur.

5. Joan Woodward, *Industrial Organization: Theory and Practice* (London: Oxford University Press, 1965).

6. See M. Scott Myers, "Every Employee a Manager," *California Management Review* 10 (Spring 1968): 9–20.

7. See Douglas McGregor, *The Human Side of Enterprise* (New York: McGraw-Hill Book Company, 1960), pp. 47–48.

8. In addition to influence from the writings of McGregor, Likert, Argyris, and others, this discussion has been influenced by "Some Assumptions About Change in Organizations," in notebook "Program for Specialists in Organization Training and Development," NTL Institute for Applied Behavioral Science, 1967; and by staff members who participated in that program.

9. For a discussion of the "linking pin" concept, see Rensis Likert, *New Patterns of Management* (New York: McGraw-Hill Book Company, 1961).

10. Warren G. Bennis sees three major approaches to planned organizational change, with the behavioral scientists associated with each all having "a deep concern with applying social science knowledge to create more viable social systems; a commitment to action, as well as to research . . . and a belief that improved interpersonal and group relationships will ultimately lead to better organizational performance." Bennis, "A New Role for the Behavioral Sciences: Effecting Organizational Change," *Administrative Science Quarterly* (Sept. 1963), 157–58; and Herbert A. Shepard, "An Action Research Model," in *An Action Research Program for Organization Improvement*, pp. 31–35.

11. Bennis, "A New Role for the Behavioral Sciences," p. 158.

12. For a discussion of some of the problems and dilemmas in behavioral science research, see Chris Argyris, "Creating Effective Relationships in Organizations," in Richard N. Adams and Jack J. Preiss, eds., *Human Organization Research* (Homewood, Ill.: Dorsey Press, Inc., 1960), pp. 109–23; and Barbara A. Benedict, et. al., "The Clinical Experimental Approach to Assessing Organizational Change Efforts," *Journal of Applied Behavioral Science* (Nov. 1967): 347–80.

13. For further discussion of action research, see Edgar H. Schein and Warren G. Bennis, *Personal and Organizational Change Through Group Methods* (New York: John Wiley & Sons, Inc., 1966), pp. 272–74.

14. William Foote Whyte and Edith Lentz Hamilton, *Action Research for Management* (Homewood, Ill.: Richard D. Irwin, Inc., 1964), p. 2.

15. Jeremiah J. O'Connell appropriately challenges the notion that there is "one best way" of organizational change and stresses that the consultant should choose his role and intervention strategies on the basis of "the conditions existing when he enters the client system" *(Managing Organizational Innovation* [Homewood, Ill.: Richard D. Irwin, Inc., 1968], pp. 10–11).

16. For further discussion of organization diagnosis, see Richard Beckhard, "An Organization Improvement Program in a Decentralized Organization," *Journal of Applied Behavioral Science* 2 (Jan.-March 1966): 3–4; "OD as a Process," in *What's Wrong with Work?*, pp. 12–13.

17. For example, see Floyd C. Mann, "Studying and Creating Change," in Timothy W. Costello and Sheldon S. Zalkind, eds., *Psychology in Administration—A Research Orientation* (Englewood Cliffs, N.J.: Prentice-Hall, Inc., 1963), pp. 321–24.

See also Delbert C. Miller, "Using Behavioral Science to Solve Organization Problems," *Personnel Administration* 31 (Jan.-Feb. 1968), 21–29.

18. For a description of feedback procedures used by the Survey Research Center, Univ. of Michigan, see Mann and Likert, "The Need for Research on the Communication of Research Results," in *Human Organization Research,* pp. 57–66.

19. This phrase probably came from a management workshop sponsored by NTL Institute for Applied Behavioral Science.

20. For a description of what goes on in team-building sessions, see Beckhard, "An Organizational Improvement Program," pp. 9–13; and Newton Margulies and Anthony P. Raia, "People in Organizations—A Case for Team Training," *Training and Development Journal* 22 (August 1968), 2–11. For a description of problem-solving sessions involving the total management group (about 70) of a company, see Beckhard, "The Confrontation Meeting," *Harvard Business Review,* 45 (March-April 1967), 149–55.

21. For a description of actual organization development programs, see Paul C. Buchanan, "Innovative Organizations—A Study in Organization Development," in *Applying Behavioral Science Research in Industry* (New York: Industrial Relations Counselors, 1964), pp. 87–107; Sheldon A. Davis, "An Organic Problem-Solving Method of Organizational Change," *Journal of Applied Behavioral Science* 3, No. 1 (1967): 3–21; Cyril Sofer, *The Organization from Within* (Chicago: Quadrangle Books, Inc., 1961); Alfred J. Marrow, David G. Bowers, and Stanley E. Seashore, *Management by Participation* (New York: Harper & Row, Publishers, 1967); Robert R. Blake, Jane S. Mouton, Louis B. Barnes, and Larry E. Greiner, "Breakthrough in Organization Development," *Harvard Business Review,* 42 (Nov.-Dec. 1964), 133–55; Alton C. Bartlett, "Changing Behavior as a Means to Increased Efficiency," *Journal of Applied Behavioral Science* 3, No. 3 (1967), 381–403; Larry E. Greiner, "Antecedents of Planned Organization Change," ibid. (1967), 51–85; and Robert R. Blake and Jane Mouton, *Corporate Excellence Through Grid Organization Development* (Houston, Texas: Gulf Publishing Company, 1968).

22. From Bradford, "Biography of an Institution." See also Kenneth D. Benne, "History of the T-Group in the Laboratory Setting," in Bradford, Jack R. Gibb, and Benne, eds., *T-Group Theory and Laboratory Method* (New York: John Wiley & Sons, Inc., 1964), pp. 80–135.

23. Schein and Bennis, p. 37.

24. For further discussion of group composition in laboratory training, see Schein and Bennis, pp. 63–69. NTL-LABS now include the Center for Organization Studies, the Center for the Development of Educational Leadership, the Center for

Community Affairs, and the Center for International Training to serve a wide range of client populations and groups.

25. Chris Argyris, "T-Groups for Organizational Effectiveness," *Harvard Business Review,* 42 (March-April 1964), 60–74.

26. Based on discussions with NTL staff members. One estimate is that the incidence of "serious stress and mental disturbance" during laboratory training is less than one percent of participants and in almost all cases occurs in persons with a history of prior disturbance (Charles Seashore, "What is Sensitivity Training," *NTL Institute News and Reports* 2 [April 1968]:2).

27. Ibid., 1.

28. For a description of what goes on in T-groups, see Schein and Bennis, pp. 10–27; Bradford, Gibb, and Benne, pp. 55–67; Dorothy S. Whitaker, "A Case Study of a T-Group," in Galvin Whitaker, ed., *T-Group Training: Group Dynamics in Management Education,* A.T.M. Occasional Papers, (Oxford: Basil Blackwell, 1965), pp. 14–22; Irving R. Weschler and Jerome Reisel, *Inside a Sensitivity Training Group* (Berkeley: University of California, Institute of Industrial Relations, 1959); and William F. Glueck, "Reflections on a T-Group Experience," *Personnel Journal* 47 (July 1968), 501–4. For use of cases or exercises based on research results ("instrumented training") see Robert R. Blake and Jane S. Mouton, "The Instrumented Training Laboratory," in Irving R. Weschler and Edgar H. Schein, eds., *Five Issues in Training* (Washington: National Training Laboratories, 1962), pp. 61–76; and W. Warner Burke and Harvey A. Hornstein, "Conceptual vs. Experimental Management Training," *Training and Development Journal* 21 (Dec. 1967), 12–17.

29. Robert J. House, "T-Group Education and Leadership Effectiveness: A Review of the Empiric Literature and a Critical Evaluation," *Personnel Psychology* 20 (Spring 1967), 1–32. See also Dorothy Stock, "A Survey of Research on T-Groups," in Bradford, Gibb, and Benne, pp. 395–441.

30. House, ibid., pp. 18–19.

31. John P. Campbell and Marvin D. Dunnette, "Effectiveness of T-Group Experiences in Managerial Training and Development," *Psychological Bulletin* 70 (August 1968), 73–104.

32. Ibid., 100.

33. Ibid., 101. See also the essays by Dunnette and Campbell and Chris Argyris in *Industrial Relations* 8 (Oct. 1968), 1–45.

34. On this point, see Larry E. Greiner, "Patterns of Organization Change," *Harvard Business Review* 45 (May-June 1967), 119–30.

35. See Sheldon A. Davis, "An Organic Problem-Solving Method."

36. See Rensis Likert, *The Human Organization: Its Management and Value* (New York: McGraw-Hill Book Company, 1967).

Chapter 13 New Roles for Proactive Administrators

THE MANAGEMENT OF IDEAS

Melvin Anshen

A profound change in the main task of top management is emerging as a result of the accelerating dynamics of technologies, markets, information systems, and social expectations of business performance. If this projection is correct, the threat of obsolescence of managers will pass swiftly from today's conversational shocker to tomorrow's operating reality. Executives best prepared to survive this challenge may turn out to be those equipped to think like philosophers—a type of intellectual skill not ordinarily developed in business schools or by the common work experiences of middle management.

The roots of this radical transformation of the general management job can be identified in recent business history:

Resources

Up to about the last two decades the main task of top management could fairly be described as the efficient administration of physical resources. The focus was essentially short-range and unifunctional, and the dominant decision criteria were economic. The highest demonstration of management skill was the successful manipulation of revenues and costs in the production and distribution of materials, machines, and products.

People

Beginning in the 1930's this concern with managing physical things was enlarged by a growing interest in managing people. This was enlargement, rather than change, because the ultimate goal of effective people management was still effective thing management, with top executives extending their grasp over resources by means of their ability to organize and motivate people. The focus of management attention remained within short-term horizons and unifunctional activity.

Money

After World War II, in a business environment marked by rapid growth in corporate size, product and market diversification, accelerated technological development, and shortened product life cycles, the principal task of top management evolved from concentration on physical and human resources to a major concern with money. This shift was accompanied by an extension of planning horizons and a transition from a unifunctional to a multifunctional view of a company's activities.

In contrast to physical resources, money is inherently neutral; to be used it must be transformed into physical and human resources. Money also is flexible through time, that is, capable of expansion and contraction, as well as of rapid shifts in the forms, risks, and costs of financial instruments. These characteristics of neutrality and flexibility encouraged a broader management view that encompassed many functions within a company as well as longer-term planning horizons.

Ideas

We are now beginning to sense that a focus on managing money, although broader than the earlier focus on physical and human resources, still fosters a dangerous sort of tunnel vision. The world of management is in a revolutionary phase. Within the company, racing technologies destroy both their own foundations and intertechnological boundaries. Outside the company, the environment is moving faster (in market evolution and consumer behavior), exploding in geographic scope (from nation to world), and reflecting the demands and constraints of a new society in which the traditional role of private business and traditional criteria of management performance are challenged by new concepts and standards.

At the same time, new analytical techniques, largely quantitative and computer-based, are presenting a management opportunity that is unique in at least two important ways. First, they provide an administrative capability without parallel in breadth, depth, and speed. Second, for their full and efficient utilization they press management to establish a unified command over the totality of a business, including the dynamic interface of external environment and internal activities. These changes are defining a novel view of management itself as a universally applicable resource, readily transferred from one business to another, from one industry to another, from one technology to another, from one country to another.

In this emerging management world, what will be the main task of management, common to top-level administrators in all types and sizes of companies? I suggest a combination of spatial and temporal intellectual vision, with the ability to transform vision into operating results through the flexible administration of physical, human, and financial resources

in any environment. This might be described as applied conceptualization—or, more simply, as the management of ideas.

Central Focus for Ideas

Skill in generating and manipulating ideas is precisely the skill of the great philosophers—the ability to universalize from here and now to everywhere and always. If it is true that top executives in the years ahead are going to be tested above all by their ability to manage ideas, then they are going to have to understand what it means to think like philosophers and develop skill in doing it. This has implications for management education, training, and selection, especially at the higher levels of administration. It also carries a substantial threat of obsolescence for managers now holding broad responsibilities whose talent, education, and experience have not equipped them to use their intellects in this manner.

The implications are not limited to the purely intellectual demands placed on general managers. They also extend to corporate purpose, organization, and function. A business devoted to the identification of central ideas and the formulation of strategies for moving swiftly from ideas to operations will differ in structure and activity from a business primarily concerned with management of money, or of physical and human resources.

Management of ideas is a broader concept than either management by objectives or long-range planning. The use of objectives and planning are techniques equally relevant for any major management task, whether it be a focus on physical resources or money, or a principal concern with ideas.

Management of ideas also goes beyond the concept of strategy. Just as there are alternative strategies for attaining an objective, so there are alternative strategies for executing an idea that defines the central purpose of a business. Focusing on the management of ideas contributes to more realistic planning, more appropriate objectives, more relevant strategies.

Ideas for Technology

One example of how an idea may be viewed as the central focus for management attention can be found in industries characterized by advanced, dynamic technologies.

Soft Answers

In this arena, it is attractively easy to frame a soft answer to the hard question of how to organize resources for maximum effectiveness. A typical soft answer: "In our fast-moving technological environment, the big winners will be those companies with large investments in research and development, because out of R&D come the new products that capture markets and generate high return on investment. Therefore we should invest every available dollar in R&D."

The inadequacy of this operating design is suggested by the common management complaint in these industries that it is difficult to establish rational control over investment in and performance of R&D, difficult to measure payback on R&D investment, and difficult to concentrate research efforts on projects with high potential payoffs.

Hard Answers

However, there are a few companies in high-technology industries in which such complaints rarely arise. These are the companies whose top managers have done the thinking that develops hard, rather than soft, answers. They have observed that a commitment to R&D without a specific central concept for total organization effort is a clumsy, even a meaningless, commitment. But by resolute probing, they have found an opportunity for defining a core idea around which total company effort can be designed. This opportunity can be described in terms of three specific idea options:

1) To mobilize all of a company's resources around the concept of becoming a creative technological leader—the first in the industry to discover, develop, and market new products at the leading edge of moving technology.
2) To organize resources around the central idea of becoming an early imitator and adapter of the successful innovations of the industry's creative leader.
3) To become a low-price mass producer of established products, sacrificing the high margins (and high risks) of innovation for the high volume (and limited risks) of low-price imitation.

Each of these options carries specific implications for the kind of investment in product and market research, as well as for organization structure, information network, scale of activity and risk, and many other aspects of a company's physical, personal, and financial resources. In short, out of each of these idea options can be derived a total scheme for operating a business. This total scheme will be uniquely determined by the central idea and will represent the top management choice among alternative strategies for executing the idea throughout the business.

Ideas for Conglomerates

Another example can be found among diversified or conglomerate companies. Here, too, there have been many soft answers, framed around a generalized acquisition drive. Economic pressures have revealed the inadequacies of this course. In contrast, some managements have exploited opportunities to select as a base for a total enterprise commitment a central idea from several identified options:

1) A structure of unrelated or accidentally related companies anchored to a central core of unusual management competence, both general and functional, available to strengthen the performance of each satellite company.
2) A designed diversification aimed at exploiting complementary technologies, production resources, or market systems.
3) A diversification aimed at balancing high-risk and low-risk ventures, fluctuating and stable industries, and cyclical and seasonal variations.

As with the high-technology idea options, each of the diversification models carries specific implications for every element in a business and for the goals and strategies by which the elements are activated.

Other Examples

Still other examples of central ideas may be cited briefly:

1) A shift in the definition of a business from one concerned with the sale of a product to one concerned with the delivery of a complete system of customer values—as in airlines' marketing of packaged vacations, computer manufacturers' marketing of systems to solve customers' information problems, and consumer hard-good companies' marketing of assured lifetime performance of products.
2) The discovery, almost the invention, of new industries—such as environmental hygiene and control, education as a lifespan need, and the profit-oriented performance of traditional public services such as urban redevelopment or even urban creation.
3) The abandonment of accepted notions of industry boundaries—as in the transformation of a steel company into a materials company or of

a petroleum company into an energy company.
4) The evolution of "scrambled merchandising" in retail stores which focus on a pattern of consumer needs and buying habits rather than on historic product categories such as groceries or drug products.

Each of these ideas is the energized core of a unique design for a business. The exploitation of each idea requires a comprehensive intellectual grasp of the totality of a business viewed as an interacting system that includes both internal resources and functions and external distribution systems and markets. From such a comprehensive vision will issue a flow of strategic options for products, services, costs, prices, technology, organization structures, responsibilities, information networks, and motivations for all levels of management.

New Ways of Thinking

Thinking in terms of such ideas, from initial concept through full implementation, is a difficult intellectual task. It is no assignment for second-rate minds, or even for first-rate but narrowly oriented minds. Moreover, it demands the special intellectual ability to visualize the translation of ideas and strategies into controlled operating systems responsive to dynamic change.

The need for these unusual talents is the inevitable outcome of radically new conditions within and outside the corporation. The critical new condition is an acceleration in the rate of change of such magnitude that change itself becomes the central object of management attention. Up to now, with rare exceptions, the administration of change has been handled as a supplement to the administration of established ongoing activities. In this context, the future evolves from the present at a controllable pace, and it is reasonable for managers to concentrate mainly on targets of efficiency and to treat adapting to market challenges as a subsidiary element within a larger administrative responsibility.

Only a few companies have been in a position to report to stockholders such dramatic news as that "50% of our sales in the past year and 75% of our profits were generated by products that we did not handle five years ago." When many companies report such news, or make equally startling observations about short-term penetration of new markets or new technologies (whether from internal development or acquisitions), the fact of change moves to the center of the stage and all else is peripheral.

Preparing for Change

At this point, it becomes more important to make correct decisions about the direction, timing, and implementation of change than to attain a high level of efficiency in administering steady-state operations. However, few business organizations have been designed to give primary support to this unfamiliar ordering of goals. In most companies the values, organization, responsibility, control systems, information networks, and performance standards are not well adapted to this requirement.

Most companies, including many with reputations for being well managed, are organized primarily to administer yesterday's ideas. Investments and operations are measured by efficient performance, with relatively short-term targets for achievement, and a primary focus on taut administration of existing resources and markets. This was an appropriate corporate design concept when the rate of changes within and outside the company was slow.

The weakness of such organizations is revealed, however, whenever a new opportunity or a forced adaptation is sensed by a single department. Rapid exploitation of new markets usually increases production costs, and is therefore resisted by managers whose performance will be ad-

versely affected in any shift in ongoing efficient activities. Less common, but equally possible, is resistance from the marketing people to innovation in production technology with its risk of cost, quality, and delivery uncertainties.

But even this view is simplistic. For in spite of the current touted commitment to a marketing orientation in management, the performance record in many companies suggests that leadership by the marketing function frequently generates little more than better adaption of existing products to better defined existing markets. This may be a move in the right direction in the short run. But it is not good enough in a period when new technology may erode established market positions or capture untouched markets "overnight."

Inherent in the concept of core ideas for top management is a total business orientation, rather than a market-oriented administration (or a technology-oriented or any "other-oriented" administration). A total business orientation views the company as a system of physical, financial, and human resources in dynamic interaction with a changing environment. It views swift response to opportunities and problems as more important for long-run success than efficient control of current operations. It values the future above the present. Such an orientation has revolutionary implications for many management designs and tasks.

New Organizational Patterns

Consider, as one example, the way companies assign authority and responsibility. Whatever the shape of a company's organization tree, it shares certain characteristics with all organization structures. First among these, and most visible because it is specifically charted, is some type of cluster design that gathers together a prescribed set of related activities. The design may focus on patterns of functions, products, geography, or projects. Whatever the pattern, the task performance is substantially influenced by the prescription of the pattern itself, and the pressures of the perceived reward criteria.

With one exception (the project cluster), all of these cluster patterns inevitably develop a built-in resource and emotional investment in the continuance of the established design. Since there are no defined time limits for the exercise of responsibility within the cluster, the accumulating managerial bias must be toward preservation of existing activities and status.

In such an environment, it would be extraordinary if radical change claimed a dominant share of management attention. Thus we see the common practice of establishing a long-range planning function at a single, usually remote, location in the organization tree, with the resulting problems of working through informal channels to bring ideas about the future into contact with current operations.

In these structures, radical change is painful. It is viewed as disruptive and costly by managers committed to the present and appraised by their administration of the present. In their constrained sighting they are right. They resist change because it is in their perceived economic interest to resist and because change threatens their status and their intellectual and emotional commitments.

This may go a long way toward explaining why so many of the major conceptual innovations—the great new ideas—are introduced and initially exploited by companies other than the corporate giants. (It should be noted, however, that this conclusion has nothing to do with the development and application of technological progress which is one of the prime accomplishments of large research-oriented companies.)

The single organization pattern that is free from this built-in bias is the project cluster. While there may be difficult administrative problems associated with project-oriented structures, they offer the important advantages of tailor-made design to fit unique tasks, flexible resource commitments, defined termi-

nation points, and an absence of enduring commitment that encourages resistance to radical innovation.

The project pattern suggests important clues for the characteristics of an organization structure focused on the management of ideas in a dynamic environment. One principal requirement will be unconstrained adaptability to new tasks, with easy transitions across technological, product, and market boundaries. Another will be performance measurement and motivation that give substantial encouragement to future-oriented management thinking. A third will be an ability to bring multifunctional considerations quickly to bear on opportunities that appear initially in the field of vision of a single function.

All of these requirements suggest a fluid concept of organization structure marked by short-lived, specific-assignment clusters, flexibility in job definitions, and a high degree of vertical and horizontal teamwork. Thus *both* middle and top management must accept and adjust to this fluid concept. This means critical demands on both the quality of managers' intellectual resources and the ways in which managers are motivated to use these resources. None of these demands can be met by fiat. They call for the creation of a new way of life for which many executives are ill-prepared by education and experience.

Information Revolution

A further example of revolutionary change in administrative design can be found in the area of information generation and use.

A few words about computers are in order at the outset. The history of computer applications in the 17 years [as of 1969] since their introduction to the business market reveals two distinct stages in management concepts of their potential.

1) Initially, most managers viewed computers as electronic clerks. The

primary use of computers was therefore in familiar tasks.

2) Recently, a second stage of management thinking can be discerned. This has been marked by a superficial popularization of the concept of the integrated information system which calls on the storage, retrieval, and manipulative capability of large computers to bring the total information requirements of a business within an integrated decision network. (This does not imply a computerized decision system, but simply an organized information system, computer-based, to assist comprehensive human decisionmaking.)

While the notion of the integrated information system has been widely described and explored in technical and management journals, several probes of management practice suggest that few companies have made a sustained attempt to operate in this way, and few managers have any real grasp of what the concept means in either theoretical or operating terms. There is, to be sure, a growing number of fractional, single-function information systems, such as those linking production, inventory, and procurement activities. And there is a growing disposition to talk about comprehensive management information systems. But the operational application is a long way from the discussion, with many unresolved conceptual and technical problems in between.

It would be a gross misconception to view this gap as the familiar one between software and hardware. The primary task ahead is not to develop programs that will utilize the capabilities of the machines. Rather it is to develop management concepts that define integrated systems. It will then be possible to describe the principal data requirements to make such systems operational, including clear delineation of relationships among the components of a dynamic system responsive to external and internal feedback. The next step will be the design of computer programs to store and manipulate data for management needs.

At present, most top managers have yet to approach even the initial stage of developing basic concepts. The skeptic may be inclined to say:

But this can't be true! Managers are running companies, and this means that they are running systems, with whatever crude tools, including the human brain, they may have at hand.

To which the appropriate reply is:

True enough, managers are running companies. But examination of the typical management decision process reveals that what is happening is in no sense total system analysis. Problems are usually fractionated within the total company system—partly to reduce them to a size and order of simplicity that are manageable with available analytical tools, and partly to follow familiar routines and utilize familiar rules of thumb.

What is defined here is not a technical requirement, but an intellectual requirement. This is essentially a command of logical design. The basic design building blocks are:

1) Identification of critical areas of initiating change that generate effects in one or several operating areas.
2) Rough measures of the magnitudes of the primary cause-effect relationships.
3) Identification of the principal feedbacks.
4) Rough measures of these feedbacks.

For purposes of concept formulation and testing, the degree of precision ordinarily required is modest because this is not primarily a quantitative exercise. One does not need numbers to design a business system. In fact, the truth is quite the reverse. One first needs a concept of a system in order to identify the kinds of numbers needed to work the system.

Furthermore, it is unlikely that any comprehensive business system can be completely quantified in the sense of converting all decision inputs into a set of manipulatable numbers. The objective is limited and practical. It is simply to use both quantitative and qualitative analysis to extend management's decision horizon to the total business viewed as a dynamic system, and thereby to improve the quality of decisions. The improvement will be reflected in the ability to make decisions that are broadly consistent with the basic concept of the business, sensitive to impacts and feedbacks throughout the business, and rapidly and flexibly adaptive to changing conditions within and outside the company.

Focus on the Future

A third example of the impact of revolutionary change is the need for upgrading management's ability to forecast the shape of things to come. During the last 20 years economic forecasting has made the transition from favorite parlor game of professional economists to favorite reading matter of professional managers. The prognostications of accredited economic forecasters are a mandatory item on every trade association agenda, while discussions of the economic outlook clog the pages of management magazines.

But economic change is only one of several environmental areas important to managers. Three other areas are equally significant: technological change, social change, and political change. Few companies and few individual managers have addressed themselves in a serious and organized way to the problems of forecasting trends in these areas. Yet changes in the years ahead, coming more rapidly than ever before, will be loaded with opportunities for the forewarned, and with threats for those who have not cast their minds forward and formulated offensive and defensive strategies.

The requirement is for more than a freshened interest in the future. The evolution of economic forecasting to its present significant role in management planning resulted from the invention of sophisticated tools of analysis. One cannot predict economic trends with a useful level of confidence until the significant economic variables have been identified and their interacting dynamics at least roughly measured. Forecasting of technological, social, and political changes (including both trends and rates of movement) will require a comparable intellectual achievement. Large rewards will be realized by organizations that can anticipate developments in these areas with enough confidence to incorporate their forecasts in strategic planning.

Technological Forecasting

In the area of technology an essential conceptual adaptation must be to extend management thinking beyond the base to which it is commonly tied, that is, the view that improvements will be regularly generated from developments in the technologies that have been their historical foundation. This is an understandable but limiting and risky framework for forecasting.

Analysis of recent technological advances clearly identifies two related phenomena of great importance to management. One is the application of "foreign" technologies in process and product areas where they have played no significant prior role. The other is the erosion, often the disappearance, of traditional industry and product boundaries. Together, they lay down a requirement that technological forecasting be treated broadly.

It will not be safe for a manager to project the shape of technological changes by extrapolating trends in existing applications. Some of the most significant developments affecting both production and marketing are likely to be spawned within technologies that are not currently applicable in his industry and company.

Technological forecasting of this breadth and sophistication will not progress far without the development of a new kind of professional expertise, comparable to that of professional economists. It will be a prime responsibility of enlightened managers to encourage qualified scientists and engineers to address themselves to the assignment, and to build their own ability to communicate with and guide this new corps of professionals.

In addition, just as the sophisticated manager needs the skill to translate economic forecasts into signals of opportunity and threat for his company's future operations, so will he need a parallel skill to translate technological forecasts into meaningful guides for business strategies. This task cannot safely be left to the technicians. There should be little need to emphasize this warning to managers who have grasped, often after painful experience, the need to guide the work of computer specialists to assure that they mobilize information specifically relevant for management control and decision.

A prime ingredient in translating technological projections into business applications will be a thorough understanding of the difference between technical feasibility and economic feasibility. Technology determines what can be done. Economics determines what will be done. Managers must be familiar with this distinction. Many of today's naïve forecasters of the technological outlook who are writing in the popular press certainly are not.

Social Forecasting

Forecasting of social trends covers such topics as changing social structure (including racial and ethnic components), evolution of living patterns and related spending patterns, and shifting values and priorities (for example, between work and leisure, between risk assumption and security).

The full implications of the opportunities presented by recent social trends have been grasped by few companies. For instance, managers of a number of financial institutions reveal a persistent preoccupation with superficial economic phenomena of consumers' saving and investment patterns, rather than a probing analysis of the financial service needs of a society marked by widespread affluence, multiple options in discretionary spending, confidence in long-range income security, and rising concern about permanent inflation.

A well-known example of the powerful application of social (appropriately combined with economic) forecasting is the course pursued by Sears, Roebuck and Co. since World War II. The dramatic divergence of this company's performance from that of its direct competitor, Montgomery Ward & Co., Inc., needs no description for a management audience. But the important contribution made by a projection of fundamental social changes and the translation of that forecast into market opportunities deserves to be noted.

Sears made an aggressive exploitation of social perspective through a core institutional idea. The results have been as spectacular as was the comparable grasp of a new business opportunity evoked by socioeconomic change evidenced in the implementation of a core management idea by General Motors under Alfred P. Sloan's direction in the 1920's.

The extension of management's conceptual competence in the area of social dynamics calls for knowledge and perceptiveness that have not been required hitherto. As in the field of technology, managers will be dealing with professional specialists whose work must be directed and interpreted. Competence in doing this will build the confidence to use social projections in designing business strategies that open the way to radical innovations in organization and operations.

Political Forecasting

The principal business element in political forecasting is the shifting boundary between the private and public sectors of the economy. Until recently, the prevailing management view of this area was a superficial conclusion that a transfer of activities was occurring from the private to the public sector, directly by intervention or indirectly by control.

Current developments are beginning to suggest that this is a naïve judgment. Movement in the opposite direction can also be discerned, for example, in education, research, and construction. New, mixed public-private enterprise forms, such as Comsat, are being invented. More developments of this sort may be anticipated. Moreover, changes in the domain of private enterprise, in pure or mixed form, are not totally a result of decisions taken within government. Business initiative can open the door to private expansion, particularly where the public performance has been lethargic, unimaginative, or grossly inefficient.

The pejorative descriptive phrase, "socialization of American society," indiscriminately applied to developments in such diverse fields as health, insurance, transportation, housing, or even protection of consumer interests, has a dangerous potential for stultifying thinking about the central issues. A more open view might recognize that an industrialized, urbanized, high-technology society, in which a dramatically visible gap appears between the actual and the potential quality of life, is a society ripe for changes in traditional public-private relationships.

The changes may move in either direction: toward public invasion of the private sector or toward private invasion of the public sector. The direction and rate of these changes will be powerfully influenced by managers who can deal confidently with new ideas in areas where businessmen have seldom allowed their minds to be engaged. The political environment, there can be little doubt, will be redesigned. But those who believe that environment is created by forces outside their control will not be in an intellectual position to participate in the redesign. An environment will be imposed on them

which, however reluctantly, they will be compelled to accept.

On the positive side, a rising interest and skill in forecasting political relationships will identify opportunities for private enterprise to invent new environmental concepts. Formulating these concepts, and relating them to profitable resource investment, will require an intellectual adventure in the world of ideas such as few managers have so far experienced. Part of the process will surely be fresh definitions of the words "private" and "public," which, as applied to business and government activities, have been largely emptied of meaning by emotional abuse.

As in forecasting social change, it is not easy to perceive shifts in the private-public balance, or potential for inducing shifts by initiatives from the private sector. We lack even the professional discipline to generate the knowledge and develop a reliable analytical base for management thinking. Traditional political science is oriented toward the problems of governing men and the performance of institutions for public legislation and administration. The new issues are closer to those implied by the classic term, "political economy," and involve concepts of social design on the grand scale.

Philosopher-Executive

The emerging dominance of ideas as a central concern for top management raises critical questions about the education, selection, and development of candidates for high-level assignments in the years ahead. Neither business school education nor in-company experience is presently structured to emphasize the manager-as-philosopher concept. Rather, the principal thrust in school and company environments is toward new analytic techniques, both quantitative and qualitative, and their application in rational decisionmaking and control.

There is good reason to doubt that students in professional schools are at a stage of their intellectual development where they would benefit from a major emphasis on the role of central ideas in top management responsibilities. Moreover, the relevant technical input to their education is so important and growing so rapidly that any sharp curtailment would constrain their ability to handle management tasks in junior executive positions.

The education of middle-level managers is another matter, however. There are opportunities at this stage to expose selected high potential executives to the significance of core ideas in the design of long-range corporate strategies and in the adaptation of organization and resources to their implementation. The opportunities arise in planned job experiences and management education programs, both in-house and university. Imaginative action at this level will produce two important benefits. One is the preparation of a cadre of potential top executives for the broad new responsibilities that the future business environment will thrust on them. The other is a new selection criterion for top-level positions, based on specific performance in mid-career assignments

where the ability to think conceptually and to relate ideas to applied management can be tested.

Today's development programs give principal emphasis to new techniques for analysis and control in functional areas, and to strategic planning of resource utilization at the general management level. It would be desirable to curtail the technical content to some degree and introduce material on dynamic environmental change (markets, technologies, social, political), on the role and manipulation of ideas, and on the impact of change on corporate strategy.

A related effort to enrich idea-management experience on the job and test executives' abilities would require more opportunities below the top management level for assignments that require imaginative projection, assessment of the total environmental outlook, and relevant strategic decision. Corporations which move in this direction will fortify their management ability to cope powerfully and speedily with a radically new business world.

THE EXISTENTIALIST EXECUTIVE

Anders Richter

The debacle of the Vietnam War has manifested a number of massive and startling effects, including the fall of the Johnson government four years after its great affirmation of power, a systemic weakening of the American economy, aggravation of the hostility of our Negro and poor citizens, and alienation of the best part of our youth. Now it has become apparent that these are not temporary fissures in the body politic, but that we are in a process of rapid change heralding the demise of American conservatism which, since 1898, has so success-

fully maintained the power and prosperity of a "have" nation. The revelations of the war—a supine Congress, a leadership incapable of change in ideology or behavior, indeed, all of the "Emperor-has-no-clothes" phenomena—have indicated a probability that this process will be revolutionary in character.

Revolution from the Top

A most remarkable figment of the present sociopolitical situation is that, if it comes, the revolution well may be from the top. It may be a peaceful revolution of the bureaucracy, in time to forestall a violent revolution from the bottom. I was moved to this surmise during eight weeks as a student executive at the Federal Executive Institute in Charlottesville, Virginia. In this gentlemanly ambience, successive classes of middle-class, middle-aged federal executives are steeped in a heady brew of iconoclastic portents. Though no solutions are prescribed, it is suggested that more temporary organizations will be created to deal with the problems of a rapidly changing environment. I concluded that traditional institutions, such as religion and family, will provide less support for normative choices, and that even the most basic values will be challenged in a fluid society. Rather than looking to given standards of value and behavior, the new executive will be forced to rely on his self-created norms and interests in coping with a world of change. It will follow that the personal responsibilities thus imposed will cause him to experience anxiety about himself and his actions. Though perhaps not intended, and though doubtless pragmatically derived, these notions nevertheless bear a close resemblance to those of existentialism.

In reading the existentialist literature 15 years after its first vogue in America, I discovered that one can descend in a line from the seminal philosophies through what is called both existential and humanistic psychology, directly into management texts. To do so is to take a plunge in obscure terms: *Dasein*—phenomenology—self-actualizing—eupsychian—proactivert. *Dasein* is interesting for its compound meaning: *Da,* meaning there, in this context referring to the human psyche, with *sein,* or being, which in German has the active meaning of becoming, posits the elemental detachment-involvement enigma (or absurdity) of human existence. One first wonders, what does the word existentialism mean? Sartre's classical definition, the cryptic "Existence precedes essence," is not very helpful for the bureaucrat. For the philosopher, it proposes sub-

jectivity as the point of departure to experience and knowledge. The world is deduced from consciousness—is revealed in the play of light which is consciousness. Existence lies outside consciousness, while the human subject, itself in a state of "there-being," forms concepts about the world only through experience. The field between thought and the outside world is where the individual maneuvers in personal venture and experience. It is an area of fundamental ambiguity, where confusion reigns as to what is endogenous and what exogenous. This ambiguity, known to existentialists as the human condition, is unescapable; it is best met with the ancient and humanistic dogma "Know Thyself."

The reason our existential age is one of anxiety is that it is possible for man to suddenly and shudderingly perceive himself as object. He can die, and he is subject to chance. Existentialists call this a feeling of contingency. Religion is man's attempt to escape his contingency, but it won't wash: Nietzsche killed God in 1884. No matter: Latter-day existentialists offer a positive antidote to despair. They say that consciousness is not passive, but is intentional—that it seeks out experience, as it were, and thus gives meaning to our percepts of the world. Our ability to do this is our inner freedom. Most of us, however, reject this freedom quite stringently and allow our everyday consciousness to present the world to us in familiar stereotype. But insights, intuitions of our freedom and power, intrude continuously to tell us that our everyday consciousness is a deceiver. Moments of encompassing clarity, common though unpredictable, reveal the true nature of consciousness, as do psychedelic experiences which may be induced. They are called peak experiences by humanistic psychologists.

According to the existential psychiatrist Rollo May, man's psyche exhibits a decisive attitude toward existence. This allows the existentialists another striking cliché, i.e., decision precedes knowledge. That is, commitment is a necessary prerequisite for seeing the truth. "The points of commitment and decision are those where the dichotomy between being subject and object is overcome in the unity of readiness for action."[1]

Action

Now we have arrived at something the executive can grasp: the notion of action. In truth, existentialism, which is life view rather than doctrine, is the most activist of all philosophies. Sartre himself writes that "man is nothing else but what he makes of himself."[2] The key is man's conscious intentionality, for this is what commits him to action, and his actions determine what he is, his being. People (as opposed to machines) are uniquely self-activating; that is, they initiate the getting of knowledge from their environments, which knowledge leads to immediate and suitable actions. Where we fear to know, we fear to act, as with those Germans who chose to be ignorant of the Nazi persecutions of the Jews.

Men of action have long been our acknowledged leaders. In his appraisal of the leaders of antiquity, Machiavelli remarked that "they owed nothing to fortune but the opportunity which gave them matter to be shaped into what form they thought fit."[3] The ideal for modern public administration is leadership which assumes the responsibility of changing organizations through action, and which maintains the welfare of society by remaining considerate of the purposes and behavior of others.

The conscious separation from what exists, and self-projection toward what is intended, give the existentialists a definition of man's freedom. Such liberty is the indispensable condition of all action. It is not a property of human nature in the sense that I can excuse my actions as determined by human nature. Nor can I find religious sanctions for my actions if God is a cop-out and does not exist. Freedom, in short, is absolutely individual and unfettered. It thus bestows an awesome responsibility. Man is responsible for what

he is, and determines what he is by his actions. This is difficult enough, but Sartre goes further, and says that when a man is responsible for himself, he is thereby responsible for all men. The doctrine of personal responsibility is inherently fraught with danger to the state, and while occasionally it is expounded by a disestablishmentarian such as Thoreau, it rarely finds its way into proclamations of government. One landmark exception was the determination of war guilt made by the Nuremberg Tribunal. "The official position of Defendants, whether as heads of State, or responsible officials in Government departments, shall not be considered as freeing them from responsibility, or mitigating punishment. . . . The fact that the Defendant acted pursuant to order of his Government or of a superior shall not free him from responsibility. . . . "[4] This is the stuff of existentialism, and of arresting significance to every executive engaged in execution of the United States war policy for Vietnam.

Choice

Throughout the existentialist literature, there is a dominant theme: choice. All leaders know the anguish of choice; Sartre gives the example of a military officer accepting responsibility for an attack—a responsibility to himself and to others which cannot be evaded. Failure to act is also choice, and the officer may choose to be a coward. That is, he is choosing his own being. There is no compulsion; if a man fails to act one way it is because he prefers certain other values, such as conformity or the good opinions of others. It is no good for Eichmann to say that he was not responsible for his acts; every administrator is fully responsible, for if he is passive it is because he has chosen passivity. The confrontation with choice is a never-ending, existential process. Choice and consciousness are one and the same thing.

What is the nature of choice? Optimism: Even in times of the darkest uncertainty, our choices are the best that seem possible. And at those times when his goal beckons clearly, man is most enterprising and resourceful. Openmindedness: The existentialist executive must be prepared to alter his choices as he receives fresh information from his environment. Empathy: On the basis of our own subjective feelings of making choices, we also impute choices to others. Finally, choice has the quality of altering the personality of the chooser. Observers of management frequently have discerned significant changes of behavior as a consequence of individuals making decisions. This has been marked especially within teams organized for so-called project systems, where involvement in decisionmaking has resulted in personal commitments which produce high yields of output.

The management term for choice is decisionmaking. A decision is required when something is blocking the intentionality of the administrator or the purposeful activity of the organization. Choices then must be made among different ways of dealing with the blockage. According to the management specialist Bertram Gross: "An important decision is invariably a huge cluster of sequential choices in which the earlier choices help determine the alternatives available."[5] He then contends that this can lead to a synergistic creativity, because the sequential steps lead to the formulation of significant new questions, which in turn create new and productive alternatives for the decision maker.

Are we federal executives conscious of our freedom to choose? The existential novelist Colin Wilson believes that all men would engage in more creative acts of conscious freedom if they were more aware of their elemental intentionality. Because of laziness and passivity, we submerge our freedom in the unconscious. We are then too secure, we become bored, and lose our sense of action. We make a habit of limited perception. We establish a high threshold of indifference to protect ourselves from disturbing events in our environment; but this is a fallacy, for the environment acting inexorably on man is a myth. As Sartre says: "The environment can act on the subject only to the exact extent that he comprehends it; that is, transforms it into a situation."[6]

The federal bureaucrat finds many excuses for his rejection of choice. He is uncomfortable with intentionality, and lacks even good ordinary language to deal with organizational purposes; hence, the glittering generalities in which official purposes are typically phrased. The true purposes of the organization often are submerged beneath what management analysts call code observance. This is most pronounced in hierarchical organizations, where the code seems to require different behavior from individuals at different levels. Code compliance is manifested in either a grim or a bland, but always a tenacious, attachment to the system. The watchwords cooperation, extended to support of the status quo, and feasibility are invoked repeatedly to stifle deviant action. In recent years, still another excuse has succored the passive bureaucrat; the myth that man is a creature of technology. But the Great Blackout of 1965 was caused by man's inaction, not by technology. Seymour Melman argues that political interests, not technical requirements, have determined the character of our military establishment as well as the very design of its weapons: "A most important demonstration of the socially determined nature of technology was the decision by the United States in 1961 to build an overkill force of over 1,000 intercontinental ballistic missiles."[7]

Perhaps the most persistent bureaucratic cop-out is the old Pendleton Act principle about elected officials making policy, while appointed officials only execute. The appointed agency head who is an energetic policymaker, but who cannot translate his decisions into action through an inert career (i.e., Civil Service-protected) management, is in a familiar Washington pickle. Increasingly common is the converse situation, in which an activist middle-level manager is frustrated in his desire to execute a legislated program by the repressive forces of Congress or his agency superiors. One augury of the bureaucratic revolution is that Nader obtains much of his evidence of program failure from individuals engaged in program execution. It is reasonable to suppose that federal executives soon will attempt their own Nader-style identifications of breakdowns and will seek political support for their remedial actions.

Objectivity

A behavior of choice imposes on its practitioners a sense of objectivity—a more or less exact appreciation of where-I-am-now and how-I-can-get-where-I-am-going. This requires a certain discipline in viewing one's impulses from above. It requires, also, a hardnosed acceptance of the fact that one is the way one acts. For example, Sartre tells us that there is no such thing as a cowardly constitution;[8] a man makes himself a coward by his acts, and is fully responsible for his cowardice. For the individual, objectivity means an understanding of the consequences of one's behavior; for the organization, it means a critical examination of its culture, that is, the values and processes in its environment. No organization can isolate itself, for its very members are individuals drawn from the environment who impose their values on the organization.

The enemy of true reality is ultrapracticality. The managerial class has long given its homage to pragmatism; the method of prior formulation, recurrent testing, and optimal decisionmaking. Such scientism is inevitably impersonal, because models formulated for testing cannot encompass the complexities of people problems which, accordingly, are considered unprofessional. Hence, large-scale organizations tend to lose, both inside and outside, their rapport with people—that is, their objectivity. Those who would uphold people interests are dismissed as utopians, while decisionmaking is delegated to ex-

perts. Alas, how often have these experts—be they highway engineers, economists, or geopoliticians—made the wrong choices? The expert's refuge and security is in rationalism. When threatened by the chaotic world-as-it-is, he defines his terms, states his assumptions, applies his rigorous logic, and sticks by his conclusions through the thin of aloof superiority and the thick of catastrophic failure. Thus has it been with Vietnam, both in the high reaches of the National Security Council and in the hamlets, where the second looey, entrapped at the end of someone else's logic train, could rationalize that "we had to destroy that village in order to save it." The old Whiteheadian aphorism is ever apt: "Life is larger than logic."

Following a book of rules may result in the most bizarre irrationalities because it suppresses recognition of nonroutine problems. It is irrational, also, to believe that administrators can conduct their affairs in the same manner that scientists conduct research. Indeed, there is much hogwash even concerning the infallibility of the scientific-technological process, in which there is at all times a good deal of magic. In physics, Heisenberg's uncertainty principle has demonstrated a fundamental limit to our ability to know or predict the world of matter; while in mathematics, queen of the sciences and the very fount of rationalism, Godel's upsetting theorem has presented us with ultimate conditions of absolute insolubility. Man cannot escape his finitude or give over his problems to a giant computing machine.

The words of Gross are especially useful in laying the myth of administrative rationality:

Because of its multidimensionality, there are few administrators capable of considering the rationality of an organization's entire purpose pattern. . . . Moreover, no matter what elements they may be concerned with, most administrators develop a personal style of comparative weighting among desirability, feasibility, and consistency. . . . When there are enough administrators in an organization to provide complementary representation for these various dimensions of reality, the conditions are ripe for the synthesis of these limited approaches into a broader pattern of rational action. Such a synthesis usually comes, it may be added, not in technical documents or in policy conferences but in the heat of action itself.[9]

I have . . . [emphasized the last phrase], because this culminating phrase is purely existential.

A behavior of choice requires further of the executive a willingness to take risks which is endowed, in many cases, by a sense of commitment—but not of commitment to the organization. Bailey, after questioning two dozen company presidents, found them remarkably disposed to put their jobs on the line in support of important decisions.[10] Moreover, this readiness to accept consequences seemed to give the presidents an inner serenity, as if it were an ultimate safety valve allowing them to labor over critical problems free of anxiety for their personal futures. Less and less, in the society of American organizations, do professionals and executives see their careers in terms of one firm or agency. And, in choosing to join or leave an organization, the existentialist executive is more and more governed by the values and purposes upheld by the organization.

Yet a host of federal bureaucrats remain limited in their freedom to make choices by devotion to job security. Indeed, many of our bureaucratic evils—conformity, flight from conflict, code observance, the myth that administrators do not make policy—may be rooted in the fear of job loss. An entrenched system of legislated tenure allows the career administrator in the federal government to be secure in his job and in his passivity; he may raise higher the safe walls of everyday consciousness. It means, further, that he is pseudoseparated from the consequences of his acts. By bland noncompliance and inaction, or through cynicism, the federal bureaucrat can and does

subvert changes promoted by political appointees, thus mindlessly and free of risk perpetuating his habit of routine and boredom. Yet in so doing, he paradoxically subverts his own standard of nonauthority for policymaking; for, even as the existentialists say, he cannot evade the responsibility of his choices: by demolishing policy, he makes policy.

Authenticity

Perhaps the prime quality of a behavior of choice is what the existentialists call authenticity. Wilson writes that "authenticity is to be driven by a deep sense of purpose," in awareness of "a standard of values external to everyday human consciousness."[11] In more homely terms, it is behaving the way you are, in place of posing in a role. It means getting rid of irrelevant emotional garbage which, in Freudian context, is usually associated with the past; existentialists start with the here-and-now. It means honesty about one's self, and directness with others. Authenticity is telling it like it is. The management analysts Beatrice and Sydney Rome have derived, from their Leviathan methodology, a description of the authentic organization:

A hierarchical organization, in short, like an individual person, is "authentic" to the extent that, throughout its leadership, it accepts its finitude, uncertainty, and contingency; realizes its capacity for responsibility and choice; acknowledges guilt and errors; fulfills its creative managerial potential for flexible planning, growth, and . . . policy formation; and responsibly participates in the wider community.[12]

The psychologist Abraham Maslow refers to "living by illusions" as a sickness which is widely shared.[13] One cannot live in Washington, D.C., without feeling depressed by the prevailing phoniness of federal officialdom. There is an essential arrogance in bureaucratic behavior (though frequently its actors attempt to mask it with servilities to "the taxpayer"), for what often provides administrators with feelings of importance is their provision of services, not the need of others for them. In truth, the inauthentic bureaucrat is a pitiable hypocrite. According to the psychologist Hubert Bonner:

In him the anxiety which is the lot of all of us is a function not of his awareness of life's imperfectibility or of the awesomeness of human choice but of the fear that others will see through his counterfeit choice. . . . He cannot choose or make decisions, for these entail risk regarding the unpredictable future.[14]

The present aspect of Washington is bleak, but the situation is ripe for the revolution from the top. That the contemporary literature of management is suffused with existentialism is only an indication of the historical forces which presently favor rapid change. According to Sartre's interpreter, H. J. Blackham:

When there is prevailing confidence in established values and authorities, the primordial, absolute, and solitary responsibility of the individual is regarded either as a meaningless platitude or as a dangerous thought: [I]n less settled times, it may come vividly home to some as a sharp and searching truth.[15]

These are less settled times. The nation is imperiled. Those who scoff at the suggestion of violent social revolution are retreating from the signs. Much more are we threatened with the extinction of our species.

The assumed inevitability, probability, or possibility of a third world war has become a guiding principle for the operations of a very considerable number of members of directorates, top managers, bureaucrats, and trade union leaders. This possibility is so much taken for granted that people who talk about the necessity for peace or disarmament are looked upon with a suspicion. . . .[16]

The fact that Gross wrote this in 1964 is itself cause for hope, because it seems less true today. A grand abstraction, such as peace, gains strength in the polity when its relationship to survival is so immediate. It is a truism that the citizenry become concerned about government to a greater degree when the state fails to serve basic human needs. The challenge of survival is not for the United States Congress, which has lost its republican character and abdicated its responsibility to curb a reckless Executive. In such an institutional vacuum, an enlightened class of federal administrators may achieve a new estate. The federal establishment must descend into the hands of gifted generalists whose expertise resides in the ability to improvise in the presence of a superb new technology. We must discover proactive administrators who possess the objectivity with which to make responsible choices. The fact is, existentialism emphasizes many human qualities which can be identified with traditional virtues, which is further cause for optimism. Energy, the characteristic of the man of action; honesty; sense of responsibility; committedness—such attributes are not likely to be rejected by the conventional ethics of the American public.

Even more will an existentialist revolution in government appeal to the present young generation who are the coming executive class. Young men and women, in an increasing degree, reject money as the measure of achievement. Many young intellectuals will reject academia for its inability to act, or because of its corruption of scholarly prerogatives with opportunism. Many will continue to choose the professions, but many more than in the past will go where the action is, into government, the arena of greatest confrontation with problems of moment and opportunity for effective action. They will bring with them a strong infusion of existentialist values—most emphatically a commitment to action, a readiness to accept the consequences of their acts, and an abhorrence of phoniness. These qualities are evident in today's campus rebels, and they will be the motive forces for the revolution of the bureaucracy.

The prospect of our government in the hands of such innerdirected administrators may be disquieting for the average American. What saving social ethic is present to curb these self-actualizing choice makers? Ernest Hemingway is said to have remarked that "morality is what you feel good about after you've done it, and immorality is what you feel bad about after you've done it." Does the ethic of existentialist choice reduce to that?

Tolerance

Existentialism is not a prescriptive behavior for the individual, nor is it a social doctrine. Tolerance, following choice, is a second keystone of existentialism. The existentialists are not dedicated to conversion; they only seek liberation of the individual by showing him his essential freedom and by eliminating the poison of moralism. The concept of Moral Law is inimical to existentialism, for that way lies coercion and the evil of dictatorism. "Indeed," writes May, "compulsive and rigid moralism arises in given persons precisely as the result of a lack of sense of being."[17] If, instead, man is aware of his elemental purposiveness, he instinctively acts in protest against the present and its values. He especially rejects the value of social conformity, which often is no more than a false mode of self-esteem. This emphatically does not mean, however, that existentialism is unlimited self-gratification (which is, in the final analysis, like moralism conducive to personal aggrandizement and tyranny). Existential philosophy is explicitly attentive to the freedom of others. Sartre writes:

. . . in wanting freedom, we discover that it depends entirely on the freedom of others, and that the freedom of others depends on ours. . . . Consequently, when, in all honesty, I've recognized that man is a being in whom existence precedes essence, that he is a free being who, in various cir-

cumstances, can only want his freedom, I have at the same time recognized that I can only want the freedom of others.[18]

Philosophically, an individual's freedom is limited by his condition as an object to others. Simone de Beauvoir states it thus: "To be free is not to have the power to do anything you like; it is to be able to surpass the given toward an open future; the existence of others as a freedom defines my situation and is even the condition of my own freedom."[19] Yet—and this is the critical paradox—recognition of the freedom of others does not in itself limit one's own freedom. The limitations are present in the given interpersonal condition; they are not imposed by others as prohibitions, and every man is free to realize himself through his experience.

The existentialist executive makes his own choices, and at the highest level this has been seen as the "terrible isolation" of the American presidency. But, in the process, various and contending interests are weighted. Gross writes that one of the great virtues of making choices is that, in the act, "a magic common denominator is somehow or other found that cuts across all the pro's and con's. . . . "[20] The usual means of resolving conflict through decisionmaking is not by relying on compromise alone, but by widening the agenda of attention to encompass a new basis for the solution. For this reason the generalist, better than the expert, will fill the role of proactive administrator, a role which requires a broad perspective toward life and a varied acquaintance with the total environment. Some assurance has been obtained from empirical studies of proactive people which show, according to Maslow, that they are "quite spontaneously identified with the human species, with other people," and that they are "especially concerned with duty, with responsibility," and "with a kind of intrinsic ethics or morality which they do not learn by precept. . . . These characteristics appear as a by-product of their personalities, as an epiphenomenon. It would appear that it is not necessary to teach these virtues."[21] If this is true, then Hemingway's definition of morality, though illogical because it assumes moral people, may be applicable to existentialist administrators.

In respect to organizations, the Romes tested their hypothesis that "authentic organizations" are more effective than others in system performance. "On the basis of evidence," they wrote, "it appears that our hypothesis . . . has received preliminary but vivid experimental corroboration."[22]

Every person within an organization is responsible for his own choices. Personal responsibility is, however, multidirectional. The nexus of personal responsibilities and behavior is the determinant of moral tone throughout the organization. It is a huge leap of understanding to think that federal executives may literally preserve the planet by discarding pseudo-attitudes and phony behavior—as a beginning, at least. The existential proactivert will readily believe it and act on it.

References and Notes

1. Rollo May, co-ed, *Existence: A New Dimension in Psychiatry and Psychology* (New York: Basic Books, Inc., Publishers, 1958), p. 88.

2. Jean-Paul Sartre, *Existentialism and Human Emotions* (New York: Philosophical Library, 1957), p. 15.

3. Niccolo Machiavelli, *The Prince* (Oxford: Oxford University Press, 1906), chapter VI.

4. *Trial of the Major War Criminals Before the International Military Tribunal* (Nuremberg: International Military Tribunal, 1947), volume 1, pp. 223–24.

5. Bertram M. Gross, *The Managing of Organizations* (New York: Free Press, Div. of The Macmillan Company, 1964), p. 764.

6. Sartre, op. cit., p. 77.

7. Seymour Melman, "Who Decides Technology?" *Columbia University Forum* (Winter 1968).

8. Sartre, op. cit., p. 34.

9. Gross, op. cit., p. 757.

10. Joseph C. Bailey, "Clues for Success in the President's Job," *Harvard Business Review* (1967).

11. Colin Wilson, *Introduction to the New Existentialism* (Boston: Houghton Mifflin Company, 1967), p. 153.

12. Beatrice and Sydney Rome, "Humanistic Research on Large Social Organizations," in James F. T. Bugental, ed., *Challenges of Humanistic Psychology* (New York: McGraw-Hill Book Company, 1967), p. 185.

13. Abraham Maslow, *Toward a Psychology of Being*, 2d ed. (New York: Van Nostrand Reinhold Company, 1968), p. 16.

14. Hubert Bonner, "The Proactive Personality," in James F. T. Bugental, op. cit., p. 64.

15. H. J. Blackham, *Six Existentialist Thinkers* (London: Routledge & Kegan Paul, Ltd., 1952), p. 155.

16. Gross, op. cit., p. 87.

17. May, op. cit., p. 45.

18. Sartre, op. cit., pp. 45–46.

19. Simone de Beauvoir, *The Ethics of Ambiguity* (New York: Philosophical Library, 1948), p. 91.

20. Gross, op. cit., p. 531.

21. Abraham Maslow, "Power Relationships and Personal Development," in A. Kornhauser, ed., *Problems of Power in American Democracy* (Detroit: Wayne State University Press, 1957).

22. Rome and Rome, op. cit., p. 192.

MANAGERS FOR TOMORROW: SURVIVAL AND GROWTH IN A CHANGING WORLD

Rohrer, Hibler & Replogle

Change is as inevitable as the morning sun, but neither survival nor growth can be predicted with certainty in managerial circles. Some managers will be required to run as fast as they are able just to keep even, just to hang on the edge of a fast-moving, ever-shifting economic order. Some—only a few, the wisest, most thoroughly trained and most skillful executives—will be able to outrun the parade, to anticipate impending changes and thereby make adaptations that lead to growth as well as survival.

What is likely to concern the manager for tomorrow? What will he become involved in? What will he strive for? Will his purposes have to become more precise? Must he articulate his values more clearly? Will his total commitment encompass the full range of responsibilities appropriate to his position?

How can we part the curtain veiling the future of this rapidly moving process? It is our privilege as we have indicated throughout this book to live closely with industrial leaders, which gives us an insight into their purposes, dreams, and goals. We have drawn upon these perceptions in formulating and in sharing with you a glimpse into the future. Our purpose in this chapter is to summarize some of the significant implications for managers who will be concerned with survival and growth.

Not everything changes. We believe that there are some basic continuing requirements necessary to the sustenance of corporate vitality and continuity in a rapidly changing world. There are some elements of corporate strength in our present economic order that continue to be fundamental. On the other hand, as we shall suggest, there are some human or psychological areas of interaction that will need better solutions tomorrow if progress is to be our objective.

Obviously, no one has sufficient wisdom to predict all of the problems that tomorrow's managers will face. But experience leads us to believe that many dimensions of the human equation in successful management may be even more important tomorrow than they are today. We know, for example, that the development of appropriate managerial behavior typically lags behind technical development. It is imperative for the future to find ways to reduce this lag by accelerating human development so that managers can cope successfully with the everyday problems involved in the various phases of human enterprise.

Vitalizing the American Way

Business is indisputably dependent on the society of which it is a part. It is unthinkable that those governments which hide behind political iron curtains would espouse free enterprise. Freedom cannot be applied to one segment of society and withheld from another.

We know, of course, that business is conducted in a social context determined by community, church, state, and nation, as well as by business itself. Business and society are not discrete entities in a community; they *are* the community. Our values, our philosophies, our way of life—these produce both social climate and business enterprise. Yet, every so often, political action and governmental responsiveness suggest that the supportive climate for free enterprise is diminishing. We seem to act as though government can closely control our social life while, at the same time, it supports a free industrial economy. We forget that free enterprise is dependent on free men and that restricted mobility, controlled thinking, and managed social orders are the paths to conformity, lassitude, and sterility.

We observe too many businessmen who speak with feeling about their inalienable rights, but who reveal little awareness of their concomitant responsibilities. They feel satsified to enjoy the benefits of a climate that permits free enterprise, without feeling obligated to feed new vitality into this climate. Businessmen, moreover, are prone to assume that their values are commonly shared by all and are, somehow, self-perpetuating. But, hopefully, today we see the beginnings of individual effort to preserve and propagate the values and processes on which our system of free enterprise rests.

This growing awareness among businessmen of their social responsibility is reflected in their generosity toward worthwhile causes. Corporate giving to service institutions has reached a level unknown in any society. The trouble is, the universality of such giving suggests that many corporate executives feel that they have fulfilled their community and civic responsibilities when the monies have been delivered. Indeed, in some instances, when the purpose behind such giving is clear, it is narrowly confined to patronage or public relations. Sponsorship (or underwriting) by industrial organizations is becoming more prevalent in many significant areas of community life. Corporate giving is likely to increase in our society, but as it does the purposes of such giving should be more sharply defined and the results more carefully evaluated. We should remind ourselves that neither today nor tomorrow can a major civic undertaking be consummated without the financial backing of business enterprise.

Money Versus Leadership

Money is freely given—as it should be—both by individuals and by corporations. But there is insufficient personal involvement in the activities and values of the recipients of this money. The role of the manager today seems to be essentially that of making funds available—through his company, his efforts in community drives, and the efforts of his organizations and associations. His rewards appear to rest in personal prestige or in a public relations function for his company. Unquestionably the business leader of tomorrow should do more. He should invest *himself as an individual* in the communities of which he is a part. He should enunciate, live, and teach the basic values on which our society—as well as our business community—is built. Thereby, through his swag and his sweat, he will provide the supportive climate in which free men can live—a climate in which a competitive business enterprise will continue to plow back into the community a significant portion of its profits.

Freedom to compete is not a one-way street. If a manager wants freedom, he must breed freedom. He must recognize also that those who are managed also want freedom. They want the freedom *to be, to belong, to become.* These freedoms seldom emerge in a business environment of controlled thought, controlled action, and controlled destiny. People who are *told,* who must *obey,* have little incentive, and they seldom become involved in a company's problems or in its objectives. They have lost their interest in responsibility. They

don't want to "stick out their necks." They make only safe decisions, often limited to "Yes, sir." They become masters at second-guessing. They get little done, but their record is clean. They avoid new ideas because they avoid criticism. Yet, new ideas and adventurous decisionmaking are the stuff on which free enterprise rests. Controlled thoughts produce few innovations.

Freedom to discover requires freedom to roam. Many managers today claim to want creative men around them; yet, many of them do not know what to do with creativity when they stumble upon it.

Psychological Climate

The values held by the manager with respect to the men he manages psychologically condition the climate in which both he and they work. If the manager thinks of his central function as that of coordinating people around a task, the people quickly conclude that the company is interested only in what it can get out of them. The individual's needs for growth, initiative, self-reliance, and self-actualization become submerged in a mass of performance data purporting to tell the manager how he is doing. Is it surprising that people who accept this concept of themselves on the job, and who "let others do the thinking," find it easy to accept this concept in all segments of their lives—in the community, at the polls, and in the state? Why should they vote for freedom of any kind when they have so little of it on the job where they spend most of their energy? Free enterprise is permanently wed to personal enterprise. If we desire one, we must cultivate both.

If the manager believes that he should be as strong as possible and that his subordinates should be as compliant as possible, he has set the stage for power over incompetence. When subordinates realize that their leader expects compliance (when what they had hoped for was investing some initiative), their drive is blunted and their productivity thwarted. Under wraps goes any stimulus for growth in personal competence necessary to meet new challenges and ever-increasing responsibility. Such subordinates give only what is demanded—nothing more.

What is it that we are so desirous of preserving in our way of life? Basically, our values: our regard for individuals and individual enterprise; our esteem for the democratic principles on which our country and its economy rest; our regard for freedom—individual, corporate, and political; and our belief in integrity and in those spiritual values that enable man to rise above his human urges in dealing with his fellow man and in ordering his personal destiny.

Inescapably, the manager of tomorrow will be required to assume, along with his responsibility for running a business, greater obligations for a way of living. In matters dealing with personal and business ethics, economic and political integrity, business and public concerns, he can no longer avoid letting his subordinates know *what he believes is right,* and he has the obligation to clarify his own thoughts before he attempts to influence others. When leadership is uncertain, the structure wobbles. Further, there can be no dynamic survival without a sense of shared values and common purposes between a company's management and its employees. Shared values are the rivets that hold our social structure together.

Let us look briefly at what one company president is doing to share and preserve the basic concepts and values of our free-enterprise system:

Frank became president of a company his father had spent a lifetime building. As he came to know the thinking and attitudes of his management group, he became alarmingly aware that these men did not really understand the implications of the economic trends, business practices, and political climate in which their company was having to conduct its business.

Frank began to probe the thinking of his people to verify his suspicions. When he asked their opinions, many freely admitted that they had no firm convictions. Some indicated they had not given those things a

thought. It was apparent to Frank that his key people were, in reality, woefully ignorant about our system of free enterprise.

He set to work to remedy this regrettable situation. He rented, for a weekend, a secluded guest ranch some eighty miles from the city. He obtained the services of two experts in the free-enterprise field to serve as a faculty nucleus in developing a basic frame of reference. He talked up his project for several weeks to develop an interest in his people.

When the time came, every key man was on hand. They spent the weekend listening to informative talks and engaging in provocative discussion. When it was over, nearly everyone was impressed by what he had learned. Everyone realized also, that his education was not complete. More sessions of this kind were needed.

Since then, Frank has provided, at company expense, a second weekend "school" for his management group. And the reaction he has received from them indicates that they are "waking up," both inside and outside the company. Frank plans to continue his educational project as long as enthusiasm lasts.

This is what can happen to a group of men under the leadership of a concerned president. They are discovering that they, as individuals, must do something to perpetuate and improve the way of life they enjoy and have taken for granted.

Developing Human Resources

We often forget that technological development of improved products and services does not in itself improve men. It is, in fact, the other way around. Industrial growth results, not primarily from increased capital, but from technological improvements brought about by significantly improved men. Thus, the fundamental task of managers in the future will be the same as it is now—to provide for the development of the company's human resources. This central task carries an unusual obligation because of one practice that is becoming widespread in industry. Top management positions are more frequently being filled by men with technical training and experience. On the surface, this practice makes sense because of the value of technical knowledge in making business judgments. But a deeper look reveals a potential source of trouble. For as a group, men with highly technical backgrounds know a great deal about "things," but they may know little about people. Their level of awareness and insight into human behavior in a work situation often lags behind their comprehension and skill in dealing with technical matters. The more rigorously they are trained as specialists, the greater the likelihood that they have had little time to learn even the fundamentals of human behavior. When they manage, they tend to rely upon their scientific methodology buttressed by policies and procedures. They are likely to assume that the human factors will fall into place as they move toward their objectives.

Is there a danger that technological specialization among top managers will move us toward a "push-button" concept of management? Technology is an inadequate substitute for an understanding of the human equation involved in organized effort. Since the effectiveness of any group results inevitably from the quality of the relationship between the leader and the led, we may be heading toward serious managerial ineffectiveness when leaders lean too heavily upon their specialized technology.

Greater Understanding

In fact, managers in the future will need a much greater understanding of human behavior in order to provide the type of leadership demanded to achieve the goals of both the business enterprise and the people who comprise it. As indicated in former chapters, men work most productively when the pattern of organized human relationships satisfies reasonably well some of the more basic needs of employees. Our experience indicates that four of these basic human needs are often ignored in superior-subordinate relationships:

1) *Work That Has Meaning.* Every human being has a need to engage in meaningful, productive activity. He is often expected by his superiors to be productive without being provided with any purpose or meaning. He is then denied the opportunity to know about the end results of his effort. This need is met when he feels that he has some voice in what he does.

2) *Respect That Is Mutual.* For two or more people to work together productively, there should be shared interest, mutual confidence, and trust. A person feels respected and worthwhile when he experiences an acceptance of himself and when he feels secure enough to express a differing or minority point of view without fear of reprisal. Respect between individuals includes recognition and acceptance of feeling as well as thoughts and ideas. Trust is highly important to productive joint effort because solving problems produces friction, tension, and sometimes conflict among highly involved people searching for a solution. When mutual respect and trust are evident, an atmosphere exists in which problems can be solved most expeditiously.

3) *Communication That "Levels."* Leveling involves being open and honest with others, especially in communicating feeling. For working relationships to be truly productive, human beings need to be open to each other, about each other, and to face reality together. People need and want to reduce the factors that keep them separated. They would rather be truthful than be false. They prefer to express freely their actual thoughts, feelings, and attitudes. Often feelings are withheld in business communications, especially negative interpersonal feelings, for fear of rejection or retaliation. When people can level with each other, they are able to listen, to recognize, and to understand each other's needs. They are able then to minimize misunderstandings which

create difficulties in exchanging ideas and solving problems.

4) *Learning That Is Continuous.* Every person has a deep need to learn something that develops his potential. A human being is always in process of becoming; he is never static. To be otherwise is to stagnate. A person needs to be challenged by opportunities to develop, to gain knowledge and skills, to be involved and committed.

These four basic human needs— *meaningful work, mutual respect, honest communication, continuous learning*—are the ingredients that stimulate men to improve in personal competence and meet the future with confidence. When these needs are suppressed, human resources dry up; men become only a fraction of what they could be. Meeting these needs determines the pattern of leadership required to achieve the goals of business enterprise. Skill in developing human competence requires as much insight as skill in developing technical competence. It is important to remember the fact that improved management stems only from improved men.

The executive of the future, in addition to understanding the individual and how to relate to him, will be required to understand organization as a process of human interaction, as well as a means for achieving a corporate goal. He will be expected to understand how to maintain the conditions under which men work most productively. Since knowledge is becoming vast and complex, multiplying year by year, no one man can know all he needs to know about any field. This fact requires more collaborative effort and teamwork. To lead this kind of human activity, executives will have to become practical behavioral scientists, rather than merely human-relations exponents.

Developing Men

Management means developing men. When we actually think about it, it is easy to see that, as in the past, the quality of human performance is the key to the future in a competitive enterprise. Profits will depend upon human alertness to opportunity and to problems, the efficient use of human capabilities, the keen assessment of risks and the willingness to take them. Profits will depend increasingly upon the human factors of a business.

Competition, both at home and abroad, is expected by every alert manager to increase in severity and challenge. Increased competition will put a premium on those human attributes that build success into a business: imagination, skill in communication, and effective leadership.

The manager of tomorrow in exercising leadership will be acutely aware of human interaction. He will tap both individual and group resources. He will set an example by striving for excellence in all things that matter. He will arrange conditions that release hidden potential, since undeveloped resources provide his main hope for surviving successfully.

Preparing for Change

We are certain of one more thing in life— change. And change calls for innovation. The willingness to innovate has been the taproot of free enterprise. As business conditions change, perhaps drastically, companies must rely upon human inquiry and perception for innovation. These behavioral changes will require flexibility of thinking, as well as an acute awareness of the objectives sought. Changes affecting business enterprise may well be so dynamic and continuous that managers will have to rely upon the processes of problem solving instead of rigid habit patterns that often have been their guide to action.

Today's shortage of forward-looking managers may well increase. Companies will be required to look harder to find these capable men.

A high premium will be placed on the manager who develops and uses human resources in management practices. The manager who demonstrates that he can assess, develop, and use the abilities of people with a minimum of waste will be in great demand.

The men who manage will be expected to devote more working time to developing the company's next generation of managers. This task is the next imperative direction in management.

Management Problems

Corporate management will face increased psychological problems in many administrative areas. For one thing, rapid technological change will increase the pressure for innovation in order to stay ahead of obsolescence. Managing the processes of innovation, and the human reactions that will be derived from them, will require increased insight and skill to cut down lag time in getting desirable change established. Making sound decisions involving great risk will place managers under increased intellectual and emotional strain. Managers for tomorrow will be required to develop new insights to cope constructively with conflict. For example, a reconceptualization of labor-management negotiations may reduce conflict by getting both sides off the hook of a win-lose approach. Developing business statesmanship adequate to cope successfully with government encroachment and control will require levels of thinking and patterns of behavior not yet applied by top management.

There will be increased psychological stress arising from organizational growth in size and complexity. More and more mergers of companies will provide considerable threat to the employees involved. The use of more complex technological equipment will require better-trained men. Larger corporate organizations will create more complex lines of communication, thereby increasing the importance of effective communication. The individual employee will tend to feel smaller, less important, more isolated from the mainstream of company life. Keeping such an employee stimulated to high quality productivity will require a level of insight into human behavior and into the sources of work satisfaction that

management heretofore has not generally demonstrated.

In the past, management has been concerned with how people could be organized, controlled, and directed to achieve high production, rather than how to release human potential to achieve high production. Somehow people have been expected to do what they "ought to" in achieving company goals with little understanding of the thinking behind the established objective. Such expectations will be unrealistic. The human dimensions of corporate management will be more important in the years ahead if American business continues to prosper.

Probably the basic concept that runs through all these problems, and others like them, is that of change or innovation for the better. It is a relatively simple act to force change by management edict; it is a relatively complex process to obtain human acceptance and support for innovation. Management, in general, has insufficient understanding of the process of change since innovation usually amounts to changes in human behavior. These changes do not come about easily even when human behavior is taken into consideration in planning for change. Behavioral science has much to contribute to management at this point. Hence, we believe that use must be made of these contributions in the future.

President of the Future

How will a rapidly changing world affect the corporate president of tomorrow? What will be some of the significant changes in his function? What personal qualities of the man will move into greater prominence?

The president will probably be required to be a generalist, not a specialist, since management know-how is distinct from technical and specialized knowledge. To be an effective generalist, the president must acquire the behavioral insights and leadership skills needed to make more productive use of all kinds of specialists. He will keep abreast of the broad picture and share his observations with his specialists to keep them focused on the big objectives. They, in turn, abreast of their specialized fields, will share with the president their resources in accomplishing the company's objectives.

The chief executive will have to get more done in less time. There is only one way he can do this successfully. He will strive to become less involved in the operational end of his company and more concerned with the human dimensions of corporate effort. He will seek to become aware of the conditions necessary for men to do outstanding work and to specialize in the skills needed to bring these conditions into being.

The president will assume a broader obligation in using his status and authority. He is already accepting broader obligations to the community and the state in which he lives and to the industry of which he is a part. Too frequently in the past he has been reluctant to become involved in partisan issues involving basic principles in which he believes. He has chosen to remain aloof. He is now finding he can no longer afford this position. It is also becoming clearer to him that the future of the ideology and practices of our free-enterprise system lies in his hands and not in the public educational system of our country. As president of a successful company, he is the best authority in the country on free enterprise. He must therefore become more articulate and speak out to a wider audience than company employees. With his heritage of free enterprise, he has an obligation to preserve its best features by teaching them to the next generation.

In general, the president of tomorrow will be a person with higher potential who can develop faster than did his predecessors. The demands made upon the president as his role becomes more clearly understood will indicate the kind of person he must be. He will need to be confident and flexible, a person who can adapt to changing tides with relative ease. In addition to the basic human values, he will have to be able to develop a set of "tentatives" to guide his day-to-day decisions, rather than rely on a fixed set of "tenets."

Our experience with presidents who rise to new demands, build strong companies, and get things done, suggests that they have these personal qualities in common:

1) They exhibit the *forcefulness* of persons who have well-integrated, *powerful convictions.* They have an anchor point that keeps them stable, even calm, in the midst of stress and storm. They have an inner compass that points the way. They recognize the difference between wheat and chaff, the significant and the insignificant.

2) They have *a humility that is eloquent.* This deep core of strength derived from being able to search out reality and to face it lends an ongoingness to these men. Their people believe in them and follow them with trust and confidence. They are men who face truth and facts and use these as a standard for their action.

3) They possess *the security of resourcefulness.* They never seem to fear or become overwhelmed by what the future may present to them. They have a built-in competence. While they may not have an answer to a problem at a given moment, it does not occur to them that one will not be forthcoming. They specialize in asking good questions of their management team rather than becoming preoccupied with giving good answers. They are flexible and adapt themselves to the bumps in the road.

4) They possess the strength and *power of a great faith in people.* These men trust other people in spite of occasional disappointments. They have an understanding and acceptance of people who are different from them—in ideas as well as personality. They build a team of powerful leaders because they stake their faith in them, and they do not abandon them when they are down. The ability to place great faith in a group of people creates great power in that group. This ability makes them conscious of the fact that one of the greatest satisfactions, the

greatest fun, is working with the right group in a joint effort.

Beyond Survival

Those presidents who succeed in leading their companies beyond survival into real growth in the changing world will be characterized by the spirit of having fun while grappling with a tremendous challenge. Truly to succeed, a president must have fun!

So we recommend these convictions and practices:

1) Invest a great amount of your time in *a few good men.* There is great wisdom in this practice. In order to make things happen, you have to bet heavily on a few people. Live and think with them.

2) Invite these few good people with you on *a rugged adventure.* Dream with them. Build a vision with them. Let them see how tough this adventure is going to be. Help them understand that the journey may get a lot rougher before it gets better.

3) Weld this small group of good men into *a strong team.* Integrate them around difficult, firm, clear-cut goals. Help each person find his place of greatest contribution. The way of the delegator is selfless. Derive your satisfaction from choosing, coaching, and delegating.

4) *Challenge* them to master difficult situations. Focus on the things that make each man reach for something that exceeds his grasp.

5) Require *intellectual honesty.* Begin with yourself; practice it alone and with your top team. Settle for nothing else from your group. Permit no one, including yourself, to become involved in duplicity. To win, men must face reality as it is, not as they wish it to be—and they must face it on a sound ethical basis.

These then are the convictions and practices out of which winners are forged. We recommend them to you as you face the challenge of the future.

Chapter 14 Organization Research and Policy Development

SOCIAL SCIENCE AND SOCIAL POLICY

Scott Greer

Social science is, in a profound sense, the business of creating social fact. That fact may be crude and erroneous but it is finally a necessity for any public policy; since it is a basis for important policy decisions, it is a critical input into human destiny. William the Conqueror relied upon that census reported in the Domesday Book for data useful in exploiting his new possession; the United States relies upon the estimates and interpretation of Kremlinologists, experts on Russia, in making major foreign policy decisions. It does no good to protest that these facts are not solid; they have solid consequences in the destiny of nations.

To be sure, we do not often consider the matter in this light. Our everyday discourse assumes a simple "finding of facts," which lie out there in the world. Facts are those assumed existential realities of stability and change underlying the belief that a problem exists as well as that effort to intervene in the flow of things we term policy. Thus social action is always dependent upon such regularities. Since this is the case, an early contribution of social science to policy lies in introducing "data quality control" to improve the accuracy of social fact. If a decision to intervene in a neighbor's revolution depends upon whether it is defined as a civil war or an invasion by enemy forces, no amount of argument can substitute for accurate data. (Assuming, of course, that one has an adequate definition of civil war versus invasion.)

Much of what is taken for social fact is, when measured by the standards dis-

cussed earlier, weak indeed. Take the case for marijuana control. It rests upon two assumptions: that marijuana is a dangerous, addictive drug, driving people mad; and that the way to prevent the use of drugs is to outlaw them. Both are patently false; both were built into a policy of control.

Marijuana is made from Indian hemp, a crop grown commercially in this country for many decades. In the years before it was outlawed, laborers in the harvest fields of Indiana smoked it as they gathered the crop; to the Mexican-Americans of the Southwest, it was a staple of cheap, mildly euphoric parties. (It is, when legal, much cheaper than alcohol; its suppression may be one more aspect of the class war over vice. In this war the issue is: Whose vice is virtuous?) But a propaganda campaign linking ethnicity, horror at hallucinations, and exaggerated stories of dementia and violence resulted in its suppression. The penalties for selling, owning, and smoking the hemp were made very drastic indeed.

There were a number of predictable results. First, users of marijuana who had been law-abiding citizens were now "vicious criminals." Such was the social fact created. (One creates law-breakers by making a law.) Second, by outlawing the drug the authorities created a market quickly entered by those specialists in illegal products, the organized criminals. This market, protected by legislation, resulted in much higher prices; what had been very cheap became expensive. Third, the organizations selling marijuana

421

often did not want a buyer's use to stop there; marijuana is not addictive, so it cannot develop lifetime consumers who will pay any price for the commodity. Consequently, some peddlers concentrated on introducing novices to the heavy narcotics that are addictive. Outlawing marijuana placed some of those who used it in a position to interact with the international underworld of narcotics traffic.

Thus the result of the policy to suppress marijuana was the exact opposite of its aims. New customers were introduced to addictive drugs, and drug addiction increased thereby. Whatever one thinks of drug addiction (and judgments vary immensely over time and cultures), the point is that social policies should not produce results exactly opposite from the stated goal. Hospitals should not spread disease; drug control policies should not spread addiction. With defective social fact we cannot have a meaningful debate of public policy, for we all inhabit the same (hallucinatory) symbolic system.

One can see such corrupt social fact as reflecting merely conspiracy on the part of the makers of law. It is sometimes the case, for social facts are weapons and are used as such. More often, however, it reflects an unthinking acceptance of the cliché at hand—and that cliché is usually out of the conventions and moralities of earlier societies where it may even have served as adequate. (One accompaniment of the "disenchantment of the world" is an increasingly higher standard for fact—not a trivial gain.)

Thus older policies with respect to poverty in the United States reflected the ethos of the nineteenth century small farmer and shopkeeper. Since for such folk all had opportunity, poverty was an indication of incompetence and/or immorality. This secular version of the doctrine of predestination only left room for the exercise of the Christian charity complex on the part of the state. With new circumstances, however, as the poor became increasingly unprofitable for the economy as a whole, the "facts" behind poverty were examined in a more empirical way. The resulting treatment of the problem saw poverty as a result of social learning (and not learning), of weakness in the relationship between family and economy, of the position of the aged and the ethnic in American society. Defined in such commonplace concepts of social science, the problem became amenable to action in the same terms.

But the creation of an improved set of facts which are effective in the origin and design of social policy is not an easy matter. To begin with, there are enormous hiatuses in our social science theory, and the propositions we can derive from it are often vague and contingent. Lloyd Rodwin has discussed the situation of the British planners in these terms:

The fact is that the town planners' intellectual lines have been overextended: [T]heir base needs strengthening; their supplies are limited; they are operating in unknown terrain; and their key personnel are not well enough equipped for many of the problems that lie ahead.

Under such circumstances almost any application of social science is apt to be in some degree "premature," and there is a real danger that it will be oversold. Officials may expect a kind of efficacy impossible without long and careful experimentation.

Two directives seem to follow from this situation. First, it is necessary that more energies be committed to developing and testing basic theories of social science—those powerful generalizations that, once discovered, illuminate a wide range of situations. And, equally important, it is necessary for the social scientist to speak the truth about the state of the art when commenting on policy issues. To do so, he must abnegate the mantle of professional charisma and adopt the role of the craftsman of social fact; this is where his real authority lies. In the process he may be able to educate other social actors to the differences between normative and empirical theory, as well as the variable truth value of the latter. In short, his effectiveness finally depends upon the intellectual comprehension of social science among his audience or clients.

For his social facts are potentially dangerous. He may add to confusion, as his tentative formulations are turned into dogmas. Thus today there is an ongoing and complex debate over the nature of community politics in the United States; yet battle lines are often drawn between "the movement" and an assumed "community power structure" that may be quite imaginary. (In the process one *may* create such a structure.) In a similar fashion, our urban policy is couched in terms of an outgrown metaphor that compares cities to trees, sees neighborhoods as "blighted," and chronicles population change in neighborhoods as "invasion and succession" of different species. The generalizations of the social scientist have a way of turning into social fact some decades after they have been abandoned by the discipline.

Even when theories and tools are adequate, social science may be ignored in favor of the conventional wisdom. Thus the 1964 Republican candidate for the American Presidency relied upon an "invisible conservative majority" that had been rejecting all previous candidates as too liberal. Any competent political scientist could have demonstrated that he was in error; he was not convinced until his campaign was dead. Men of affairs prefer to rely on folk thought and the formulations they learned long ago in the universities of another epoch; as Keynes noted, the "practical" politician is usually obeying the words of some defunct economist. They are not alone in this.

There is a spurious assumption of authority in the conventional wisdom. After all, it probably came from unimpeachable sources, and much of our acceptance of theory is based wholly on authority. And in a simpler society where change moves slowly, folk thought may have been enough for the individual to survive and prosper. Our case is different, and for most of our catastrophic issues there are few precedents in the past. Thus willynilly the practical men must ask the social scientists for answers, not because they have them but because somebody has to formulate the situation. Premature application of social science is an inevitable result of cultural complexity and change. At an extreme, the social scientist may be little more than an "uncertainty absorber"—a planner who designs zoning ordinances because somebody must do it, an administrative analyst who designs a school district in a given manner because it must be designed in some fashion.

However rational and specific a policy may be, however congruent with dependable social science, it must still be instituted through a political process of some sort. In that process there is typically confusion between what is desirable and what is possible, the aims of a program and the weight of political power. In the process of bargaining off votes, critical parts of an integrated plan may be distorted or omitted, leaving the resulting "package" an unworkable monstrosity. Thus urban renewal, as a program to improve housing, may result in the destruction of hundreds of thousands of dwellings in "slums," but without a new supply of "standard" houses at low cost to replace them, have the unintended effect of raising the price and lowering the quality of housing for the poor. Without new public housing, urban renewal fails, but the goal of public housing is politically unpopular, the slum clearance program popular, and the result is again 180 degrees away from the goal. We destroy the housing of the poor.

Once a program has been accepted politically, it still remains only legitimated aspiration until it is organized in the actions of men. Here again, the administrative structure may distort and delete important parts of a whole. Based as it is upon precedent, protocol, antiquated theory, and political adroitness, administration may have the effect of sabotaging the most rational programs. If the theory behind the policy is not understood and accepted by those who implement it, they may unwittingly make nonsense of policy; the ward attendants at the psychiatric hospital, in constant attendance on the patients, may effectively define the purpose of the hospital. No matter what psychiatric theories the therapists use, the attendants create the atmosphere and fact of a prison. (Their theories about the causation of mental illness may be the folk notions of possession by demons or moral turpitude, their treatment repression and punishment.)

We tend to exaggerate greatly the rationality of the society and thus our ability to make rational policy. For looking at the whole through time, it is clear that much of the collective results of decisions amounts to inadvertency, with accident, ignorance, and mistake—the real demiurges of our histories. Yet underlying our behavior there is obviously a massive order, as in our thoughts and in various degrees in our actions. A continental power grid, space travel, and catastrophic wars require and produce systems for ordering the behavior of men, materials, and messages in fantastic scope and precision.

But it is a partial order. Within a given segment of society there may be a precise fitting of means to ends and highly predictable operations over time; yet the rationality of scattered parts does not mean a comprehensive order for the whole. Indeed we may purchase a small order at the price of a greater disorder. Labor unions and management may resolve their conflicts at the price of an unrepresented third party—another firm, another union, consumers of their joint product. To be sure, one can simply describe the society as it exists and call it ordered, but this is not a rationalized order. It is more aptly described as a symbiosis among organizations, with various systems competing, conflicting, flourishing, and dissolving.

The social order is partial for a more profound reason. As we have noted earlier, any given order, rationalized or not, applies only to aspects of the individual; other aspects may be ordered by other norms and belief systems, or they may be practically autonomous with respect to society. Even if we would, we could not participate in an order comparable to that of the social insects; the process of symbolization, the origin of our rationality, is also the origin of our irrational and arational action. Scattered individuals are able to be rational about some aspects of their experience, but rationality, interpreted strictly as a self-conscious fitting of means to ends, is probably more rare than is generally believed.

But social science may easily drift into a view of man that assumes him to be much more socially determined in his behavior than is the case. Harsh walls of custom, contract, dominance, and law certainly constrain much of our behavior; but these limits are not impermeable, and there is always some slippage in the system of control. If much of our life is spent in what Santayana called "normal madness," unthinking conformity to the social surface of things, some is still spent in questioning limits and devising surfaces more conducive to what we hope for.

The Uses of Social Science

What, then, can social science do for social policy? We have already noted that it can improve social fact—it can help us to achieve whatever ends we have stated in general terms, in the context of specific empirical situations. This endeavor is certainly worth doing, but it is limited; it treats social science as simply instrumental, the social scientist as a "gun for hire." This aim is a far cry from the great ideologists who promulgated a view of history and the future, a place for the individual in a cosmos.

And indeed we can go further. Social scientists have no mandate to prescribe the ends of a society, but they can certainly evaluate those ends against the means at hand. They can demonstrate a range of truth values for policy from the impossible to the likely success. And in the process they can demonstrate the costs of the policy. For though one may be quite unable to put values to such di-

mensions as esthetic satisfaction and social justice, it is frequently possible to
"solve for" these values by calibrating
what they would cost in terms of material
sacrifice.

They can also indicate kinds of cost
that may have escaped the eye of the
policymaker. By choosing given means to
an end, we are always incurring two sorts
of cost. First, we are incurring "opportunity costs," the things we foreclose by
choosing a given route to the goal. What
have we lost when we adopt rote learning
as the best means of inculcating mathematics in young children? Probably the
opportunity to interest them in the operations they have memorized. Second, when
we choose a means to an end, we are incurring costs in the side effects, created
like wakes from the sides of a boat. Thus
the use of punishment in teaching children
(whether in school or at home) has the
effect of creating hostility directed against
the teacher; he then has two problems,
and handling hostility may tax his capacity more than the job of instruction.

In short, cost-accounting social policy
in a more inclusive and systematic way
requires a broad frame of reference, one
that sets the policy problem in a complex
social context. This requirement means
the social scientist should be able to aid
policy formation by using his particular
vision to indicate alternative courses of
action; his training should result in a point
of view free from the intellectual ruts of
the specialist at politics, just as his base
in another discipline (and usually, organization) frees him from the political
pressure that, often unconsciously, makes
certain ideas taboo. In short, social scientists, used to a complex view of an interacting society and to treating the given
regularities as at least intellectually problematic, may be fertile sources of innovation. They know that it can be done differently, for it has been elsewhere.

The group of social scientists who proposed the guaranteed annual income is a
case in point. They demonstrated how little it would cost to see that all citizens
had adequate money for subsistence—

trivial in terms of the total income of the
United States. In reaching the conclusion
that this scheme would work, however,
they assumed an intellectual tradition that
included the knowledge of societies in
which work is not so separated from play
as in our puritan citadel—societies such
as the Trobriand Islands, where men
worked without the continual pressure of
the threat and the bribe. And at a less
esoteric level, they were aware of modern
large-scale societies, such as Norway,
where the creation of security for all had
not caused an attrition of industriousness.

My concern is not to argue for such a
policy but to indicate the way social scientists can bring new ideas into a political
arena. Whether a policy is made the law
of the land is, however, beyond the competence of political scientist or economist
to decide. Policymaking is *choice* and
must remain a choice. Requiring normative theory as well as empirical theory, it
rests finally upon the rank order of values, which can and does vary immensely
among the citizenry and their representatives. Thus there is no scientific way to
determine whether you want a society to
support those who are inept and unproductive. Many Americans probably
think such a policy immoral, a threat to
the very nature of morality. What is the
value of such beliefs? That can only be
settled through the political process, for
there is no means of reaching universal
agreement on this kind of fact. Thus politics is absolutely inescapable; in whatever
guise, it is the way that we resolve our
normative differences.

Social science can, however, improve
the level of discourse. By showing the implicit assumptions underlying the arguments, it is often possible to clarify the
nature of differences—sometimes they
disappear. Intellectual somnambulism is a
dangerous thing for governments that increasingly hold the very existence of the
world in their hands. One cannot decide
by scientific means what is right, but he
can, frequently, show implications and
significances that allow the policy to be
better related to reality. It has been said

that the British acquired an empire in a fit of absentmindedness—a degrading way to make policy.

Finally, a brief for policy as a resource for social science. We have noted earlier that social policy may approximate the classical experiment if we know what the situation is before action, what the action signifies in a theoretical frame of reference, and what the consequences are. Such research allows us to use the society as a laboratory without confusing normative and empirical thought. But we may go further; if research were systematically built into all action programs, it would be possible continually to adjust both the procedures of the action agency and the theories of the social scientist. These latter usually include a time element; continuous monitoring and evaluation of such radical innovations as urban renewal and the efforts to eliminate poverty should allow an increasing specification of theories, increasing understanding of processes, and, at the same time, a closer fit between means and end, action and goal.

SOCIETAL FEEDBACK

Raymond A. Bauer

Feedback and Planning

Planning demands a reasonably long time perspective. Without that time perspective, there is no point to planning. Similarly, planning demands that the planner have reasonable confidence in his ability to control his own fate or, at least, that planning and relatively deliberate control will improve his prospects enough to be worth the cost. Finally, planning demands that one have the resources to bring to bear to implement one's plans. These necessary conditions are met in modern American society, despite such notable failures or stalemates as the Vietnam war and the race problem.

Stimulants to planning and control, beyond the necessary conditions cited, are the rapidity of change and the increasing interrelatedness of our society. Perhaps the most concrete manifestation of the pressure for planning and control arising from the interrelatedness of our society is pollution of various forms. What one man does to the air, water, and sound in his environment affects other men, and the volume of such effects has risen to the point where they can no longer be ignored.

But the nature of planning and control has also changed. For decades, the Soviet Union was the established model of a planned and controlled society. What distinguished the Soviet model was the assumption that a blueprint for a desired future state could be drawn up, together with the necessary steps to the achievement of that state, and that one could then proceed literally to "carry out the plan" in full and reach that state. The Soviet experiment demonstrated that a limited amount of social action can be carried out according to this model but that it is a costly way of proceeding. All social action produces unintended consequences, some of which may be regarded as incidental cost, some of which may be unexpected benefits, and others of which represent substantial inversions of the original purpose. To the extent that one can avoid adverse unintended consequences, one operates more efficiently.

A modern version of planning and control places a much higher premium on early detection of the consequences of one's actions, with a consequent adjustment of one's plan. Detection of these consequences may cause one to take different steps toward the goal and to alter that goal or goals. To a large extent, this view of planning and control is influenced by the cybernetic model of electrical engineering, which stresses the importance of feedback to correct errors resulting from one's actions. While the cybernetic model has undoubtedly had a strong impact on our view of planning and control, it does not per se provide for the reassessment of one's goals—namely, for the correction of one's course toward an established goal. Probably the most profound contribution of cybernetics to our thinking is the establishment of error as a systematic inevitable feature of all action.

The notion of adjustment of goals comes from an approach to planning and control that stresses the plurality of future possible states and consequences of one's actions. Probably the best known proponent of this view is Bertrand de Jouvenel, director of the French *Futuribles* project.[1] The version presented here is a more familiar one, which was developed in connection with our book *Social Indicators*.[2] To my knowledge it may differ from that of de Jouvenel only in some slight preferences in terminology.

The term "prediction," commonly associated with planning, is misleading in that it connotes the identification of a single most probable state of affairs and an implication that the probability of this state of affairs may approach certainty. While it may be argued that a "prediction" need not and should not be treated as though it were made with certainty, in practice it seems that concentration on a single most probable future state deflects proper attention away from alternate possible states. For planning purposes, it is preferable to employ the concept of "anticipation" (de Jouvenel uses "conjecture"). One uses whatever information and stimulants to one's imagination that are available to anticipate that range of future states of reasonable possibility and importance that might flow from one's ac-

tions. (De Jouvenel calls these "conjectured" future states *futuribles*.) One then decides which of these future states one wants to make most probable. (A highly desirable state may appear difficult to attain and therefore a less desired state may be aimed at.) Having chosen such a target future state, one then devises and inaugurates a course of action aimed at increasing the probability of its occurrence. Having inaugurated that course of action, one takes readings of the consequences of those actions, reassessing the probable future states and the probability of their being attained and making the adjustments of action and goals referred to above.

Clearly, in this version of how one should plan and act, a high premium is placed on accurate and rapid information about the existing state of the system on which one is acting and on one's ability to relate those states of the system to actions already completed. It could be contended both that no model of planning and control ever devalued information and that the model, as sketched, is one which is seldom if ever used. To the extent that this model is approximated, feedback becomes a more crucial element.

Several authors state that the aim of control is to assure that the results of operations conform as closely as possible to plans. . . . To the extent that middle management can make decisions that are better than those implied in the plans, top management wishes to do so. . . . Since no one can foretell that future precisely—that is, since people are not clairvoyant—it follows that in some respects actual events will differ from the assumed events that the plans are designed to meet. . . . Therefore top management does not necessarily want operations to conform to plans. . . . Furthermore, since people are not omniscient, their plans do not necessarily show the best course of action; they merely show what was thought of as best when the plan was made.[3]

Views such as these are obviously, philosophically and practically, radically at variance with early stereotyped notions such as a Five-Year Plan which it was expected would be adhered to rigidly and which was changed only grudgingly. Error is considered inherent in planning and action; change of plan and action is a central part of the process; and, of course, feedback is vital.

Formal Information Systems

In recent years, "information systems" have come into considerable vogue as a management tool in business. But, in practice, at the time this is being written, the number of sophisticated information systems in operation is apparently very small. Despite this, the logic of their use is so persuasive that this use is bound to spread. An information system is no more than a formal set of procedures for gathering, storing, retrieving, and reporting data relevant to the decisions and actions that must be taken in an organization. In their prototypic fashion, information systems may actually take over some of the decisions and actions ordinarily done by people, by feeding the relevant data directly into a machine or other mechanism for action. Thus, sales or shipping records may be fed into an inventory system which will automatically order additional production to fill the inventory or order shipments to retail outlets to replace items which have been sold.

Such systems for the control of routine operations have been in existence for more than a decade. They have applied, however, *only* to such situations in which decisions and actions can be routinized and generally where optimum courses of action can be calculated. Of more interest to us, and of more recent origins, are information systems which are designed to serve those situations in which human judgment is essential. This latter class of situations is a large one. And while many of the decisions and actions in which

human judgment is presently involved may become routinized in the future, there will always be some irreducible number of situations for which this is neither possible nor desirable. These are situations in which the decision is unstructured, which is to say that the problem with which one is confronted demands the invention of new courses of action and/or demands tradeoffs of values. A structured decision is one in which, for all practical purposes, the full range of actions is known; the consequences of the actions are known with substantial accuracy; and there is agreement on the value to be maximized.

Quite obviously, there are very few important issues in the public arena which involved structured decisions of this sort. At a minimum, there is no clear agreement on the weight to put on the various values involved or on whose interests are to be preferred over others, and usually there is the need for the invention of some unique course of action that will reconcile a sufficient coalition of interests. The logic of what a formal information system does for a person in such a situation is not new. It is substantially what the military have done for centuries in presenting generals with up-to-date position statements, displaying, in as appropriate a fashion as possible, information on his own and his enemy's situation. Furthermore, war games and simulated war games, such as chess, gave him a basis for anticipating the probable consequences of the various courses of action open to him.

What a modern computer-based information system does is to make available more information, more rapidly, and in many forms. In its most developed form it includes (1) ongoing data series such as the "social indicators" . . . ; (2) stored data that an executive may want to use, for example, the demographic characteristics of the population a hospital serves, past records of illness in various segments of the population, and the results of experiments which have been carried out; and (3) a simulation model of the system on which the executive wishes to act. This model might, for example, be a model of the market for toothpaste, which will tell him the probable reactions of consumers and of competitors if he does something such as change the price of his product or the amount of his advertising.

We have, of course, precedents for such models in the public arena. The economic models used for control of the economy in the past two decades actually predated the computer-based simulation models used in business. The economists have, of course, updated their own models as the state of the art advanced.

Granting that there are earlier precedents or approximations for each of its components, the image of a modern, sophisticated information system *suggests* the possibility of planning and control of a sort that would have been impossible in the past. I have not mentioned yet, for example, the notion of a "real time" system which, for practical purposes, presents a man with a picture of the state of the world in which he is interested, with no time lag. Thus, sales of a company's products from wholesale houses, or potentially even from retail outlets, can be recorded directly in a computer as they are made so that a sales manager could know within a matter of minutes the precise state of sales of his product on a company-wide basis, by region, by city, or in any combination he chose. He could also know the state of his own organization, if he wanted to: the rate of production of various products, cash available, or, if he cares, the health of the labor force or the existence of unusual skills. Whether this is a good thing or not can be discussed separately.

The image referred to above is, then, that of a man with virtually instantaneous feedback of many of the consequences of his actions or, at least, instantaneous feedback of those things which he has chosen to measure. (There will be an organizational lag between his own actions and the impact of the organization's ac-

tions on the environment; for example, it may take many months for a program of inoculation to be organized and executed, and to have its effect on incidence of a disease.) In any event, he has a very up-to-date and complete picture of the world in which he operates and of the state of his own organization. Furthermore, his ability to anticipate the consequences of his possible future actions is improved by trial runs on a simulation model.

An information system of this sort is the logical tool for the type of planning and control which is described above. It in no way changes the rationale. The use of a simulation model to make trial runs is no more than a refinement of the process of "anticipation," but does not reduce the need for feedback. Since simulation models are based on historical data and are, of necessity, simplifications of the real world, they can only reduce, but never eliminate, the errors which will inevitably result from any course of action.

Systems of this sort have, of course, their own difficulties. For example, a person whose feedback system is "perfect" may react too rapidly to changes in reactions to his actions and cause great damage. The tendency of executives to overreact to information is a real and serious one. Also simulation models must, of necessity, make assumptions to bridge our gaps in information and in our understanding of the state of the world, and some of these assumptions turn out to produce seriously erroneous answers at times. And, of course, the information system does not tell one what courses of action are conceivable. Man himself must conceive them.[4]

Whatever its limitations, a formal, computer-based information system is a good prototype of the sort of system one might want for planning and control. It is also a good point of departure for consideration of the limitations of a societal informational system for planning and control in the public arena.

We may now move from this idealized world to the real one.

Limitations of Formal Information Systems

This section is devoted, in part, to an explication of the inherent limitations of formal information systems and, in part, to the extent to which a societal information system cannot, at this point in time, achieve the degree of sophistication that seems possible for the informational systems of single-purpose institutions such as the military, health systems, or business firms.

The primary limitation of any information system is that it is finite. But on the other hand, if it were not finite, it would be impossible to use, even if cost and effort were no consideration. The goodness of an information system is dependent on the extent to which it is efficient in serving the informational needs of specifiable individuals in an organization. Ordinarily, the development of an effective information system begins with an analysis of the decisions made by various persons in the organization, their preferences in the use of information, and the like. The purpose of this analysis is, in the first instance, to make sure that these individuals will get the information they need and want; but, in the second instance and equally important, that they will not get information that they do not need or want. The need to sort out unrequired information not only produces inefficiency but may even have the worse result of tempting a person to meddle in organizational affairs which are "none of his business." For example, the chief executive of a business firm who gets daily reports on sales in specific cities may begin interfering in tactical maneuvers that are properly the affair of the regional marketing director.

We may begin to differentiate a societal information system from that designed to serve a single institution by noting the multiplicity of users of the societal system. Not only must a vastly larger number of *actors* be served, but a societal system must also serve as a vast array of *evaluators:* the public, the Congress, the press, and future historians, for example.

It must be aimed at comparability over a very long time span. Hence, its data series cannot be closely designed to serve one clientele.

The most efficient information systems must, of course, contain some surplus information. If the flow of information to a man were restricted to only that which he was *certain* to need, it would inevitably miss information which probably would be useful to him. The amount of potentially surplus information to include is a difficult matter to decide, but the proper answer lies somewhere between "everything" and the certainly useful. This decision obviously can be made more sensibly for repetitive types of problems. The immediate corollary of this is that formal information systems are less useful for broad strategic problems than for routine ones.

Strategic or policy decisions are, by definition, responses to major opportunities or threats which could not entirely be anticipated. The first sign that a major threat or opportunity exists *may* manifest itself in some sharp discontinuity in regular data gathered for routine purposes, or in some shift in the relationship of two or more data series. One of the standard features of formal systems is "exception-reporting," which notifies the relevant person that some one indicator has deviated beyond some pre-established limit. Generally speaking, however, such changes of pattern will indicate merely that "something is happening" and thereby serve as a stimulus to search for pertinent data. It is just as likely that the signal for a strategic or policy decision will come from some source entirely outside the formal information system—a newspaper story, a conversation with an informed person, or some other. This matter of how strategic information is sought out will be dealt with in more detail later. At this point, it should be established that formal information systems are, by their nature, better suited to servicing relatively narrow repetitive problems than broad, unique ones. They can indeed be very valuable for servicing broad, unique policy problems, but such problems demand additional activities which will be discussed below.

We can get additional perspective on the limitations of a societal information system if we review the broad functions for which one would expect an information system to be useful. (Note that the word "serve" was not used. This was to avoid the implication that an information system could, even under ideal circumstances, be expected to do the entire job.) These broad functions are: (1) detection of the state of affairs; (2) evaluation; (3) diagnosis; and (4) guide to action.

Social indicators, like any other series of trend data, are per se means for detecting the state of affairs.

For some matters, the job of evaluation may be virtually automatic in that there is a strong consensus that some states of affairs (for example, health) are "good," and others are "bad" (for example, sickness). However, in the majority of instances, evaluation depends on the system model one holds, whether that model be explicit or implicit. For example, a setback in educational opportunity for Negroes might be viewed favorably if one thought that revelation of the situation would create such a feeling of indignation that it would create unprecedented support for increasing opportunities for Negroes. If the reader thinks that this type of reasoning is far-fetched, it rests on logically the same type of process as that behind the frequently used argument that the pace of Negro progress should be contained for fear that the white backlash would more than offset the gains.

What is important, however, is that, in many instances, evaluation is not self-evident. And the difficulties of evaluation do not rest solely on personal differences in taste or values, but on empirical questions as to what will be the eventual consequences of the state of affairs that has been detected. It is here that the adequacy of the model one has, and consensus on a model among parties, becomes most relevant. It is gratuitous to say that, whatever difficulties one may have in develop-ing a model of a market for a business firm, the difficulties of developing one for the United States social system, or even that of a metropolitan area, are infinitely greater.

The absence of consensus on a model, of course, poses problems at the very point of selection of what indicators to measure. What one has to look to is consensus on the indicators independently of consensus on a model of the society. For example, most of the relevant parties can agree that unemployment is something that we want to have information on, even though they do not agree as to what conclusions they will draw from the data.

The steps from detection, to evaluation, to diagnosis—let alone to prescription for action—are usually taken too blithely. Few, if any, of the social indicators proposed in these volumes will tell us *automatically* what caused a given state of affairs. Accurate data may, however, spoil one of our favorite sports of invoking preferred explanations of dubiously existent phenomena, for example, blaming an "increasing" crime rate on the collapse of our moral fiber. Actual causal relations must be inferred, with the gaps of inference being narrowed by ad hoc research designed to establish the linkage. We may infer, for example, that the white backlash has been caused by some combination of the advances of the Negro community, anxiety over threats to their own position on the part of whites, moral indignation, guilt, or what have you. Research directed to this issue can, with varying adequacy, sort out the plausible causes.

Any information system requires provision for ad hoc research directed toward two ends: (1) diagnosis, for example, exploration of the causal origin of trends reflected in regular social indicators or of any other observable important social changes, and (2) measurement of the impact of discrete events whose impact may be expected to be reflected in regular data series only partially, indirectly, or with some delay.[5] Included in the latter category is the study of unexpected events such as a presidential assassination but, perhaps more importantly, as a regular matter, program evaluation. The evaluation of public programs demands rapid feedback, and it also demands measures of phenomena that one would not ordinarily think of including in regular indicator series. We may take as an example Project Headstart of the current poverty program. If it achieves its goal of increasing the opportunities of underpriviledged children, this ultimate objective will be detectable only some years from now in the educational and occupational performances of such groups as Negroes. The immediate traceable impact may be found in such things as the degree of enthusiasm for the program on the part of parents and children (this at least will ensure their continued participation) and some improvement in the motivation and social skills of the children, which may be the preface to an improvement in learning ability and in learning itself and *subsequently* to improved educational and occupational performance.

While such measures are necessary in any information system, they play an increased role in a broad-gauged, multipurpose system of social indicators. Or to put the matter in reverse, the more closely a system is tailored to a limited set of objectives, the higher the proportion of relevant effects which will be included in regular data series and the fewer will be the steps of inference required to establish causation. This is probably a tautology, but it underscores the general need for such ad hoc research in a societal information system.

Finally, any presently constructed societal information system will suffer from the *relative* lack of models with which to test out the consequences of possible courses of action. This lack is, of course, relative. Economists can test out the probable consequences of economic policies. One can also predict that a frontal attack on infectious diseases will almost certainly result in an increase in such diseases as heart trouble and cancer. On the whole, however, we lack dynamic models of most of the areas of our society which will help us to "anticipate" the consequences of programs we might introduce. This circumstance dictates the relative importance of feedback, of being able to detect these consequences as rapidly as possible after their occurrence.

In sum, formal information systems, like all of man's creations, have inherent limitations, and these inherent limitations get accentuated in anything we might contemplate in the way of a societal information system. Information systems are most adequate for handling repetitive, routinized problems and to the extent that the system is tailored closely to the needs of a limited range of problems. While societal information systems are useful for routine operating purposes, they are most pertinent for the handling of broader policy problems of an unprogrammed nature. Furthermore, a societal information system applies not only to a wide range of problems, but also to a variety of interests. It is not merely a tool for action for those who must devise and carry out actions (as in a business firm or health system) but also for those people who evaluate such actions. And a societal information system must be designed with a relatively poor model of the society.

The result of all these conditions is that the parameters to be measured must be selected only on the basis of a general agreement that they are "important," even though their importance cannot be justified *via* reference to an agreed-upon model. Furthermore, measures of such parameters must be, in general, oriented toward multiple usage. On the whole, this means, in turn, that the problems of evaluation and of diagnosis and of drawing inferences for action are based on complex inferences. Such a system will be relatively unusually dependent on the quality of the inferences drawn, on ad hoc research to establish casual connections and evaluate the effects of discrete events such as public programs, and on feedback to detect the consequences of actions which can only inadequately be anticipated.

Scanning for Strategic Information

Formal information systems become increasingly less adequate as we are concerned with policy or strategic problems, as contrasted to repetitive operational problems. It is clear that the writers of all the chapters in [Bertram M. Gross, ed., *Social Intelligence for America's Future: Explorations in Societal Problems* (Boston: Allyn & Bacon, Inc., 1969)] are primarily concerned with broad problems of evaluating trends in the society, of the impact of broad programs, and of the need for revising programs or adopting new ones. We are concerned with the national welfare, but, in this context, not with the day-to-day problems of operating a local welfare office.

The difficulty in saying anything systematic about the procurement of strategic policy information is simply that it is an amorphous, complex topic about which little of a systematic nature has been said.[6]

One thing that is certain is that strategic policy problems must involve persons in high positions who are simultaneously concerned with operating problems which tend to saturate their attention.

We noted how routine, immediate, familiar, and programmed considerations tend to crowd out strategic, long-range, unfamiliar, and unprogrammed considerations.[7]

This, of course, is recognized in most organizational arrangements by the provision of specific staff functions. On the national level, it is the function of the Council of Economic Advisors to review the evidence bearing on policy questions and to report the evidence and recommendations for action. The proposal of Senator Mondale for a Council of Social Advisors[8] reflects a realization that establishing a staff function to review evidence beyond the strictly economic will ensure greater attentiveness to noneconomic social matters.

The provision of a staff function for reviewing a wider range of information is one thing. The process of this viewing is another. Scanning the environment for strategic information can, to some extent, be systematic, to the degree that it involves the monitoring of regular data series for evidence of discontinuity or changes of pattern. Thus, one might find, on the one hand, a sharp jump or a sharp drop in unemployment or, on the other hand, a shift in balance of the aspirations and achievements of Negro youth. Either of these circumstances might signal the existence of an imminent new threat or opportunity.

However, there is a large random element in scanning for strategic information. Unprogrammed problems manifest themselves in unexpected places and unexpected forms. The work of Keegan[9] suggests two further generalizations that may be cited.

The first of these is that one can better decide *where* to look for strategic information rather than *what* to look for. The executives he studied were much more likely to report that they had found strategic information by monitoring a source known in general to be useful rather than by deliberate investigation or by research.

The second is that a high proportion of strategic information is transmitted by personal, usually face-to-face communications. Various sources of evidence suggest to me that this may be due to the fact that matters of broad policy importance are, to some extent, only vaguely sensed in their early stages. The person who senses that "something is in the air," who "makes a connection," has difficulty in coding his perceptions into words which he knows will be relevant to his potential audience. He may also be reluctant to put into writing or into print that which may make him look foolish. However, when he meets a potential user of his, still only partially formulated, "information" he can explore, in a transactional fashion, what it may mean, with someone equipped to assess its meaning.

The last of these generalizations obviously implies a fairly well-accepted generalization, namely, the usefulness of personal contacts.

Out of all of this, can any specific suggestions be made? Two seem straightforward and have been implied above. Provision should be made for an explicit function of scanning the environment for evidence that policy changes might be in order. And there must be sufficient organizational slack to provide for a certain amount of directed random behavior—monitoring of selected channels of information in which strategic information may occur and the maintenance of a network of interpersonal contacts.

Less straightforward, but also implied in preceding pages, is the importance of the social system model which one has. The richer that model, the greater the likelihood that the potential implications of a given item of information will be seen.

How to Use Information

The question of what data to gather and how to use it is one which has been addressed in detail in each of the papers in these volumes. Most of the decisions which have to be made are matters of judgment, and judgment must be specific to the situation in which it is applied. Granting this, some general comments may offer some guidance to the application of the necessary judgment.

. . . The United States is not suffering from a glut of information of adequate quality in the various areas of concern. We may expect the expansion and refinement of existing data series. This expansion and refinement will unquestionably take place as a function, not only of the need for such series but of the bargaining power of those who propose them and of the technical resources that they can bring to bear.[10]

Some centralization of decisionmaking on statistical series can be helpful in assuring that criteria of relevance play as much a role as possible. The Bureau of the Budget has, to some extent, played such a mediating role. The existent Social Indicators Panel of the Health, Education, and Welfare Department will have some ad hoc impact. A Council of Social Advisors, such as that proposed by Senator Mondale, would unquestionably play such a role. Such a centralized group must weigh the relative priority of general, overall social needs for information against the urgency of the needs of particular parties, especially those who require information for direct operational purposes. This balancing off of immediate, specific needs against broader long-term needs is a matter on which one cannot prescribe at a distance, except to point out that staff persons (such as those who are likely to be setting such priorities) are likely to be biased in favor of the broader, long-range problems while line operators will have a selective preference for the most specific, short-range data. In business organizations, the line operator tends to control the organization and is generally able to have his way. In the government, the line operators are likely to have the ear and sympathy of the Congress which appropriates funds. These circumstances are relevant.

However, decisions as to what measures to take are not simply a matter of priorities. The decision to observe a phenomenon implies a decision to be responsible for it, if such responsibility is within one's power. On the one hand, the decision to observe can be used constructively and positively as a way of commanding attention. This is obviously one of the intentions of Senator Mondale's proposals. But whether one intends to assume responsibility or not, the knowledge that phenomena are being observed will create the expectation that such responsibilities will be assumed. For example, measurement of the aspirations of Negro youth seems to offer a valuable contribution to our understanding of the movement of Negroes into the mainstream of American life. However, the making and publication of such measurements will undoubtedly call attention to the disparity between the expectations we have created and our ability to meet those expectations. Similarly, a health information system that discloses that some segments of the population do not receive certain medical services will generate the expectation that these services be supplied.

It is wisdom, not cynicism, to urge caution in extending diagnostic measures of social phenomena beyond the system's capacity to respond to the problems which are unveiled. While it is necessary to illuminate problems for planning purposes and to stimulate the requisite actions, such illumination can also produce trouble and disillusionment. ("Why did they ask me what I wanted, if they aren't going to do anything about it?")

Another issue that must be faced is that of the level of aggregation of data. It is the ideal of a good information system that the data stored in it be disaggregated, that is, stored in the units in which it was gathered, so that it may be combined in whatever forms are desired. However, many of the newer statistical series, for example, the monthly Health Survey, and to some extent the Survey of Employment, are gathered on a sample survey basis and can provide us with estimates only for the population of the United States or, at most, for broad regions. For certain purposes, the estimates are adequate. Persons with operational responsibility for smaller units—states, towns, cities, and portions of cities—have complained of the inadequacy of such data for the tasks with which they are confronted. This is an established problem, well recognized. Less well recognized, however, is the extent to which aggregation can produce misdiagnosis. For example, if one paid attention only to overall employment figures, one would miss the extraordinary concentration of this unemployment among young Negro males. Happily, this

particular fact has been realized, and appropriate measures among Negro youth are being taken.

As long as data are available only on some level of aggregation, one cannot, of course, not know with certainty that no such anomalies are hidden behind the aggregation. Yet completely disaggregated data for the United States population on all of the data series presented in this volume are impossible. The essentiality of using sample surveys must be accompanied by acute awareness of the problem of aggregation and by ad hoc diagnostic studies when there is reason to suspect that the aggregation hides some phenomena of interest.

In some instances the problem of aggregation may suggest that one retain administratively gathered statistics available on a disaggregated basis even though the measure may be somewhat inferior to that which might otherwise be made. In other situations, such administratively gathered series might be monitored for clues to problems that might be hidden by aggregation; for example, hospital records might reveal the clustering of health problems that the sample survey does not reflect.

Finally, one must consider the organizational problems of using the information that a societal information system offers.[11] Any information on the society in which an institution exists presents potential opportunities or threats. This information will have varying values on a number of dimensions: Its clear relevance for a given institution, the degree of effort involved in responding to a threat or opportunity, the organization's capacity to respond effectively (regardless of level of effort), and the extent to which it will favor one element in the organization over another.

This latter problem of organizing to use information is one of sufficient complexity that in this brief essay it can only be touched on; the interested reader is advised to consult some more extensive treatment such as that of Anthony or of Weiss and Rosenthal, cited above.

References and Notes

1 Cf. Bertrand de Jouvenel, *The Art of Conjecture* (New York: Basic Books, Inc., Publishers, 1967). [See also Chapter 1 of this volume.]

2 Raymond A. Bauer, ed., *Social Indicators* (Cambridge, Mass.: The M.I.T. Press, 1966).

3 Robert N. Anthony, *Planning and Control Systems* (Boston: Division of Research, Harvard University Graduate School of Business Administration, 1965), pp. 28, 29.

4 Here, as at other places in this essay, the knowledgeable reader will be searching for qualifications. It is not true that an information system cannot be built that will generate possible courses of action. However, this development will generally have to wait until our understanding of human thought processes is better developed. Work on programming computers to play chess has shown that if one were to use the computers' tremendous calculational capacities to have it consider all logical possibilities, it would play an untenably long chess game. Its human opponents would have died of old age. Chess masters have heuristic devices—decision rules which simplify such enormous complexity.

5 Cf. Albert D. Biderman, "Anticipatory Studies and Stand-by Research Capabilities," in Bauer, ed., op. cit.

6 For recent exceptions to this generalization, see Francis Joseph Aguilar, *Scanning the Business Environment* (New York: The Macmillan Company, 1967); and Warren J. Keegan, *Scanning the International Business Environment: A Study of the Information Acquisition Process* (A thesis submitted in partial requirement of the degree of Doctor of Business Administration, Harvard Graduate School of Business Administration, 1967). See also Raymond A. Bauer, Ithiel de Sola Pool, and Lewis Anthony Dexter, *American Business and Public Policy* (Chicago: Aldine-Atherton, Inc., 1963), passim.

7 Aguilar, op. cit., p. 187.

8 S. 843, 90th Congress, 1st Session, February 6, 1967; introduced by Senator Mondale.

9 Keegan, op. cit.

10 For a discussion of the practical problems in introducing or refining statistical series, see Albert D. Biderman, "Social Indicators and Goals," in Bauer, ed., op. cit., pp. 95–105.

11 For an extended discussion of this issue see Robert A. Rosenthal and Robert S. Weiss, "Problems of Organizational Feedback Processes," in Bauer, ed., op. cit., pp. 302–40.

Concluding Remarks

We hope that in this book we have offered reassurance to students who have been pessimistic about the future of large, complex organizations in American society. We believe there are substantial bases for optimism on this score. This optimism cannot be justified, however, unless today's administrators and policymakers adopt a strong initiative directed toward changing many of their ways of doing things.

We anticipate, too, that we have created an awareness among our students of the possibility for proactive behavior on the part of administrators *and* organizations. Perhaps our readers will undertake to seek for themselves the route to personal proactive capability. But will today's organizations be ready to accommodate such emerging new administrators? Organizations must begin to confront their responsibilities in this regard. The trend toward new men with new values and a new consciousness is not likely to diminish. Neither is the increase in the variety of human knowledge or the enlargement of the freedom of choice. These changes are already affecting organizations, and every indication we have available today suggests that this will be more significant in the future. The value of individual freedom of choice can be expanded further through the creation of different organizations. Thus, the study of tomorrow's organizations seems not only highly desirable but inevitable for human development.

John Gardner, arguing that the individual in American society has lost confidence in government and society, calls for a "recovery of confidence." Proactive administrators as well as individuals in organizations and society must begin this recovery; it is for them to learn, to explore, and to risk new ways of doing things. Effective solutions for today's problems, as well as improved policymaking for the future, are not likely to be achieved until we develop a clearer understanding of organizational and social realities and until practicing administrators and students of organization theory develop a more sophisticated awareness of conceptual foundations, appropriate theories, and useful research methods for assessing organizational phenomena.

Any new theory pertinent to these problems may be at least partly appropriate for complex organizational situations, However, one that deals with the realities of today's social world must not only amplify existing theory but must also consider and imaginatively account the meanings and implications of the unique new problems being encountered in today's organizations—problems which are likely to be more evident tomorrow. Certainly, policy choice in the human decision process must realistically incorporate conditions of the social world (the "real world") if organizational policy is to be implemented in that world.

All of this is simply to emphasize the point which is central to our purpose in this book: that tomorrow's organizations must continuously learn from new theories and new knowledge; that man learns from new experiences, develops and uses new values and searches for new goals; that humanism and pluralism are enhanced by less structured perceptions of reality, by a diversity of values; that there are many ways to think and do, many possible organizations, many possible societies. We believe we may fairly argue that more effective use of multiple theories about human behavior, organizations, and social phenomena will improve the quality of human and social development, thereby strengthening our position as we confront the paradoxes and ambiguities in tomorrow's different world.

Bibliography

General Introduction

Argyris, Chris. *Integrating the Individual and the Organization.* New York: John Wiley & Sons, Inc., 1964.

Bennis, Warren G. *Changing Organizations.* New York: McGraw-Hill Book Company, 1966.

Berger, Peter L., and Thomas Luckmann. *The Social Construction of Reality.* Garden City, N.Y.: Doubleday & Company, Inc., 1967.

Blake, Robert R., and Jane Srygley Mouton. "A Behavioral Science Design for the Development of Society." *The Journal of Behavioral Science* 7, no. 2 (March-April 1971): 146–63.

Bosserman, Phillip. *Dialectical Sociology: An Analysis of the Sociology of Georges Gurvitch.* Boston: Porter Sargent, Inc., 1968.

Buckley, Walter. *Sociology and Modern Systems Theory.* Englewood Cliffs, N.J.: Prentice-Hall, Inc., 1967.

Bugental, James F. T., ed. *Challenges of Humanistic Psychology.* New York: McGraw-Hill Book Company, 1967.

Etzioni, Amitai. *The Active Society: A Theory of Societal and Political Processes.* New York: Free Press, Div. of The Macmillan Company, 1968.

Drucker, Peter F. *The Age of Discontinuity: Guidelines to Our Changing Society.* New York: Harper & Row, Publishers, 1969.

Katz, Daniel, and Basil S. Georgopoulos. "Organizations in a Changing World." *The Journal of Applied Behavioral Science* 7, no. 3 (1971): 342–70.

Katz, Daniel, and Robert L. Kahn. *The Social Psychology of Organizations.* New York: John Wiley & Sons, Inc., 1966.

Lauer, Quentin. *Phenomenology: Its Genesis and Prospect.* New York: Harper & Row, Publishers, 1965.

Lawrence, Paul R., and Jay W. Lorsch. *Developing Organizations: Diagnosis and Action.* Reading, Mass.: Addison-Wesley Publishing Company, Inc., 1969.

Likert, Rensis. *The Human Organization: Its Management and Value.* New York: McGraw-Hill Book Company, 1967.

Manchester Business School. "Integrated Organizational Strategy." *The Journal of Management Studies* 6, no. 1 (February 1969).

McGregor, Douglas. *The Human Side of Enterprise.* New York: McGraw-Hill Book Company, 1960.

Mannheim, Karl. *Man and Society in an Age of Reconstruction.* New York: Harcourt Brace Jovanovich, Inc., 1940.

Mills, C. Wright. *The Sociological Imagination.* New York: Grove Press Inc., 1959.

Rose, Arnold M. "Varieties of Sociological Imagination." *American Sociological Review* 34, no. 5 (October 1969): pp. 623–30.

Schutz, Alfred. *The Phenomenology of the Social World.* Translated by George Walsh and Frederick Lehnert. Evanston, Ill.: Northwestern University Press, 1967.

Silverman, David. *The Theory of Organizations.* New York: Basic Books, Inc., Publishers, 1970.

Vickers, Sir Geoffrey. *Value Systems and Social Process.* New York: Basic Books, Inc., Publishers, 1968.

Part One

Argyris, Chris. *Organization and Innovation.* Homewood, Ill.: Richard D. Irwin, Inc., 1965.

Bell, Daniel. "The Measurement of Knowledge and Technology." In *Indicators for Social Change,* edited by E. B. Sheldon and W. E. Moore, pp. 152–61. (New York: Russell Sage Foundation, 1968).

Bell, Daniel, ed. *Toward the Year 2000: Work in Progress.* Boston: Beacon Press, 1968.

Bennis, Warren G., and Philip E. Slator. *The Temporary Society.* New York: Harper & Row, Publishers, 1968.

de Jouvenel, Bertrand. *The Art of Conjecture.* New York: Basic Books, Inc., Publishers, 1967.

Drucker, Peter F., ed. *Preparing Tomorrow's Business Leaders Today.* Englewood Cliffs, N.J.: Prentice-Hall, Inc., 1969.

Ewald, William R. Jr., ed. *Environment and Change: The Next Fifty Years.* Bloomington: Indiana University Press, 1968.

Gardner, John W. *The Recovery of Confidence.* New York: W. W. Norton & Company, Inc., 1970.

Gross, Bertram M., ed. *Social Intelligence for America's Future: Explorations in Societal Problems.* Boston: Allyn & Bacon, Inc., 1969.

438

Kahn, Herman, and Anthony J. Wiener. *The Year 2000: A Framework for Speculation on the Next Thirty-Three Years.* New York: The Macmillan Company, 1968.

March, James, and Herbert Simon. *Organizations.* New York: John Wiley & Sons, Inc., 1958.

Maruyama, Magoroh. "The Second Cybernetics: Deviation-Amplifying Mutual Causal Processes." *American Scientist* 51 (1963): 164–79.

Maslow, Abraham H. *Eupsychian Management: A Journal.* Homewood, Ill.: Richard D. Irwin, Inc., 1965.

Mouzelis, Nicos P. *Organization and Bureaucracy: An Analysis of Modern Theories.* Chicago: Aldine-Atherton, Inc., 1968.

Michael, Donald N. *The Unprepared Society: Planning for a Precarious Future.* New York: Basic Books, Inc., Publishers, 1968.

Pfiffner, John M., and Frank P. Sherwood. *Administrative Organization.* Englewood Cliffs, N.J.: Prentice-Hall, Inc., 1960.

Pondy, Louis R. "Organizational Conflict: Concepts and Models." *Administrative Science Quarterly* 12, no. 2 (September 1967): 297–319.

Thompson, James D. *Organizations in Action.* New York: McGraw-Hill Book Company, 1967.

Toffler, Alvin. *Future Shock.* New York: Random House, 1970.

Wallia, C. S., ed. *Toward Century Twenty-One: Technology, Society, and Human Values.* New York: Basic Books, Inc., Publishers, 1970.

Part Two

Argyris, Chris. "Conditions for Competence Acquisition and Therapy," *The Journal of Applied Behavioral Science* 4 no. 2 (1968): 147–77.

———. *Interpersonal Competence and Organizational Effectiveness.* Homewood, Ill.: Richard D. Irwin, Inc., 1962.

Athos, Anthony G., and Robert E. Coffey. *Behavior in Organizations: A Multidimensional View.* Englewood Cliffs, N.J.: Prentice-Hall, Inc., 1968.

Baier, Kurt, and Nicholas Rescher, eds. *Values and the Future.* New York: Free Press, Div. of The Macmillan Company, 1969.

Bugental, James F. T., ed. *Challenges of Humanistic Psychology.* New York: McGraw-Hill Book Company, 1967.

Bennis, Warren G.; Kenneth D. Benne; and Robert Chin, eds. *The Planning of Change.* 2d ed. New York: Holt, Rinehart & Winston, Inc., 1969.

Blake, R. R.; H. A. Shepard; and J. S. Mouton. *Managing Intergroup Conflict in Industry.* Houston: Gulf Publishing Company, 1964.

Churchman, C. West. *Challenge to Reason.* New York: McGraw-Hill Book Company, 1968.

Committee for Economic Development. *Social Responsibilities of Business Corporations.* New York: C.E.D., June 1971.

Hampton, D. R.; C. E. Summer; and R. A. Webber, eds. *Organizational Behavior and the Practice of Management.* Glenview, Ill.: Scott, Foresman and Company, 1968.

Jourard, Sidney M. *The Transparent Self.* Princeton, N.J.: Van Nostrand Reinhold Company, 1964.

Lawrence, P. R., and J. W. Lorsch. *Organization and Environment: Managing Differentiation and Integration.* Boston: Division of Research, Harvard Business School, 1967.

Lippitt, Gordon L. *Organization Renewal: Achieving Viability in a Changing World.* New York: Appleton-Century-Crofts, 1969.

Maier, Normal R. F., and John J. Hayes. *Creative Management.* John Wiley & Sons, Inc., 1962.

Maslow, A. H. *Personality and Motivation.* New York: John Wiley & Sons, Inc., 1954.

———. *Toward a Psychology of Being.* 2d ed. Princeton, N.J.: Van Nostrand Reinhold Company, 1968.

Mohr, Lawrence B. "Determinants of Innovation in Organizations." *American Political Science Review* 63, no. 1 (March 1969): 111–26.

O'Connell, Jeremiah J. *Managing Organizational Innovation.* Homewood, Ill.: Richard D. Irwin, Inc., 1968.

Press, Charles, and Alan Arian, eds. *Empathy and Ideology: Aspects of Administrative Innovation.* Chicago: Rand-McNally & Company, 1966.

Rogers, Everett M. *Diffusion of Innovation.* New York: Free Press, Div. of The Macmillan Company, 1962.

Schmidt, Warren H., ed. *Organizational Frontiers and Human Values.* Belmont, Calif.: Wadsworth Publishing Co., Inc., 1970.

Sethi, S. Prakash, and Dow Votaw. "Do We Need a New Corporate Response to a Changing Social Environment?" *California Management Review* 12, no. 1 (Fall 1969): 17–31.

Tannenbaum, Robert, and Sheldon A. Davis. "Values, Man, and Organizations." *Industrial Management Review* 10, no. 2 (Winter 1969): 67–83.

Thompson, James D., ed. *Approaches to Organizational Design.* Pittsburgh, Penn.: University of Pittsburgh, 1966.

Turner, Arthur N., and George F. F. Lombard, eds. *Interpersonal Behavior and Administration.* New York: Free Press, Div. of The Macmillan Company, 1969.

Vickers, Sir Geoffrey. *Towards a Sociology of Management.* New York: Basic Books, Inc., Publishers, 1967.

Wilson, Colin. *Introduction to the New Existentialism.* Boston: Houghton-Mifflin Company, 1967.

Zaleznik, Abraham, and David Moment. *The Dynamics of Interpersonal Behavior.* New York: John Wiley & Sons, Inc., 1964.

Part Three

Barnard, Chester. *The Functions of the Executives.* Cambridge, Mass.: Harvard University Press, 1936.

Beer, Stafford. *Cybernetics and Management.* London: English Universities Press, 1959.

Biddle, Bruce J., and Edwin J. Thomas, eds. *Role Theory: Concepts and Research.* New York: John Wiley & Sons, Inc., 1966.

Blau, Peter. *Exchange and Power in Social Life.* New York: John Wiley & Sons, Inc., 1964.

Bosserman, Phillip. *Dialectical Sociology: An Analysis of the Sociology of Georges Gurvitch.* Boston: Porter Sargent Publishers, 1968.

Buckley, Walter, ed. *Modern Systems Research for the Behavioral Scientists.* Chicago: Aldine-Atherton, Inc., 1968.

————. *Sociology and Modern Systems Theory.* Englewood Cliffs, N.J.: Prentice-Hall, Inc., 1967.

Cadwallader, Mervyn L. "The Cybernetic Analysis of Change in Complex Organizations." *American Journal of Sociology* 65 (September 1959): 105–10.

Chin, Robert. "The Utility of System Models and Developmental Models for Practitioners." In W. G. Bennis, K. D. Benne, and R. Chin, eds. *The Planning of Change.* 2d ed. New York: Holt, Rinehart & Winston, Inc., 1969.

Easton, David. *A Systems Analysis of Political Life.* New York: John Wiley & Sons, Inc., 1965.

Etzioni, Amitai. *The Active Society: A Theory of Societal and Political Processes.* New York: Free Press, Div. of The Macmillan Company, 1968.

Gergen, Kenneth J. *The Psychology of Behavior Exchange.* Reading, Mass.: Addison-Wesley Publishing Company, 1969.

Getzels, J. W., and E. G. Guba. "Role, Role Conflict, and Effectiveness: An Empirical Study." *American Sociological Review* 19 (1954): 164–75.

Giorgi, Amedeo, et al. *Duquesne Studies in Phenomenological Psychology.* Volume 1. Pittsburgh: Duquesne University Press, 1971.

Gross, Neal; Ward S. Mason; and Alexander W. McEachern. *Explorations in Role Analysis: Studies of the School Superintendency Role.* New York: John Wiley & Sons, Inc., 1958.

Gurwitsch, A. *The Field of Consciousness.* Pittsburgh: Duquesne University Press, 1964.

Homans, George C. *Social Behavior: Its Elementary Forms.* New York: Harcourt Brace Jovanovich, Inc., 1961.

Katz, Daniel. "The Motivational Basis of Organizational Behavior." *Behavioral Science* 9, no. 2 (April 1964), pp. 131–46.

Katz, Daniel, and Robert L. Kahn. *The Social Psychology of Organizations.* New York: John Wiley & Sons, Inc., 1966.

Kahn, Robert, et al. *Organizational Stress: Studies in Role Conflict and Ambiguity.* New York: John Wiley & Sons, Inc., 1964.

Lauer, Quentin. *Phenomenology: Its Genesis and Prospects.* New York: Harper & Row, Publishers, 1965.

Likert, Rensis. "Motivation: The Core of Management." In *Management of Human Resources,* edited by Paul Pigors, et al. New York: McGraw-Hill Book Company, 1964.

McClelland, David C. *The Achieving Society.* New York: Van Nostrand Reinhold Company, 1961.

Maslow, A. H. *Toward A Psychology of Being.* 2d ed. New York: Van Nostrand Reinhold Company, 1968.

Merton, Robert K. *Social Theory and Social Structure.* Rev. ed. New York: Free Press, Div. of The Macmillan Company, 1962.

Merleau-Ponty, M. *Phenomenology of Perception.* Trans. by C. Smith. New York: Humanities Press, 1962.

Schutz, Alfred. *The Phenomenology of the Social World.* Trans. by George Walsh and Frederick Lehnert. Evanston, Ill.: Northwestern University Press, 1967.

Simon, Herbert. *Administrative Behavior.* 2d ed. New York: The Macmillan Company, 1957.

Smelser, Neil J. *Sociological Theory: A Contemporary View.* New York: General Learning Press, 1971.

Tiryakian, Edward A. *Sociologism and Existentialism: Two Perspectives on the Individual and Society.* Englewood Cliffs, N.J.: Prentice-Hall, Inc., 1965.

Wild, John. *Existence and the World of Freedom.* Englewood Cliffs, N.J.: Prentice-Hall, Inc., 1965.

Part Four

Argyris, Chris. *Intervention Theory and Method: A Behavioral Science View.* Reading, Mass.: Addison-Wesley Publishing Company, Inc., 1970.

————. *Management and Organizational Development: The Path from xa to yb.* New York: McGraw-Hill Book Company, 1971.

————. *Some Causes of Organizational Ineffectiveness within the Department of State.* Occasional Papers No. 2 Washington, D.C.: Center of International Systems Research, Department of State, 1967.

Beckhard, Richard. *Organization Development: Strategies and Models.* Reading, Mass.: Addison-Wesley Publishing Company, Inc. 1969.

Bennis, Warren G. *Organization Development: Its Nature, Origins, and Prospects.* Reading, Mass.: Addison-Wesley Publishing Company, Inc. 1969.

————. "Postbureaucratic Leadership." *Transaction* (July-August 1969): 44–51.

Blake, Robert R., and Jane S. Mouton. *Corporate Excellence Through Grid Organization Development.* Houston: Gulf Publishing Company, 1968.

————. *The Managerial Grid.* Houston: Gulf Publishing Company, 1964.

Bonner, Hubert. "The Proactive Personality." In James F. T. Bugental, ed. *Challenges of Humanistic Psychology,* New York: McGraw-Hill Book Company, 1967. Pp. 61–66.

Campbell, Donald T. "Reforms as Experiments." *American Psychologist* (1969), pp. 409–29.

Cantril, Hadley. *The Human Dimension: Experiences*

in Policy Research. New Brunswick, N.J.: Rutgers University Press, 1967.

Clark, Peter A., and Janet R. Ford. "Methodological and Theoretical Problems in the Investigation of Planned Organizational Change." *The Sociological Review* 8, no. 1 (March 1970).

Dalton, Gene W., et al. *Organizational Change and Development.* Homewood, Ill.: Richard D. Irwin, Inc., 1970.

——. *Organizational Structure and Design.* Homewood, Ill.: Richard D. Irwin, Inc., 1970.

Drucker, Peter F., ed. *Preparing Tomorrow's Business Leaders Today.* Englewood Cliffs, N.J.: Prentice-Hall, Inc., 1969.

Freeman, Howard E., and Clarence C. Sherwood. *Social Research and Social Policy,* Englewood Cliffs, N.J.: Prentice-Hall Inc., 1970.

Gawthrop, Louis C. *Bureaucratic Behavior in the Executive Branch.* New York: The Free Press, 1969.

Greiner, Larry E. "Conceptions of Organization Development in Sweden." Paper Presented at the 33rd Annual Conference of the American Society for Public Administration, New York City, April 24, 1972.

Gross, Bertram M., and Michael Springer, eds. *Political Intelligence for America's Future.* The Annals of the American Academy of Political and Social Science, Volume 388, March, 1970.

Jones, Garth. *Planned Organizainal Change: A Study in Change Dynamics.* New York: Frederick A. Praeger, Publishers, 1969.

Kahn, Herman, and Anthony J. Wiener. *The Year 2000.* London: Macmillan Co., 1967.

Lawrence, Paul R., and Jay W. Lorsch. *Developing Organizations: Diagnosis and Action.* Reading, Mass.: Addison-Wesley Publishing Co., 1969.

Leavitt, Harold J. "Applied Organization Change in Industry: Structural, Technological and Humanistic Approaches." In James G. March, ed. *Handbook of Organizations.* Chicago: Rand-McNally & Co., 1965, pp. 1144–70.

Likert, Rensis. *The Human Organization: Its Management and Value.* New York: McGraw-Hill Book Company, Inc., 1967.

McGregor, Douglas. *The Professional Manager.* Edited by Warren G. Bennis and Caroline McGregor. New York: McGraw-Hill Book Company, 1967.

Michael, Donald N. *The Unprepared Society: Planning for a Precarious Future.* New York: Basic Books, Inc., Publishers, 1967.

Sayles, Leonard. *Managerial Behavior: Administration in Complex Organizations.* New York: McGraw-Hill Book Company, 1964.

Schein, Edgar H., and Warren G. Bennis. *Personal and Organizational Change Through Group Methods: The Laboratory Approach.* New York: John Wiley & Sons, 1965.

Thompson, James D., ed. *Approaches to Organizational Design.* Pittsburgh: University of Pittsburgh Press, 1966.

Trist, E. L., et al. *Organizaional Choice.* London: Tavistock Publications, 1963.

Trist, E. L. "Sociotechnical Systems." *Tavistock Institute of Human Relations,* Doc. No. 572, November 1959.

Vickers, Sir Geoffrey. *The Art of Judgment: A Study of Policymaking.* New York: Basic Books, Inc., Publishers, 1965.

Woodward, Joan, ed. *Industrial Organization: Behavior and Control.* London: Oxford University Press, 1970.

——. *Industrial Organization: Theory and Practice.* London: Oxford University Press, 1965.

Zand, Dale. "Managing the Knowledge Organization." In *Preparing Tomorrow's Business Leaders Today,* edited by Peter F. Drucker. Englewood Cliffs, N.J.: Prentice-Hall, Inc., 1969. Pp. 112–36.

Index of Names

Index of Subjects